The Sacred Paths of the East

Third Edition

Theodore M. Ludwig

Valparaiso University

PEARSON

Prentice
Hall

Upper Saddle River, New Jersey 07458

Library of Congress Cataloging-in-Publication Data

Ludwig, Theodore M.
  The sacred paths of the East / Theodore M. Ludwig. — 3rd ed.
    p. cm.
  Includes bibliographical references and index.
  ISBN 0-13-153905-1
  1. Asia—Religion.

BL1033.L83 2006
200'.95—dc22

2004060106

VP/Editorial Director: Charlyce Jones Owen
Editorial Assistant: Maureen Diana
Marketing Assistant: Jennifer Lang
Production Liaison: Marianne Peters-Riordan
Manufacturing Buyer: Christina Helder
Cover Art Director: Jayne Conte
Cover Design: Bruce Kenselaar
Director, Image Resource Center: Melinda Reo
Manager, Rights and Permissions: Zina Arabia
Manager, Visual Research: Beth Brenzel
Manager, Cover Visual Research & Permissions: Karen Sanatar
Image Permission Coordinator: Craig A. Jones
Composition/Full-Service Project Management: Caterina Melara/Preparé, Inc.
Printer/Binder: Courier Companies, Inc.

Credits and acknowledgments borrowed from other sources and reproduced, with permission, in this textbook appear on appropriate page within text.

Pearson Education LTD.
Pearson Education Singapore, Pte. Ltd
Pearson Education, Canada, Ltd
Pearson Education-Japan
Pearson Education Australia PTY, Limited

Pearson Education North Asia Ltd
Pearson Educación de Mexico, S.A. de C.V.
Pearson Education Malaysia, Pte. Ltd
Pearson Education, Upper Saddle River, New Jersey

10 9 8 7 6 5 4 3 2 1

ISBN 0-13-153905-1

To Kathy, Kevin, Jim,
Laurie, Greg, Keith,
Amanda and Megan

Contents

Preface to the Third Edition

Events of recent years, such as attacks from terrorists who claim religious justi-fication, as well as other struggles involv-ing peoples of different religions, have made many people realize the importance of getting to know the different reli-gions of the world. This volume is designed for those who want to focus on the religious traditions of the so-called Eastern world. We look at these religions in two groupings, namely, those arising from India, including Hinduism, Buddhism, Jainism, and Sikhism; and those of China and Japan, especially Confucianism, Daoism, Shinto, and Ma-hayana Buddhism. The material in this third edition of *The Sacred Paths of the East* is also incorporated in a larger vol-ume on the whole range of the world's religions, *The Sacred Paths: Understanding the Religions of the World*, Fourth Edition (Prentice Hall, 2006).

For people just beginning to study these religions, the sheer immensity of the data—names, vocabulary, historical developments, teachings, and practices—can be very daunt-ing and overwhelming. This volume is intended to help such readers by focusing on the goal of understanding. And un-derstanding begins with a sense of what a particular religion means for the people who practice it and live by it. Of course, it is important to realize that each religious tradition is a liv-ing and growing organism stretched out over time and, thus, we pay attention to historical and cultural developments. But we also attempt to go beyond historical information and let readers find themselves in the place of the people who live by each religion—viewing the world through their sacred sto-ries, their worldview, their rituals, and their notion of the good life. The excitement and challenge of this venture will carry over, it is hoped, into a continuing engagement with understanding the complex religious traditions of the world and with the various issues raised in the academic study of these traditions.

To carry out this goal of understanding, this volume combines the necessary discussion of historical matters with a thematic approach based on general issues that arise out of human experience—questions about personal iden-tity, human existence and wholeness, and the right way to live. Since the reader can identify with such issues from personal experience, windows are opened toward an un-derstanding of the meaning and guidance people find in their particular religious traditions.

Because the discussion of each religion is structured around the key themes, readers will be encouraged to explore comparisons between the different religions. If done sensitive-ly, such comparison facilitates understanding, both of the dif-ferent religions and of the main motifs and concerns of that general dimension of human life we call religious experience.

This new edition has been revised throughout to bring material up-to-date, particularly in light of recent world events that affect people of all the religions. Some revisions are intended to provide the reader with greater clarity in discussions of complex historical and theoreti-cal materials. In particular, for each religious tradition a new section on healing and medicine has been added, inasmuch as people in all the religions are increasingly interested in their traditional practices of healing as complementary to modern biomedicine. And various bioethical issues are of deep concern within the different traditions. To help the reader clarify and review the ma-terial, a list of key terms with definitions has been added to the discussion about each religion.

The general structure and main features of the book have been retained. The same thematic structure is used in exploring each individual religion, providing opportu-nity for comparison and understanding. It is particularly important that readers have some encounter with the sa-cred texts and scriptures of each particular religious tradition—yet the comprehension and appreciation of such sacred texts are notoriously difficult for an outsider. This volume incorporates extensive quotations from the sacred texts of each tradition, providing interpretation so the reader can see the significance of these texts and comprehend what they mean for people of that religious tradition. It will be helpful, of course, if this volume is supplemented with an additional collection of sacred texts, when that is feasible.

It is important, for understanding each tradition, to pay attention to the special artistic expressions growing out of that religious experience. So this volume includes a discussion of artistic expression in the different religious traditions to help the reader see that each religion or culture has its own unique aesthetic sense. Also, this volume gives particular attention to the role of women in each tradition. Greater awareness of women's experiences and leadership roles has made possible many new understandings and insights in all the religious traditions.

Among the study features in this volume, the discussion questions for each chapter have been revised to promote review of the material as well as further reflection on the character of each religious tradition. A listing of key terms at the end of the discussion of each religion provides opportunity for reviewing and summing up the material. Other study features include maps, timelines, and suggestions for further reading for each religion.

Many have helped along the way in the development of this book and toward the completion of this third edition. And so I thank all those students and colleagues who have made so many helpful suggestions concerning ways in which this text can become a better means for understanding the religious paths of the Eastern world. Special thanks also go to the reviewers who gave suggestions for this new edition:

David Putney	Old Dominion University
Susan E. Hill	University of Northern Iowa
Donald L. Berry	Gardner-Webb University

Part 1   Exploring the Sacred Paths

INTRODUCTION

Religions, to the surprise of some, have not faded from importance in our world today. Everywhere we look, we see religious traditions, beliefs, and practices intertwined with the cultural, political, and economic activities that make up the human enterprise. That is the way it has always been, but as our global village draws ever closer together today, the need to recognize and understand the role of religions becomes vitally important.

Beginning to explore the religious traditions of the East is an exciting, though somewhat daunting, venture. There is so much to see, to sort through, and to comprehend. We are dealing with the deepest hopes and dreams, the most careful thoughts and views, and the most cherished rituals and practices of people all over the world. We are venturing onto the holy ground of others, and a humble, respectful, and grateful attitude is most appropriate.

As we begin this exploration, we need to be aware that we carry preconceived ideas and judgments with us. We may, perhaps, have a certain amount of knowledge about at least one religious tradition (our own, for example), and based on that we have some notions about what religion is. One major hurdle in understanding the religious traditions of the world is getting beyond the normal tendency to look at the religious practices of others through our own filters of understanding, our own unchallenged views and experiences.

Another hurdle comes when we become inundated with the mass of detail and diversity of forms within the Eastern religions. It is easy to become confused and bewildered, losing any coherent sense of what religion is all about. What are we looking for? The answer to that question may seem very different with each new culture that we encounter.

To help get our bearings for this exploration in the sacred paths of the East, it will be beneficial, here at the beginning of our study, to stand back and reflect more generally on the nature of religious experience, on the main themes and forms through which religious experience typically finds expression. Such an exercise can broaden our narrow vision of religion and open new windows of understanding. Thus, in Chapter 1 we begin our exploration with some reflections on the nature of religion within human life. With a preliminary, working definition of religion we then take soundings from the various religious traditions to set up a collage of themes and forms of human religious experience. It is true, of course, that each particular human community has its own unique practices and meanings, and one should exercise great care in making cross-cultural comparisons. Yet we can recognize that humans through all times and places have always experienced similar life concerns related to birth and death, family and community, survival, and all the rest. And so their attempts to construct meaning through ideas and actions—that is, their religious expressions—can be linked together in a provisional way. In this manner, we can set up a tentative structure to guide our explorations into the sacred paths of the East.

Our look at prehistoric human religious developments in Chapter 2 is somewhat brief and tentative, and rightly so, since archaeological data from ancient sites, before any written records, do not give a clear picture of religious feelings and meanings. We may feel a sense of adventure as we reflect on the immense ages during which the human species developed on this planet, surviving, experimenting, and creating cultures. Perhaps there will awaken in us a sense of indebtedness to our forebears who struggled to live, created religious meanings, and bequeathed their physical and spiritual powers to us. We need to remember that the "world religions" of today are very recent phenomena on the vast scale of humankind's religious history. We will observe how, after the last ice ages and the agricultural revolution, the ancient classical civilizations finally began to develop, providing the fertile basis from which the world religions of today began to take shape.

Chapter 1

Perspectives on the Religious Path

The human adventure can be viewed from many perspectives—and indeed there should be many perspectives, since there are many dimensions to human life, and there is not just one human story but many stories. Common to these stories is a searching for wholeness and meaning, for some connection to the larger continuity of human life. That searching has often been expressed in what we call religious structures, ideas, practices, and experiences. In this book, we are setting out on a venture of **understanding**— understanding some of those religious traditions of humankind. To do this, we need to explore their main ideas and teachings, their rituals and art, their societal structures, their whole ways of life. In all of this, we want to get to know the people who practice these religions and live their lives by them.

As we study different religious traditions of the East, we will also be attempting to understand some fundamentals of *religion* itself as a key human dimension, with similar themes and structures across cultural lines. All religion has to do with fundamental human issues and concerns. Who are we?—the basic question of identity—is crucial to our journey in life. What sense is there in life? How can we find the life that is real and fulfilling? Questions such as these reach to the depths of life concerns that are felt, vaguely or forcefully, by all human beings. Does life actually have meaning—any real meaning—or do we just live and die in the small frame of a pointless, accidental cycle of the universe?

Of course, there are many dimensions of being human, many concerns that are not directly religious ones. We are concerned about our physical makeup, our biological structure, our reasoning capacities, our languages and forms of communication, our historical memories, our

forms of society, our psychological makeup, and much more. But no matter what aspect of human existence we happen to look at, deeper questions of meaning and purpose are close at hand: Is there any sense or direction in the living of our lives? How can we be happy and secure? What responsibility do we have for fellow humans? Wrestling with such questions of meaning in their deeper aspects involves us in religious thinking and experiencing. Religion in this sense is not limited to any one dimension of human existence. Rather, it has to do with the overall meaning of human existence: Why is everything the way it is? What is the rhyme or reason behind all this?

Behind all such questions is a fundamental one: How can people be in touch with what is ultimately real, that unlimited source or sources from which they derive life and meaning? It is to that which they feel is ultimately real, the unlimited source that people within the various religions direct themselves in many different ways. We designate this focal point of the religions as **the sacred**, the ground of ultimate vitality, value, and meaning. The modes of experiencing the sacred, and the responses to this experience, are many and varied; these are the forms and expressions that make up the religious traditions of the world.

STUDYING RELIGIOUS EXPERIENCE

Two General Approaches Studying religious experience, like studying any other dimension of human life, always involves a kind of dual stance. That is, we are observers of people as they practice their religious traditions, looking from the outside and constructing our ideas about why they are doing what they are doing. But we also attempt to see and understand their experiences as they themselves do, looking from the inside, as it were, seeing their own intentions and the meaning they derive from their religious practices. Scholars of religion have elaborated theories of religion and methodologies for studying religion that focus on one or the other of these approaches, and they still debate how these approaches are to be evaluated. Both approaches are important and necessary, and both approaches have specific limitations.

In looking from the outside, the academic study of religion necessarily involves observing, describing, evaluating, organizing, and interpreting the data of religious practice. A major goal is developing theories that explain why these religious practices have developed and what function they fulfill in people's lives. Theories and methods from sociology, anthropology, political science, historical study, and many other disciplines are useful for interpreting religious data. Scholars pay particular attention to issues of class, power, and authority, as reflected in religious practices.

In looking from the inside, the study of religious practice pays close attention to what the people themselves say about the meaning and purpose of their religious practices. The attempt is to describe the phenomena as carefully as possible without evaluating them according to some outside norm or explaining them in terms of cause or function. Interpretative theories focus on meaning, value, and expectations as expressed by the people themselves. Scholars pay particular attention to issues of understanding the religious practices.

It is true that some scholars of the religions have opted exclusively for one or the other of these general approaches. Some would say that the purpose of religious studies is to create materialistic explanations of religion. That is, they would use social scientific methodology to develop theories that explain religious activities just like any other human activities, bringing out the social, psychological, political, economic, and other dynamics that motivate people in their religious practices. On the other hand, some have argued that scholars of religion should simply describe the phenomenon of religion as it actually exists and as it is interpreted by its practitioners, without imposing value judgments or explaining it on the basis of theories taken from the other human sciences.

This scholarly discussion is complex and ongoing. We might observe here that, while both of these approaches can contribute much to our overall understanding of the religions, each approach taken exclusively also has obvious limitations. For example, explaining religion strictly from the outside could lead the scholar to put forth explanations that would be unrecognized and rejected by the practitioners of that religion. But a strict insistence on describing only the meanings and interpretations put forth by practitioners would foreclose the valuable insights that can come from comparative religious studies and from other humanistic disciplines.

However these approaches are evaluated, it is clear that both the outside and the inside perspectives are important for an integral, rich understanding of the religions. In this book we take the stance that, for readers just beginning to explore the religions, the important first step is to get to know the world's religious traditions and the people who live by them. So the emphasis will be on the actual stories, teachings, and practices of the people of each religion, presented as much as possible as understood by the people themselves. Of course, we also make much use of the outside perspective in explaining the historical and social contexts of the religious traditions, in structuring our investigation around particular themes, and in attempting to understand them in the context of our own knowledge and experience.

The Task of Understanding   So our main goal in this exploration is *understanding* the religions. But that is not an easy task. Whereas many of us may have our own religious tradition, none of us belongs to all the religions. Therefore, we necessarily find ourselves in the position of being outside looking in at the intimate practice of someone else. In doing so, we miss the inner compulsion of commitment and the special meaning the religion provides for the practitioner. Furthermore, our view cannot be completely "objective," for our own personal presuppositions and beliefs stand in the way and color our perspective.

It is important, then, that we consciously make a deep effort to understand these religious traditions of others. To "under-stand" is to stand under what gives meaning to the other. It means to stand in her or his religious stance, to look at the universe of religious symbols from the perspective of being on the inside. This is not easy to do, and it is always an incomplete accomplishment. One cannot fully understand Hindu religious experience unless one is a Hindu, and the same is true of Buddhist and Shinto and Christian religious experience, as well as all of the others.

It is possible to understand at least in an incomplete way, however, if a number of important measures are taken. First, an attitude of respect and openness is necessary, a recognition of the value and importance that the religion has for the other person. Second, a conscious effort must be made to become aware of our own presuppositions, since they color our views of the religions of others. By becoming aware of our presuppositions, we can "bracket" them to some extent so they do not hinder us from entering into the worldview of the other religion. Third, it is helpful to refrain, at first, from important critical tasks such as evaluating the truth or appropriateness of religious ideas and practices, or explaining why the people follow such practices. There is a time for engaging in responsible evaluation and explanation. But it seems important first of all to *understand*, and a rush to evaluate and debate truth or to develop explanatory theories can stand in the way of understanding. Fourth, a willingness to learn from the religious experiences of others and to integrate the new information and insights is an important component of the process of understanding.

Understanding does arise from comparison. And so there is also a certain value in being able to look at several religious traditions from the outside, as it were, if this is done sensitively and with understanding. By comparing various elements in different religions, and especially by comparing what is unfamiliar with elements familiar from one's own experience, it is possible to see basic structures of religion more clearly. We can see recurrent questions and concerns about life and death, and we can survey the persistent themes in the responses provided in different religious paths. We can see common practices that give structure to life and society and, thus, develop deeper understanding of the common human needs that give rise to the various religious traditions of humankind. At the same time, seeing what is common sets the stage for reflecting on the unique characteristics of each of the traditions.

Grouping the Religious Traditions   It is a bit bewildering to look at the great variety of religions in the world, past and present. Each tribal group has its own distinctive way of life, which is its religion. And even the highly developed major religious traditions of the world are quite numerous, each with its unique ideas and practices—and there are significant divisions within many of these traditions. So that we do not get lost in the overwhelming variety of ideas,

rituals, and structures found in them, it is helpful to consider some ways of grouping the vast array of religions.

There are various ways of classifying and grouping the religious traditions, based on what we as observers consider significant and helpful. Each classification may well reveal and highlight important dimensions of those particular traditions; at the same time, other significant aspects may be obscured and overlooked. One might approach the religions with an historical scheme, for example, putting emphasis on the continuities and discontinuities as cultures developed over time. Another simple framework would be to locate some religions as indigenous and ethnic, whereas others would be considered cross-cultural or universal. A genetic or family resemblance model is particularly helpful for comparing the religious traditions; one example of this would be putting religious traditions into family groupings depending on whether they emphasize **polytheism**, **monotheism**, or **monism**. Another possible taxonomy would group religious traditions into geographic cultural circles, such as those arising in India, those arising in East Asia, and those arising in the Mediterranean world.

For the purposes of our exploration in this book, we will draw on several such classification schemes as helpful for interpretation and understanding. Our main consideration will be the so-called world religions, those that have impacted beyond local cultures. But we will also give some consideration to the local, tribal, indigenous peoples who exist today (or existed until the recent past) in areas of Africa, Melanesia, Australia, the Americas, and many other places. In the major part of the book, we will follow a geographical framework, focusing on the religious traditions arising in India, those of East Asia, and those arising in the Mediterranean world. We will note how the religions in each of these geographical areas display certain family resemblances even while having their distinctive features.

For example, religions arising in India (South Asia) share a historical development in the first millennium B.C.E. and a set of common perspectives on the world and the path to follow. These religions include the traditions known as Hinduism, Buddhism, and Jainism (Sikhism developed much later but shares some of the same perspectives). These religions tend to have a nondualistic (or monistic) worldview, the idea that somehow behind or within all the multiplicity of forms and forces in this universe there is one unified sacred reality. These religions do have gods that are important, but at a deeper level it is felt that the inner soul of reality or the truth of all reality itself is the sacred ultimate. They agree that human existence is part of the process of *samsara*, that is, birth and death over and over in an endless cycle. According to this perspective, the highest good for humans is to achieve awareness of ultimate truth through practices of meditation or devotion and to find liberation from the cycle of rebirths.

On the other hand, the religious traditions of East Asia, such as those of China and Japan, form a loose family grouping. There are many gods here, in Japanese Shinto and in the Chinese traditions, Daoism and Confucianism, but at the center is an emphasis on harmony with the divine flow of nature and reverence for the ancestors and for family. Within that harmony, human existence in the world is valued as positive and good. Chinese culture and religion have been particularly influential throughout the lands of East Asia. In particular, the Mahayana form of Buddhism has adapted the Buddhist outlook to the East Asian perspective and, thus, plays a unifying role in the cultural grouping that makes up this East Asian family of religions.

The religions of the Mediterranean world arose historically from the context of cosmic, nature-oriented religions of the ancient civilizations (Egypt, Mesopotamia, and Greece). Yet the religious traditions that eventually developed—Zoroastrianism and the three "Abrahamic" religions (Judaism, Christianity, and Islam)—constitute a family of religions whose central perspective is basically monotheistic; that is, they envision one God who created everything. Since there is one God, this God must be almighty and in charge of everything in the created world. The highest good for the creation is to fulfill the will and design of this almighty creator, and to do this, humans need revelation from God through prophets. The three Abrahamic religions have a particularly close historical relationship, arising successively from the same Semitic society of the Near East, each tracing its roots in some manner to the ancestor Abraham.

We must keep in mind that any scheme such as this can only suggest the main historical and cultural connections within the different groupings of religions. It is also true that different perspectives can be found in the same religious tradition in varying degrees. Nondualistic Hindus, for example, know a great deal about worshiping the great God who created and sustains everything, with teachings and practices that resemble monotheism. Islam, for all its

fierce monotheism, has long harbored the Sufi mystical movement, which has cultivated language that sounds much like the Hindu and Buddhist nondualist thinkers.

SOME DIMENSIONS OF RELIGIOUS EXPERIENCE

The word *religion*, of course, has a variety of meanings as it is used in the modern world. Although one might hear the question, "Do you have religion?," there is no "religion in general" but only very many practices and beliefs that have been included, at one time or another, under our term *religion*. The modern term *religion* in Western languages is based on the Latin *religio*, probably meaning a "bond" linking worshipers of a god together. In Western history the term has been associated with ideas of worshiping God or gods as well as associated beliefs, rituals, moral prescriptions, social groupings, and so on. Over the past several centuries a great many scholars have attempted to create definitions of religion that can include spiritual practices of all cultures around the world and at the same time bring out that which is distinctively common to all these practices. Since these definitions come from many perspectives—theological, philosophical, sociological, anthropological, psychological, and many more—they are widely divergent and serve to expand our sense of the possible meanings of religion. The interested reader can pursue this topic by consulting some of the many books that discuss theories and definitions of religion.[1]

For our purposes, it is important to start with an understanding of religion that is broad enough to include all cultures of the world but at the same time narrow enough to give focus and direction to our exploration. Drawing on several scholarly definitions, here is a working description of some key dimensions of religion:

1. Religion is human involvement with what is considered to be the realm of the sacred.

2. It is expressed in thought, action, and social forms.

3. It constitutes a total system of symbols with deep meaning.

4. It is a path of ultimate transformation.

Human Involvement with the Realm of the Sacred
The first part of the definition of religion suggests a relationship between two levels of experience: the limited human level and the level of that which is felt to be the sacred. Of course, we cannot examine the sacred as if it was an objective realm of reality, something to be proved or disproved. Here we are not attempting to define ultimate reality as an objective fact; we are simply exploring how people of different cultures have described their experiences of whatever it is that they consider the ultimate sacred. We see that it is the common experience of many peoples past and present that there is a sacred dimension of reality with ultimate significance, and, furthermore, that the highest good in human life has to do with relating to that dimension.

Although the idea of the sacred is distinctive in each particular religious tradition, we may perhaps discern some general outlines that resonate across religious boundaries. After all, if there are any common human life experiences throughout the different cultures of the world, we should expect some general similarities in the way people describe their experiences of what they consider to be the sacred. One suggestive perspective comes from Rudolph Otto, who studied various types of religious experience and put forth the view that basic to religious experience is a deep sense of the "numinous."[2] This is a term he coined from the Latin *numen* ("holy, sacred") to express our basic response to experiencing the sacred even before we develop rational and moral notions about it. Experiencing the numinous as ultimate mystery, people feel a strong sense of awe and reverence, at the same time being fascinated and drawn to the mysterious Other.

Drawing on Otto's suggestion, let us make some observations about experiencing the sacred. First of all, bound up with the numinous is an unlimited, primordial, overpowering quality. The sacred is ultimate, the basis of everything else, and nothing can supersede or encompass it. It accounts for everything, and it holds everything together—but it is its own basis without depending on anything else. The sacred, whether expressed as God (Islam), Brahman (Hinduism), emptiness (Mahayana Buddhism), or some other formulation, is felt to be the universal foundation of all truth, reality, goodness, and value.

We encounter the sacred as Mystery, as the Wholly Other that remains completely "other" even when experi-

Experience of the sacred takes countless forms in the religions of the world. Here a Hindu man prepares a religious offering.

enced within the human world. It cannot be completely held by humans, either with their hands or with their reason. Words can attempt to describe the sacred, but it is understood that words can only point to the mystery in a symbolic way. Every word refers to a conditioned human reality, but the sacred both encompasses and transcends human realities. For this reason, people express the experience of the sacred not only by words but also by a variety of other symbolic forms, such as sculpture, ritual actions, meditation, music, dance, silence, and so forth. On the Jewish festival of Simhat Torah, for example, dancing with the

Torah scrolls provides a deep experience of the sacred, more than words can say. Bathing in "Mother Ganges" provides a direct, nonverbal sacred experience for Hindus. After the reception of the Eucharist in a Christian church, a moment of silence is often the most appropriate way of responding to the mystery. The stillness of Buddhist meditation brings one into direct touch with the ultimate truth in a way that words can never do.

Experience of the sacred is accompanied with awe and reverence. The sacred cannot be controlled by human design; it bursts the bounds of human understanding and overwhelms with energy and demand. The human response is awe, respect, and submission. For Muslims, for example, washing the body and prostrating oneself in prayer expresses the proper human relationship to the sacred. Rudolph Otto called this quality of the sacred the *mysterium tremendum* (terrifying mystery). For the ancient Israelites, the mountain of Sinai was the awesome presence of the sacred; touching it could mean destruction. The image of a god or goddess in the Hindu tradition is full of power, so that one should not, for example, take pictures of it.

Experience of the sacred at the same time involves fascination and love; we are compelled and drawn to the ultimate origin of all that is good and true and beautiful, the source of meaning and purpose in life, the fountain of vitality and strength. The sacred is wondrous, marvelous, and compelling. Encounter with the sacred leads to the highest joy, rapture, and love. Buddhists who have experienced awakening describe it as ultimate bliss and rapture. The Muslim pilgrim is drawn to Mecca and to the experience of the sacred there as by a powerful magnet. The Hindu worshiper lovingly performs *puja* to the image of the beloved god or goddess. A Christian writer, Augustine, said that the soul is restless until it finds rest in God.

Since the sacred is the source of ultimate value, the deepest need of human life is to have an ongoing relationship with the sacred. It is this need that is met in the various religious traditions of humankind. Each religious path, in its own way, provides the context so that the human community can experience the presence of the sacred, with the power, value structures, meaning, and purpose that fulfill the religious needs of human beings.

Expression in Thought, Action, and Social Forms The second part of our description of religion suggests what goes into the making of that human involvement with the sacred. Since religion is, obviously, a human affair, it necessarily involves human forms or modes of expression. Joachim Wach[3] suggests there are three such modes of expression: theoretical (thinking, speaking), practical (doing, acting), and social (fellowship, community). These are the building blocks of religious expression, and they fit together to form a complex, unique universe of meaning, that is, a **religious tradition**.

The *theoretical* mode of expression comprises the verbal aspect of religion, what is told and described. The religious path sets forth a way of thinking about the most important, basic issues of life: how the sacred is experienced, where the world came from and where it is going, what the goal of human life is, and how we can achieve that goal. These things are talked about in two basic ways: narrative or story (myth) and theoretical statements about reality (doctrine). All religious traditions have stories or myths that put forth in narrative form the worldview and the important experiences of the sacred on which that religion is founded. Leading thinkers also express their basic perceptions in teachings or doctrines that generalize from the sacred stories to present the fundamental truths that they believe, providing intellectual guidance to the participants in that religious path.

The *practical* level of expression in religion has to do with its visible and performed side: **rituals, worship, ethics,** and so forth. Religion is not just mental but also physical, and the acting out, the performance, of the involvement with the sacred is just as important as the stories and the doctrines. Prostrating oneself before the sacred presence, going on pilgrimages, sharing in a sacred meal, chanting texts and prayers, sitting in meditation, wearing colorful robes, burning incense, observing moral rules, and hundreds of other religious rituals and types of behavior represent the acting out or performance of the religious experience.

Religion is never simply an individual affair but always is a group or communal experience involving *social forms*. It is the religious community that carries on the tradition, even before the individual was born and after he or she dies. And it is in identifying with the religious community that the individual finds personal identity. There are different structures of community depending on the type of religious experience, in family or clan, congregations, religious societies, and whole nations. And there are various types of religious leaders, such as queens, kings, priests, priestesses, sages, prophets, masters, nuns, monks, shamans, and many more. Participation in the social forms of the religious community is what gives continuity of religious experience.

A Total System of Symbols   Taken together, these modes of religious expression form a total worldview, a "map" of human involvement with the sacred, and this brings us to the third part of our definition. Religion guides and gives meaning by presenting a view of the whole order of existence. This religious map of human existence is made up of symbols—words, ideas, rituals, pictures, gestures, sounds, social groupings—that evoke the deepest feelings and most important meanings in our lives. These are the means by which a group of people expresses their perception of what life is all about. To live as part of this community is to share a whole way of knowing the world and one's place in it, a whole way of looking at life and death, and a whole set of assumptions about what is real and true and good. The system of symbols upholds deep-seated attitudes and motivations, providing a complete system of values for human life.

Let us consider a few examples of such symbols. In a Buddhist monastery, an ordinary bowl for food becomes a "begging bowl," an important symbol of the spiritual status of the monk or nun on the path toward the ultimate goal of all people in the community. A rooster and a dove are two very common animals, but used by a priest in a Daoist ritual they embody the operational forces of yin and yang and create the balance of sacred power necessary for the well-being of the human community. Common words can be powerful symbols. The words *blood* and *lamb* have ordinary straightforward meanings; but for a Christian to say "The blood of the Lamb has saved me" arouses deep religious feelings and meaning. Normal human activities often give rise to important symbolic meanings. For example, the act of eating a meal is one of the most common human activities and is often done without any particularly deep meaning. But a Jew sitting at the table celebrating the Passover seder with her family experiences deep religious meaning in that human activity. Similarly, washing oneself is an everyday human activity, but all religions have rituals that express sacred meaning in washing, such as baptism, bathing in a sacred river, or purifying oneself with water before entering a shrine.

We can envision the worldview of each religious tradition as a circle with a center. The circle suggests the totality of what the people understand as their existence in the world. It contains their universe of symbols that provides the pattern of life that is their religious path. Within the circle, then, we see the most important symbols of that religion. The meanings these symbols supply have been told in stories, painted and sculpted in art, sung and played by musicians, expressed in poems and dramas, acted out in rituals and worship, and argued and systematized by theologians and philosophers for centuries.

The various symbols fit together in a circle, for they are all related to each other in such a way as to present a comprehensive and persuasive outlook on life. Above all, the circle of symbols is centered—that is, there is a *central vision* that colors and permeates the whole circle in a pervasive way. We might suggest, for example, that for Muslims the center is the Holy Book, the Quran, whereas for Christians it is Christ. Buddhism centers on the path to nirvana, whereas the center for Shinto is the exhaustless life of the kami. Many Chinese would put the Dao at the center of their universe of symbols; other Chinese might center their world more on ancestors and family. The symbols closest to the center could be considered the *primary symbols*, those that are most essential to those of that religious path. Toward the outside of the circle appear somewhat more *secondary symbols*, those that are more inclined to change when new experiences and challenges arise, those that respond to the needs of the religious communities in different times and places. Of course, people do not always agree on whether a particular symbol is primary or secondary; diverse religious experiences lead to different emphases even within one religious tradition.

We should, therefore, keep in mind that a religious tradition is not a static, unchanging affair but rather a living, dynamic organism. Changes and transformations do occur in response to new experiences, new stories, and new challenges. Sometimes what appeared to be a primary symbol to some at one time becomes less important in later ages, whereas a secondary symbol introduced by some new religious experience shifts into a primary position. For example, Indra was one of the most powerful gods for the ancient Aryans, but he shifts to a rather small role in later Hinduism. On the other hand, Vishnu was a minor god for the Aryans, but he rose dramatically to become one of the great gods in Hinduism. For traditional Jews, the idea of bodily resurrection after death was at one time a primary symbol, but in recent times it has faded to secondary importance for some modern Jewish thinkers.

On the other hand, the Land of Israel, which was simply a spiritual idea during the medieval period, has become for many modern Jews a very primary symbol in concrete form. In spite of changes in the circle of symbols, however, there is an ongoing basic continuity, flowing outward from the central vision and maintaining the fundamental pattern of faith and life.

As we look at the issues of human life and focus on specific symbols from the religions, we must keep in mind that a particular symbol must always be viewed in its total context. Some of the symbols will, of course, appear quite similar in a family of religions, and rightly so, given the shared history and culture. The word *Dao* ("way"), for example, is used by all three religious traditions in China—Confucianist, Daoist, and Buddhist traditions—but with significant differences of meaning. Our task is to see each symbol—each teaching, idea, story, ritual, practice, or community structure—in the light that is reflected from the central vision and from the total pattern of that particular system of symbols.

A Path of Ultimate Transformation   The fourth part of our definition points out that a religious tradition is not only a system of beliefs and expressions about the relation to the sacred; it is above all a path, a way of life. Each religious tradition offers something that many humans find essential to human existence: a **path of transformation**, a path to ultimate meaning.

An important part of religious experience, it appears, is the realization of the defective or fractured nature of human involvement with the sacred, for from this arise the fundamental troubles and anxieties of existence. This awareness of the human problem is coupled with knowledge of the ideal, ultimate relationship to the sacred. One's religious practice provides a way of overcoming this fracture, of restoring the bridge to the sacred, of transforming oneself to attain the goal of life as expressed in that particular religious tradition. The path continues throughout one's lifetime, through rituals, symbols, disciplines, study, social relationships, and states of consciousness. Buddhists, for example, follow the Eightfold Path toward the ultimate attainment of nirvana. Christians follow the path of Christ to overcome sin and attain eternal life. For Hindus, the paths of action, worship, and knowledge lead toward spiritual realization and liberation from the cycle of birth and death.

Following the life of Torah for Jews is the path toward spiritual perfection. The path is a way of life, a praxis designed to restore wholeness and ultimate meaning to human existence by involvement with the source of life, the sacred.

BASIC HUMAN CONCERNS AND RELIGIOUS RESPONSES

To help in our exploration of the various religious traditions, our ground plan in this book is to take up a number of common questions and concerns about human existence and use them as windows into the fundamental views and practices of the people in each religious tradition. The goal is not to produce a synthesis of answers from all these religions, for each is unique and distinctive. We must attempt not to impose outside ideas but rather to be sensitive to the way people of each religion frame their own concerns and responses. Still, if done judiciously, looking at common human questions provides opportunities to compare the religions while seeing clearly the unique characteristics of each.

Here are some main questions and religious responses to think about as we find our way into the basic dimensions of religion. The questions and responses fall into three general areas.

1. **Sacred Story.** The important question of identity—who are we?—finds an answer especially in the **sacred stories** of each religious path, as those stories originated and were passed on through various historical dynamics to the present community.

2. **Worlds of Meaning.** Questions of meaning and understanding are answered in the main theoretical teachings of the religious tradition. What's it all about? What sense is there in life? How can we start living real life? The answers point to teachings about the sacred reality, world origins and human existence, and the path of transformation.

3. **Ritual Practices and the Good Life.** Some questions relate to practical and social aspects of life: How can we find new power for life? How should we live? The answers point to ritual and worship, on the one hand, and to communal life and ethics, on the other.

It will be helpful to explore these questions and responses in a preliminary way, drawing on examples from across the religious traditions, in order to set the stage for our look at each of the religions in the following chapters.

Sacred Story and Historical Context

One basic human concern is the question of identity: Who are we? Who am I? When a person tries to answer that question, she starts by telling the story of her life. Although there are many parts of her life story she might emphasize, one important aspect would be her religious identity: "I'm Hindu." "My family has always been Buddhist." "I can't imagine not being a Christian." "Of course, I'm Muslim." But what does that mean? It means that a person connects his or her own story with the sacred story, the master story, of his or her religious tradition—especially with those crucial events or realities of the founding of the tradition. To express his identity as a Buddhist, a person tells the story of the Buddha and the founding of Buddhism. To renew her Christian identity, a person looks to the sacred story of Christ, for that is the story—the master story—with which her own life story connects. To be a Sikh means to tie one's own life story into the master story of the Gurus who founded Sikhism. The story of the founding or the revealing of the religious path is of particular concern because it provides the divine authority for one's religious identity. In this study of the religions we devote considerable attention to the master story and also the historical changes and transformations that shaped each religion.

Myth and Sacred Story All religious traditions have master stories telling of decisive events and leaders through which the new truths and practices were inaugurated as the basis of the new way of life. These birth-giving events and leaders are told about in their stories, written about in their scriptures, sung about in their songs, depicted in their art, and remembered in their rituals. They form the central focus, the paradigm, by which the people express their religious identity.

These sacred stories, or **myths**, have a very important function in religion, for they establish the basic outlook and the way of life of the people of that religion. They tell of the central encounters of the people with the sacred, those clear episodes that illumine all aspects of life. Thus, these stories, even though they may seem in some cases to refer to distant mythological ages, are understood to be real and true, for they reveal the bridge to the sacred that is essential for human existence. Although they are presented in story form, they provide a kind of map for human life, a model that can be followed so life can be lived in the fullest way according to the design established by the sacred power. Knowing these stories means the people know how human life is to be lived in a meaningful way; not knowing the stories or forgetting them would be to live a chaotic, subhuman existence.

But knowing and remembering the sacred story are not just intellectual exercises. To perform the stories—repeating them in words and acting them out in rituals—is actually to become participants in the founding events. It is to reactualize the central happenings so they become real and powerful in human life today just as they were in the special time told about in the sacred stories.

In sum, the story provides an answer to the question of identity by making it possible to identify with those events and beings that exemplify in a clear and powerful way the relationship with the sacred that undergirds human life. The master stories may be about human sages and leaders who founded the religious path, or they may be about gods and heroes in mythological ages—or both. But in all cases the stories tell about the beginnings, the origins, of the real, authentic way of human life. And, thus, they tell us who we really are.

Some of the religions are "founded" religions in the sense that their sacred history points to specific persons who had a role in the religion's origins. Buddhism, Jainism, Sikhism, Zoroastrianism, Judaism, Christianity, and Islam may be cited as examples, though the view of the founders may be quite different among these traditions. Since these religions focus on founders who lived in a particular age amid crucial events of human history, the stories tend to dwell more on actual historical events and human personalities than do the stories of religions that do not have central founding events and leaders.

Peoples of indigenous, tribal societies, even though they often do not remember a particular "founder," have their myths about the sacred beings and ancestors of the "time of the beginnings" who performed the crucial actions to create life the way it is. These myths are repeated in festivals so the power and vitality they tell about can become real once more for the people. Also, religious traditions such as Hinduism and Shinto, even though they have no particular founding events or leaders, have their stories about the gods and the cultural heroes, stories that provide the foundation of the authentic way of life.

In presenting and interpreting the stories of these communities, we rely on scholarly work that has clarified the origins and early history of each of the religions, providing a historical context for the stories. It is also our intention, however, to see each story as it is told and interpreted by that religious community. We are, after all, not dealing with history strictly speaking but with sacred history. And that sacred history is expressed not by archaeological finds or history books but in the stories told in the worshiping communities.

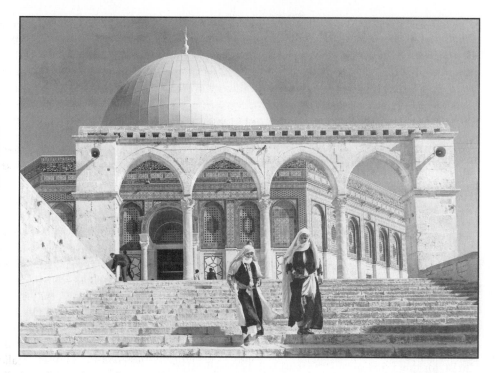

According to the Muslim story, the Dome of the Rock in Jerusalem marks the spot from which Muhammad was taken on a journey to heaven. The mosque stands above the foundation of the Jewish temple, which Christians also consider a holy place.

Change and Transformation in the Religious Tradition

The history of the religious tradition does not end with the sacred stories of the beginnings. Each religion is a living organism that changes and develops in new situations and experiences. Understanding this dynamic quality of religious tradition is important, for it is the "passing on" (*traditio*) of the story through many generations of people that finally shapes the religious identity of present-day followers of the path. They receive and interact with the story through the tradition that has brought it to them.

For example, one cannot understand Buddhism in the world today without taking some account of the Mahayana perspectives and also the various developments in Southeast Asia and in East Asia. Judaism has been transformed by the teachings of the rabbis, the medieval persecutions, the emancipation, and most recently the experience of the Holocaust. To understand modern Christianity one must take into account the transformations brought about, for example, by the establishment of Christianity as the religion of the Roman Empire, the medieval synthesis of doctrine and life, and the Reformation and the Counter-Reformation. And it would be most difficult to understand Chinese religion without considering the rise of Daoism, the development of the state cult of Confucius, the importation of Buddhism, and so forth. So it is with each religious tradition. Although in this book we cannot focus extensively on the historical developments of each religious tradition, it is important to become aware of the major transformations and the effect they have had on the understanding and practice of that tradition.

Our modern era in particular has been a time of drastic challenges and far-reaching transformations for many of the world's religions. The rise of science has brought forth questions about traditional religious worldviews, scriptures, and long-accepted teachings. Political and economic turmoils often have caught religious communities up in divisive power struggles or pushed them toward nationalism or revivalism. Immigrations and population shifts have resulted in many people living as religious minorities in diaspora situations, where traditional religious supports are limited. Most people have become much more aware of religious pluralism, and religious communities are struggling with the challenge of living together with people of many faiths. And so, as we look at each religious tradition, we will pay attention to their responses to the challenges of the modern world.

Worlds of Meaning: Theoretical Teachings

Sacred Reality   What's it *all* about? Confronted with the maze of human life in a mind-boggling universe, we wonder how we can make sense of everything that is. How does it all hold together? The answer presented in each religious tradition, in its own distinctive way, is what we call *the sacred*, the ground of all, the ultimate reality. Each tradition has appropriate terms to point to this ultimate reality: God, Goddess, Brahman, nirvana, Dharma, Dharmakaya, Dao, Heaven, and many more. Without such a vision of sacred reality, religious people feel there would be no center, no order, only a chaos of things and events occurring haphazardly without rhyme or reason. And so since the beginning of human life on this planet, people have always sought after sacred reality as the source and support for this world and human existence within it.

What are some of the ways people think about the sacred? Some people, especially in the ancient world and among indigenous peoples of today, have understood the sacred to be experienced in numerous forms and powers. Some speak of an impersonal sacred power that penetrates and interacts with everything. Wherever we turn, in nature and in society, we encounter Power. Often the sacred is personified as gods and spirits, who are immanent in the various aspects of the world: One god shows power in the rain and storm, another in the healing and creating power of the sun, another in pregnancy and childbirth, and so forth. This view, often called *polytheism*, means power is shared, with no one sacred being having unlimited sway. Many of these religions do have a supreme god who is the primordial creator and has ultimate authority, but this god delegates the functions of the world to other gods and goddesses. This general vision of the sacred can also be found to be widespread in Asia, within the Hindu, Buddhist, Daoist, and Shinto traditions. It is generally understood, of course, that such divine beings are not ultimate in power or status.

Another general view of the sacred is *monotheism*, the view that there is one sacred reality, a personal God who created and supports this world and everything in it, with no alternates, no competitors. There is one God and one world, the creation. However, God is not a part of this world. God is transcendent, that is, above and beyond the created world, holy and eternal. At the same time God is present in a personal way to the created world. God encounters us especially in historical events, giving us guidance and challenging us to fulfill the divine will. The three Abrahamic religious traditions are strong advocates of this perspective on the sacred, but it can be found in modified forms in Zoroastrianism, Sikhism, and even special Hindu and Buddhist groups.

Still another conception of the sacred is sometimes called *nondualism* or *monism*, a broad category of thought and experience with an emphasis placed on the unity of all reality. **Nondualism** means that there is no real difference between the ultimate reality and the phenomenal world. **Monism** is the view that all reality is one unified divine reality. There may still be many personal gods, but they may be understood, for example, as facets of the one sacred reality, or as beings on a higher level of the rebirth cycle. Within these traditions, it may be emphasized that the sacred is our inner true self; it may be the suchness of reality; it may be the state of ultimate consciousness; it may be the principle that is found in all reality. This kind of perspective on the sacred ultimate is present in some forms of the Hindu, Buddhist, Daoist, and Neo-Confucianist traditions. Tendencies toward monism can also be found in certain mystical movements in Judaism, Christianity, and Islam, as well as in some philosophical thinkers in the Western tradition, such as Plotinus, Spinoza, and Hegel.

So the sacred can be experienced as many in nature, or one beyond nature, or one and many both in and beyond nature, and more. Depending on which vision is dominant, the religious path to the sacred has distinctive features in each particular religion. The crucial question is, how do we encounter the sacred? Is the sacred found in the forces of nature and society? Is the sacred encountered in history and events? Is the sacred met within as one's real self? Is the sacred experienced as a personal being or as impersonal reality? Is the sacred known as the ultimate truth of reality?

In each of the religions, people have opted for a particular vision of the sacred and, thus, each has a distinctive religious path. Yet people in each religion often explore the other possible perspectives as well in order to add depth to their own vision and experience.

Of course, religious perceptions change over time, and the modern secular worldview has influenced the view of the sacred in most religious communities. In ancient times it was a common assumption of almost all peoples that this world and human life are supported by divine power or powers, although various peoples differed in their conception of the divine realm. In modern times, however, far-reaching questions have been raised in people's minds about the traditional beliefs concerning the sacred. As science and technology have developed all around the globe, notions of sacred reality have gradually been eased out of the picture. We live our lives in a very secular way, that is, without paying attention to the sacred in most aspects of our existence. Is there really a God who controls all events? Do Vishnu and Shiva actually have power in the world? Is nirvana real? Is it true there is an underlying principle of all reality? Questions about God have bothered Jews and Christians ever since the Enlightenment, but today people of all religions are facing the challenges that modernity and secularity pose for the traditional concepts of the sacred.

In spite of these developments, adherents of the religions still find meaning in the depth dimension of the sacred. There are, of course, questions and problems that have to be dealt with, and modern people cannot easily go back to conceptions of sacred reality as a heavenly grandfather who watches lovingly over all his children, for example, or as gods, goddesses, and demons who cause all good and bad things to happen. Yet it is the experience of many people of the different religions today that a sense of the sacred still is essential and can be retrieved in the tradition and practice of their religious path. How can we find again a way to experience the sacred present and powerful in our lives? Take up the path and see, they would answer.

World Origins and Human Existence   What sense is there in life? And why are we here? Why is there so much evil and suffering in the world? Questions such as these are at the heart of all religious experience, for they pertain to the deepest needs of human life—the need to understand our own existence within the world and society, the need to feel a purpose or destiny, and the need to integrate evil and death into our view of life without despairing.

The religious traditions deal with questions like these especially in their **cosmogonic** stories, that is, their stories about the creation and maintenance of the world and of humans within it. For it is in knowing the origins of the world that we know its real essence and character.

In the creation stories of the peoples of the world, the origin of the world is attributed to many causes. Often a variety of gods and divine helpers create the world, remaining as ongoing powers within the world. Sometimes the creation of the world is seen as a battle between the various divine forces, and humans get caught up in the conflict. The monotheistic religions insist that the entire creation results from the one creator God. Again, especially among the religions of India, the origin and the operation of the world may be viewed as an eternal recurring process, like waves on an ocean, emanating from the sacred reality.

The cosmogonic myths or stories telling of origins also provide important views about the nature of the world and the role of humans within it. Some of the ancient peoples and indigenous peoples teach that the world is controlled by many divine forces, expressing their wills in the functioning of nature; therefore, the most important role of humans is to serve and propitiate these gods. People of the Abrahamic religions teach that because there is one God, the creator and preserver of all things, this world makes sense as a good and purposeful creation. And humans are to assist God to care for this world, fulfilling God's design. Other, such as Hindus and Buddhists, teach that the world as we experience it is somewhat illusory and passing. The most important thing for humans to do is to get in touch with that which is ultimate rather than the changing and transitory world. Again, it is sometimes taught, as in the Chinese religions and in Hinduism, that there is a universal world order or harmony into which everything fits, and humans do best by living their lives according to this order.

It seems that all religions have some view of human failure and imperfection. This follows from their vision of what the ideal is. The ideal human existence is sometimes expressed in creation stories, in descriptions of the origins of the world and of humans. There was an age of innocence, for example, a paradisiacal state when people lived peacefully and in harmony. The original human state is looked to as a kind of standard of what we ought to be. And juxtaposed to that is the realistic view of how things actually are: fractured and estranged because of human imperfection and failure. Of course, the extent to which we are thought to be alienated from the good, ideal state differs in the various religions. But it is commonly accepted that humans are not what they can or ought to be. Naturally, much evil happens without our choice. But in our experience we know that people sometimes do things that are destructive and violent. In our own lives we recognize that we sometimes do things that are hateful and ugly, and we fail to do the things we ought to do—why? There is a big shadow of failure and imperfection cast over human existence.

The religious traditions of the world give differing reasons for human failure and evil. Some African tribal religions, for example, have myths of origin in which the first humans live in a paradisiacal state with the supreme god, represented by the heavens, close to them on earth. Because of some fault in the humans—such as being too greedy for food—the supreme god moves far away, with the result that human life becomes full of pain, death, and evil. The three Abrahamic religions teach that God, although making humans as the crown of creation, also gave them of all creatures a dimension of freedom. And within that freedom comes the possibility and the reality of rebellion, unbelief, and fracturing of the loving relationship with God.

Another way of looking at the human problem is found in the Hindu and Buddhist traditions, where human existence is often seen as a kind of trap. Because of the fire of desire that leads us to cling to false ideas of self, we are trapped in an infinite cycle of material existences full of pain and suffering. We cling to the sensual ego-centered illusions, and by doing so we fall under the causal law of karma: We reap exactly what we sow, experiencing the fruits of our clinging actions. The general view among Confucianists, Daoists, and Shintoists is that the highest human good is to be in harmony with the universal order of the cosmos and the flow of sacred powers of the world. When we act in ways to cause disharmony, whether in society or in nature, we experience the resulting fractures and discords as evil and suffering.

Sometimes the problem is put in the form of a question: Is human nature fundamentally good or evil? If human nature is evil through and through, then what else can we expect except violence and destructive behavior any time that humans are free to act unchecked? But some would say that humans are basically good and peaceful by nature. Then the violence and evil must be the result of other forces, such as possession by evil spirits, the corrupting influence of society, or oppression by tyrants. Or human evil may arise from our human tendency to forgetfulness and ignorance.

Is human nature fundamentally good or evil? To put the question thus is certainly an oversimplification, for most religious thinkers emphasize human moral responsibility. Somehow humans must be free to make their own choices in decisions of behavior, or they would not be responsible for anything they do. The realities of human existence lead most people to conclude that there is within us a struggle concerning choices about good and evil. Outside forces perhaps influence us; perhaps there are inner inclinations toward good or evil. But finally—in the view of most religious teachers—the choice is authored by the person herself or himself, who bears the final responsibility for it.

What this unsettling state of imperfection, ignorance, struggle, discord, or sin does, when realized against the standard of sacred design and law for human existence, is to impel us toward some change: repentance, seeking help from sacred powers, following a new path to transform our incomplete human existence.

The Path of Transformation and Wholeness   How can we start living real life? Where are meaning and peace to be found? How can we be healed? Questions such as these arise when we come face to face with the existence of failure, imperfection, and evil in our lives, knowing at the same time that this is not the way things should be. These are questions about the possibility of **transformation**. Many different terms are used in the various religions: salvation, liberation, enlightenment, purification, healing, perfection, and more. This religious transformation in all religious paths means wholeness and rightness—a transformation away from the fragmentation, alienation, sin, and ignorance we feel in our lives, a movement toward peace, health, wholeness, and perfection. Transformation as taught in a particular religious tradition responds to the way in which the human problem is understood and experienced. For example, sin must be transformed by forgiveness, pollution by purification, ignorance by knowledge, fracture by healing, and wandering by guidance on the straight path. All religions offer some means by which such transformation can be possible.

Functioning as a means of transformation, a religious path provides methods of interaction with the realm of the sacred. This is the ultimate source of life and meaning, and the basic human problem arises when this source is cut off for one reason or another. The first need is for some kind of restoration of this contact so that sacred power can transform life.

Although people of all religions agree that it is the power of the sacred that transforms humans, there are different visions as to how this power arises and operates in restoring the relationship. People in some religions emphasize human depravity and helplessness; in this view, all power and salvation must come from a source outside oneself. A good example of such an approach is Japanese Pure Land Buddhism, which stresses the notion of complete human degeneracy and helplessness in this "age of the end of the Buddhist law." This means that the only hope for humans to escape an endless series of rebirths in the suffering realms is to rely totally on help from the compassionate Buddha, Amida. On the other hand, some religious teachers emphasize an approach to the means of transformation that relies on power within oneself. Also in Japanese Buddhism, Zen adherents say there is no need to look to Amida Buddha for help or salvation. Each person has the transcendent Buddha nature in herself or himself, and through the practice of meditation each person can awaken to that Buddha reality and reach enlightenment.

These two opposite extremes are from the same religious tradition, namely, Japanese Buddhism. This would suggest that even within one religion we might expect to find both the "outside power" and the "self power" emphases. And this is the case. In Hinduism, for example, one finds both a tradition of worshiping the gods in reliance on their grace, and also a tradition of passing beyond the gods to pure realization of the sacred through discipline and meditation. It is true that people of some religions, such as Christianity, speak more about "grace" (outside power); and people of other religions, such as Islam, place more emphasis on human responsibility for action (self power). But the relation to the sacred is always a two-way relation. Even if salvation comes totally from the sacred power, still humans receive it and live it out in human religious structures. And even if the whole emphasis seems to be on one's

own power in terms of performing disciplines, still these disciplines draw on deep sources of sacred power. One of the distinctive characteristics of each religious tradition, in fact, is its particular vision of the interaction between human practice and sacred gift.

The means of transformation or salvation that a religious tradition offers will involve all three levels of human expression: theoretical, practical, and social. On the theoretical level, the myths and doctrines are to be understood and accepted by faith and/or reason, so that the person's whole outlook on life can be transformed. On the practical level, ritual, discipline, and practice are means of transformation. Such activities would include praying, baptism, acts of repentance, sitting in meditation, studying, keeping rules of purity, acts of self-discipline, and the like. Means of transformation on the social level would include participating in social structures such as families, congregations, sacred peoples, priesthoods, monasteries, and the like, so that the new way of life can be lived fully as a lifelong practice.

Together, these various means of transformation make up a path to follow. This path of transformation is a dynamic process that goes on throughout life in greater and smaller rhythms. It continually involves a double movement: a distancing and separating from the situation that is fractured and wrong, and a restoration and renewal of the state of wholeness and harmony with the sacred. The movement of separation includes acts such as repentance, vows of abstinence, withdrawal of thoughts from outer things, and rituals of washing and purifying oneself. The movement of restoration and renewal comes through acts such as retelling sacred revelation, feelings of ecstasy in worshiping one's god, receiving assurance of forgiveness, and awakening the mind in enlightenment.

Furthermore, the path of transformation is both a means and an end in itself. As a means it is a praxis, a method of moving toward a goal: transformation or salvation, restoration of the relationship with the sacred. In one sense, that goal is never fully reached within human life, for the problems of human failure and sin remain until death. For that reason many religious traditions have ideas of the future human state in which the ideal goal is perfectly and completely consummated. There may be some model person who achieves that goal now, such as a savior, saint, prophet, samnyasin, buddha, arhat, or jina. But for the rest

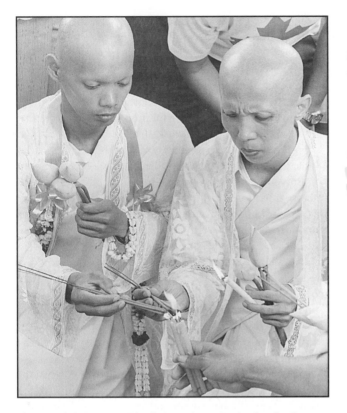

Thai men light incense sticks during solemn rituals of ordination as Buddhist monks.

of us, the path is a means toward a goal of transformation that will be a complete, perfect reality only in a transcendent state or a world or lifetime to come.

However, seen from another point of view, the path of transformation is itself the experience of transformation. There is an "already, even though not yet" quality to the experience in following the path. The path is itself the means we have of experiencing contact with the sacred. Zen Buddhists express this most strikingly. Master Dogen insisted that practice (sitting in meditation) and enlightenment (experiencing the Buddha nature) are the same thing, with no difference at all. Other religious teachers would perhaps not identify the path so closely with the transformation it brings. But all would agree that following the path is not just a means to reward in another state or world to come; the goal of transformation is already at least partially present right now as we follow the path.

Ritual Practices and the Good Life

Religion by its very nature is practical and social. Theoretical teachings about the sacred and about life need to be lived, not just believed. And the path provides a structure of life within a religious community. It is never just an individual affair but always involves the person in a larger community of people going on that religious path. The religious community provides daily life with a structure including both **sacred time** and sacred life. That is, the ordinary time of one's existence is punctuated by special times of ritual and festival. And the ordinary living of one's daily existence becomes the arena of the good life in fulfillment of the sacred design for the whole community.

Making Time Sacred Through Ritual, Worship, and Art

Where can we find new power for life? How can we feel more in touch with what is real? These questions and many more like them have to do with our need regularly to renew the meaning and purpose of our lives, day by day, year by year, in family and in community, through ritual, devotion, and worship.

Mircea Eliade[4] has suggested that, looked at in a completely profane or secular way, human life would be a self-contained, closed system with intervention by sacred power logically excluded. There would be no "breaks" to the sacred, no special or strong (sacred) times that can provide centers of meaning and, thus, give structure and order to life.

Since humans cannot tolerate such a meaningless chaos of existing, we seek out special or strong times. In traditional religious contexts, these are the sacred celebrations, the festivals, holy days, and rituals that periodically punctuate and renew the ordinary day-by-day passage of our existence. Even modern, secularized people who have little use for traditional religious rituals have not transcended the need to have sacred times. Breaks in time, centers of meaning and renewal, are widely sought after in such forms as vacations, national holidays, parties, sports, entertainment, and the like. The purpose of such sacred times is "re-creation," that is, the renewal and enlivening of our otherwise humdrum routine of existing.

Religious communities have found that the power that motivates life needs constantly to be renewed. Life-power tends to run down, to become exhausted and weak. There is need regularly to move into sacred time, the time in which the realities of the sacred story are experienced as new and present once again. Ordinary time is transcended, and the people of now become contemporary with the gods and the founders and heroes of the Beginning Time. The rituals and festivals provide a rhythm of periodic renewal.

Rituals and festivals are also sources of orientation for life, centers around which all else makes sense. They establish a pattern of living, derived from the sacred story, that can extend out and sanctify the ordinary hours and days of existing. They make real again the identity shared by the community and the incorporation of the individual within it.

Ritual worship connects the sacred with the common elements of human life. Fundamental to religious ritual is the sense of sacred presence in the most vital areas of human experience: eating, sexuality, birth, death, work, play, family, community, water, earth, sun, and so forth. The materials for ritual celebration stem from these basic elements of the human context. A meal is a most universal form of religious ritual, for example. So also is washing by water, or burying in the earth, or dancing and singing, or offering products of one's labor—the list of religious rituals is as long and diverse as the vital aspects of human life.

Ritual worship not only incorporates the vital human aspects, but it also "returns" them, now sanctified, to life. By the offering of the first fruits of the harvest, all the harvest is sacred. Through the ritual uniting of a woman and a man, all their sexual life is consecrated. By means of the rites of puberty initiation, boys and girls are incorporated as men and women of the community. Ritual washing means all the body is pure and sanctified. Ritual worship, thus, transforms human life by lifting it up, connecting it with the sacred, and returning it, now sanctified and empowered, to daily existence.

Ritual celebration of sacred time, as an activity on the path of transformation, has a movement or structure for renewal. First of all, there needs to be a **kenosis,** an "emptying out."[5] With the recognition that power has run down and become exhausted comes the need for an emptying out of the old situation, a distancing so that the renewal can take place. This kenosis takes many different forms in religious practice. Among the most common rituals would be those that symbolize washing or cleansing, removal of impurity, confession and repentance, separation from the usual state, returning to a condition of chaos or disorder, and dying.

Once the emptying out has been established, the **plerosis,** "filling up," follows. Having been brought back to the original state, emptied of all exhausted powers, the renewing power of the sacred can be experienced. Rebirth and new life are symbolized by rituals such as emerging from the waters, putting on new clothes, sharing in a meal, receiving a new name, incorporation into a community, singing and dancing, and the like.

Very often the two movements of kenosis and plerosis are connected by an in-between **liminal** state (from *limen,* "threshold"). This liminal state can be seen, for example, in puberty initiations. Young boys and girls may be separated from their mothers and removed to the bush (kenosis) before being incorporated back into the community as young men and women (plerosis). During that time in the bush they experience a liminal, threshold state; they are "betwixt and between," having died to their childhood existence but not yet reborn as adults. In this liminal state they return in a sense to a prebirth existence. Everything may be stripped from them; they may experience ritual death and receive sacred revelations. After this critical threshold experience, they are reincorporated into the community as new, reborn people.

Such a liminal experience can be observed in many rituals and festivals. The New Year festivals of many cultures, for example, typically have a time of cleansing and purifying (kenosis), which leads into a liminal condition of "antistructure" or chaos; finally renewed structure and order are created (plerosis). The Christian ritual of baptism involves a distancing from evil (renouncing the works of the devil), a liminal passage of symbolic death in the waters, and a renewal ritualized by a new name, white garment, and a burning candle. The ritual of pilgrimage, important in traditions as different as Hinduism and Islam, includes symbols of distancing through a long journey, vows, and a special garment. The liminal period covers several days full of intense rituals and experiences. And the pilgrim has a new spiritual and social status upon completion of the pilgrimage.

Festivals and Rituals of Passage Religious communities generally structure their lives by following ritual calendars, some of which are quite elaborate. Among the most common rituals are those that occur periodically, such as seasonal festivals. They follow the rhythm of the year and celebrate different aspects of involvement with sacred power. Many of these seasonal festivals have some connection with the cycle of sacred power in nature: spring renewal festivals, fall harvest festivals, and the like. In some religious traditions, the seasonal festivals are associated with events in the sacred story. For example, the spring festival of Passover celebrates the deliverance of Israel from slavery in Egypt, the spring festival of Easter celebrates the resurrection of Jesus from the dead, and a spring festival in Buddhism commemorates the birth of the Buddha. All of these festivals, although they emphasize events in human history, retain symbolism of liberation of nature's forces from the captivity of winter.

Another very common type of festival occurring periodically is the holy day, a particular day singled out for commemorating and celebrating some aspect of sacred power. These may be lucky or unlucky days determined by the astrological calendar; they may commemorate the birth or death of some great saints or religious founders; they may be critical points in the transitions of the annual seasons, such as the winter solstice; or they may follow a repeating pattern, such as every seven days (Jews, Christians, and Muslims), every nineteen days (Baha'is), or bimonthly on the lunar pattern (Buddhists).

Some rituals recur every day, such as morning devotions for Brahman Hindus or ritual worship at their family kami altar for a traditional Japanese family. And certain rituals even take place periodically throughout every day, such as the five daily periods of prayer in Islam or the daily hours observed by Christian monks and nuns.

These seasonal festivals, periodic holy days, and regular ritual times offer a plenitude of sacred centers in the living of human life, a rhythm of recurring renewal to sustain the community and the individual within the community.

Another major type of ritual celebration is that associated with the vital passages of human life, especially birth, puberty, marriage, and death. These **rites of passage**[6] are focused on the individual within the context of the community, serving to transform the person into the new stage of life and to integrate her or him into the community at that new spiritual level. Each of these passages of life is liminal—that is, it involves crossing a threshold from one state of existence to another. Each passage is critical to the full human development of the person and to the welfare of the community and, therefore, religious rituals accompany and actualize the passage.

To move from one stage of life to another means, first of all, to put an end to the old stage. Thus, rituals of kenosis, such as separation, distancing, or dying, are most appropriately used as the first movement in the cel-

ebration of passage. The end of an infant's prebirth state may be ritualized by burying the afterbirth or washing the infant for the first time. Children to be initiated into adulthood are typically separated from their homes and parents as the beginning of their initiation. Carrying a bride-to-be away from her home to the marriage hall shows the end of her state of maidenhood. Funeral rituals typically include the removal of the body from the normal life surroundings.

Separated from the old stage, which is now completed and thus done away with, the person enters into a state of liminality, "betwixt and between." Having moved back to the precreation state, rituals of liminality bring the person into direct contact with sacred power. These include rituals of death and burial, suspension of time and identity, encounter with the ancestors, and so forth. Mother and newborn baby are often confined for a period of time during which various birth ceremonies take place. Children in indigenous societies die symbolic deaths during their initiation rituals, have their sexual organs cut, or engage in battles with mythical monsters. Marriage passage rites often include a period of betrothal during which the man and woman are neither single nor yet joined as one. In funeral rituals, the newly dead person is often felt to be in an in-between state, and the family and community observe a "wake" or sometimes a lengthy mourning period before the dead one is fully incorporated as an ancestor.

Finally, rituals of plerosis, such as rebirth, empowering, and reincorporation into the community, complete the passage. The person has left the previous state, passed over the threshold, and now is recognized and welcomed at the new level of life. The infant is named and, thus, incorporated into the community. The young people now speak a new language and take their places as adults. The marriage is consummated and rituals of establishing a new home take place. The dead one is welcomed back as an ancestor and is enshrined on the family altar.

Other rituals of passage have to do with spiritual rebirth; they follow the pattern of rites of passage but are not necessarily connected with the physical development of human life. Christian baptism, for example, is not simply a birth ritual but also a ritualization of the death of the "old one" and the resurrection of the new spiritual being in whom Christ lives; thus, people of all ages receive baptism as the ritual of entry into the Christian community. In some traditions, initiation into secret religious societies follows the pattern of the rites of passage. Religious specialists such as shamans, yogins, priests, monks, and nuns enter into their new spiritual level of existence through passage rituals of ordination or consecration, with all of the symbolism of death and rebirth.

Healing Rituals and Practices for Wholesome Life   For traditional peoples, physical health has always been connected with spiritual resources. Today, of course, modern Western scientific medicine, with its power to combat sickness and disease of every kind, has become essential among all peoples of the world. But in many societies, traditional practices of healing and medicine also continue to play an important part in the health and well-being of the people. Although Western medicine developed scientifically without obvious connections to religion, traditional **healing rituals** are interconnected with the views and practices of the respective religious traditions.

Virtually all religious traditions have spiritual practices intended to help bring healing and wholeness to those who are sick. Although there is great diversity in these practices, corresponding to the worldview of each religion, basic dimensions of religion are involved. Prayer on behalf of the sick is widespread in most religious traditions. The sick one is not left to pray alone, but the community engages in prayer—family, friends, pastor, shaman or shamaness, congregation. Sacred time is created, and the sick one is connected to the sacred by telling the sacred story and performing rituals to reactualize the creative, healing power. Sacred place has an important role in healing. In most traditional societies, the home is the place most conducive to healing, or a shrine, church, or other sacred place to which a healing pilgrimage may be made. A modern hospital can be experienced as an alien environment. So the family and the community attempt to create sacred space, through visits to the hospital room, use of the chapel, congregational prayers to connect the person to the church or temple, and the like. These healing activities create an overall framework in which the illness as well as the healing can be understood, both by the individual and by the community of which he or she is part.

Healing practices in each religious tradition grow out of their worldview, their sense of how sacred power operates. Whatever cause lies behind sickness (unhappy spirits, imbalance of powers, or even medical disease in the scientific sense), religious people believe that their traditional heal-

ing rituals can contribute to healing. Navajo people, for example, chant Blessingway and perform sandpainting rituals to connect the sick one with the Holy People of the beginning and their healing powers. Hindu healing specialists perform the intricate Ayurvedic system of traditional medicine, balancing the three doshas (humours) that, according to their sacred texts, make up all life. Chinese medicine relies on the ancient Chinese worldview, with its elaborate techniques (such as acupuncture) of balancing the yin and yang forces and the five agents that operate in the body, to bring healing and wholeness. Traditional African Christian groups such as the Zionists practice prayer and laying on of hands to expel disease-causing spirits and fill the sick person with the power of the Holy Spirit.

In recent years, in all the major religious traditions there has been much renewal of interest in holistic, faith-based healing rituals and practices. And so Jews, Muslims, Anglicans, Catholics, Baha'is, Buddhists, and all the rest turn to meditation, prayer groups, healers, healing pilgrimages, sacramental blessing, and much more. These spiritual resources are seen as complementary to modern medical treatment, providing real *healing* that supplements and goes beyond the curing offered by modern medicine.

Artistic Expression and the Sacred   In our discussion of sacred time and ritual practices, we need to include some consideration of the arts. In the broad sense, we can consider the arts as all human activities and creations that express the aesthetic sense of beauty and meaning, especially the visual, literary, and performing arts. Art is closely tied to celebration and ritual. Religious experience is expressed largely through **aesthetic** media, for our contact with the sacred must be grounded in our perception (*aesthesis*) of reality. People of the different religious traditions have always known that the sacred is experienced through the things of the world and of human existence. Although interior, direct contact with the sacred is also known, the outer forms through which the sacred is experienced have been lovingly cultivated into artistic forms.

As used in religious practice, art forms symbolize the sacred. That is, they point beyond themselves to some dimension of the sacred or of human relationship with the sacred. They are not mere signs or pointers, however. To symbolize the sacred means to share somehow in the sacred reality, to convey the power and the presence of the sacred. A statue of the Buddha on the altar is not itself, wood or stone, that to which Buddhists direct worship. But it conveys the presence of the Buddha to the worshipers and, thus, participates in the reality to which it points.

Some art is designed mainly to represent the sacred; other art intends actually to "present" the sacred. Art that represents the sacred may be instructional, providing guidance and bringing the sacred to the minds and hearts of the people. A drama acting out the sacred story might have the goal of instructing the people. Images and statues on Hindu temples and Christian cathedrals function as a kind of visual narrative of the story of the religion.

Other art more directly presents the sacred for a worshipful, transformative religious experience. Use of the arts in worship and ritual is often of this more presentational type, evoking and creating the experience of the sacred. In Hindu puja (worship), the god is invoked into the image and worshiped. The artful ritual actions, objects, and chanting of the Shinto priest in a shrine festival present the blessing and power of the kami directly to the worshipers. Of course, art can combine both types. The dramatic Jewish Passover meal (seder), for example, educates by narrating the story, but it also creates the religious experience of being present at the great deliverance of the exodus from Egypt.

From the religious point of view, all aspects of human existence have the possibility of being open to the sacred. Therefore, the religious impulse is to involve all possible human arts, especially in worship and ritual. Since the arts are highly expres-

sive, they can evoke experiences of the sacred at deeper levels than the rational and logical. For example, all the various literary arts make use of the rational structure of language. But there is a difference between a precise philosophical proposition of faith that attempts to define (and, thus, limit) the sacred, and a liturgical poetic expression that makes the sacred powerfully present. The great power that people find in the scriptures of their religion is related to the artistic quality of the sacred literature. The aesthetic sound of mantras (sacred formulas) in Hinduism and Buddhism conveys power even if the literal meaning of the words is not understood.

Visual presentations of the sacred and of the sacred story are used in many religious practices, although there is also reluctance in some religious traditions to portray divine realities in representational visual form. Iconography (pictorial imagery) presents important aspects of the sacred, but it also imbues the sacred with sensuous form—and, thus, limitations. Painting, sculptures, small figurines, and symbolic abstract designs all serve to evoke a sense of the sacred full of aesthetic power and beauty with form, color, and texture.

The art of music has been found to be a powerful presenter of the sacred in almost all religions. The beautiful sounds of music—gripping rhythm, haunting melody, special qualities of different instruments—reach to deep levels of aesthetic sensibility and express many different aspects of the experience of the sacred. It is particularly powerful when words are wedded to music in sacred chants, mantras, hymns, and the like. The art of music, whether a solitary flute or the ringing Hallelujah Chorus of Handel's *Messiah*, gathers and directs spiritual emotions and evokes the sacred presence as no other art form does.

Expression of the sacred in art: woodcut of Christ on the cross, by Paul Gauguin. Paul Gauguin, French, 1848-1903 'Christ on the Cross' ca. 1900. Woodcut, printed in brown ink. 15 7/8 x 5 3/8 in. The Metropolitan Museum of Art, New York. Harris Brisbane Dick Fund, 1929.

Another art form widely cultivated in religious practice is dance, the aesthetic and spiritual expression of body movements. Closely associated with dance would be drama and liturgical rituals. The ritual actions of a Daoist priest very much involve arts of movement and drama, as do the Shinto kagura dances, the Muslim art of ritual prayer, and the Hindu dance-drama festivals.

The sense of sacred place is artistically expressed in different religious traditions by distinctive forms of architecture. Temples and shrines symbolize the *axis mundi*, the center of the world, providing a center of orientation for all the rest of space. The sacred building is often thought of as a microcosm of the cosmic world. The aesthetic quality of architectural forms expresses essential dimensions of the vision of the particular religious tradition. Soaring Gothic cathedrals reaching toward heaven, Muslim mosques filled with openness and light, Hindu temples with their dark and mysterious inner room, simple wooden Shinto shrines in Japan—all give expression to particular spatial-local qualities of the experience of the sacred.

Since artistic forms can evoke deep feelings with powerful presentations of the sacred, occasionally they can be experienced as destructive or demonic. People can look to the art form itself as ultimate, a situation called idolatry ("worship of an idol") in some of the religious traditions. People in all religions know, however, that the art forms, no matter how beautiful or powerful, are symbols of the sacred. They point beyond themselves to the sacred; they convey and present the sacred; but they are not themselves the ultimate sacred. Still, many art forms have been resisted or banned in the history of the different religions. Poetry has been considered the work of demons. Music of certain types raises dangerous emotions. Dance can become too sensuous and ecstatic. Iconography—imaging the sacred in visual form—has been a controversial art in some religions, because people fear it leads to idolatry or to seeking to gain control over the sacred.

People of each religious tradition choose special aesthetic forms as the most appropriate, sometimes resisting others as useless, misleading, or even dangerous. We might say that each religion or culture has its own distinctive aesthetic sense, closely related to the deep insights of that spiritual vision. To really understand a culture, we must look at its literature, poetry, dance, visual portrayals, architecture, music, and the rest. For example, the Hindu experience of

countless gods within an ultimate unity opens the way for the cultivation of all the arts. And the Muslim reluctance to link God together with likenesses of any kind has led to a restriction on representational visual arts and a flowering of decorative and verbal arts. Some religious arts are more conducive to meditation, others to celebration and ecstasy. In broad terms, the religious traditions of South and East Asia have stressed intuitional, meditative aesthetic experiences, whereas the traditions of the West have often emphasized an aesthetic sense connected with the word, intelligence, and logic. But these differences can easily be overstressed, for the shape of the aesthetic vision is often a matter of emphasis. Even within one religious tradition, significant differences can be found.

Sacred Life: Social Structure and the Good Life   Where do we belong? How should we live in wholeness? What is our responsibility to human society? Religious experience carries with it an imperative to live in a way that conforms to one's religious identity. A person is always a part of a group, a community, and the good life is structured in that community context. Acting according to one's religious identity involves, in many religions, a sense of responsibility and mission to others in the world.

As we saw earlier, each religious tradition has a master story that gives identity and purpose to the religious community and sets the model for the right kind of life. The story tells about the original people, special and sacred. These people are set apart for special identity, for special life, and for a special role in the world. The Japanese Shinto myths, for example, tell how the Japanese islands and the Japanese people descended from the kami (the divine beings). The emperor descended from the highest kami, the sun kami Amaterasu. This mythology has supported a sense of the Japanese people as a sacred community and the emperor as the divine head of the nation. Buddhist stories tell how the Buddha, after his enlightenment, gathered a band of disciples into a monastic community of monks and nuns, the sangha. The lay people participate in this religious community by supporting and honoring the sangha. In traditional China, ancient teachings support the strong notion that the clan or extended family is the center of meaning for each individual, and beyond that there are the hierarchically organized village and state within which the individual finds religious identity.

The organization and structures of the religious community are grounded in the sacred history and traditions of the religion. Of course, these structures reflect the configuration of power and authority in the community, and so they may change over time. Provision is made for some kind of religious leadership. Sometimes the religious leaders function by virtue of the power of their office, like kings and priests. In other cases, religious leaders are recognized by virtue of their personal charisma and power, as in the case of sages, prophets, shamans, healers, and diviners. The community also has social structures involving clan relationships, congregations, lay groups, secret societies, masters and disciples, apprentices, and the like.

Gender Issues in Religious Leadership Every society has its traditional roles defined for women and men. Since almost all societies have been structured patriarchally, women have everywhere been subordinated to men and have had limited access to leadership roles. Yet we know that women have always been deeply involved in religious activities and experiences in all the traditions. Unfortunately, their intimate, private religious participation has generally been neglected or glossed over by the male-dominated official stories and sacred writings. This makes it all the more important for us to search out material on women's lives in the different religions and to take note of their important roles.

Looking at the religious traditions from the point of view of women's experiences leads to new understandings. The significance of women's perspectives relates to all aspects of religious tradition—how the sacred history is told, the concept of the sacred, ethical precepts, and all else. For example, taking sensitive notice of women in the ancient Israelite tradition—seeing not just Abraham in the stories but also Sarah and Hagar—provides new questions for the sacred story. Where was Sarah during the sacrifice of Isaac? What was Hagar's understanding of God's plan when her husband Abraham abandoned her and his son Ishmael in the desert? Sensitivity to women's perspectives in interpreting the Bible elicits new maternal images for understanding God's presence, new relational perspectives for interpreting the covenant relationship, and so forth. To realize that one strong and long-ruling Chinese emperor was a woman (Empress Wu), also a powerful Buddhist leader, forces us to rethink our usual images of the subordination and powerlessness of women in the Chinese religious traditions.

Furthermore, we need to see the increasingly active leadership roles of modern women in all these societies, as they find religious resources for breaking out of traditional limitations, helping to renew and transform their societies in the process. In traditional societies as widely different as Hindu, Muslim, Jewish, or Buddhist societies, women have emerged as strong leaders, even heads of state. Women scholars, theologians, masters, and gurus are revitalizing their traditions, creating new models and possibilities for the future, not only for women but also for men at the same time.

Sacred Space, Sacred Land The ideal of authentic, wholesome life for the people is often tied together with stories about a sacred land or territory: the sacred islands for the Japanese, the tribal land and burial grounds for the African tribes, Jerusalem for Jews, the pilgrimage sites and sacred rivers in India, and the like. Sacred space is established by the presence of the sacred and, therefore, it is experienced as the center of the world (*axis mundi*), as Mircea Eliade has elucidated.[7] This center may function, for example, as the connecting point between the human realm and the divine realm. Once the center is established, it provides orientation and a sense of being at home in the world. Sacred space can be a whole land, or it may be a village, mountain, shrine, temple, altar, or even a home. This is the strong space that provides meaning and identity. It gives a feeling of rootedness; cut off from it we feel lost in the chaos of foreign, meaningless space. And so religious communities have always cultivated their bonds with their traditional sacred spaces and have created new sacred spaces as new circumstances arise.

Of course, as religious communities grow and spread, the sense of sacred space is also transformed. Over history, some of the world's religions (such as Buddhism, Christianity, and Islam) have spread throughout the world, creating new sacred spaces and sacred lands in the process. Obviously, in modern times there have been drastic changes that have seriously eroded the sense of sacred land for many people. Around the globe indigenous peoples have been uprooted from their ancestral lands, wars and famines have caused many refugees and displaced persons, and widespread migrations have created diaspora communities that live as religious minorities in new lands. It is important to see how these peoples have continued to struggle with the need to create a sense of rootedness even away from their traditional sacred lands.

The Moral Pattern for Authentic Life   The moral pattern for the good life is usually presented in the sacred history, for there we learn what the gods did in the mythological age, or the rules laid down by the ancestors, or the examples provided by the founders.

It is the conviction of people of each religious tradition that this pattern for life is "natural" in a deep sense. It is the way of life that most fits our original nature, as we were intended to be before we turned away or forgot that pattern. Whereas rewards may be promised for living the moral life and punishments threatened for neglecting it, the fundamental motivation for following the ethical guidance of the religion is deeper. This is the model for authentic human life, that which harmonizes with the greater spiritual forces and patterns of the cosmos. To many indigenous peoples, real human life is to do what the gods did in the Time of the Beginning. According to Hindus, living according to the Code of Manu corresponds to the eternal Dharma (cosmic order), and that is right and brings happiness. The Five Classics, according to Confucianists, express the sacred pattern of life according to the will of Heaven, as exemplified by the ancient sages, and, thus, studying and following these Classics will bring peace and harmony. The Shari'ah law code, in Islamic thought, follows perfectly the universal pattern of God's creation and, thus, it brings peace and harmony.

The ethical life has something to do with how we should be and, therefore, it is based in the religious vision of creation and human nature. The law of morality is often thought to be an authority outside oneself, usually recorded in scripture and tradition, to which one submits. But the religious teachers also talk about how that law becomes internalized, transformed into the inner motivation for right living, so that one naturally does what is right—thus, there occurs a sanctification of life.

It takes practice to live as one ought. Confucius taught that to transform ourselves into people of humanity (*ren*), it is most helpful to take up the discipline and practice of the principles of propriety (*li*). Hindus believe that following the Path of Action, doing one's duty according to one's place in life without desire for reward, is a way of reaching higher spiritual perfection and better rebirths. The thing that makes

Jews distinctive from others is their willingness to take up the discipline of the commandments (*mitzvot*)—not for the reward that this will bring but because the very doing of the mitzvot is itself the good life. Even Christians and Pure Land Buddhists, with their basic mistrust of the idea of merit coming from good works, know of the sanctification of life, of the careful cultivation of the good tree that bears good fruit.

The religious tradition provides guidance in all areas of life. In personal behavior, often the stress falls on self-control and moderation. One should not be controlled by the passions and desires, but rather these passions and desires should be controlled and redirected toward transformation of self. The religious tradition also spells out the relation of the individual to others and indicates the right and wrong ways of treating others in various situations. The ethical life is lived for the welfare of the community. In following the code of life, strife and competition are avoided and healing and harmony are promoted. The religious traditions usually teach motivations of compassion and sacrifice, giving oneself for the good of the community.

Technically speaking, *ethics* is the activity of thinking about moral decisions on the basis of the tradition. The religious tradition provides ethical guidance about many or most of the crucial questions in life. But the individual and the community, living in concrete situations with changing circumstances, also continually make ethical decisions about a variety of possible actions. In modern times, the ethical decisions have become increasingly numerous and difficult, involving such questions as abortion, homosexuality, serving in the military, adopting Western customs, and reforming deeply embedded social injustices. Many burning questions today revolve around changing roles for women and men. Thousands of questions like these face people in all the religions today, and as they think about the possible decisions on the basis of the religious tradition, they are engaging in ethical thinking.

Some religions are tribal, which means the people generally have limited opportunity to express solidarity with humans outside the tribe, though they often have codes on how to treat outsiders. People of tribal religious traditions often have a strong sense of relation with the natural world. They promote the welfare and continuation of the whole world that supports human society, made up of vegetation, animals, and the earth itself in a kind of primal ecology, based in a feeling for the sacredness of all life.

Within the world religions there has developed more awareness of the universality of the human race and of the common human welfare in the world. Thus, all the world religious traditions have some vision of the nature and purpose of all humankind and of their own role or mission in the world. In the context of world society, many people of the different religions have developed a sense of responsibility for the good of the larger world, especially in areas such as social justice, education, and relief for the poor and hungry. In recent times, concern for reconciliation and peacemaking has come to the fore in many religions. Today, people in all religious traditions see the need for peace and harmony between different cultures, especially in view of the drastic threat of modern warfare, economic exploitation, ethnic conflict, and all the other ills of the global society.

Inherent in every self-conscious religious tradition is the claim to be the truth, and, thus, the ideal way of life. Whereas tribal peoples generally do not attempt to spread their religious practices beyond the borders of their own tribe, all religions that have a sense of universality also have some feeling of responsibility to share their vision with other peoples of the world. This does not necessarily mean trying to convince others to convert to this religion. This responsibility may simply be having a special role within the world that is of benefit to all, as is expressed in the Jewish idea of a special covenant history within the world. Others, such as Hindus, have a tolerant attitude toward truth embodied at different levels, so they are usually not motivated to promote their religion to other peoples.

The concern that the truth must be shared with all peoples is especially strong in the so-called missionary religions: Christianity, Islam, and to some extent Buddhism, and also some newer branches of the older traditions, such as Baha'i, Nichiren Shoshu, and the International Society for Krishna Consciousness. People of these religions feel a mission, for example, to Christianize all peoples, Islamicize the world, spread the Dharma, and so forth—for the ultimate welfare of all. For people of these religions, this kind of mission is also an important part of their self-understanding and identity. Apart from Buddhism and some of these new religious movements, the religious traditions of the East generally have not actively tried to convince others to convert to those religions. But as the world shrinks and communication between peoples of the globe increases, Hindus, Sikhs, Daoists, Shintoists, and others increasingly

are presenting their visions of truth to be heard and understood by the peoples of the world.

Concern for the welfare of the world, and the realization that people of other religions also have visions for the world and claims to truth, have led to conversation and cooperation among people from different religions. Many people today recognize that religions and ideologies have contributed a great deal to the conflicts in the world. In recent years a new movement of dialogue and cooperation among people from various religions has become a part of the religious happenings of the world. At the very least, there is a widespread sense that peoples of different religious traditions need to work together against the forces of exploitation, violence, and secularization that threaten human society today in an unprecedented way.

DISCUSSION QUESTIONS

1 Do you think questions such as "Who am I?" and "What is the purpose of life?" are universal human concerns, or are they the product of modern Western thought?

2 What are some aspects of the experience of the sacred that seem to be shared by people of different religious traditions?

3 Give some examples of how symbol systems change over time.

4 What is implied in calling religious practices a "path"?

5 How can a story or myth from ancient times still provide identity for people today? Give some examples.

6 What do cosmogonic stories reveal about the way a particular people look at the world and human existence?

7 What is meant by speaking of "transformation" or "salvation" in the various religious traditions?

8 What is meant by saying that participation in sacred times or festivals brings renewal of human life? What do the ritual phases of kenosis and plerosis mean?

9 What is the difference between art that *represents* the sacred and art that *presents* the sacred?

10 Do you think that living the good ethical life is something natural or unnatural?

11 Do you think a sense of universal truth and mission is something essential to a religion?

KEY TERMS:
EXPLORING THE SACRED PATHS

aesthetic concerning beauty or artistic perception, important for religious expression

cosmogonic myth sacred story that tells of the creation or founding of the world and of basic human realities

ethics thought and study about moral decisions on the basis of traditions of right and wrong

healing rituals religious rituals devoted to promoting health, often complementary to modern medical practices

kenosis "emptying out"; in ritual, the movement of separation or doing away with the old state; *see* plerosis

liminal in ritual, the state between separation (kenosis) and restoration (plerosis)

monism view that all reality is one unified divine reality

monotheism belief in one almighty God, separate from the world

myth story about sacred beings in the beginning time, telling how existence came to be as it is and providing the pattern for authentic life

nondualism view that ultimate reality and the phenomenal world are not different

path of transformation practice in a religious tradition that changes one from the wrong or inadequate state to the ideal state

plerosis "filling up"; fulfillment or restoration movement of ritual; *see* kenosis

polytheism belief that many divine powers share in the world's operation

religious traditions sacred stories and basic ideas and practices that religious communities "hand over" from generation to generation; that which is handed over (Latin *traditio*) is thought to maintain a recognizable unity even while changing over time

rites of passage rituals connected with the critical changes or passages in a person's life, especially birth, puberty, marriage, and death

rituals activities of many kinds that connect people with sacred realities, including prayer, sacrifice, chanting, pilgrimage, festivals, disciplines of meditation, and much more

sacred space space that is made special by connection with the sacred, providing orientation and rootedness for a people

sacred story master story of a religion, providing identity for the adherents; *see* myth

sacred time special time of ritual and festival, when mythic events are made present once more

sacred, the what is experienced as ultimate reality, the mysterious Other that is the ground of ultimate value and meaning

symbols words, pictures, ideas, rituals, and so on that evoke deep meanings by connecting with sacred reality

transformation the act of reaching the ideal state of wholeness, perfection, or salvation

understanding "standing under" another's way of thought and life, comprehending it by reference to one's own experience

worship respectful ritual activity in special times, directed toward sacred beings or realities of ultimate value

Chapter 2

Beginnings of the Human Religious Adventure

Where did the worldviews and religious practices of the world religions come from? We know they must have a very long history. The world religions of today, highly developed and encompassing large populations, are relatively modern phenomena, all of them having reached their classical form within the past three thousand years. That means we humans lived for hundreds of thousands and even millions of years—perhaps 99.9 percent of our human story in length of time—prior to the development of these world religions. Although we have no way of knowing the mental and spiritual outlook of the earliest humans, we may at least assume that religious ideas and practices have been part of humankind's experience for as long as humans have had thinking, reflecting, and imagining capabilities. Furthermore, up to the nineteenth and twentieth centuries, large numbers of people in various parts of the world remained outside the domain of our present world religions. Surely all of this accumulated religious experience is an important part of our human story. Our identity today as human beings is deeply indebted to these sacred experiences from other times and places.

There is great diversity among these ancient religious traditions, and within their vast domains it is possible to find almost all symbols and forms of religion that have come to expression in the world religions of today. A great many of these religious traditions of course are **prehistorical**, existing before there were written records or existing in a culture that had not developed writing, and, thus, we know only a small fraction of them through archaeological research. Other religions of the past belong to the great **ancient civilizations**, peoples who did produce written records and texts; even though they no longer live, we can know about them through their literature and other artifacts. We note also the religious paths of *contemporary indigenous peoples*, those who have lived to the present day or at least to the recent past at a premodern level of tribal economy and society, having continued their archaic traditions for countless generations.

Perhaps one common characteristic among these religious traditions of prehistorical, ancient, and indigenous peoples is their tribal or ethnic character. The people do not envision their religious practices as having universal application but as the mark of themselves as a particular people. However, certain thinkers in some of the ancient civilizations, such as in China, India, Greece, and Rome, did push toward a kind of intellectual universality. And religious ideas and practices often crossed ethnic and linguistic boundaries. Another common element among prehistoric, ancient, and indigenous peoples is the general acceptance of the plurality of sacred powers emanating from the cosmos—that vision we sometimes call "polytheism." Yet again we must qualify that statement. Some Greek and Roman thinkers articulated a vision of sacred unity encompassing all of nature (pantheism); there were stirrings of monotheism in ancient Egypt, Persia, and Israel; some Vedic hymns from ancient India explore the one reality behind all the gods; and many indigenous peoples today have ways of speaking of the "One" behind all the plurality of sacred forces.

Ancient peoples and contemporary indigenous peoples tend to have a very natural involvement with the sacred in their ordinary lives. They are open to the interweaving of the sacred within their social and political life, food-producing activities, birth, sickness, death, and all the rest. Mostly these peoples do not even have a word for "religion," since religious activities are completely integrated with their traditional way of life. This is not to say that archaic and indigenous peoples are naive and simplistic, for they are capable of sophisticated intellectual activity and excel in practical wisdom. But they, unlike many of us who are drenched in modernity and secularity, are open to experiencing the sacred in all the vital dimensions of life.

Here in this chapter we provide a brief look at humankind's early religious adventure, climaxing in the great civilizations of the ancient world. We will have occasion to further explore some of the ancient civilizations and their religions later as we study the beginnings of the world religions in India, China, and Japan.

STORY OF HUMANKIND BEFORE HISTORY

With each of the major world religions, we will begin by looking at the sacred story that gives identity to the people of that religious tradition. Here at the beginning it is appropriate to sketch out a story of early humankind, not as it is told in any religious tradition, of course, but as scholars have reconstructed the religious history of humanity. This is not really a sacred story, for we do not tell it through myth and ritual as the basis for our identity. But still we can feel respect and indebtedness to our human forebears who transmitted the spirit of life and whose religious visions have somehow over millennia contributed to our own humanity.

The Origin of Religion: Theories   Scholars of religion have long been interested in the question of the "origin" of religion—how did religion begin and where did it come from? If we could answer the question of origins, they have felt, we would have some notion of the "original form" of religion and, thus, presumably we could explain why there is religion and what its nature is. In the late nineteenth and early twentieth centuries, many theories of the origin of religion were proposed, trying to explain why humans would somehow start having religious ideas and practices.

For example, the early anthropologist and ethnologist Edward B. Tylor (1832–1917) argued in his influential *Primitive Culture* (1871) that religion originated in **animism** (from *anima*, "spirit"). As primitive people thought about their experiences of death and of dreams, they reflected on where life goes when a person dies and how deceased people can still be seen in dreams. They came up with the notion that people and things have spir-

its that can leave their respective bodies and carry on a separate existence. People started worshiping the more important spirits, and religion was born. Eventually they turned their worship to the powerful spirits of nature (polytheism), and finally religion evolved into the belief in one supreme God over all (monotheism).

Another early anthropologist, James Frazer (1854–1941), followed Tylor's basic theory but added an earlier stage. He collected massive materials from the various ancient and indigenous cultures (which he published in the twelve thick volumes of *The Golden Bough* [1915]). On the basis of this material, he argued that the earliest human response to the world was **magic**, the attempt to control and manipulate the forces of nature. Finding that magic did not deal effectively with the sacred forces, primitive humans turned to religious rituals and prayers directed to personal gods.

Other scholars looked for the origin of religion in psychological or social factors among primitive people. Sigmund Freud (1856–1939) constructed a number of psychoanalytic theories about the origin of religion. In *Totem and Taboo* (1913), he described the "primal horde" of primitive humans, in which the band of brothers kill their father and possess his wives—and then, consumed with guilt, they started worshiping the totem animal as a substitute for their father. And in *The Future of an Illusion* (1927), Freud put forth the theory that belief in God is a psychological projection of our father figure, growing out of the human need to feel protected and secure.

The early sociologist Emile Durkheim (1858–1917) developed an elaborate theory of the origin of religion based on sociological analysis, published in *The Elementary Forms of Religious Life* (1912). He looked at social life among the Australian aborigines, for he considered them to be a truly simple community. He noted that each of their clans was identified with a totem animal, plant, or object as symbolic of the sacred and he concluded that the sacred reality actually was the clan itself, totally identified with its totem. From this totemic principle all religious ideas and structures have arisen—souls, spirits, gods, rituals, and all the rest. All are expressions of the sacred reality of the society itself. Thus, for Durkheim, religion is not itself primary but originates as a projection of the society's sacred identity.

These scholars attempted to explain the origin and nature of religion through theories that came from their scientific disciplines, such as anthropology, psychology, and sociology. None of them considered religion itself to be a primary human dimension. Rather, they reduced religious experience to something else by explaining it as nothing more than intellectual, social, or psychological projection. Many scholars today hold that, although religion does have intellectual, social, and psychological functions, it is important to pay attention to the religious dimension for its own sake, as it is experienced and described by its practitioners. However, there are other modern scholars who argue that social scientific methodology is the only proper approach to religious studies and that the goal of such study should be to explain religion in the context of social, political, economic, or psychological activity. And the debate goes on today.[1] Almost all scholars do agree, though, that religion is multi-faceted and that many approaches are needed to arrive at a comprehensive understanding of the religious traditions.

However, seeking to identify the *origin* of religion is probably a futile venture. The interest in finding the origin of religion arose in the heyday of evolutionary theories of culture, and it suggests that we might find some particular point in human development at which religion began. The data necessary for such an investigation are simply not available. Furthermore, since religious values and practices seem to form an important dimension in human life, it may be supposed that religious feelings and experiences have been present as long as there have been human beings who could think, imagine, and reflect on themselves and their world. So perhaps the more appropriate question of origins is this: How long have there been human beings to express themselves through religious experience?

Origins of Religion: Early Human Species   The answer to how long there have been human beings depends on the consensus of paleoanthropologists about recent discoveries. Many scholars feel that an early human species—as distinct from other animal species—existed two to three million years ago or even earlier in parts of Africa. These early hominids were of several types, but they displayed the human characteristics of walking erect and making simple tools. It is true that their brains were smaller than humans today, though still much larger than other animals. But the presence of artificial tools, including tools for making tools, is particularly important, suggesting a human level of imagination and symbolic thought. A distinctly human type among these early hominids appears

to have begun gathering and sharing food and living in campsites for periods of time. Somehow these unknown ancestors carried the human spirit forward, through immense difficulties. We, of course, have no way of knowing the feelings and ideas these early humans had about themselves and their world, but it is fascinating to sense our shared humanity across that vast stretch of time and imagine their spiritual needs and longings—not that different from our own—in relation to food, companions, children, birth, and death.

Certainly, full humanity becomes recognizable with the type of humans that emerged about one million years ago in a variety of places in Africa, Europe, and China—a type that has been called **Homo erectus**. One of the outstanding discoveries of this human type was in a limestone-filled cave near Beijing, where skeletons of some fifteen individuals were found. By about half a million years ago these humans were exhibiting distinct human tendencies, with a brain size nearly that of modern humans. Living in small communities in caves and rock shelters, they learned the use of fire for domestic purposes, for warmth, and for cooking food. They made many stone tools, cooperated in big hunts of animals such as elephants, rhinoceroses, and deer, and, thus, no doubt had developed some forms of human speech to communicate with each other. Clearly they were thinking, imagining, and symbol-creating humans. The archaeological remains that have been discovered, however, are still too scanty to provide much firm evidence of their distinctively religious practices and ideas.

Finally, clear archaeological evidence of religious ideas and practices comes with the **Neanderthal** type of humans, living in parts of Europe, China, and Iraq in the Middle Paleolithic period, around 100,000 to 35,000 years ago. Neanderthal humans, contrary to popular prejudice, had developed a sensitive, complex culture, living in communities with many tools and some forms of art. A number of finds in their burials suggest they had religious ideas associated with death and afterlife. For example, at one burial site flint tools had been placed near the hands of the dead; at another, a skull was surrounded with a ring of stones; and in another burial a group of skulls had been immersed in red ochre, perhaps a symbol of blood and life. Often bodies were laid on the right side with the head toward the east, and in at least one burial the body was surrounded with flower blossoms. There is evidence here that death was looked upon as a passage to another kind of life, and they had developed rituals to surround this passage. What we have suggested about earlier human species now is manifest in the Neanderthal archaeological record—these early humans definitely had religious ideas and practices.

Humans in the Upper Paleolithic Period   It is still debated whether Neanderthal humans were directly related to the line of descent of later humans or whether they were a separate offshoot of the human species. In any case, around 35,000 years ago some dramatic changes begin to appear, particularly new kinds of tools made of thin, slender stone blades, and a variety of representational art, both sculpted and painted on walls. In this Upper **Paleolithic** period, the modern species of **Homo sapiens sapiens** developed, equal to modern humans in physical appearance. Communities of these humans now are found in various places of the world—in Europe, Siberia, Southwest Asia, parts of Africa, and even, by about 20,000 years ago, in Australia and North America. All we humans of the world today are descended from these Upper Paleolithic human communities.

Now there is abundant evidence of religious beliefs and practices. Many burials from this period show careful treatment of the bodies, with red ochre sprinkled on the bones, probably symbolizing life-power. Some corpses are buried in a huddled-up position, symbolizing returning to the womb for rebirth. Often bodies are lined up together in the same direction, and special treatment of the skulls is indicated. Necklaces and other personal ornaments and implements are buried with the body, showing that the dead live on in some way. All of these are ritual practices associated with death, and they point to the religious conception of death as a passage to new life. They show that the people are concerned about their continuing relationship with their dead family and community people.

Religious concerns of our ancestors in the Upper Paleolithic era are also evident in impressive artistic drawings, paintings, figurines, and other artifacts. For example, while the last ice ages still held sway in much of Europe, in the far recesses of caves in France and Spain, artists of the Cro-Magnon peoples drew paintings on the walls, many having to do with animals such as bears, deer, and birds. Numerous scenes appear to display hunting motifs. Some paintings depict certain animal-human forms, which appear to

be shamans or mythological figures such as masters or mistresses of animals (as known from indigenous hunting cultures of today). Similar artistic motifs of animals and humans have also been found in Upper Paleolithic rock shelters in Africa. It seems clear that there were rituals connected with these paintings and drawings, promoting the continuance of life-power and reflecting the close connection felt between humans and animals, especially related to hunting activities. From these various archaeological remains, we can conclude that these prehistorical hunting peoples, perhaps as early as 35,000 years ago, had well-developed religious ideas and practices, not unlike those of the hunting peoples who have continued their traditional way of life into the nineteenth and twentieth centuries.

A great many figurines have been found in these early human communities. The majority depict the human female form, often with exaggerated breasts and buttocks, sometimes conspicuously pregnant. One of the best known of these figurines is the so-called Willendorf Venus, from Willendorf in Austria. Made of soft limestone, this figurine is 4.4 inches high and is sculpted with ample body proportions and large breasts. Other finds also seem to focus on female symbolism, such as sculptured breasts perhaps used as pendants, abstracted images of vulvas, and female images painted on cave walls in connection with animals. Perhaps some of these finds were associated with religious ideas about a **great goddess** or goddesses as a primary source of life-power. Worship of life-giving goddesses may have been one of the earliest and most widespread forms of religious practice. Of course, these numerous figurines and female symbols reflect the beliefs and practices of many different communities, with a great variety of cultural traditions, economic systems, and languages. So the meanings of goddess worship also no doubt have significant variety. The figurines may represent sacred female powers associated with pregnancy, birth, fertility, and the menstrual cycle. The goddess may be understood as mother or mistress of animals, goddess of the dead and the underworld, mistress of the land, protector of the dwelling, goddess of the regenerative powers of nature, and more.

These Upper Paleolithic people had language and art and, thus, it is clear that they engaged in imaginative, symbolic thinking. We know there were artists among them who painted the pictures and sculpted the figurines based on their sacred traditions. No doubt there were shamans and shamanesses telling sacred stories about the first people and animals and the origin of the hunt. Certainly they had ideas and concepts about the sacred, perhaps personified as goddesses and gods of nature, animal masters, spirits, and ancestors. Life concerns were very real—food, protection, children, sickness, death, afterlife, ancestors, and so forth. They participated in rituals and practices to promote wholeness in life, continuing in death. To be part of a family and community certainly was vital for them, and so they had social structures as well as notions and regulations about living the good life together in their community. We can recognize these people as our fellow humans, with a full range of religious experience.

Religious Changes in the Agricultural Revolution   Humans of the Upper Paleolithic era continued, like humans for hundreds of thousands of years before them, to live as hunters and gatherers, with their religious experience shaped by that kind of focus. By the end of the last ice age, around ten thousand years ago, human communities lived in virtually every part of the globe, although, of course, in many places the population was sparse.

But now, in this **Neolithic** period (ca. 8000–3000 B.C.E.), a major transformation in human culture took place. Due perhaps to climatic changes as well as human cultural creativity, people in certain areas of the world began to discover how to assist the earth in producing plants for food and, finally, how to cultivate crops such as barley and wheat for their own food. Soon some of these peoples also learned how to domesticate herds of animals, such as sheep, goats, pigs, and cattle, to ensure a regular food supply. The earliest agricultural transformations

From late Paleolithic times, a stone figurine known as the Venus of Willendorf, possibly representing a goddess of fertility and life.

arose in the eastern Mediterranean areas (such as Palestine, Syria, Iraq, Iran, and Anatolia) and in southeastern Europe. Other areas where agriculture developed in this Neolithic period include the western Mediterranean regions, northwestern Europe, the Sahara, the Nile Valley, China, and Mesoamerica.

This great **agricultural revolution** changed the shape of human life and religion forever. Producing their own food meant that people could settle down, creating villages, towns, and cities. They could develop societies in which some people could produce the food while others could attend to other important activities, such as making pottery, creating art, and engaging in commerce.

Religious concerns were very apparent among these early farmers. In some settlements there were shrine rooms in some of the dwellings. In larger settlements there were communal shrines and cult centers with altars, figurines of gods and goddesses, murals depicting ceremonies and rituals, and many other indications of religious activities. Humans now became more attuned to the powers and cycles of the earth in producing vegetation. A large number of female figurines and other female representations attests to the widespread worship of the life-giving powers of goddesses associated with the cyclical death and rebirth of the vegetation. Concern for the dead and afterlife is very apparent in these communities, with a variety of burial practices—under the floor of the dwelling, in special cemeteries, collective burials in megalith tombs, ritual use of skulls of their ancestors, and the like.

RELIGIONS OF THE GREAT ANCIENT CIVILIZATIONS

As the agricultural-urban revolution spread, the changes in human culture began to come much more rapidly, into the Bronze Age (ca. 3200–1200 B.C.E. in the eastern

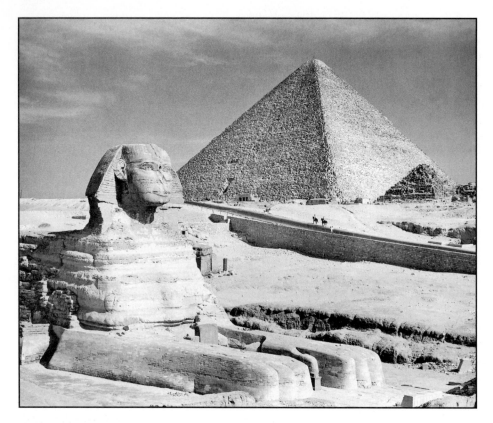

The Sphinx and the Chops Pyramid at Giza near Cairo provide colossal expression of the sacred from the ancient Egyptian civilization.

The new perspectives associated with agriculture and settled life continued to develop in countless farming communities, villages, towns, and cities around the globe. The depth and richness of humankind's story now can be seen especially in the great religious systems of some of the more highly developed civilizations.

In the eastern Mediterranean area were the ancient Egyptians, with over two thousand years of kingdoms and dynasties, with spectacular cultural creations and elaborate religious practices. Likewise highly developed were the empires of Mesopotamia, including the Sumerians, the Babylonians, and the Assyrians. Smaller kingdoms developed in the Syro-Palestinian region, including the Canaanites and the Israelites, well known both from archaeology and from the biblical texts.

Mediterranean areas) and the Iron Age (starting ca. 1200 B.C.E.). Towns and cities continued to develop, kingdoms evolved, and great ancient empires emerged with their city-state religions. Now the invention of writing begins to play a significant role in human culture. A great variety of written texts, along with various art objects, implements for food production and industry, houses, public buildings, monuments, and many other remains and artifacts have allowed scholars to reconstruct these civilizations in elaborate detail. So now we come to the end of the prehistorical period and the beginning of the historical period of the human story, at least in many areas of the world. Now we can put a personal human face on these peoples and begin to get a clear sense on their religious yearnings, conceptions, and practices.

In South Asia, the inhabitants of the great fertile region of the Indus River developed a highly organized agricultural-urban society; this Indus valley civilization was contemporary with the great Egyptian and Sumerian civilizations. In East Asia, the ancient Shang dynasty and the early Zhou dynasty in China ruled over great civilizations, cultivating elaborate ritual practices to ensure harmony with ancestors and the forces of nature. In ancient Japan, the introduction of rice cultivation created an agricultural society, and an elaborate imperial state developed, even before the introduction of writing from China.

Many ancient civilizations stemmed from that migratory group of peoples that scholars call **Indo-Europeans**. Originating perhaps in the steppes of Asia, these peoples migrated westward throughout Europe and eastward to Persia and India. They were pastoralists, but wherever they settled down they developed agricultural societies and interacted with the indigenous populations. In this long process, eventually the great European civilizations emerged, such as the Greeks and the Romans with their extensive empires, as well as the Celts, the Germanic peoples, the Slavs, the Balts, and more. Eastward, the migrating Indo-Europeans contributed to the development of the Persian civilization, where Zoroastrianism developed. The Indo-Europeans who migrated to India called themselves Aryans, contributing to the great civilization there from which Hinduism, Buddhism, and Jainism eventually developed.

Among the ancient agricultural-urban civilizations, we may also include city-state peoples of the Americas, such as the Mayas and the Aztecs in Mesoamerica and the Incas in South America.

Of course, there was a great variety of cultural and religious perspectives among these many civilizations. But in general we can say that they all were agriculture-based societies, most of which evolved complex city-state societies. They are characterized by belief in many great gods of nature, sacred kingship, elaborate priesthoods, sacred stories, and written texts (or oral texts written down later). Most characteristic of these religions is the strong ritual component, for it is through the highly complex rituals that the crops, the society, the state, and even the cosmos are sustained.

In terms of total human history, the agricultural revolution, with the cultural and religious developments that have accompanied it, is a very recent event, one that still permeates our worldview today. Even though most of these ancient cultures did not survive into the modern world, they made deep contributions to the human religious adventure. For it is in these ancient civilizations that we see the initial stirrings of the present-day world religions. In the course of this book, we will see numerous examples of these ancient religions as we investigate the beginnings of the world religions. We will look at the Indus Valley civilization and the Aryans in India, the Shang and early Zhou peoples in China, and the ancient Japanese peoples.

DISCUSSION QUESTIONS

1 Discuss the concept that the vast majority of our human ancestral history took place before the beginning of our world religions of today. What significance might that have for human self-understanding today?

2 Do the theories about the origin of religion put forth by Tylor, Frazer, Freud, and Durkheim make sense to you? To what extent do you think religion can be explained through social and psychological theories?

3 What is the nature of evidence for religious practices from the Lower and Middle Paleolithic periods (*Homo erectus* and Neanderthal humans)?

4 What major religious ideas and practices are known from our human ancestors of the Upper Paleolithic period (Cro-Magnon people in Europe), about 35,000 to 10,000 years ago?

5 What kinds of changes in religious ideas and practices were occasioned by the Neolithic food-producing revolution (ca. 8000–3000 B.C.E.)?

6 What are some common characteristics of the religions of the ancient agricultural, city-state civilizations?

KEY TERMS: BEGINNINGS OF THE HUMAN RELIGIOUS ADVENTURE

agricultural revolution the widespread changes in human culture when ancient humans learned to produce their own food in Neolithic times

ancient civilizations the great civilizations that developed after the agricultural revolution, with cities, temple cults, kings, commerce, and often systems of writing

animism belief in spirits; theory that religion originated in reverence for spirits of living beings and inanimate objects

great goddesses feminine sacred beings, source of life and power, worshiped at least as early as the Upper Paleolithic period (starting ca. 35,000 B.C.E.)

Homo erectus human species about 500,000 years ago; lived in communities, had many stone tools, and engaged in cooperative hunts

Homo sapiens sapiens modern human species, dating back to Upper Paleolithic period

Indo-Europeans groups of pastoralist peoples who migrated from the steppes of Asia and founded ancient civilizations in Europe, Persia, and India

magic attempt to control forces of nature through rituals and incantations

Neanderthal human species ca. 100,000 to 35,000 years ago, with clear archaeological evidence of religious activities

Neolithic period beginning after the last ice age (ca. 10,000 years ago) when planting was discovered and villages and cities founded

Paleolithic Old Stone Age; in the Upper Paleolithic period (ca. 35,000 to 10,000 years ago) the modern species of *Homo sapiens sapiens* appeared

prehistorical before written records

Part 2   Religions Arising from India

INTRODUCTION

The South Asian subcontinent, the broad cultural area known historically as India (including present-day Nepal, Pakistan, and Bangladesh), has been a fertile spawning ground for world religions. The story of these religions reaches back to ancient indigenous peoples such as those of the Indus valley civilization, and it includes the Aryans who came in from outside to establish Aryan religion and culture in India. From these ancient streams have arisen the religious movements known as Hinduism, Buddhism, Jainism, and—much later, after Muslim influence became strong in India—Sikhism. In spite of wide ethnic diversity in this vast region, this group of religions does share some strikingly similar religious ideas and practices.

There is, of course, a close historical and geographical relationship among these religions. Hinduism, Buddhism, and Jainism all took shape at approximately the same time in north India. Hindus trace their sacred story to the earlier Aryans with their Vedic scriptures, and Jains reach back to Parshva (ninth century B.C.E.) and earlier. But certainly one of the most formative periods for each religion was around the sixth century B.C.E. In Hinduism, the Upanishads were being composed as the foundation of the Hindu perspective. Siddhartha Gautama was following the way to enlightenment and founding the first Buddhist community. And Mahavira also was walking the path to enlightenment as the leader of the Jains. There was some interaction among members of these three movements, and they grappled with many of the same issues as they created three distinct paths. It was not until about two thousand years later that Sikhism was founded, but still this movement grew up in India and drew on the religious visions and practices of devotional Hinduism and Islam in creating a distinctive Sikh way of life.

For all of them, the south Asian subcontinent has been "Mother India," not only historically but also culturally and spiritually. Most of these religions have been content to stay within the bosom of India, with little attempt to spread and translate their spiritual wisdom into other places and cultures. Only Buddhism has become a missionary religion, losing its status in India but spreading the truth of the Buddha throughout South Asia, Southeast Asia, and East Asia. Even though Buddhism does not have a lot of adherents in India today, Buddhists still look to India as the sacred source, since their early history happened there and most of their scriptures were composed there.

What are some elements of the common vision shared among the peoples of these South Asian religions? The people of these religions of India tend to start from experience in the world. Their common perception of human existence is that it goes in cycles, lifetime after lifetime, world age after world age. The human individual stands now, but many existences before have brought about the present state of affairs, and many existences to come are being caused by this existence. Furthermore, the whole universe goes in cycles, without beginning or end, in recurrent evolutions and devolutions like the waves on the sea.

One of the big questions that arises in this context, then, has to do with what is *real* and ultimately significant. It cannot be only the passing phenomena, whether of the world or of oneself. The vision of India says that the real is unified and absolute, beyond the changes and cycles of existence. The sacred is generally not seen in personal, historical terms—although, of course, the sacred can be revealed or reflected in such forms. The ultimate sacred reality is often conceived as impersonal, transcending historical processes, not an individual creator God involved personally in the historical events of the world. Yet there is room, in this religious vision, for personal gods and goddesses as well.

In this view, the real essence of humans is not really our life in this passing world, but rather what connects us with the sacred. Our true nature is somehow to be identified with the ultimate sacred, and the goal of religious practice is to bring this truth to realization. And so each religious tradition leads its adherents to discipline themselves to withdraw attachments to the passing world, blocking up the causes that will bring about future existences. There are religious practices, especially meditation, to help in seeing the sacred within, leading to spiritual fulfillment and liberation from the cycle. Devotion to spiritual beings and ethical disciplines often assist in achieving this religious goal.

But perhaps we have said too much already about the common vision, for Hindus, Buddhists, Jains, and Sikhs bring much more to their own visions, interpreting these basic ideas in distinctive ways, developing their own worlds of symbols that guide and structure life. Many of these symbols look similar, of course, as we would expect among closely related religions. But in each religion the symbols reflect the truth of the religious vision in a characteristic way, and it is that special, unique path of each religious tradition that we seek to understand.

With respect to Buddhism, we should note that from India, Buddhists spread their teachings widely throughout Sri Lanka, Southeast Asia, and East Asia, and in each of these areas Buddhism has developed distinctive forms. But all forms of Buddhism retain a basic continuity with the community that first arose in India. Here in Part 2, Buddhism in China and Japan will be discussed only briefly, since those forms of Buddhism will be further explored in Part 3, Religions of China and Japan.

Hindu Sacred Story and Historical Context

Hindus today make up some 82 percent of those who live in the state of India—that means there are over 800 million Hindus in India, plus several million who live in what is called the Hindu diaspora (in the Americas, Europe, South Africa, and other areas).

But who is a Hindu? The term *Hindu*, of course, is a Western designation for this religious tradition of India, which derives from a Persian word meaning "Indian." Although some question today whether this term is appropriate, it seems commonly accepted by Hindus themselves as an inclusive term to designate their various religious practices. Some scholars today choose to speak of Hinduisms to signal the great variety of traditions and practices. And those who live in the Hindu diaspora seem to be creating yet new Hindu identities.

In any case, Hindu identity is indeed very broad and inclusive. It almost seems that being a Hindu is the same as being a person of India. To be Hindu implies accepting and respecting the ancient traditions of India, especially the Vedic scriptures and the social class structure with its special respect for Brahmans (the priestly class). Thus, except for several dissenting Hindu groups, the only people of India who are really excluded from this Hindu identity are those who do not accept the authority of the Vedas and the special place of the Brahmans—that is, Buddhists, Jains, and Sikhs, together, of course, with Indian Muslims, Christians, and Parsis (the small community of Zoroastrians in India). The Vedas and the social class system—and the sacred realities of which they are a part—provide the center of the Hindu story. Surrounding that center, the rich texture of Hindu identity is filled out by a vast realm of sacred texts, teachings, stories, ritual practices, forms of behavior, and deep personal experiences.

FOUNDATIONS OF THE HINDU TRADITION

Unlike the other religions arising from India and unlike Judaism, Christianity, and Islam, the Hindu religious tradition has no specific founders involved in historical events that gave rise to the religion. The Hindu sacred history places relatively little emphasis on what we normally think of as historical events or persons, and it shows only slight interest in historical sequences. Most things happen in a transcendental kind of time frame. The Vedic scriptures, for example, are considered timeless and eternal. With respect to the narrative epics, Hindu tradition suggests that the events told in the *Ramayana Epic* take place in the *treta-yuga* (the second of the four mythic world ages), hundreds of thousands of years ago measured in human time. And the *Mahabharata Epic* tells of events at the end of the *dvapara-yuga*, still ages before the present world age, the *kali-yuga*. The sacred reality is reflected in all these ages and cycles, but it also transcends them. So the stories about the gods and goddesses, the heroes and heroines, are not particularly concerned about how they fit in the human history of our age. Hindus do not seem to worry about the "historical" Krishna, for example, in contrast to Christian interest in the historicity of Christ. The great gods, goddesses, kings, and heroes the stories tell about are important because they are models of deep, eternal religious truth and value.

So the sacred history is not so much about the founding of Hinduism as it is about the *foundations* of Hinduism—that is, the sacred realities that form the pattern for Hindu life and meaning. As we look at the Hindu story, we need to provide some historical orientation, which includes events such as the migration of the Aryans into India around 1500 B.C.E., the composing of the Upanishads, the development of city-states and the Hindu social order, and the like. But we must take care not to confuse the historical orientation with what Hindus consider to be the real sacred story: the ancient sages hearing and transmitting the eternal Vedas, the legendary and mythological events about gods and heroes described in the epics, and foundations of essential practices such as yogic meditation and devotion to gods and goddesses. Although we need the historical orientation, we also need to understand that the real meaning of the sacred history, for Hindus, is in those events that transcend our historical age.

The Formative Period of Hinduism

As the foundation of Hinduism, the Hindu sacred story highlights the people called the Aryans and their sacred texts, the Vedas. From scholarly research we know that the Aryans were related to Indo-European peoples who probably came into India from outside and eventually became the Hindus. But we also know that there were indigenous peoples in India prior to the Aryans, in particular the people of the Indus valley civilization that had reached its zenith around 2500 B.C.E. It appears that sometime after 2000 B.C.E., the Aryans, migrating into India from the northwest, eventually became dominant—but in the process some of the indigenous peoples and their religious ideas eventually were absorbed into Hinduism as it developed over a number of centuries. Here—as in the case of the ancient Israelites settling in Canaan—took place a fascinating encounter of very different cultures, for the Indus valley people were basically agriculturalists, and the Aryans traditionally had been pastoralists. We do not know much about the details of the interaction between the Aryans and the various indigenous peoples, unfortunately, but the resulting creation was the richly textured religion of Hinduism.

The Indus Valley Civilization Among the indigenous peoples of ancient India, the **Indus valley civilization** stands out as particularly advanced and impressive. Coming to full bloom by about 2500 B.C.E. and flourishing for a thousand years or so, this civilization stretched for a thousand miles along the valley of the Indus River. It was comparable in many ways with the two other great river valley civilizations that existed at the same time, ancient Egypt along the Nile and ancient Sumer along the Tigris and Euphrates rivers. Like them, the Indus valley people lived by agriculture with domestic animals, developed a system of writing (unfortunately, not enough remains to be deciphered), and built many towns and cities. Two of the cities, Mohenjo-Daro and Harappa, were quite large and appear to have been religious and administrative centers. There is a most striking uniformity of culture throughout the whole civilization, from the cities to the several hundred towns and villages thus far discovered, suggesting rigid control by powerful rulers. For example, the cities were all carefully laid out on the same plan, with major streets crossing each other at right angles. Houses were supplied with water and had bathrooms from which water drained out into a drainage system.

Archaeological investigations have turned up a number of things suggestive of the religious vision of these people. One striking point is that they had a great reverence for water. In addition to the bathrooms in individual houses, apparently for ritual purposes, a large bathing tank has been found in the great platform mound of Mohenjo-Daro, flanked by dressing rooms and arcades. It seems they considered water to have important purifying powers, an idea that we find also in later Hinduism.

The archaeological finds include a large number of clay figurines of animals, women, and men. As befits an agricultural civilization, there appears to have been emphasis on the fertility of mother earth. Many terra-cotta figurines depicting females have been discovered, clearly associated with powers of fertility and the growth of plants. Mythic scenes depicting fertility powers appear on many small personal soapstone seals. There is a series of scenes, for example, portraying an ensemble of goddesses, trees, tigers, and water buffaloes. On one seal there appears to be a horned goddess amid the branches of a pipal tree (sacred in later India), worshiped by a figure on bended knee. The kneeling worshiper presents before the goddess an animal that is a composite of buffalo hindquarters, ram horns and forepart, and a large masklike human face. Lined up in a row are seven figures with tunics, pigtails, curved horns, and bangled arms. It may be that later Hindu traditions of the great goddesses and of the recurring patterns of death and life were influenced by the fertility religion of these ancient people.

Another religious emphasis has to do with male creative powers. Many figurines and seals depict powerful male animals—bulls, tigers, rhinoceroses, antelopes, elephants, and unicorn-type animals. A two-tiered incense stand is often set before the single-horned animal, showing that these male animals represented sacred power to be worshiped. A number of phalluses, models of the male sexual organ, have been found in the excavations, suggesting some ritual worship of male fertility power. A most fascinating figure is depicted on several seals: what appears to be a male person seated in a kind of yoga posture with legs drawn up and heels together, similar to the posture used in yoga meditation in later Hinduism. In one seal, the god (assuming the figure represents sacred power) is surrounded by an elephant, a tiger, a rhinoceros, and a buffalo, and beneath his stool are two deer. He wears a headdress of two horns, with a plant growing between them, and there appears to be a phallic emphasis. The combination of symbols is striking: fertility of plants and animals, yogic meditation, and male sexual energy. Differing interpretations have been suggested, but this figure is at least suggestive of themes in later Hinduism, especially those associated with the great god Shiva, who is known as the great yogin and often symbolized by the lingam (phallic symbol).

Worship was probably carried on both in homes and in public shrines. At the domestic level there would have been ritual votive offerings involving fertility figurines, bathing, and ritual purity. On the public level, worship was probably associated with the raised platform mounds, perhaps involving animal sacrifices.

The Indus valley civilization began to decline around 1900 B.C.E., dying out slowly because of desiccation of the lower Indus basin, perhaps fragmenting into smaller regional communities. This civilization no doubt had some connections with earlier preurban cultures of India and related areas, as part of a broader cultural complex in pre-Aryan times. No historical documentation exists to show the impact these cultures had on the development of Hinduism, and certainly Hindus do not usually count the Indus valley people as part of their sacred story. But we—looking now from the outside—may surmise that the Indus valley civilization, along with other pre-Aryan peoples in India, contributed to some of the characteristic Hindu ideas and practices, especially those associated with water, the cyclic pattern of existence, yogic meditation, and the great goddesses and gods.

Aryan Religion: The Vedic Period   The group of people who migrated into the Indus Valley from the northwest sometime after 2000 B.C.E., perhaps around 1500 B.C.E., called themselves **Aryans** ("noble ones"). Some Hindu scholars, it is true, feel these Aryans developed within India over a longer period of time. In any case, they were related to the larger grouping of Indo-European peoples who migrated in various directions from the original Indo-European homeland, probably in the steppe land that stretches from Eastern Europe to Central Asia. Some of these original Indo-European peoples migrated westward into Europe and became the Greeks, the Romans, the Germanic peoples, the Slavs, the Balts, and so forth. Others of these peoples migrated eastward and became the Persians (Iranians), the Armenians, and the Aryans. The language spoken by the Aryans, which later evolved into Sanskrit, was closely related to the other Indo-European languages, as was their culture and religion. Wherever the Indo-Europeans went, of course, they interacted with indigenous peoples and created distinct cultures and religions.

The Aryans were pastoralists (cattle herders), grouped in a number of tribes, each headed by a chieftain. Their society was divided into three classes: the warriors, the priests, and the herders or producers. They were fierce warriors, having domesticated the horse and invented the chariot, and they were skilled in metallurgy and weaponry. After settling in India, the Aryans continued to develop their own traditions for several centuries, gradually absorbing local, non-Aryan practices and beliefs into their fundamentally Aryan religion.

Although the Aryans did not have a writing system, from early times they composed hymns and ritual verses called *Veda* (knowledge), transmitting them orally in priestly families. Hindus understand the Vedas to be timeless, eternal truths "heard" by the *rishis*, the seer-poets of old; they are the original foundation of Hinduism. Special place is accorded to the four **Samhitas** (collections), also simply called Vedas. The *Rig Veda* is the oldest and most important collection, with over one thousand hymns. The *Sama Veda* contains verses arranged to be sung by the musical specialist during the sacrifice, and the *Yajur Veda* supplied short formulas spoken by the priest who performed the physical operations in the sacrificial ritual. The fourth collection, the *Atharva Veda*, contains incantations for priests to use for various needs such as childbirth, illness, securing the affection of a lover, and much more. These Vedic hymns were recited, chanted, and performed as sacred liturgy.

The religion that is expressed in these Vedic hymns and formulas centers on worship of gods by means of sacrifice, petition, and praise. The gods are many, residing in the three realms (sky, atmosphere, and earth) and showing their powers in the various processes of nature. The word for *god* in Sanskrit is *deva*, meaning "shining" or "auspicious." And that is what the gods are—the powers that create life and growth, that are present in wind, fire, water, speech, consciousness, and all facets of existence. The gods include Dyaus Pitar (god of the sky), Prithivi (earth goddess), Ushas (dawn, daughter of heaven), Surya (the shining sun), Savitar (the sun as generator), Rudra (destroyer and healer), Mitra (the sun), Tvashtar (the heavenly blacksmith), Vayu (the wind), and very many more. As examples of these gods, let us look briefly at four of those most frequently mentioned in the *Rig Veda*, namely, Varuna, Indra, Agni, and Soma.

Varuna is god of the vault of the sky, sometimes described as creating the world, whose function it is to guard the cosmic order (called *rita*). In that capacity Varuna is the god who sees humans in their wrongdoings and catches them in his noose, punishing them with disease. Thus, he must be petitioned to remove those offenses.

> For the emperor [Varuna] I will sing a splendid, deep prayer, one that will be dear to the famous Varuna who struck apart the earth and spread it beneath the sun as the priest who performs the slaughter spreads out the victim's skin. He stretched out the middle realm of space in the trees; he laid victory in swift horses and milk in the dawn cows, intelligence in hearts and fire in the waters. Varuna placed the sun in the sky and Soma on the mountain. . . . If we have cheated like gamblers in a game, whether we know it or really do not know it, O god, cast all these offences away like loosened bonds. Let us be dear to you, Varuna.

(*Rig Veda* 5.85.1–2,8)[1]

Indra is a god of the atmosphere, a storm god who shows himself in the lightning and thunder. Like Thor among the Scandinavians, Indra is a boisterous warrior god, drinking soma (a hallucinating, invigorating drink) and leading people in battle against their enemies. Many hymns tell of Indra's cosmic battle with the demon Vritra, who has shut up the waters and the sun; after a fierce battle, Indra slays him and releases the life-giving forces.

> Let me now sing the heroic deeds of Indra, the first that the thunderbolt-wielder performed. He killed the dragon and pierced an opening for the waters; he split open the bellies of mountains. He killed the dragon who lay upon the mountain; Tvastr fashioned the roaring thunderbolt for him. Like lowing cows, the flowing waters rushed straight down to the sea. Wildly excited like a bull, he took the Soma for himself and drank the extract from the three bowls in the three-day Soma ceremony. Indra the Generous seized his thunderbolt to hurl it as a weapon; he killed the firstborn of dragons.

(*Rig Veda* 1.32.1–3)[2]

Of the many gods of the third realm, earth, **Agni** (Fire) assumes special importance as the god of the sacrificial fire. The power of Agni is centered especially in the fire sacrifice, Agni being the sacred power that accepts the offerings and transports them to the realm of the gods. For that reason, Agni is addressed in nearly one-third of the Rig Vedic hymns, as in this hymn that opens the *Rig Veda*:

> I pray to Agni, the household priest who is the god of the sacrifice, the one who chants and invokes and brings most treasure. Agni earned the prayers of the ancient sages, and of those of the present, too; he will bring the gods here. Through Agni one may win wealth, and growth from day to day, glorious and most abounding in heroic sons. Agni, the sacrificial ritual that you encompass on all sides—only that one goes to the gods. . . . To you, Agni, who shine upon darkness, we come day after day, bringing our thoughts and homage to you, the king over sacrifices, the shining guardian of the Order, growing in your own house. Be easy for us to reach, like a father to his son. Abide with us, Agni, for our happiness.

(*Rig Veda* 1.1.1–4,7–9)[3]

Throughout all periods of Hinduism, special importance has been attached to the ritual of fire sacrifice—and, thus, to the god Agni as the priest of the gods.

Another god of the earth realm who is prominent in the Vedic hymns is Soma, a god whose power is known in *soma*, an intoxicating drink offered to the gods in sacrifice and drunk by the worshipers. "We have drunk the Soma; we have become immortal; we have gone to the light; we have found the gods," a hymn celebrates (*Rig Veda* 8.48.3).[4] Soma symbolizes both ecstasy and the special power of consciousness experienced through this divine power.

In the early Vedic conception, then, power for running the world and human existence derives from the gods. How humans live and relate to the gods is important; properly

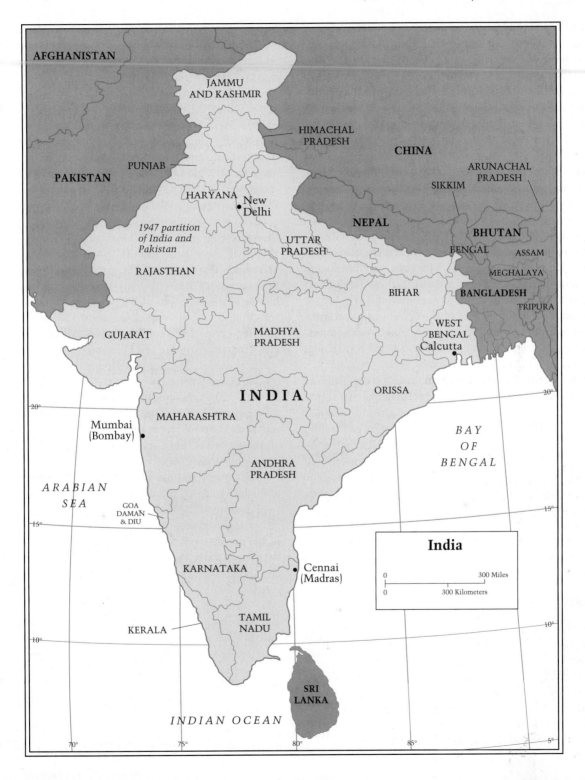

AFGHANISTAN

JAMMU
AND KASHMIR

HIMACHAL
PRADESH

CHINA

PUNJAB

ARUNACHAL
PRADESH

PAKISTAN

SIKKIM

HARYANA

New
Delhi

*1947 partition
of India and
Pakistan*

NEPAL

BHUTAN

UTTAR
PRADESH

BENGAL

ASSAM

RAJASTHAN

MEGHALAYA

BIHAR

BANGLADESH

TRIPURA

GUJARAT

MADHYA
PRADESH

WEST
BENGAL
Calcutta

INDIA

ORISSA

20°

20°

MAHARASHTRA

Mumbai
(Bombay)

*BAY
OF
BENGAL*

ANDHRA
PRADESH

*ARABIAN
SEA*

GOA
DAMAN
& DIU

15°

15°

India

KARNATAKA

Cennai
(Madras)

0   300 Miles

0   300 Kilometers

TAMIL
NADU

KERALA

10°

10°

SRI
LANKA

INDIAN OCEAN

70°   75°   80°   85°   5°

serving the gods results in wealth, long life, many sons, and a happy life after death. The Aryans thought of human life as centered in the *atman* (breath, soul), which lived on after the death of the body. At death, the atman, by means of the funeral fire sacrifice, with help from the person's meritorious deeds, is transported to the heavenly realm of the fathers to enjoy the continued blessings of life.

In the early Aryan system, the most important way of serving the gods was sacrificing to them by means of the fire sacrifice ritual. Daily the head of the household performed domestic sacrifices to Agni and to the sun god, and periodically much more elaborate sacrifices were performed with the aid of the priestly class. The larger sacrifices were performed in the open field. Priests built sacrificial fires, poured ghee and soma on them, and chanted sacred hymns and formulas. The gods were invoked to come and sit with the worshipers on the grass at the holy place, to listen to the hymns and petitions, and to enjoy the ghee and soma. The purpose of the ritual was to promote happiness, health, long life, many offspring, wealth, remission of guilt for wrongdoing, and generally the good things of life.

The basic idea behind the sacrificial cult is the vision of the Vedic seers that humans need to participate in sacred power by sustaining and reinvigorating Agni and the other gods so that the gods will continue their work of creating and bringing blessings to the world and to human existence. Although this Vedic perspective on the centrality of sacrifice underwent development in the next centuries, the fact that humans are partners with the gods in continuing the creative processes of the world by sacrifice is a basic presupposition of Hindu thought and ritual. And the Vedic hymns and daily sacrifices are still considered essential to the Hindu community today, performed by priests and people of the upper classes.

Searching for the One Reality Behind All This   In the story of how Hinduism developed, there appears an important speculative period leading from the early Vedic religion toward the classical flowering of Hinduism. We can see beginnings of this speculative period already by about 1000 B.C.E. with some of the later hymns in the *Rig Veda* (e.g., some of those in Book 10), followed by the **Brahmanas**, ritual manuals and interpretations (ca. 800 B.C.E.), and then finally the **Upanishads** (starting ca. 600 B.C.E.). In these texts we find important new ideas about sacred reality and human existence. Whereas there is no way of demonstrating the origin of these new ideas, it might be supposed that some of them came about in response to pre-Aryan, indigenous religious ideas and practices.

That something new is happening is evident by a new style used by the seers: They turn to questioning and speculation. "Which god should we worship with sacrifices?" is the refrain of one hymn that attempts to probe the origins of everything and find one reality behind all the gods (*Rig Veda* 10.121). No longer satisfied with the traditions about the power of the individual gods, the sage speculates that some power prior to the gods is the origin of everything. In a similar way, another hymn even questions the power and the knowledge of the traditional gods: "Who really knows? Who will here proclaim it? Whence was it produced? Whence is this creation? The gods came afterwards, with the creation of this universe. Who then knows whence it has arisen?" (*Rig Veda* 10.129.6).[5] What the sages are searching for is the sacred center of all, the unified One from which all derives. In their tentative speculations they give different names to this One and describe it in different ways. The poets say that this One is the one life of all the gods, the reality who encompasses all the worlds (*Rig Veda* 10.121.7, 10). One graphic description envisions the One as a gigantic person (*purusha*) who pervades the whole universe, from whom everything, including all space and all time, derives. Even the gods form part of the one Purusha (*Rig Veda* 10.90).

This last-mentioned hymn to Purusha shows that, along with the vision of the One, a number of related notions were coming to the fore. It is when Purusha is *sacrificed* that all of the universe comes into existence. The early Vedic idea of the sacrifice reinvigorating the gods is now extended to the whole universe. This primordial sacrifice of the One creates everything (including the gods); this means, by derivation, that each time a priest performs the ritual sacrifice he is repeating this primordial sacrifice and, thus, creating and sustaining the world. It is significant that this hymn to Purusha includes the Hindu social order as part of the universe created in the primordial sacrifice. The mouth of Purusha became the Brahmans (priestly class), his two arms were made into the Kshatriyas (warriors), his two thighs became the Vaishyas (merchants, workers), and from his two feet the Shudras (servants) were born. This first mention of the basic Hindu social class system in the Hindu sacred texts is noteworthy in that, first of all, it considers these four classes to be part of the cosmic order initiated in the primordial creation. But it also shows that by now the warrior class has lost its superior standing and has been replaced at the top by the Brahman class. The priests, after all, are the ones who know how to perform the sacrificial rituals that uphold the world and even the gods and, thus, their authority has by now become all-important.

Another tendency during this period is the increased emphasis on the importance of knowledge. Finally, the sages conclude, it is not so much the outward performance of the sacrifices that upholds the world and provides blessings, but it is the knowledge of the inner reality. One text from the Brahmanas explains the great public sacrifice known as the Building of the Fire Altar—made of materials collected over the course of a whole year. The text interprets the real meaning of the building in terms of the upholding of the whole universe:

> Verily, this brick-built Fire-altar (Agni) is this terrestrial world. The waters (of the encircling ocean) are its circle of enclosing-stones. The men its Yagushmatis bricks, the cattle its Sudadohas. The plants and trees are its cement-fillings (between the layers of bricks). . . . Thus this comes to make up the whole Agni, and the whole Agni comes to be the space-filler. And, verily, whosoever knows this, thus comes to be that whole (Agni) who is the space-filler. But, indeed, that Fire-altar is also the air; the junction of heaven and earth (the horizon) is its circle of enclosing stones. . . . But, indeed, that Fire-altar also is the sky. . . . But, indeed, that Fire-altar also is the sun. . . . But, indeed, that Fire-altar also is the Year. . . . But, indeed, that Fire-altar also is the body. . . . But, indeed, that Fire-altar is all beings, all the gods.

But the interpretation of this ritual makes it clear that the important thing is not just the performance of the ritual; rather, the *inner knowledge* is the power that leads to the world of blessing:

> Regarding this there is this verse: "By knowledge they ascend to that state where desires have vanished; sacrificial gifts go not thither, nor the fervid performers of rites without knowledge." For, indeed, he who does not know this does not attain to that world either by sacrificial gifts or by devout practices. Only to those who know does that world belong.

(*Shatapatha Brahmana* 10.5.4)[6]

Searching for the One, raising the power of sacrifice to cosmic levels, developing the class system with the Brahmans as supreme, and putting an emphasis on inner knowledge—with these developments there begin to emerge some of the basic lines of Brahmanism, as this early form of Hinduism is sometimes called. These ideas are worked out more fully in the Upanishads (some as early as 800 B.C.E., later ones ca. 600–200 B.C.E.), and still more ideas are added to form the foundation of thought for classical Hinduism.

Speculation and Knowledge: The Upanishads   There is no clear break between the Brahmanas and the Upanishads; some of the earlier Upanishads (called Aranyakas, Forest Treatises) were composed as part of the Brahmanas. Hindus consider the Upanishads to be the revelation of the same truths as the Vedic hymns and the Brahmanas, and all of these texts are collectively called **Vedas**. In this transitional period, the earlier Vedic rituals and sacrifices were being continued by many people. The ritual manuals called Brahmanas had multiplied the sacrificial ceremonies and made them extremely complex and complicated—in keeping with the idea that the order of the whole world is upheld by the proper performing of the ritual sacrifices. But there were some teachers and disciples who continued searching and probing after the inner truth of all reality, the cause of human problems, and the possible solutions offered by knowledge and meditation. The Upanishads resulted from this search. The word *upanishad* perhaps refers to teachings passed from a teacher to a disciple sitting near the teacher (*upa*, "near"; *ni*, "down"; *sad*, "sit"), and the setting given in many of the Upanishads is just that: a teacher answering the disciple's questions, a father teaching his son, or a sage instructing an assembly.

Some of the Upanishads talk about ritual and sacrifice, but these acts are both cosmosized and internalized. The *Brihad-aranyka Upanishad*, for example, refers to the great horse sacrifice, but then it proceeds to show how this ritual is really an internal act of meditation by which the whole world is sacrificed. The worshiper is instructed to meditate on the dawn as the head of the sacrificial horse, the sun as his eye, the wind as his breath, the year as his body, the sky as his back, the atmosphere as his belly, the earth as the under part of his belly, and so forth. "He [who knows this] wards off repeated death, death obtains him not, death becomes his body, he becomes one of these deities" (*Brihad-aranyka Upanishad*, 1.2.7).[7]

The motivation for this speculation seems to be a new conception that had been developing in some circles, perhaps influenced by the Buddhist and Jain movements.

Now, instead of the early Vedic optimistic view of life in this world and the next, there is increasing concern about "repeated death"—that is, death ending not only this life but also the future life. Some way to escape this re-death needs to be found, and this is beyond the power of rituals and sacrifices to the gods. In the Upanishads, this idea of re-death was broadened to a cyclical view of human existence: being born in this world is the result of dying in another life, and on and on in a never-ending wheel of existence. The way to understand the human problem, according to the Upanishads, is to see that it is *samsara*, an endless round of birth and death.

What causes samsara? Tied together with the notion of samsara is the discovery of *karma*, the law that every action has its effect. *Karma* literally means "action," and the sages knew from experience that what one does causes consequences to happen. The idea of karma already had religious implications, in the notion that the action of the sacrifice causes results for the gods and for humans. The teachers of the Upanishads explained that the soul (**atman**) that dwells in the body has reached its present state because of actions (karma) performed in previous lifetimes, and that the actions performed in this lifetime will lead the atman after death to be born into another body, and then another—and the circle of **rebirth** goes on and on.

If all this world, including the gods, is caught up in samsara, where can liberation from this cycle be found? The Upanishads continue the earlier speculation about the One, that which is truly real and the source of all, and the importance of knowledge more than ritual and sacrifice. Although many terms had been used, many teachers of the Upanishads finally settle on *Brahman* as the designation of the One, the Real. Earlier, the term *brahman* had meant the sacred words used in the sacrificial rituals. Now Brahman is extended to identify that one power, the inner source of all, that which is absolute and eternal and prior to all that is known as samsara.

Finally, according to these teachers, it is knowledge of Brahman that brings liberation (*moksha*) for the atman from the cycle of samsara. The means for attaining this liberating knowledge is meditation on the atman and the Brahman. No longer the outer rituals and actions, it is the inner knowledge that leads to the source that brings the power of transformation and transcends the trap of samsara. The Upanishads, and the sages who continued to practice this way of knowledge, devised disciplines and techniques of meditation designed to bring about this transformation and, thus, final liberation (moksha) from samsara.

Whereas the vision of the Upanishads is complex and the goal practical only for those who are spiritually advanced, the basic ideas of the Upanishads have become foundational for Hinduism. The reality of Brahman and atman, the problem of karma and samsara, the goal of moksha—all Hindus recognize these as fundamental to the Hindu religion.

The texts of the Upanishads complete the sacred writings collectively called Vedas, as they were regularized according to the Brahmanical tradition. All of these texts—the Upanishads, together with the early Vedic hymns (Samhitas) and the Brahmanas, are known collectively as the *Shruti* (that which is "heard" by the sages), the eternal revelation of the truth. These Shruti writings may not be easily understood, but they are considered the eternal truth, and being a Hindu means respecting them as such and honoring those who study and recite them.

The Many Faces of the Hindu Tradition

During this long period of development, the Indo-Aryans had gradually settled into villages and towns, and a city-state culture developed in northern India. There was considerable disunity, with many small kingdoms and tribal groups, and one center of developing Hinduism moved eastward out of the Indus valley, toward the Ganges River valley. Starting in the sixth century B.C.E. political and religious unrest brought challenges and changes to the Brahmanical tradition. The Persian Empire established a province in western India, opening the door to Persian influence in India. And throughout northern India smaller kingdoms and tribal groups, which had provided support for Aryan rulers and Brahmanical ritualism, were being absorbed into larger political units. In this unrest, a number of alternative, non-Vedic movements rose to challenge the dominance of the Brahmanical tradition.

Two such alternatives that had a lasting impact were the Jain and Buddhist movements. Both Mahavira, founder of the Jains, and Siddhartha Gautama, the Buddha, rejected the sacrifice-oriented Vedic ritual system, teaching instead a more direct, personal solution to the problem of endless rebirths in the cycle of life. The Jains put the emphasis on rigorous asceticism, ridding the self of karma through fasting, mental control, and physical austerity. The Buddhists emphasized discipline, meditation, and knowledge that would lead to enlightenment and breaking the chain of samsara. Other movements likewise advocated ascetic disciplines of yoga, while popular cults devoted to gods and goddesses gained followers.

Adding to the unrest came Alexander the Great's invasion of western India in the fourth century B.C.E. Stimulated by these incursions, the Maurya family established a dynasty in northern India that eventually grew to include most of central and southern India as well. The Mauryan rulers were not especially devoted to the Vedic traditions, often giving their support to the non-Vedic groups such as Jains and Buddhists. King Ashoka (ca. 269–232 B.C.E.), in fact, became a devout Buddhist and promoted Buddhism throughout his empire and beyond. After Ashoka, the Mauryan Empire broke up into disunity once again, but in the meantime the traditional Brahmanical system of Vedic sacrifices and priestly control lost ground among the people. Finally, after a lengthy period of rival foreign kingdoms in northwestern India and regional kingdoms elsewhere, under the Gupta dynasty (320–467 C.E.) there was a return of political unity.

In response to these changing situations, a variety of religious tendencies were being developed in the Brahmanical tradition in this creative period from about 400 B.C.E. to 400 C.E., which is sometimes designated the epic era of Hinduism. Some of these tendencies go back to earlier ideas and practices; others probably represent non-Aryan forms surfacing in the Hindu synthesis. These tendencies began to focus in a number of directions, later designated as *margas* (paths). These included practical forms of meditation and seeking release from samsara, including practices of withdrawal and yoga; concerns for the duties of the societal classes and the ongoing life of society; and a flourishing of interest in worship (bhakti) of the gods old and new. Overall, this long epic, classical period led to a unification and consolidation of Hinduism.

During this time a great many new sacred writings were composed, expressing the new ideas and practices. To distinguish these new writings from the Shruti scriptures, they are usually referred to as the *Smriti* (remembered) writings, the tradition. Major Smriti scriptures composed in this classical period include the Yoga Sutras, especially the *Yoga Sutras of Patanjali*; the Dharmasutras and the Dharmashastras, especially the *Law-code of Manu*; and the great *Ramayana* and *Mahabharata Epics*, including the *Bhagavad Gita*. Whereas these scriptures do not have the same status or universal respect as the earlier Smriti ones, to many Hindus these writings provide the most immediate guidance in the sacred story of Hinduism.

Development of Practices of Withdrawal and Yoga
The practice of withdrawing from the world and practicing asceticism and meditation is ancient in India, mentioned already in the *Rig Veda* (*Rig Veda* 10.136). The Upanishads talk about sages like Yajnavalkya who live a detached life as hermits in the forest to practice mental disciplines. These disciplines involve bodily discipline and controlling the mind to realize the true inner atman and reach moksha. A famous image is that of the chariot representing bodily life and the charioteer as the soul; as the charioteer controls the chariot to reach his destination, so the soul should control the various forces of the body, disengaging the atman from its temporary sojourn in a bodily existence (*Katha Upanishad* 1.3.3–9).

A related technique to reach liberation that developed was called *yoga* (from the same root as "yoke"). It is by controlling one's attachment to the outer world and withdrawing inward, withdrawing even from mental activity, that liberation can be attained. Classical Hinduism developed many forms of yoga. Indeed, almost every Hindu movement has some form of yogic discipline; physical bodily control, mental discipline, ways of performing actions, even worshiping the gods can all be called yoga. The best-known form of classical yoga is described in the *Yoga Sutras of Patanjali* (ca. 200 C.E.?), and these writings have the status of scripture for many. Patanjali devised an eight-step method of discipline and control leading to transformation and liberation. This "royal yoga" as set forth by Patanjali (discussed later) became the basis of one of the later schools of philosophy, and it has guided much of the development in yogic practice ever since.

Compilation of the Dharma Scriptures   Another stream of Hindu thought and practice, also reaching back to ancient times, is the emphasis on the eternal order of everything and of human life within that order. In early Vedic times Varuna was looked to as the guardian of this eternal order (*rita*). In the classical period, the eternal order of everything was called *Dharma*, and sages were busy composing writings that spelled out what this order was all about, especially for society and for the individual within society.

These Dharmashastras (Dharma texts) picture an idealized society that is in conformity with the eternal truths of the Vedas. In fact, what Westerners call "Hinduism" is to Hindus simply the "Eternal Dharma." It is true that some tension exists between the goal of moksha, liberation from the world of samsara, and the concern of Dharma, maintaining the good of the social order. But Hinduism is built on that tension, and most religious practices acknowledge the duty both to support the social order and to seek the goal of moksha.

Basic to this vision of Dharma is the idea of karma and rebirth, as taught by the Upanishads. Everyone is born into a particular place in society because of the karma accumulated in past existences. The role of the individual, thus, is determined by birth, and she or he is expected to perform the actions (karma) appropriate for that particular role. The best known of the Dharma texts is the writing called the *Law-code of Manu*, traditionally thought to be given by Manu, the originator of humans and the first lawgiver. This extremely influential writing spells out the Dharma especially in terms of class (*varna*, or "color"), giving detailed descriptions of the duties of people born as Brahmans, Kshatriyas, Vaishyas, and Shudras. These Dharma laws, thus, consolidated a variety of practices in society, influenced perhaps by the development of Buddhism and Jainism with their monastic/lay structure of society. Probably the periodic disunity in India and the incursions of barbarian peoples into northwestern India spurred on these attempts to structure Hindu society in an orderly way in conformity with religious ideas. This idealized varna system later developed into the so-called caste system, in which there are hundreds of subcastes linked with these four classes, and it has continued to exercise great influence over Hindu society.

The *Ramayana* and *Mahabharata* Epics An important development in the Hindu tradition is the use of popular stories to convey religious meaning. In fact, for many

Rama, divine hero
of the *Ramayana Epic.* Rama, India, Tamil Nadu; Chola period, 11th century. Copper alloy. H. 37 3/4 in. (95.9 cm.). Photograph by Susuma Wakisaka, Idemitsu Museum of Arts, Tokyo. The Asia Society, New York, Mr. and Mrs. John D. Rockefeller 3rd Collection.

Hindus, the part of the story they are most familiar with involves the great epics, the *Mahabharata* and the *Ramayana*, for these tell the stories of the gods and the heroes of old who provide models for the Hindu way of life. The epics combine interest in the path of knowledge and liberation with support for the values of Dharma and action in society. They also provide a broad foundation for bhakti, that is, worship of the gods. The epics developed over many centuries but probably reached their final form between 200 B.C.E. and 200 C.E. The events described in these epics are not historical in the same sense as the rise and decline of the Mauryan dynasty, for example; rather they are legendary and mythological events. Yet the Hindu tradition considers these events, as ideal types and models of eternal truth, to be a more significant "history" than the confusing, fleeting realm of day-to-day historical events.

The story of the *Ramayana Epic* is the cosmic battle between the great God Vishnu and the demonic forces of evil, and it establishes the paradigm for human conduct according to the notion of Dharma. The main hero of the story is **Rama**, a prince who is an *avatara* (incarnation) of Vishnu, and his opponent is Ravana, the demon king of the island of Lanka. Rama fought a great war to defeat Ravana and rescue his wife Sita who had been abducted, getting help from a race of monkeys, with the god Hanuman as their chief. In the process, Rama set the model for honest and proper conduct, ruling as a righteous king. Even before he became king he showed high ethical qualities, accepting fourteen years of exile rather than question his father's rash promise that gave the kingship to his younger stepbrother. After he had finally established order and a righteous kingdom, he again demonstrated the highest ethical conduct by banishing his pure, beloved wife Sita from the kingdom because some subjects questioned her chastity while she had been under the demon's power. Besides providing a model of Hindu morality and self-control, this story also presents the god Rama as a divine hero to be worshiped. Throughout northern India, the cult of Rama is very popular, with a great autumn festival called Ramlila, in which the story of Rama is recited and acted out.

The *Mahabharata* is an immensely long and complicated epic poem (nearly 100,000 verses long) dealing with conflicts between two related clans in northern India in a previous world age. The issues have to do not with good and evil forces but with questions of the dharma of warriors, the goal of moksha, and the importance of devotion to the gods. The heroes of the epic are the five Pandava brothers, who have a conflict with their cousins over who will rule northern India. In this rambling, fascinating story, the most famous section is a chapter called the *Bhagavad Gita* (song of the beloved one). As the two armies prepare to meet on the battlefield, Arjuna, the most renowned warrior of the Pandavas, sees that the ranks of the enemies include relatives, friends, teachers, and the like, and he is overcome with grief. He drops his weapons and says that it would be better to be killed than to inflict such suffering on others. His charioteer is **Krishna**, an avatara (incarnation) of the great God **Vishnu**, who proceeds to teach Arjuna—and all of us—the truth about existence, providing a synthesis of Hinduism that to this day remains the most popular scriptural presentation of the way of Hinduism.

Arjuna really is raising a fundamental question of human life: Is it always best to do one's duty? His duty as a warrior is to fight and kill, but wouldn't it be better for everyone if he did not fight? In answer, Krishna first teaches that, although the body is destroyed, the atman is imperishable and simply takes itself to a new body, much like a person discarding old clothes and putting on new ones—therefore, one should not grieve over death. Second, Krishna explains, action done without desire for its fruits, that is, done simply because it is one's duty, is higher than nonaction. The key is to perform actions without attachment and desires: "When he renounces all desires and acts without craving, possessiveness, or individuality, he finds peace" (*Bhagavad Gita* 2.71).[8] In this way Krishna synthesizes both paths: seeking liberation and performing one's duty in society.

But the real focus of the *Bhagavad Gita* is **bhakti**, devotion to one's god. The highest path, Krishna teaches, is the path of selfless action and wisdom through loving and surrendering to Krishna as the supreme Lord. Krishna really is none other than the great God Vishnu, creator and preserver of the whole universe. And those who worship him can

find the highest liberation: "Keep me in your mind and devotion, sacrifice to me, bow to me, discipline your self toward me, and you will reach me!" (9.34).[9]

So the *Gita* presents a grand synthesis of Hinduism, putting forth the ideas of different paths or margas that became important in later Hinduism. In particular, the *Gita*, by emphasizing the worship of Krishna, opened the way for a great flourishing of bhakti, devotion to the gods, in the next centuries. In this great poem, beloved by Hindus of all persuasions, we see most clearly the foundation for what it means to be Hindu.

The epics describe other gods also, besides Vishnu and his incarnations, Rama and Krishna. The *Mahabharata* tells stories of the other great God of classical Hinduism, **Shiva**, the divine mountain yogin who as the creator of all beings is associated with the lingam (phallic pillar). The epic also refers to the virgin goddess Durga who delights in wine and animal sacrifice and slays the buffalo demon. By the end of the epic period, the great Goddess **Devi** rises to central importance for many Hindus, representing the creative power of *prakriti* (primal matter or nature). She is worshiped alongside Vishnu and Shiva with the same basic rituals. Over the next centuries, the growing bhakti practice tends to cluster around these theistic traditions associated with Vishnu, Shiva, and Devi, the great Goddess.

So with all these elements of the story—the Upanishads and the Yoga Sutras with their emphasis on meditation and release, the Dharmashastras outlining the proper way of life in society, and the epics summing it all up and emphasizing devotion to the gods—we can see the basic outlines of Hindu identity.

CONTINUING TRANSFORMATIONS IN THE HINDU STORY

The master story of any religion is always somewhat open-ended; the creative events continue to have effect even to the present time. Often, however, there is a sense of closing the age of the sacred story. For example, Christians determined the limits of the canon of scripture as the foundation of Christian teaching, and Muslims consider the source of truth to be the revelation through Muhammad as the final prophet, with no more to come. What happens afterward is historical transformation of the story. In Hindu tradition, however, the sacred story continues in further historical transformations without any clear break. Even after the great epics, more sacred writings continue to come forth, expanding the stories of the gods and the possibilities of truth and ritual, throughout much of the long period from the end of the epic classical period up to the beginnings of the modern age (ca. 400–1800). Philosophical schools developed to explore the deep truths of Hinduism. And a substantial impact came from the Muslim invasion and dominance over much of India.

Shaping the Sacred Ways: Puranas and Tantras

Major developments in worship and ritual took place in this medieval period, shaping Hinduism in new ways, creating visions and practices that have remained a major part of Hinduism until the present day.

The Flowering of Bhakti: Puranas and Sectarian Hinduism

A great flowering of devotional cults took place, a movement that came to dominate all of Hinduism with its gods and goddesses, puja (worship of divine images), temples, festivals, and the like. The new line of kings that reunited northern India in 320 C.E., the Guptas, gave strong support to worshiping the gods, especially Vishnu, raising theism to the level of a state religion, supporting devotional groups and building temples. And this great bhakti synthesis really became constitutive of mainstream Hinduism from this time on.

The gods had always been worshiped in India, but gradually some of the Vedic gods were eased out of prominence, whereas other gods—some perhaps non-Aryan in origin—came to dominate or were combined with Vedic gods. The great epics provided a broad foundation on which bhakti could flourish, and in the centuries following, a series of *Puranas* (ancient stories) were composed describing the various gods and devotion to them. Many devotional cults sprang up, focused on Vishnu or Shiva or Durga and the gods and goddesses associated with them, and poets and singers never tired of creating a wealth of joyous, ecstatic devotional literature.

A number of bhakti scriptures—for example, the *Vishnu Purana*, the *Harivamsa*, and the *Bhagavata Purana*—provide extensive materials related to worshiping Vishnu,

together with his wife Lakshmi, goddess of beauty and wealth, and his delightful avatara, Krishna. Krishna of the *Bhagavad Gita*, as an avatara of Vishnu, taught Arjuna the essence of the way of Hinduism. These Puranas elaborate the story of Krishna greatly, focusing on Krishna Gopala, the lovable baby and young man among the cowherd people of Vrindavana. In festivals, devotees performed the stories of Krishna's love affairs with the cowherd girls and especially with Radha, his favorite—stories that demonstrate the highest form of loving God.

The delight of worshiping Krishna and Rama forms the theme of much religious poetry composed by saint-singers throughout the medieval period, as, for example, in Jayadeva's *Gitagovinda* (twelfth century), one of the world's most beautiful love poems. In the sixteenth century, a great revival of Vishnu bhakti swept northern India, especially Bengal, led by the famous saint Chaitanya (1486–1533). He introduced the practice of devotees parading around the streets publicly singing and chanting and dancing in praise of the lord. He and his followers established Krishna temples and systematized the theology of Krishna worship. Chaitanya himself was widely regarded as an incarnation of both Krishna and Radha (Krishna's lover) in one body. This tradition of ecstatic Krishna worship has continued to the present and even has been introduced into America through the International Society for Krishna Consciousness (popularly known as the Hare Krishnas).

The stories of Shiva in the Puranas have quite a different mood from those of Vishnu. There is no connected life story for Shiva, as there is for Krishna and Rama, but there are abundant stories revealing one aspect or another of this great God. Shiva combines all dualities in himself, so the stories tell about his powers of life and death, his passionate pursuits and his ascetic withdrawal, his love and his anger. He is sometimes pictured in images as half-male and half-female, uniting the cosmic generative forces, and his most typical symbol is the *lingam* (phallic symbol) placed in a *yoni* (symbol of the female organ). He is the creator and nourisher of existence, but at the same time he is the great destroyer.

Throughout the medieval period, Shaivite movements cultivated the bhakti of this great God in his various aspects. Since Shiva is the great divine yogin, among those devoted to him were a variety of ascetics (sadhus) and yogins. Worship of Shiva became especially dominant in southern India, and poets sang praises of him in Tamil. The largest group of Shaivites, the Shaiva Siddhanta, consider their ritual texts, called Agamas, to be equal in value to the Vedas. Another important group, Virashaiva, developed in the twelfth century as a kind of countercultural movement, its founder refusing to go through the sacred thread initiation ceremony. Known as the Lingayats because they wear a small stone lingam on a chain around the neck, they protested against the caste system, worship of images, and many other Hindu beliefs and customs. In their poems in praise of Shiva, written in Kannada, they insist on a Shiva monotheism.

Associated with the Shaivite tradition, there developed the worship of Shiva's female aspect called his *Shakti*, for Shiva perfectly embodies the divine powers both male and female. This Shakti can be seen as Shiva's energy and power, or Shakti can be personified as the wife of Shiva, under names like Parvati and Uma. Or this Shakti can become the focus of worship in her own right as the great Goddess, usually under the names of Devi, Durga, and Kali. The relationships of these goddesses to each other and to Shiva is by no means clear in the Puranas. What is clear is that both Durga and Kali are ferocious, terrifying goddesses, expressions of the terrible energy and destructiveness of the sacred. The central sacred story about **Durga** relates how she delivered the world from the vicious attack of the buffalo-demon Mahisha. In the *Devimahatmyam* ("Glorification of the Goddess," probably composed about 400–600 C.E. and included in the *Markandeya Purana*), the Goddess Devi emerges fully as the Divine Mother, worshiped by her devotees, the Shaktas.

Perhaps the part of the sacred story most strange to non-Hindus deals with the dark goddess **Kali**. When battling demon armies, the story goes, Durga became furious and her face turned black as ink; from between her brows emerged the terrible Kali, brandishing a sword and carrying a noose. She wears a garland of human heads and a girdle of severed arms, causing the world to tremble with her bloodthirsty cries and frantic dancing. Yet this terrifying goddess became the focus of bhakti for some groups in Hinduism, especially in Bengal, that found ecstasy and fulfillment in worshiping God also in her destructive aspects. The worship of Kali, the terrifying, destroying mother, forms an important though difficult-to-understand strand of bhakti Hinduism.

We should note that, in general, most Hindus still today see their identity intimately connected with these devotional traditions that developed in medieval times. Some families have traditionally been devotees of Vishnu and the gods and goddesses associated with this great God—they are called Vaishnavites. Other families have long been Shaivites, devotees of Shiva and his associated gods and goddesses. Whereas most Hindus follow one of these two great theistic traditions, others devote themselves to the great Goddess Devi, known under different names such as Durga, Kali, or Lakshmi. It is important to understand that, while bhakti seems to presuppose a great number of gods and goddesses, devotees tend to focus on one of the great Gods or Goddesses as the source of ultimate sacred power. To a Vaishnavite, Vishnu is all, the creator, preserver, and destroyer of the universe. Shiva is everything to a Shaivite, and a devotee of the great Goddess Durga likewise is "monotheistic" in outlook. At the same time, there generally is a tolerance for the other traditions of bhakti and a sense that God shows herself or himself in many forms.

The Development of Tantrism Closely related to the worship of the great Goddess was a small but significant movement called **Tantrism**, and to complete the sacred story of Hinduism we must take note of this complicated and somewhat controversial form that arose in the medieval period. The goal of Tantra is moksha by means of elaborate ritual and yogic practices focusing on the power of the great Goddess. Tantra emerged as a vast collection of ideas and practices, expressed in a variety of ritual scriptures. They centered on the inseparability of Shiva and Shakti, of male and female, of divine and human, of the macrocosmos and the microcosmos. Since the body is a microcosmos, there is a sacred geography in the body, and through ritual practice it is possible to activate the sacred forces latent in the body, bring about the union of Shiva (passive, pure intelligence) and Shakti (active, creative energy), and achieve a spiritual transformation.

The Tantrists distinguished between a right-handed and a left-handed path. The right-handed path was considered to be for all Tantrists and employed mantras (sacred sounds), mandalas (cosmic diagrams), and yogic-ritual techniques such as breath control to activate Shakti within, to rise and be united with Shiva within. The left-handed path was considered appropriate only for advanced

Tantrists, for it included a special ritual called circle-worship (*cakra-puja*), using elements normally forbidden and associated with the lower bodily senses. These are called the "five M's" (each begins with the letter M in Sanskrit) and involve the use of wine, meat, fish, parched grain, and sexual intercourse. It was particularly the use of sexual impulses as ritual yoga to unite the powers of Shakti and Shiva that characterized this form of Tantra. More orthodox Hindus strongly criticized left-handed Tantra for this seeming perversion of traditional morality. But Tantrists insisted that the ritual practice must be done only by advanced adepts in the context of purity, self-discipline, and devotion to the goddess, under the guidance of a Tantric guru, not as gratification of desires but as the redirection of those desires into worship and transformation.

Rethinking the Vedic Truth: Philosophical Systems

Another important development in Hindu tradition during these centuries was continuing philosophical discussion of the Vedic truths. In a dialogue between student and teacher, written by the great philosopher Shankara, the student asks these kinds of questions: How can I be released from samsara? Is this suffering my own nature, or does it result from some cause? What is the cause, and what will remove it? What is ignorance, and what is knowledge?[10] Such questions have provided the grist for Hindu philosophy for over two thousand years.

The intellectual underpinnings of Hindu tradition go back to the sages of the early Vedic hymns and the teachers of the Upanishads, and the quest for intellectual understanding never halted. Alongside ritual systems and practices of meditation and yoga, there developed elaborate, highly sophisticated systems of doctrine and speculation based on the Vedic scriptures. These systems were exegetical in nature, expressed mainly in the forms of commentaries on the Vedic scriptures and on primary texts called Sutras. Often concerned with questions of grammar and logic, these systems put forth ideas about liberation (moksha) as their primary purpose. A major topic of speculation was the relationship between the one and the many, that is, between the absolute One reality as suggested in the scriptures and the human experience of the world as manifold and diverse.

Eventually, six orthodox schools (**darshanas**, "viewpoints") of philosophy came to be recognized (orthodox because they recognize the authority of the Vedas and Upanishads), in addition to unorthodox philosophies such as Buddhism and Jainism. Two of these schools, Nyaya (the school of logic) and Vaisheshika (the atomistic school), were concerned chiefly with logic and cosmology as a means to liberation. The Mimamsa school occupied itself with showing how the Vedas are eternal and how the Vedic rituals are important for religious duty (dharma) and attainment of salvation. The most influential schools have been the Samkhya-Yoga pair and the Vedanta school.

We mentioned the practice of yoga earlier, focused on the eight-stage path taught by Patanjali. The Yoga philosophical school with its path toward higher release developed in close relation to the **Samkhya** school's "map" of the cosmos and the causes of bondage. Samkhya taught a dualism of pure nature or matter (*prakriti*), out of which develops the whole person with mind and senses, and pure spirit (*purusha*), which is the transcendent consciousness. The problem is that the embodied mind mistakes itself for purusha, which causes bondage in the samsara cycle. And so the goal of yogic practice is to disentangle purusha consciousness from the material self and mind and bring about liberation.

The **Vedanta** school has been particularly influential in Hindu intellectual developments. Philosophers of Vedanta (end of Veda) were especially interested in the teaching of the Upanishads concerning Brahman as the one ultimate reality and the self as identical with Brahman. Their key emphasis was on the correct knowledge (*jñana*) of Brahman and the atman that is of primary importance for liberation. Many Hindus look to the brilliant philosopher **Shankara** (788–820), of the Nondualist Vedanta school, as the outstanding thinker of the Vedanta school. Shankara, from southern India, became a samnyasin as a boy and died at an early age, but in those few years he wrote very influential commentaries on the Upanishads and the *Bhagavad Gita*.

Shankara starts with insistence on the nondual character of reality: There is only Brahman, the ground of being, without qualities, unchanging. Furthermore, Brahman is identical with the eternal, unchanging atman (soul), which underlies all individuals. Moksha (liberation) means the knowledge that one's atman is the eternal Brahman itself.

But our problem, according to Shankara, is that we commonly view the world as changing, full of different realities, persons, and things, including our own soul as an individual reality. The way out of this illusion, Shankara says, is not through rituals, actions, or worship, but through knowledge attained through meditation, knowledge that I and Brahman are one.

Shankara's philosophical system, called **Advaita** (nondualist) Vedanta, has repercussions for traditional Hindu ideas and practices. One is forced to conclude that there really are no permanent individual selves and that even the samsara cycle and release from it are ultimately illusions. Most radical, perhaps, is the implication that devotion to a personal god cannot bring liberation—for even the gods must be illusions! But—and this has been most influential in shaping Hinduism—Shankara allowed that there are different levels of truth, corresponding to one's spiritual development. At the lower levels of truth, devotion to one's god can be of benefit for spiritual transformation. But one who reaches the highest knowledge realizes that there is only one Brahman; such a one transcends gods, rituals, Dharma, and scriptures.

Influential though Shankara was, some later Vedanta philosophers disagreed with his radical nondualism focused on Brahman. **Ramanuja** (ca. 1017–1137), a leading theologian among the Vaishnavites, wrote commentaries in which he brought devotion to God back to center stage, rejecting Shankara's idea of a lower and a higher truth. His system was called Vishishtadvaita (qualified nondualist) Vedanta, for he argued that within the one eternal reality (Brahman), there is a qualitative distinction between the self and God. Thus, the devotee could worship Vishnu as the supreme world-soul. And later in the thirteenth century, the Vaishnavite theologian Madhva went all the way to a dualism in his so-called Dvaita (dualist) Vedanta, holding that scripture maintains an eternal distinction between the individual self and God.

In spite of such disagreements between the philosophical schools and even within the Vedanta tradition itself, these philosophical systems exemplify the intellectual foundation of the fascinating diversity of what we call Hinduism. How can both an atheistic philosopher and an ardent lover of Krishna—and everyone else in between—all be considered Hindus? Shankara's philosophy in particular suggests that there are many levels of spiritual development and each soul proceeds at its own pace toward the goal of liberation.

Muslim Presence and Impact in India

Further shaping of the Hindu traditions in the medieval period came through the vigorous presence of Muslims in India. The great expansion of Islam that swept through much of Asia and northern Africa continued on into India, with the first Muslim incursions coming in the eighth century. By the thirteenth century, Islam dominated northern India, and the Muslim Mughal dynasty controlled most of India from the sixteenth until the eighteenth centuries. Over the course of many centuries, tens of millions of Indians (Hindus and Buddhists) converted to Islam. Many clashes did, of course, occur between these very different religions, with Islam's radical monotheism quite at odds with Hindu bhakti. Muslim invaders of northern India in the eleventh century destroyed many Hindu temples in a crusade to wipe out idolatry and establish Islam. Aurangzeb (r. 1658–1707) of the Mughal dynasty enforced restrictive laws against the Hindus and destroyed famous temples of Krishna, Rama, and Shiva, replacing them with Muslim mosques.

But there was also mutual influence. For example, some Muslim rulers developed a toleration for Hindu practices and beliefs. The outstanding example is Akbar (1542–1605), who encouraged the practice of Hinduism as well as Islam, married Hindu princesses, and even promulgated a statement called *The Divine Faith* in which he set forth a religious framework that synthesized ideas from Islam and Hinduism as well as other religions. Hindu devotionalism and saints inspired the Muslim Sufis in India, and the Sufis in turn inspired many devout Hindus with their religious ideas and practices. In the area of Benares in northern India, the poet-saint Kabir (ca. 1440–1518), from a Shudra subcaste that converted to Islam, was inspired by Vaishnava devotionalism and composed bhakti poetry that was widely sung in northern India. Kabir is unique in that he is highly revered as a saint and mystic by Hindus, Muslims, and Sikhs alike. And Nanak (1469–1539), from a Hindu warrior-class family in the Punjab, expressed a loving devotion to the one God in a way that combined aspects of

Hindu bhakti with Islamic Sufism. He emerged as the great religious leader Guru Nanak who founded the Sikh religion.

By the eighteenth century, Mughal power faded and the British entered to take control of India. But Muslim presence in the South Asian subcontinent has remained enormous—representing the largest population of Muslims anywhere in the world today. And the culture and religions of India, including Hinduism, have been influenced in many ways by Muslim ideas and practices.

THE MODERN ERA: RENAISSANCE AND RESPONSE TO THE WEST

Under the British Raj, many changes took place in South Asia. The British East India Company dominated Indian economic and political life. There was a shift to a new language (English) as the language of commerce, government, higher education, and other cultural institutions. While Christians had been present in India since the early Christian missionaries went there in the second and third centuries C.E., Christian presence came in a stronger way in connection with the colonial rule. Although Christianity remained a small minority in India—less than 3 percent of the population today—its teachings of love and its demonstration of social responsibility in opening schools and hospitals and caring for the poor had a strong impact on modern Hindu thinkers. Western culture also brought new democratic political ideas, together with modern science and technology.

Reform Movements and Thinkers

Western ideas brought to India by the British helped to raise questions among some Hindus about certain aspects of their own tradition, especially the caste system and the sense that the world is the realm of samsara from which the goal is to escape. As Hindus learned Western thought, there arose attempts to reform Hindu society and to bring Hindu thought into the modern world.

Brahmo Samaj and Arya Samaj   One of the important early movements of reform was started by Ram Mohan Roy (1772–1833), who had worked for the East India Company. He spoke out against what he considered abuses in the Hindu system, such as polytheism, worship of images, neglect of women's education, and the practice of burning a widow alive at her husband's cremation (called sati or suttee). Influenced by Christianity but unwilling to accept the idea that Jesus was God, Ram Mohan studied the Vedas and Upanishads and found that they also taught a simple monotheism. In 1828, Ram Mohan founded the Brahmo Samaj (Society of Brahman) as a religious society advocating a rational, humanistic religion without all the Hindu rituals and customs. The members of the society would meet weekly to study the Upanishads, pray, and sing hymns.

Later, led by Debendranath Tagore (1817–1905), the Brahmo Samaj broke away from orthodoxy by asserting that reason and conscience, not the Vedas, are the final authority in religion; the truth of the scriptures is to be confirmed by the inner light, which all possess. The society revised the old rituals to excise references to the many gods, and they pressed for laws against child marriage and polygamy. Weakened by divided opinions toward the end of the nineteenth century, the Brahmo Samaj's religious ideas did not carry the day in modern Hinduism, but the society effected a significant change of attitude among Hindus with respect to the unquestioned rule of tradition.

In 1875, the Arya Samaj was founded by Swami Dayananda Sarasvati (1824–1883), representing another attempt to restore the original purity of Hinduism. Dayananda had been a Shaivite devotee, but under the influence of a fiery teacher who accepted only the oldest Vedic scriptures, he came to reject the Puranas and all the popular gods of Hinduism, together with image worship and the caste system. In his book, *The Light of Truth*, he held that Hindus should rely on the early Vedas alone (the Samhitas) for all religious truth. Other religions, such as Islam, Christianity, and bhakti Hinduism, have corrupted this pure truth. The early Vedas are also the source of all scientific truth. Furthermore, the caste system made up of numerous subcastes should be abandoned. Anyone can study the Vedas. Women should be educated, widows should be allowed to remarry, and child marriage should be abandoned.

Thus, the Arya Samaj moved in somewhat the same direction as the Brahmo Samaj in social reforms, but it differs in rejecting Western influences and in calling for a strict return to the early Vedas as supreme religious truth. Advocating Hindu laws for India, the Arya Samaj rejected the modern secular constitution of India and engaged in intense opposition to all non-Hindu elements in India—Muslims, Christians, secularists, even Hindu groups that were perceived to have non-Vedic traditions. They founded schools (gurukulas) to promote Vedic culture and Hindu unity. The influence of the Arya Samaj can still be seen in contemporary Indian cultural life, and they provided a strong impetus in the development of Hindu nationalistic politics.

Although the Brahmo Samaj and the Arya Samaj operated with quite differing religious visions, they both helped to revitalize Hindu pride in the face of Western dominance and laid the groundwork for a Hindu spiritual revival by reasserting Hindu tradition as the source of value for modern society.

Ramakrishna and Vivekananda As movements in India revived the sense of pride in India's spiritual heritage, many leading thinkers who had been influenced by the West began to turn to their own heritage for guidance in the modern world. Of the many who contributed to this task, we might single out **Ramakrishna** Paramahamsa (1836–1886) and his disciple, Swami Vivekananda (1863–1902).

Ramakrishna was a God-intoxicated Hindu who revitalized the Hindu tradition and channeled it into new directions. A temple priest of the goddess Kali who communed with her in trancelike meditation, he also worshiped other gods such as Krishna and practiced the nondualist Vedanta type of meditation. He also followed disciplines of Christianity and Islam, experiencing visions of Christ and Muhammad; on that basis he came to believe that the ultimate reality may be approached by any tradition of worship. Thus, Ramakrishna was able to develop an expansive Hinduism, not by pruning it but by incorporating into it Western religious ideas and experiences, remaining all the while devoted to the Hindu tradition. Already in his lifetime he was widely regarded as a great Hindu saint and even an avatara of the divine.

One of the disciples of Ramakrishna was Swami Vivekananda who, after Ramakrishna's death, organized the Ramakrishna Order and the Ramakrishna Mission. He came to the United States to speak at the Parliament of Religions at the Chicago World's Fair in 1893 and excited many with his presentations on Hinduism. Thereafter he traveled about lecturing on Hinduism, founding **Vedanta Societies** to continue the work of teaching the Hindu tradition in America. In India, the Ramakrishna Mission was dedicated to a wide variety of charitable, missionary, and educational activities for the masses. By his example, Vivekananda established a new samnyasin model, a holy man actively engaged in social concerns.

Independence and New Visions: Gandhi and Aurobindo

As the Hindu renaissance represented by these movements brought Indians a new sense of pride and peoplehood, an independence movement arose that, under the leadership of people like Mohandas **Gandhi** (1869–1948), brought India independence from British rule. The motivation to work for independence came from many sources, of course, including many ultranationalists fighting for a "Mother India" purified of all Muslim and British influences. The man who became the leader, however, was a new kind of religious leader in Hinduism. Gandhi was born in the Vaishya (merchant) class and was not particularly learned in the Vedic texts and tradition, studying law in England and working for many years in South Africa

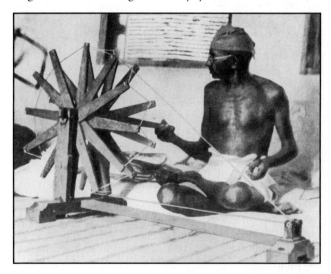

Mahatma Gandhi at his spinning wheel, a symbol of national self-reliance.

before returning to India to lead the independence movement. His favorite Hindu scripture was the *Bhagavad Gita*, which he felt taught nonviolence and selfless action for the welfare of society, and he was also much influenced by the Sermon on the Mount in the Christian Bible. Drawing on these religious sources, he developed the philosophy and technique of *satyagraha* (holding to the truth), by which he meant a style of nonviolent resistance that awakens in the oppressors a sense of wrongdoing. It is wrong to seek personal victory over opponents, he taught; one must rather purify oneself of all selfish motivations and act without any violence and without any sense of anger. He was totally confident that this way of love and nonviolence (*ahimsa*) will always win out in any situation.

Gandhi became a kind of samnyasin, establishing a community that lived in simplicity and daily work—his spinning wheel became the symbol of his movement. Living in celibacy with his wife, wearing only the traditional loincloth of the samnyasin, exerting his energy to purify India of the sin of having made one class of people the "untouchables," and bringing the British to their knees in India by nonviolent resistance, Gandhi represented a spiritual moral force drawn from Hinduism that has had great impact, not only on India but also on the whole world.

Of the many other modern Hindu thinkers who have expressed a new and vital Hindu perspective, we might single out Sri Aurobindo (1872–1950), who lived through the same years as Gandhi but took a somewhat different course. Educated at Cambridge University in England, he got involved in the nationalist movement in India and was imprisoned in 1910. Discovering through visionary experiences that real human liberation went far beyond the political liberation of India, he chose thereafter to withdraw from the world and established an ashram (retreat) in the French enclave of Pondicherry for the practice of Tantric yoga. In his writings, *The Life Divine* and *Synthesis of Yoga*, he drew on India's ancient wisdom to develop the view that human life can be transformed into the highest forms of spiritual reality by the practice of an all-encompassing discipline of yoga. The divine forces are within us, though we are ignorant of them. If we search within and master these divine forces, making them pervade and transform all dimensions of our life, we will be able to live in the highest possible divine way. Society itself should be reshaped so that it is conducive to this human evolution into the divine life. Although Aurobindo draws on traditional Hindu ideas and techniques, what makes his vision a modern one is the way he integrates individual yogic means with the transformation of social conditions.

Hinduism in the World Today

Today, there is a renewed sense of religious vitality among Hindus, both in India and in the Hindu diaspora throughout the world. Problems abound, of course, as in all the world's religions today. There are social tensions between castes and between ethnic groups. Political struggles continue, as between the states of India and Pakistan, or in the Punjabi separatist movement. Religious conflicts develop between Hindus and Muslims, or between Hindus and proselytizing Christian groups. And a strong dose of secularism accompanies modernization and westernization for many people. But overall, Hindus are feeling pride in their religious traditions and a desire to continue these spiritual practices in their lives today. We take brief note of several important developments today: the rise of Hindu nationalism, the increasing interest in global Hinduism, and the attraction Hindu practices have for Western followers.

Hindu Nationalism   Together with the revival of Indian self-consciousness and pride, recent years have seen the development of a number of Hindu nationalist groups, wishing to promote India as a Hindu rather than as a secular state. This notion of Hindu national identity is a very modern one, linked as it is with the idea of India as a modern nation-state, and projecting that identity into the past. Drawing on the nationalism of the Arya Samaj, a number of Hindu political parties and cultural organizations have developed that attempt to uphold Hindu rights and establish a Hindu value system in India. The important Hindu nationalist political party called the BJP (Bharatiya Janata Party), for example, has attracted wide support particularly from India's educated classes, as it upholds what are considered traditional Hindu values while advocating the rights of all Hindus. At times, communal violence has been associated with some of the more extreme Hindu nationalist groups, although it should be remembered that most leaders of these groups advocate political change rather than violence as the means to achieve their goals.

Global Hinduism   Yet a different vision of Hinduism is espoused today by Hindus who, following the tradition of the Brahmo Samaj, Vivekananda, Gandhi, and others, emphasize universal values of the Hindu tradition that are beneficial for the spiritual transformation of humankind. This kind of global Hinduism has wide appeal to many in India, but particularly also for the Hindu diaspora communities—that is, the growing numbers of Hindus living in the Americas, in Europe, in Australia, and in many other parts of the world. These Hindus still think of India as the center for Hinduism, and many of them hold to traditional values and ideas such as respect for the Vedas as ancient revelation, belief in reincarnation, acceptance of a transcendent divinity manifested in various forms of Hindu gods and goddesses, and acknowledgment of the value of practices of ritual and meditation. But these Hindus tend to stress the aspects of Hinduism that transcend national barriers, deemphasizing the importance of caste, for example, giving more space to women's influence and leadership, and advocating the idea that Hindus share truths found in other religions. After the terrorist attacks of September 11, 2001, and the heightened fear in Western countries of those ethnic groups that appear different, Hindus have been concerned that others learn better to understand these universal values and teachings of Hinduism.

Western Followers of Hinduism   Even though Hinduism has never been a missionary religion, the renaissance of Hinduism in India together with the growing Hindu diaspora communities have brought this religion of the Eternal Dharma to the attention of many Westerners. We noted previously the Ramakrishna Mission, which established Vedanta Society centers in various places in America and has for the greater part of a century been providing Americans with solid knowledge of Hinduism. In the 1920s, Paramahamsa Yogananda (1890–1952) came to America and founded the Self-Realization Fellowship, initiating Westerners into his yogic practices.

In recent years, a variety of other Hindu movements have been transplanted to the West, including yoga, meditation, and bhakti of various sorts. Many Westerners are familiar with yoga for exercise and fitness purposes. But increasing numbers are being drawn to the deeper aspects of yoga philosophy and spiritual practice. And so they join yoga meditation centers or study with teachers of yoga, seeking mental and spiritual health and peace through these practices. In recent years, many Westerners have gotten interested in Hindu medicine and healing practices as an alternative to Western medicine. So they turn to practitioners of Ayurveda, the Hindu system of medicine that offers health and wholeness through healing techniques, herbal medicines, and spiritual disciplines, based on the ancient Hindu worldview (see pp. 114–116).

We may look briefly at two specific Hindu religious movements that emphasize meditation and bhakti and became widely influential in the West: Transcendental Meditation and the International Society for Krishna Consciousness.

Maharishi Mahesh Yogi (b. 1917) studied Shankara's Nondualist (Advaita) Vedanta meditation, but unlike the many other practitioners of this type of meditation, he came to America and popularized this system for Westerners. Commonly known as **Transcendental Meditation** (TM), this practice emphasizes each person's inner divine essence and the creative powers that can be harnessed when this inner source is realized through meditation. TM is a natural process, the Maharishi emphasizes, employing the normal desire of the self to seek joy and happiness. Although some traditional Hindu forms are used, this type of meditation fits well with the American desire for personal success and well-being; by practicing meditation, a person can find health and happiness in all areas of life.

A very different form of Hinduism is the Krishna bhakti group known as the **International Society for Krishna Consciousness** (ISKCON), a movement that has brought Chaitanya's Bengali Krishna worship into the streets of America's big cities. Swami A. C. Bhaktivedanta Prabhupada (1896–1977) became a samnyasin late in life in India and was sent by his master to bring Krishna Consciousness to the West. Arriving in New York City in 1965, he began to chant the names of Krishna in a park and in 1966 opened the first ISKCON center in New York. Soon the movement spread to all parts of the United States and to other countries as well. Prabhupada has also written many studies of the *Bhagavad Gita*, the Puranas, and Chaitanya's writings, through his books making an impact on Western knowledge of Krishna Hinduism.

Although there are many lay devotees and many Hindus from India who feel at home at the festivals held in Krishna temples, the devotees who live in the temples and devote their whole lives to Krishna Consciousness form the heart of the movement. Their day begins about 3:45 A.M. and involves a full schedule of personal and corporate rituals, study sessions, chanting in public places, worship of Krishna and the other deities, and so forth. The Hare Krishnas, with shaved heads and saffron robes, chanting in ecstasy and inviting others to join in the delights of Krishna, have become a familiar touch of Hinduism in the West.

There are many other Hindu-related gurus and movements in the West today. Some of the more bizarre ones get much media attention, whereas others cultivate a traditional type of Hinduism in a Western context. Recently a kind of re-enculturation effect can be noted, in that some of these gurus and movements in the West now are being adopted by urban Hindus in India.

Continuing Vitality of Hinduism   It is clear, from the vital movements in India today, the continuing adherence to Hinduism by people in the Hindu diaspora, and new groups of Western followers, that Hinduism is alive and well and contributing to the future of humankind's religious experience. Already significant dialogue has been taking place between Hindus and people of other religions, especially Christians, Muslims, and Buddhists. In the opinion of some scholars of such matters, Hinduism, because of its expansive conception of religious truth at many different levels, can be a resource for mutual understanding and cooperation between these very different paths we call the religions of the world.

DISCUSSION QUESTIONS

1   Who is a Hindu?
2   Discuss the relationship between the history of Hinduism in the modern Western sense of "history" and the traditional Hindu story as told especially in the epics. Which is more important to Hindu identity?
3   What were some important features of the Indus valley civilization, and what influences did this culture have on Hinduism?
4   Discuss the main features of Aryan religion in the Vedic period.
5   Explain the new ideas of the authors of the Upanishads about Brahman, the atman, karma, and rebirth. Do these ideas seem to fit together as a religious worldview?
6   In the *Bhagavad Gita*, what kinds of advice does Krishna give to the warrior Arjuna? How is this a synthesis of Hindu teaching?
7   What are the main devotional cults that developed in the medieval period with the Puranas and other writings?
8   Compare the Brahmo Samaj and the Arya Samaj as modern reform movements.
9   What new vision of Hinduism has emerged from the work of Ramakrishna and Vivekananda?
10   What were Gandhi's main ideas and activities? Why did he attract such attention worldwide?
11   What new visions seem to be developing in the global Hinduism advocated by some in India and in the Hindu diaspora?
12   Why do you think some Westerners are so attracted to Hindu practices today?

Hindu Worlds of Meaning

Chapter 4

THE ULTIMATE REAL: BRAHMAN, GOD/GODDESS

What's it all about? What is really ultimate, the center of all? Hindus have a long tradition of asking such questions, a tradition going back at least three thousand years. A hymn from Book 10 of the *Rig Veda* (ca. 1000 B.C.E.) puts it this way:

> Who really knows? Who will here proclaim it? Whence was it produced? Whence is this creation? The gods came afterwards, with the creation of this universe. Who then knows whence it has arisen? Whence this creation has arisen—perhaps it formed itself, or perhaps it did not—the one who looks down on it, in the highest heaven, only he knows—or perhaps he does not know.

(*Rig Veda* 10.129.6–7)[1]

Answering these questions, the Hindu traditions have put forth many proposals and experimented with many conceptions of ultimate reality, from the gods of the early Aryans to the modern Hindu's God or Goddess, from the power of the fire sacrifice to the eternal cosmic order, from Brahman of the Upanishads to the Shakti of Tantric ritual. In our brief look at these traditions several thousand years in the making, we note that the answers have tended to go in two directions. One vision emphasizes the ultimate as impersonal, eternal, all-embracing, called Brahman by the sages. The other vision focuses more on the personal qualities of the ultimate, whether called Brahman or Ishvara, or by another name of the great God or Goddess. These answers, as we by now have come to understand, are not exclusive, of course.

Brahman as Sacred Ultimate

Since the time of the Upanishads, there has been a tradition of designating that which is ultimate as "**Brahman**." As noted earlier, the term *brahman* in early Vedic times referred to the powerful words spoken by a priest in the ritual of fire-sacrifice. The priests who spoke the words were called Brahmans (sometimes spelled Brahmins) and the manuals about the ritual are the Brahmanas. Increasingly the term *Brahman* was used to refer to the sacred power that pervades and maintains all things. For a major portion of the Hindu tradition, Brahman is ultimate reality.

Brahman as the One Reality Even within the Upanishads there are differing ways of describing the reality of Brahman, personal or impersonal, beyond the world or immanent in the world, and other ways. But one major theme about Brahman is oneness in contrast to multiplicity. A student once asked the sage Yajnavalkya how many gods there are, and Yajnavalkya answered that, as mentioned in a hymn, there are 3,306 gods. "But," the student presses on, "just how many gods are there?" "Thirty-three," is the answer. "Yes, but just how many gods are there?" "Six." "Yes, but just how many gods are there?" "Three." The student is still not satisfied: "Yes, but just how many gods are there?" "Two." "Yes, but just how many gods are there?" "One and a half." "Yes, but just how many gods are there?" Finally Yajnavalkya answers, "One," and he explains that all the gods are but various differentiated powers of the One who is called Brahman (*Brihad-aranyaka Upanishad* 3.9.1–9).[2] Brahman is the one life of all the gods, the one soul of the universe, the one source of all.

As the One, Brahman is primordial, prior to all forms and divisions. Brahman is without qualities and limiting attributes, transcending this universe. Yajnavalkya once was challenged by the renowned Gargi Vacaknavi about his idea of Brahman. Posing a deep mind-puzzle, she asked him to define that across which all reality, all past and present and future, even all space is woven, like warp and woof. "That, O Gargi, is called the Imperishable," he answered. "It is not coarse, not fine, not short, not long, not glowing, not adhesive, without shadow and without darkness, without air and without space, without stickiness, odorless, tasteless, without eye, without ear, without voice, without wind, without energy, without breath, without mouth, without measure, without inside and without outside." Brahman is the ground of all the universe, Yajnavalkya explained, and further it is the ground of personal existence. "Verily, O Gargi, that Imperishable is the unseen Seer, the unheard Hearer, the unthought Thinker, the ununderstood Understander. Other than It there is naught that sees. Other than It there is naught that hears. Other than It there is naught that thinks. Other than It there is naught that understands" (*Brihad-aranyaka Upanishad* 3.8).[3]

As the ultimate ground of all reality, that from which everything else is derived, Brahman cannot adequately be described, for any description would have to reduce Brahman to something else. But Brahman is the subject of all reality and, thus, is beyond speech and concepts. Yajnavalkya explains,

> For where there is a duality, as it were, there one sees another; there one smells another; there one tastes another; there one speaks to another; there one hears another; there one understands another. But where everything has become just one's own self, then whereby and whom would one see? then whereby and whom would one smell? then whereby and whom would one taste? then whereby and to whom would one speak? then whereby and whom would one hear? then whereby and of whom would one think? then whereby and whom would one touch? then whereby and whom would one understand? whereby would one understand him by means of whom one understands this All? That Soul (Atman) is not this, it is not that (neti, neti).

(*Brihad-aranyaka Upanishad* 4.5.15)[4]

Although as the ground of reality Brahman cannot be described adequately, still it can be known directly. For Brahman is immanent, permeating all things, humans, gods, the physical universe, space, and time. "Verily, this whole world is Brahman" (*Chandogya Upanishad* 3.14.1).

Most importantly, according to the Upanishads, one's own true self (atman) is none other than the Brahman:

> This Soul of mine within the heart is greater than the earth, greater than the atmosphere, greater than the sky, greater than these worlds. Containing all works, containing all desires, containing all odors, containing all tastes, encompassing this whole world, the unspeaking, the unconcerned—this is the Soul of mine within the heart, this is Brahman. Into him I shall enter on departing hence.

(*Chandogya Upanishad* 3.14.3–4)[5]

Since the inner atman is really the Brahman, a central path toward liberation in Hinduism, as we see later, is to acquire knowledge of this inner atman, to fully realize, as the Upanishads say many times, that "This Atman is the Brahman" (*Brihad-aranyaka Upanishad* 2.5.19).

Two Levels of Knowing Brahman   To know Brahman as the ultimate is the goal—but that requires high spiritual understanding. Hindu thinkers have a long tradition of speaking of two levels of truth. One seer, for example, tells of two forms of Brahman, the formed and the formless. The formed Brahman is different from the wind and the atmosphere and, thus, is personal and worthy of worship. The formless Brahman is the wind and the atmosphere and, thus, is impersonal, described only by "Not this, not this" (*neti, neti*) (*Brihad-aranyaka Upanishad* 2.3.1–6). Generally, both ways of describing Brahman—as personal and as impersonal—are found in the Upanishads.

The Vedanta philosopher **Shankara** spelled out the two levels of knowing Brahman with characteristic thoroughness:

> Brahman is apprehended under two forms; in the first place as qualified by limiting conditions owing to the multiformity of the evolutions of name and form (i.e., the multiformity of the created world); in the second place as being the opposite of this, i.e., free from all limiting conditions whatsoever.[6]

Brahman without qualities he called the *nirguna* Brahman; this is the very ground of existence, prior to any limiting characteristics, which can only be described negatively and known intuitively—the highest truth of Brahman, the ultimate. Brahman with qualities, the *saguna* Brahman, is the creative power of the universe, the foundation of the phenomenal world. Shankara considered saguna Brahman to be experienced as God in a personal sense, for whom he used the term *Ishvara*, the supreme Lord personified as deity; this Lord of existence can be described and known and worshiped.

To explain how Brahman is one all-encompassing reality, and yet we experience the world and ourselves and even God as distinct realities, Shankara taught the doctrine of *maya* (illusion), a word used in the Vedas for divine creative magic. From the point of view of the lower level of knowledge, the empirical world and all that is in it do exist and are really experienced. However, from the point of view of the higher knowledge, the world experienced as made up of distinct entities is an illusory projection, maya, superimposed on the one Reality, the Brahman.

To help people understand this puzzle, Shankara used the illustration of a snake and a rope. Seeing a coiled-up object lying on a path, one jumps to the conclusion that it is a snake—and one experiences it with all the emotion, fear, and anxiety associated with encountering a snake. It is real. But upon closer examination, it turns out to be a rope coiled up, lying in the path—and now one's subjective experience of it totally changes. It really is a rope. In much the same way, we out of ignorance project our experience of the multiformed world onto the one Brahman. Now Shankara is not arguing that we should treat the world and ourselves and other selves as though they did not exist or have no value. Rather, he wants us to see that this is the way the Real is experienced under the conditions of our sense organs and minds—under the conditions of maya. From the viewpoint of the higher knowledge, all these distinct realities, with the associated subjective experiences of them, fade away in the unity of the Brahman. From the viewpoint of *nirguna* Brahman, then, even *saguna* Brahman is the result of maya.

There are, of course, still other perspectives on Brahman as ultimate reality in Hinduism, as not all Hindu thinkers adopt Shankara's nondualism. As we saw earlier, Ramanuja taught a qualitative distinction between the highest Lord and the world, and Madhva abandoned the nondualist vision altogether in holding the world and individual selves

Divine image with three heads, representing the great Gods Brahma, Vishnu, and Shiva.

as eternally distinct from Brahman. And the Samkhya philosophers argued an ultimate distinction between eternal *prakriti* (the ultimate material principle from which the whole world evolves) and *purusha* (eternal pure consciousness, ultimate self, equivalent to the Brahman).

But we can look to Shankara's nondualism as a very influential perspective on Brahman as ultimate reality: nirguna Brahman as the impersonal, ultimate ground of all with no limiting characteristics; and saguna Brahman as the creative power and foundation of the universe.

God as Supreme Sacred Reality

Down through the centuries, while philosophers were arguing about Brahman, people continued their worship of the gods. Spurred on by the stories of the gods in the great epics, theistic Hinduism came to be more widely accepted and practiced even by the scholars and philosophers, who participated in the great sectarian movements and developed new interpretations about God (gods) as the ultimate reality.

To Shankara, *saguna* Brahman (personal God) is known at a lower level of truth, but to those Hindu thinkers who are devoted to their God, the argument is equally valid that God is the highest level of truth. One philosopher who argued this most persuasively was **Ramanuja** (1017–1137), a leading thinker among the Vaishnavites of southern India who worked out a theology of Vaishnavism that bridged Shankara's nondualist philosophy of Brahman and his own devotion to the great God Vishnu. Ramanuja, interested in promoting bhakti, held that whereas Brahman is one unified reality, there is *within* the one Brahman a qualitative distinction between the soul, the world, and the highest Lord. Using the analogy of soul and body, Ramanuja taught that, as body and soul are united and yet different, so the Lord is the soul of one's soul in a personal relationship that includes both identity and difference, so that one's soul can worship its lordsoul. Ramanuja put forth an intellectual system in which God (Vishnu) is the ultimate reality, and worshiping God, therefore, is the highest truth.

Similar theological sentiments have been expressed by devotees in the other sectarian bhakti movements, showing that alongside the vision of an impersonal Brahman there is a strong and lasting tradition of expressing the ultimate sacred reality in personal theistic terms—as the great God Vishnu, or the great God Shiva, or again as the great Goddess Devi.

The Great God Vishnu   As we know, the *Bhagavad Gita* revealed Krishna to be a form of Vishnu. The *Gita* presents **Vishnu** as the highest Lord of all, transcending the cycles of samsara, evolving worlds forth from his own essence and absorbing them back again. The theophany (divine manifestation) revealed to Arjuna in Book XI of the *Bhagavad Gita* stands as one of the most impressive descriptions of God in religious literature. Arjuna prays to see Krishna's divine form, and the resulting vision of Krishna in his "All-Form" as the great God Vishnu is so awe-inspiring that Arjuna's hair stands on end.

> I see the gods
> in your body, O God,
> and hordes
> of varied creatures:
> Brahma, the cosmic creator,
> on his lotus throne,
> all the seers
> and celestial serpents.
> I see your boundless form
> everywhere,
> the countless arms,
> bellies, mouths, and eyes;
> Lord of All,
> I see no end,
> or middle or beginning
> to your totality. . . .
> only boundless strength
> in your endless arms,
> the moon and sun in your eyes,
> your mouths of consuming flames,
> your own brilliance
> scorching this universe. . . .
> You are the original god,
> the primordial spirit of man,
> the deepest treasure

> of all that is,
> knower and what is to be known,
> the supreme abode;
> you pervade the universe,
> Lord of Boundless Form.
> You are the gods of wind,
> death, fire, and water;
> the moon; the lord of life;
> and the great ancestor.
> Homage to you,
> a thousand times homage!
> I bow in homage to you
> again and yet again.
> (*Bhagavad Gita* 11:15–16, 19, 38–39)[7]

All beings emerge from Vishnu, and he is the dissolution of all. His abode is far beyond the worlds of samsara. Vishnu as the universal lord concerns himself with cosmic stability. He is foremost the creator and preserver of the world, and his consort is Lakshmi, the goddess of wealth and abundance. When the world is periodically threatened by demons, he embodies himself in an avatara (incarnation) to restore cosmic order, a factor that has become very important in Vaishnavite theology.

The best-known incarnations of Vishnu are Rama, hero of the *Ramayana Epic*, and Krishna, divine teacher of the *Bhagavad Gita*. The form of God as Krishna is amply filled out in the Puranas, where delightful stories are told about his lovable nature and his exploits as a baby and as a young man among the cowherd people, as we saw earlier. Reflecting on God's incarnation in Krishna, Ramanuja says,

> [God's] divine form is the depository of all radiance, loveliness, fragrance, delicacy, beauty, and youth—desirable, congruous, one in form, unthinkable, divine, marvelous, eternal, indefectible, perfect. His essence and nature are not to be limited by word or thought. He is an ocean of boundless compassion, moral excellence, tenderness, generosity, and sovereignty, the refuge of the whole world without distinction of persons. . . . [By his incarnation] he can be seen by the eyes of all men, for without putting aside his [divine] nature, he came down to dwell in the house of Vasudeva, to give light to the whole world with his indefectible and perfect glory, and to fill out all things with his own loveliness.[8]

For Vaishnavites following Ramanuja's theology, Vishnu is the one supreme reality encompassing all gods, displaying that divine radiance to the whole world through his incarnation, Krishna.

The Great God Shiva Many Shaivites have a theistic vision similar to the Vaishnavites but consider **Shiva** to be the great Lord of all, the ultimate One. Yet the theology of Shaivism is quite different from that of Vaishnavism. When we think of what is really central to all existence, what holds everything together, we have to think of evil as well as good, pain and death as well as birth and growth. Divine creativity involves death and rebirth; life coming into this world means life leaving this world. Many in India, strong-minded and dedicated to truth as it is really experienced, feel that ultimate reality is best experienced through Shiva and his Shakti (feminine side). Many, of course, worship Shiva and Shakti along with many other gods. For some single-minded visionaries, Shiva is the One, the ultimate form of the sacred.

The stories portray Shiva as the greatest, supremely powerful god. A story in the Puranas relates how Brahma the creator god, before creation was complete, met Vishnu and the two argued over who was greater. Suddenly a great pillar of flame shot up out of the darkness below and rose out of sight. Deciding to investigate this pillar, Brahma took the form of a swan and flew upward, and Vishnu took the form of a boar and pushed downward. A thousand years later the two gods returned, unable to find the top or the bottom of the pillar. The sacred sound *OM* began to issue from the pillar, and Shiva himself came forth from the pillar and received worship from Brahma and Vishnu. The pillar was none other than Shiva's lingam, the infinite source of the whole universe.

Some Shiva devotees moved toward a kind of Shiva monotheism. For example, the Virashaivites, in their poems in praise of Shiva, sometimes mocked other practices as people worshiping a stone as a god,

or a pot as god, or fire as a god—so many gods that one cannot find a place to stand. They strongly assert that Shiva, with his many different names, is the one God.[9]

Shiva is the power connected with the lingam and yoni, the power of yogic meditation, and the dancing divine energy. Central to the theology of Shiva is the encompassing of all dualities—male and female, good and evil, creation and destruction, eroticism and asceticism. As the cosmic generative power, Shiva is the very sap of existence, the vigorous creative power that permeates all life. As the divine model of yoga or the antisocial madman haunting cremation grounds (as in some myths), Shiva beckons people to search for the ultimate truth of liberation from the world. As the divine dancer, Shiva expresses the ultimate truth that sacred power is continually creating and destroying the world. In Shiva, these opposites are reconciled in a higher unity. Shiva's lingam is the axis of the universe and also extends infinitely beyond, showing that even the temporal and the eternal are united in him, as are manifested existence and unmanifested Brahman.

Great Goddess: Mother and Destroyer As we saw earlier, some theistic Hindus turn to a great Goddess as supreme in their bhakti. There are many great Goddess forms in India, such as Durga and Kali, for example, associated with Shiva but also worshiped as the one ultimate by single-minded devotees. Other great Goddess personalities are linked with the Vishnu tradition, such as Lakshmi, Vishnu's consort, or Radha, lover of Krishna.

As an example of these great Goddesses, consider **Durga**, widely worshiped for her power in combating demons and protecting the world. A well-known account tells

The great God Shiva Nataraja dancing out the continued creation, preservation, and destruction of the world. Shiva as Lord of the Dance (Shiva Nataraja) India, Tamil Nadu; Chola period, 12th century. Copper alloy. H. 29 1/4 in. (74.3 cm) 1979.29. Photograph by Susuma Wakisaka, Idemitsu Museum of Arts, Tokyo. The Asia Society, New York: Mr. and Mrs. John D. Rockefeller 3rd Collection.

how the demon Mahisha performed austerities and became invulnerable to all opponents except a woman, so he defeated all the gods and took over the universe. In desperation, the gods assembled and emitted their fiery powers into one great mass, which congealed into the body the beautiful goddess Durga. The parts of her body were formed from the male gods (face from Shiva, arms from Vishnu, etc.), and each of the gods gave her a special weapon. Thus, Durga is the embodied strength of all the male gods, and she roars and causes the earth to shake as she defeats Mahisha and all other demons. On the battlefield she often creates powerful goddesses from herself, such as **Kali**, who emerges from her brow as the embodiment of Durga's fury and power. Yet Durga also turns her vast powers to creative ends, blessing, protecting, and nourishing the world.

Some Hindus came to believe that there is one unified great Goddess that is revealed in all these diverse goddesses. Although known by many names, she is often called simply **Devi** ("Goddess") or Mahadevi ("great Goddess"). The term *Shakti* ("power") is applied to her, for she is the active dimension of divine reality, the power that underlies all creating activities. This theological perspective sees the different goddesses all as manifestations of the unifying cosmic principle that is female, powerful, and active, the divine energy from which all creative processes derive. With her inexhaustible creative powers, the great Goddess actively constitutes the material world. So she is the divine mother, guarding and nurturing all her children. Creation and preservation also have their destructive side, and the divine mother kills and destroys her creation as well. But this dark, destructive, and bloodthirsty side is seen as a natural part of the total order of the world, with its positive and necessary interaction of creation and destruction, life and death.

The nineteenth-century Hindu saint Ramakrishna, a lifelong devotee of the goddess Kali (Shakti), expresses this vision of the divine mother as ultimate reality, one with Brahman:

> Thus Brahman and Shakti are identical. If you accept the one, you must accept the other. It is like fire and its power to burn. . . . Thus one cannot think of the Brahman without Shakti, or of Shakti without Brahman. One cannot think of the Absolute without the Relative, or of the Relative without the Absolute. The Primordial Power is ever at play. She is creating, preserving, and destroying in play, as it were. This Power is called Kali. Kali is verily Brahman, and Brahman is verily Kali. It is one and the same Reality. When we think of It as inactive. . . . then we call It

Brahman. But when It engages in these activities, then we call it Kali or Shakti.[10]

Ramakrishna's words show that Hindus can encompass both nondualism and theism in thinking about ultimate reality. The truth of one ultimate Brahman does not forestall the experience of the ultimate in personal form as the great Goddess Shakti/Kali.

EXISTENCE IN THE WORLD: DHARMA AND SAMSARA

What sense is there in life? Why are things the way they are? The Hindu vision of the nature of the world and of the situation of humans within it is complicated and varies from one period to another, from one group or community to another. One key idea found throughout most of the traditions is that somehow, behind all this multifaceted world of existence, there is a unitary source from which all evolved in a creative process. The nature of the world and of humans involves two levels or contexts: the phenomenal world with its ongoing process, and the underlying sacred source and its realization. Problems in human existence arise at both levels, because of our ignorance and selfishness. We fail to fulfill our place within the order of things, and we neglect the realization of the eternal source, with the result that existence becomes a wheel of suffering and repeated death.

The World and Human Nature in Hindu Thought

Throughout the three thousand years of Hindu sacred literature, many versions have been presented of the creation of the universe, its nature and duration, and its dissolution and recreation. And the human role within this picture has been a prime concern of the sages. Finally, as we already know, the role of humans is to seek moksha, liberation from the whole conditioned world of samsara. But we need to see that as the *ultimate* goal, not as the only thing to be said about the world and humans. Whatever the ultimate truth about the world, there is at least a penultimate truth: The world is here, it is real, it functions by the eternal Dharma, the gods work to keep it going, and humans have the duty to contribute to its welfare. There is more to be said, but we can at least begin with that.

Eternal Dharma Although Brahman may be the highest reality, in the context of understanding the world and living life the way one should, Hindus look to **Dharma**—not the underlying source and essence of reality, not a god to be worshiped, but the eternal order of things to be followed.

The word *Dharma* comes from a Sanskrit root meaning "sustain, support," and in Hinduism it comes to mean the essential foundation of things in general. Originally it was closely related to the Vedic notion of *rita*, the universal harmony in which all things in the cosmos and in human society have their proper place and function. Dharma is something like the law of nature, eternal and unchanging. Following our dharma means living in accordance with reality. And it has as its correlate the law of karma, the law that there is an unfailing result that comes from every action. The whole world is supported and continues to exist on the foundation of Dharma and karma. The *Bhagavad Gita* says that even the great God Vishnu has his dharma to fulfill: It is to perform the work (karma) of originating and sustaining the world, and then to absorb it into himself again (*Bhagavad Gita* 3:22–24). Like all the world, humans also have their dharma, conditioned as we are by our own past karma—the works that follow us from lives lived long ago into our life in the present. The dharma we have in our present class and circumstances is part and parcel of the eternal Dharma.

The eternal Dharma stands in a certain tension with Brahman as ultimate. To realize Brahman means moksha, withdrawing and being liberated from the world of samsara. But to live according to one's dharma means supporting and sustaining the samsaric world. Withdrawing from the world or working in the world—this creative tension is built into the religious paths of Hinduism, and it provides much of the dramatic interest in the stories of the epics and Puranas, where the values of moksha and Dharma often conflict.

Paradigms of World Creation Pictures of the creation of the world in the sacred texts vary from a mechanistic self-evolving process to a more theistic view of God or gods creating the universe. We have already mentioned the very influential Hymn to Purusha in the *Rig Veda*, which described the whole universe created from the sacrifice of the gigantic primordial reality, Purusha. From the one sacred, through the power of sacrifice, come all the orders of the universe. We can mention two other well-known paradigms of creation, one from the Upanishads and the other from the *Vishnu Purana*.

The Upanishads elaborate on the creation of the world from the one sacred reality. One version runs like this:

> In the beginning this world was Soul (*Atman*) alone in the form of a Person. Looking around, he saw nothing else than himself. He said first: "I am." . . . Verily he had no delight. Therefore one alone has no delight. He desired a second. He was, indeed, as large as a woman and a man closely embraced. He caused that self to fall into two pieces. Therefrom arose a husband and a wife. . . . He copulated with her. Therefrom human beings were produced. . . . She became a cow. He became a bull. With her he did indeed copulate. Then cattle were born. . . . She became a she-goat, he a he-goat; she a ewe, he a ram. With her he did verily copulate. Therefrom were born goats and sheep. Thus, indeed, he created all, whatever pairs there are, even down to the ants. He knew: "I, indeed, am this creation, for I emitted it all from myself."

(*Brihad-aranyaka Upanishad* 1.4.1–5)[11]

Atman (Brahman) is the original solitary reality. This text and others tell how the primordial one desired to be many, and in the heat of that desire evolved itself into many, entering into and becoming this whole creation. The world is multiformed, but its sacred source is still the one dwelling in it all. The whole universe, then, is self-evolved from the primordial Brahman.

Let us, for one more paradigm, turn to a more theistic vision of creation from the *Vishnu Purana*. Here the great God Vishnu is the supreme lord, identical with Brahman, unified but containing the potential entire universe in his own nature. He unites within himself the primordial forms of spirit (purusha), matter (prakriti), and time (kala). Stirring himself, he engages in play to create the whole universe with these forms, evolving them into a vast egg resting on the cosmic waters. He enters the cosmic egg as **Brahma** (the creator) and creates the three worlds of sky, atmosphere, and earth, populating them with gods and all living beings. Then Vishnu becomes the preserver, supporting the world through its great time cycles (yugas) for millions of years until it is exhausted. Now Vishnu becomes the destroyer and burns up the world in a great conflagration, bringing down rain until all is one vast ocean. Vishnu now sleeps on the coiled body of his great serpent (a setting often depicted in art), until he once again creates the world for another world cycle.

In this grand cosmic vision, in addition to the idea that the whole universe evolves from the one reality, we see that creation is really the "play" of the great God—suggesting both the exuberant divine energy and the temporary nature of the creation. We also learn that creation is a cyclical process of evolution and destruction over and over, a theme firmly set in the Hindu vision. Commonly, this picture of cosmic time cycles has smaller cycles (yugas) set within larger cycles (kalpas). It is said, for example, that the period from the beginning of creation to its destruction is one kalpa, but within each kalpa are 1,000 mahayugas ("great" yugas), each lasting 4,320,000 human years. Each mahayuga is made up of four lesser yugas, which progressively degenerate until a renewal takes place in the new mahayuga. The whole kalpa, made up of 1,000 mahayugas, is called one day of the Brahma, and it is followed by an equally long night of the Brahma in which Vishnu sleeps, until he again creates the universe for a second day of the Brahma. These kalpas continue for a lifetime of the Brahma, which is 100 years of 360 days and nights of the Brahma. Then at last the whole process is reversed until Vishnu alone remains in his primordial state of spirit, matter, and time—until he again decides to play and set the whole cosmic process in motion again.

Humans: Eternal Atman Within Changing Worlds
What are we, and what is our place within this whole world? The quest for understanding the self is as old as the human race, and Hindus have done their share of speculating on this question. It is important, Hindus believe, to make a distinction between the *real* self and the empirical self that appears to live in this phenomenal world. The empirical self is made up of the physical body composed of the gross elements (earth, water, light, wind, and ether), and it also includes the subtle body made up of the vital breaths, the organs of action, and the organs of knowledge, mind, and intellect. This empirical self seems to be the "real me," for it has all my physical characteristics, and my distinct personality, my habits, my way of thinking also rest in this self. Isn't this the real self?

Hindu wisdom says no. The real self is something other: The *atman*, eternal and formless, in essence is none other than the Brahman. A famous dialogue in the Upanishads between a father and son emphasizes this point. The wise father, Uddalaka, instructs his son Svetaketu, who is conceited about his knowledge of the Vedas, but doesn't know the secret, inner truth. Uddalaka tells his son:

> "Place this salt in the water. In the morning come unto me."
> Then he did so.
> Then he said to him: "That salt you placed in the water last evening—please bring it hither."
> Then he grasped for it, but did not find it, as it was completely dissolved.
> "Please take a sip of it from this end," said he. "How is it?"
> "Salt."
> "Take a sip from the middle," said he. "How is it?"
> "Salt."
> "Take a sip from that end," said he. "How is it?"
> "Salt."
> "Set it aside. Then come unto me."
> He did so, saying, "It is always the same."
> Then he said to him: "Verily, indeed, my dear, you do not perceive Being here. Verily, indeed, it is here. That which is the finest essence—this whole world has that as its soul. That is Reality. That is Atman (Soul). That art thou, Svetaketu."
> (*Chandogya Upanishad* 6.13.1–3)[12]

"That art thou"—this is one of the most fundamental statements of identity. "That"—Brahman that is the essence of all—is the same as your own true self, the atman. That self is eternal, formless, pure consciousness. That real self is the birthright of all living beings, and knowing it means attaining supreme bliss.

This is the highest self. Yet the lower realities of life are not unimportant. This real self, atman, is attached to the empirical self made up of physical, mental, and psychological aspects, and it is in this condition that we live out our countless existences. Hindu wisdom teaches that the eternal atman is embodied according to the working of the law of **karma**. The actions the atman performs in one lifetime, depending on their moral quality, create the conditions for the next embodiment of the atman. "According as one acts, according as one conducts himself, so does he become. The doer of good becomes good. The doer of evil becomes evil" (*Brihad-aranyaka Upanishad* 4.4.5).[13] The law of karma works neutrally and it inexorably metes out the results of one's actions, **rebirth** after rebirth. There are countless living beings—each one embodying an atman—and countless levels of rebirth, from those in the hells to plants, animals, humans, and gods. One's evil karma may bring rebirth at lower levels, even as an animal or plant; one's good karma may bring rebirth at a higher human level or even as a god or goddess.

This whole process is **samsara**, the rebirth cycle, which is beginningless and endless. Since, as we saw, there is an eternal Dharma that prescribes the role of all things, every atman within samsara at any given time has its own dharma and, thus, its own role to fulfill. One's dharma involves duties according to sex, caste, and so forth—all this is considered part of the nature of reality and is the basis for the operation of karma. If I am born as a servant, that is the karmic result of my previous lifetimes. In accordance with my dharma as a servant, my actions in this lifetime as a good servant or a bad servant will cause the level of my next rebirth.

People in some other religions talk about the nature of the world as good, or as evil, or as a mixture of good and evil. In the Hindu vision, the world, evolved from the primordial One or created as play by the great God, is really neither good nor evil but neutral. On the highest level, the ultimate goal is to seek moksha, liberation from samsara altogether. But on another level, our role is to live our lives according to Dharma, the eternal law of the world, promoting the welfare of all beings in the interrelated cycle of life—and living on again and again in the cycles of samsara because of our karma. That's the way things are.

Samsara and the Problem of Existence

Why do things seem not right? Why is there so much pain and suffering? Whereas to outsiders the idea of living another lifetime after this one might seem attractive, Hindus know that another lifetime—and countless more after that—means more of the same pain and death endlessly. Not that everything about life is unhappy—far from it. The dharma of Hindu householders, for example, includes the duties of pleasure and accumulating wealth. Hindus do not have an unduly pessimistic view of life in the world. But the Hindu tradition does stress the relative, transient quality of life clearly: It is not the lasting, most authentic state of the soul. Seen in the eternal perspective, one searcher discovered, this passing bodily life really is nothing to rejoice about and cling to:

Sir, in this ill-smelling, unsubstantial body, which is a conglomerate of bone, skin, muscle, marrow, flesh, semen, blood, mucus,

tears, rheum, feces, urine, wind, bile, and phlegm, what is the good of enjoyment of desires? In this body, which is afflicted with desire, anger, covetousness, delusion, fear, despondency, envy, separation from the desirable, union with the undesirable, hunger, thirst, senility, death, disease, sorrow, and the like, what is the good of enjoyment of desires? . . . In this sort of cycle of existence (samsara) what is the good of enjoyment of desires, when after a man has fed on them there is seen repeatedly his return here to earth? Be pleased to deliver me. In this cycle of existence I am like a frog in a waterless well.

(*Maitri Upanishad* 1.3–4)[14]

The very heart of the human problem, according to Hindus, is ignorance. I don't know who I really am. My true self really is the atman, eternal and identical with Brahman—but I think this living, breathing, thinking, feeling, desiring, socializing, personalized body is who I really am. As we saw, the philosopher Shankara provided an astute analysis of our human problem. We commonly view the world as changing, full of different realities, persons, and things. But this arises from *maya* (illusion). Although there is one absolute Brahman, we in the process of maya superimpose false notions on Brahman, notions of separate individual realities and selves. This maya then blinds us so that we react to that illusion as if it is real, and so we live our lives as if we are individual egos in relation to all the separate things of the world. In a cryptic statement, one teacher of the Upanishads said,

By the mind alone is It to be perceived.
There is on earth no diversity.
He gets death after death,
Who perceives here seeming diversity.
(*Brihad-aranyaka Upanishad* 4.4.19)[15]

If I am ignorant of the unity of the Brahman—that is, if I think of myself as different and see this world as made up of various things—I get "death after death," trapped endlessly in the rebirth and redeath of samsara. Why? Because out of ignorance that sees many rather than One, desire arises, and from desire comes the impulse to selfish action (karma). The law of karma is such that actions performed out of desire have evil repercussions in the next lifetime, bringing a state of suffering and pain for the embodied atman.

Ignorance, desire, karma, rebirth—that is why there is suffering in the world, that is why life isn't what it should be. It is a vicious circle, as the sage teaches:

According as one acts, according as one conducts himself, so does he become. . . . As is his desire, such is his resolve; as is his resolve, such is the action he performs; what action he performs, that he procures for himself. On this point there is this verse:

> Where one's mind is attached—the inner self
> Goes thereto with action, being attached to it alone.
>   Obtaining the end of his action,
>   Whatever he does in this world,
>   He comes again from that world
>   To this world of action.

So the man who desires.

(*Brihad-aranyaka Upanishad* 4.4.5–6)[16]

What one does now, out of ignorance and desire, creates conditions for one's next lifetime under which one will continue to act in ignorance and desire—a vicious circle that is likely to spiral downward. That is why the sages of India have generally regarded samsara as a trap of existence, with the ultimate goal being **moksha**, liberation from samsara.

But that final goal of moksha requires great spiritual knowledge and perfection, and at best it is many lifetimes away for most people. And so we ought at least strive to live the good life, doing good deeds instead of evil, so that our karma will create the conditions of a higher rebirth or at least not a lower one. But even knowing that, we find it difficult to get away from selfish actions time after time, desiring other things, experiencing feelings of anxiety and regret when we lose something. How can one keep from despairing over being trapped in samsara? How can one keep ignorance and selfish desires from bringing ever lower rebirths? The Hindu answer is to follow the path of transformation at the level appropriate to one's spiritual status.

THREE PATHS TO TRANSFORMATION AND LIBERATION

How can we start living *real* life? How can we reach liberation? At first glance the answers to this question given within the Hindu tradition seem almost countless. We find almost every conceivable religious pursuit being practiced by someone or other. One devotes herself to a particular god or goddess; another studies the Vedas and performs sacrifices; another goes on pilgrimages. Then there is another who is

deeply skeptical of these practices and prefers speculation and philosophy. One tries to fulfill moral duties and works for the good of the community. Yet another abandons his family and community and wanders about, seemingly uninterested in society and even in the gods. It's a bit confusing! What is the path of transformation for Hindus?

Following the model set in the *Bhagavad Gita*, Hindus traditionally have grouped these various ideas and practices into three basic paths (*marga*) of transformation: the **Path of Knowledge** (*jñana-marga*), the **Path of Action** (*karma-marga*), and the **Path of Devotion** (*bhakti-marga*). These three are broad paths and intersect at many points. Typically a Hindu may be following practices associated with all three paths, and the emphasis may change at different points in a lifetime. But each path does have a special focus and structure, and depending on a person's particular spiritual level and progress, attention is given more to one or the other of these paths.

The Path of Liberating Knowledge

The theoretical basis of the path of knowledge was first worked out in the Upanishads, although perhaps the roots of this path go back to more ancient times, including non-Aryan sources. And it no doubt was influenced by Buddhist and Jain practitioners. The focus is on self-realization through disciplines of meditation and withdrawal. Some Hindus consider the path of knowledge to be the highest path toward transformation, because it is the one that most directly can bring the searcher to the final goal of moksha (liberation).

Moksha, the Realization of the Real Atman   "Whoever thus knows 'I am Brahman!' becomes this All" (*Brihad-aranyaka Upanishad*, 1.4.10).[17] So the final goal is to "know" that I am Brahman. This is what brings moksha, the full and unconditioned release from the bondage of karma and samsara.

We should not be deceived by the simplicity of this answer. Knowledge here, of course, involves knowing the scriptures and the philosophical commentaries. But it is much more—not a merely intellectual knowing but rather a deep, experiential realization of the ultimate ground as one's true self. It far transcends the intellect and the mind, which are aspects of the subtle self involved in the rebirth cycle. The intellect can assist in reaching this knowledge, but eventually even the intellect is transcended in the pure consciousness of the true atman. This knowledge is to be felt, experienced, and lived, knowledge that transforms one's whole being.

How is it that knowledge can be transforming and liberating? We need to recall that ignorance is the root of the human problem. Because I am ignorant of my real atman, I take my empirical self to be my real concern and the focus of my desires. I look upon the other things in this world as separate objects, and I perform actions (karma) out of a desire to enhance my self, perpetuating the cosmic process that keeps me tied to the samsara cycle. But if I know that my true self is indeed the Brahman, and that Brahman includes within itself the entire universe, then there is nothing for me to desire for my "self," for I already am all. "If a person knew the soul (*Atman*), with the thought, 'I am he!,' with what desire, for love of what would he cling unto the body?" (*Brihad-aranyaka Upanishad*, 4.4.12).[18] Since this knowledge destroys all desires and, thus, all karma, there will be no more rebirths once this knowledge is fully and completely realized.

> What is soundless, touchless, formless, imperishable,
> Likewise tasteless, constant, odorless,
> Without beginning, without end, higher than the great, stable—
> By discerning That, one is liberated from the mouth of death.
>
> (*Katha Upanishad* 3.15)[19]

When the body dies, the subtle self of mind and the vital breaths do not draw together around the atman to lead to a new rebirth; the true atman is liberated. "Being very Brahman, he goes to Brahman" (*Brihad-aranyaka Upanishad*, 4.4.6).[20]

Moksha is described in various ways in the Hindu tradition. Sometimes it is pictured as a dissolving of the atman into the one Brahman. Just as a lump of salt dissolves when thrown into water, leaving no salt to grasp but making the water salty wherever one may taste it, so the atman becomes one with the Brahman. The individuality characterized by the empirical self—the physical body and the traits of mind and personality—comes to an end in the pure oneness of the Brahman. Moksha, however, is not annihilation or extermination of the atman; it is rather expansion, becoming all by transcend-

ing the limited self of mortal existence. So other descriptions of moksha portray it as pure bliss, peace, freedom, and joy. It is endless and unlimited.

Renunciation, Yoga, and Meditation To follow the path of knowledge and reach moksha requires a high level of spiritual perfection and understanding. Therefore, the path of knowledge is necessarily an elite path, although it is beneficial even for those at lower spiritual levels to devote some attention to it. A person who really wants to follow the path of knowledge to its end in moksha is advised to take the prior steps of self-discipline and preparation by becoming a **samnyasin**, a renouncer. By cutting off all ties to this world, by giving up possessions, family links, and all worldly concerns, one will have the freedom necessary to devote oneself to attaining the knowledge that will liberate from samsara.

But even prior to becoming a samnyasin, dedicated women and men engage in practices of renunciation and spiritual disciplines to move along on the path of knowledge. A variety of ascetic and spiritual practices, often called yoga and meditation, form the heart of this path. Yoga typically involves moral restraints, bodily exercises, breath control, withdrawing senses inward, and numerous meditation exercises (see pp. 110–111). Meditation itself is perhaps the most characteristic activity on the path of knowledge, for it is by looking inward that one finds the true self, the atman. Many types of meditation have been developed in India, but in general the process is to withdraw one's consciousness from the outer sensual reality and turn it inward, by stages, until all dualities and conditions dissolve and one experiences the pure, unified consciousness of the Brahman.

One meditation described in the Upanishads can suggest the general direction of meditation practice. The *Mandukya Upanishad* suggests a four-stage process, based on the mantra OM (in Sanskrit, AUM). OM is often used in meditation, for it is considered the sacred sound that encompasses all sounds and, therefore, fittingly symbolizes the Brahman. The letter *A* of AUM corresponds to the waking state, with consciousness turned outward. *U* corresponds to the dreaming state, with consciousness turned inward but still not unified. *M* symbolizes the deep-sleep state, which is a blissful, unified, massive consciousness—but still not the final goal. The fourth state, experiencing the real atman, corresponds to the silence that precedes and follows the saying of the mantra AUM. This state is neither cognitive nor noncognitive; it is indescribable and unthinkable. It is the unified, tranquil, blissful experience of the atman as Brahman. "He who knows this, with his self enters the Self—yea, he who knows this!" (*Mandukya Upanishad* 12).[21] This universal self is eternal and changeless, and knowing it as one's real self, one transcends death and rebirth completely.

This path of knowledge is available to all seekers and provides rewards of spiritual growth and transformation. Eventually, by becoming a samnyasin and following the path of knowledge to the higher spiritual levels, ultimate transformation can be attained, according to Hindu wisdom. One reaches moksha, the fullest type of existence, and, if that moksha is complete and perfect, when this lifetime ends there will be no more rebirth. Being Brahman, one attains Brahman.

The Path of Action

Although it might be recognized that the path of knowledge is the path that leads finally to complete moksha, most people are a long way from that kind of spiritual perfection. Whereas practices such as meditation are beneficial, there are other religious pursuits that provide help along the way. Since the human problem has to do with desire and the resultant action (karma) that binds us in the rebirth cycle at ever lower levels, it makes sense to work toward the lessening of desire and the cultivation of actions that will move us upward in the rebirth cycle. To a great many Hindus, following the path of action (karma-marga) is what Hinduism is all about as a way of transformation.

We learned that karma (action) was the cause of the samsara cycle. How can karma be the basis of a path of transformation? Hindus point out that there are different kinds of karma. Many—probably most—of the actions we do result from desire, from wanting something for ourselves. Action done out of desire or passion produces a "hot" kind of karma that has adverse effects in the future. We become as we desire, the Upanishads teach. This karma will bring fear and anxiety into our lives. And a whole lifetime filled with actions done out of passion and desire will inevitably result in rebirth at lower levels.

But there is another kind of karma, that is, action done without desire, "cool" karma. This kind of karma produces effects, of course, but these are good and beneficial effects. This kind of karma brings peace to life, and it will result in rebirths at higher levels in the samsara cycle. With enough good karma one can even be reborn as a god—though this, of course, is not yet moksha. Eventually, after many lifetimes, a person will reach the level of spiritual perfection in which she or he can follow the path of knowledge and reach ultimate liberation.

So the crucial question for a Hindu is, how can I eliminate action rooted in desire and cultivate action done without desire? The classical Hindu answer is simply to do what is expected according to one's dharma, one's place and role in the eternal order of things. For example, if my karma has caused me to be born as a warrior, I should go about my duty of protecting people, not out of desire or hope for reward, but simply because it's my dharma. If I'm a woman, I should be a good woman; if a slave, I should simply serve others without desiring to be something else. The whole system worked out in the *Law-code of Manu*, which we discuss later, provides guidance for the path of action: Caste, sex, and stage of life make up the essential elements of one's dharma, and by performing that role properly, without desiring some reward, it is possible to move forward on the path of transformation. The *Bhagavad Gita* teaches that such detached carrying out of one's dharma leads toward the good:

> He incurs no guilt if he has no hope,
> restrains his thought and himself,
> abandons possessions,
> and performs actions with his body only. . . .
> Always perform with detachment
> any action you must do;
> performing action with detachment,
> one achieves supreme good.
> (*Bhagavad Gita* 4.21; 3.19)[22]

In a sense, the path of action is a universal path for Hindus, for everyone is born into it, and most Hindus keep practicing it until the end of their lives. Only some world-renouncers and devotees of certain gods claim to transcend the laws of eternal Dharma. The path of action is a way of transformation through discipline, ritual, and morality. Performing one's duty without desire leads to the higher spiritual levels.

The Path of Devotion

There is yet another way. Only few can attain the liberating freedom of the path of knowledge. The path of action does not promise liberation and poses many problems itself, as we see in the great epics in which examples of people caught between duty and love abound. Arjuna grieves for his slain relatives and wishes to avoid his duty as a warrior. King Yudhishthira mourns the countless lives sacrificed in the great battles and wishes he could renounce the world. We all know what our duty is; yet desires, longings, and even what appear to be higher values constantly keep us from performing our duty in a completely unattached way. Is there no other way? Yes, there is: the path of **bhakti** (devotion).

How Can God Liberate Us? Generally in the Hindu system of thought, the gods, though powerful and blessed, are understood to be within the cycle of samsara and, therefore, not ultimate. From ancient times, in India, various gods were worshiped for all kinds of benefits. And still today, Hindus perform rituals of worship for various reasons, such as worshiping Sarasvati to attain learning and art, Ganesha for success in business, Lakshmi for wealth, and the like. But how can such gods provide salvation? How can they liberate us from the effects of our karma?

We saw earlier how several great theistic movements developed in Hinduism, one centered on Vishnu, another on Shiva, and yet another on the great Goddess Devi, in each case looking on the great God or Goddess as the personal sacred power of the universe. Unlike the descriptions of Brahman in the Upanishads, these great Gods are personal and present; they pervade all reality, they are present within the soul, and they can be worshiped and loved. Since, according to devotees, Vishnu, Shiva, and Devi are supreme and in fact none other than the Brahman, they can be sources of saving power, not only bringing limited benefits but also transforming us and liberating us from bondage to samsara. It is not only knowledge of the inner Brahman, realized by the spiritually elite, that brings liberation; God, the lover of my soul, to whom I can abandon myself no matter what my spiritual status, can help me to liberation.

Bhakti means to love and devote oneself to one's God, fully and completely. By such self-abandonment, all desires and wants and needs are turned to God rather than to the self. United with the great God of the universe who is also the inner soul of one's heart, one rises above the bondage of karma and finds joy, peace, and ecstasy in the power of the Beloved One.

The Vaishnavite Path of Bhakti The transforming power of Vishnu can be experienced in different ways by the bhaktas (devotees), whether through Vishnu's presence in the universe as creator, preserver, and destroyer, or through Vishnu's avataras Rama and Krishna. The important factor is the love and the self-surrender on the part of the worshiper. In the *Bhagavad Gita*, for example, Krishna emphasizes this self-surrender:

> Keep me in your mind and devotion,
> sacrifice to me, bow to me,
> discipline your self toward me,
> and you will reach me!
> (*Bhagavad Gita* 9.34)[23]

Our bondage to the conditions of karma—whether high caste or slave, woman or man, pure or sinful—is overcome in the power of God's love. Women and Shudras were excluded from performing Vedic rituals, but everyone, including women and Shudras, can worship Krishna and find salvation in him (9:32). Even those who are devotees of other gods and worship them are actually worshiping Krishna (9:23)! Since Vishnu transcends even the samsara cycle, in loving union with the Lord we too can rise to salvation:

> Even in Brahma's cosmic realm
> worlds evolve in incessant cycles,
> but a man who reaches me
> suffers no rebirth, Arjuna.
> (*Bhagavad Gita* 8.16)[24]

The theme that God is lovable and invites our love is emphasized as the Puranas fill out the story of Krishna with much more detail. A demon king by the name of Kamsa, the story goes, has seized rule of Mathura, and his power threatens even the gods. In answer to their appeal, Vishnu tells of his plan to be born into the world as the eighth son of King Vasudeva and his wife Devaki. King Kamsa, learning of this plan, kills the first six children of Devaki. Her seventh son is an incarnation of Vishnu, Balarama, who is transferred to the womb of Vasudeva's second wife and, thus, saved. When Krishna is born as Devaki's eighth child, he is exchanged for the newborn daughter of the cowherd woman Yashoda—and, thus, Krishna and his brother Balarama grow up among the cowherd people of Vrindavana.

Yashoda and the other cowherd people are filled with wonderful joy and love through the presence of the beautiful baby, dark as the lovely blue lotus petal. His playfulness and mischief endear him to everyone—untying village calves, mocking his elders, teasing babies, stealing butter and sweets, playing tricks on the villagers, dancing and sporting with his brother Balarama and the village boys—all of this brings the love of God to the people. How joyful to love God as a baby, as a free and playful child! God is present in spontaneous, tumultuous power, at the same time approachable and adorable. In the child Krishna, we can see that God's very nature is to sport and play, inviting us to share in the divine self-delight.

Child Krishna grows up and becomes young man Krishna—still adorable and beautiful and playful, now irresistible to the gopis, as the young women among the cowherd people are called. When he goes out to the forest and plays his flute, the divine sound is too enticing to resist, and the women leave their chores, husbands, and families and come out to be near Krishna. Krishna dances and plays with all of them, multiplying his form so that each can experience his love. It is a festival of love, full of intoxication, joy, and abandon. One Purana describes this great romance:

> Some of the cow herdesses . . . out of fun forcibly took away the flute from the hands of Lord Krishna. Then they pulled his yellow dress. Some passionate girl denuded him of his clothes, took away his yellow garment and then in jest returned it to him. . . . Some danced and sang with Krishna in the centre; others forcibly caused him to dance. Krishna also out of fun, dragged the clothes of some milkmaid, made her naked and then returned the clothes to her.[25]

The scene grows more tumultuous, and Krishna, surrounded by this group of impassioned gopis, makes love to them all, a celebration that even the gods assembled to watch. Among the gopis, Krishna's favorite is Radha, and the stories delight in telling of the many facets of the love affair between the divine lover and his beloved. They are drawn to each other passionately, they grow jealous and quarrel and make up, they consummate their love in ecstasy and abandon and bliss. Krishna plays and delights him-

self, and Radha and the gopis are drawn into this divine delight. Here all duty and obligation are forgotten, and the gopis and Krishna are drawn together out of sheer divine passion and delight.

Here, some say, is the highest form of loving God. We can love God as a father or mother, as a brother or friend, as a beautiful baby—but to love God as a lover means totally forgetting self and surrendering to the ecstasy of divine joy and delight. And that experience helps the devotee toward transformation and liberation.

The Shaivite Path of Transformation   Shiva appears to be a very different god from Vishnu; he is all-holy, fiercely destructive, impetuous, and even his creative powers wreak havoc. Yet his devotees, like those of Vishnu, experience transformation and liberation in worshiping him. In Shiva, the creative and the destructive powers of the sacred are held closely together, along with other dualities such as male and female, desire and asceticism, and life and death.

Shiva is often portrayed as bringing fierce destruction because of his quick temper and outrageous behavior. He is wild and unpredictable, often called "Madman" by his devotees. Sexually attracted to Parvati, daughter of the mountains, he marries her but then practices asceticism and refuses to impregnate her. They have a tempestuous relationship. For example, Parvati has a son **Ganesha**, born from the dirt she removed from her body while bathing. Ganesha guards the bathhouse, but one day Shiva forces his way in and, enraged that Ganesha tried to stop him, cuts off Ganesha's head with a mighty blow. Parvati's anger now threatens to destroy the world, so Shiva agrees to restore Ganesha's life, taking the head of the first living thing that came by—an elephant—and placing this on Ganesha's body. Shiva's violent act is the origin of the extremely popular elephant-headed god Ganesha, worshiped as the bringer of prosperity and good fortune.

Shiva also is worshiped as the creator, nourisher, and preserver of existence. Stories tell how he made it possible, for example, for the heavenly Ganges River to descend gently over the Himalayas to water the earth, cushioning the river's descent with his own divine head. Another well-known story tells how the gods and the demons were churning the vast milk ocean to obtain the nectar of immortality. They used the great serpent Vasuki as the

A seventeenth-century temple hanging showing the gopis (cowherd women) searching for Krishna in the night. 'The Rainy Season (Varsha)'. India, Gujarat or the Deccan; late 17th century. Temple hanging (pichhavai); opaque watercolor, gold, and silver on dyed cotton 80 3/4 x 86 /2 in. (205.1 x 219.7 cm) Photograph by Otto Nelson. The Asia Society, New York, Mr. and Mrs. John D. Rockefeller 3rd Collection.

driven by desire for Parvati. His male powers are evident in that his semen is the seed from which the whole universe arises; yet he retains his seed and refuses to give in to Kama's enticements. A famous passage describes how Shiva destroyed Kama by burning:

> Kama assumed the form of a very subtle creature and entered Shiva's heart. Then Shiva was heated by a desire for sexual pleasure, and he thought of Devi, and his perfection vanished. . . . Then he saw Kama in his heart, and he thought, "I will burn Kama out of my body by means of withdrawal from worldly objects. . . ." [Kama] shot the arrow of Delusion into Shiva's heart, and in anger Shiva burnt Kama to ashes with the fire from his third eye.[26]

With Kama destroyed, of course, all life and fertility are threatened, and the gods beg Shiva to restore Kama. Finally, in his desire for Parvati, he brings about a revival of Kama, and life can go on.

churning rope and a great mountain as the churning rod, but after a thousand years of furious churning, a terrible poisonous venom began to gush from the thousand mouths of the serpent. Now the lives even of the gods were threatened, so Shiva agreed to accept the poison as if it were the nectar of immortality, saving the gods and all the world from destruction. His supreme power kept him from harm, although the venom left his throat a dark blue color, still seen on artistic representations.

Shiva embodies the tension between erotic powers and ascetic powers. A central story in the Puranas is the conflict between Shiva and Kama, the god of desire. As the great ascetic, Shiva is the epitome of chastity; yet he is constantly

Based on stories and perceptions like these about Shiva, those devoting themselves to him often involve themselves in yogic austerities and meditation practices. Worshipers of Shiva may smear ashes on their bodies and haunt cemeteries in their quest for union with Shiva. Poet-saints cultivate love for Shiva in monotheistic tones, expressing an extreme sense of unworthiness in the face of the all-holy God, and a deep sense of guilt and pain in separation from Shiva. Through love and service, Shiva devotees have vivid personal experiences of the gift of divine knowledge, purification of the soul from delusion, and infinite bliss in oneness with Shiva. They revel in the overpowering holiness of the presence of Shiva. Devotees call on Shiva, "Oh madman with moon-crowned hair," and they experience divine ecstasy:

But me he filled in every limb
With love's mad longing, and that I might climb there
    whence is no return,
He showed his beauty, made me his. Ah me, when shall I go
    to him? . . .
Thinking it right, sin's path I trod;
    But, so that I such paths might leave,
And find his grace, the dancing God,
    Who far beyond our thought doth live,
O wonder passing great!—to me his dancing shewed.
Ah who could win that which the Father hath bestowed?[27]

Shiva pervades the whole universe and is manifest within it through his Shakti (power, female energy). Therefore, attunement of one's self to Shiva, who is present in the blissful throbbing waves of divine consciousness in the breast, is a means of ultimate transformation.

Transformation Through the Great Goddess   The great Goddess (Devi) likewise brings transformation to her devotees. As we saw, great Goddesses are worshiped in many forms and localities for a variety of benefits, but there are some who single-mindedly devote themselves to one of these forms as supreme. To them, devotion to Devi is a way of salvation. The many faces of the Goddess—grace, cruelty, creation, destruction, love, indifference—express the endless energy active at the heart of the world. So worshiping her, through meditation, Tantric rituals, and ecstatic devotion, can bring liberation through her gracious power.

Even the ferocious goddess Kali is worshiped by some strong-minded ones as source of salvation. Tantric ritual practitioners confront her head-on as the source of fear, terror, as death itself, and in doing so they overcome the bondage of fear and death and transform Kali into a vehicle of salvation. Other devotees look to Kali as their mother and adopt the posture of the helpless child; even though the mother is fearsome and terrifying, the child has no choice but to cling to her. For example, the great Bengali poet Ramprasad Sen (1718–1775) was a lifelong devotee of Kali, and he often expressed this sense of struggle and pain in trying to hold on to mother Kali—even though she beats it, the child clings to its mother, crying "Mother." Being Kali's child means to suffer—but somehow through

that suffering the realities of desire, suffering, and death are confronted, and, thus, Kali helps the devotee to liberation. So Ramprasad sang the praises of mother Kali, intoxicated with her many names—Devi, Durga, Uma, Dark One, Crazy Kali. Kali plays, tortures him, deludes him, brings misery and death—but in the end he finds that her divine energy, symbolized by her wild hair, brings grace and mercy.[28]

The modern Hindu saint **Ramakrishna** (1836–1886), together with his disciples, often sang to Durga-Kali-Shakti in group devotion, as in this example:

Thy name, I have heard, O Consort of Shiva, is the
    destroyer of our fear,
And so on Thee I cast my burden: Save me! Save me,
    O kindly Mother!
Out of Thy womb the world is born, and Thou it is that
    dost pervade it. . . .
Thou art the Primal Power, O Mother! She whose senses
    are controlled;
The yogis meditate on Thee as Uma, great Himalaya's
    daughter.
Thou who art the Power of Shiva! Put to death my cease-
    less cravings;
Grant that I never fall again into the ocean of this world.[29]

For such devotees, Kali as the great Goddess grants the boon of unconditioned freedom and release from concern over the samsara world. In worshiping her, one confronts death head on, giving oneself over to her play, singing and dancing with the abandon and ecstasy of liberation.

Ramakrishna not only followed the path of devotion but also he brought it together with the path of knowledge. He practiced meditation, and his deepest trances came as he focused on his beloved Kali. Once again we remind ourselves that these three paths of liberation in Hinduism are not exclusive, and it is more than likely that any given Hindu will be following at least two of them at the same time. Within these three paths are possibilities for all people, no matter how high or low spiritually or socially, to move toward transformation and liberation.

DISCUSSION QUESTIONS

1 Outline some of the main aspects of Brahman seen as ultimate reality, including the difference between nirguna Brahman and saguna Brahman.

2 What is meant by different levels of knowing Brahman as proposed, for example, by Shankara? How does the idea of maya fit in?

3 Sketch out the main theistic visions of the ultimate associated with Vishnu, Shiva, and the great Goddess Devi. How do theists relate their God to Brahman?

4 What is the Hindu conception of Dharma, and how does the notion of karma relate to this? How does one know what his or her dharma is?

5 What are some of the ways Hindu scriptures talk about the creation of the world?

6 Explain the Hindu notion of great world cycles of time. Is there a beginning and end to the world?

7 What is samsara, and how does the Hindu tradition view this condition of existence? Is life in samsara something to escape from, or should one affirm and better this life?

8 What is moksha? Is this anything like "salvation" in other religions?

9 Explain the main practices in the Hindu path of knowledge. How does knowledge lead to liberation in the Hindu view?

10 What is the main purpose of the path of karma as a path of transformation? How can performing karma lead to spiritual progress?

11 Explain the main rationale of the path of devotion. How do the qualities of this path differ in the Vishnu, Shiva, and Devi traditions?

Chapter 5

Hindu Ritual and the Good Life

RITUALS AND SACRED TIMES OF HINDUISM

The Hindu paths toward transformation focus on knowledge, action, and devotion. Within these paths there is a wide range of activities, some directed more to ritual and devotion, others directed more toward ethical duties and disciplines. First we will look at traditional Hindu ritual practices, and then we will turn our attention to the ethical notions and practices that make up the good life according to Hindu wisdom.

How can we find new power for life? How can we get in touch with what is real? Part of the Hindu answer is to participate in the exciting, colorful rituals and festivals so close to the heartbeat of Hinduism. Some spiritually advanced Hindus, withdrawn from the world and approaching the goal of moksha, feel little need for festivals and worship of the gods, but they still practice rituals of meditation and yoga. Other Hindus would say that everything they do, following the traditional law-codes of Dharma, is worship and piety. But for most Hindus, a central part of Hindu life is worship of the gods, rituals and pilgrimages, festivals, and life-cycle ceremonies. Religion is not so much something to theorize about or even to believe; rather, it is something to be done.

Vedic Rituals and Puja

One important observation to begin with is the centrality of the notions of pollution and purity in the Hindu way of life. Interaction with the sacred powers is essential for human welfare and spiritual transformation; yet the limiting conditions of human life often make that interaction difficult or even dangerous. The highest gods must be worshiped by

Brahmans who are in a pure state; polluted by contact with people of lower castes, for example, a Brahman cannot offer the Vedic sacrifices, and the whole community suffers. A woman who is menstruating should not prepare food to be offered to the gods. The ordinary biological processes of the body are polluting, so morning devotions should be preceded by a purifying bath. Rituals, ceremonies, and festivals always begin with the people purifying themselves.

Vedic Rituals and Sacrifices   The fire sacrifices and other rituals prescribed in the Vedas and other ancient texts enjoy great prestige, just as the Vedas themselves do. In earlier times, powerful and wealthy individuals hired Brahman priests to perform great public sacrifices, offering food and drink to the gods to strengthen them and harness their powers for the welfare of the world and of the people. Today, many Hindus still believe in the efficacy of these ancient rituals; they organize them for various purposes, sometimes in public for a communal cause, and sometimes in private for a personal concern. A simple form of the fire sacrifice is the domestic ritual performed by the householder, offering a sacrifice in the sacred household fire. But the larger fire sacrifices involve the participation of Brahman priests, setting up three to five fires, making offerings of grains, butter, ghee, or other vegetables, chanting Vedic mantras, and invoking Vedic gods. These larger sacrifices can last from a few hours to several days, and they are used to promote the fertility of the land, encourage wealth and industry, assist in bringing peace, and whatever other concerns there are for the community.

For example, one might see Vedic rituals in drought-stricken villages in rural India in the scorching days of summer, the dry season. The ground is dried up, water is rationed, food is running low, and famine threatens the community. Government agencies are busy sinking deep wells in the drought-afflicted region and bringing water in from elsewhere to avert calamity until, they hope, the refreshing rains of the monsoon season finally come. But the people of the village are most interested in the group of Brahman priests who go from village to village, chanting Sanskrit mantras from the Vedas and offering fire sacrifice. They are the real "experts" in this crisis, and the people hope and believe that the sacred vibrations set loose in their chanting and their sacrifice will bring rain and benefit to the struggling community. By participating in these Vedic sacrifices, humans share in the ongoing processes of creation and recreation of the world, nourishing the gods and goddesses, and continuing the sacred power that has been made present for thousands of years through the Vedic mantras and sacrifices.

One ancient Vedic prayer that is very important to many Hindus is the verse called *Gayatri*. These are the first words of Veda transmitted to a student by his teacher, and they are considered the concentrated power of Veda, the gateway to the divine. Typically, the head of the household arises at dawn, purifies himself with water, makes offerings, and concentrates his mind. Raising his arms to the rising sun, the brilliant symbol of Brahman, he chants the mantra:

> OM. Earth, Atmosphere, Sky.
> We meditate on the radiant
>   splendour of the divine
>   Source.
> May that One enlighten our
> intellect.
>
> (*Rig Veda* 3.62.10)

The mantra OM, the imperishable syllable, represents all of reality and Brahman itself. The Sanskrit words for Earth, Atmosphere, and Sky are world-creating utterances that support the whole

Ten-armed image of Ganesha, god of wisdom and remover of obstacles. Ganesha. India, Uttar Pradesh; 8th century. Sandstone. H. 49 1/2 in. (125.7 cm). Photograph by Lynton Gardiner. The Asia Society, New York: Mr. and Mrs. John D. Rockefeller 3rd Collection.

universe. This Gayatri, recited morning and evening, destroys the effect of bad deeds, drives away darkness, and harmonizes one's mind and life with the spiritual force of the universe.

Puja: Celebrating the Powerful Presence of God
Whereas Vedic rituals are restricted to the higher classes (Brahmans, Kshatriyas, and Vaishyas), there is no such general restriction on **puja**, the acts of worship paid to a god or goddess, usually in the presence of the divine image at a temple or domestic shrine.

The image of the sacred being plays a central role in most puja. The image is made by craftspeople according to the special iconographic tradition for that particular god, and then a ritual calls down the vitalizing presence of the god into the image. All worshipers, of course, know that the image is not the whole manifestation of the god. The god, especially if it is a form of Vishnu or Shiva or the great Goddess, pervades the whole universe, and the image is simply one local center for the operation of the sacred power.

There is a great variety of images of the gods and goddesses. A most common symbol of Shiva is the **lingam** (phallic pillar) placed on the yoni (female generative symbol). Another favorite image is the Dancing Shiva. Vaishnavites favor the shalagrama, a black stone with fossil ammonite, or Vishnu reclining on his serpent Sesha, or images of Rama or Krishna. Shaktas might focus on the ferocious image of Mother Kali. Hindus often have small images of the gods and goddesses in their home shrines and devote acts of puja to them in their home ritual devotions. In temples, the divine images are carefully and lovingly attended to. Large temples have rituals of putting the god to bed at night, waking the image in the morning, dressing, feeding, and entertaining her or him like a great queen or king, and taking the image out for joyous processions.

Puja at a temple generally begins with purification, invoking the presence of the god, and greeting the god with respect. The goddess (or god) is honored with **kirtana**, devotional worship that includes singing songs, playing auspicious music, dancing, offering items such as garlands of flowers and food, pouring water on the image, marking the forehead of the goddess with sandal paste, circling the goddess with incense, and waving lights. Worshipers hold their hands over the fire that has been offered before the goddess, then touch the hands to the forehead. The devotees are particularly intent on taking **darshana** (seeing) of the goddess or god, a ritual accompanied with intense feeling and emotion in the large temples. It is particularly by the ritual "seeing" of the goddess or god, and being "seen" by the god, that the worshiper feels united with the divine power and energy.

Another important ritual is the taking of **prasad**, sacred food. The food that was prepared to be offered to the god or goddess is also given to the worshipers, a tangible form of divine grace. By eating the food that the goddess has "eaten," the worshipers are accepting the blessing of the goddess and sharing in her power. Puja, especially as done in temples and at festivals, is a joyful, emotional, and exciting event, transforming both the individual and the community. For many Hindus, puja is the central religious activity of their lives.

Ascetic and Meditational Practices: Yoga

From the basic Vedic ritual of fire sacrifice, ancient Hindu tradition developed traditions of speculation and meditation on the inner power and meaning of the sacrifice. Such meditation was linked to the practice of asceticism (*tapas*), internalizing the heat and the power generated by the fire sacrifice. Many different types of ascetic and meditational practices developed over time, and still today these practices are considered by many to be at the heart of Hindu religious life.

Many forms of meditation, especially those involving ascetic disciplines, are commonly spoken of as *yoga*. Yoga, related to the English word *yoke*, has come to mean a discipline that harnesses spiritual power. In fact, almost any spiritual practice in Hinduism has been called a yoga:

bhakti yoga, karma yoga, jñana yoga, tantric yoga, and more. Many Hindus practice these meditative and yogic rituals of self-transformation. These are generally individual rituals, often performed under the guidance of a guru or master, designed to master one's physiological system and tap into the deeper spiritual resources. The rituals are varied, including the yogic practices of bodily posture and breath control, ritual chanting of mantras, sitting within a circle of fire, and much more.

But what has come to be considered the classic form of yoga is the eight-stage system developed by the ancient sage Patañjali in his *yoga Sutras*, the eight stages illustrating the movement from external distraction to inner knowledge. Pantañjali's system of yoga has been enormously influential in Hindu tradition.

This classical form of yoga is directed toward achieving discriminative knowledge, a transforming knowledge that distinguishes between a person's physical and mental reality (prakriti) and his or her true nature as pure spiritual consciousness (purusha). In this view, we experience suffering because of afflictions of body and mind that arise from ignorance of one's true purusha nature. And so the yogic practice cultivates body and mind through various disciplines in order to reach discriminating knowledge and, thus, the experience of liberation and wholeness. We can group the eight stages of Pantañjali's Yoga into three areas: ethical values, physical practices, and cultivation of consciousness.

Ethical Values

1 Moral Self-Restraints (yama), getting one's life in moral order through nonviolence, truthfulness, nonstealing, sensual restraint, and nonacquisitiveness

2 Moral Commitments (niyama), laying the moral foundation of purity, contentment, self-discipline, self-education, and dedication to God

Physical Practices

3 Postures (asana), involving steadiness, endurance, equilibrium, relaxation of effort, and meditation on the infinite

4 Regulation of Vital Energy Through Breath (pranayama), controlling the energy of the mind–body system by breath exercises

5 Withdrawal of Senses (pratyahara), eliminating mental distraction from the sense-organs so that all powers of consciousness can be focused inward on the source of being

Cultivation of Consciousness

6 Concentration (dharana), one-pointed mental concentration on a single object of thought

7 Meditation (dhyana), sustained attention to the object, stabilizing the mind in an uninterrupted state of contemplation

8 Meditative Trance (samadhi), the culminating experience in which the object of meditation vanishes and the mind swells to encompass a limitless reality. Plural things and plural souls are no longer recognized, and there is a consciousness of absolute freedom and liberation.

Ceremonies, Festivals, and Pilgrimages

The rhythms of sacred time in India come in daily, weekly, monthly, and yearly cycles. Sacred times also have regional emphases, although certain great festivals are celebrated all over India. The same is true of the important practice of pilgrimage to holy places, sacred rivers and mountains, and the like. These are usually set during sacred periods and provide a dramatic experience of sacred time and renewal.

Daily Rituals Depending on individual inclination, and also on caste and family custom, Hindus practice a rich daily series of ceremonies. A pious person rises before sunrise to meditate on the qualities of his or her god, bathe, and offer puja before eating the morning meal. If he or she is a Brahman, the daily Vedic rite is to be performed twice during the day, at sunrise and sunset, purifying oneself with water, making offerings, and reciting mantras to the fire god (Agni) and to the sun god. Orthodox householders of the upper classes perform the five great sacrifices daily: studying the Vedas, giving food offerings to the gods, offering water to the ancestors, giving food to Brahmans and students, and offering food to all beings. In modern times, many Hindus do not find time for all these rituals. But almost all Hindus observe the ceremonies of purification, bathing in flowing water or pouring water on oneself

(never bathing in a closed container, which retains the pollutions).

In many Hindu homes, the traditional rituals of cooking, serving, and eating daily food are carefully observed. The kitchen is the citadel of the household, maintained with ritual purity against intrusions of pollution from the outside. In Hindu tradition, the serving of food is really an act of puja; the food is encircled with drops of sacred water while a mantra is recited. Thus, the food is first offered to the god and the family meal becomes a form of prasad, eating food offered to the god.

Many families also have a household shrine, perhaps located near to the pure kitchen area. Images of the gods of special importance to the family are kept there, and worship rituals are performed daily, at least by the devout.

Festival Calendar Certain days of the week and of the month, such as the new moon and the full moon, are times for special ceremonies and celebrations. Most characteristic of Hinduism is the annual festival cycle; a typical village in northern India, for example, has over forty ceremonial occasions based on the lunar calendar of the year. Hindu religious life passes through seasons with various festivals and fairs, depending on the caste and sectarian affiliation of the community involved. Individual gods and goddesses all have their special festival times and seasons, far too many to attempt to describe. Here are three brief examples.

One great festival time throughout much of India, coming in the fall at the end of the rainy season (September–October), is **Durga** Puja, celebrating the triumph of good over evil and remembering especially the goddess Durga's victory over the buffalo demon, Mahisha. This is a ten-day festival to the great Goddess, with gala processions and dancing with lights and music. In the Belur Math temple in Calcutta (famous because of Ramakrishna's vision of Kali there), for example, a huge statue of Durga is consecrated and dressed, and prayers and songs ask Durga to drive away evil and bless the good. Another emphasis during this fall festival time are the Ram-lila plays, celebrating the victory of Rama over the demon Ravana, acted out in dramatic fashion by actors representing the divine heroes and demons, followed by communal celebrations.

Divali, which means "cluster of lights," comes in October–November and is one of the most festive times of the year. The central ritual is the lighting of row upon row of lamps all over, outside the house and on the roof, as many as possible, for lights symbolize prosperity. Lakshmi, the goddess of prosperity, is a main patroness of this festival, and she is invited to come inside the house to a temporary altar containing symbols of wealth—coins, ornaments, and shells. The people perform puja with sweets and milk, and these are then passed around the family as sacred food. It is a time of housecleaning and refurbishing, a general renewal of life. This festival is especially important to merchants, beginning the new business year.

Probably the most popular festival in northern India is **Holi**, celebrated on the full moon at the beginning of spring (February–March). For days the anticipation of the festival grows as people roam the streets seeking wood and combustibles for the Holi fire—with the accepted rule that everyone must contribute something for the fire. The fire is associated with the story of Prahlada, a virtuous young man who persisted in worshiping Vishnu even though his wicked aunt Holika tried to burn him in the fire. Holika had been given the divine boon of indestructibility by fire, so she held Prahlada on her lap in the flames—but Rama intervened and the lad emerged unscathed, whereas the demoness Holika was destroyed. With the rising of the full moon, the great fire flames up, and people of all castes circle it, throwing cakes of cow dung into the flames, shouting obscene phrases of vituperation toward the blaze representing Holika.

The great fire signals the beginning of "Holi play," representing the play of Krishna and Radha, and a carnival atmosphere rapidly develops. Boys run about splashing people with mud, colored water is thrown around on everyone, erotic dances take place, many people drink bhang (marijuana) mixed with sweetened milk, and every street reverberates with hymn singing and shouts of Holi joy. Holi is a time of license and frenzy, negating the tight structure and rules of ordinary society, providing a catharsis for high-born and low-born alike. Marriott offers this interpretation:

> The dramatic balancing of Holi—the world destruction and world renewal, the world pollution followed by world purification—occurs not only on the abstract level of structural principles, but also in the person of each participant. Under the tutelage of Krishna, each person plays and for the moment may experience the role of his opposite: the servile wife acts the domineering husband, and vice versa; the ravisher acts the ravished; the menial acts the master; the enemy acts

the friend; the strictured youths act the rulers of the republic. . . . Each may thereby learn to play his own routine roles afresh, surely with renewed understanding, possibly with greater grace, perhaps with a reciprocating love.[1]

Sacred Geography of Mother India To be a Hindu is to live in India and celebrate the presence of sacred power at the various holy places. Some holy places are naturally beautiful or awe-inspiring sites, such as rivers and mountains; others commemorate the exploits of gods and saints—and often the two types coincide. Like people of other religions, Hindus find it very spiritually rewarding to make pilgrimages to these holy places. A pilgrimage is a passage from the ordinary world of daily life to the world of the sacred. The pilgrimage begins with rituals of separation: shaving the head, putting on special clothes, and physically leaving the familiar neighborhood for a perilous journey. The journey itself represents a liminal, in-between state when the ordinary structures of social life are removed. People walk in groups with little attention to social status and caste. Hymn-singing, popular religious recitations, and sleeping in makeshift tents all contribute to the sense of crossing the threshold from the profane to the sacred. At the pilgrimage center, the pilgrims appropriate the sacred power through rituals and through the very fact of being there, receiving the darshana (seeing) of the deity or deities enshrined there. They gain personal merit and derive special benefits such as healing or expiation for wrongdoing. And when they return home they are reincorporated in their own community with an enhanced personal status.

All over India there are thousands of these sacred places, some visited regularly, some only at certain times—the famous Kumbha Mela festival in Allahabad, for example, is held only once every twelve years, when it attracts millions of pilgrims. Important among the sacred places known as Dhamas (abodes of god) is Mt. Kailasa high in the Himalayas, the celestial abode of Shiva and Parvati. Another is Puri, on a beach on the Bay of Bengal, the abode of Krishna as Jagannath (Lord of the World). The great car festival at Puri commemorates Krishna's journey to Mathura to slay wicked Kamsa. To have darshana of the great image on the chariot (a chariot some forty-five feet high and supported by sixteen wheels each seven feet in diameter) provides great power for salvation.

There are also many sacred cities for pilgrims, the most sacred perhaps being Banaras (Kashi), the City of Light.

Banaras is especially holy as the residence of Shiva and Parvati, but Vishnu and almost all the gods and goddesses are also present within the circle of this city. And the River Ganges flows through the city. Mother Ganga, the River of Heaven, agreed to flow on earth for the restoring of human life; Shiva caught the Ganges in his hair as she fell so the earth would not be shattered by her torrential force. Coming to Banaras, taking darshana of the sacred places of Shiva, Vishnu, and the other gods and goddesses, and bathing in the waters of the sacred Ganges provide great blessing, the salvation of the dead, and the purification of the living. Another of the sacred cities is Mathura, loved by millions of Hindus as the birthplace of Krishna.

Ritualizing the Passages of Life

The critical changes in life, such as birth, puberty, marriage, and death, are times when special rituals are needed to bring blessing and renewal. For this purpose, Hindus have a series of **samskaras**, rituals of the rounds of life, focused on the individual's life changes but involving the community as well. These changes are not simply physical and social, for the individual passes to a new identity within the eternal Dharma. Although there are many samskaras (sixteen by some traditions), they tend to cluster around birth, initiation, marriage, and death.

Samskaras: Rituals of the Life Cycle   Among the many prebirth rituals, some Hindus observe a rite for a healthy pregnancy called the "parting of the hair": the husband parts his wife's hair and applies a mark of red cosmetic powder as protection from malevolent spirits. About ten days after birth comes the important naming rite, and at about three years there is the first haircut, leaving only the sacred tuft, which some high-caste Hindus do not cut for the rest of their lives.

The great event for Hindu boyhood (for males of the upper "twice-born" classes) is the **upanayana** (initiation) ceremony. Traditionally this is performed when the boy is between eight and twelve, although it can take place as late as twenty-four years of age. The initiation ceremony is the ritual introduction of the boy to his Vedic teacher (guru), who drapes the sacred thread over the boy's left shoulder and chest, to be worn thereafter as the mark of a twice-born Hindu. The boy is taught the important Gayatri mantra, which he should recite daily thereafter, and he learns how to perform the ritual of fire sacrifice. The boy is now qualified to begin study of the Vedas, having died to the world of childhood and been reborn to the realm of responsibility. The initiation ritual is a joyous family and communal affair.

Although not recognized by the orthodox brahmanical tradition, there are also puberty rites of initiation for girls in various Hindu communities, based on oral and folklore traditions. For example, the Aiyar Brahman women of Tamilnadu have their own rites of passage, including a first menstruation ritual in which the girl is isolated for three days, followed on the fourth day by a ritual bath, a joyful feast, and a visit to the temple.[2]

One of the most important family and communal celebrations is marriage (vivaha), consisting of a series of rituals symbolizing this important passage of life. The Law-code of Manu suggests that marriage is a young woman's equivalent to the upanayana ritual, that serving her husband is similar to Vedic study, and doing the household work is equivalent to the fire sacrifices (2.67). Parents arrange a suitable match and solemnize it with a betrothal and other premarriage ceremonies. On the wedding day, chosen with the help of an astrologist, the bridegroom and relatives go to the bride's house, where the bride and groom sit side by side on a wooden bench while Brahman priests perform sacrifice and chant Vedic mantras. Following the traditional wedding pattern, the groom holds the bride's hand before the sacred fire and says, "I seize thy hand for the sake of happiness, that thou mayest live to old age with me, thy husband. . . . The Heaven I, the Earth thou. Come let us marry." The bride places her foot on a grinding-stone to symbolize firmness, and the ends of their garments are knotted together. The most binding part of the ceremony is the seven steps around the fire, during which the husband says, "May you take one step for sap (or force), second step for juice (or vigor), third step for the thriving of wealth, fourth step for comfort, fifth step for offspring, sixth step for seasons, may you be my friend with your seventh step!"[3] The husband touches his bride over the heart and paints the vermilion cosmetic mark on her forehead. In the evening they go out under the sky to look at the unchanging Pole Star, a symbol of faithfulness in their marriage.

The last samskara, called antyesti (last sacrifice), takes place at death. In a traditional Hindu family, after a

Hindu wedding ceremonies are celebrated with elaborate rituals. The bride and groom are draped with garlands of flowers.

person dies, he or she is washed, anointed with sandalwood paste, and freshly clothed. Then quickly relatives and friends form a procession with the body to the cremation grounds, led by the eldest son of the deceased. The body is placed on a pyre of wood and the son sets it aflame with an ancient prayer to **Agni** to convey the soul to the place of the ancestors. The mourners recite verses urging the dead person to join the ancestral spirits, leaving sin behind and avoiding the dogs of Yama. After the cremation, the mourners depart without turning around and take a purifying bath before entering their homes. Three days later is the bone-gathering ritual, and the eldest son will take them to the River Ganges or some other water symbolic of the Ganges. The final rituals are the shraddhas, the offering of cakes of rice and water together with the recitation of sacred verses, constructing a body for the departed on the journey to the realm of ancestors. These rituals continue for ten days, symbolizing the embryo's gestation over ten lunar months, after which the next-worldly body of the deceased is thought to be completed and moves into the realm of the ances-

tors. The funeral rituals reflect, perhaps, the ancient Vedic notion of the creation of the deceased person's body in the realm of the ancestors, an alternate conception of the afterlife that has continued in ritual practice alongside the Brahmanical teaching about the reincarnation of the soul.

Ritual of Spiritual Passage For some few who have reached a high spiritual level of perfection, an important ritual of spiritual passage is the act of becoming a **samnyasin**, the fourth and final stage of life in the traditional system, the dramatic spiritual break that comes when a person decides it is time to renounce the world. He or she gives away all possessions and performs the personal funeral rituals, shaving the head, clipping the nails, and taking a purifying bath. Performing the householder rites for the last time, the renouncer bids farewell to family and friends and walks away without looking back—never to mention or think of them again. Now the newly realized samnyasin lives as a wandering beggar, roving about freely. To help reach final perfection, the samnyasin may take a guru who contributes a final impetus on the path, tearing off the sacred thread and cutting the tuft of hair—no longer is the samnyasin bound by rules of caste or duties of social position. Now the one duty is to seek **moksha**, liberation.

Healing and Medicinal Practices: Ayurveda

Hindus and other South Asians are familiar with a variety of traditional healing practices that are closely linked with their religious worldview. Many, of course, look to practices of meditation and yoga as helpful for maintaining health, as well as a variety of rituals, sacred places, and holy people that traditionally have provided healing.

Of particular importance in India is the well-known holistic system of medicine called **Ayurveda**, which since ancient times has been associated with Vedic scriptures and written medical treatises. In modern times, Ayurveda has become quite popular, with the upsurge of interest in India's national heritage. The government of India has set up a special Department of Indian Systems of Medicine and Homeopathy to regulate and promote Ayurveda and the other traditional systems of medicine. Of course, Western biomedicine is important to everyone in India, especially for acute diseases, but many Hindus believe Ayurveda also is helpful as an alternative, for maintaining health and dealing with ordinary disorders and chronic conditions. In fact, with government support, India now has approximately as many recognized Ayurveda medical practitioners as physicians of Western medicine. Many South Asians living in the Western world take interest in Ayurveda, and this system of medicine is becoming increasingly popular among non-Asian Westerners as an alternative health practice.

The Ayurveda system of medicine is based on the traditional Hindu worldview. One key point is that everything in the world has its particular characteristics through the interaction of three universal qualities or *gunas*, namely, sattva, rajas, and tamas. *Sattva* is white and bright, bringing clarity of perception; *rajas* is red, bringing passion, emotion, sensation, and movement; *tamas* is dark and causes heaviness, inertia, and confusion. From these three qualities and their interaction derived all characteristics of the world and of humans. For example, people who are high in sattva qualities tend to be pure, truthful, creative, and intelligent. People in whom rajas qualities are strong are ambitious, controlling, jealous, and loving to those who help them. And people with strong tamas qualities tend to be lazy, greedy, irritable, and loving of food and sleep.

In addition to the makeup of such temperaments and mental characteristics, a person's health is determined by the harmony of the various elements and energies that make up the body. Each person's body is structured by the five basic elements (space, air, fire, water, and earth), each one produced by a particular combination of the three gunas. *Space* permits the flow of intelligence between cells; *air* is the vital force that governs all sensory stimuli and motor responses; *fire* regulates body temperature and is re-

sponsible for digestion and absorption of food; *water* exists as the body fluids, carrying energy from one cell to another; and *earth* is present in all solid structures and tissues.

Within this body structure, the actual functioning of the body is governed by the three *doshas* or biological energy forces: *vata* (from space and air), *pitta* (from fire and water), and *kapha* (from earth). These energy forces are present throughout the body, in every cell, tissue, and organ, and differ in their combinations in each person. Ayurveda physicians distinguish seven body types: vata prevalent, pitta prevalent, kapha prevalent, dual vata-pitta, dual pitta-kapha, dual kapha-vata, and equal vata-pitta-kapha. Now, *vata* is the energy of movement; it is dry, light, cold, active, astringent. That means a vata-type person would have dry skin and hair, a light body frame, cold hands, poor circulation, tending toward constipation, active, with emotions of anxiety and insecurity. People with unbalanced vata are susceptible to diseases involving air, such as pneumonia, emphysema, arthritis, or nervous system disorders. *Pitta* is the energy of digestion or metabolism; it is hot, sharp, light, sour, oily, and bitter. Thus, a person with strong pitta has warm skin, a strong appetite, perspires easily, has sharp features and mind, oily hair, moderate body frame, and an aggressive personality. People with unbalanced pitta tend to have diseases involving the fire element, such as fevers, inflammatory diseases, ulcers, colitis, and sore throat. *Kapha* is the energy that forms the body's structure; it is heavy, slow, cool, dense, static, sweet, and salty. A person in whom kapha dominates has heavy bone and muscles, puts on weight, has cool and clammy skin, a slow mind, and is loving and compassionate. People with unbalanced kapha tend to have diseases related to the water principle, such as sinus congestion, influenza, diabetes, excess weight, and headaches.

Now, the Ayurvedic notion of health is a well-balanced state of this total body–mind matrix that includes the three energy forces (doshas) as well as the five elements and the mental temperament. Clearly, this is a holistic notion of health involving physical, mental, social, emotional, and spiritual well-being. Disturbances in this natural harmony, whether they come from within or without, cause imbalances that, if not corrected, build up toxins and lead to disease. The progression of the disease begins with an accumulation of the aggravated dosha in its location: kapha in the stomach, pitta in the small intestine, and vata in the colon. If not treated, it begins to provoke the surrounding organs, settles in a weak tissue, and produces toxins that lead to a particular disease.

Ayurvedic physicians have many diagnostic techniques involving the whole person and environment, such as questioning about life history, observation of the body, palpating, pulse diagnosis, and examination of the tongue as well as urine, feces, skin, nails, eyes, voice, and so on. The goal of the prescribed treatment is to help restore the healthy balance of the whole body matrix. Some treatments alleviate the disease by balancing the doshas and burning the toxins; these treatments involve herbal medicines, fasting, yogic stretching, and breathing exercises. Other treatments cleanse out excess doshas and toxins from the body through enemas, therapeutic vomiting, nasal medicine, and blood cleansing. Once the doshas are in balance again, the physician prescribes therapies to promote strength and vitality through diet and exercise as well as meditation and spiritual exercises.

Hindus and Sacred Art

As in other traditional cultures, so also in Hindu society nearly all art is religious to some extent. The nondualistic Hindu vision means that the sacred is present in everything, so the function of art is to help us "see" the sacred. Hinduism is a strongly visual and sensuous religion. The sacred is present in this world and, thus, all the senses can be means of experiencing it. We see the sacred in the image, we touch the sacred by feeling the image, we hear the sacred sounds, we taste the sacred in the prasad and liquid offerings, and we smell the sacred by means of flowers and incense. Hindu religion is the cultivation of aesthesis, "perceiving" the sacred through sensuous forms. Furthermore, Hindu art excels in elaboration and embellishment to express the divine reality of the world in its full, ideal, perfected form.

The literary arts have been central to Hindus since the ancient Sanskrit poems of the Vedas, and the art of chanting the sacred sounds is still important. The epics and mythic literature, telling of the deeds of the heroes and the gods and goddesses, have been a vast artistic treasury from which Hindu artists have drawn their inspiration for many centuries. The literary art has flourished especially in devotional poetry, in the poems and hymns of God-intoxicated poets and saints, both in Sanskrit and especially in the vernacular dialects. There is a vast assortment of Sanskrit hymns of

adoration and supplication embedded in the epics, puranas, tantras, and other sacred works, or arising independently. Composed all over India, the poems are addressed to forms of Vishnu, Shiva, and Devi, and also many other gods and goddesses. For example, Jayadeva's *Gitagovinda* (late twelfth century) is a Sanskrit masterpiece, unfolding the drama of love between Krishna and Radha. Poet-saints in southern India roamed the countryside with Tamil poems in praise of Shiva or Vishnu. In northern India, Hindu bhakti poetry in Hindi and Bengali is widely known. Chaitanya (1486–1533) popularized the practice of singing ecstatic songs in praise of Krishna/Vishnu, and Ramprasad Sen (1718–1775) composed powerful poems to the great Goddess.

Very characteristic of Hindu art is the sculpture or painting of the gods and goddesses. The creation of an image is an act of religious discipline or yoga on the part of the artist. The artist must see into the divine so that he or she can present the sacred in visual form, that others can take darshana—see and experience the sacred presence. The divine image (murti) is the instrument that allows the believer to catch a reflection of the deity who transcends what the eye can see but who is present during worship. A most popular artistic creation is the image of Vishnu as he lies sleeping on his cosmic serpent in the period prior to the creation of the world for the new world cycle. The artistic portrayal represents the endless cycle of the worlds, inhaled and exhaled as it were by Vishnu, who is represented as relaxed and serene, the eternal sacred reality.

In another well-known portrayal, Vishnu stands erect, with his four arms (most Hindu images have more than two arms) holding his four main symbols: the conch, wheel, mace, and lotus. The conch, a shell from the deep ocean with its structure spiraling from a single point, represents the origin of the universe. The lotus flower stands for the universe unfolding from the waters of creation. Time, with its cycle of seasons, is represented in the wheel; and the mace symbolizes powerful knowledge. The four attributes are placed differently in different images (a total of twenty-four varieties), defining the special emanations of Vishnu for the needs of the worshiper.

Another class of iconography includes many images of **Shiva**, visualizing both his grace and his destructive terror. He is pictured as the great Yogin, as the protector of all animals, as the celestial bridegroom embracing his consort, and as the great Lord of wholeness whose right half is male and left half female. Other images portray Shiva as a naked young beggar or, again, an emaciated skeletal god. A favorite image is the dancing Shiva, Nataraja, the great God simultaneously dancing out the destruction and the creation of the world. He dances in a fiery circle, with a drum and flame in his upper hands—the drum sound symbolizing the beginning of creation, and the flame representing the destruction of the world. His raised foot shows freedom from gravity and all limitations.

Devi, the great Goddess, the energy and power of all gods, is often portrayed wielding weapons. A widely known image is that of Durga beheading the mighty buffalo demon, her archenemy. Some images show her in divine beauty. Others portray her in a shape of horror as the bloodthirsty **Kali**, with a necklace of heads and a girdle of severed arms, wielding a bloody sword and holding the severed head of the demon.

Such artistic images, in countless forms throughout India, present the divine realities for us to "see," without words of explanation. Fiercely ascetic and terrifying images, voluptuous and colorful paintings—there is no limitation on presenting the sacred through images in Hinduism.

Another important art form for Hindus is dance drama, in which the actors pattern their movements on the gestures and movements of the gods and goddesses. In the great religious festivals, they perform the lila (play) of the gods to the audience in tangible form, identifying with the divine models they portray. Through this artistic creation the audience is able to experience rasa, the flavor of sacred presence within our human world.

Performances of Ramlila, dance-drama celebrating the life cycle of **Rama**, are widespread in India. His birth, his coronation, the banishing of Sita his faithful wife, and other aspects of Rama's life are enacted nightly over a period of twenty days. The young boys playing the parts of Rama and his brothers are treated as divine images for the duration of the drama.

Dramas enacting the Krishna stories are very popular in India, with Krishna, Radha, and the cowherdesses (gopis) played by young boys, or, in other cases, young girls. New episodes are presented every day in this lila, culminating in the rasa, the ancient circular dance with Krishna standing in the center and the cowherdesses surrounding. The rasa provides a highly ecstatic experience, and members of the audience prostrate themselves before the young dancers, worshiping them as icons of Krishna and Radha.

A very characteristic Hindu art form is the temple, the sacred architecture that fixes the sacred centers of the world, functioning as earthly dwellings of the gods and goddesses. Hindu temples are designed on the model of the square, reflecting the final perfection and order of divine space in contrast to the temporary, changing earthly spaces. A typical temple has a holy center or garbha (womb), which houses the image from which power radiates. The rest of the temple surrounds that center just as the human body surrounds the inner soul or **atman**. Many temples have great towers, representing a cosmic mountain to which one might ascend to the presence of the sacred. Other temples lead the worshiper into the depths, to the womb or navel of the cosmos from which the god sends out sacred power.

SOCIETY AND WHOLESOME LIFE

How should we live? When someone says she is Hindu, this means she belongs to Hindu society by birth, finding her place in that complicated, stable structure of society that all Hindus instinctively understand. So important is the Hindu societal system that it was long believed one could not really be a Hindu outside India—that is, outside traditional Hindu society. It is within this society that one finds one's place and knows how to live the good life. Today, of course, many living in the Hindu diaspora throughout the world are searching for ways to maintain their Hindu identity and way of life even while living in other societies.

Structure of Hindu Society

Well known throughout the world is the unique Hindu social structure, the so-called caste system. It is certainly one of the distinguishing marks of Hinduism, rooted in the ancient scriptures and made prolific through many centuries. Though caste discrimination is officially outlawed in modern times, for many Hindus this social system still is a powerful and stable structure in their lives.

Origins and Development of the Class System
Whereas the caste system is well known throughout the world, it is often misunderstood. What is sometimes simply called the "caste system" is really made up of two social structures merged together: the **varna** (color) class divisions and the **jati** (birth) caste divisions. There are

only four (or five) classes (varnas) but over two thousand castes (jatis) in Hindu society. Let us look first at the traditional class system.

As we noted earlier, one reason Hindu social structure is so highly respected and remains unchanged is that its origin, according to the Vedic scriptures, is in the eternal **Dharma**, the order of the world. The four classes, into which all people enter according to their birth, are defined in the sacred texts in terms of their religious and social duties.

The **Brahmans** are the highest varna; their duty is primarily to study and teach Vedic learning and preside over the important rituals and sacrifices. The traditional duty of the **Kshatriya** (warrior) varna is the protection of the people and the administration of a beneficial government. Today in India, the Rajputs, for example, represent this class. The **Vaishya** (producer) varna is to provide for the economic needs of the community. Today, Vaishyas are mainly businesspeople. These three upper classes are "twice-born" in that boys go through the initiation ceremony and receive the sacred thread. Thus, all three classes are expected to study the Vedas.

The lowest class is the **Shudra** varna, the menials, whose one profession is to serve the upper three. They are often domestic servants, doing work that is forbidden for the other classes. They cannot hear or study the Vedas, but they are permitted to participate in the path of bhakti. Hindu tradition places a fifth class below these four classes, called the untouchables or outcastes, people without varna. These people generally are to live outside the boundaries of cities and perform extremely polluting activities. Untouchables have to avoid contact with people of higher castes lest they pollute them; their occupations include fishermen, hunters, leatherworkers, sweepers, handlers of dead bodies, and the like.

The Structure of Castes (Jati)   Another social structure has grown up superimposed on the class system to make up the characteristic subdivisions within Hindu society. This is the jati (birth) system of castes, subdivided into at least two thousand jatis, some very large, others little more than a group of families in a village. Each jati by tradition belongs to one of the four classes or the untouchable class. A jati is usually characterized by three restrictions on its members: endogamy, commensality,

and occupational exclusivity. A jati is almost always endogamous; that is, one is permitted to marry only within one's own jati—a rule that is still very widely observed today throughout traditional Hindu society. Commensality means eating only with others of one's caste. And these castes are usually occupational groups, following a particular calling that has been handed down over the generations within the families that make up the caste.

One of the primary religious concerns in daily life is to maintain ritual purity, especially for the higher castes; otherwise they cannot perform their religious duties. There are complex rules about contacts between the castes, and settlement patterns are set up to minimize such contacts. When contact must be made, as at a village council meeting, seating is arranged so that the higher castes are elevated and distant from the lower castes.

All this seems very complicated. But Hindus seem to know rather clearly where they belong in the caste system, and moreover they know how the castes are to be ranked and how people of each caste relate to the other castes. Each of the varna classes contains a large number of castes. There are perhaps hundreds of Brahman castes, for example, engaged in various occupations, and they rank each other, giving rise to the saying that where there are seven Brahmans there will be seven cooking fires, each one believing himself or herself higher in the caste system and, thus, refusing to eat with someone lower.

For all its negative features, especially for the lower castes and the untouchables, Hindus often say that the caste system provides a sense of security and identity. People know for sure where they belong. Their caste gives them a definite place in society, protects them, and makes it unnecessary for them to compete for higher places. Since it is accepted that one's caste is determined by one's past karma, there is no reason to be bitter about one's lot or to envy others.

Living According to Dharma

How should we live? Hinduism is suited for people with different temperaments and spiritual abilities. There is a place for everyone, with appropriate duties and ethical requirements. The concept of Dharma, as discussed, is central to the Hindu understanding of society. Dharma comprises comprehensive precepts having to do with the material sustenance and the spiritual welfare of human society and of the individual. Human life based on this pattern is spelled out in the classical writings and commentaries called Dharmashastras, the best known of which is the *Law-code of Manu*. Furthermore, both the *Mahabharata* and the *Ramayana* epics provide a broad and deep foundation for living out these Hindu ethical values.

Hindus are aware of universal ethical values that apply to everyone, of course. For example, there are certain acts forbidden to everyone, such as stealing or doing injury to others. And there are obligations that are common to all by reason of the human status, such as the obligation to respect one's parents. But Dharma touches most concretely where we live and work in society, as it organizes our life through well-defined social classes and through stages of individual life. The *Bhagavad Gita* states, "Better to do one's own duty (dharma) imperfectly than to do another man's well; doing action (karma) intrinsic to his being, a man avoids guilt" (18.47).[4] In its narrow sense, Hindu tradition has often equated Dharma with Varna-Ashrama-Dharma, that is, the ordained duties (dharma) of the different classes (varnas) as they live through the four stages of life (**ashramas**).

Ethical Life Based on the Classes and Castes   How should we live? The first answer is very direct: one should live in the way expected of one in the particular class and caste. The Law-code of Manu spells out in detail the duties of the four traditional classes. The duty of living according to one's class (varna) is commonly extended to include also the obligations, requirements, and prescriptions that belong to the particular occupational caste (jati) into which a person was born. The good life means abiding by the rules of one's caste about marriage, dining, occupation, and clothing. It also means to avoid polluting the purity of one's caste and of the larger community by wrongful contact with those of other castes.

The ethical vision expressed in the caste system is widely misunderstood by non-Hindus. A chief ingredient in this system is the idea of maintaining caste purity, and it is true that this purity has a hierarchical order, for one brings pollution on one's own caste by contact with someone of a lower caste. But it is important to understand that purity is a vital possession of the whole community, not just of one caste. Brahmans do have a special responsibility for maintaining the purity of the community because they study and teach the Vedas and perform the Vedic rituals—an activity of extreme importance for the whole society—and it is felt they cannot perform this service if they are polluted by contact with lower castes. But the purity of the community is also maintained by the people of lower jatis, such as the Shudras and untouchables who wash clothes, cut hair, carry away garbage, and remove dead animals. The whole community is diminished by a breakdown of purity in its midst, but likewise the whole community is enriched by the purity, solidarity, cooperation, and contribution structured through the traditional caste system.

It is widely recognized by modern Hindu leaders that aspects of the caste system, such as the obligation to engage in the occupation of one's father or the practice of untouchability, are in conflict with the basic Hindu ethical vision. Modern Indian law does not permit discrimination on the basis of caste, and untouchables are permitted to enter temples, sit in movie theatres, and eat in public restaurants. **Gandhi** took particular care for the untouchables in his movement to reform India, calling them Harijans (children of God) and himself engaging in unclean jobs reserved for the untouchables. Today efforts are being made to help those of the lower castes to improve their lot in modern society. But the Hindu ethical system remains based on the fundamental truth that one's birth is not an accident. It was determined by karmic causes from one's past existences in the samsara cycle. I am where I belong. Therefore, the good and noble life consists of living according to my dharma, following the life prescribed for me by my caste.

This is not to say that life is completely free of ethical conflicts. The *Mahabharata Epic* contains the famous story of King Yudhishthira, the king of Dharma, who feels bitter inner conflict over his duty as a warrior-king and his higher vision of nonviolence and detachment. Yudhishthira wants to withdraw from life in the world and become a forest-dweller, for he knows that if he continues to live in the world as king he will have to inflict violence and pain on others. But King Yudhishthira did fulfill his duty, encouraged to do so by none other than Lord Krishna, waiting until he had grown old before he finally abandoned the world. So Hindus respect the duties assigned by birth, knowing that the path of liberation ultimately leads beyond duties of class and caste.

Four Stages of Life Another key to living the good life is to be observant of the duties and opportunities incumbent in the different stages of life. Hindu tradition recognizes that the principles that bring a healthy and fulfilled human life change throughout the course of a lifetime and, thus, the Dharma scriptures put forth the ideal of four stages of life (ashramas), at least for males of the higher three classes. In the traditional system, the Shudra and untouchable classes do not participate in the movement through different stages of life. Women also did not traditionally move through these stages in a direct way, at least not the student stage. But women certainly share in these stages insofar as they are related to the males in their families. The four stages of life are the stages of student, householder, forest-dweller, and renouncer (samnyasin).

The first stage of life is that of being a student, with the obligations of studying the Vedas, cultivating respect for one's teacher, developing self-control, and learning to be a contributing member of Hindu society. Brahman boys of eight years of age, and Kshatriya and Vaishya boys of eleven or twelve, are to begin their student life with the ritual of initiation, after which traditionally they go to study with their teachers. In past times, girls were educated in the home to be wives, mothers, and homemakers. The student stage is a rigorous way of life, learning rituals, values, duties, and patterns of behavior. The student is to remain celibate, ritually pure, begging for food, and acting as personal servant to the teacher.

Upon completing the period of being a student, the person moves on to the stage of householder, the keystone of Hindu life and society and an essential stage of personal spiritual development. Some few, it is true, seem spiritually prepared to omit this householder stage and pass immediately to the ascetic rigors of the renouncer stage of life, close to final liberation. But for almost all people, the householder stage is necessary and beneficial. During this major period of one's life, Hindu ethics require a happy, productive, ritually observant way of life. People should marry and raise children to continue the line. As householders they perform the proper sacrifices and rituals, maintain a ritually pure home, and engage in economic and political activity.

In the householder stage, the woman's role, according to the Dharma scriptures, is significantly different from the man's role. The wife is subject to the husband and should serve him, not presuming to eat, for example, until after he is finished. At the same time, the husband is required to honor his wife and protect her. The Law-code of Manu states,

> Women must be honored and adorned by their fathers, brothers, husbands, and brothers-in-law who desire great good fortune. . . .
>
> Her father protects her in childhood, her husband protects her in youth, her sons protect her in old age—a woman does not deserve independence.
>
> The father who does not give away his daughter in marriage at the proper time is censurable; censurable is the husband who does not approach his wife in due season; and after the husband is dead, the son, verily, is censurable, who does not protect his mother.
>
> The husband should engage his wife in the collection and expenditure of his wealth, in cleanliness, in dharma [religious rituals], in cooking food for the family, and in looking after the necessities of the household. . . .
>
> Women destined to bear children, enjoying great good fortune, deserving of worship, the resplendent lights of homes on the one hand and divinities of good luck who reside in the houses on the other—between these there is no difference whatsoever.[5]

Deserving no independence and serving her family, on the one hand, and being honored as a goddess on the other—these are the two sides of the woman's role in traditional Hinduism. The pressure for offspring and for marrying off daughters led to marriages involving child-brides. And the notion of self-sacrifice for one's husband sometimes led to the practice of young widows immolating themselves on the funeral pyres of their husbands—becoming thereby **sati** (sometimes called *suttee* in Western languages), a true woman who sacrifices bodily existence for the higher spiritual duty. Modern reforms have made this practice illegal, but occasionally there still are reports of a widow performing sati, whether by choice or by coercion.

"When a householder sees his skin wrinkled and his hair gray and when he sees the son of his son, then he should resort to the forest."[6] Having reached the end of the productive householder stage, one should go into spiritual retirement and become a "forest-dweller." That is, a man together with his wife retires to a forest retreat (ashrama), or at least to quiet quarters within the family residence, to devote themselves to self-discipline, study, and meditation. The responsibilities of home management and business are turned over to the children, though the retirees may still be available for consultation. Abstaining from sex is recommended for this stage, as the withdrawal from householder life becomes more and more complete.

The final stage of life is that of the samnyasin, the "renouncer" who breaks all ties to enter the last part of the path toward liberation. "Having thus passed the third part of his life in the forest, he should renounce all attachments to worldly objects and become an ascetic during the fourth part of his life. . . . He should always wander alone, without any companion, in order to achieve spiritual perfection."[7] Those few who reach this stage of spiritual perfection have dissolved all sense of selfish needs and desires and, therefore, although beyond caste and not involved in society, they demonstrate the highest ethical values as a model for all others.

> He will patiently bear with hard words, despising none, nor out of attachment to the body will he bear enmity to anyone. To one who is angry with him he will not show anger in return, and him that curses him he will bless, nor will he utter any untrue word. . . . By curbing the senses, by destroying affection and hatred, by doing no harm to any living thing, he will conform himself to deathlessness.[8]

Most people will not reach the stage of samnyasin in this lifetime, but having that model before our eyes helps us to live out our own roles in the proper ethical perspective.

Four Aims of Human Life Hindus have traditionally summed up the vision of the good life by speaking of the four aims of human life (purusharthas). These four good values of life that we should seek after are Dharma, material prosperity (artha), pleasure (kama), and liberation (moksha). This is a well-balanced ethical structure, verified by centuries of experience, designed to balance the concern for good life and happiness with the concern for spiritual development and liberation.

Of course, the balance of these four aims of life differs depending on one's particular stage of life. Fulfilling the Dharma is something that should always be central, for this is the key to how the individual's life in its different stages fits into the total order of reality. Seeking material prosperity is especially important at the householder stage, for involvement in business and politics is the foundation on which the whole society rests. Likewise, seeking pleasure and happiness is most directly appropriate at the householder stage, for without sexual pleasure and physical happiness the life of the family could not go on. Liberation (moksha) is understood to be the spiritual goal throughout one's life, but it becomes a more central concern in the forest-dweller stage of retirement, and for one who reaches the samnyasin stage it becomes the total and exclusive concern.

Religious Leaders in Hindu Society Even though many people of the Brahman class pursue secular occupations, the Brahman class is honored with special religious functions. Those Brahmans who become priests have an important

Devout Hindus bathe in the sacred waters of "Mother Ganga," the Ganges River.

function for all in Hindu society, according to the Vedas. Even though some classes and castes cannot hear the Vedas or participate in Vedic rituals, the chanting of the Vedas and the performing of the rituals bring benefit across the board, maintaining the order of the world and society. Some Brahman priests are household priests; that is, they perform rituals and important ceremonies for various families. Other Brahmans are temple priests, making their services available for the rituals and festivals centered in the temple for the benefit of the community. Another important function for learned Brahmans is in teaching the Vedas.

Religious leaders in Hinduism include many other holy men and women who pursue the higher path of knowledge and who teach others in the many ashramas (retreats) scattered throughout India. The **guru** or learned person is one who has come to have deep insight into the truth and perhaps has attained a high level of spiritual realization, sometimes even recognized as God-realized or as an incarnation of one of the great Gods. The widely revered saint Ramakrishna, for example, was one such spiritual master. Sri Aurobindo, a modern religious thinker, also founded an ashrama for the study of yoga. In general there is high respect for those holy men and women who leave the world to advance their own spirituality and seek enlightenment. Even if they are simple wanderers seemingly doing nothing of benefit for the rest of society, they are supplying a continuous model and reminder of the high path toward moksha.

Women in Religious Leadership　It is abundantly clear, from our discussion so far, that women generally play a subordinate role in Hindu society and, therefore, leadership roles tend to be restricted to spheres like family and specifically women's roles and rituals. Yet this is not completely the case. There certainly are some powerful divine models for women's active participation in ultimate matters. There is Devi, the great Goddess, in all her powerful forms, the energizing power of all the gods, the nurturer and the destroyer together. Draupadi, wife and queen of the five Pandava brothers in the *Mahabharata Epic*, is wise, courageous, and powerful in both the domestic and public spheres. Radha, beloved of Krishna, and Sita, loyal wife of Rama, provide additional models for virtue and strength of character manifested by women.

There have been numerous women gurus and spiritual leaders—even some who have performed priestly roles,

much to the consternation of the more traditionally minded. Sarada Devi was not only the wife of the well-known nineteenth-century saint Shri Ramakrishna but also his disciple and spiritual partner. He taught her how to initiate people into the sacred **mantras** for the worship of the great Goddess, and after his death she was looked to as spiritual guide for the disciples of the Ramakrishna Order.

Today in India there are numerous women who are revered and consulted as spiritual teachers and gurus. In Madras, for example, a well-known woman guru is Shri Jnanananda Saraswati, called Ma ("mother") by her disciples and devotees. She is also called Satguru ("true guru"), in recognition of her high spiritual status as a guru who is also a samnyasin, a fully realized spiritual teacher. While there are gender differences between men and women, according to her, they do not relate directly to the attainment of full realization. Charles White reports on the kind of spiritual leadership she provides, for both men and women:

> . . . Satguru granted me a great privilege in allowing me to sit with her on the first of two evenings while she gave darshan to her Indian disciples individually or in small, mainly family, groups. In all, I saw and listened to about forty persons during these exchanges. At least for now Ma is able to see personally most of the people who approach her. What an experience of relief this intimate discussion of problems must be to hard-pressed individuals who discover Ma, the loving mother, in the torturing crosscurrents of Indian life! Nevertheless, she does not always say what one would prefer to hear. For Satguru may also be regarded by her disciples as the incarnate goddess, Rajarajeshwari. . . . Her motherliness, therefore, is in a different category altogether from ordinary human motherliness.[9]

Among the many people who took darshan of the Satguru and received spiritual counsel from her were a young man with job difficulties, a young woman in a deep depression, a middle-aged woman whose daughters-in-law had thrown her out of the house, an athletic young man who worked for the Defense Department, an intellectual who could not bring himself to surrender completely, and a young society girl who rushed in to see Ma Jnanananda between jet flights.

Many women in India today are spiritually accomplished, with education and public life more available to them. For example, in this male-centered society, Indira Gandhi (1917–1984) rose to the highest political and moral leadership as prime minister, internationally known and respected as a compelling leader and spokesperson for India, until her assassination by extremists. As women's lives and women's leadership become more central, the promise of Hinduism as the eternal Dharma, the path that leads toward wholeness and ultimate liberation, will become more practical and available to women as well as men.

Hindu Visions for Society and the World

It is sometimes said that Hindus have no concern for the betterment of society, since the Hindu tradition places so much stress on withdrawal from the world of the senses and on individual meditation and pursuit of liberation. And it is true that nowhere in the Hindu tradition did there develop the notion of having a mission to the whole world in the sense of spreading Hinduism to all. Yet the Hindu tradition does in its own way display deep concern for the welfare of the whole social order, and some modern Hindus have utilized those resources to improve the lot of all in society. The Hindu values of peace and nonviolence have made an impact on the whole world, and in modern times some Hindu thinkers have taken up the mission of transmitting the spiritual wisdom of India to the rest of humankind.

Toward the Betterment of Human Society One perspective sees all life caught up in endless cycles of samsara, each lifetime determined by the karma of preceding ones, with the final goal being liberation from the whole cycle. This is the perspective of moksha. But another perspective complements this one, the perspective of Dharma. This present order has its own value and importance, and to maintain and promote the Dharma of this world is to enhance the welfare of all beings.

This is why the householder stage is so central, for the proper fulfillment of this role contributes significantly to the preservation and happiness of the whole community. The fact that one of the four aims of life is material success (artha), involvement in the economic and political life of the society, shows that working toward the general welfare of all is a central Hindu concern. In fact, all the basic values and duties, such as respect for parents and maintenance of caste purity, prevent social breakdown and corruption and, thus, work toward the welfare of the whole society.

In modern times, reform movements have drawn on the spirit of the Hindu tradition to better society by doing away with some evils that had developed within the tradition, such as child marriage, widows burning themselves, the subordinate role of women generally, and the cruel lot of the lower castes and the untouchables. Mahatma Gandhi and others worked tirelessly against the evil of untouchability. Gandhi thought the class system, however, could still be the structure of society, for the classes are duties, not privileges, and those of the higher classes are more responsible for the welfare of all. The hallmarks of Gandhi's ethical vision are simplicity, austerity, and nonviolence, and he felt these values could create the good life not only for Indian society but for other societies as well:

> There are two aspects of Hinduism. There is, on the one hand, the historical Hinduism with its Untouchability, superstitious worship of sticks and stones, animal sacrifices and so on. On the other, we have the Hinduism of the *Gita*, the *Upanishads*, and Patanjali's *Yoga Sutras*, which is the acme of *Ahimsa* [nonviolence] and oneness of all creation, pure worship of one immanent, formless, imperishable God. *Ahimsa*, which for me is the chief glory of Hinduism, has been sought to be explained away by our people as being meant for the samnyasi only. I do not think so. I hold that it is the way of life and India has to show it to the world.[10]

The possibility of reconciliation and peace through nonviolent means and through spiritual discipline and practice, as demonstrated by Gandhi and many others like him, has made a powerful impression on people of other cultures who are searching for a way to reverse the escalation of violence and materialism in the world.

Hindu Wisdom for the World Hinduism is not a missionary religion. It is fundamental to Hinduism to believe that there are many spiritual paths, appropriate to different peoples depending on their own past karma and spiritual perfection, and the idea of converting others to Hinduism does not fit with this. Yet Hindus do believe that the Vedas, as the Eternal Wisdom, present the truth in an ultimate way not found in any other religious path.

In modern times, under pressure from other religions such as Islam and Christianity, some Hindu thinkers have attempted to reassert the primacy of Vedic Hinduism. For example, Dayananda Sarasvati, founder of the Arya Samaj, not only rejected many aspects of Hinduism that he felt conflicted with the Vedas but also took an aggressive and militant approach to other religions. He argued that Christian belief was logically inconsistent and that the Quran presents a God unworthy of worship. Some members of this group engaged in attempts to gain Hindu converts from among Muslims.

On the other hand, other modern thinkers, such as Sarvepalli Radhakrishnan, have responded to the challenge of Christianity and other religions by seeking out the universalist aspects of these religions that would be in keeping with the Vedantic teachings. Radhakrishnan argued that whereas Hinduism is the ultimate truth of religion, it is a truth that can be universally accepted by all. He brought his Hindu philosophy to the West through lectures and books, teaching that each religion is valid to the degree that it helps its followers achieve spiritual realization:

> If the Hindu chants the Vedas on the banks of the Ganges, if the Chinese meditates on the Analects, if the Japanese worships on the image of the Buddha, if the European is convinced of Christ's mediatorship, if the Arab reads the Quran in his mosque, and if the African bows down to a fetish, each one of them has exactly the same reason for his particular confidence. Each form of faith appeals in precisely the same way to the inner certitude and devotion of its followers. It is their deepest apprehension of God and God's fullest revelation to them. The claim of any religion to validity is the fact that only through it have its followers become what they are.[11]

Some Hindu groups today, such as the **International Society for Krishna Consciousness**, take the stance that Hinduism is the exclusive highest truth, and they bring it to the West as part of their commitment to this truth. Other modern Hindu thinkers follow the tradition that truth is found in many paths. Convinced that Hinduism still is the highest of these many paths, many Hindus do feel a responsibility to help peoples in the rest of the world to become acquainted with the ancient wisdom, come to understand it, and incorporate its basic truths into their lives also. The world society will become enriched, they feel, more spiritual, and more peaceful if the perspective of Hinduism is better understood and appreciated.

DISCUSSION QUESTIONS

1 Why do the Vedic sacrificial rituals have such great prestige, even though people of the lower classes cannot perform them?

2 What is puja, and why is it so central to many Hindus?

3 What kind of religious experience is darshana? How is this important in activities such as festivals, pilgrimage, and art?

4 Outline the main samskaras associated with the passages in life: the initiation ceremony, marriage, and the funeral rites.

5 Show how Ayurveda medicine fits in the traditional Hindu religious worldview.

6 What is it about Hinduism that promotes such a wealth of artistic practices? Explain some of the ways in which Hindu arts give expression to various qualities of sacred experience.

7 Explain the class (varna) and caste (jati) systems and how they fit together in Hindu society.

8 Discuss how the story of King Yudhishthira (in the *Mahabharata*) illustrates the tension often expressed in Hinduism between doing one's duty (dharma) and seeking liberation (moksha).

9 Show how the Hindu sense of the good life is summed up especially in the four stages of life and the four aims of life.

10 Discuss women's traditional roles in Hindu society. Are any changes taking place today?

11 Some modern Hindu thinkers believe the Hindu tradition has valuable insights to offer to the whole of human society. What might these be?

KEY TERMS: HINDUISM

Advaita nondualism, Shankara's school of Vedanta, emphasizing the all-encompassing one ultimate reality, Brahman

Agni Vedic god of fire

Aryans peoples related to the Indo-Europeans, who migrated into India in ancient times

ashramas the four stages of life for higher-class males in Hinduism: student, householder, forest-dweller, and renouncer; ashrama is also a hermitage or place for meditation

atman the soul or self, considered eternal

avatara descent or incarnation of a god, as Krishna and Rama are avataras of the great God Vishnu

Ayurveda traditional system of medicine in India

Bhagavad Gita important scripture from the *Mahabharata*, containing Krishna's teaching to

Arjuna and summing up the fundamental ideas of Hinduism

bhakti   devotion, self-surrender to one's god

Brahma   designation for the creator god in Hindu thought

Brahman   Hindu term for ultimate reality; the divine source and pervading essence of the universe

Brahmanas   ritual commentaries, part of the Vedas

Brahmans   highest-ranked, priestly class in Hindu society

darshana   in Hinduism, the ritual act of being granted the "seeing" of a sacred image, person, or place; also, the six "viewpoints" or traditional schools of philosophy

Devi   Hindu term for goddess, sometimes meaning the great Goddess, often under many other names

Dharma   the cosmic order, social duty, and proper behavior

Divali   autumn festival of lights and good fortune in India

Durga   great, fierce Hindu goddess, often considered a form of Devi

Gandhi   leader of the Hindu independence movement emphasizing spiritual preparation and nonviolent resistance (1869–1948)

Ganesha   son of Shiva, popular elephant-headed Hindu god who overcomes obstacles and brings good fortune

guru   spiritual guide and master

Holi   popular festival in northern India with a carnival atmosphere

Indra   Vedic storm-warrior god

Indus valley civilization   urban-agricultural civilization that flourished in the third millennium B.C.E. in the Indus River valley and influenced Hinduism

International Society for Krishna Consciousness   new Hindu movement, founded by Swami Bhaktivedanta Prabhupada (1896–1977), worshiping Krishna as the supreme manifestation of the divine; known as ISKCON, this movement has drawn many Westerners as devotees

jati   "birth"; one's caste or closed social group as determined by birth in India

Kali   goddess of death and destruction in Hinduism, often considered a form of Devi

karma   "action," law that all deeds and thoughts, according to one's intentions, will have set consequences, including rebirth

kirtana   devotional group worship through song and dance

Krishna   avatara of the great Hindu god Vishnu; hero of the *Bhagavad Gita* and popular god in Vaishnavite devotional movements

Kshatriyas   the warrior class in Hindu society

lingam   phallic pillar that symbolizes the great God Shiva

Mahabharata   one of the two great epics of Hinduism

mantra   powerful sacred words, formula, or verse chanted as a focus for meditation and devotion

maya   appearance, illusion; term to indicate that which prevents one from seeing truly

moksha   liberation from bondage to samsara and karma; the goal of Hindu spiritual practice

Path of Action (karma-marga)   Hindu path toward liberation based on acting according to Dharma, without desire for the fruits of action

Path of Devotion (bhakti-marga)   Hindu path toward liberation based on devotional practices directed toward one's god

Path of Knowledge (jnana-marga)   Hindu path toward liberation based on knowledge, emphasizing meditation

prasad   gift from the deity consecrated in ritual, especially food, shared by the devotee

puja   ritual worship of the image of a god by offering food, flowers, music, and prayers

Puranas   late Hindu scriptures that developed from popular theistic devotional movements

Rama   avatara of Vishnu, divine hero of the *Ramayana*

Ramakrishna   modern Hindu holy man (1836–1886) whose teachings were brought to America by his disciple Vivekananda (1863–1902), who established the Ramakrishna Mission (Vedanta Society)

Ramanuja   Hindu philosopher and advocate of the Vaishnavite bhakti tradition (ca. 1017–1137)

Ramayana   story of Rama, one of the two great epics of Hinduism

rebirth   belief that after the death of its body the soul takes on another body, determined by karma

Rig Veda   the earliest and most important collection of Vedic hymns

Samhitas   "collections" of early Vedic hymns and verses; there are four collections: *Rig-Veda, Sama-Veda, Yajur-Veda,* and *Atharva-Veda*

Samkhya   one of the classical schools of Hindu philosophy stressing an absolute distinction between matter and spirit

samnyasin   one who has renounced the cares and concerns of the world; samnyasa is the fourth stage of life in Hinduism

samsara   the rebirth cycle of existence

samskaras   rituals performed at the critical changes and passages of life

sati self-sacrifice of a widow on her husband's funeral pyre; outlawed in modern times

Shakti divine energy, personified as a goddess; female aspect of a god, especially of Shiva

Shankara great philosopher of Advaita (nondual) Vedanta (788–820 C.E.)

Shiva one of the two great Gods, symbolized by the lingam; focus of the Shaivite devotional movement

Shruti "that which is heard," the eternal truth, that is, the Vedas

Shudras classical servant class in Hindu society, the fourth class

Smriti "that which is remembered," the tradition, that is, the scriptural writings after the Vedas

Tantrism movement using initiation, rituals, imagination, and sexual symbolism as spiritual practices leading toward liberation

Transcendental Meditation Hindu meditation movement founded in America by Maharishi Mahesh Yogi (b. 1917), emphasizing simple meditation techniques for practical benefits

upanayana initiation of high-class boy into the student stage of life; he is given a sacred cord to wear over his left shoulder and taught the appropriate mantras

Upanishads collection of teachings about the self and ultimate reality that makes up the last part of the Veda (Shruti)

Vaishyas the classical producer-merchant class in Hindu society

varna "color," term for the classes in the system of Hindu society

Varuna Vedic god of the heavens

Vedanta Societies Hindu groups in America and Europe following the teaching of Swami Vivekananda (1863–1902) and Sri Ramakrishna (1836–1886)

Vedanta "end of the Vedas"; influential school of philosophy based especially on the Upanishads

Vedas most important scriptures of Hinduism, the Shruti; they consist of the Samhitas, Brahmanas, Aranyakas, and Upanishads

Vishnu one of the two great Gods, worshiped also in his avataras Rama and Krishna

Chapter 6

Buddhist Sacred Story and Historical Context

The traditional Buddhist world sweeps from India and Sri Lanka and Southeast Asia, up through central Asia and Tibet and China, all the way up to Mongolia and Korea and Japan in the north of Asia, encompassing a vast array of peoples and cultures and languages. One thing they all have in common is reverence for the Buddha.

What we call Buddhism today is a broad, multifaceted religious tradition made up of several related paths, sharing a similar goal but diverging somewhat in teachings and practices. We meet up first with those on the Theravada path, orthodox and traditional, adhering closely to the words and practices of Siddhartha Gautama the Buddha. But then there is the variety of Mahayana paths such as Zen and Pure Land, with single-minded emphasis on meditation and devotion to Amida Buddha, respectively. Yet another approach comes in the Vajrayana or Tantric path, where practitioners engage in elaborate ritual and intense sensual meditative experiences. Yet this variety of people all call themselves Buddhists, following the way of the Buddha toward the goal of nirvana or enlightenment.

The Buddhist religion, born in India but grown to become the light of much of Asia, shares many things with Hinduism. But the wisdom taught by Siddhartha Gautama turned in a different direction, leading away from the idea of the eternal Brahman and atman (self), the authority of the Vedic scriptures, the caste system of society, and even for the most part the importance of worshiping the gods. Growing from similar roots, Buddhism turned from the Vedic tradition to create a spiritual perspective very much like its sister Hinduism in so many ways—but so different in still more crucial ways. Buddhists and Hindus today can certainly recognize a family resemblance between themselves. But like relatives who have long gone in different directions, the things held to be most important are often those things that are different.

STORY OF THE BUDDHA

To be a Buddhist, to be on the Path of the Buddha, means to derive one's identity from the story of the **Buddha**, Siddhartha Gautama, who lived about 2,500 years ago in India, and from the truth taught by him and by many teachers after him.

Unlike Hinduism, Buddhism is a "founded" religion; sacred stories about a particular person and the things he did and said help to provide the foundation of the religion. In that sense Buddhism is like Judaism, Christianity, and Islam, with the story of the founder at its heart. While the Buddha was not divine or a prophet of God, he was like these founders in the sense of being the teacher and the model for the lives of his followers.

An important difference with those other founded religions is the special sense that Buddhists have of history in relation to ultimate reality. The fact that God is revealed in unique historical events and works through specific persons is important to Jews, Christians, and Muslims, and, thus, the historical events and persons take on a special significance. Buddhists see the historical events of this particular world age in the context of the great world cycles of samsara. While Siddhartha Gautama's lifetime 2,500 years ago is indeed crucial as a model and guide, it is not necessarily the complete, one-time focus of revelation and truth. The Buddha existed many lifetimes before this, for example, and there have been other Buddhas. Historical events are part of the story, but equally important are mythological stories and revelations of eternal truth.

We do not know for certain when the first scriptures of Buddhism were composed or written down; Buddhist tradition says they were transmitted orally by disciples after the **parinirvana** (passing away) of the Buddha. The most important biographical accounts of the Buddha's life, such as the very influential one by Ashvaghosha, were not written until about five hundred years later (ca. first century C.E.). Thus, it is not possible to unravel the "historical" details from mythological elements. We cannot find the historical Buddha any more than the historical Jesus or the historical Moses. In our discussion we will, of course, make use of scholarly historical research to provide orientation in the beginnings and development of Buddhism. At the same time, one of our primary interests is to see how the sacred story is understood by Buddhists themselves as a central paradigm giving meaning and identity, and for that purpose the legendary materials as to what the Buddha said and did are as important as the historical facts. The story is more than just a history of certain people. For Buddhists, it reveals the true path of life.

Sacred Biography of the Buddha

The Buddha lived in northeastern India in the sixth century B.C.E., at the time when fellow sages were composing the Upanishads and, thus, helping to create Hinduism. This was an age of social and political instability, as small communities were giving way to larger political states. At this time some sixteen small independent states existed in northern central India, but within a century after the life of the Buddha, only one empire, the Magadha, would rule this whole area. This was a most creative period, for at the same time the early Jain leaders were developing their religion, and there were other movements with new interpretations of the Vedas.

Important religious figures in this northeastern part of India were wandering ascetics who had withdrawn from society and lived in the forests. These hermits (shramanas) stood in a certain tension with the Brahmans, who represented the Indo-Aryan establishment. The shramanas often went about in groups, following a recognized teacher, practicing austerities, and discussing various theories

about the truth of human existence. The ideas they were discussing were similar to those being expressed by the teachers who were at this time composing the Upanishads: karma, samsara, rebirth, the relation of the soul and the supreme reality, liberation, and the like. It was a time of searching, experimenting, and debating about the ultimate truths of human existence.

Among these wandering ascetics we find Siddhartha Gautama (and also Mahavira, leader of the Jains). Siddhartha searched for the truth for some years, experienced a great awakening, and became the Buddha, or "enlightened one"; then he taught a community of disciples for some forty-five years until he died. His life was in many respects not unlike that of other holy men of his time. But this teacher was different, as attested in the sacred biography. In his career and teaching, Buddhists believe, the ultimate truth for all human existence is found.

Birth of the Buddha-to-Be   Siddhartha was born about 563 B.C.E., according to the chronology accepted by many Western scholars today (other scholars prefer a date around 448 B.C.E.). Buddhist traditional dating has generally placed his birth around 624 B.C.E. In any case, he was born in a tribe in northeastern India called the Shakyas, who also used the traditional name of Gautama. So Siddhartha is often simply called Gautama or **Shakyamuni** (wise one of the Shakyas). His parents were royalty, King Shuddhodana and Queen Maya of Kapilavastu (located in present-day Nepal). There he grew up, married, and had a child, until his spiritual experiences led him to go forth at about age twenty-nine to become a wandering ascetic, searching for the truth—a story not unlike many others of his time, but this one was different, as the tradition makes clear. The story of the Buddha, like those of other great religious founders, is larger than life, and the story is told with many elaborations in Buddhist literature and art. That one human lifetime is connected with transcendental power and meaning. The birth of Siddhartha comes as the result of aeons of preparation, and his lifetime and teachings have ramifications for people of all times and places.

Reaching beyond the boundaries of human finitude, many stories tell of the previous lifetimes of the Buddha in which he achieved merit and wisdom leading finally to Buddhahood. For example, the Buddha told his disciple Ananda about a wise and compassionate prince named

Mahasattva who lived in the remote past. One day, strolling in a forest, he came upon a tigress surrounded by seven small cubs. The tigress was exhausted from giving birth to the seven cubs and was weakened by hunger and thirst. Mahasattva realized that if she found no fresh meat and warm blood, she would die, so he resolved to sacrifice his own body, which, he reasoned, was doomed to perish in the end anyway. Taking a vow to sacrifice himself to win enlightenment for the welfare of the world, he threw himself down in front of the tigress. But she was so weak that she could do nothing, so he cut his own throat with a sharp piece of bamboo. Finally, when she saw his body covered with blood, she ate up all his flesh and blood and was strengthened. Concluding this story, the Buddha told Ananda: "It was I, Ananda, who at that time and on that occasion was that prince Mahasattva."[1] So through many lifetimes, the Buddha-to-be grew in compassion and perfected himself in wisdom.

But finally the decisive moment came. After a lifetime in the Tushita heaven, he decided to enter the womb of pure Queen Maya of Kapilavastu to be born one final time as a human and to reach Buddhahood. In a dream, Queen Maya saw four guardian angels carry her away to the Himalayan Mountains and purify her. Lying on a couch, she saw a superb white elephant approach and seemingly enter her body so that she conceived. When the time came for Maya to give birth, she went out to the beautiful Lumbini grove, accompanied by many attendants. She gave birth from her side standing up, and four guardian kings placed the baby on a golden net and washed him with heavenly fragrant warm water. At the birth of the Buddha-to-be, the heaven and earth greatly shook, a great light shone throughout the universe, flowers fell from heaven, evil and suffering temporarily ceased, and many other signs appeared showing that an event of world significance had happened. The young child stood, took seven steps, and said, "I am born to be enlightened for the well-being of the world; this is my last birth."[2] Learned sages saw the auspicious signs on his body and said that he was certain to become either a universal monarch or the perfectly enlightened one.

> Should he be a great, earthly sovereign, he will rule the entire world with courage and righteousness, leading all kings, as the light of the sun leads the lights of the world. If he seeks deliverance by living in a forest, he will acquire true wisdom and illumine the entire world.[3]

The Going Forth Siddhartha's mother Maya died seven days after bearing him, and King Shuddhodana married Maya's sister Prajapati, who brought up the young prince as his foster mother. His father the king, of course, wanted him first to be a mighty king and then, perhaps, retire to the forest in his old age. So he provided education and martial training for Siddhartha, who quickly excelled in all his endeavors. His father surrounded him with luxury and pleasure, built three beautiful palaces for him, and arranged for him to marry the lovely maiden Yashodhara, who in time bore him a son, Rahula.

According to the story, however, the gods knew that the time for Siddhartha's enlightenment was drawing near, so they intervened by presenting **Four Sights** to the Prince. When Siddhartha was out on an excursion in his golden chariot, the gods created an old decrepit man, and Siddhartha exclaimed, "O charioteer! Who is this man with gray hair, supported by a staff in his hand, his eyes sunken under his eyebrows, his limbs feeble and bent?" And the charioteer had to explain old age to Siddhartha, who then asked, "Will this evil come upon me also?" And the answer: "Advanced age will certainly come upon you through the inescapable force of time, no matter how long you may live."[4] The young prince sat looking at the old man for a long time, disturbed that this human process of old age indiscriminately destroys beauty and strength, and yet people in the world are not changed from their selfish pursuits by such a sight. Again, on a second excursion, the gods created a diseased man, and then thirdly a dead man, with the same shattering effect on Siddhartha. Finally he saw a hermit monk, one who has withdrawn from the world and, thus, is in some way above all this. And Siddhartha moved toward his own decision to withdraw to the forest and devote himself fully to searching for the truth.

But, as we all know, such decisions are not made without a struggle between conflicting values and loyalties. Siddhartha was now twenty-nine, with a wife and a son, heir to the throne of the kingdom. His father, sensing Siddhartha's inner struggle, attempted to persuade him that his duty was to fulfill the role of a householder first before withdrawing from the world in his old age. But Siddhartha countered with a metaphor that has become famous in Buddhist literature: "It is not right to hold by force a man who is anxious to escape from a burning house."[5] The king made one final attempt to keep Siddhartha from going forth to become a wandering hermit, providing the most pleasurable entertainments with dancing girls and lovely music. Siddhartha was unmoved, and as the night wore on all the women fell asleep in distorted postures and shocking poses—"some with their bodies wet with trickling phlegm and spittle; some grinding their teeth, and muttering and talking in their sleep; some with their mouths open; and some with their dress fallen apart so as plainly to disclose their loathsome nakedness."[6] Seeing all this the prince was filled with disgust and determined to go forth that very night. He bid a silent farewell to his sleeping wife Yashodhara and son Rahula. Mounting his faithful horse Kanthaka, with his servant Chandaka he rode to the edge of the forest, the gods having opened the palace gates that had been secured tightly by orders of his father. He cut off his hair and beard and put on the robe of a monk in place of his princely robes, instructing Chandaka to bring his jeweled turban and other articles back to his father. Thus took place the crucial turning point in the Buddhist story, the Great Renunciation.

Unlike Christianity's founder Jesus, who was born in poverty, Siddhartha was born and grew up in riches, luxury, and power. But it is precisely these things—which all humans strive for—that keep us from seeing the real nature of human existence. When Siddhartha did finally see human existence as it really is, stripped of the veneer of luxury and pleasure, he realized that the princely life was an illusion and he cast it aside, going forth to search for the truth as a forest monk.

The Attainment of Enlightenment   For the next six years Siddhartha wandered about, begging for his food and searching for the truth. He followed two teachers who taught him yogic knowledge and techniques, but, although he quickly mastered these disciplines, after a time he came to feel that this was not the path to the ultimate truth he was seeking. Then for a time he practiced the path of extreme self-mortification, like that followed by Mahavira and the Jain monks, fasting and depriving himself of even the bare necessities of life in an attempt to attain victory and release. Five other ascetic monks were attracted to his struggle, and they practiced fasting and other disciplines with him. However, near starvation, Siddhartha came to an important realization: "This is not the way to achieve passionlessness, enlightenment, liberation. . . . How can it be reached by a man who is not calm and at ease, who is so exhausted by hunger and thirst that his mind is unbal-

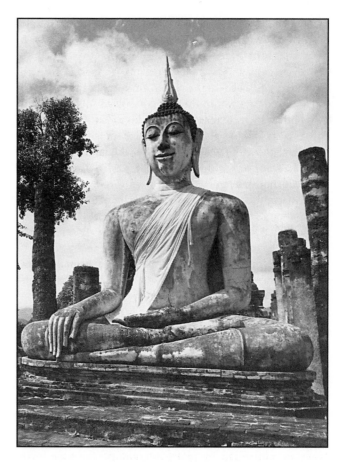

Images of the Buddha express various qualities of enlightenment. Elongated earlobes are among the auspicious marks that designate a Buddha, as on this image in Sukhothai, Thailand's 700-year-old royal capital.

anced?"[7] Mind and body are united in this search; weakening the body means weakening the mind also. So Siddhartha resolved to follow the "middle path," avoiding the extremes of riches and luxury, on the one hand, and self-mortification on the other.

At just that moment, inspired by the gods, a cowherd woman named Sujata brought milk-rice and offered it to the Buddha-to-be. He accepted it, bathed himself, and ate it to nourish himself for his attainment of enlightenment. The five monks abandoned him because it appeared he had given up the search, but Siddhartha went alone to sit cross-legged in meditation under a wisdom (bodhi) tree at **Bodh Gaya**, making the mighty resolution, "Never from this seat will I stir, until I have attained the supreme and absolute wisdom!"[8] The struggle was on. Representing the forces of passion and death, the god Mara (Death) entered the picture to attempt to thwart the attainment of Buddhahood. Mara is the god of worldly desires; seeing that Siddhartha was passing beyond his control, Mara tried to entice him with his three daughters, but Siddhartha's heart remained pure. Then Mara brought his battle legions to overwhelm the Siddhartha, frightening even the gods. But all his awesome powers were rendered harmless by the strength of Siddhartha's meditation. Now Siddhartha pointed to the earth, calling upon it to be witness to his merit and his right to achieve Buddhahood, and the earth responded with such a deafening roar of assent that all Mara's hosts were scattered and defeated.

Siddhartha continued in the power of his meditation, and on the night of the first full moon he attained Buddhahood. In the first watch of the night he reviewed all his former existences, and then he turned his compassionate mind toward the sufferings of all beings in the unending wheel of rebirth. In the second watch of the night he attained the divine eye by which he saw the entire world as in a spotless mirror, with all beings impelled by their deeds to undergo repeated death and rebirth, and he grew in compassion. Siddhartha turned his meditation in the third watch of the night to the real nature of this world, understanding the causes of all rebirth, suffering, and death, beginning with ignorance and yearning for existence, and, thus, he also perceived the path leading to the cessation of all this.

He knew what was to be known : he became a Buddha
awoke from his meditation and saw a self nowhere in the world
   gained the highest peace by the eightfold noble path
I have attained this path : I have fulfilled this path
   which the great seers followed
   (who knew the true & the false)
   for the benefit of others
And in the fourth watch, when dawn appeared
   and the whole world was tranquil
He gained omniscience : the imperishable state
& the earth trembled like a drunken maiden when he was
   enlightened
the heavens shone with his success
   and kettledrums sounded in the sky[9]

Turning the Wheel of the Dharma For some time the Buddha stayed there at Bodh Gaya, looking into his own mind and knowing he had found freedom. But now the

question arose as to whether this enlightenment should be shared with others. Some stories tell how the Buddha was thinking at first that humans would not be able to understand his teaching. But the god Brahma came and pleaded with him, persuading him that some beings would understand. The Buddha surveyed the whole world with his Buddha eye, and he had compassion for all living things, deciding to teach this way of liberation to the world. Making his way to Sarnath near Banares, he sought out the five ascetics who had earlier abandoned him and preached to them, turning the wheel of the **Dharma** (truth). He told them that the two extreme ways of life, living in luxury and practicing total self-mortification, were useless; it is the "middle path" that leads to enlightenment. Then he proclaimed the **Four Noble Truths:**

> And this is the Noble Truth of Sorrow. Birth is sorrow, age is sorrow, disease is sorrow, death is sorrow; contact with the unpleasant is sorrow, separation from the pleasant is sorrow, every wish unfulfilled is sorrow—in short all the five components of individuality are sorrow.
>
> And this is the Noble Truth of the Arising of Sorrow. It arises from craving, which leads to rebirth, which brings delight and passion and seeks pleasure now here, now there—the craving for sensual pleasure, the craving for continued life, the craving for power.
>
> And this is the Noble Truth of the Stopping of Sorrow. It is the complete stopping of that craving, so that no passion remains, leaving it, being emancipated from it, being released from it, giving no place to it.
>
> And this is the Noble Truth of the Way which Leads to the Stopping of Sorrow. It is the Noble Eightfold Path— Right Views, Right Resolve, Right Speech, Right Conduct, Right Livelihood, Right Effort, Right Mindfulness, and Right Concentration.[10]

The vision of life and its goal of transformation expressed in these four truths is profound, and we look at it more closely later. The Buddha retained the Indian view of life as samsara, a series of deaths and rebirths caused by karma. He saw that this whole existence involves "sorrow," that is, suffering, discontent, frustration, and the anxiety of being death-bound. He had seen that all this sorrow arises from clinging, grasping, holding onto the self. But he had also experienced the liberation that comes when clinging is totally done away with and, thus, sorrow ceases—this liberation he called *nirvana*, which means ending the samsara cycle and reaching complete freedom. And the way to reach this, he taught, was the noble **Eightfold Path**, a lifetime of disciplines focused on knowledge, ethics, and meditation, designed gradually to root out all clinging and bring about the transformation of existence, the attainment of nirvana, the imperishable and absolute state beyond all this. It is this new Dharma (truth) that the Buddha proclaimed.

Founding the Sangha   The five hermits accepted the Buddha's Dharma and were ordained as the first monks (Pali: bhikkhus), and with that the Buddha created the *sangha*, the community following the path to enlightenment. A tradition says the Buddha went to Kapilavastu and preached the Dharma to his father, who was overjoyed, and even went to the heaven where his mother dwelt and preached the Dharma for her and the gods there. He spent the rest of his long life, some forty-five years, traveling about northeastern India, teaching the Dharma and gathering many disciples into the community of the sangha. Starting with the five hermits who became the first monks, under the Buddha's guidance some of these disciples reached enlightenment and attained the state of nirvana. The Buddha called these enlightened monks *arhats* (Pali: arahants), meaning "worthy ones," and they became the leaders of the new community, the sangha.

When he had a community of sixty enlightened monks, the Buddha sent them out as missionaries to travel about and bring the Dharma to all beings, and many converted to this path. The Buddha accepted all classes of people without regard to race or social status, thus breaking away from the Indian caste system. At the request of his foster mother Prajapati, combined with urging from Ananda, he also accepted women into the sangha in a separate order of nuns (Pali: bhikkhunis), with Prajapati and her attendants as its first members. The Buddha taught that women as well as men could reach enlightenment, and the scriptures tell of a number of nuns who did in fact attain to the state of full enlightenment. However, the Buddha did, according to scriptural texts, establish additional rules for nuns that in effect subordinated them to the monks in the sangha.

As the Buddha organized the sangha into a monastic community, he established the main guidelines for monastic life, including the basic precepts such as chastity, having no possessions, begging for food, and nonviolence toward all living things. Whereas the early monks and nuns were basically wanderers, the Buddha did establish the custom of retreats during the summer monsoon season, often gathering in caves in northern India. Eventually the conversions got so numerous that the Buddha gave the monks permission to ordain new monks wherever they went and, thus, the sangha spread as a kind of republican society of monastic communities in various places.

The Buddha also accepted lay adherents to the path—kings, princes, merchants, and others, teaching them to observe the basic moral precepts and attain merit by supporting the monastic community. He also insisted that the monks and nuns teach their lay supporters and help them live meritorious lives. So the sangha has four divisions: monks (**bhikkhus**), nuns (**bhikkhunis**), laymen, and laywomen.

With the founding of the sangha, the Buddhist identity is complete. All Buddhists down to the present day have expressed this identity by saying the formula that is used for entry into the Buddhist community: "I take refuge in the Buddha, I take refuge in the Dharma, I take refuge in the Sangha."

Death of the Buddha: Parinirvana   After a long, full lifetime of teaching, the Buddha knew the end of his human existence was near. According to one text, he said to Ananda and the other monks,

> I am old now, Ananda, and full of years; my journey nears its end, and I have reached my sum of days, for I am nearly eighty years old. . . . So, Ananda, you must be your own lamps, be your own refuges. Take refuge in nothing outside yourselves. Hold firm to the truth as a lamp and a refuge, and do not look for refuge to anything besides yourselves.[11]

Ananda wept at the prospect of the teacher leaving him, but the Buddha told him not to grieve, reminding him that it is in the very nature of things that we must sever ourselves from all things near and dear to us. After ascertaining that none of the monks had any doubts or perplexities about the Buddha, the Dharma, the sangha, or the path, the Buddha spoke his last words: "All composite things must pass away. Strive onward vigilantly."[12] And in the midst of his final meditation he passed into parinirvana, complete liberation without any ties remaining to pull him back for another lifetime in samsara. At the passing of the Buddha, legends say, the earth shook, thunderbolts crashed, rivers boiled with water, and the tree over the Buddha's couch showered his golden body with flowers.

The grief-stricken laypeople of the area, the Mallans, honored the Buddha's remains for six days. Then they carried his body on a bier to a great funeral pyre, and fire consumed all but his bones. The bones and other relics of the Buddha were kept in golden jars and taken to the village hall, where they were venerated for seven days. Rulers of the neighboring regions also wanted relics of the great teacher so they could establish shrines, and after some resistance the Mallans allowed the relics to be divided into eight parts and taken by the kings of the region, who built stupas (memorial mounds) over them. The relics provide a sense of the ongoing presence of the Buddha, who is beyond existence in the state of parinirvana.

Tripitaka: **Word of the Buddha**

The Buddha had told the monks that the Dharma (the truth) would be their leader, and so they looked especially to his sayings and teachings as the source for the Dharma. During the first rainy season retreat after the Buddha's parinirvana, the story says, five hundred **arhats** (fully enlightened monks) assembled in the **First Council of Buddhism** at Rajagriha and collected the sayings and teachings of the Buddha so that the Dharma might abide. Though the Buddha was no longer present, having entered into the state of parinirvana, the Dharma itself would be the ongoing presence of the Buddha.

Since Ananda was the one who heard the Buddha speak most often, they asked Ananda to recite the Buddha's sayings. So Ananda recited the words that the Buddha spoke in his sermons and dialogues (the sutras). Another monk, Upali, recited the various rules that the Buddha had given to regulate the life of the monks and nuns (the vinaya). Thus arose two of the main parts or "baskets" (pitaka) of the scriptures, the *Sutra* (Pali: *Sutta*) *Pitaka* and the *Vinaya Pitaka*, containing the Dharma of the great teacher. Somewhat later, disciples produced a set of scholarly treatises on points of doctrine, the *Abhidharma* (Pali: *Abhidhamma*), also considered to derive from the word of the Buddha. These three

sets of writings are the *Tripitaka* (Pali: *Tipitaka*), the "Three Baskets," the scriptures of Buddhism. Scholars of today think the formation of the scriptures was a longer and more complicated process than the tradition says. The sayings were passed on orally by different groups, interpreted and added to, and eventually written down in the Pali language centuries later. But what the Buddhist story emphasizes is that the Dharma of the scriptures derives directly from the teachings of the Buddha. The *Tripitaka* is "word of the Buddha."

In the story of the Buddha, then, one finds the paradigm for what it means to be a Buddhist. The Buddha, the Dharma, and the sangha are not just historical artifacts to be researched and reconstructed; they are living realities in which all Buddhists of all ages can participate. Furthermore, the life story of the Buddha is in a real sense the life story of every Buddhist, showing how the path proceeds from ignorance and worldly attachment to knowledge, detachment, and complete liberation.

HISTORICAL TRANSFORMATIONS: SHAPING THE BUDDHIST WAY

The story of Buddhism, although it centers on the historical life of Siddhartha Gautama, is actually very open-ended. The ultimate truth can be expressed in many other persons and realities. For example, as we noted earlier, the Buddha himself had many previous lifetimes. And there have been other Buddhas in the great aeons of the past and there will be other Buddhas in the future. So the story came to be expanded greatly as Buddhism developed in its various historical transformations.

Ashoka, the Second Founder of Buddhism

For two centuries, Buddhism spread mainly in the Ganges Valley area of eastern India. But in the middle of the third century B.C.E., it burst forth and spread throughout India and southward to Sri Lanka. One of the primary agents of this expansion was the great King **Ashoka** (r. ca. 272–236 B.C.E.), one of the most important rulers in Indian history and a zealous Buddhist. At the beginning of the third century B.C.E., the Maurya dynasty was engaged in extending control over much of India.

The third Maurya king was Ashoka, who conquered Kalinga in northeastern India, the last area to be subdued. But in the process, the extensive bloodshed and destruction filled Ashoka with remorse, and he began to study the Dharma of Buddhism. He became a lay follower and even lived in a monastic community for a while, giving up the royal pastime of hunting because of the Buddhist precept not to harm living things.

Some five years after the bloody conquest of Kalinga, Ashoka proclaimed the new policy of the peaceful Dharma conquest. In a series of fourteen edicts engraved on rocks throughout his empire, he proclaimed that all people are his children and that they should live by basic Buddhist precepts: they should do no injury to any living things, they should be obedient to parents and elders, reverent to teachers, and the like. He abolished animal sacrifice and regulated the slaughter of animals for food, provided for the welfare of the common people, built thousands of stupas, supported the monastic communities, and worked to have the developing sects of Buddhism recognize and tolerate each other. King Ashoka is fondly remembered by Buddhists as the "second founder" of Buddhism, establishing the model of the Buddhist layperson and the Buddhist state, complementary to the ideal of the sangha monastic community.

One of Ashoka's edicts says he sent Dharma-envoys to the Greek rulers of Syria, Egypt, Macedonia, Cyrene, and Epyrus, although these missionaries apparently did not have much success. Closer to home, however, in addition to spreading the rule of Dharma throughout India, Ashoka sent his son Mahinda and his daughter Sanghamitta as missionaries to Sri Lanka, and the two of them converted the king and the women of the court to Buddhism.

Theravada and Mahayana

In the course of its development, Buddhism came to be divided into two main branches: **Theravada** (Path of the Elders) and **Mahayana** (Greater Vehicle). Through complex historical developments, Theravada came to be dominant in South Asia and Southeast Asia, whereas Mahayana spread throughout the lands of East Asia. A third branch, **Vajrayana** (Diamond Vehicle) or **Tantrism**, was accepted in Tibet and in one Japanese Buddhist school.

Early Buddhist Schools   In the first three or four centuries after the Buddha's death, there was much debate as Buddhists attempted to define the Buddha's most central teachings. By 200 B.C.E., reports indicate the existence of seventeen or eighteen "schools," each with a particular way of interpreting the path taught by the Buddha. It is important to understand that no actual schisms developed among these early Buddhists, for they all adhered to the basic rules of the sangha, and monks belonging to different schools of thought often lived together in harmony in the same monasteries. Yet they had vigorous debates over points of doctrine, and two more general councils were held to try and sort out the disagreements. One school was the group that called itself Theravada (way of the elders), claiming to follow closely and to transmit the original teachings of the Buddha. Another early group was known as the Mahasanghikas (Great Sanghites), who admitted lay followers to their assemblies and taught that a transfigured Buddha exists with endless life beyond the world, appearing at different times and places. They also, of course, claimed that they carefully preserved the teaching of the Buddha. Other schools promoted somewhat differing views on issues such as the concept of a person, whether things have only a momentary existence, how to explain karma, and other key questions.

All of these early Buddhist schools of thought splintered and eventually died out, with the exception of the Theravada school. The Theravadins established themselves especially in Sri Lanka, and they preserved the Buddhist scriptures, the *Tipitaka*, in writing in the Pali dialect. In general, it may be said that the Theravada school did maintain the central teachings of early Buddhism, together with the structures of monastic orders and lay supporters, and they have continued to represent this early form of Buddhism in the Buddhist world down to the present day. Some of the teachings of the Mahasanghikas, it seems, were taken over and continued in the Mahayana movement that developed in India.

Rise of Mahayana   Pressure for changes that came to fruition in the Mahayana movement came from several sources. In the sangha, the arhats (enlightened monks) tended to form an elite guild and insisted that only they knew the true Dharma, alienating many other monks and laypeople, so in some communities there was a movement

Burmese Buddhists meditate before Buddha statues in Rangoon's Shwedagon pagoda.

to include all, even laypeople, as equals on the path. The influence of Hindu bhakti (devotional) movements began to be felt, with many people desiring ways of expressing devotion and worship, even though they were Buddhists. And the philosophical searching and speculation characteristic of thinkers in India led some Buddhists to explore the nature of reality in a more systematic, philosophical way, contributing new perspectives on the original Buddhist vision. These tendencies came to fruition in Mahayana Buddhism.

In keeping with the new Mahayana ideas that were being formed, during the second and first centuries B.C.E., new scriptures, now in Sanskrit, were written expressing this vision. The expanded story now came to incorporate new conceptions of the sangha, the scriptures, the ideal saint, and the Buddha.

Great Sangha and New Sutras   A major Mahayana innovation was to open the path to all people, monks and lay alike. The word *Mahayana* means "greater vehicle" or "greater course," and one implication of this new name is that the narrower concept of the arhat as the one reaching the goal was being broadened to include others, even

laypeople. All can be equally on the path toward achieving Buddhahood. Of course, Mahayana communities continued to recognize monastic discipline as especially important in cultivating the higher virtues, but the path was thought to be within the reach of those who chose not to withdraw from the world and become monks or nuns. Mahayanists expressed criticism of the traditional form of Buddhism, designating it as **Hinayana**, the Lesser Vehicle, since it offered salvation only to the few.

The Theravadins in turn criticized the Mahayanists for developing these new ideas rather than relying only on the Dharma of the Buddha. The new writings composed in Sanskrit by Mahayanists were not just commentaries on the older Pali scriptures; they were claimed to be the secret teaching that the Buddha himself had given to his most advanced disciples. Mahayana, thus, taught a kind of progressive revelation of the truth; to those with lesser understanding, the Buddha had revealed the preliminary truth embodied in the *Tripitaka*, the scriptures of Theravada, but to those with deep understanding he revealed the full truth, which was passed on orally and eventually written in the Mahayana sutras. All of these are still "word of the Buddha." Important early texts of Mahayana include writings like the *Sadharmapundarika* (Lotus), *Prajñaparamita* (Perfection of Wisdom), and the *Sukhavati* (Pure Land) sutras. In the following centuries a great number of additional sutras were added to the Mahayana corpus, filling out and refining the new understandings of the Buddha and the path.

The Course of the Bodhisattva   Mahayana is really the "great course" of the **bodhisattva** (one becoming a Buddha). It was one of the main innovations of Mahayana to teach that the Great Course leads directly to Buddhahood, whereas the Lesser Course (Theravada) leads only to arhat-ship. The Theravadins, it is true, had an idea of the bod-hisattva path toward liberation, but they associated it with a few special beings like Gautama. But Mahayanists began to teach that the course of the bodhisattva is the higher path that leads to Buddhahood and which, furthermore, is for all to follow, open even to laypeople. Thus, in a signifi-cant shift of focus, Mahayana Buddhists started looking be-yond the arhat, who reaches nirvana with great discipline and effort, as the supreme spiritual model. For them, rather, the ideal model now is the bodhisattva, an enlight-ened being who reaches nirvana but voluntarily remains in the samsara existence, rebirth after rebirth, for the purpose of helping others.

Some bodhisattvas are celestial beings, living in the heavens and working to help and save all beings. These bodhisattvas can be worshiped and prayed to for help, bringing the element of bhakti into Mahayana Buddhism. One such heavenly bodhisattva is Manjusri, who appears to humans in dreams. Hearing his name subtracts many aeons from one's time in samsara, and those who worship him are protected by his power. Another widely worshiped bodhisattva is Avalokiteshvara, who is described in the *Lotus Sutra* as an omnipresent savior rich in love and com-passion, taking many different forms to help living beings. Those who worship him and call on his name will be saved from all dangers, whether drowning in water, bound in prison, or burning in a fire. He grants women their desire for a daughter or son. In China and Japan the names Guanyin and Kannon are used for this bodhisattva, whose images are often represented as a compassionate woman, a "goddess of mercy."

The Mahayana Conception of Buddha

The Mahayana group also expanded the conception of who or what the Buddha is. They emphasized that the Buddha is really the eternal power of the Dharma, and that this "Dharma Body" of the Buddha is transcendent and universal, yet for-ever active in the world. The Dharma Body has lived for countless ages in the past and will continue to live forever in the future. This Dharma Body is the only real body of the Buddha; it is ultimate reality.

But the Dharma Body has various manifestations for the welfare of living beings. Some manifestations are in human form, such as Siddhartha Gautama, to teach and guide humans. Other important manifestations are the heavenly Buddhas who preside over Buddhalands in which all the inhabitants are assured of attaining enlightenment. Moreover, some of these heavenly Buddhas can also be worshiped by people still living in this world, sharing merit with them so that they can be saved from a variety of suf-ferings and ultimately be reborn into one of the heavenly Buddhalands.

Mahayana Schools: Madhyamika and Yogacara

As Mahayana thinkers speculated on the meaning of these new ideas about bodhisattvas and Buddhas, a new philo-sophical perspective emerged to become characteristic of the Mahayana approach, formulated especially by the **Madhyamika** school and its famous thinker, **Nagarjuna** (ca. 150–250 C.E.). The Madhyamika thinkers came up with the dramatic new idea that, since all things in the world come into existence as a result of causes and conditions, they do not have an independent existence and, thus, are "empty" (shunya). This whole phenomenal world of sam-sara is characterized by emptiness (**shunyata**). Taking this one step further, the Mahayana thinkers proposed that nir-vana also is empty, since it is devoid of all definitions and discrimination. This means that the phenomenal world of samsara and the realm of nirvana are both empty and, thus, they may be equated with each other. Rather than see-ing nirvana as the opposite of samsara, nirvana is to be un-derstood as the realization that all things are really empty and, therefore, there are no dualisms. One who under-stands this fully is enlightened and realizes the Buddha-nature within himself or herself.·

Nagarjuna is famous for his logical reduction-to-absurdity method to show that every concept contains contradictions in itself and, therefore, is unreal, proving that the whole phenomenal world is empty or unreal be-cause it is based on contradictory relations. The purpose of this method, he points out, is to free our minds of all theories and enable us to realize the unconditioned truth, beyond all words and concepts.

The other important Mahayana philosophical school, Yogacara, focused on how the mind creates and experi-ences the illusory world as real. With its slogan, "Mind only," this philosophical school worked out a complex the-ory that the experienced world is nothing but a perceptual construct. They identified emptiness with what they called the "storehouse consciousness," the basis of all existence. Later philosophers of this school equated the storehouse consciousness with "the womb of the Buddha" (tathagata-garbha), that is, the womb from which all Buddhas are born. Furthermore, it is the embryo Buddha-nature that is present in all things. This idea implies that all beings possess Buddhahood and that the goal is to realize that Buddhahood. If that is so, then many possible paths toward realizing that Buddhahood open up, from meditation and yogic practices to devotion and worship of the Buddhas. And in fact, especially in China, many Mahayana Buddhist schools developed to cultivate the different paths toward realizing Buddhahood.

Buddhist Tantra: Vajrayana Yet another form of Buddhism developed in India, influenced by Tantric aspects of Hinduism, which used many rituals, **mantras** (sacred words), **mandalas** (sacred diagrams), ritual sexual intercourse, and the like, to achieve realization of Buddhahood. Eventually the Tantric Buddhists produced new scriptures; these are manuals for rituals and meditations designed to lead directly to the realization of Buddhahood. These Tantras purported to come directly from the Buddha passed on secretly to his most advanced disciples, and they were written in a kind of code language so the uninitiated would not understand. Called Vajrayana (Diamond Vehicle), this form of Buddhism greatly extended the Buddha pantheon by adding many new Buddhas, bodhisattvas, feminine consorts, gods, and goddesses, representing the whole cosmos. Tantrists also believed that this sacred cosmos is replicated in the human body; that is, all these Buddhas and bodhisattvas reside within us, so with the proper rituals and meditation one can visualize or identify with these powers and realize Buddahood. Vajrayana, later influential especially in Japan and Tibet, thus developed a path by which one could achieve Buddhahood even within this very lifetime.

Great Expansion of Buddhism in Asia

Unlike Hindus, who stayed mostly in the context of India, Buddhists from early times on considered the Dharma to be the truth for all living things and, therefore, one of the important duties in following the path is to make it possible for others to share in the benefits of that Dharma. Buddhism spread to several major cultural areas and in transforming them was itself transformed, taking on a distinctive flavor in each region. First, Buddhism spread throughout India and to Sri Lanka at the time of King Ashoka. Then with the Indianization of Southeast Asia it also became dominant in those lands. Since the Theravada form of Buddhism was strong in India during these expansions, those lands became Theravada countries, with indigenous cults and traditions still in place. When the expansion to central and East Asia took place, Mahayana was in the ascendency, so East Asia emerged predominantly Mahayana.

Within India itself, Buddhism remained fairly strong in most regions up to the seventh century, but over the next centuries a slow decline set in. By about the thirteenth century, Buddhism had virtually disappeared from the land of its birth. One element in the demise of Indian Buddhism was perhaps the extent to which monastic Buddhism, with landed estates and royal grants, had grown unresponsive to the needs of the people. The general populace found their needs met more by theistic Hinduism and increasingly turned in that direction, incorporating some Buddhist worship and piety into popular Hinduism. Another factor in the weakening of Buddhism in India was the onslaught of outside invaders. Beginning with the White Hun invasions of the sixth century, the Buddhist monasteries of northwestern India were devastated. Later Muslim invaders and Muslim rulers continued to demolish Buddhist temples and monasteries, along with Hindu temples. Hinduism, depending on village Brahmans and devotional cults, survived, but Buddhism, focused on the monastic communities, weakened and eventually disappeared. But by this time Buddhism had already become the light of many other parts of Asia beyond its homeland.

Expansion to Sri Lanka and Southeast Asia Beginning when King Ashoka's son and daughter converted the rulers of Sri Lanka, Buddhism has flourished there for over two thousand years, the longest continuity of Buddhism anywhere. At times there has been Mahayana influence in Sri Lanka, along with Hindu cults, but Theravada eventually became dominant. Sri Lanka boasts a tree said to have grown from a shoot of the tree of Bodh Gaya under which the Buddha reached enlightenment; the tree shoot was brought to Sri Lanka by King Ashoka's daughter. And a special temple in Kandy houses a tooth of the Buddha. From the beginning, the sangha was strongly supported by the rulers of Sri Lanka. Buddhist kings were patrons of Buddhist art and learning, and they built many temples and monasteries, even helping to regulate the affairs of the sangha.

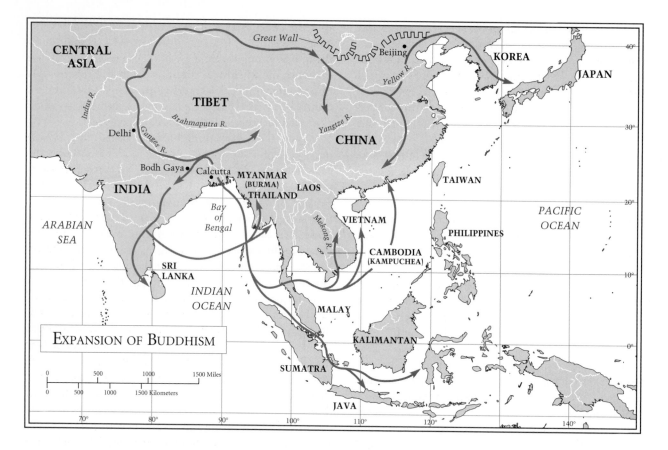

EXPANSION OF BUDDHISM

Since Burma provided a trade gateway for India to Southeast Asia, Indian merchants were bringing Buddhism with them into Burma already in the third century B.C.E., and some monks were also sent by Ashoka. Over the next centuries, Buddhist influences continued, and gradually Burma became a flourishing center of Buddhist life. For a while, Mahayana and Tantric influences were strong, but during the period of the Pagan kingdom, King Anawrahta (1040–1077) turned to Sri Lanka for inspiration; thus, Burma became a thriving center of Theravada Buddhism, retaining a pure form of Theravada ordination and tradition. Lay Buddhism in Burma took on a special character by adopting local cults of spirits (nats), so that side by side with the monastic community are found shamanistic practices involving women possessed by nats healing people and providing benefits for them.

A mixture of Mahayana Buddhism and Hinduism spread into Cambodia, Thailand, and Laos from about the fourth century C.E. onward. The Theravada form of Buddhism did not come to Cambodia until the twelfth century, when it supplanted both Mahayana and Hinduism. The Thai states developed in the thirteenth century and accepted Theravada from Burma, although Thai kings used Hindu law and Brahmanical ceremonies. The first Laotian state developed in the fourteenth century and the Khmer missionaries from Cambodia introduced Theravada Buddhism, which became the official religion of Laos. Vietnam, though a part of Southeast Asia, received strong influence from China and has been predominantly Mahayana in orientation. Indonesia was Hinduized by the fifth century C.E., but Buddhism was also introduced and existed side by side with the cult of Shiva. At Borobudur, on the island of Java, was built the greatest and most glorious of all stupas, in the shape of a great mandala in stone representing the pilgrim's search for enlightenment.

Characteristic of the development of Buddhism in Sri Lanka and Southeast Asia is the interrelationship between the monastic community and the laypeople. The monks and nuns pursue the path toward nirvana, of course, and the laypeople carry on householder life in the cities and in rural areas. But each group lives in a certain dependence on the other. The monks need the support of the laypeople in terms of food, buildings, security, and the like. The laypeople need the services of the monks in terms of teaching, chanting scriptures, and providing spiritual power for the community.

Development of East Asian Buddhism As early as the first century C.E., Buddhist monks and laypeople made their way along the silk routes into central Asia. For a time, both Theravada and Mahayana flourished in central Asia (present-day Afghanistan), until Buddhism was stamped out by the Muslim advance around the tenth century C.E. Scholars today are only beginning to recover the impressive achievements of Buddhists in central Asia, including temples, great sculptures of the Buddha, and important translations of Indian Buddhist texts.

From central Asia, monks and missionaries brought Buddhism to China, where in its Mahayana form it rose to become one of the three great religions of China, along

Buddhist monk ringing the monastery bell during the New Year celebration in Japan.

with Confucianism and Daoism. Buddhism contributed to many transformations in Chinese society and religious thought, and in the process Buddhism itself took on characteristic Chinese forms. Particularly important was the development of special lineages or "schools" of Chinese Buddhism, each with important writings and practices. The **Tiantai** school, for example, focused on the *Lotus Sutra*, and the **Huayan** school made the *Garland Sutra* its principal scripture. Eventually two Buddhist schools became the most widespread in China. There was **Pure Land**, which centered on the worship of the compassionate Buddha Amitabha and promised rebirth in the Pure Land paradise. The second school was **Chan** (meditation) Buddhism, which worked out methods of awakening to one's innate Buddhahood through emptying the mind in meditation. These Chinese schools of Buddhism will be discussed further in Part 3.

From China, Buddhism spread to Vietnam, Korea, and Japan, with the result that these cultures became predominantly Buddhist. Vietnam was influenced both from India and from China, but it was Chinese Mahayana especially in the Chan form that finally prevailed. Later Pure Land Buddhism came to dominate village-level Buddhism in Vietnam, whereas the monasteries remained predominantly Thien (Chan).

Buddhism was brought to the northern part of Korea in 372 C.E. by a Chinese monk, spreading throughout the rest of the land by the sixth century. Korean religion had been a form of shamanism, which still survives today as a cult of spirits. When Buddhism came in, the common people were much attracted to Pure Land Buddhism with its promise of salvation in the next world. During the eighth and ninth centuries, Chan (in Korean, Son) was introduced from China, and this became the most popular form of monastic Buddhism in Korea. The Buddhist scriptural canon was printed in Korea twice, as Korean Buddhism made a particularly important contribution to the spread of Buddhism.

From Korea, Buddhism spread to Japan, beginning around the year 550 when Korean kings sent gifts of Buddhist sutras and Buddha images to the Japanese emperor. Buddhism in Japan was first adopted by the court and ruling families as a means of unifying the nation, but later it became an important part of popular Japanese life. Important schools of Buddhism developed in Japan, as in China, continuing their vitality up to the present time. **Tendai** (the

Japanese form of Tiantai) and Shingon (esoteric or Tantric Buddhism) became widespread foundational Buddhist movements in Japan's classical Heian era (974–1185). And in the upheavals that accompanied the beginnings of the feudal period in Japan, Pure Land and **Zen** (the Japanese form of Chan) became widely popular, together with the movement founded by the charismatic Japanese Buddhist leader, Nichiren. Japanese Buddhism is discussed in more detail in Part 3.

The Special Shape of Tibetan Buddhism   In the seventh century C.E., Buddhist missionaries from India began to press northward to a new region in central Asia, the isolated Himalayan Mountains of Tibet. The indigenous religious practice of Tibet was called Bon, and it focused on many spirits both good and hostile. Shamans communicated with these spirits by going into trances, and the people offered animal sacrifices. Since, during this period, Tibet also had contact with central Asia and China, Chan Buddhism was successful in Tibet for a while, but at the same time the Tantric form of Buddhism, Vajrayana, was being imported from India. Toward the end of the eighth century, a Tibetan king staged a remarkable international debate between Chinese Chan monks and monks from India. According to the Tibetan version of the story, the Chinese were defeated and expelled from the country, after which the Tibetans definitely turned toward India and Vajrayana Buddhism.

Under support from the Tibetan kings, Vajrayana missionaries from India entered Tibet to teach, translate Sanskrit scriptures into Tibetan, and found monasteries. One missionary remembered in a host of legends was Padmasambhava, who arrived in Tibet in 747 and used his Tantric powers to subdue all the Bon demons who were hostile to Buddhism; after being subjugated, they were included in the Tibetan Buddhist pantheon as protectors of Buddhism. Under royal patronage, Indian and Tibetan monks translated a vast number of scriptures into Tibetan, virtually creating the Tibetan literary language in the process. Many monasteries were established where scholar-monks practiced the disciplines of monastic life and mastered the classical Vajrayana doctrines. And countless wonder-working Tantric yogins wandered about, often married and with families.

Tibetans, with their background in the popular shamanistic religion, accepted Vajrayana Buddhism from India but shaped it in their own way, enriching the pantheon with Buddhist saints, Tibetan gods and goddesses, demons, local heroes, and the like. The pantheon included many female figures, such as the bodhisattva Tara who became a kind of universal protectress worshiped by both monks and laity. Monks and nuns participated in popular Buddhism, but they also cultivated esoteric practices involving yogic meditation and Tantric rituals, with the goal of transforming the consciousness into the absolute Buddha reality. The religious specialists were the **lamas**, spiritual masters, often thought to be living gods, and under their direction the disciplines and rituals were practiced.

With this admixture of Tantric and popular rituals and teachings, there developed a number of schools or lineages of Buddhism in Tibet, which exist up to the present day. Three of these schools began to develop in Tibet around the eleventh century: the Nyingma-pa, the Sakya-pa, and the Kagyu-pa. The Nyingma-pa (ancient school) is the school that traces its line most directly to the tradition of Padmasambhava, with its strong emphasis on Tantric texts and magic rituals, including admixtures of Bon elements. A decisive influence for shaping and reforming Buddhism in Tibet was the scholar-monk Atisha (982–1054), who came from India in 1042 and helped to purify the sangha in Tibet, emphasizing celibacy and proper understanding of Buddhist doctrines. His influence led to the formation of an important monastic order, the Kadam, which emphasized a high standard of scholarship and strict adherence to monastic discipline.

The Tibetan master Drok-mi (992–1072) studied the Tantric practices in India, and under his influence a monastery was founded at Sakya; this Sakya-pa adopted the Kadam monastic disciplines together with its own Tantric practices. The leader of this school married in order to continue his line, as the Sakya-pa became dominant in Tibetan politics in the thirteenth and fourteenth centuries.

Another Tibetan master who studied the Tantric practices in India was Marpa (1012–1096). On returning to Tibet, Marpa married and, as a householder, revealed his Tantric practices only to a chosen few. His chief disciple was the famous Milarepa (1040–1123), beloved in Tibetan legend as a wanderer of the Himalayas and a wonder-worker for the people. The school that arose from Marpa's influence is the Kagyu-pa (whispered transmission school), featuring a complex yoga system and secret instructions from master to disciples.

An important reform movement beginning late in the fourteenth century was called the Geluk-pa (virtuous school), also known as the Yellow Hats. Tsongkhapa (1357–1419), founder of the Geluk-pa, wrestled with the problem of finding order in the welter of teachings and practices that had found their way into Tibetan Buddhism. He developed a comprehensive system in which all Buddhist teachings are seen as mutually reinforcing rather than contradictory, thus laying the foundation for the great monastic universities. The Geluk-pa stressed learning, discipline, and celibacy, advocating a return to the traditional Buddhist monastic life and also a modification of some of the Tantric magical practices. It should be noted that these four traditional schools—Nyingma, Sakya, Kagyu, and Geluk—are not rigid sects with hard and fast divisions between them. Rather, they are related movements within the larger stream of Tibetan Buddhism that have separate identities but have continued to influence each other up to the present day.

In time, the Geluk-pa achieved political leadership in Tibet. Tsongkhapa's third successor as head of this school, Sonam Gyatsho (1543–1588), converted the Mongol ruler Altan Khan to Buddhism, and eventually the peoples of Mongolia, northern China, and southern Russia also came to follow Tibetan Lamaism. The Khan bestowed on Sonam Gyatsho the title of **Dalai Lama** (Ocean of Wisdom Teacher), a title that was then retrospectively granted to his two predecessors so that he became known as the Third Dalai Lama. This tradition grew out of the idea that certain lamas could intentionally be reincarnated in a child who would then become the next lama. Furthermore, the Dalai Lama was recognized as an incarnation of the bodhisattva Avalokiteshvara, adding to the prestige and authority possessed by this figure. The Fifth Dalai Lama established himself as ruler of all of Tibet, setting the stage for the Geluk-pa to rule the country until well into the twentieth century. Since lamas are recognized as incarnations in a continuing series, after the death of a Dalai Lama a search party would go out to find the new Dalai Lama, who would be an infant born forty-nine days later (the period of the intermediate stage). The searchers would be guided by the dying lama's indications and other pertinent signs, and once the right child was found, he would be brought to Lhasa to be educated for his role while regents ruled temporarily. The present Dalai Lama (b. 1935) is the fourteenth in this line.

BUDDHISM IN THE MODERN ERA

Developments in the modern era have often been disruptive to Buddhism as to other religions. Even before the modern era, as we saw, Buddhism disappeared in its motherland India. The upheavals of the modern era have posed many challenges as well as opportunities for Buddhists.

Challenges from Without and Within

Colonialism and Western Missionaries   Starting in the mid-sixteenth century, Western colonialism and missionary work posed challenges to traditional Buddhist societies throughout Asia. In Sri Lanka, for example, the Portuguese attempted to convert the people to Catholicism, destroying Buddhist temples and relics and executing monks found wearing the yellow robe. Under British colonial rule in Sri Lanka and Burma, missionaries continued to disparage Buddhism as a religion of the ignorant and superstitious. Since Buddhism in these countries had been supported especially by kings and rulers, colonial rule meant the sangha lost much of its support.

Under colonial rule, Western medicine, science, and education were introduced, and the traditional functions of Buddhist monks as doctors and teachers for the people were diminished.

Nationalism, Communism, and Political Upheaval Nationalistic and ideological movements have also created difficulties for traditional Buddhist communities in Asia. For example, Japan's strong Buddhist institutions were seriously weakened by the rise of Japanese nationalism and the creation of the state cult of Shinto in the late nineteenth and early twentieth centuries, as most Buddhist temples were closed and all Buddhists were required to participate in the state cult. And the difficulties were compounded by the devastation brought by World War II—opening the door for massive Westernization and secularization in the postwar period in Japan. Many Japanese drifted to a secular lifestyle that relegated Buddhist practices to the realm of funerals and memorials for the dead.

The spread of communism in Asia has proved to be a drastic challenge for Buddhists, with communist rulers coming to dominate much of the area that had for centuries been the heartland of Buddhism: China, Mongolia, North Korea, Tibet, and the Southeast Asian countries of Vietnam, Laos, and Cambodia. Mongolia, taken over by a Soviet-inspired communist government in the early 1920s, replaced Buddhist teaching with communist ideology and stripped the Buddhist political leaders of their power. In China, the Maoist procedure was to close the monasteries and force monks and nuns to return to secular life, gathering the remnants of Buddhism into a state-run Chinese Buddhist Association. The Chinese conquest of Tibet caused great disruption in this traditional Buddhist culture, which had not even experienced a period of modernization; the Dalai Lama and thousands of others fled the country in 1959, and the Chinese took over the administration of the monasteries, with serious curtailment of Buddhist activities. Buddhists in China and Tibet suffered greatly during the Cultural Revolution (1966–1976), when monasteries and temples were closed and monks and nuns were persecuted.

Communism and political upheaval have seriously weakened the Buddhist institutions in Southeast Asia as well. Vietnamese Buddhists suffered from devastation during the Vietnam War and from communist rule, resulting in the closing of many monasteries and temples. Following the American bombing in Cambodia, the fanatical Khmer Rouge regime killed many monks and forced others to disrobe. In Laos, some monks were forced to work with the communist-backed Pathet Lao, while others fled to Thailand. Still today in Sri Lanka, continuing civil war has made life difficult for Buddhists, and some have resorted to violence and acts of terror. And harsh military rule in Myanmar (Burma) has kept the venerable Burmese sangha in a suppressed state.

Though the glorious days of Buddhism in central Asia (Afghanistan) ended a thousand years ago, still the flagrant destruction of great rock-carved Buddha statues by the Taliban government sent shudders through Buddhists and all people who advocate religious tolerance. It was a chilling reminder that Buddhists, like people of other religions, face hatred and persecution in some areas of the world even today.

Revitalization of Buddhism Today

Scholars and Reformers   Yet there is a sense of revitalization among Buddhists today. Buddhists in many lands have responded to the various challenges of the modern age with a revival of Buddhist activities, reforming Buddhist institutions, revitalizing Buddhist practice for monks

and nuns as well as laypeople, working for peace and equality in their societies, and producing a large amount of scholarly work.

Within Buddhist lands there have been many reformers who have redirected the monastic life toward constructive religious and social roles. In Thailand, for example, Buddhadasa Bhikkhu (1906–1993) established a forest meditation center where he developed a balanced program of meditation and study. He severely criticized popular Buddhist practices as well as capitalism, which pits one person against another in a struggle for personal gain, thus promoting selfishness and egoism and leading to personal and social suffering. Through many books and talks, Buddhadasa influenced many monastic as well as lay Buddhists to return to the pure, compassionate Buddhist life, working together for personal and social transformation. In Taiwan, Chinese Buddhism has become a vital influence in society, with thousands of Buddhist temples and organizations. Over ten thousand monks and nuns have been ordained since the Republic of China was established, and of these new monastics, over 60 percent are women. Many of these Buddhists in Taiwan are active in organizations that engage in social action to build a better society and world.

Throughout the Buddhist world, much attention has been given to increased activity of the laypeople in Buddhist affairs through education, religious activities, and lay Buddhist associations. Interest in the revitalization of worldwide Buddhism is seen in the founding of the World Fellowship of Buddhists in Sri Lanka in 1952 to unite Buddhists of all nations. And in connection with the 2,500th anniversary of the Buddha's enlightenment, a two-year-long Sixth Great Council of Buddhism was held in Rangoon in the 1950s.

In motherland India, there have been some inklings of a revival of Buddhism. Small groups of Indian intellectuals have been attracted to Buddhism because it suits their ideas of social reform and rational spirituality. Refugees from Tibet live in communities in India and Nepal, continuing the traditions of Tibetan Buddhism. And in 1956, Dr. B. R. Ambedkar (1891–1956) and his wife, leaders of Maharashtra's untouchables, converted to Buddhism, having become convinced that the Buddhist Dharma speaks to the suffering conditions of the untouchables in India and could bring about a social transformation in India. Within five years, more than three million untouchables followed Ambedkar's lead and con-

verted to Buddhism. Since then the number of Buddhist converts has reached about five million, most of them in the western state of Maharashtra, constituting a significant presence of Buddhists in India.

To meet the challenge of modern secular values, Buddhist scholars have been working to retrieve the sources of their own traditions and are reformulating Buddhist doctrines to address modern questions. Buddhadasa Bhikkhu (mentioned previously), the Dalai Lama from Tibetan Buddhism, Thich Nhat Hanh from Vietnam, and many other scholars and leaders are engaged in a revival of Buddhist scholarship and thinking that seeks to provide spiritual and moral guidance to Buddhists and to all in our world. Some Buddhist thinkers, such as Japanese philosopher Nishida Kitaro (1870–1945) and others of the renowned Kyoto School, have been influential in relating Buddhist ideas to Western philosophical and scientific modes of thought.

Expansion of Buddhism in the West Another significant aspect of Buddhism today is its expansion in the West. Thriving communities of immigrant Buddhists have been established, with temples, monasteries, and training centers. These ethnic communities tend to be strong especially in such places as Hawaii and California, but increasingly they are growing in other areas as well, in the United States, Canada, England, Germany, France, Italy, Australia, and many other countries. While early immigrants tended to come from the Chinese and Japanese Pure Land school of Buddhism, in recent years immigrants from other parts of Asia—Korea, Thailand, Vietnam, Tibet, and others—have strengthened the Buddhist presence in the West. Today virtually all Buddhist sects from Asia have adherents in the United States, Europe, and other areas of the Western world.

Along with immigrant communities of Buddhists, there are also significant numbers of Westerners who have become Buddhist. This trend started especially as teachers such as D. T. Suzuki interested many in Zen Buddhism through writings and lecturing, and a number of Japanese Zen masters established Zen centers in the larger American cities. Then in the 1960s came a surge of interest in Tibetan Buddhism and the establishment of training centers for all four traditional schools of Vajrayana. Since then, Theravada masters from Thailand as well as Mahayana masters from China, Korea, and Vietnam have attracted Western disciples.

So today there are many Westerners in America, Europe, and elsewhere who practice Buddhism, whether in the Zen tradition, or one of the Tibetan schools, or Theravada, or Nichiren Shoshu or others. A very significant development is the ordination of Western successors to Asian Buddhist masters, indicating a basis for the continuation and growth of these fledgling Buddhist communities in the West. These Western Buddhists have been especially active in what has been called "socially engaged Buddhism," promoting Buddhist principles and actions to work for peace, social and economic justice, equality for women, and other such transformations of society.

DISCUSSION QUESTIONS

1 According to the traditional Buddhist story, what was Siddhartha's early life like? Why did he decide to go forth to seek the truth?
2 Describe Siddhartha's attaining of enlightenment. What was the role of Mara and of the gods?
3 What was the content of the Buddha's first sermon given at Sarnath near Banares?
4 How did the Buddha go about teaching and gathering disciples? Describe the different orders that make up the sangha.
5 How, according to tradition, was the *Tripitaka* compiled? What are its contents?
6 Why is King Ashoka called the second founder of Buddhism? Do you think it is possible to govern a nation with non-violence?
7 Explain the important new developments in the Mahayana movement: the greater sangha, new sutras, the idea of the bodhisattva, and the expanded idea of the Buddha. What do you think led to these new ideas?
8 Outline the expansion of Buddhism in Asia and account for its virtual disappearance in India. Would you call Buddhism a missionary religion?
9 What are some unique characteristics of Tibetan Buddhism?
10 What have been some major problems for Buddhism in the modern period? What are some indications of Buddhism's revitalization today?
11 Why do you think Westerners are attracted to Buddhism?

Chapter 7

Buddhist Worlds of Meaning

THE ULTIMATE: DHARMA, NIRVANA, BUDDHA

What's it all about? What is really ultimate in our existence? Buddhists, like Hindus, do not fall back on a simple single answer like God. God and gods, like everything else, are part of the samsara cycle and, therefore, cannot be ultimate. One of the central Buddhist teachings about reality is that everything is impermanent and conditioned; there is nothing, even God, that is eternal and absolute. Does this mean, then, that Buddhists have no sense of the ultimate at all?

Such a view would be misleading, for Buddhists for many centuries have found ultimate meaning and transformation in the path of the Buddha. What is really ultimate? There is considerable diversity among those who are following the Buddhist path, with different philosophical systems and practical disciplines. Yet there is a common shape to the Buddhist vision of the ultimate. Perhaps we can get a sense of that vision as it is expressed in the universally used **Three Refuges** formula: "I go for refuge to the Buddha, I go for refuge to the Dharma, I go for refuge to the sangha." The Buddha as a human being is not ultimate, of course; but he reached the ultimate truth and, thus, is the exemplar of enlightenment. The Dharma is the transcendental absolute truth itself. And the sangha is the community of those who follow the Dharma and are focused toward the experience of nirvana, the unconditioned state of liberation.

The Ultimate as Unconditioned Truth

So, as a start in understanding the Buddhist vision, we can say that it is the Truth, the Dharma, that is ultimate. Now it might appear to someone on the outside that Buddhists worship the Buddha as God, as sacred reality.

They build temples dedicated to the Buddha, perform rituals before statues of the Buddha, revere relics of the Buddha, and the like. Buddhist religious rituals and festivals can be as colorful and dramatic as any other. But, most Buddhists insist, they are not worshiping the Buddha or any other object as ultimate reality, for the Buddha is beyond existence in the unconditioned state of nirvana, and all other objects of worship are conditioned and limited like everything else. Whereas it is beneficial to bow before a statue of the Buddha or invoke a guardian goddess, these objects of devotion are not ultimate and unconditioned. What then is ultimate and unconditioned? It is the Dharma as the truth of reality and nirvana as the unconditioned state of knowing that truth. The Buddha attested to this, and the sangha experiences and lives it.

The Ocean of Dharma As we saw earlier, before the Buddha died he counseled Ananda and the other disciples that they should hold fast to the truth (Dharma) as a lamp and a refuge, and they should not look for refuge to anything besides themselves. The Dharma is to be found in the word of the Buddha transmitted in the scriptures. Of course, the scriptures themselves are conditioned, but the Dharma is not. It is the eternal truth that transcends even this world age, taught by all the Buddhas and known directly by those attaining enlightenment.

The word *dharma* was taken into Buddhism from the broader traditions of India, where it came to mean, as in Hinduism, the universal ordering principle that penetrates everywhere and is operative in everything. As such, it is equated with things as they really are, and so the word *dharma* in Buddhism comes to mean ultimate truth, the knowledge of what really is. It is this truth that was realized by the Buddha when he reached enlightenment. Dharma is the truth about the way existence really is: the truth about the nature and function of the world, and the truth about liberation from the bondage of samsara. The story of the Buddha's enlightenment reveals the basic content of this Dharma. It tells how he saw the whole chain of his previous existences and then he saw the whole universe as in a mirror, with the operation of the law of karma and rebirth. He perceived the Four Noble Truths about reality. Finally, according to Ashvaghosha's account of his enlightenment, he realized the principle of "dependent co-arising" (*pratitya samutpada*) as the last step to enlightenment and release from samsara.

Dependent co-arising is essentially a doctrine of causality, showing the interconnectedness of everything. There is no god who causes everything, but it is also false to assert that everything happens randomly by chance. Rather, the truth is that everything and every event are caused by something prior in an interrelated process. Every condition contributes to the next, but it is itself conditioned by countless other determining conditions. This universal truth is often expressed in the well-known statement from the *Majjhima Nakaya*: "When that is, this comes to be; on the arising of that, this arises. When that is not, this does not come to be; on the cessation of that, this ceases."

Dependent co-arising is, thus, the most real knowledge about the world, and it is often simply equated with the Dharma—whoever sees one sees the other, and understanding it is tantamount to enlightenment. Since this Dharma was realized and taught by the Buddha, the Dharma is also often equated with the teaching of the Buddha. At the Deer Park in Sarnath, the Buddha first preached the truth and "turned the wheel of the Dharma."

The Dharma is not simply some mechanical law about reality. It is a transcendental principle immanent and operative in the world that is real, valuable, and normative; at the same time it is infinite and eternal. The Dharma is alive in a sense; how well the sangha lives out its vocation in the world has an effect on the Dharma. When unhappiness and trouble come upon society, it is assumed that the ruler and the sangha have disrupted the Dharma by unfaithfulness. When the future Buddha Maitreya arises, Dharma will be stirred up again so that humankind will again know and live the truth. When monks chant scripture for the laypeople, they are unleashing the power of the Dharma for the benefit of the people.

The Dharma is a central aspect of ultimate reality to Buddhists. It is not a supernatural being or god. But, as unconditioned truth, the Dharma takes on a character of awesomeness, protection, and deliverance. It should not only be respected but also worshiped and sought as a refuge. The hall of meditation in a monastery is often called the Dharma hall, the seat where the teacher sits is the Dharma seat, and the rule of King Ashoka is the reign of Dharma.

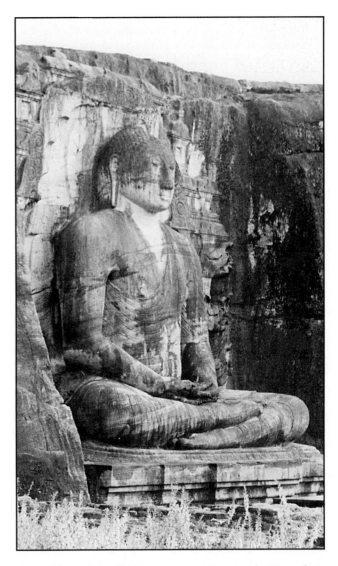

The Buddha in the meditation posture, a statue carved into a rock at Anuradhapura in Sri Lanka.

The Unconditioned State of Nirvana Closely related with the Dharma is the unconditioned state of nirvana. For those following the path in the sangha, the importance of the Dharma is that it brings the reality of nirvana; fully realizing the Dharma means achieving nirvana. Nirvana is not a place like heaven or the realm of the gods, for all of these are part of samsara and, thus, conditioned and impermanent. Nirvana is freedom from samsara and, therefore, is a permanent, unconditioned state. The Buddha speaks about nirvana:

> O bhikkhus, there is the unborn, ungrown, and unconditioned. Were there not the unborn, ungrown, and unconditioned, there would be no escape for the born, grown, and conditioned. Since there is the unborn, ungrown, and unconditioned, so there is escape for the born, grown, and conditioned.[1]

As in this description, nirvana is often described negatively, for it is unlike anything else in our human experience. But how can such a negative idea be thought of as ultimate reality? The fact that nirvana is often described in negatives has led some outsiders to think of it as annihilation or as unreal. But this is a misunderstanding, for the Buddhist tradition applies many positive concepts to nirvana. Edward Conze draws from various texts some of the things that can be said in describing nirvana:

> [in the texts] we are told that Nirvana is permanent, stable, imperishable, immovable, ageless, deathless, unborn, unbecome; that it is power, bliss and happiness, the secure refuge, the shelter and the place of unassailable safety; real Truth and the supreme Reality; that it is the Good, the supreme goal and the one and only consummation of our life, the eternal, hidden and incomprehensible Peace.[2]

Such descriptions contain many attributes that people of other religions might apply to God, and they show that nirvana does function as ultimate for Buddhists. Yet nirvana is not in any sense like God, for it is not a sacred power outside oneself, operating in the world. Nirvana is a reality experienced within, as it were, a state of unconditioned freedom.

Still, nirvana is real. It is eternal, absolute, unconditioned, and ultimate. Therefore, it is highly desired and looked to by every Buddhist as the supreme goal of human existence, even though it may be thousands of lifetimes away.

Emptiness and Suchness: Mahayana Perspectives Mahayana Buddhists go further in their view of the unconditioned real. Reflecting philosophically on the ultimate qualities of nirvana, they tend to emphasize terms like "**emptiness**" (*shunyata*) or "suchness" (*tathata*), which they see as positive and creative perspectives on the ultimate.

Emptiness is a complex and yet extremely simple perspective on reality. Early Buddhism taught that everything is a conglomeration of elements or "dharmas"; the chariot, for example, is only the sum of its parts and, therefore, not real, although its parts are real. A distinction was then made between all these **dharmas** or conditioned things, and the one *unconditioned* dharma, namely, the state of nirvana. But Mahayana philosophers began to teach that emptiness (shunyata) is actually the common predicate of all dharmas, whether conditioned or unconditioned. Emptiness means the *absence of "own-being,"* where "own-being" means something existing through its own power and having an immutable essence. So emptiness is really the same as the truth of dependent co-arising. But Mahayanists point out that not only are all conditioned dharmas (that is, the phenomenal world of samsara) empty, but also the unconditioned reality of nirvana is empty. This leads to the startling idea that, because both nirvana and samsara are empty, there is no essential difference between them. As the great philosopher Nagarjuna concluded, "Nirvana is samsara."

The fact that emptiness is a predicate both of nirvana and of samsara and that these two are, thus, identical, means a revaluation of living in the world. To Mahayanists, nirvana is not a state found by fleeing from this world, but it is experienced precisely within this world. There is a nirvanic quality that can be experienced in life if we but awaken to it, because of the emptiness that characterizes all reality. Nirvana is precisely awakening to emptiness, seeing the world as it really is in its "suchness."

So among Mahayanists, especially in East Asia, emptiness is considered a positive and powerful basis of reality. It is true that "emptiness," especially to Westerners, may sound like a lack or a deprivation. But actually it is more the supreme affirmation or fulfillment, for emptiness is really the codependence, the cooperation of all. Emptiness is actually the womb (*tathagata-gharba*, womb of the Buddha) that gives birth to all reality, the creative source of all that is. In more practical terms, it is the silence that surrounds and supports every sound, the stillness that is the foundation of all movement, the pure consciousness that is the ground of all thought.

So, what's it all about? The Dharma. Nirvana. Emptiness. These concepts together, all basically indefinable, point to the shape of ultimate reality in Buddhist thinking.

Going for Refuge to the Buddha

Along with the Dharma and nirvana, it seems that the Buddha has always had some place related to the Buddhist idea of ultimate reality. It should be clear by now that the Buddha, Siddhartha Gautama, is not God, although he did live as a god in one of the heavens in a previous existence. He is not "supernatural" in the sense of a power that comes from beyond to save people. The Buddha was, in his final lifetime, a human being like the rest of us humans, and he remained a human being for forty-five years after becoming the Buddha, until he died and reached the state of parinirvana, beyond existence and nonexistence. His great achievement was done at the human level and, thus, it is a goal that all living beings can reach, since all living beings have the possibility of being born at the human level.

The Perfections and Powers of the Buddha   Still, as a human being the Buddha was "supernormal," for he achieved all those supreme spiritual qualities that are far beyond the capabilities of most. Over countless lifetimes he reached the ten perfections, achieved miraculous powers, and attained complete omniscience, not to mention various other higher powers. Yet all these attainments and powers, which might appear to outsiders as possible for God alone, do not make the Buddha a god. Rather, they make him, still a human being, into the *Tathagata*, the "one who has arrived there," the victorious one, the very embodiment of the Dharma.

To put the Buddha in the proper perspective, we need to remind ourselves that there have been and will be other Buddhas in the infinite cycles of the rise and fall of the universe. And they will all reach the same perfections and powers and teach the same Dharma. The story of Siddhartha Gautama is the story of a being who, through a long series of lifetimes as a bodhisattva, made such spiritual progress that becoming a Buddha was inevitable, and he was born as a human at the time and place of his own choosing, to achieve the great breakthrough and become

the Buddha, the world savior to whom Buddhists in our world-age go for refuge.

So then, it is appropriate to chant in devotions every day, "Adoration to him the blessed one, the worthy one, the fully enlightened one." Whereas Buddhists know that the Buddha is not alive today as a god or savior, the powers he achieved are real and present in our world, symbolized by his images and relics, present in his words and teachings, experienced in meditation, and actualized in those who follow his path.

The Mahayana Vision: Dharmakaya and Heavenly Buddha   Mahayana Buddhists go much further than Theravadins in their visions of the Buddha reality. The ultimate reality seen in the Dharma, in emptiness, and in the achievement of the Buddha is brought together in the Mahayana notion of "Buddhahood," expressed especially in the **Three Body** (*trikaya*) teaching. The doctrine of the Three Bodies of the Buddha, as worked out by philosophers of the Yogacara school, is a way of formulating the dimensions of ultimate reality in terms of Buddha. There are three "bodies" (kaya) or dimensions of "Buddha": the Dharma Body (*Dharma-kaya*), the Bliss Body (*Sambhoga-kaya*), and the Transformation Body (*Nirmana-kaya*).

The idea of Buddha now moves far beyond the historical human Siddhartha Gautama, the teacher. The Buddha is really the eternal power of the Dharma. The *Dharma Body* of the Buddha encompasses all aspects of ultimate reality. Just as the Dharma is universal, eternal, and ultimate, so also is the Buddha. Just as nirvana is unconditioned and absolutely free, so is the Buddha. The Buddha is the same as suchness and emptiness. It is the Buddha-source identified as the Womb of the Tathagata, innate to all living beings, irradiated by the pervading power of Buddhahood. Mahayana thinkers, with their notion of a supermundane, universal Buddha essence, bring into Buddhism something like Brahman in Hinduism—an underlying ultimate reality. The Dharma Body is the fundamental Buddha-essence, which permeates and supports all things.

The human form of Buddha (*Transformation Body*) now is seen as a kind of magical-appearance body by which the eternal Dharma Body of the Buddha appeared in our age to lead humans on the path to enlightenment. Siddhartha was really an apparition that took on the characteristics of human life and reached enlightenment as a model and guide to other living beings in this age. Likewise, the Buddha reality has shown itself through Transformation Bodies in countless other ages and worlds. In the innumerable long periods of the past, says the *Lotus Sutra*, there have been an infinite number of Buddhas saving people, hundreds of trillions of kinds.

Furthermore, it makes sense that the Dharma Body, characterized by eternal, all-powerful compassion, should be manifest in bodies in all times and places in the universe, to respond to the needs of living beings everywhere. And so Mahayanists believe that the universe is filled with heavenly Buddhas (*Bliss Body* of the Buddha) who use all kinds of means to lead all living beings to enlightenment and salvation, functioning almost like gods and saviors.

One of the most widely worshiped of the heavenly Buddhas is **Amitabha** (Unlimited Light). Countless aeons ago, Amitabha was a monk named Dharmakara who decided to become a Buddha. He was taught by the Buddha for ten million years and practiced meditation for five aeons, concentrating all the qualities of Buddhahood on the creation of one Buddhaland, the Pure Land. He vowed that his Buddhaland would contain no evil destinies, that all those reborn there would be destined for nirvana, and that all who meditate on him could share in his merit and, thus, attain rebirth in this paradise. After practicing as a bodhisattva for a trillion years, Dharmakara became the Buddha Amitabha, presiding over the Pure Land of the West, sending out unlimited compassion to all who call on him.

Another important heavenly expression of ultimate Buddhahood is **Mahavairochana** (great Shining Out), widely worshiped as the sun Buddha. One view is that Mahavairochana is actually the cosmic Dharma Body of the earthly Buddha. Important especially in Vajrayana (Tantric) Buddhism, Mahavairochana's body is really the whole cosmos, and his mind and power permeate the universe.

Some Buddhists of the Pure Land school and the Tantric school look to Amitabha or Mahavairochana as the ultimate reality, virtually identical with the Dharma Body of the Buddha, and thus express a kind of monotheism or cosmotheism. But most Mahayana Buddhists recognize that these various heavenly Buddhas are not themselves the ultimate reality; rather, they are manifestations of the Buddha-nature in different times and places to help people with various means, leading them toward enlightenment.

We need to understand that since truth is experienced at different levels, Buddhism can include the worship of heavenly Buddhas and much more, including bodhisattvas, gods, goddesses, and a variety of local spirits. And this is true both in Mahayana and in Theravada lands. For many people these various divine forces are direct sources of help in various situations of need. For the spiritually advanced, these forces can be seen as expressions of the universal Buddha-nature or simply as divine beings operating within the samsara existence.

EXISTENCE IN THE WORLD

What is this world all about anyway? Such a question is often taken to refer to issues about origin and purpose. The *origin* of the world is not as important to Buddhists as is the *nature* of the world and of ourselves. Questions about origin and purpose could imply a beginning and an end, and Buddhists think more in terms of a beginningless, endless process. On this question the Buddha is reported to have said, "O bhikkhus, this cycle of continuity [samsara] is without a visible end, and the first beginning of beings wandering and running round, enveloped in ignorance and bound down by the fetters of thirst is not to be perceived."[3] Of more concern than the origin and purpose of life are the following questions: What is the nature of reality? And what is one's own nature? Long wrestlings with these questions have produced both deep intellectual speculations and single-minded practices.

The Nature of the World

Origin of the World and of Humans   Buddhists, like Hindus, think of the universe as virtually endless both in space and in time. According to descriptions in the scriptures, the universe is an incredibly vast *trichiliocosm*, three sets of thousand world-systems. Each world-system is full and complete in itself. Horizontally it resembles a platter surrounded by a ring of very high iron mountains, with vast oceans containing four inhabited continents, and at the center an enormous mountain called Meru. It is said that the diameter of the world-system is 1,200,875 yojanas, that is, about 10,807,875 miles across. Vertically, Mt. Meru towers 80,000 yojanas (some 720,000 miles) high and reaches equally far down into the waters. All 31 realms of rebirth are layered in this world, from the hells deep down through the animal and human realms on the continents, up the slopes of Mt. Meru with the realms of lower gods, and the realms of the higher gods far above the peak of Mt. Meru. Now, a set of a thousand such world-systems makes up a small chiliocosm, and a thousand small chiliocosms make up one large chiliocosm, and finally a thousand large chiliocosms make up the whole universe, the trichiliocosm—a mind-boggling one billion worlds in all.

Just as the universe is virtually endless in space, so also is time. One illustration, for example, says that the amount of time this universe has existed is innumerable times greater than how long it would take to wear down to sea level a vast, high mountain by touching it lightly with a piece of soft Banaras silk once every hundred years. The Buddhist traditions agree with the Hindu view that there are periodic creations and destructions of the universe, like the rhythm of waves on the sea. As the various worlds are destroyed and evolve again, beings are born from one into another because of karma. The Buddha told a story about this process in which he skillfully refuted the traditional idea of creation of the world through the god Brahma.

> There comes a time, my friends, sooner or later, . . . when the world is dissolved and beings are mostly reborn in the World of Radiance [one of the heavens]. There they dwell, made of the stuff of mind, feeding on joy, shining in their own light, flying through middle space, firm in their bliss for a long, long time.
>
> Now there comes a time when this world begins to evolve, and then the World of Brahma [a lower heaven] appears, but it is empty. And some being, whether because his allotted span is past or because his merit is exhausted, quits his body in the World of Radiance and is born in the empty World of Brahma, where he dwells for a long, long time. Now because he has been so long alone he begins to feel dissatisfaction and longing, and wishes that other beings might come and live with him. And indeed soon other beings quit their bodies in the World of Radiance and come to keep him company in the World of Brahma.
>
> Then the being who was born first there thinks: "I am Brahma, the mighty Brahma, the Conqueror, the Unconquered, the All-seeing, the Lord, the Maker, the Creator, the Supreme Chief, the Disposer, the Controller, the Father of all that is or is to be. I have created all these beings, for I merely wished that they might

be and they have come here!" And the other beings . . . think the same, because he was born first and they later.

> And it might well be that some being would quit his body there and be reborn in this world. He might then give up his home for the homeless life; and . . . he might attain such a stage of meditation that with collected mind he might recall his former birth, but not what went before. Thus he might think: "We were created by Brahma, eternal, firm, everlasting, and unchanging, who will remain so for ever and ever, while we . . . are transient, unstable, short-lived, and destined to pass away."

"That," said the Buddha, "is how your traditional doctrine comes about that the beginning of things was the work of the god Brahma." [4] So the idea of creation of the universe by Brahma is an illusion. Really, the world and all living beings, including the gods, go on through successive stages of evolution and devolution, without beginning, without end—in all the billion worlds that make up the trichiliocosm.

According to the Buddhist tradition, there is a typical pattern in this recurring process of world development. The *Aggañña Sutra* describes how, when this world-system begins to reevolve, certain beings, to work out their karma, fall from the Realm of the Radiant Gods (one of the heavens) to come again to this world. They are self-luminescent, made of mind, feed on joy, and move through the air. Eventually they begin to eat an earth essence and, thus, become dependent on subtle morsel food, their bodies becoming more substantial. Then they start eating a rice-pap sort of food, and male and female characteristics appear, and soon they indulge in sexual acts. They begin gathering and hoarding the rice and, thus, the earth-human society evolves to include private property with individual rice plots. This leads to stealing, lying, violence, kings, taxes, punishments, and so on, and our human historical era begins—over and over again.

The Real Nature of the World and of Humans   Like all the peoples from India, Buddhists accept the basic ideas of **karma** and **samsara**. There is a wheel of existence, both for the whole world and for the individual, and it is propelled by karma. But what is distinctive about the Buddhist view is the emphasis on **impermanence** and *no-self* as doctrines about the nature of the world, together with the underlying truth of dependent co-arising.

What is there to really hold on to in this world? Nothing. For there is nothing that is permanent, lasting, and absolute. Everything is impermanent, in a process of flux, coming into being and passing out of being endlessly. Even God and the gods, even the world itself, come and go. Even Brahman, central to Hindu belief as absolute reality, cannot be an eternal, unchanging reality. Whatever exists is a stream of becoming and fading. A beautiful, fragile blossom is often used to exemplify this view. It blooms in beauty momentarily, but then it is driven to the ground by the rain or wilted by the sun. That is not particularly tragic or to be regretted; that is the nature of existence.

One aspect of the doctrine of impermanence regards one's own self. What is the real self? From Hinduism we learned that inward of the empirical self is the real atman, eternal and indestructible, which is embodied in existence after existence but itself does not change. The Buddha says there is no atman (an-atman), no permanent reality we can call the self. Rather, that which we call the self or the person is really a changing process made up of a series of five *skandhas* or aggregates combined together for a lifetime. This process of aggregates includes physical matter, sensations, perceptual activities, impulses to action, and bits of consciousness. These aggregates come together for a lifetime, constantly changing, and they dissipate when the lifetime ends. Where, beyond these aggregates, asks the Buddha, do you see a permanent self? There is none.

For understanding the changing process of the world and especially the **no-self** teaching, it is important to remember the central Buddhist concept of dependent co-arising, which shows the interconnectedness of everything. Everything is conditioned by other things, but it is false to assert that everything happens randomly by chance. Thus, there is some continuity even in this world of change. For example, is an old man the same person he was when he was a baby? On the one hand, he obviously is not, for everything about him has changed since babyhood. On the other hand, he still is the same because of the common stream of conditions that has made him what he is.

So it is the idea of dependent co-arising that makes it possible to understand how there can be **rebirth** cycles and yet no permanent self. Hinduism teaches that the eternal atman passes from one lifetime to the next. The question for Buddhism is: What is it that goes through the rebirth cycles if there is no atman? The answer is that *nothing* goes through the rebirth cycles. Rather each rebirth is caused by the previous existences in a chain of causation. It is like touching the flame of one candle to the wick of another

Thai Buddhist monks outside Marble Temple in Bangkok.

and lighting it. Nothing is passed from the one candle to the next; there is no "candle-soul" or substance transmitted, yet the first burning candle is the cause of the burning of the second candle. It is the heat from the first flame that combusts the second candle, and likewise, it is the karma from one lifetime that "combusts" the next lifetime.

Whereas the highest truth about the world consists in these doctrines of impermanence, no-self, and conditioned co-arising, there is still ample reason to carry on life in the world in a constructive, beneficial way. That I am no real self is the highest truth, to be realized by those reaching high spiritual perfection. Yet "my" life-process goes on, interrelated with all other living beings, and further teachings about reality provide guidance on the ideal way to live. One important idea is the interrelationship of all things: all beings are one in the ocean of life. What affects one affects all. Another important facet of reality is the nature of karma. As explained by the Buddha, the law of karma has a volitional aspect; it is not the working of a merely mechanical fate, but it involves will and desire. I am who I am now because of past existences, but every moment I have the freedom to perform moral rather than immoral actions, thus changing the flow of karma and my own future existence.

Mahayana Buddhists, as we have seen, have additional things to say about the nature of the world and human existence. For example, Mayahana cosmologies envision

Buddha-realms throughout the universe, presided over by heavenly Buddhas. Since the essence of all reality is the Buddha-nature, the very truths of impermanence and no-self point to this. That is, the samsara cycle of birth and death is Buddhahood; all things interpenetrate all else, and all are the Buddha-nature. What is thought to be the self is illusory, but one's true nature is Buddhahood. So the goal in life is to realize the Buddhahood of the world and one-self. Whereas Mahayanists share the fundamental Buddhist outlook on the world, these additional doctrines give a somewhat different color to their view of the goal and the problem of human existence.

The Human Problem: Clinging

The evolutionary cycles of the world, the stream of karma and rebirth, the impermanence and interdependence of all things—these are neutral facts of existence. That's the way things are. So what's the problem?

The Truths of Suffering and Clinging   The problem, the Buddha said in his first sermon, is *dukkha*, suffering (the first Noble Truth). All existence is permeated with suffering. The Buddha was not a grim-faced doomsayer or even overly pessimistic about human life. He allowed that people do experience moments of happiness and joy. But there always is that sense of anxiety and uneasiness, knowing that we are going to lose what we have, knowing that finally we will lose even our selves in death. So the problem is a matter of how we experience our existence, constantly fearful of losing what is important to us.

Why do we feel this kind of suffering and anxiety? It is because of *clinging*, answers the Buddha (the second Noble Truth). We try desperately to cling and hold on to things like happiness, to life itself, to ourselves. But the truth is that there is nothing to cling to, since everything is passing, so we lose what we try to hold on to, and in the process we experience suffering.

Buddhists have gone to great lengths to illustrate these truths of suffering and the cause of suffering. Once, according to a poem by Ashvaghosha, a relative of the Buddha named Nanda became a monk but was about to leave the order because of his longing for his wife. The Buddha took him to the paradise of King Indra, a heaven of indescribable beauty where beings who had built up much merit as humans now live happily as gods, perpetually young and free from suffering. Beautiful celestial nymphs reward all who come to this paradise by virtue of their previous austerities. Seeing the ravishing beauty of the nymphs, Nanda forgot his wife, and the world of humans seemed to him no better than a cemetery. So, having seen this paradise, Nanda resumed his austerities in order to reach this reward. But his fellow monk Ananda warned him that living in paradise is only temporary, and that one day the gods there also will fall to be reborn on earth—and just think of the tremendous suffering they will feel because of the great delights and pleasures they will finally be losing! It is better, Ananda counseled, to strive for final release, for even the gods, with all their might, come to an end and fall.[5]

Trapped in Ignorance   Why is it that we are enmeshed in an existence in which we are constantly desiring and, therefore, constantly suffering? To account for the arising of these conditions, Buddhists apply the principle of dependent co-arising to human existence. They picture a series of twelve conditions of becoming, each condition causing the next condition. Frequently these twelve causes are pictured in the form of a twelve-spoked wheel, since there really is no beginning or end to the process. The hub of the wheel, the driving force, is made up of hatred, delusion, and greed. And the twelve groups of conditions are:

1 Ignorance, causing volitional actions
2 Volitional actions, causing consciousness
3 Consciousness, causing personal existence
4 Personal existence, causing the mind and the senses
5 Mind and senses, causing mental and sensorial contact
6 Mental and sensorial contact, causing sensations and feelings
7 Sensations and feelings, causing craving
8 Craving, causing grasping
9 Grasping, causing new becoming-forces
10 Becoming-forces, causing rebirth
11 Rebirth, causing aging and dying
12 Aging and dying, causing ignorance again

And the wheel rolls on and on. Buddhist art has developed a graphic form of this wheel, held in the claws and mouth of the demon Mara (Death), the ruler of samsara who tries to keep anyone from being liberated from this wheel of life.

Artistic depictions of the wheel of existence show how the wheel leads to the six realms or destinies of rebirth. The most degrading realms of rebirth are the hells (age-long but not eternal punishment), next the realm of the hungry ghosts, then the realm of animals. Fourth is the human realm, fifth that of the demigods, and the highest realm is that of the gods. Remember that even the gods, when their traces of karma run out, suffer death and lower rebirth, because they lack sufficient merit—and losing their heavenly joys causes indescribable suffering. In practical terms, only in the human realm can virtue and wisdom be increased, to proceed toward the goal, to transcend the wheel entirely.

So the whole wheel of life is really a trap, founded especially in ignorance, the delusion that I am a self and, therefore, I need things for myself. "I am—therefore I want." Our faint stirrings of morality, compassion, and goodness are quickly swallowed up by hatred, delusion, and greed, and the wheel of selfish existence rolls on.

To stop this wheel of existence takes something more than desire and selfish struggle—it takes getting on the path of transformation.

THE PATH TO NIRVANA AND BUDDHAHOOD

How can we start living real life? Where are peace and liberation to be found?

Paradoxically, the Buddha taught that the only way to find real life is to withdraw from life as we normally perceive it, to work toward cessation of those attachments that keep existence going. Some, therefore, have thought of Buddhism as a negative, world-denying religious path designed to lead to extinction. But that is to misunderstand Buddhism. The path leads to cessation of attachments so that true life and meaning can be experienced—that which is called nirvana or Buddhahood.

Nirvana and the Noble Eightfold Path

The human problem, as we saw, is depicted in terms of suffering caused by craving or clinging in a universe that is characterized by impermanence. At the heart of the problem

is human ignorance and the illusion of a permanent self. The Buddha described the human problem only to show the way out, the means of conquering and reaching liberation.

The Truth of Nirvana   In his sermon at Deer Park in Sarnath, after enunciating the first truth that human existence is suffering and the second truth that the cause of suffering is craving, the Buddha presented the third Noble Truth: "And this is the Noble Truth of the Stopping of Sorrow. It is the complete stopping of that craving, so that no passion remains, leaving it, being emancipated from it, being released from it, giving no place to it."[6] The suffering and frustration of our existence can be removed! They are removed by eliminating that which causes them, namely, craving. All craving can be eliminated by removing all the conditions on which it depends. The conditions on which craving depends are, we remember, depicted in the twelve-spoked wheel of existence: ignorance, wrong intentions, impure consciousness, the illusion of self, and so forth. Eliminating these conditions and, thus, eliminating craving will bring cessation of suffering. And this is the state of nirvana.

Nirvana, as we saw earlier, is not the extinction of existence, nor is it a state to be experienced only after death. Nirvana (blowing out, cooling off) is the experience of full life and meaning achieved by eliminating all forms of grasping and attachment. In an early Buddhist text, the venerable monk Nagasena helps King Milinda understand the reality of nirvana and the path that leads to its realization:

> That principle of Nirvana, O king, so peaceful, so blissful, so delicate, exists. . . . And if you ask, "How is Nirvana to be known?," it is by freedom from distress and danger, by confidence, by peace, by calm, by bliss, by happiness, by delicacy, by purity, by freshness. Just, O king, as a man being burnt in a blazing furnace heaped up with many faggots of dry sticks, when he has freed himself from it by great effort and escaped into a cool place, would experience supreme bliss—just so whosoever orders his life aright, he by his careful thinking will realize the supreme bliss of Nirvana, in which the burning heat of the threefold fire [desire, hatred, and delusion] has all gone out.[7]

Nirvana is complete freedom from conditions and limitations, permitting life to be lived in the full richness of the present moment, without fear or anxiety. Since the causes of bondage have been eliminated, one who attains nirvana will not experience further rebirths in the samsara cycle; the liberation is complete.

It sounds simple. But as we all experience over and over, eliminating craving is an awesome thing, and even the most painful results of our craving do not induce us to give up that craving. How can this state of nirvana be attained?

The Noble Eightfold Path   The Buddha was more concerned with practical spiritual results than with philosophical speculations about existence. He thought of himself as a physician or therapist. He showed people their symptoms (suffering), presented a diagnosis of what causes the suffering (craving), made a prognosis that suffering can be stopped by stopping the cause (nirvana), and finally offered the prescription: the Path.

Not all the Buddha's disciples were satisfied with this practical approach. The monk Malunkyaputta felt the Buddha had left unanswered a whole set of important questions, like whether the world is eternal, whether it is infinite, whether the self and the body are identical, and whether one who reaches nirvana exists after death. So he challenged the Buddha, saying that he would leave the monastic life unless the Buddha would answer these questions. The Buddha reminded Malunkyaputta that he had never promised to answer such questions, and further he pointed out that the questions rested on so many assumptions and distinctions that they could not be answered in a lifetime. But, most important, these questions are simply beside the point.

> Suppose, Malunkyaputta, a man were wounded by an arrow thickly smeared with poison, and his friends and companions, his kinsmen and relatives, brought a surgeon to treat him. The man would say: "I will not let the surgeon pull out this arrow until I know whether the man who wounded me was a noble or a brahmin or a merchant or a worker." And he would say, "I will not let the surgeon pull out this arrow until I know the name and clan of the man who wounded me; . . . until I know whether the man who wounded me was tall or short or of medium height; . . . until I know whether the man who wounded me lives in such a village or town or city; . . . until I know whether the bow that wounded me was a long bow or a crossbow; . . . until I know whether the shaft that wounded me was wild or cultivated; . . . until I know with what kind of feathers that shaft the wounded me was fitted; . . . until I know with what kind of sinew the shaft that wounded me was bound; . . . until I know what kind of arrow it was that wounded me—whether it was hoof-tipped or curved or barbed or calf-toothed or oleander."

All this would still not be known to that man and meanwhile he would die.[8]

This kind of speculation does not profit, nor does it have to do with the fundamentals of the religious path. Whether the world is eternal or not, there still remain birth, old age, death, and suffering. The important thing is to get on the Path.

The noble Eightfold Path sets forth a whole way of life leading progressively to higher levels of spiritual transformation. It consists in:

1 Right understanding } Wisdom
2 Right intention
3 Right speech
4 Right action } Moral Conduct
5 Right livelihood
6 Right effort
7 Right mindfulness } Contemplation
8 Right concentration

These eight norms are not separate steps, as if one followed the other in succession. Rather one should cultivate a way of life in which all eight norms are followed together, for each supports all the others. The eight are traditionally grouped in the three basic axioms of the path, namely Wisdom, Moral Conduct, and Contemplation.

First, Wisdom involves both some basic understanding of the nature of existence and also the intention to act in accord with this understanding. *Right understanding* would include knowing the four noble truths of existence, the doctrines of impermanence and no-self, the teaching of the conditionedness of all existence, and the like. Whereas understanding deepens as we follow the Path, some understanding is necessary to reverse our ignorance and motivate us to start on the path in the first place. This leads to the *right intention* of freeing ourselves from the conditions of craving by cultivating the virtues of selflessness, goodwill, compassion, and love for all beings.

Next, Moral Conduct results directly from Wisdom. *Right speech* is telling the truth, speaking in kindly and friendly ways, and saying only what is helpful. *Right action* means not killing or hurting living things, no stealing, and no wrong sexual activity; positively it fosters the welfare of all living beings. *Right livelihood* involves avoidance of occupations that bring harm to others, accepting only those occupations that promote peace and well-being.

Finally, Contemplation is made possible when all the other norms are in place, and it involves a steady discipline of mind that leads to awareness and insight. *Right effort* means achieving a strong will that prevents and gets rid of wrong states of mind and creates and develops wholesome states of mind. *Right mindfulness* means being carefully aware of what goes on in the body and in the mind, attentively mindful of all sensations, feelings, and thoughts. And, finally, *right concentration* is the attainment, through meditation, of higher stages of mental awareness by direct insight and enlightenment. Here all sense of self and selfishness drops away, and ignorant grasping is replaced by peace and total freedom. The "I am" conceit is rooted out, and nirvana is experienced.

The Practice of Meditation   As we can see, there are a great many practices and disciplines that make up the Buddhist path of transformation. There are steps here both for the beginning layperson and for the advanced nun or monk. The attainment of wisdom needs to proceed on many levels, reading the scriptures, listening to Dharma talks, practicing meditation, and other disciplines. Pursuing moral conduct means setting one's whole life in order, systematically removing the sense of selfishness that seems so naturally connected with speech, job, treatment of others, and all the rest. There is plenty to occupy oneself with for a lifetime—or for many lifetimes.

Among all these steps and disciplines, it is most characteristic of the Buddhist path of transformation to consider meditation to be an important means toward making progress on the path. There are different types of meditation, of course, as Buddhists point out. One type, called *samatha* or "calm" meditation, involves concentrating and focusing the mind on an object or idea, leading to the calming of the mental processes and even to higher states of trance and supernormal psychic experiences. Whereas this type of meditation can be useful, the movement of meditation that leads toward nirvana involves developing insight and awareness, for finally it is "seeing" reality as it really is (the truth of dependent co-arising) that brings the nirvanic experience. So the Buddha taught *vipassana*, "insight" meditation, an analytic method based on mindfulness, observation, and total awareness of reality as it is.

The Buddha suggested that such insight meditation might profitably deal with four areas of life: the body, the feelings, the mind, and intellectual subjects. For example, the meditator might simply become totally aware of the bodily breathing process, watching and observing every minute aspect of breathing in and breathing out. Or, again, the meditator might observe and become mindful of sensations and feelings. A Buddhist scholar, Walpola Rahula, explains the process and the goal:

> First of all, you should learn not to be unhappy about your unhappy feeling, not to be worried about your worries. But try to see clearly why there is a sensation or a feeling of unhappiness, or worry, or sorrow. Try to examine how it arises, its cause, how it disappears, its cessation. Try to examine it as if you are observing it from outside, without any subjective reaction, as a scientist observes some object. Here, too, you should not look at it as "my feeling" or "my sensation" subjectively, but only look at it as "a feeling" or "a sensation" objectively. You should forget again the false idea of "I." When you see its nature, how it arises and disappears, your mind grows dispassionate towards that sensation, and becomes detached and free.[9]

So through meditation one becomes totally aware of the operation of the mind, knowing the mind with lust as being with lust, the mind without lust as being without lust, the mind with hate as being with hate, the mind without hate as being without hate, and so forth, through all states of mind, cultivating total awareness and with it the cessation of attachment and clinging. Furthermore, one may meditate on the truths about reality—the Four Noble Truths, the five aggregates, and so on. By becoming totally aware and, thus, seeing reality directly as it is, one facilitates the cessation of clinging and false sense of self, moving toward the experience of nirvana.

Arhats and Laypeople on the Path   Following the Path is a lifelong affair, indeed, a many-lifetimes affair for all but the most spiritually advanced. Because of the disciplines involved, to follow the Path fully one must leave society and become a nun or monk. Among the monastic community, various levels of attainment traditionally were recognized. At a high state of spiritual perfection a monk or nun was recognized to be a "stream-winner," destined to have only a limited number of rebirths before reaching nirvana. Higher yet were the "once-returner," who will experience only one more rebirth, and the "nonreturner," who will achieve nirvana in this lifetime. The final stage was the arhat (worthy one), one who has already achieved nirvana and lives the completely enlightened, free life. Even though that traditional scheme may not be defined so precisely today, the goal held out is victory over the world, the elimination of the illusion of self, the attainment of nirvana.

What about the laypeople in Buddhism? How can they follow such a strict, detached religious path? In Theravada Buddhism, it is true, the laity cannot expect to reach the goal of nirvana without eventually becoming a monk or nun. But laypeople can still get on the path and cultivate the important virtues of generosity and moral conduct. Besides deepening their understanding and intention, such disciplines also build up merit to counterbalance their store of bad karma. Merit can bring about more favorable rebirths; sufficient merit can even bring about rebirth as a god. The final goal of such merit, of course, is a lifetime in which the pursuit of nirvana will be possible. But that may be a long way off, and in the meantime it is better to be reborn in a happy state than in a despicable state. Theravadin laypeople do perform rituals and practice meditation, of course, which also builds up merit.

Statue of a bodhisattva, probably Avalokiteshvara, from thirteenth-century Nepal. 'Bodhisattva'. Nepal; Early Malla period, 13th century. Gilt copper with inlays of semiprecious stones. H. 18 3/4 in. (47.6 cm). Photograph by Lynton Gardiner. The Asia Society, New York, Mr. and Mrs. John D. Rockefeller 3rd Collection.

The Mahayana Enlargement of the Path of Transformation

Whereas Mahayana Buddhists accept the basics of the path as described previously, their expanded vision of the sangha and the Buddha allows for additional possibilities on the path. Nirvana is understood as realizing one's Buddhahood, and this path is open to laypeople as well as monastics. The model to follow on the path is the bodhisattva rather than the arhat. And new possibilities of help from heavenly Buddhas and of realizing the inner Buddha-nature make this a much broader path of transformation. Yet it still is, we must remember, the same path of the Buddha.

Becoming the Buddha: The Broad Path Since Mahayanists believe the Dharma Body of the Buddha is the source and essence of all reality, the goal of the path can be rephrased in terms of realizing one's Buddha-nature. Furthermore, since Buddha-nature (or nirvana) is not a state apart from this life but is in fact identical with the samsara world, the goal is to awaken to the Buddha-nature of this very life. The basic problem, as understood by Mahayanists as well as Theravadins, is ignorance. We do not see the real Buddha-nature, and instead we cling to our illusory nature—and we suffer in this lifetime while creating an equally suffering future lifetime by our karma. How does one start living the real Buddha life?

The place to start is certainly the discipline of the Eightfold Path. But since the emphasis is on realizing the Buddhahood of all beings, the path stresses the awakening of the thought of enlightenment and the cultivation of compassion. Monastic disciplines are still important, but even laypeople can attain the realization of Buddhahood.

In a significant shift on the path of transformation, Mahayana Buddhists do not look to the arhat, reaching nirvana with great discipline and effort, as the supreme spiritual model. Rather, the Mahayana path is really the course of the bodhisattva.

Inherent in Buddhism from the beginning was an emphasis on compassion, the sense of oneness with all living beings. But monastic religion seemed to some to place a great emphasis on striving for individual salvation. The arhat is one who perfects himself or herself through spiritual disciplines, roots out all clinging, and finally attains nirvana, liberation from the sufferings of the rebirth cycle in which all other beings are trapped. Whereas the arhat cultivates compassion as a virtue, the ultimate goal is release from samsara. But the bodhisattva, according to the Mahayana vision, is a great being who aeons ago grasped the thought of enlightenment and took vows to work incessantly for the welfare and salvation of all living things, thus starting on the bodhisattva course. Through countless lifetimes, the bodhisattva cultivates the ten perfections, eliminates all defilements, and reaches enlightenment and supreme Buddhahood. But having reached the goal, the bodhisattva delays entering into nirvana, continuing in the rebirth cycle in order to work for the salvation of all beings, in accordance with the bodhisattva vow.

An important factor in the idea of the bodhisattva is the Buddhist notion of merit, which is built up by moral, selfless deeds. The bodhisattva builds up a tremendous amount of merit in his or her long course, especially in voluntarily being reborn in samsara even after reaching enlightenment. And this merit can be transferred to others in need, delivering them out of physical distress and even helping them to rebirth in one of the paradises. One bodhisattva vow says:

> With the good acquired by doing all this as described, may I allay all the suffering of every living being.
>
> I am medicine for the sick. May I be both the doctor and their nurse, until the sickness does not recur....
>
> May I be an inexhaustible treasure for impoverished beings. May I wait upon them with various forms of offering.
>
> See, I give up without regret my bodies, my pleasures, and my good acquired in all three times, to accomplish good for every being.
>
> Abandonment of all is Enlightenment and Enlightenment is my heart's goal. If I must give up everything, better it be given to sentient beings.
>
> I make over this body to all embodied beings to do with as they please. Let them continually beat it, insult it, and splatter it with filth....
>
> I am the protector of the unprotected and the caravan-leader for travellers. I have become the boat, the causeway, and the bridge for those who long to reach the further shore.
>
> May I be a light for those in need of light. May I be a bed for those in need of rest. May I be a servant for those in need of service, for all embodied beings.[10]

The bodhisattva may be born in the world, appearing as an ordinary person, to help others. Although she has penetrated to the true nature of reality, yet she appears like one of those who are blinded by ignorance. It is through her compassionate skill in means for others that she is tied to the world. For the bodhisattva vows that she will take upon herself the burden of all suffering: she resoves to abide in each single state of woe for numberless aeons, to help all beings to freedom. The bodhisattva pursues a path of transformation based on the cultivation of compassion, of sharing merit with others, as the highest virtue that finally transforms one. The path of the bodhisattva is a model for all, showing the infinite transformations ahead on the path and the shape of the final goal.

Two Ways on the Path Because of the idea of the universal Buddha-nature, in Mahayana there can be a number of approaches toward this path of transformation. It is possible, on the one hand, to practice meditation and see directly into one's Buddha-nature and the Buddha-nature of all reality. On the other hand, the compassionate nature of the Buddha reality makes it possible to receive help along the path from various bodhisattvas and Buddhas who are dedicated to the salvation of all beings. Frequently the path can be a combination of these two impulses.

Meditation plays an important role for many on the Mahayana path, as in Theravada. Practices of meditation are especially important in some East Asian Mahayana schools such as Tiantai (Tendai in Japan) and Chan (Zen). A special emphasis in Mahayana meditation is the realization of emptiness, that is, seeing the nirvanic quality of all reality. In Chan meditation, for example, it is felt that the main barriers to experiencing one's innate Buddha-nature are the mind-blocks that we normally place in the way. The mind is ever active, like a monkey flitting about from tree-limb to tree-limb, and so it creates a secondary dualistic reality that blocks the mind from seeing directly the Buddha reality. Therefore, by emptying the mind in meditation, the dualistic barriers are overcome and one "sees directly" the Buddha-mind. After all, if one's real nature is the Buddha-nature, then transformation occurs by overcoming the illusion of separate selfhood and awakening to the Buddha-nature within. In this sense, one can "become Buddha" even within this very body and life—that is, awaken to one's innate Buddha-nature and, thus, live life in a transformed way. And this awakening is available for all people, not only for monks and nuns, for all people equally possess the Buddha-nature.

The meditation practices of Vajrayana (Tantric) Buddhism have often focused on the potential each person has for realizing the inner Buddha-nature through ritual practices. In Tibetan Buddhism, for example, one important ritual technique is visualization. Since the cosmos is filled with Buddha-nature, it is possible through ritual meditation using sounds, movements, and pictures to visualize and so mentally create that cosmic Buddha reality and to identify oneself with it. In this way, one is transformed ritually and becomes one with the cosmic Buddha-nature.

The strong Mahayana ideas about the universal Buddha essence, the virtue of compassion, and the model of the bodhisattva mean that the path of transformation can include reliance on power from Buddhas as well as self-power for transformation and salvation. If one cannot follow the holy path of discipline and meditation to reach nirvana, and if one cannot even build up sufficient merit to hope for a better rebirth, there still is another way: one can rely on the power of the merciful Buddhas and bodhisattvas for help and salvation. This path has become very popular in East Asian Buddhism, both for laypeople and for monks and nuns.

This view is often associated with the notion that the world has degenerated progressively over the different ages and we now live in an age of increased evil and suffering. So the question is, how can we, sinners that we are and living in this degenerate age, have assurance of salvation from these lifetimes of suffering and evil? The Pure Land school would answer: have firm faith and recite the powerful name of Amitabha Buddha. If people practice this as a discipline and make it the center of life, they will receive spiritual assurances and growth in this life and salvation in paradise in the next life. Most Pure Land Buddhists acknowledge that rebirth in the Pure Land is not yet Buddhahood—but those reborn there will never again be born at lower states of woe, and they will achieve Buddhahood in just a few more lifetimes.

Can this "easy path" still be called Buddhism? Behind this path is the basic vision of Mahayana: all beings are one in the ocean of life, and merit achieved by one can be shared with others. Through faith the mind and heart lie open to the presence of the Buddha power. Reciting the sacred name actualizes that power and transforms us, breaking the bonds of past karma and bringing us to realization of the Buddha-nature. In these Mahayana Buddhist schools, the path of salvation is not a matter of an individual struggling on his or her own merits to reach liberation; it is rather a path in which the individual can tap into the communal resource of saving power made available through the supreme Buddha power.

We see, then, that the path of transformation in Buddhism is multicolored. There is the nirvanic path followed by Theravada monks and nuns, leading to arhatship. But the laypeople follow the karmic path of building up merit for better rebirths. In some Mahayana schools the path of Buddhahood-realization is followed through meditation and ritual. And still other Mahayana Buddhists follow the path of salvation through saving power. Though they seem quite different, one can still recognize the basic Buddhist accents in all these paths.

DISCUSSION QUESTIONS

1 Discuss the Buddhist sense of the ultimate as unconditioned truth. What is signified by "dependent co-arising"? What happens to God in this view?

2 What is nirvana? Should one desire to reach nirvana?

3 Describe the Mahayana notion of emptiness (shunyata). How can "emptiness" be a positive basis of reality?

4 What is the Mahayana teaching about the Three Bodies of the Buddha? Compare this with the Theravadin notion of the Buddha.

5 Describe Buddhist ideas about the origin of the world and of humans. Is there a creator of all this?

6 Explain the Buddhist teachings about impermanence and no-self. How can there be rebirth if there is no self?

7 What, according to Buddhism, is the basic problem in human existence?

8 Explain the workings of the Noble Eightfold Path, showing how it leads toward nirvana.

9 Describe the role of "calm" meditation and "insight" meditation on the Buddhist path.

10 What is a bodhisattva? How would you recognize one?

11 In Mahayana Buddhism, what are the two general ways toward realizing Buddhahood? Can one participate in both ways?

Buddhist Ritual and the Good Life

RITUAL AND DEVOTION IN BUDDHIST LIFE

To find new power for living, to get in touch with what is real, to make merit and progress on the path, Buddhists have a rich store of ritual practices, devotional activity, and observance of sacred times. While there is considerable variety in particulars across the extensive Buddhist lands and schools, the main features of ritual and devotion are recognizable and fairly constant.

First we should note that Buddhists have a strong sense of individual mindful effort as the means of transformation, and so Buddhist thinkers often express a relativizing attitude toward ritual and worship. The goal of ultimate transformation, that is, nirvana, can be reached only by individual discipline and mindful meditation, not by acts of worship or ritual directed toward sacred beings. Yet there still are many reasons and goals for worship and ritual in Buddhist practice, even for spiritually advanced monks and nuns. Many rituals are commemorative, remembering and respecting the Buddha and the great saints of the past. Rituals can also be expressive, a way of showing emotions of thankfulness, respect, and devotion to the Buddha, the Dharma, and the sangha. Performing such rituals can guide people in their practice of the path, and they can help to create the refreshed and peaceful mental attitude necessary for mindful meditation and meritorious action. Meditation itself often is performed in a ritual way.

Many Buddhists believe that ritual and devotion are also instrumental in bringing about blessings in life and even inner spiritual transformation. Devotional rituals can be beneficial in concerns like health, wealth, rainfall, coping with crises, passing through stages in life, and the like. And worship can contribute toward happy rebirths, because of the merit involved in making offerings to the Buddha and also because worship creates a favorable mental state—and it is the mental state at death that largely determines the nature of one's next existence. Sacred rituals like ordination as a monk, chanting the scriptures, and making pilgrimages can produce merit and help to bring about important inner spiritual transformation.

Central Rites and Ceremonies of Buddhists

The Structure of Buddhist Ritual　For all the variety of ceremonies in different places of the Buddhist world, there are several basic rites that Buddhists perform no matter where they are. They always include some form of giving or offering in worship. Making offerings with the proper attitude and motivation serves to bring merit, and it is especially appropriate to show homage to the Buddha by making offerings of lighted candles, flowers, water, and food. In Mahayana Buddhist communities, offerings are made before the images of the various Buddhas and bodhisattvas. Of course, the Buddha does not need or receive these offerings, for the state of parinirvana is beyond all this. But making the offerings brings merit for the future and blessings for this life; it reminds one of the Buddha and his teaching so as better to contemplate his attributes; and it helps on the way toward selflessness and compassion. Offerings are also made to monks and nuns to show honor and veneration and to bring merit.

Another rite that all Buddhists perform is bowing before the Buddha image, the pagoda in which Buddhist relics are kept, or other symbols of Buddhas and bodhisattvas. A person may bow to the rosary and to the cushion used for meditating. And parents may bow to their ten-year-old son who has just been initiated as a temporary novice monk. This ritual of bowing is not that of a humble sinner petitioning a holy God for pardon and blessing. Rather, it shows respect for the Buddha, the Dharma, the sangha, parents, teachers, and all beings on the path. By bowing a person experiences the truth of no-self, symbolically turning away from self-centeredness to the real Buddha-nature of compassion and love.

In their worship and ritual, all Buddhists use words of prayer, devotion, commemoration, and petition. For example, they often begin their devotion with the threefold recitation of the Three Refuges formula: "I take refuge in the Buddha, I take refuge in the Dharma, I take refuge in the sangha." A widely used Buddhist common prayer runs like this:

> I beg leave! I beg leave! I beg leave! By act, by word, and by thought, I raise my hands in reverence to the forehead and worship, honor, look at, and humbly pay homage to the Three Gems—the Buddha, the Law, and the Order—one time, two times, three times, O Lord [Buddha]! . . . By this act of worship may I be free from the four States of Woe [in hell, as an animal, a ghost, a demon], the Three Scourges [war, epidemic, and famine], . . . the Four Deficiencies [tyrannical kings, wrong views about life after death, physically deformed, dull-witted], and the Five Misfortunes [loss of relatives, wealth, health, proper belief, morality], and may I quickly attain Nirvana, O Lord! [1]

Since love and compassion are central to Buddhist spiritual life, in words of prayer they share merit with all others, especially wishing love for all beings:

> May all creatures, all living things, all beings, all persons, all individuals, all males, all females, all Aryans, all non-Aryans, all gods, all mankind, all spirits be free from enmity, from care, and from oppression. May they all live happily. May they all be free from trouble and adversity. May they all enjoy prosperity. May they all help themselves through the law of karma. [2]

Monks and nuns often chant words of scripture in ritual settings, releasing merit for the benefit of the whole community.

Meditation, of course, is one of the central Buddhist practices, especially for monks and nuns but also for spiritually advanced laypeople. Whereas meditation is not necessarily a part of all Buddhist worship and ritual, typically it is done in a ritual context. Before Buddhists sit to meditate, they bow to the image of the Buddha and perhaps to images of bodhisattvas and other masters, and they chant scriptures together. After meditating, they offer incense and bow

The great stupa at Sanchi in India. The gateway has important early Buddhist artistic depictions.

again. Whereas meditation takes one beyond outward ritual to the higher truths, the ritual context is beneficial for calming the mind and developing the proper will and intent.

Universally used objects of ritual attention include Buddha images in sculpture or painting as well as images of bodhisattvas, protective guardians, and founding masters. For some centuries after the Buddha's death no images of him were used. Instead people paid homage to symbols of the Buddha such as an empty throne, a pair of footprints, a wheel, or a lotus plant—symbols still used in Buddhist art. Later, Buddhists began creating images of the Buddha in many different forms and postures, and today people will almost always turn to such an image as they worship. Other widely used objects of worship include relics of the Buddha, such as the famous Buddha tooth at the temple of Kandy in Sri Lanka, and sacred tablets or scrolls inscribed with names of Buddhas, bodhisattvas, or mantras.

Daily Rituals and Worship Traditional, pious Buddhists usually have a small shrine in their home, perhaps a simple shelf with a small Buddha image and a vase for offering flowers. The first act in the morning and the last act in the evening is ritual worship, offering fresh flowers and/or food offerings, lighting a candle, bowing, reciting prayers, and sometimes saying the rosary of 108 beads.

Monks and nuns, on the path toward victory, of course, have a much more demanding ritual schedule throughout the day. Many of the common daily activities are accompanied with rituals of devotion and homage to the Buddha and the other sacred realities. Typically, from 3:00 A.M. until 10:00 P.M. there is a busy schedule of chanting scripture, meditating, making offerings to the Buddha, bodhisattvas, and founding masters, saying prayers, reciting the Three Refuges and the monastic rules, listening to talks on the Dharma, participating in the communal tea ceremony, and much more. Even daily work like gardening and cleaning can be ritual opportunity for spiritual transformation, as practiced especially in the Chan (Zen) monasteries of China and Japan.

One might also, as the need arises, perform ritual worship any day at temples or at street-side Buddhist shrines. Such visits might be part of one's daily routine, or they might grow out of personal needs such as a crisis at work, relief from sickness, showing compassion for an aborted infant, preventing senility in old age, and much more.

Holy Days and Festivals

The rhythm of renewal follows a regular pattern on certain days of the month and the year, with variances, of course, in different Buddhist lands.

The Uposatha Holy Day   Although Buddhists do not have a weekly holy day like Saturday or Sunday for communal worship, many do observe a similar type of regular holy day called *uposatha*. This rhythm is based on the lunar calendar, celebrating the days of the full moon and the new moon and, less importantly, the half moon days. On these days the monks and nuns have special observances, such as reciting the whole set of rules for monastic training and practice. And these are appropriate times for laypeople to visit the monastery or the temple for worship. This is not something required as a religious duty, and there is no demerit in not observing this worship—many good Buddhists only keep this day occasionally. But there is merit and benefit in going to the monastery or temple to

show respect to the monks and nuns, present food and other offerings, hear them chant scripture, receive the precepts, and listen to instruction. This is an opportunity for laypeople and monastics to meet together and share spiritual benefit.

These holy day observances provide an opportunity for some devout laypeople to live temporarily according to the rules of monastic life. A person who has a job and a family normally takes only the **Five Precepts** for laypeople (to refrain from taking life, from stealing, from wrong sexual relations, from wrong speech, and from drugs and liquor), but on this holy day the person can take the Eight Precepts, which include some of the additional precepts followed by monks and nuns (not eating after noon, refraining from music and entertainment as well as personal adornment, and not sleeping on a high comfortable bed). And the layperson can stay overnight in the monastery, practicing the discipline of a novice monk or nun, before returning to normal householder life the next day.

The Great Annual Festivals   Perhaps not a lot of Buddhists participate in the uposatha holy day, but the great annual holy days and festivals are central to the rhythm of religious life, providing occasions for many people to gather at the temples and holy places. These annual festivals often commemorate events in the life of the Buddha or the great bodhisattvas, and celebrating them provides an opportunity to renew the sacred story and make it real once more. Other festivals have to do with the seasonal changes in monastic life and with the veneration that is due to the ancestors. Among the most important and most widely celebrated festivals are the New Year's festival, the Buddha's birthday, the beginning of the Rainy Season Retreat, the presentation of robes to the monks, and the Ullambana festival celebrated in China and Japan.

In Theravada countries, the New Year comes at the end of the dry season and the beginning of new life in nature, falling in the month of April. It is a time of cleaning up, washing away the demerits of the past, and starting afresh. To begin the festival, houses are thoroughly cleaned, and scented water may be poured over Buddha images and over monks' and elders' hands. This may be followed by a carnival-like water festival, with water thrown good-naturedly on all. In some localities, sand stupas are built in temple precincts or on river banks; the dispersal of the sand the next day symbolically cleanses away the bad deeds of the past year. Then comes a time for rededication to the Buddhist path, worship at the temples, taking the precepts, and giving offerings. It is especially meritorious on this festival, as on other festivals, to set animals and fish free into enclosures or ponds where they will be safe from harm for the rest of their lives. Since the release of the animals is accompanied by a monk or priest reciting the Three Refuges and the Precepts, the animals become "children of the Buddha" and have increased advantage of better rebirths.

The **Birthday of the Buddha** is a joyful celebration, usually observed in May on the full moon day (on the eighth of April in China and Japan). In Southeast Asia, this is the grand festival of **Vesakha**, celebrating the Buddha's birth, enlightenment, and parinirvana. People decorate their houses with garlands and paper lanterns, and there are many displays of painting of the Buddha's life. Monks lead the people in circumambulating the temple or the Buddha image. In China, this festival is marked by the ritual of washing the Buddha image—a ceremony based on the tradition that the Buddha was bathed with scented water poured down by the gods after he was born. Another important ceremony is the procession of Buddha images, amidst the cheering and shouting of the people setting off firecrackers, burning incense, scattering flowers, and the like.

In Theravada communities, the beginning of the three-month **Rain Retreat** (*Vassa*) is an especially important sacred time. The practice of the Rain Retreat goes back to the Buddha's time in India, when monks gathered in caves during the rainy season for intensified spiritual practice. During the Rain Retreat, the monks and nuns stay at their home temples, dedicating themselves to study and meditation, and the laity present specially prepared candles to the monastery to burn throughout the retreat. Other special offerings of food, money, and items of personal use are also made to the monks. At the full-moon celebration marking the end of the Rain Retreat, the monks chant and meditate while wax drips from a burning candle into a bowl of water, which is then sprinkled on laypeople to bless them with the monks' merit built up during the Rain Retreat. This is followed by a festival of lights, when houses and monasteries are specially illuminated. During the month at the end of the Rain Retreat (October–November), the laypeople perform the ritual of presenting newly made yellow robes to the monks and nuns, together with other elaborate gifts. High government officials also participate in

these ceremonies, showing that the continued presence of the monastery is essential for the welfare of society.

A most popular Buddhist festival in China and Japan is the Ullambana festival (All Souls' festival) for ancestors, which will be discussed in Part 3. There are many special festivals held in sacred places in addition to these widely observed festivals. For example, the Temple of the Tooth in Kandy, Sri Lanka, has a big ten-day celebration in August, featuring a procession of great elephants carrying the precious relic of the Buddha's tooth. All over the Buddhist world, communities celebrate the birthdays or other special days of Buddhas and bodhisattvas. Pilgrimage to the sacred places often takes place in the context of festivals.

Rituals of the Changes of Life

Buddhist people, like other humans, have many special rituals for the critical passages in life. But the Buddhist spiritual path itself does not focus on human concerns like birth and growth and marriage; rather it is concerned with spiritual transformation in life and the critical passage of death.

Rites of Passage Throughout the Buddhist lands, families and communities observe many prebirth and birth rituals. Some rituals ensure safety during pregnancy, and others are directed to the health and welfare of the baby: the first head-washing, placing into the new cradle, naming, and so forth. Puberty and coming of age rituals are also plentiful and varied, reflecting the people's concern properly to initiate their girls and boys into adulthood in the family and community. These birth and puberty rituals are observed according to local tradition with little specifically Buddhist context, although monks and nuns may bring blessing to the family by their presence. Often these rituals are connected with indigenous traditions of worshiping the gods and spirits. For example, in Myanmar (Burma), birth rituals such as the ritual during labor to assure a safe delivery or the ritual of placing the baby in a cradle are accompanied with prayers to propitiate the nats (evil spirits) and to call for protection from the deva (gods). In Japan, a baby is presented to the kami (gods) at the local Shinto shrine thirty days after birth, and the coming of age ritual on January 15 is a colorful and joyous Shinto festival for young people who have turned twenty.

Likewise, Buddhist communities in different cultures have a great variety of marriage customs and wedding rituals. In a typical Thai wedding, the main officiant is a layman called a "spirit doctor," who summons the spirits to bless the couple and ties a piece of string around the wrists of the bride and groom, with relatives and guests following suit. This "tying of the spirits" represents the union of the bride and groom on both physical and spiritual levels, as well as the communal significance of the marriage. Chinese weddings focus on Confucian and Daoist rituals and values, symbolically transferring the bride from her own clan to her husband's clan. Most Japanese Buddhists turn to traditional Shinto wedding ceremonies, sealing their marriage by exchanging o-sake cups in the presence of the kami. Overall, then, these various wedding rituals have little reference to Buddhist concerns, and Buddhist monks and nuns do not usually attend the actual wedding ceremonies. They, of course, may be invited to chant sutras for the safety of the new home and to be fed by offerings from the family. Buddhists recognize that birth, growth, sexuality, and happiness in life are important, and it is all right to perform rituals dedicated to those gods and spirits who provide these blessings. But the world is transitory, and the deeper Buddhist truth teaches one to keep all this in perspective by cultivating detachment and preparing for a holy death.

More important, as far as Buddhists are concerned, are the rites of passage that focus on the higher truths. In many Theravada communities, the ritual of initiation of young boys into novice monkhood is one of the most important events of community life. The initiation corresponds to a puberty rite of passage, but its meaning is a spiritual transformation: The young boy becomes a novice monk for a temporary period. Typically this ceremony is carried out amid great festivities, the family inviting many relatives and friends for a joyful celebration complete with food, songs, dancing, and the like, in honor of the young prince decked out in his finest. In some Burmese communities, an ear-boring ceremony is performed for young girls at the same time as a coming-of-age ritual, although this ceremony does not indicate spiritual passage in the Buddhist sense. It is after all these festivities, when most of the guests have left, that the real ceremony takes place. Some monks assemble, the boy's head is shaved, and he takes the vows of the monastic life. Now he spends the night in the monastery and, when he goes out begging the next day, even his parents bow to him to honor his elevated spiritual

state. After a few days or weeks, the boy may return to normal life, but now he is spiritually an adult and may reenter the monastery sometime in the future.

All things are impermanent. So Buddhists believe they should keep death in mind always, and funerals are times to remember most directly the transitory nature of existence. Buddhists also believe that a person's rebirth is determined at least in part by his or her state of mind immediately before death, so preparation for death is vitally important. And if the departed person is reborn in one of the states of woe, as a hungry ghost or in one of the hells, it becomes important for the descendants to offer prayer and merit to ease the sufferings and make deliverance possible.

To help the dying person to a peaceful, unattached, calm state of mind, Buddhist devotions are recited at the death bed, and monks may come to recite sutras. Pure Land Buddhists recite the name of Amida Buddha over and over, on the basis of Amida's vow to save all beings who recite his name. After death the body is washed and the head shaved. Many friends and relatives come to call, and on the day of the funeral a Buddhist service is held in which the priests chant scriptures and burn incense. Then the body is taken in a procession to the crematorium or to the burial ground, and the memorial tablet may be taken back to the house and placed in the household shrine. A variety of rituals during the funeral may offer food to hungry ghosts, keep the soul of the deceased from returning to the house, and transfer the merit of the monks to the departed one. After the funeral, special rites are held on the seventh day and at regular intervals thereafter, including annual anniversaries of the death. Although rites for the dead differ widely among areas such as Myanmar, Thailand, Tibet, China, and Japan, they all symbolize that this most critical passage of life is taken seriously and affects everyone, the living as well as the dead. Hope for a favorable rebirth is a central concern. Yet at the same time, Buddhists believe we should think of the higher truth that our own life with its karma causes rebirth and that ultimate liberation from the rebirth and redeath cycle is the final goal.

The Great Spiritual Passage of Life   These natural passages of life have spiritual importance. But the highest passage in spiritual significance is that critical step of leaving normal life with all its cares and clingings, passing through the narrow passage to become a mendicant to follow the higher path of the Buddha. Ordination into the monastic life is, therefore, a very important community affair, and those who bear its expense build up a considerable amount of merit. Some Buddhist communities, especially in China, traditionally had a tonsure ceremony that preceded ordination. The candidate was accepted by a spiritual master, who performed the head-shaving ceremony and thus established the candidate as a trainee, learning the discipline to be a monk or nun. In Theravada lands, it is customary for ordination as a novice to come before full ordination. The novice takes the Three Refuges and the Ten Precepts in the "going forth" ceremony.

Full **ordination** (**upasampada**) as a monk or nun is a drastic step and not to be taken lightly. Much training and preparation are involved. For the ordination ceremony, there must be an assembly of at least ten monks. For women candidates, there must be an additional assembly of ten nuns—a requirement that contributed to the eventual cessation of full ordination for nuns in Theravada communities, when the numbers of nuns dwindled. In Mahayana regions, full ordination for nuns has continued to the present. The candidate, head shaven and dressed in a yellow robe, petitions the assembly for admission to the sangha. The candidate is questioned to ascertain that he or she is free from certain diseases, is of free birth, debtless, exempt from military service, at least twenty years old, and furnished with parental permission. The candidate then kneels and asks the assembly for ordination. Silence indicates assent, and the interrogation is repeated a second time. The proclamation is made: "If any approves, let him be silent. If any objects, let him speak." If silence follows three repetitions of the proclamation, the tutors announce that the candidate has received ordination, noting down the date and the hour of the ordination into the sangha, since seniority is determined not by age but by time of ordination. Then the new monk or nun is given an exhortation to the effect that from now on his or her four reliances are to be alms for food, old rags for clothing, the shade of a tree for shelter, and cow's urine for medicine.

Healing and Medicine in Buddhist Tradition

The Buddha's description of life as suffering (dukkha) pointed especially to the mental and psychological symptoms and causes: anxiety, unhappiness, and anguish, caused by ignorance, desire, and attachment. But the Buddha also taught that mind and body are totally interdependent, so that suffering involves bodily conditions also, and the path to the cessation of suffering (nirvana) brings healing and wholeness for the whole person. The Buddha called himself a physician, and he presented the Four Noble Truths in the form of diagnosis and therapy for suffering in life. So Buddhists have always considered their spiritual practices to be conducive to health as well as spiritual progress.

The central Buddhist practice of meditation, involving calming and emptying the mind, can promote wellness by reducing stress and engaging one's mental energies in the healing process. In traditional Buddhism, other spiritual and ritual practices for diagnosing and healing diseases were also cultivated, such as recitation of sutras and healing formulas, astrology and divination, use of amulets, and exorcism. Most traditional Buddhist societies had shamanistic healing practitioners, who usually combined Buddhist practices with indigenous folk practices. Buddhism as a religious path does not negate the usefulness of traditional indigenous practices, whether supernatural or natural, that are considered to bring benefits for living a healthful life in this world.

The diversity and multiethnic character of Buddhism prevented a single traditional system of medicine from developing. In India, Buddhists as well as Hindus contributed to the development of Ayurvedic medicine, and traditional medicine in Buddhist lands such as Sri Lanka and parts of Southeast Asia is influenced by Aryuveda. In East Asia, Buddhists have long participated in traditional Chinese medicine and its variant forms in Korea and Japan.

Tibetan Buddhists, with their unique culture influenced by the indigenous Bon religion as well as Buddhists from India and China, developed a system of medicine, complete with written texts, that has some similarities with Ayurveda. A central feature of Tibetan medicine is the theory that every form of existence depends on the interaction and balance of three energies or elements: space (movement), digestive energy, and material. Physical, emotional, and spiritual health is a state of well-functioning balance, whereas disease results from disruption of this balance. In diagnosing illness, the physician examines the whole appearance and mental-emotional state of the patient, also using a complex pulse reading as well as examination of the urine. Illnesses are treated with diet, herbs, yogic breathing exercises, massage, and moxa treatment (burning a moxa herb above the skin to apply heat), as well as religious rituals and spiritual disciplines. Spiritually empowered medicine can be obtained from lamas and monasteries.

Many Buddhists today, of course, especially those living in the West and in urbanized, developed areas of Asia, depend on Western forms of medicine, even while respecting some of the traditional methods. Even in using Western medicine, however, Buddhists have needs and concerns related to their beliefs and teachings, and they raise questions about certain uses of Western medicine. For example, Western medicine seeks to eradicate suffering, even by heavy sedation if necessary. Yet Buddhists feel that suffering itself has spiritual benefits, for it is the recognition of suffering that impels one to seek liberation by following the path. Furthermore, the idea of karma may lead Buddhists to take a resigned attitude toward sickness and dying. It is particularly important to have a peaceful and calm mind when approaching death, so Buddhists ideally want to avoid analgesics and sedatives so that their mind can be filled with wholesome thought, perhaps aided with Buddhist rituals and scriptures.

Certain modern medical practices, such as abortion, euthanasia, organ transplantation, and definition of brain death, raise special concerns for Buddhists. Since harming or taking life is contrary to the First Precept, Buddhists generally stand against abortion and euthanasia. Not only is killing involved, but also the natural working out of karma is thwarted. Western definitions of brain death are based on the assumption that the brain is the only determinant of life, but in Buddhist thought, life is interdependent with many other factors and conditions. Because they don't accept the brain-death definition of death, Buddhists have concerns about organ transplantation from still-living bodies. Yet, some modern Buddhists make the point that pledging to donate one's organs is a bodhisattva-type of act done out of compassion. They refer to the story about how the Buddha, in a previous lifetime, gave his own living body to be eaten by a starving tigress, establishing a model of great compassion.

Artistic Practice Among Buddhists

With its focus on escaping the world and reaching nirvana, it might seem that Buddhists would hardly be attracted to art's sensuous, earthy aspects. For example, monks and nuns vow to wear no ornamentation and to go to no shows or music. But Buddhists, like people of most other religions, have harnessed the various human creative activities to produce art expressive of the Buddhist vision of life. Though the emphasis is on enlightenment and nirvana, the path proceeds *through* human life with its many activities and arts. And the aesthetic expressions that most deeply and compellingly express the real meaning of human life are those that arise from the creative power of one who has awakened to the Truth by following the path.

Since the Dharma rests on the word of the Buddha, it is fitting that Buddhists have always cultivated the literary arts. From the very beginning up to the present the sacred words have been memorized, recited, reiterated, elaborated, written, chanted, and sung with an enormous inlay of artistic power and creativity. The narrative art has been especially important: the creation of stories about the previous lives of the Buddha, elaborations on the events in the Buddha's life, stories about many other Buddhas and bodhisattvas, and stories about saints to provide inspiration and a model to follow.

Poetry is another characteristic Buddhist literary art, for the sense of oneness with all beings and the immediacy of insight into the truth can be especially well expressed in a poem. From the earliest disciples of the Buddha come poems like this, from the collections called *Songs of the Nuns* and *Songs of the Elders*:

> I am thin
> I am sick & weak
> but leaning on my stick I go
> climbing the mountain
> I lay aside my robe
> turn my bowl upside down
> lean against a rock
> & smash the mass of darkness

Poems of early Buddhist nuns often describe their own very vivid personal experience that guided them to take up the nun's life:

> I was drunk with my beauty
> with my form & with my fame
> I was still with youth
> I despised other women
> I adorned this body
> for the delight of fools
> I stood at the whorehouse door
> like a hunter laying a snare . . .

today I went to beg for alms
shaven & dressed in robes
I sat at the foot of a tree
& attained to nonthinking
all bonds are loosed
human & heavenly
I have destroyed all drunkenness
I have become cool : quenched[3]

Poetry is a favorite art form in all cultures penetrated by the Buddhist path, in their various national languages. In Tibet, for example, the great poet Milarepa (1052–1135) is said to have composed 100,000 verses, expressing how his life experiences crystallized his enlightened sense of impermanence—contributing greatly to the Buddhist arts and also to the Tibetan national cultural heritage.

Probably the most characteristic Buddhist art form is the Buddha sculpture, omnipresent wherever there is a temple, shrine, or altar. In the early centuries, Buddhists refrained from creating images of the Buddha, possibly reflecting the transcendence of the Buddha, plus the practical consideration of educating the people not to worship him as they were accustomed to worship Hindu gods. The Buddha's presence was symbolized by motifs such as the throne of enlightenment, the begging bowl, his footprints, or the Bodhi tree under which he sat to attain enlightenment.

Beginning around the first centuries B.C.E. or C.E., artists began creating statues of the Buddha, illustrating different qualities of Buddhahood. The statues would be standing, seated, or reclining in the parinirvana symbolism, often with several of the thirty-two auspicious marks that designate a Buddha—such as elongated earlobes, wrinkles on the neck, or gold skin coloring. Many statues are truly colossal in a variety of media, chiseled in cliffs, cut in stone, cast in bronze, or modeled in clay. Most typical is the Buddha seated in meditation, legs crossed, on a throne, depicted in various local Indian, Thai, Chinese, Tibetan, and other styles. Such local styles concretely indicate the universality of the Buddha presence.

Of particular importance are the hand gestures (*mudras*) on the statue. Of the many gestures, these might be mentioned: the mudra of the fulfilling of the vow, with the palm lowered and turned outward in a gesture of offering; the mudra that grants the absence of fear, with the hand raised, palm facing outward; the mudra of appease-ment or teaching the Dharma, hand raised, palm outward, with thumb touching the end of the index finger; the mudra of touching the ground, with right hand pointing downward; and the mudra of concentration, with the hands in the lap.

A seated Buddha statue will often be placed on an altar as the central focus of devotion in a temple. Other statues will depict the Buddha in various postures—walking, standing and teaching, fasting as an ascetic, or reclining in parinirvana. In Thailand, for example, temples and shrines often have a set of statues of the Buddha in different postures, one for each of the days of the week.

Buddhist art includes sculptures and paintings also of the heavenly Buddhas and bodhisattvas of Mahayana, and also monks, masters, founders of schools, and guardian gods. One significant type of painting is the mandala, a symbolic depiction of the whole universe emanating from the cosmic Buddhas. These mandalas, used widely in Vajrayana for purposes of meditation, may typically focus on the great Sun Buddha (Mahavairochana) at the center, radiating outwards with Buddhas in all directions, the cosmos filled out with many more Buddhas and bodhisattvas.

Buddhist architectural expressions include the early **stupas**, royal burial mounds that housed the relics of the Buddha and many other artistic symbols. These memorial stupas developed to incorporate cosmic symbolism, such as the egg-shaped dome and the vertical axis or pillar. As a symbol of the Buddha's presence, stupas became objects of devotion, and later they were enclosed in a large hall, also providing shelter for worshipers. Shelters for monks and nuns were also added, and throughout the Buddhist world are found large temple compounds, with fitting architecture to serve the needs of both the monastics and the laypeople.

A grand expression of Buddhist architecture is the great stupa at Borobudur in Java, from the eighth century. It is a giant mandala in stone, representing the Buddhist cosmology, with its five square terraced galleries and its three upper circular terraces set with many perforated stupas and crowned by a solid stupa. The pilgrim path, representing the search for enlightenment, is adorned with more than two thousand sculptures. Throughout Buddhist lands, the Buddhist temple takes many forms, influenced by the different indigenous cultures, from the pagoda form in Southeast Asia to the massive temples of China and Japan that follow the pattern of imperial palaces.

The Sri Mahatat Temple in Bangkok.

BUDDHIST SOCIETY AND THE GOOD LIFE

How should we live? To be Buddhist is to take the Buddha's story as one's own, to find one's place in the community of those on the path of the Buddha, that is, the sangha, following the ethical precepts given by the Buddha.

Structure of Buddhist Society

The Sangha and Religious Leadership   In one sense the sangha is restrictive, focused in the community of monks and nuns. But in another sense it is wide open—open, that is, to all who genuinely search for the truth. The Buddha rejected the caste system of Hinduism and accepted people of all classes and castes and of both sexes into the sangha. The major requirement is that people enter voluntarily and in good faith, willing to dedicate themselves totally to seeking enlightenment.

The main purpose of the monastic community is to strive for nirvana. This means that the social ideal for

monks and nuns is radical world renunciation, for nirvana can be achieved only by the extinction of all attachments to the world and its vanities. It might seem that the sangha monastic community, the ideal social order for Buddhists, is antisocial in its very essence. The monk or nun rejects many normal social values, begs instead of working, does not marry or have a family, and cannot participate in politics or the defense of the community. If all people joined the sangha, there could be no society!

But the sangha does have a most constructive role in society. First of all, its very presence is a constant reminder to all Buddhists of the ultimate goal of the Buddhist path—to transcend attachment to the world and reach nirvana. Only a small percentage of the people in society join the monastic community, of course. But for all of the laypeople the monastic life represents the final goal of the path. Furthermore, the monks and nuns perform valuable spiritual services for the laypeople, even though they recognize this is not their primary function. For example, the temple-monastery complex contains halls where the laity can participate in the ceremonies and school buildings where the local boys and girls can be instructed. Monks and nuns regularly chant scriptures and perform rituals at the temple and in people's homes. The basic idea is that some of the purity and merit built up in the monastic life can be channeled into the community for the benefit of all.

In terms of religious leadership, Buddhist society focuses on the religious adept, the virtuoso who, like the Buddha, has experienced the truth at a high level and can thus be a model and illuminator for others. It is, of course, within the monastic community that these religious leaders are generally found. The social structure of the monastery is hierarchical, from the young novice at the bottom to the abbot of the monastery at the top. Seniority is determined by how many years the person has worn the monastic robes, with the abbot and the senior monks or nuns providing leadership for the monastic community. For the laypeople, the monks and nuns provide spiritual leadership by instructing, performing ceremonies, and chanting scriptures. In Mahayana communities, the ordained monks are often thought of as "priests" as they serve the local people in various ways.

Of particular importance, especially in the Mahayana tradition, is the "master" who founded the spiritual lineage and who passed on his authority to designated Dharma successors. The head of a monastery will be recognized as a Dharma successor of the founder, and he in turn may choose one or more monks or nuns to be his successors. The relationship between master and disciple is like that between parent and child, forming an important social structure within Buddhist religious society.

Outside the realm of "official" Buddhism, there are in some Buddhist lands additional religious specialists who perform a variety of rituals and exorcisms, dealing with the spirits and gods who affect the immediate welfare of the people. This has nothing to do with the goal of nirvana, so generally monks and nuns pay little attention to such things. But for the people involved with concerns of birth and sickness, marriage and wealth, such religious specialists can offer immediate help and benefit.

Women in Religious Leadership The Buddha made it clear from the beginning that caste, class, and gender differences are of no importance on the path, and he did set up the order of nuns for women who want to retire from social life and focus on the path. But his ambivalence in doing so has characterized women's status in monastic life ever since.

According to traditional reports, the Buddha's aunt Prajapati, who had raised him after his mother's death, made an earnest request that women be allowed to enter the monastic life, but she was sent away in tears. Even though the Buddha admitted that women as well as men can attain enlightenment, he denied Prajapati's request. It was only after his close disciple Ananda pleaded with him numerous times that the Buddha acceded to Prajapati's request and set up the bhikkhuni sangha, the order of nuns. But he also added eight stipulations designed to subordinate the order of nuns to the order of monks, so that even the most senior

nun would be inferior to the most junior monk. And he gave a dire prediction that the acceptance of women into the monastic life would bring about the early decline of the Buddhist Dharma. Scholars debate whether these stipulations actually came from the Buddha himself or reflect later views in the male-dominated monasteries. Yet it is abundantly clear that in all Buddhist lands, women, including nuns, have been subordinate to men and have had minimal opportunity for religious leadership roles. The idea gained ground widely in Buddhist circles and even in some texts that women have to be transformed into men or be reborn as men in order to reach Buddhahood!

Much of this subordination of women is surely cultural, deeply imbedded in the social practices of India, Sri Lanka, Thailand, China, Japan, and all the other societies that embraced the Buddhist path. But one unfortunate result has been lack of recognition and support for orders of nuns, and over the years nuns' orders have lapsed in most Buddhist societies. While full ordination for nuns has been retained in Buddhist societies related to China, religious women in the Theravada societies have had to be content with a kind of novice status rather than full ordination, thus not receiving the respect or economic support that should be due them as nuns.

Yet it remains true that the fundamental Buddhist perspective places women equal with men on the path, and there are many positive models for women's leadership in the Buddhist tradition. One such figure includes the feminine form taken by the great bodhisattva Avalokiteshvara in East Asia, that is, Guanyin in China and Kannon in Japan, widely worshiped as a savior figure by women and men alike. Another widely worshiped feminine figure is the goddess Tara in Tibetan Buddhism, a female Buddha known as the Great Protector. She is a personification of motherly compassion and mercy, close and available to all people no matter what their class or status. A popular Buddhist sutra, *The Lion's Roar of Queen Shrimala*, tells of Queen Shrimala, portrayed as an ideal layperson and esteemed teacher, teaching others about the *tathagata-garbha*, the inner Buddha-nature that all carry within themselves. In this sutra, the Buddha predicts that Queen Shrimala will attain enlightenment and preside over a great Buddha land.

The order of nuns, even with its checkered history, has had a strong impact on religious and cultural affairs in the various Buddhist lands. From early on some nuns received renown for their spiritual achievements, learning, and skill in teaching the Dharma. An early collection of poetry, *Songs of the Nuns*, preserves poems of seventy accomplished women practitioners. Some of the poems show that it was their experience as women that led them to enlightenment, and they sing of their liberation from former sorrow and attachment, their freedom from constraints of gender. In spite of deprivation and lower status in Theravada societies, courageous women in Thailand, Burma, Sri Lanka, and elsewhere have dedicated themselves to the religious life and served selflessly, often engaged in alleviating the sufferings of the poor and needy. In Tibet, there have been many well-known holy women who became siddhas, enlightened and highly respected spiritual masters. And there have been numerous outstanding and influential Buddhist nuns in Chinese, Korean, and Japanese history, as we will note in Part 3.

Today the Buddhist world knows many educated and able women sharing in religious leadership in numerous ways. Western Buddhist communities have taken the lead, with women in prominent positions as scholars, spiritual masters, and lay leaders. For example, it was a woman roshi, Jiyu Kennett Roshi, who founded the Shasta monastery in the United States. Change has come more slowly in the traditional Asian Buddhist communities, but there have been attempts to revive and strengthen the orders of nuns, and there are promising signs of women taking leadership roles among laypeople.

The Role of the Laypeople in Buddhist Society Buddhist laypeople generally do not focus on the *nirvanic* goal; rather, they pursue the *karmic* goal of a good life and better rebirths. This means they strive to live in accordance with the Buddhist moral precepts, which we will discuss on pp. 169–171. Laypeople, of course, participate in the various structures of society, including family life, economic activity, and politics, areas to be avoided by monks and nuns. One of the most important roles of the laity is to support and maintain the sangha, making it possible for the monks and nuns to strive for nirvana. Supporting those who are on the monastic path brings a good deal of spiritual merit. It might be said that, whereas in some other religions the clergy serve the people and help them reach transformation and salvation, in the Buddhist path the people serve the monks and nuns to help them attain nirvana. In the process, the people build up merit for their own benefit and better rebirths. The sangha, we might say, is the team struggling for victory on the field of the Dharma. The laypeople are the backers of the team, supporting them so that they can devote themselves fully to the struggle and reaping the benefits of having a victorious team in the community.

Buddhist Vision of the Good Life

So how should we live? Since the doctrine of no-self is fundamental to the Buddhist conception of existence, the ideal way of life would be one that demonstrates as little attachment to self as possible. This may sound like a negative approach to life, but really it aims to bring out the fullest potential. This task is not easy, of course, and the Buddhist tradition offers many guidelines and practices to help one move toward that kind of good life. It is recognized that not everyone is at the same grade of spiritual development, however, and so the ethical life needs to be expressed at different levels. While it is the same ethical life, the forms it takes differ somewhat for the monastic life and for the life of lay householders.

The Life of Love and Compassion Among the many traditional subjects for meditation for Buddhists is one that has to do specifically with relationship to others, that is, with ethics. This meditation is on the four "sublime states," which are (1) boundless love, (2) boundless compassion, (3) sympathetic joy, and (4) limitless equanimity. These four states give expression to the way Buddhists cultivate their own inner life with respect to others, and so they reflect the Buddhist ethical vision. They all spring from the enlightened wisdom that knows there is no separate self and that all beings exist in interdependence.

Boundless love (*metta*) is related to friendliness. But many of our experiences of friendly love are intertwined with feelings of need, dependency, lovability of our friend, and so forth. Buddhists cultivate love that is unconditioned and unlimited, based on the knowledge that all are one in the ocean of life. The well-known *Sutra on Boundless Love* states that one should direct one's thoughts by reflecting in this way:

May all beings be happy and secure; may their minds be contented.

Whatever living beings there may be—feeble or strong, long, stout, or medium, short, small, or large, seen or unseen, those dwelling far or near, those who are born and those who are yet to be born—may all beings, without exception, be happy-minded!

Let not one deceive another nor despise any person whatever in any place. In anger or ill will let not one wish any harm to another.

Just as a mother would protect her only child even at the risk of her own life, even so let one cultivate a boundless heart towards all beings.

Let one's thoughts of boundless love pervade the whole world—above, below and across—without any obstruction, without any hatred, without any enmity.

Whether one stands, walks, sits or lies down, as long as one is awake, one should maintain this mindfulness. This, they say, is the Sublime State in this life.[4]

If one has anger in one's heart, one takes it out on all, regardless of who or what they are. So also, when one's mind is filled with thoughts of boundless love, that love radiates out to all, regardless of who they are or whether or not they are deserving of love.

The second sublime state, boundless compassion (*karuna*), is the intense fellow-feeling one should have for all living beings who suffer pain, anxiety, ignorance, and illusion. It was Siddhartha Gautama's compassion that led him, after achieving enlightenment, to devote the rest of his life to teaching the way to liberation for the benefit of all beings suffering in the ocean of life. Compassion is knowing that when one living being suffers, we also suffer, for we are not separate from any being but are one with all. Mahayana Buddhists have raised this sublime state of compassion to a supreme virtue as displayed by the bodhisattva who takes a vow to devote himself or herself unceasingly to bearing the sufferings of others and sharing merits for the salvation of all others. Out of compassion the bodhisattva vows:

> All creatures are in pain, all suffer from bad and hindering karma . . . so that they cannot see the Buddhas or hear the Law of Righteousness or know the Order. . . . All that mass of pain and evil karma I take in my own body. . . . I take upon myself the burdens of sorrow; I resolve to do so; I endure it all. I do not turn back or run away, I do not tremble. . . . I must set them all free, I must save the whole world from the forest of birth, old age, disease, and rebirth, from misfortune and sin.[5]

Of course, this is the vow of the highly perfected bodhisattva. But then all Buddhists are "Buddhas-in-the-making"

(bodhisattvas), and so these sentiments of compassion can be cultivated by all.

Whereas compassion is sometimes thought to dwell on the negative aspects of human existence, sharing the suffering and pain of all, the third sublime state of sympathetic joy (*mudita*) moves one to seek out the prosperity and happiness of others and rejoice with them. Strangely, this is difficult to do, for in selfish inclination people seem more ready to gloat over the misfortunes of others. However, when the sense of our needy, grasping self is extinguished, we no longer need to feel superior and, therefore, can genuinely not only promote the welfare of others but also join in sympathetic joy in their material and spiritual happiness.

The final sublime state, equanimity (*upekkha*), is in the mind of some Buddhists the culmination of these four states. It expresses that sense of nonattachment to self and to the world that the arhat achieves by following the path of transformation and rooting out all desire and clinging. In terms of the ethical life, equanimity is that fundamental sense of impartiality that makes it possible to treat all others equally with love, compassion, and joy, with no aversion to them and no desire to win their approval. Unthreatened by the evil vibrations of others, not seduced by the bribes or temptations offered by others, one can radiate love, compassion, and joy to all beings equally.

Ethical Steps on the Path   These four sublime states portray a high-minded ethical vision of selflessness and giving. But is it practical? Who can live according to such principles in the real world? Buddhist teaching is above all practical teaching, and the emphasis is on the actual practice of these ideals. There are many scriptures that spell out practical guidance and concrete disciplines for the good life. The *Dhammapada*, for example, offers over four hundred statements to give direction in how to live. Here are three samples:

> "He abused me, he beat me, he defeated me, he robbed me"; the hatred of those who harbour such thoughts is not appeased.
>
> One should not pry into the faults of others, into things done and left undone by others. One should rather consider what by oneself is done and left undone.
>
> Conquer anger by love, evil by good; conquer the miser with liberality, and the liar with truth.[6]

To get a feeling for the practical dimension of Buddhist ethics, we can concentrate on the Five Precepts, recited often and respected as a model for life by all Buddhists. The Five Precepts are:

> To refrain from taking life;
>
> to refrain from taking what is not given;
>
> to refrain from wrong sexual relations;
>
> to refrain from wrongful speech; and
>
> to refrain from drugs and liquor.

Through these precepts Buddhist ethical ideals are put into everyday practice.

The principle to refrain from destroying life is especially central to the Buddhist vision; this is the principle of nonviolence (*ahimsa*), shared in common with Hinduism and Jainism. The concept of not taking life and not harming life does not apply only to human life but also to animal life, and so it has always been the Buddhist principle to refrain also from killing animals, even for food, thus making vegetarianism the ideal way of sustenance. It is true that, given the reality of the natural world order with its continual struggle for existence, some provision has been made in Buddhist teaching for laypeople to eat meat and even for monks and nuns to eat meat if it is received as a gift—provided that they did not see the killing of the animal and that the animal was not killed for their sake. But the positive side of the principle is important: One should do all possible to promote and support the well-being of fellow humans and of all living beings, assisting them, whether near or far, to live with honor, dignity, and security. It is particularly meritorious to save animals from harm and death by setting them free in a safe place.

To refrain from taking what is not given—that is, stealing—means also, of course, to avoid all forms of cheating or dishonest dealings to gain an advantage over others. Rather, putting away selfish motivations, one should share with them and promote ways in which they can lead a peaceful and secure material life.

When the Buddhist precept teaches to refrain from wrongful sexual behavior, it does not mean that everyone should totally avoid sex. That is true, of course, for monks and nuns on the higher path of perfection. But the Buddha had many lay followers also. It is expected that lay householders should indeed marry and have sexual intercourse in a rightful way. But the sexual impulse is one of the most powerful human drives and, therefore, it can easily upset one's self-control. It can lead one to take advantage of others, harming both them and oneself.

To refrain from wrongful speech goes far beyond just avoiding lies and only telling the truth. It does, of course, mean to avoid all falsehoods, because they are always harmful to others and to oneself as well. The Buddha said that there is no evil that will not be done by one who is not ashamed to lie. But right speech means also to refrain from all slander and recriminations that would bring about hatred, enmity, and disharmony among people. It means to avoid all abusive, harsh, rude, and impolite language, for this is offensive to others. And it means to stay away from all gossip, all disparaging of others, and all idle and useless babble. Avoiding these kinds of wrong and harmful uses of words, one's conversation with others will deal with the truth, with that which is friendly, pleasant, meaningful, and beneficial to others.

To refrain from drugs or liquor is important, for these tend to cloud the mind and make insight and awareness difficult, thus hindering one's progress on the path. Furthermore, intoxication can lead to reckless behavior and violence of various kinds to others, thus leading to the breaking of the other precepts.

These Five Precepts form an ethical guide to the kind of profession and social involvement that would be consistent with the virtues of love and compassion. Obviously one should avoid any activity that, directly or indirectly, brings harm to others. This would certainly include professions that have to do with harming and killing people, such as making or trading in arms and lethal weapons, serving in military forces, or even supporting the making of weapons and military actions by our taxes. Occupations having to do with killing animals are also to be avoided—slaughtering animals, hunting, working in leather, and the like. Since intoxicating drinks and drugs are harmful to the minds and lives of people, one should avoid activities that promote or use such harmful materials. It is not justified to claim only to be a middleman or to argue that what others do with what one has produced is not one's responsibility. To earn wages by engaging in activities that contribute to causing harm to living beings is inconsistent with the Five Precepts. Rather, one's personal livelihood should at the same time be service for the welfare of the community of living beings.

These Five Precepts are practical, down-to-earth principles for leading the good life of compassion, love, and fulfillment. In the wisdom of the Buddha, however, they are at
the same time steps along the way to transformation. The
more one practices these disciplines, the more it is possible
to root out clinging and become self-giving and loving.

Ethical Life for Monks and Nuns The Buddhist path of
transformation is such that one becomes a nun or monk to
pursue the higher stages—and, thus, there is a higher ethical life also, that of the mendicant. The basic principles of
boundless love, boundless compassion, sympathetic joy,
and limitless equanimity are the same, simply intensified in
practice. The main difference is that the monk or nun has
gone beyond normal society and practices a high level of
detachment from those material, economic, and social attachments that characterize life for laypeople. Yet the presence of these mendicants within society helps to set the
ethical tone for the community: they are the conquerors,
near to the goal, and their lifestyle is the model to approxi-
mate whenever possible.

The ethical life of monks and nuns is characterized first
of all by the Ten Precepts, which they take at their ordination as novices. The first Five Precepts are taken by laypeople also, but they are intensified by monks and nuns. The
Ten Precepts are to refrain from (1) taking life, (2) taking
what is not given, (3) sexual misconduct, (4) lying, (5)
drugs and liquor, (6) eating after noon, (7) watching
shows, singing, and dancing, (8) using adornments of garlands, perfumes, and ointments, (9) sleeping in a high bed,
and (10) handling gold and silver. These basic principles
are elaborated in the *Vinaya* scripture as the rules of discipline for monks and nuns. Over two hundred rules define
categories of offenses, prescribe punishments, and regulate
the conduct of the monks and nuns. The two dominant
ethical concerns are not harming life and sexual conti-
nence, but many other matters are dealt with as the code
defines the proper mendicant lifestyle.

The code defines the four most serious offenses that
warrant expulsion from the order: sexual intercourse, theft,
intentionally killing a human being, and falsely claiming
spiritual attainments. Many rules deal with improper sexual conduct; for example, a monk is put on probation if he
intentionally ejaculates, touches a woman, speaks sugges-
tively to a woman, urges a woman to gain merit by yielding

to a monk, or serves as a go-between in arranging a meeting between a man and a woman. Other serious offenses
meriting probation include false accusations against another monk, causing divisions in the monastic community,
and refusing admonishment from other monks. Some offenses require forfeiture and expiation, such as accumulating more than one begging bowl or buying articles with
gold or silver. There are quite a few offenses that require expiation, such as lying, stealing another monk's sleeping
place, digging in the ground, destroying any vegetable, taking animal life, drinking liquor, or going near an army
drawn up for battle. Whereas many of the rules may seem
trivial and quaint, taken together they shape a lifestyle designed to facilitate the rooting out of clinging and desire
and to promote love and compassion for all living beings.

Dharma Model for Society and the World

With the highest ideal being withdrawal from society and
the world, how do Buddhists have anything to offer for the
betterment of human society? The Buddha likened life in
the world to a burning house from which one should escape as soon as possible. Isn't it the Buddhist position just
to let the house burn itself down?

Of course, Buddhists, like other peoples, have a vision
for the betterment of society. It is true that much attention in the scriptures is given to the role of the monks and
nuns, and relatively little is said about laypeople and their
lives in society. But from the beginning the Buddha did
have lay disciples and he did give them guidance on life in
society.

Society in the Buddhist Model The earliest Buddhist
societal reform was the sangha itself. Whereas Indian society was stratified into the different classes, the Buddha accepted people from all classes to be in the sangha. He
argued that biologically all humans are of one species and,
therefore, the different classes were simply convenient des-
ignations for different occupations. When some Brahmans
tried to maintain the superiority of their class, he asked,
"Do the brahmans really maintain this, when they're born
of women just like anyone else, of brahman women who
have their periods and conceive, give birth, and nurse their
children, just like any other women?" And he went on to

assert that people from all classes can equally live the high spiritual life. He asked his questioner,

> And if [a person] avoids grave sin, will he go to heaven if he's a brahman, but not if he's a man of the lower classes?
> No, Gautama. In such a case the same reward awaits all men, whatever their class.
> And is a brahman capable of developing a mind of love without hate or ill-will, but not a man of the other classes?
> No, Gautama. All four classes are capable of doing so.[7]

The Buddhist view of ranks in society is summed up in this passage:

> No brahman is such by birth.
> No outcaste is such by birth.
> An outcaste is such by his deeds.
> A brahman is such by his deeds.[8]

Essential to the Buddhist vision for society is the fundamental principle that all types of people are equal and that honor depends not on circumstances of birth but on moral and spiritual achievement.

But what about life in family, in community, in society? Don't Buddhist masters seem to downgrade the importance of this? In one important discourse the Buddha set forth great respect for family and social life, saying that one should "worship" parents, teachers, wife and children, friends and counselors, slaves and servants, and ascetics and Brahmans. There should in fact be mutual honor and care and help from children and from parents, from students and from teachers, and so on. With respect to the relation between husband and wife, the Buddha taught:

> A husband should serve his wife . . . in five ways: by honoring her; by respecting her; by remaining faithful to her; by giving her charge of the home; and by duly giving her adornments. And thus served by her husband . . . a wife should care for him in five ways: she should be efficient in her household tasks; she should manage her servants well; she should be chaste; she should take care of the goods which he brings home; and she should be skillful and untiring in all her duties.[9]

The Buddha occasionally spoke about the needs of material, economic life. He clearly stated that poverty is the cause of immorality and crime; this cannot be suppressed by punishment, but rather the economic condition of the people needs to be improved. When a layperson asked him how laypeople can improve their welfare, the Buddha told him that there are four things conducive to welfare. First, a person should be skilled in his profession. Second, he should protect the income that he has earned righteously. Third, he should have good and helpful friends. And, fourth, he should spend reasonably, in proportion to his income, not hoarding and not being extravagant. But along with this, of course, the person should cultivate spiritual values, keep the precepts, be generous, and develop wisdom. Wealth is not bad, according to Buddhist teaching; in fact, proper care for economic security can be conducive to a peaceful and spiritually minded society.

What about political power and the necessary force to keep order in society? The Buddhist scriptures do not say a lot about states and government, but one text does put forth these ten duties of the king: he should be generous, of high moral character, sacrificing everything for the good of the people, honest, gentle, austere, free from hatred, nonviolent, patient, and not opposing the will of the people. A government based on these principles would surely contribute to a happy, peaceful nation. Actually, the great Buddhist King Ashoka (r. ca. 272–236 B.C.E.) put many of these principles into practice as he ruled according to the Buddhist Dharma, treating people with forgiveness, extending his kindness also to animals. One of Ashoka's edicts states: "For this is my rule—to govern by Righteousness, to administer by Righteousness, to please my subjects by Righteousness, and to protect them by Righteousness."[10] Describing how painful his earlier bloody conquests were to him now, Ashoka publicly declared that he would never draw his sword again for any conquest; from now on the only conquest would be that by righteousness. At the zenith of power, Ashoka renounced war and violence and turned instead to nonviolence and peace.

Following Ashoka's model, Buddhists often are pacifists, not abandoning the world to its self-destruction but seeking to conquer violence and terror by kindness and righteousness. While there are conflicts and examples of violence in some Buddhist societies today, generally Buddhists are at the forefront of movements for peace in the world. The Buddhist aim would be to create a society in which the ruinous struggle for power and supremacy is renounced and where hatred is conquered by kindness.

Spreading the Dharma to the World The missionary impulse in the Buddhist tradition derives from the Buddha himself, from the compassion he felt after his enlightenment as he surveyed the whole world and saw suffering, ignorant beings everywhere. He preached the first sermon and began the turning of the wheel of Dharma. And when there were sixty enlightened monks, he sent them out to proclaim the Dharma for the benefit of all, out of compassion for the world, for the welfare of humans and of gods. The human condition analyzed in the Dharma is universal, and the path put forth in the Dharma is universal—so the motivation to bring the Dharma to others naturally arises out of the Buddhist sense of compassion.

This does not mean that Buddhists are intolerant of other peoples' beliefs and religious practices. Many Buddhists acknowledge that the other world religions recognize something of the fundamental problem of human ignorance and clinging, and that those religions also incorporate many elements of the path of transformation in their own various ways. On one of his rock edicts King Ashoka engraved this message, referring to various sects within India:

> The Beloved of the Gods [King Ashoka] . . . honors members of all sects. . . . But he does not consider gifts and honors as important as the furtherance of the essential message of all sects. This essential message varies from sect to sect, but it has one common basis. . . . Whoever honors his own sect and disparages another man's, whether from blind loyalty or with the intention of showing his own sect in a favorable light, does his own sect the greatest possible harm. Concord is best, with each hearing and respecting the other's teaching.[11]

Not all Buddhists, of course, demonstrate this religious tolerance toward others as stated by King Ashoka, especially when threatened by aggressive members of another religion. One can point to numerous episodes of intolerance in Buddhist history, as in other religious history. But with their emphasis on love and compassion, and with their insight that it is finally the mind, not faith, that brings one to liberation, Buddhists have generally chosen the style of spreading the Dharma by rational explanation, practical advice, and personal example.

One important consideration for the spread of the Buddhist Dharma is the flexibility allowed in matters that religions traditionally focus on. There is plenty of room in traditional Buddhist cosmology for gods and goddesses, demons and devils, ancestors, nats, shen, gui, kami, and whatever other spiritual beings people believe they have to deal with to live a happy life. As the Buddhist path spread from people to people, many of the traditional religious practices were left intact—for finally they have little importance, positively or negatively, for the Buddhist path of liberation. Let the nat wives, the shamanesses, the exorcists, and the ritualists ply their trade and deal with the supernatural world for the material welfare of the people. The path of liberation is a different matter, and when one advances far enough in the Dharma one will find oneself beyond these gods and spiritual beings. Different concerns arise, of course, when religious claims for ultimate liberation and salvation are made on the basis of worshiping one supreme God, as in world religions such as Judaism, Christianity, and Islam. And so some Buddhists of today have entered into dialogue with members of other religions, showing respect and tolerance, yet affirming the ultimacy of the Dharma.

DISCUSSION QUESTIONS

1 With the Buddhist idea that mindful meditation is the means toward higher transformation, explain the meaning and purpose of worship and ritual practices.

2 What typically goes on in Buddhist ritual worship?

3 Describe several important annual Buddhist festivals.

4 Which passages in the human life cycle have the greater spiritual significance for Buddhists? Why?

5 Describe the ordination ritual (*upasampada*) for becoming a monk or a nun. Why is this so important to Buddhists?

6 Why do Buddhists find artistic expression through poetry particularly meaningful? Describe some ways of representing the Buddha through sculpture and painting, and explain what this means to Buddhists.

7 Why would Buddhists want to avoid sedation when approaching death? Why do Buddhists have concerns about certain modern medical practices such as abortion, euthanasia, and organ transplantation?

8 What is the sangha? How can there be both nirvanic and karmic goals on the path?

9 Explain how, according to the scriptures, the Buddha established the order of nuns and the additional prescriptions he set forth for them. Can you give any reasons why the Buddha would have subordinated nuns in this way, or why the monks would have reported that he did so? What effect has this had in the history of the bhikkhuni order?

10 Interpret the ethical vision expressed in the "four sublime states" used in Buddhist meditation.

11 Explain the significance of each of the Five Precepts in terms of the basic Buddhist ideal of non-selfishness.

12 What do you see as key precepts and rules that guide the ethical life of monks and nuns?

13 What basic principles of the Buddhist path do you think would be helpful for the betterment of human society?

KEY TERMS: BUDDHISM

Amitabha heavenly Buddha who presides over the Pure Land Buddha realm

arhat (Pali: **arahant**) "worthy one," a perfected saint who has reached nirvana and will be released from samsara at death

Ashoka great Buddhist king in India (r. ca. 272–236 B.C.E.), the "second founder" of Buddhism

bhikkhu, bhikkhuni Pali terms for Buddhist monk and nun (Sanskrit, bhikshu, bhikshuni)

Birthday of the Buddha joyful festival usually celebrated in May (in April in Japan). *See also* Vesakha

Bodh Gaya the place where Siddhartha Gautama attained enlightenment

bodhisattva being who is intent on becoming fully enlightened; in Mahayana Buddhism, one who reaches enlightenment but vows to continue rebirths in samsara to assist others

Buddha "Enlightened one"; Siddhartha Gautama (ca. 563–483 B.C.E.) became the Buddha for our present age

Chan school of meditation Buddhism in China, Korea, Vietnam, and Japan (Zen in Japan), influential in the arts

Dalai Lama head of the Geluk Tibetan Buddhist school, traditionally recognized as spiritual and political leader of Tibetans; the current Dalai Lama (b. 1935) is the fourteenth

dependent co-arising (pratitya-samutpada) central Buddhist teaching that everything is conditioned by something else, that all reality is interdependent

Dharma in Buddhist usage, the truth; the teaching of the Buddha

dharmas the most basic constituents of all phenomena

Dukkha "sorrow," characteristic of all conditioned reality as stated in the First Noble Truth of Buddhism

Eightfold Path the fundamental path toward nirvana as taught by the Buddha, involving eight interrelated practices: right views, right resolve, right speech, right conduct, right livelihood, right effort, right mindfulness, and right concentration

emptiness *See* shunyata

First Council of Buddhism held at Rajagriha shortly after the Buddha's parinirvana, where, according to tradition, the Buddha's sayings were recited and compiled

Five Precepts the basic Buddhist moral precepts: to refrain from destroying life, from taking what is not given, from wrongful sexual behavior, from wrongful speech, and from drugs and liquor

Four Noble Truths basic teachings presented in the Buddha's first sermon: the truths of sorrow, of the cause of sorrow, of the overcoming of sorrow, and of the path to follow

Four Sights sickness, old age, death, and a wandering hermit; seeing these motivated Siddhartha Gautama to seek enlightenment

Hinayana *See* Theravada

Huayan a Chinese school of Mahayana Buddhism based on the *Garland Sutra*

impermanence basic Buddhist doctrine that change is characteristic of everything that arises

karma "action," law that all deeds and thoughts, according to one's intentions, will have set consequences, including rebirth

karuna Buddhist ideal of compassion

lama "master" or spiritual leader in Tibetan Buddhism

Lotus Sutra important early scripture of Mahayana Buddhism

Madhyamika early school of Mahayana Buddhism that emphasized shunyata (emptiness)

Mahavairochana the great sun Buddha

Mahayana the "great vehicle," form of Buddhism that arose in India beginning in the second century B.C.E. and eventually spread to East Asia

mandala painting of cosmic Buddhas or a symbolic cosmos, used especially in Vajrayana Buddhist ritual and meditation

mantra powerful sacred words, formula, or verse chanted as a focus for meditation and devotion

mudra hand gesture or pose with symbolic meaning

Nagarjuna important philosopher (ca. 150–250 C.E.) of the Madhyamika school of Buddhism

nirvana "blowing out" the fires of life, liberation from suffering and rebirth, the spiritual goal of Buddhist practice

no-self (an-atman) the basic Buddhist doctrine that there is no permanent, absolute self

ordination *See* upasampada

parinirvana full nirvana; complete liberation attained at the death of a Buddha

Pure Land Mahayana school of Buddhism focusing on worship of Amitabha Buddha, with hope of rebirth in the Pure Land Buddha realm

Rain Retreat (*Vassa*) important three-month time of study and discipline for Theravada Buddhist monks and nuns, when lay people also make offerings and perform service for the monastics

rebirth belief that after a person's death, the accumulated karma will cause another rebirth to take place

samsara the rebirth cycle of existenc

sangha the communities of Buddhist monks and nuns

Shakyamuni a title of Siddhartha Gautama the Buddha: the wise one of the Shakya clan

shunyata "emptiness," Mahayana Buddhist teaching that all things are devoid of any substantial or independent reality

skandhas "heaps" or aggregates; the Buddhist teaching that a person is really a changing process in five aggregates: physical matter, sensations, perceptual activities, impulses to action, and bits of consciousness

stupa memorial Buddhist shrine or reliquary

Tantrism *See* Vajrayana

Tathagata title for the Buddha meaning the "Thus Come One," that is, the perfected one

Theravada "teaching of the elders," term for the early Buddhist tradition and practice still followed in South and Southeast Asia. Theravada is generally used in place of the term *Hinayana*, "lesser vehicle," a pejorative term that Mahayana Buddhists applied to the early Buddhist sects

Three Body Teaching Mahayana teaching of three dimensions of Buddha: Dharma Body (universal Buddha essence), Bliss Body (heavenly Buddhas), and Transformation Body (human manifestations of Buddha)

Three Refuges the ritual formula, "I take refuge in the Buddha, I take refuge in the Dharma, I take refuge in the Sangha"

Tiantai (Tendai in Japan) a school of Mahayana Buddhism in China and Japan, based on the *Lotus Sutra*

Tipitaka *See Tripitaka*

Tripitaka (Pali: *Tipitaka*) the scriptures of the Pali Canon of Buddhism, meaning "Three Baskets"; they include the Vinaya Pitaka, the Sutra Pitaka, and the Abhidharma Pitaka

upasampada ordination, important Buddhist ritual marking the beginning of life as a monk or nun

uposatha fortnightly Buddhist holy day when temple meetings for teaching, ritual, and meditation are held

Vajrayana Diamond Vehicle, the Tantric tradition of Buddhism especially in Tibet and Japan, using initiation, rituals, imagination, and sexual symbolism as spiritual practices leading toward liberation

Vesakha in Theravada communities, a grand festival in May celebrating the Buddha's birth, enlightenment, and parinirvana

Vinaya texts containing rules for Buddhist monastic life and discipline

vipassana central Buddhist meditation practice focusing on calming the mind and seeing true reality

Zen *See* Chan

Chapter 9

The Path of the Jains

Compared to the other religions that arose in India, the Jains are a relatively small segment of the population of India today. However, their values and practices are widely admired, and they have contributed significantly to Indian art, literature, education, and professional life. Significant numbers of Jains are now found among the general Indian diaspora population in Western countries. Many Westerners are aware of Jains particularly because of their strong advocacy of a vegetarian lifestyle and of the ideal of nonviolence.

SACRED STORY AND HISTORICAL CONTEXT

To call oneself a Jain means to participate in one of the world's most ancient religious paths. It means to follow the teaching and model of the **Jinas**, the "conquerors." The Jinas, also called "Ford Builders" (**Tirthankara**), are those who have conquered by reaching liberation from the wheel of existence and who show the way across the ocean of suffering. The most recent Jina in our present world cycle is **Mahavira**, whose story, though 2,500 years in the past, provides in a very direct way the model of life for Jains.

Mahavira Becomes the Jina for Our Age

Jains conceive of the universe as a vast structure subject to endless cycles of time, each cycle consisting of a progressive half-cycle and a regressive half-cycle. It is taught that twenty-four Jinas (Tirthankaras) will arise in each half-cycle as teachers, leading others to attain liberation. The first Tirthankara of our present half-cycle was Rshabha,

who established civilization, including the Jaina path. The twenty-third Tirthankara was **Parshva**, who lived in the middle of the ninth century B.C.E. and established an order of mendicants. Mahavira became the twenty-fourth and last Jina of our cycle, with no more to come for many thousands of years. He brought about certain reorganizations and reforms in the community that had been established by Parshva, thus setting up the Jain community in the basic form that has endured to the present time. Whereas Jains pay worship to all twenty-four Tirthankaras, it is Mahavira who is the most recent Jina and, thus, the central model for following the path.

Sacred Life Story of Mahavira   The stories about Mahavira differ slightly between the two main sects of Jainism, the **Shvetambaras** (whose mendicants are white-clad, that is, clothed), and the **Digambaras** (whose mendicants are sky-clad, that is, unclothed). But the general outline of his life is accepted by all, centering around the five auspicious moments that Jains still celebrate: his conception, birth, renunciation, enlightenment, and final death (nirvana).

Mahavira is said to have been born in 599 B.C.E. (modern scholars suggest about 540 B.C.E.) in northern Bihar, India, at Kundagrama near modern Patna, to parents of the Kshatriya (warrior) class who were followers of Parshva. His father, Siddhartha, was a warrior chieftain, and his mother, Trishala, was the sister of a ruler. Stories about his birth make it clear that this child was intended for a high destiny. For example, his mother had a series of fourteen dreams involving things like a white elephant, the rising sun, a lake adorned with lotuses, and an enormous heap of jewels, dreams that are still celebrated in ritual and art. Within the womb, the Jina-to-be showed the virtue of **ahimsa** (nonviolence), lying still lest his kicks should cause his mother pain. The birth was attended by numerous marvels and the child was named Vardhamana, "he who brings prosperity," as his parents' wealth had grown abundantly during his mother's pregnancy. Other names and titles were given to him later, especially Mahavira, "Great Hero." As a child he had remarkable spiritual power; one story tells how he calmed a terrifying snake with his own powerful courage and aura of compassion. He married the princess Yashoda and had a daughter (the Digambara sect says he remained a bachelor) and, even though he wanted to renounce the world, he fulfilled the duties of a householder until both his parents died.

When he was thirty, certain gods appeared and urged him to make the great renunciation, to pursue the path for which his many previous lifetimes had prepared him, telling him to awake and establish the teachings of the holy path for the benefit of all living beings in the universe. The story says Mahavira was adorned with garlands by the gods and carried on a palanquin to a large park. There he fasted, renounced all possessions, removed all his clothing, pulled out his hair by hand, and set forth on the mendicant path. The Shvetambara sect says he wore a loincloth for thirteen months until it accidentally caught on a thorn bush and was pulled off, after which Mahavira went about unclad. Mahavira's Great Renunciation is celebrated as a glorious occasion for all renunciants in Jaina communities even today.

He joined a group of hermits for a while, but then he came to believe one must practice a more severe form of asceticism to win release, and he went wandering about and practicing extreme austerities for the next twelve years. He begged only for the most minimal food, and often he practiced complete fasting, that is, abstaining from both food and water for long periods of time, sometimes as long as a week. Furthermore, he was convinced that a most essential practice was ahimsa, nonviolence toward every living thing. He walked carefully to avoid stepping on living things and did not travel during the four-month rainy season when the paths teemed with living things. Insects and other things gathered on his body and caused pain, but he did not wash or scratch so as to avoid hurting them. In the cold he sought out cold places to meditate, and in the heat he sat in the sun.

After twelve and one-half years of the harshest self-deprivation, Mahavira reached the highest enlightenment (**kevela**), the infinite, supreme, omniscient state, with full knowledge of all the world, past, present, and future. And,

thus, he became the twenty-fourth and final Jina of the present world cycle.

Jina Mahavira and the Jaina Community   Digambara stories say that after his enlightenment Mahavira was completely free from all defects of human existence—hunger, thirst, disease, and so forth. He engaged in no mundane activities but sat in omniscient meditation in a special hall created by the gods. Disciples were attracted to his victorious nature, and the Jaina community was thus established. Other stories from the Shvetambara sect say he preached to the gods, then converted three brahman priests who were offering a Vedic sacrifice. These were Indrabhuti Gautama and his two brothers, who with their followers were taken into the new order. Soon eight other Brahmans were converted, completing the inner circle of eleven chief disciples (ganadharas), who with their followers made up the Jaina community. Mahavira set up one of the first structured religious communities (tirtha) in India, with four orders: monks, nuns, laymen, and laywomen. By the time he died, Jain tradition says, the congregation had grown to 14,000 monks, 36,000 nuns, 159,000 laymen, and 318,000 laywomen.[1]

Whereas Mahavira primarily demonstrated for his followers a way of life to reach liberation, some basic teachings about the nature of reality and human existence guided his followers. Although the soul has infinite knowledge, bliss, and energy, because of actions the soul becomes enmeshed in karmic matter, which causes false views of reality and improper conduct and leads to embodiment at the level appropriate on account of the past actions. Fettered with karma of passion and desire, the soul commits more such actions, leading to more and more rebirths. Every soul passes through tens of thousands of incarnations, which may include fire, mineral, air, and vegetable bodies to animal, human, and god bodies. In most of these existences the soul experiences great suffering, and so the goal of liberation from the whole cycle is the most important thing, according to Mahavira's teaching. The path toward liberation involves an awakening of knowledge, faith in liberation, and conduct that will lead finally to that liberation.

Death of Mahavira and Life of the Community   When he was seventy-two years old, Mahavira passed into nirvana, thus becoming fully liberated, forever free of rebirth and embodiment, old age and death. And, thus, he became the model for all Jains ever since. All eleven of Mahavira's chief disciples attained enlightenment either during the master's lifetime or shortly thereafter. His closest disciple, Indrabhuti Gautama, was so deeply attached to his master that he could not attain this goal. On the last day of his life Mahavira exhorted Indrabhuti not to linger on the path, reminding him that human life is short like a dewdrop clinging to the top of a blade of grass. Now that Gautama has crossed the great ocean, why would he halt so near the shore? Mahavira died that day soon after giving this exhortation, and Gautama attained enlightenment also that very day.

The Jain story says that when Mahavira preached, his words took on a divine sound, and this divine sound was translated into the scriptures by the chief disciples, especially Indrabhuti, who passed them on through oral transmission. The main content was incorporated in the later scriptures called the **Agamas**, although there is some disagreement between the Shvetambaras and Digambaras over the scriptural canon. These scriptures provide Mahavira's teaching on conduct for monks and nuns, basic teachings, false doctrines to avoid, and exhortations for the laity. Many secondary scriptures arose in the course of Jain history, and Jains also composed numerous commentaries and philosophical writings interpreting the teachings of the enlightened Jina.

Historical Transformations in Jainism

The Great Division: Digambaras and Shvetambaras
After Mahavira's time, Jain communities spread south and west, and they were supported by a number of rulers. It is said that the first Maurya emperor, Candragupta Maurya (grandfather of the great Buddhist king Ashoka), fasted to death as a Jain adherent. But starting shortly after the time of Mahavira, differences of opinion over a number of points led eventually to a schism into two major sects. The dispute seems to have begun about 300 B.C.E., when one part of the mendicant community fled southward in the face of a great famine. After twelve years they returned, but they found that the northern group had prepared a recension of the sacred texts containing many things that were unacceptable to them. Furthermore, according to them, the "northern" monks had taken up the wrong practice of wearing clothes.

The full split came sometime in the first century C.E. The Digambara (sky-clad) group of mendicants insisted

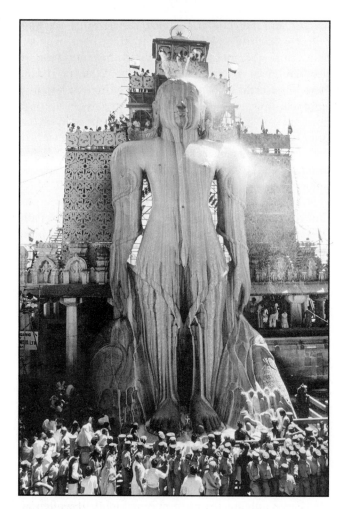

Colossal, thousand-year-old statue of Bahubali at Karnataka in Shravanabelagola. The statue is anointed every twelve to fourteen years in a great festival.

that the mendicant vow of nonpossession meant giving up clothing and going totally unclad as Mahavira reportedly had done, for clinging even to a loincloth is to be seen as a form of attachment. This group also insisted that women could not be allowed into the full monastic life; they can become monks and reach enlightenment only after rebirth as men. The other group called themselves the Shvetambaras (white-clad), holding that clothes are requisites for maintaining the mendicant life and are not possessions. The Shvetambaras allowed women into the monastic community and felt they also could reach enlightenment.

In fact, according to the Shvetambaras, the nineteenth Tirthankara, Malli, was a woman.

Eventually the two communities also became separated geographically, the Digambaras moving to the south and the Shvetambaras to the west. The schism between the two main groups has not lessened through the centuries, although there have been attempts at cooperation in modern times.

Jains and the Culture of India   In the course of history, Jains spread throughout all regions of India. They became assimilated with the people of the various regions in which they lived, greatly enriching these cultures with their own contributions. Jain adherents have tried to strike a balance between perpetuating orthodox faith and practice, on the one hand, and fruitful intercourse with Hindu society, on the other. Jains incorporated the legends of Hindu gods, such as Rama and Krishna, with appropriate adjustments to Jain values. They took over in a modified manner the use of mantras, holy fire, and rituals of the passages of life. Over the course of centuries they erected over forty thousand temples, many renowned for their architectural beauty.

To be a Jain means above all not harming any living thing—thus, there are some occupations that Jains avoid, occupations that involve taking life or making a profit from the slaughter of living things. So Jains have generally avoided being soldiers, butchers, leatherworkers, or even farmers. Because of this, Jains have tended to enter commercial professions, where their reputation for honesty and morality has made them quite successful. They have also made significant contributions to the public welfare by founding institutions such as public lodgings, public dispensaries, and schools. They have established libraries and contributed to Indian literature and philosophy.

The basic principle of nonviolence has become firmly embedded in Indian tradition, also in Hinduism and Buddhism, partly because of the persistent Jain adherence to this principle of ahimsa. Mahatma Gandhi, who successfully put this principle into practice in modern times in the movement leading to India's independence and brought it into the moral recognition of the whole world, acknowledged that he had been strongly influenced by Jains, especially the saintly layman Raychandbhai Mehta (1868–1901).

Tensions of Life in Today's World   Today it is estimated that there are some 3.5 million Jains living in India, with a significant number of Jains dispersed in the Western world.

Perhaps six thousand Jains are engaged in the monastic life as monks and nuns. Conditions of life in today's world, modernized and westernized, make it difficult to follow the rigors of traditional Jain life. And Jains, like people of all religions, worry that young people are drifting away from Jain identity and practice. Yet—even living in the West—Jains find ways to practice vegetarianism and engage in occupations and activities that promote ahimsa (nonviolence)—hallmarks of their traditional identity.

JAIN WORLDS OF MEANING

Ultimate Reality: Eternal Universe, Liberation

What's it all about? What is really the center that holds everything together? In their view of the universe, Jains appear to be decisively atheistic. Yet—as we have learned in India—there is not just one way. Many Jains also worship the Jinas and a number of gods.

Jains do not believe in a supreme being who creates and runs the universe. Rather, the world process operates according to its own innate laws, in world cycles of evolution and degeneration without beginning and without end. This eternal universe is real, with its laws of operation and its constituents of space, motion, rest, time, matter, and infinite individual souls. What is really central and permanent on the Jaina path is the pure state of blissful omniscience achieved by the soul that reaches complete liberation from the embodied condition of samsara. But even this liberation process is controlled by the laws that are inherent in the universe. According to the laws of the eternal universe, in each world half-cycle there will arise twenty-four Jinas, conquerors, who attain complete omniscience and, thus, can teach the truth for others to follow. In a sense, then, ultimate reality is the truth taught by those Jinas who attained this state of omniscience and liberation.

Since our world age has already seen its twenty-four Jinas, the last one being Mahavira, there will be increasing degeneracy until the end of our age. Thus, no one will even be able to attain enlightenment (the last one who did so was a saint who lived shortly after Mahavira).

Even with this worldview, Jain thinkers still talk about worshiping God—not a creator God but God as representing the totality of all the Jinas and other perfected souls. So it is proper to worship and venerate the Jinas, not as saviors who hear our prayers and help us, but as conquerors whose souls now enjoy the bliss of eternal liberation and omniscience. God is also worshiped under names such as Ishvara, Vishnu, Brahma, and Mahadeva. These gods, worshiped for various benefits, are souls who have attained rebirth in the god-realm but who still must in some future rebirth become humans in order to achieve liberation.

Karmic Matter and Eternal Souls

What is this world all about? The Jain view of the world resolutely rejects any creator or any beginning or end to the process of the universe. Jain writers through the ages have raised deep questions about a theistic idea of creation:

> If God created the world, where was he before creation? If you say he was transcendent then, and needed no support, where is he now? . . . If he is ever perfect and complete, how could the will to create have arisen in him? If, on the other hand, he is not perfect, he could no more create the universe than a potter could. . . . If out of love for living things and need of them he made the world, why did he not make creation wholly blissful, free from misfortune? . . . Know that the world is uncreated, as time itself is, without beginning and end, and is based on the principles, life and the rest. Uncreated and indestructible, it endures under the compulsion of its own nature.[2]

Jains believe that the eternal principles by which the world operates are congruent with the findings of the modern physical sciences. For example, the Jain worldview posits the operation of karmic particles everywhere in the world, and these karmic particles can be investigated and substantiated by modern particle physics.

The Jaina Universe and Human Existence   The Jain view of the world and human nature is very complex. Jains envision the universe, eternal and uncreated, as a vast three-dimensional structure, often pictured as a man or woman with arms and legs apart, with three levels. The lower level contains numerous hells, the middle level houses worlds in which humans and animals live, and in the upper level live the gods, who are always young and beautiful. Crowning the whole structure, beyond the celestial realms, is the crescent-shaped abode of the liberated souls. Surrounding the cosmic structure is absolute

nothingness. The complex physical structure of the universe is further complicated by the idea that the areas occupied by human beings in the middle regions are subject to endless time cycles. Each cycle contains a progressive half-cycle followed by a regressive half-cycle. The progressive half-cycle moves through six stages from an extremely unhappy to an extremely happy stage, and the regressive half-cycle moves through six stages from extremely happy to extremely unhappy. Only in the middle portions of each half-cycle—when conditions are neither extremely happy nor extremely unhappy—can beings be moved to seek enlightenment.

All existents can be divided into two groups: souls (jiva) and nonsoul (ajiva) entities. The nonsoul entities include matter, and also space, motion, rest, and time. Space contains an infinite number of immaterial, eternal souls whose essential nature is pure consciousness, bliss, and energy. But all these souls—except those who have attained liberation and dwell in the pure state in the highest realm—are embodied in matter and always have been so. Existence in an embodied state is accompanied by desire, which causes more karma to accumulate, leading to further defilement and endless embodiments in the cycles of rebirth (samsara).

The possibilities of **rebirth** are enormous, from the crudest life forms to the most exalted gods. The four main categories of birth destinies are as gods, humans, hell beings, and animals and plants. These four categories have from earliest times been illustrated in Jain art by the swastika-shaped wheel of life. The animal–plant category is almost infinite, including even microscopic creatures with only the sense of touch and single-sense organisms whose body is air, water, fire, or earth.

The Bound Soul: Karma   Why is one's soul bound like this? The Jain view of **karma** and how it affects the soul is distinctive among the religions, for Jains see karma as a subtle form of matter. The universe is filled with tiny imperceptible particles of material karma, floating about freely until attracted to an embodied soul. Because of its defilement, the soul's inherent energy creates vibrations that attract the karmic particles. Because of the passions of desire and hatred, the soul is "moistened" and the karmic particles stick to it, clouding its pure consciousness, giving rise to more desire and hatred, which attracts more karma, and on and on.

The influx of karma leads to an actual change in the soul, as drinking wine involves an actual alteration in one's internal chemistry. Some forms of karma cause the soul to become confused and desirous, whereas other karma obstructs the qualities of the soul, and still other types of karma bring about embodiment and determine the precise type of embodiment (whether the soul will be born human or plant, male or female, and so on) and also the duration of that embodiment. The effect of the karma depends on the type of act that attracted it. For example, if greed leads to robbery, the attracted karma will eventually cause loss of one's own possessions; and if I slander someone else, the karma I attract will cause me to be slandered sometime in the future.

The rebirths caused by the accumulated karmic matter adhering to the soul include not only the relatively pleasant life of humans and the blessed life of the gods, but also the untold lifetimes spent as hell-beings and as incarnations in animal, plant, even air and water bodies. The intense sufferings experienced by the soul in these unimaginably vast numbers of lifetimes are portrayed with deep feeling by the young prince Mrigaputra as he begs his parents to allow him to take up the life of a mendicant to cut the bonds of suffering once and for all:

> From clubs and knives, stakes and maces, breaking my limbs,
> An infinite number of times I have suffered without hope.
> By keen-edged razors, by knives and shears,
> Many times I have been drawn and quartered, torn apart
>   and skinned.
> Helpless in snares and traps, a deer,
> I have been caught and bound and fastened, and often I have
>   been killed.
> A helpless fish, I have been caught with hooks and nets;
> An infinite number of times I have been killed and scraped,
>   split and gutted.
> A bird, I have been caught by hawks or trapped in nets,
> Or held fast by birdlime, and I have been killed an infinite
>   number of times.
> A tree, with axes and adzes by the carpenters
> An infinite number of times I have been felled, stripped of
>   my bark, cut up, and sawn into planks.
> As iron, with hammer and tongs by blacksmiths
> An infinite number of times I have been struck and beaten,
>   split and filed. . . .
> Ever afraid, trembling, in pain and suffering,
> I have felt the utmost sorrow and agony. . . .
> In every kind of existence I have suffered
> Pains which have scarcely known reprieve for a moment.[3]

When we remember that one can only seek liberation when born on the human level, we realize that, passing up the chance in this lifetime, it may be millions of lifetimes before we again are born as humans. That's why Jains—laypeople as well as monks and nuns—are intent on following the path of transformation.

The Path of Liberation

How can one reach liberation? The Jain view of the human problem, as we saw, seems quite bleak: eternal souls trapped for millions of lifetimes because of karmic matter, born in material bodies mostly at lower levels full of suffering. There is a path of transformation available to all, however. This path consists of a process of purifying the soul, both stopping the karmic influx and expelling previously accumulated karmic matter, so that the soul can move upward toward the highest state of enlightenment (kevela) and ultimate liberation. There is no possibility that this can be accomplished in this lifetime, for according to Jain doctrine we are now in the degenerate part of this world half-cycle when no one can any longer reach enlightenment. Still, the consequences of passing up this human lifetime with no strenuous efforts at purifying the soul would be drastic, trapped ever again at lower rebirth levels. So there is strong motivation to follow the path, not only for monks and nuns but also for laypeople.

Jains reject the idea that a divine power from outside can help the soul, and they also reject the idea that the soul is hopelessly trapped with no possibility of changing its fate. Rather, the soul, even in its defiled state, retains certain capacities that can change the effect of the karmas, especially the central capability to start, under certain conditions, in the direction of knowledge and liberation. The soul has an innate tendency toward self-improvement, and time and again it progresses to higher states only to fall back again because of onrushing karmas. But, Jains believe, a moment can come when two factors coincide: the soul both is in a relatively pure state, and it encounters a set of outside conditions that activates the energies of the soul toward liberation—the outside conditions could be, for example, an encounter with a Jina or his image, or hearing the Jain teachings. That transforming event completely redirects the soul toward moksha so that, no matter how many lifetimes it may take, it never falls back; the bonds of samsara begin to unravel, and ultimate liberation is assured.

Once started on the ladder upward, the soul progresses on fourteen rungs (stages of purification) until it reaches ultimate liberation and pure consciousness at the top of the universe. Every embodied soul dwells at the first stage (ignorance) until the great shift occurs, the first awakening when the soul, blind until now, has its first glimpse into its true nature. The soul achieves certain attainments of knowledge and energy that eliminate masses of accumulated karmas, melting away like ice before a flame, and the soul, with growing insight and energy, eventually reaches the fourth stage on the ladder, the stage of true insight. The significance of this stage is that the soul now is irreversibly on the path to moksha. It will fall back to lower stages, for the deluding karmas have been suppressed but not entirely eliminated yet. But even in falling back, the soul retains true insight and will eventually make its way upward again. It is said that the soul that has reached true insight will remain in bondage no longer than the time it requires to take in and use up one-half of the available karmas in the universe—which may seem a tremendous time but really is tiny compared with what the soul has already endured. Before reaching this stage of true insight, following the religious path is not possible.

After reaching the stage of true insight, to progress further requires voluntary restriction of activities tying one to the material world, and for this purpose the Jains have two paths, that for mendicants and that for laypeople. The path for both is ascetic, and all focus their attention on the "three jewels" of Right Faith, Right Knowledge, and Right Practice.

To be a Jain monk or nun means to observe a whole series of **restraints** and other disciplines on a path of total renunciation. Monks and nuns take the five Great Vows or Restraints (*Mahavrata*), to refrain from injuring life, false speech, taking what is not given, unchastity, and possession—and they observe these restraints in total fashion. In the case of not injuring life, for example, nuns and monks extend this principle to *all* living things, even one-sense beings. Thus, they cannot dig in the earth, bathe or walk in the rain, light or extinguish fires, fan themselves, or touch a living plant—for all of these activities harm delicate one-sense beings who have earth, water, fire, air, or vegetation as their bodies.

Monks and nuns take on many such restraints and disciplines. For example, they possess only things like a begging bowl, a whiskbroom, scriptures, and a loincloth. Digambara monks remain unclad and carry no begging bowls. By ob-

serving all the restraints in a comprehensive way, they reduce activities in the world that would generate the influx of karmas and the rise of fresh passions. Rigorous meditation techniques are used to attain deeper insight, and finally, after a lifetime of such thorough disciplines, the monk or nun in ideal situations may attain the highest spiritual state of enlightenment, which is identical with omniscience.

But even then the last step remains to be taken: elimination of those activities that accrue to embodiment. Just before death the enlightened one enters a trance in which he or she stops all activities of mind and body, including even heartbeat and breathing, so that the soul, now freed from all embodied activity, may at the moment of death dart upward to liberation at the top of the universe, and remain there eternally free from all karmic bondage.

Laypeople follow a similar ascetic path but at an appropriately less rigorous level. They take twelve "partial" vows or restraints, among which the first five correspond to the five vows taken by mendicants: to refrain from violence, lying, stealing, illicit sex, and attachment to possessions. The other restraints include limiting the area of one's activities and also ritual activities such as meditation, fasting, and giving alms to mendicants. In addition to their ascetic disciplines, laypeople participate in rituals such as worshiping the Jinas, keeping holy days, and going on pilgrimages. Laypeople can progress spiritually until their religious disciplines are almost as rigorous as those of the monks and nuns.

RITUAL AND THE GOOD LIFE
Ritual and Worship Among the Jains

How can we find new power for life in our everyday existence? Jain teachers have traditionally taken a skeptical attitude toward ritualism and worship of the gods. Still, Jains live in the context of India with its long traditions of ritual, bhakti, and festivals. And so the Jain tradition recommends that people worship the Jinas, perform the rites of the life cycle and the festivals, and above all engage themselves in prayer and meditation. There is, of course, considerable difference between the worship life of mendicants and that of laypeople, but it is a difference of degree, not of substance.

Jains are sometimes called atheistic, and to some extent that is true, as they do not accept an ultimate creator god to whom they should direct their worship. How then can one worship, and whom does one worship? It is beneficial, according to Jain tradition, to practice the ritual of worship directed to the "supreme ones." These are not gods, of course, for Jains believe that final perfection can happen only at the human level. These worshipful ones are humans who have reached perfection or are well on the way toward perfection. The most important of these "supreme ones" are the Arhats, that is, the Jinas or Tirthankaras who have conquered and who are no longer to be seen in their embodied state. Statues of these Jinas are installed in temples to remind Jains of the spiritual attainments for which they are adored. These great ones can be worshiped—not because they hear prayers and grant favors but because it elevates one's soul to dwell on their ideal perfection.

It is also customary for the laypeople to worship gods and goddesses who control and protect various aspects of human existence. This kind of worship can be distracting, of course, since these gods are not ultimate. Yet many Jains do find it helpful to worship, for example, the guardian gods of the regions, Sarasvati (the goddess of learning), and the spiritual guardians who are attendants of the Jinas. It is true that there are influential subdivisions of the Shvetambaras, namely the Sthanakavasis and the Terapanthis, reformist groups that do not worship any images either of the Jinas or of the gods. Hence, their rituals are restricted to meditations, confessions, and so forth.

Daily worship (puja) for Jains involves bathing in the morning and repairing to the temple, standing respectfully in front of the statue of the Jina, reciting sacred formulas, and making some offerings of food or flowers. They may also say the rosary of 108 beads and devote a few minutes to the study of the scriptures. If more time is available, such as on festival days, devotees may bathe the image of the Jina with pure water and make more elaborate offerings, symbolizing the desire to attain eventually to the status of the Jina. Jains might conclude the daily worship with this prayer for peace:

> May Lord Jinendra bestow peace on the land, the nation, the city and the state, and welfare on all the citizens, may the rulers and administrators be strong, law-abiding and righteous, the rains be timely and adequate, all the diseases and ailments disappear, no one in the world be afflicted with famine or scarcity, with theft, loot, plunder and devastation, nor with epidemics, even for a moment: Peace to all!!![4]

Jains observe many fasts and festivals along with visits to temples and pilgrimages to holy places. Since the practice of austerities is important, there are various fasts, such as the important fast of Paryushana, which lasts for eight to ten days in the month of Bhadra (September/October). On these days the people assemble at the temple in the mornings, perform worship and study, and fast to their abilities—some taking no food at all for these days, others eating only once a day. It is especially important during these fast days to prevent any animal life from being taken. Other festivals include events such as the nine-day saint-wheel worship done twice a year by Shvetambara Jains, the birthday of Lord Mahavira (the only festival commonly celebrated by all sections of the Jain community), the day of worshiping the sacred books, and great Indian festivals such as Divali observed by Jains along with Hindus.

Holy places for the Jains are the beautiful temples built for the worship of the Jinas. In these temples laypeople can come near to the statue of the Jina, just as some in ancient times encountered a living Jina sitting in omniscient glory. The image can be a tangible aid to visualization of this sacred being, stirring up the soul for awakening. The most renowned temples are the lovely marble temples of Vimalasaha and Vastupala.

Rituals of the passages of life observed by traditional Jains are many. Shvetambaras list some sixteen ceremonies for the layperson, beginning with a ritual for the protection of the mother and the child in the embryo, and ending with the death rituals. Many ceremonies surround birth, naming, and tonsure of the child. The initiation ceremony comes at about age eight when the child adopts the cardinal virtues and becomes a student. The marriage ceremony, of central importance in the life of a householder, is generally similar to the Hindu rite. A person on his or her deathbed ideally offers final prayers, does repentance, and dies in meditation. The body is cremated and the ashes thrown into a river, while the family meditates on the transitory nature of life. No specific rituals (such as the ritual offering of food to the manes) in honor of the dead person are observed.

Jains, of course, practiced and contributed to the Aryuveda system of traditional medicine in India, and in modern times they have embraced modern medicine, with many Jains becoming physicians and medical practitioners. The basic principle of ahimsa (nonviolence) colors their approach to healing and medicine, most importantly in

Jain saddhus worhipping at the foot of the huge statue of Bahubali at Shravanabelagola.

been created from all kinds of materials, to be consecrated in temples and worshiped by the faithful. These sculptures—sometimes colossal in size, radiant in selfless contemplation, epitomizing the perfection of the saint who has conquered—provide the main focus for Jain worship and pilgrimage. Jain temples with their richly carved and sculptured pillared chambers have contributed significantly to Indian architecture and art. The way of Jainism, leading far beyond the world, still is grounded in the basic stuff of this world through ritual, art, and architecture.

avoiding any form of killing of animals or using animal products as food. Jains are strong advocates of total vegetarianism, arguing that the natural diet of humans is vegetarian, which can supply all nutrition and promote natural health. Meat products from animals bring fat, cholesterol, and harmful chemicals, harming not only the body but also the mind. In fact, according to Jains, even allowing violence into one's thinking can bring ill effects that disturb mental health as well.

The principle of nonviolence brings many concerns to Jains related to medical practice. Obviously, any medical procedure that harms life such as abortion or mercy killing cannot be condoned. And Jains work strongly to end practices of harming animals in medical research. In the complex modern age, Jains engage in interesting discourse over the practical employment of their principle of ahimsa. Do you think, Jains asked each other in a recent discussion, that viruses are living beings? The answer was left open for the time being.

For sacred times and rituals, Jains have created art and architecture that rank in the forefront of the cultural heritage of India. The most distinctive contribution is in the area of icon-making. Innumerable images of Jinas have

Society and Ethics

The Jain Community: Mendicants and Laity   The Jain community, which Jains believe to be the oldest continuous religious community in the world, has never grown large by standards of the other religions. Yet Jainism did survive in India and maintained its distinctive features, whereas the other non-Vedic movements (like Buddhism) did not.

One reason for the vitality of the Jain community has been the close association of the monks and nuns with the laypeople. Monks and nuns do not withdraw to monastic centers of learning far removed from the laypeople. Rather they stay in close contact and in effect simply practice a more radical and austere form of the same path that the laypeople are following. The role of the laity is to support the monastic community.

It is interesting that the number of women in monastic life has always been very high from the beginnings of the Jain community. Buddhists also, of course, allowed women into the mendicant life, but orders of Buddhist nuns have been very small in number, and the fully ordained order of nuns no longer exists in Theravada communities. As noted previously, the mendicant community founded by Mahavira contained two and a half times as many female ascetics as male. And still today there are more than twice as many Jain nuns as there are monks. It is true that, among the Digambara, nuns have a lesser status than monks since they cannot enter the state of ascetic nudity, but Shvetambara nuns take the same vows as monks do and are, thus, regarded as equal in status. Many of the nuns are widows who have entered the monastic community later in life, it seems, but the numbers still show a striking participation of women in the highest levels of the path to liberation.

Whereas the role of women in the Jain community differs from Hindu communities, some Jains (notably the Digambaras in the south) have adopted some aspects of the Hindu social caste system, especially the caste of Jain-brahmans. However, Jains interpret the origin of the castes not as stemming from the eternal order of things, as in the Hindu understanding, but as simply necessitated by events. According to Jain tradition, Rshabha, the first king and the first Jina of our world half-cycle, originated the organization of human society. All humans belonged to a single jati (birth), but Rshabha, while still a layperson, took up arms and became a king to curb the excessive lawlessness, thus establishing the Kshatriya caste. As he invented new means of livelihood and various arts and crafts, the Vaishya and Shudra castes also arose. It is said that Rshabha's son Bharata honored people who refused to walk on fresh flowers and sprouting grain by giving them the sacred thread and calling them divine Brahmans. In Jain society, those of the Shudra class generally have been excluded from the full mendicant life, but they can perform nearly all the lay ceremonies and can attain to a quasi-mendicant status.

How does one become a Jain monk or nun? The distinction between advanced laypeople and the mendicants comes about with the formal assumption of the great vows in the **diksha** (initiation) ceremony. The new monk or nun casts off all lay possessions and abandons his or her former name. The relationship between the laity and the mendicants is demonstrated in the initiation ceremony, which is supported financially by laypeople. Besides renouncing everything (even a loincloth in the case of a Digambara) and receiving a whiskbroom for gently removing insects, Jains enter the mendicant status by slowly pulling hair from the head in five handfuls. On the day following the initiation there is great excitement as the new monk or nun goes begging for the first time. The householder who provides these alms is considered to earn great merit.

The Jain View of the Good Life: Nonviolence   The Jain vision of the good, ethical life is strongly shaped by the underlying idea of karma, which attaches to the soul through certain types of deeds. The Jinas are the conquerors who by strenuous self-discipline, asceticism, and meditation, mastered the flesh, annihilated all karmic forces, and attained the highest spiritual perfection. The path they taught is for everyone to follow, and it involves the same kinds of self-discipline and asceticism practiced by the Jinas. Perhaps the best way to approach an understanding of Jain ethics is to consider the five vows or restraints taken both by laypeople and by mendicants—the laypeople observing them less strictly, the mendicants observing them with stringent completeness. The five vows are nonviolence, abstaining from falsehood, nonstealing, celibacy, and nonpossession.

Of these vows, the one that stands in the forefront of Jain ethics is nonviolence (*ahimsa*). In fact, nonviolence is the driving principle in almost every aspect of Jain conduct. It is intentional violence toward living organisms that causes karmic matter to adhere to the soul, so the most important ethical principle would be to abstain from such violence in any form. Violence is understood to be doing any kind of harm or injury to any living organism—including the billions of microscopic organisms of one or two senses. A distinction is made between violence done with intention and nonintentional violence; intention here means through selfish motivation but also through pleasure, wantonness, or avoidable negligence. It is permitted for laypeople to harm one-sense organisms (such as vegetable life), for the obvious reasons of providing food for society, but they are strictly enjoined from harming animals and, thus, they practice vegetarianism. Monks and nuns avoid doing harm to all organisms, even to one-sense organisms. For example, they carry a whiskbroom to clear the space on which they sit or sleep so they do not inadvertently step on microscopic creatures, and they strain their water before they drink it. Some orders of monks and nuns even wear a cloth over their mouths so they do not harm air bodies (one-sense organisms that have the air as their body) by sudden rushes of air while breathing. Many laypeople, too, will consciously avoid treading on growing plants, and they will never leave a vessel with liquid uncovered, lest insects rush in and be killed.

Nonviolence is not just something negative. One Jain saint, Samantabhara, said that nonviolence is the highest bliss known to beings in the world. Ahimsa (nonviolence) is the highest religion that has evolved in the world. Violence not only causes pain to other beings but also it results in calamity for oneself in this world and in future existences. But nonviolence brings blessings and bliss. It means showing benevolence toward other beings, feeling joy at the sight of virtuous beings, showing compassion toward the suffering, and displaying tolerance toward the ill-behaved. The Jain path is really the path of total nonviolence.

The second vow, speaking truthfulness, is related to nonviolence, since all lying is motivated by the passions and damages the soul. Furthermore, particular care should be taken not to use any speech acts, even if true, that cause harm or damage to living beings. This requirement, of course, may lead to complicated situations. For example, when asked by a hunter where a deer is, a layperson should probably mislead the hunter rather than cause destruction to the deer by his or her speech. Nuns and monks, of course, must observe this vow perfectly and, thus, could only keep silence in the face of the hunter's question.

The third vow is not to steal, that is, not to take anything not given, since doing so always arises out of greed and causes violence. Necessarily, then, a person should not engage in any activities involving gain at the expense of others, such as substituting inferior goods for the original, using underhanded measures, accepting stolen goods, and the like. Even finding and keeping something that has been lost by another person is wrong.

The fourth vow, sexual restraint, means for the layperson refraining from all illicit sexual activities, practicing moderation in sexual behavior strictly within marriage, and avoiding all types of sexual contact with persons besides one's spouse. As laypeople progress toward higher spiritual development, they may late in life take the more stringent vow of complete celibacy. Monks and nuns, of course, avoid all sexual feeling, since that is always accompanied by the passions, and avoid all sexual contact.

The fifth vow is nonpossession or nonattachment, and for monks and nuns that means giving up all possessions entirely—even clothing, as we noted, for monks of the Digambara sect. Merely thinking about possessions is damaging to the soul. For laypeople, some possessions are necessary for the welfare of society in general, but one should not be overly attached to one's possessions. Rather, people should impose restrictions on themselves so as to check their greediness; ideally, once they have the amount of pos-

sessions they need for a decent life, they should voluntarily refrain from further acquisitions. If they accumulate more than they need, they are enjoined to use it for charities, distribution of medicines, the spread of knowledge, and feeding the poor and hungry.

Welfare of the World   Jainism envisions a human society based on the central principle of nonviolence with its related corollaries. Whereas ethical practice is primarily directed toward the end of perfecting the soul and finally reaching liberation, Jains have always been concerned about the welfare of the whole society and of the entire ecological sphere with its countless billions of living organisms. Some modern Jain thinkers have pointed out that the basic Jain principles of nonviolence can make a great contribution to world society. The Jain ethical vision has an answer to the modern problems of racism, economic inequality, the inadequacies of both capitalism and communism, the disastrous destruction of our ecology, modern sexual exploitation, overpopulation, intolerance, and above all, warfare.

Jains are not missionaries out to convert the world. But leading thinkers clearly articulate for all thinking people the universal benefit of following the Jain principles, as in these words of Jyotiprasad Jain:

> And, it is today, more than ever, when suspicion and distrust are vitiating the atmosphere of international peace and brotherhood, when the world is filled with fear and hate, that we require a living philosophy which will help us to discard them and recover ourselves. Such a living wholesome philosophy, bearing the message of love and goodwill, ahimsa and peace, internal as well as external, personal as well as universal, is the Jaina philosophy of life. It is this system of Jaina religion, thought and culture that stands for the highest and noblest human values, moral elevation and spiritual uplift, eternal and universal peace and happiness.[5]

DISCUSSION QUESTIONS

1 What is a Jina or Tirthankara?
2 Describe how Mahavira became a Jina. Why is his story, of all the Jinas, of particular importance to the Jains?
3 Describe the two major mendicant groups within Jainism.
4 What is the Jain conception of the universe? Does this view seem to you in accord with modern science?

5 Describe the particular Jain notion of the working of karmic particles.
6 What insights into the Jain perspective do you find in the poem by young prince Mrigaputra?
7 How does the soul move upward on the path of transformation?
8 Show how the practice of nonviolence (ahimsa) is central to Jain life.
9 Do you think Jainism has answers for some of the crucial problems in the world today?

KEY TERMS: JAINISM

Agamas main scriptures of the Jains
ahimsa "nonviolence," one of the most important Jain principles; also emphasized in Buddhism and Hinduism
Digambara "sky-clad," renouncing the use of clothing; one of the two major groups among the Jains
diksa initiation ceremony for Jain monks and nuns
Jina "conqueror," Jain idea of one who has reached total liberation; *see also* Tirthankara

karma Jain idea of subtle form of matter that clings to the soul because of the soul's passion and desire, causing rebirths
kevela the highest state of enlightenment, according to Jainism
Mahavira the twenty-fourth and last Jina of the present world half-cycle, who according to Jain tradition lived from 599 to 527 B.C.E.
Parshva the twenty-third Jina of the present world half-cycle, who lived in the mid-ninth century B.C.E.
rebirth in the Jain tradition, belief that after the death of its body, the accumulated karma causes the soul to take on another body from the almost infinite range of possibilities, including one-sense bodies
restraints the Jain vows of nonviolence, not lying, not stealing, refraining from wrong sex, and nonpossession or nonattachment
Shvetambara "white clad," accepting the use of clothing; one of the two major Jain groups
Tirthankara "ford builder," Jain idea of one who has reached total liberation and shows the way across the ocean of suffering; *see also* Jina

The Way of the Disciples: The Sikhs

Sikhs, many sporting turbans and beards, are highly visible in the world today, both in India and in Western societies. They are active in government, business, medical professions, education, science, and the like, respected for their honesty and hard work. The Sikh religious tradition combines devotional love for God with a practical sense of virtuous engagement in society.

Sikhism, beginning in the sixteenth century C.E., is the youngest of the major religions to arise in India, coming into being at a time when major bhakti movements were active in Hindu communities of northern India. The early Sikh leaders were influenced by the interaction of Hinduism with Islam, that strongly monotheistic religion from outside of India that seems so opposed to the Hindu vision of life but that became such an important factor in Indian culture and religion. In a remarkably fertile religious and intellectual climate, spiritual forces from these differing religious paths were drawn together in Sikhism, the path of the disciples of the Gurus. Sikhism provides an Indian way, still within the worldview of samsara and rebirth, to find salvation by union with the one God, through love experiencing the person of God dwelling within and responding with the heart to the voice of the Divine Guru.

SACRED STORY AND HISTORICAL CONTEXT

To be a **Sikh** means to be a "disciple," a disciple of the **Guru**. And who is the Guru? Of course, it is Guru **Nanak** and the other gurus, ten in all, through whom God's Word is present. But then the Guru is also the Holy Book, the *Adi Granth*. In the final analysis, God is the Guru. The identity of Sikhs is tied up with the sacred story about the Gurus, the Holy Book, and God.

Nanak and the Other Gurus

The time for the founding of this new religion of India came when the great bhakti (devotional) movement was in full swing. This movement had begun in the Tamil country in the south, but in the fourteenth and fifteenth centuries it spread all across northern India. These devotees maintained that God is the one and only divine reality, though known by many names, and that all the rest is illusion (maya). They felt that one should serve God through complete submission to God's will, as known especially through the guidance of a *guru* or spiritual mentor. Furthermore, it was agreed that the best way to salvation is by approaching God in love, meditating and singing God's name in hymns of love and praise to reach inner union with God. Leaders of this bhakti movement were called *sants*, those who know the truth; often the sants were mystical poets who brought their teachings to the popular level through hymns and stories.

Although most of these sant-poets were worshipers of Vishnu, there were also other devotional groups. Some people found spiritual fulfillment in devotional attachment to God in the form of Shiva. In this time Islamic spiritual influences were also strong in India and contributed to the overall bhakti movement. The Muslim Sufis were cultivating a similar path of mystical love and devotion to God, with emphasis on the master who guides the devotional meditation. In this spiritual climate, there was a tendency among the sants to ignore traditional differences in sectarian beliefs and caste social status. Under whatever name, God is one, and men and women of any social status can attain unity with

God through meditation and singing the hymns of love and praise.

Among the Hindu sants, an important predecessor of Nanak, the founder of Sikhism, was the poet **Kabir** (1440–1518), who did not accept the authority of the Vedas and who combined Hindu and Muslim ideas in his syncretistic approach. He felt that he was inspired by the one God, the Sat Guru (True Guru):

> The grandeur of the Sat Guru is infinite, infinite is his
>   bounty,
> He opened my eyes to the Infinite and showed me Infinity.
> I was just tagging along in the wake of the world and the
>   Veda,
> the Sat Guru met me on the path and he put a lamp in my
>   hand.[1]

Kabir taught that everyone should worship this one God. But images and rituals such as pilgrimages provide no help; rather, the simple love of God that captures the heart is sufficient to free one from the wheel of rebirth. There still is a group today in India, the Kabir Panth (community of Kabir), that follows the path of Kabir. And Sikhs look to Kabir for spiritual inspiration—in fact, many of his hymns and verses appear in the *Adi Granth*, the Sikh holy book.

Nanak Becomes the Guru   Nanak was born in 1469 in the village of Talwandi near Lahore (in present-day Pakistan) to a Hindu Kshatriya (warrior) family. His father was a revenue officer for the Muslim overseer of the village, and Nanak received a Hindu upbringing along with considerable exposure to Islam. Whereas Sikhs consider Nanak's writings in the *Adi Granth* to be the only completely authentic information about him, they have many other popular stories about his life. He was a precocious youth, a poet by nature, more given to meditation and searching for religious truth than to the business affairs his father tried to interest him in. In this heavily Muslim area he explored Islamic religious ideas and practices, and he took every opportunity to talk with holy persons of any sect. He was married at an early age and had two sons, and he worked for a while for a Muslim official in the nearby town of Sultanapur. He became close friends with a Muslim family servant, Mardana, who played the rebec, a stringed instrument, and together they sang the hymns that Nanak composed, gradually attracting a small community of seekers.

When Nanak was thirty there came a crucial, intense religious experience that transformed his life. One morning after bathing in the river he disappeared in a forest and experienced being carried up to God's presence, where he was given a cup of nectar and a divine call, telling him to rejoice in God's Name and to teach others to do so. Emerging from the forest three days after he disappeared and had been thought drowned, Nanak was silent for one day, and then he said, "There is neither Hindu nor Muslim, so whose path shall I follow? I shall follow God's path. God is neither Hindu nor Muslim, and the path which I follow is God's."

Now Nanak was a guru, one who drives away darkness and teaches enlightenment, giving voice to the word of God who is the true Guru. Traditional stories tell how he pursued his divine calling by spending many years traveling about India, Sri Lanka, and Tibet, often accompanied by Mardana, teaching and singing evangelistic hymns in marketplaces, street corners, and open squares. Some stories say he and Mardana even traveled to Mecca, Medina, and Baghdad. To emphasize his pronouncement that there is neither Hindu nor Muslim, he often would wear the traditional garments of Sufis or samnyasins. In these various travels and encounters, he always emphasized the one God, the unity of the different religious paths, and the futility of relying on traditional rituals and practices. One story, for example, recounts how he was invited to join in prayer in the mosque with Daulat Khan Lodi and the Qazi of Sultanpur. However, while they were performing the bowing and prostrations of the prayer, Nanak simply remained standing. Questioned as to why he had not joined them in the prayer ritual, he replied that he was the only one who had really been praying, for the qazi's mind had been filled with worry that his newborn filly might fall into the well, and the prince's mind was set on purchases in Kabul—and they had to acknowledge that their thoughts had been thus occupied during the prayer.

After many years of traveling, in about 1521 Nanak decided to settle down with his family, establishing a Sikh religious center in Kartarpur and devoting the rest of his life to teaching and serving this community. He adopted the common garb of a householder, to show, perhaps, that his religious path did not mean abandoning the world. Here he established his home and built a dharmasala, a room for Sikhs to gather for devotional singing. This became a common feature of Sikh homes wherever they lived—each house became a place where devout Sikhs gathered to sing the guru's hymns.

Thus began the important concepts of *sangat* (congregational gathering) and *kirtan* (devotional hymn-singing) that became characteristic of the growing Sikh community.

Guru Nanak's teachings revolved around God as the sole reality who is formless and beyond all conceptions, whose self-manifestation is the whole creation so that in a sense everything is in God. Yet the transcendent, unknowable God is experienced as personal through love and devotion. One of the most important passages in the *Adi Granth*, the first part of the *Japji* (recited by Sikhs in every morning devotion), was composed by Nanak immediately after his enlightenment experience. It well expresses his experience of God:

> There is one God,
> Eternal Truth is His Name;
> Maker of all things,
> Fearing nothing and at enmity with nothing,
> Timeless in His Image;
> Not begotten, being of His own Being:
> By the grace of the Guru, made known to men.[2]

The primary problem in human existence, Guru Nanak taught, is separation from God through ignorance and self-centeredness. The soul is capable of pure union with God, but in self-centeredness it turns to the world as something separate from God and allows itself to be dominated with passions and pride. The soul that is trapped in evil will have to endure countless rebirths, sufferings, and deaths. But the way to union with God is revealed by the guru, through whom God's word reverberates. By meditating on this word and on God's name, disciples are given God's grace and favor and enabled to hear his voice and open their hearts to salvation.

Since the true path is an inward preparation of the heart to receive and experience God, Nanak rejected the traditional Hindu and Muslim rituals and scriptures. And since all beings are God's creation, he rejected discriminations on the basis of sex or caste. The path Guru Nanak taught includes techniques and disciplines for preparing the heart, particularly singing God's praises (*kirtan*) and meditating on God's name, repeating it so that the divine sound fills one's whole being. Repeating the Name of the True God, Guru Nanak taught, means engrafting him in the soul.

Thus did Nanak, the true Guru, become the founder of the Sikh community, called the Panth. His teachings were embodied in the 974 hymns he composed, many preserved in written form and others still in oral form but in regular use. And the community of disciples, in Kartarpur and many other places throughout India, followed his teaching and lived the Sikh way, engaging in the householder life as a way of divine service, gathering to sing the hymns and to meditate on the divine name. From these beginnings arose the Sikh Panth that continues still today.

The Ten Gurus and the Sikh Community   The Sikh community focuses on the Word of God as it is present through the guru—and so Guru Nanak's last act was to ensure the ongoing presence of the guru for the community. His two sons were not inclined for such a role, but Lehna, a former devotee of the goddess Durga, had become a follower of Guru Nanak and demonstrated high spiritual ability and obedience to the divine message. So before his death in 1539, Guru Nanak named Lehna to be his successor as head of the Sikh community, renaming him Guru Angad ("part of me"), implying that Angad did indeed possess Nanak's own spirit. Henceforth God's word would continue to come through Guru Angad and the following gurus, leading the community to union with God. For a succession of nine gurus after Nanak, the same Guru continued on, Sikhs say, as a single flame can be transmitted from one torch to nine successive torches.

When the third guru, Amar Das, began collecting the Sikh scriptures, he included not only hymns of Guru Nanak but also hymns composed by Guru Angad, himself, and a number of non-Sikhs such as Kabir, for they all were regarded as transmitting the voice of God. This developing holy book became known as the *Adi Granth* (Original Collection) and is also often called **Granth Sahib** (Sacred Collection), itself called Guru. Guru Amar Das also created a system of Sikh parishes and established rituals and festivals for Sikh observance in place of Hindu celebrations.

Ram Das, the fourth guru, enjoyed the favor of the tolerant ruler Akbar, and he set up the village Amritsar near a pool of water that had been especially beloved by Nanak. Amritsar became the religious center for Sikhs and their most holy city. One interesting story tells how the great ruler Akbar came to visit the guru; instead of a royal reception, he was asked first to sit on the ground and eat a common meal with the other visitors—the custom of the *langar* (free kitchen), which became a key mark of Sikhism, continuing to the present day.

Now the guruship became hereditary. Before he died in 1581, Guru Ram Das appointed his son **Arjan** to be the next (fifth) guru, and all the remaining gurus were direct descendants of Ram Das. Under Guru Arjan, the Sikhs began to build the important **Golden Temple** at Amritsar. Guru Arjan also gathered the hymns of the first four gurus and other inspired hymns and poems, including some of his own, into the final, authoritative edition of the sacred book, *Adi Granth*. This sacred text was enshrined in the Golden Temple, to be from that time the central focus of Sikh faith and worship.

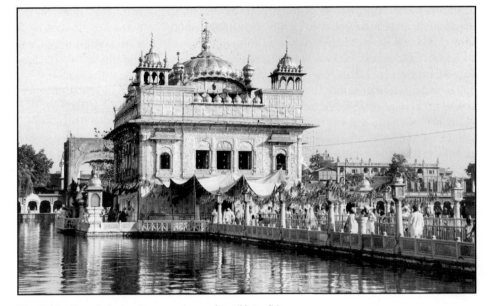

The Golden Temple in Amritsar, most sacred in Sikh tradition.

But now political adversity comes into the story. The Mughal successors to Akbar were less tolerant and began persecuting non-Muslims, and Guru Arjan had to choose between accepting Islam or death. Choosing death, he became the first Sikh martyr in 1606. But before he died, Guru Arjan sent a message to his son Hargobind, the sixth guru, telling him to sit fully armed on his throne. So at his investiture, Guru Hargobind girded himself with two swords, symbolizing both spiritual authority and worldly authority. Thus began a new outlook of military struggle and defense for the young Sikh community. Clashes with the Mughals and other local insurgents continued under the seventh guru, Har Rai, and the eighth guru, Har Krishan, who died while still a child. In still more tumultuous times, the ninth guru, Tegh Bahadur, was executed in Delhi by the Mughals in 1675 because he refused to become Muslim. These struggles, and especially the martyrdoms of Guru Arjan and Guru Tegh Bahadur, have become a very important part of the Sikh sacred story and are remembered in festivals.

Yet another important component of the story comes under the tenth guru, **Gobind Singh** (1666–1708). Part of a male Sikh's identity is his long hair, special dress, and his name **Singh**; and when Sikhs worship together they glorify the *khalsa*. What is this all about? As we saw, the Sikh community had begun to realize that it needed to develop military preparedness to defend itself, and so the gurus were trained as military leaders. The tenth guru, Gobind Singh, in preparation for a momentous struggle for Sikh survival, founded the khalsa military society in 1699. According to the traditional story, Guru Gobind addressed an assembly of Sikhs on New Year's Day and stressed the seriousness of the times and the need for strength, unity, and loyalty to the guru. With his sword uplifted, he called for five volunteers to come forward to die for the Sikh cause to show their loyalty and conviction. After a fearful silence, one Sikh came forward and was led into the guru's tent. Guru Gobind emerged with his sword dripping with fresh blood and asked for more volunteers. One by one four more brave Sikhs came forward and were escorted into the tent. In a dramatic climax, Guru Gobind emerged from the tent with all five Sikhs still alive; he had substituted a goat for the sacrifice of the five men.

Now Guru Gobind performed a ceremony of initiation of the Five Beloved Ones, as they are called. Mixing nectar in water with a two-edged sword, he gave them to drink of it and sprinkled it over them, initiating them into the khalsa (pure) order. Then he himself received initiation from them. As the basis of the new community, Guru Gobind proclaimed the Rahit, the khalsa code of belief and discipline. As the physical sign of the khalsa all vowed to wear the five K's: uncut hair (*kais*), a comb (*kangha*), a sword or dagger (*kirpan*), a wrist guard (*kara*), and short pants (*kachha*). The uncut hair was to be kept in a topknot under a turban.

After these first members, the guru threw open membership in the khalsa to everyone of all castes, including women. Men entering the khalsa added the common surname Singh (lion), and the women added the name Kaur (princess). The guru set up the Rahit, a special code of discipline, prohibiting such things as tobacco, eating meat of animals slaughtered in the Muslim way, and sexual contact with Muslims, but enjoining regular singing of the guru's hymns and congregational worship with men and women participating on a equal basis. Thousands of men and women were initiated on that founding day, and afterward people of all castes eagerly entered the khalsa. It seems Guru Govind Singh's intention was to make Sikhs stand out in society, so that their identity would be clear to everyone. The khalsa did sustain the Sikh community through times of grave crisis, and today the ritual of initiation, accepting the prohibitions, and wearing the five K's are still important aspects of Sikh identity. Many Sikhs may not actually become members of the khalsa or display the five K's. But they still look to the khalsa as the key community within Sikhism for maintaining Sikh identity. And so when Sikhs pray together, they often use the exclamation from the Rahit, "Raj karega khalsa" (the khalsa shall rule).

Guru Gobind's two older sons died in the struggle with the Muslim forces, and his two younger sons were executed by a Mughal governor by being bricked up alive in the city wall. Guru Gobind traveled to southern India, where he was stabbed by a fanatic. But before he died in 1708 he declared that the line of gurus ended with himself, the tenth guru. From now on, he decreed, the holy book, *Adi Granth*, would be the Guru for all Sikhs, and the Sikh Panth itself would be the ongoing corporate form of the Guru. From that time onward, except for a couple of small Sikh sects that retained human gurus, Sikhs have looked to *Guru Granth Sahib*, the Holy Book, as the continuing Guru presence that brings God's word and power to and through the Panth.

Developments, Struggles, Transformations

Religious Developments in Sikh History   As time went on and the Sikh community spread, more congregations were established, and in every locality they erected **gurdwaras**, buildings for worship and meeting together. Often these included a kitchen area (langar) where a free common meal would be served for all. This, together with the worship gatherings in which men and women participated together without priests and without class distinctions, served to maintain the sense of unity and equality in the Sikh community.

Although maintaining Guru Nanak's emphasis on a religion of the heart rather than ritual and pilgrimage, Sikhs did adopt many of the festivals of Hinduism in northern India, together with traditions and lore from the Hindu epics. Guru Gobind Singh produced a supplement to the *Adi Granth*, called *Dasam Granth* (Granth of the Tenth Guru), not considered on the same sacred level as the *Adi Granth* but still used widely for edification. Along with his own hymns, Gobind included much material from the Hindu epics, especially about the gods Rama and Krishna and their renowned exploits. He also included stories about the great goddess Durga and her victories over evil. Such heroic material could be used especially to instill bravery in the khalsa to stand firm in their faith and fight against the enemies of the Sikhs.

After the death of the tenth guru, the hostility between the Sikhs and the Mughal rulers continued to increase, and members of the khalsa took to the hills to carry on guerrilla warfare for the survival of the Sikh community. The Sikhs emerged victorious in the area of Lahore, and a Sikh kingdom was set up under Ranjit Singh (1780–1839) that controlled most of the Punjab area. But the British had taken the place of the Mughal Empire, and a period of running battles between the Sikhs and the British led ultimately to the complete surrender of the Sikhs to British control.

Because the British treated them with fairness and justice, the Sikhs turned out to be loyal subjects, serving with bravery and distinction in the armies through which the British maintained their control of India.

But the long-standing desire for freedom and an independent Sikh state could not be entirely suppressed, and the Sikhs tended to join the movement for India's independence from the British. However, they were devastated by the decision to partition their homeland, the Punjab, between the newly created Muslim state of Pakistan and India. With immense suffering and deaths, two and a half million Sikhs had to leave their homes and move across the new border to India, leaving behind rich farms and sacred places such as the birthplace of Guru Nanak.

The Sikh Community Today   Today Sikhs make up the majority in the Punjab state in India. Although the Sikh community has maintained a strong sense of unity, several divisions did develop in the course of history. Today the Singh group (the khalsa) makes up the great majority of Sikhs. A small order called Udasi is inclined toward asceticism and celibacy, going about in yellow robes with begging bowls, often with shaved head and no beards. The Sahaj-dhari group, also clean-shaven, is a non-khalsa group that refused to go along with the militant stance of the tenth guru. Within the large Singh group there are some differences as well. One faction takes a rather militant stance and carries martial implements. Another faction leans toward contemplation and scholarship.

The vision of a Sikh state has always been a part of Sikh belief. Many Sikhs have been working toward and demanding a Sikh-dominated state in the Punjab, a demand that in recent years has caused considerable violence and bloodshed, even at the Golden Temple. The Sikh community has not been able, to date, to unify itself on the question of what course to take within the extremely complicated politics of India. Some Sikhs continue to advocate resistance against the Hindu-dominated government of India, while others advocate engagement within the structures of Indian government. What they want is respect and equality and an appropriate amount of self-determination within the state of India. Some Sikhs have been very active politically and have achieved high office in the government. A Sikh has been president of India, for example, and recently Manmohan Singh has gained respect both as minister of finance and as prime minister of India.

Another problem Sikhs face today, like people of all the major religions, is the lure of secularism and the loss of tradition. Many young people abandon the khalsa emblem of unshorn hair, and there is some tendency, especially among Sikhs living outside of strong Sikh settlements, to lapse back into Hindu society. The many Sikhs living overseas in the diaspora are pressured by Western styles of life that make it difficult to adhere to the khalsa disciplines. To combat these tendencies, Sikh leaders today are promoting a revival of Sikh tradition, stressing those features that are unique to the Sikh heritage.

In general, Sikh identity appears fairly strong today. Sikh hospitals, educational institutions, and social relief agencies are flourishing in India. There have been recent celebrations of the quincentenary of Guru Nanak (1969), the tercentenaries of Guru Gobind Singh (1966) and Guru Tegh Bahadur (1975), and the tercentenary of the founding of the khalsa (1999), resulting in conferences, publications, and an increased interest in the Sikh heritage.

Sikhism is a world religion today, with perhaps eighteen million adherents in various parts of the world. The great majority, of course, still live in India, but there are many thriving Sikh diaspora communities in the United States, Canada, England, and many other parts of the world.

SIKH WORLDS OF MEANING

The Sacred Ultimate: God

What's it all about? What is really the center that holds everything together?

For Sikhs, as for Jews, Christians, and Muslims, the answer is God. Guru Nanak and the other gurus no doubt were influenced by the Muslim emphasis on worshiping the one God. But the "monotheism" of Sikhism is born of India, counting Vaishnavite theologians and poets among its sources, signaled by Guru Nanak's important teaching that God is neither Hindu nor Muslim.

At the heart of the world's existence is the one God, who is immortal, unborn, self-existent, omniscient, formless, and totally beyond human conceptions and categories such as gender or time. One of Guru Nanak's favorites terms for God is Akal Purakh, "Timeless One." God is the creator of the universe and transcendent far beyond it. At the same time, the universe is an emanation from God's being, a manifestation of God's own essence, so in a sense we can say that God is in everything and everything is in God. The world exists within the unity of God, and even the Hindu gods Brahma, Vishnu, and Shiva can be seen as manifestations of the supreme one Name. God rules over the world in the samsara cycles of existence and even over the law of karma.

But God is not simply like the Hindu Brahman, impersonal and beyond conception. Rather, God is personal, being revealed to the human heart through the word in all creation and especially through God's name, **Nam**, the dimension of God that can be known and loved by humans. The Name is the total expression of all that God is and this is Truth. "Sati Nam—His name is Truth." Sikhs believe that before the creation God lived alone in formlessness. But when God became manifest, God first formed Godself into Nam and then created nature. Nam is not different from God; Nam is the total expression of all God is, sustaining everything with the divine presence. Thus, God is the true Guru, granting self-revelation through the creation, and through grace enabling humans to hear the divine voice. Persons who thus open their hearts to God's presence and follow the path will ultimately attain complete absorption into God's being like water blending with water. In this way the Sikh experience of God as ultimate reality includes monistic and monotheistic, impersonal and personal dimensions.

Divine Creation and Human Nature

In thinking about the creation of the world and human nature, often we encounter two opposite views: belief in one creator God who creates humans for a single lifetime, or belief in world cycles with karma and rebirth as the human lot. The first is characteristic of the Abrahamic religions, and the second is typical of the religions arising from India. We have already been chastened in holding this assumption too strictly, for we found within Hinduism groups believing in one creator God. Now in Sikhism we have a religious perspective that specifically integrates elements of both these views.

The Divine Creation: World and Humans
What is this world all about? Just as Sikhs teach the ideas both of a transcendent, impersonal God and of an immanent, personal God, so also they see the world both as God's creation and as an emanation of God's being. God, formless and eternal, created all existence, and God sustains all forms of exis-

tence by dwelling in them. Originally there was darkness everywhere with only the Omnipotent One existing in abstract meditation. Then God willed, and from the word expressing the divine will the universe came into existence as a hot nebula spinning out the planets.

> Through uncountable ages,
> Complete darkness brooded
> Over utter vacancy;
> There were no worlds, no firmaments.
> The Will of the Lord was alone pervasive;
> There was neither night nor day, nor sun nor moon
> But only God in ceaseless trance. . . .
> When He so willed, He shaped the Universe;
> The firmament He spread without a prop to support it.
> He created the high gods, Brahma, Vishnu and Shiva.
> And Maya the goddess, the veil of illusion,
> Who maketh Truth dark and increaseth worldly attachment.
> To some, to a chosen few, the Guru revealeth the Lord's Word.
> The Lord creates and He watcheth His Creation;
> He made the heavenly bodies,
> Our Universe in the endless space,
> Above, below and around it.
> And out of the Unmanifested, Unmovable ground of His Being,
> To us and in us, He made Himself manifest.[3]

God creates the universe and dissolves it time and again in divine play. God sustains nature with Nam, God's own presence, and God watches with delight all he creates.

The universe is real, but it is not eternal and has no independent existence. God creates both good and evil, but the overall existence of the world is good and beneficial, and accordingly Sikhism does not advocate asceticism or withdrawal from the world. God also preserves the world according to the divine will or norm expressed in the orderly functioning of existence. In accordance with the divine norm, the *Adi Granth* says, we are born and we die, and everything, ahead and behind, is pervaded by this norm.

What is one's real self? Human souls are part of the creation emanating from God, like sparks arising from the fire. God is infinite, but the soul is finite and has its own individuality; yet it is deathless. It takes bodily form according to the will of the creator, and it gives consciousness to the body. Mind and intellect are the outer coverings of the soul; it is through the mind and intellect that the soul controls the working of the bodily senses. It is the soul that is conscious of truth or falsehood, that determines virtue or sinfulness. The soul is the basic link with God, as the receptacle of God's love. When the body dies the soul leaves and continues forever, transmigrating to other bodies in the rebirth cycle in accordance with karma. There are heaven and hell into which one can be reborn, although these are not eternal or ultimate, and we can be reborn as animals or plants. At death the soul leaves the body and appears before the God of justice. Depending on its karma, it may be sent to be reborn as an animal, a bird, or an insect. It may be sent to heaven or hell. Or it may be sent to be born again as a human being for its further development. The goal of the Sikh religious life is to attain total union of the soul with God, thus transcending heaven and hell and the rebirth cycle, enjoying uninterrupted bliss forever.

The Human Predicament   Although the world and humans were created by God and, thus, are not essentially evil, our self-centeredness and pride lead to attachment to the pleasures and concerns of the world. The result of this is separation from God and all the manifold human sufferings, including the endless cycle of rebirths.

The main human problem is the ego, that is, self-centeredness, which arises because we are enveloped in *maya*, delusion, which also is part of God's creation. It is not inevitable that humans give in to self-centeredness. Sikhs do not believe in a predestined course of the soul, nor do they hold to the belief that the soul is basically evil. The soul and the world are both good and pure. If the world is seen as God's creation, it is like a beautiful gem; and if the soul is pure, it reflects God's purity and love. But most of us give in to self-centered tendencies and turn our attentions to the pleasures of the world rather than to God. And the curse of the self-centered person is separation from God. God, the Incomprehensible, is within us, but we do not understand, because the ego hangs as a screen between. We fill our souls with self-love rather than love for God, and such a soul is trapped by the passions into a life of sin and evil.

> Those who do not cherish the Lord's Name
> Wander, deceived and bewildered;
> Without such cherishing of the Lord's Name,
> Without the love of His Eternal Being,
> Man can have no destiny except remorse and anguish.[4]

Such a person suffers further deprivation of God's love and grace, sinking ever deeper into a life of fear and anxiety.

Yama, the lord of death, uses the evil tendencies to snare those who are separated from God and lost in the world; their lot is the endless cycle of rebirths.

> O Self-love, Self-will, thou root of births and deaths,
> Thou soul of sin, thou makest a man to
> Estrange friends and increase the enmity of enemies:
> He thinketh ever of heaping up more wealth,
> And his soul exhausts itself in deaths and rebirths
> And suffers uncountable delights and agonies.
> Thou makest man to lose himself in error's dark wood,
> And thou strikest him mortally sick with covetousness.[5]

Such wanderings can stop only when we meet a true preceptor, a guru, who will guide us onto the path of transformation.

The Path of Transformation

How can we start living real life?

The human problem is selfishness, which makes one love the world rather than God, causing one to be separated from God. The answer? In Guru Nanak's words,

> What keepeth me in my detachment
> Is meditating on the Ungraspable One,
> Through the One Divine Word
> God is made real to us,
> And the saints destroy the flames,
> Of attachment to the little self.[6]

Nanak repeatedly rejected the need for various religious practices like sacrifices, pilgrimages, fasting, and the rest. Rather the path is essentially an inner spiritual discipline, with lavish attention to prayer, music, and meditation, aimed at opening the heart to God's presence. The heart needs to be purified so it can resonate to the Sat-Nam, God's true name.

Sikhs believe that God's name reverberates throughout creation as the revelation of God's own being. It is the means through which God can be known, and it reveals the path leading to union with God. It comes first of all through God's grace, awakening our minds and hearts. Guru Nanak taught that, even though karma determines the nature of our birth, it is through grace that the door of salvation is found. Every person has the capability to hear and respond to this name, for it is the revelation of God's personal being whom we can know and love. By focusing on the divine name we enter into a personal relationship with God. But how can we, selfish and forgetful, hear and respond to God's name?

Sikhs believe that to get on the path of transformation it is important to hear the word of the guru, for it is through the gurus that God channels grace to humankind. A modern Sikh scholar explains:

> To be communicable, the Supreme Being chooses one of his created men to be his vehicle and speak to humanity through that chosen vehicle in a language that man can understand. "He places himself in the Guru," the specially chosen form, says Guru Nanak.... They [the gurus] only proclaimed what was inspired in their holy beings by the Master as a command or communication. The voice thus received was recorded in human language and it, so preserved, became the eternal Guru. The voice "vibrates in the pages of the Guru Granth."[7]

The ten gurus were illuminated by the inner truth of God's word, and by their perfection they were able to be illuminators of that truth to bring others to salvation. After the death of the tenth guru, the truth that the gurus illuminated was understood to be merged into the *Adi Granth*. The path of transformation is above all to focus on the word of the guru, for that word inspires and transforms human life:

> And as music has a strange fascination for the mind, the Guru's Word is to be sung to fire one's mind with an experience that sinks in the soul, and turning the usual, habitual tide of the mind, makes the soul experience the nature of God within one's emotional self. Yea, and then this God-nature will outflow into secular activity as well, deflect man's mind from his immediate environs and personal pulls and passions, and yoke it to the service of the others in order that the Name, the all-pervading Spirit, is seen through all creation.[8]

Thus, the path involves honoring and tasting deeply the words of the gurus as they are written in the *Adi Granth*, for in this way one can attune one's inner being to the harmony and grace present in the divine name. The various spiritual practices involve "remembrance of the Name" (*nam simaran*). One very basic way to do this is to repeat again and again words or expressions that embody the meaning of the divine name, such as Sat-Nam or Vahiguru ("Praise to the Guru," often used by modern Sikhs as the name for God). In the congregational setting, the practice of remembrance of the name means *kirtan*, singing of the scriptures and various hymns, usually with musical accompaniment. Sikhs also practice meditation that reflects on the meaning of the divine name, attuning one's whole being to the grace of the Guru.

Achieving this realization naturally affects the way people live their lives. They control their desires and their sense of ego, not withdrawing from the world but seeing it as God's creation and God's revelation. As people advance in spiritual perfection and purity of mind, they move through five spiritual stages, according to Guru Nanak. The first stage of spiritual perfection is living according to the divine norms of duty and piety. Second comes the expansion of heart and mind through deep awareness and knowledge. The third stage is the realm of endeavor, where wisdom becomes profound and a deep sense of beauty prevails. The realm of grace is the fourth stage of spiritual progress, flooded with God's indwelling power. The fifth stage, then, is the realm of Truth, where the soul takes its place in God's eternal bliss. This God-realization, entering into union with God's own true, formless being, takes place in this present life, but it involves eternal bliss. The realm of birth and death, even the realm of heaven and hell, are left behind in this full liberation.

> They who think on Thee, they who meditate on Thee,
> In this dark age have their peace.
> They who think on Thee: they are saved, they are liberated;
> For them death's noose is broken.
> Those who meditate on the Fearless One
> Will lose all their fear;
> Those who have worshipped the Lord,
> In the Lord they are now mingled.[9]

A yogin once asked Guru Nanak how it was possible to live in this maya world of materialism and still become one with God. Guru Nanak gave two examples. A lotus flower cannot exist without water, yet it remains unaffected by the condition of the water, always rising pure and spotless above the surface. And a duck cannot live without water, yet since it never gets its wings wet, it never drowns in the water. In the same way, the Guru said, a person cannot live without the maya world of material. Yet a person through praise and prayer can enshrine God's name within oneself, thus crossing the ocean of the world in communion with God. In this communion is bliss, peace, and everlasting joy, a taste of the heavenly elixir.

WORSHIP AND MORAL LIFE IN SIKHISM

Ritual and Worship Among the Sikhs

How can we find new power for life? The Sikh answer is love, God's love, experienced and expressed in service, ritual, and worship. The active love and worship of God, focused on the divine revelation in the *Adi Granth*, God's presence in the gurdwara, and God's word brought through the gurus, characterize the Sikh religion. The proper way to relate to God is in prayer, submission, study of God's word, thankful praise, and a lifestyle that reflects this love.

Worshiping God   Worship starts with the **Word of God**, which is experienced concretely in the *Adi Granth*. Daily worship at home includes reading and meditating on the sacred word, the *Adi Granth*, which is kept in a special room of the house. Devout Sikhs rise before sunrise and bathe, followed by saying prayers, reciting scriptures, and concentrating on the name of the Lord. When the day is done, they again recite prayers and scriptures before retiring for the night.

Worship also means visiting the gurdwara (Sikh temple), daily, perhaps, and participating in worship there—this is

Sikhs preparing holy water for ritual use.

the heart of the Sikh religion. The central object of worship is the *Granth Sahib*, the Holy Book. In fact, a gurdwara is defined as any place that houses the *Guru Granth Sahib*. Since the divine Guru is present through the Holy Book, the gurdwara itself is treated with profound respect. The Holy Book receives the highest honor. When it is carried, it must be above the head of a Sikh, and all present stand respectfully. In the gurdwara the Book is placed on a throne, like lectern covered with clean cloths, with cushions to support the book. The book is covered with embroidered silks, with a royal canopy above. For worship, the book is ritually opened, and as long as it is open the reader or an attendant pays homage to it by waving the chauri (fan). To show honor to the *Guru Granth Sahib*, worshipers remove their shoes, cover their heads, and sit on the floor.

Sikhs bathe themselves before worshiping in the gurdwara. After entering the gurdwara, they walk solemnly to the Holy Book, kneel and touch their foreheads to the floor, and place a small offering before the Book. Then they move back to sit on the carpeted floor with the rest of the congregation. They greet the other assembled Sikhs with the salutation, *Vahiguruji ka khalsa, Vahiguruji ki fateh*, "Hail to the Guru's khalsa, Hail to the Guru's victory!" Since there are no priests or ordained worship leaders in Sikhism, each person is free and empowered to perform the rituals of worship. Women as well as men lead worship rituals and read from the scriptures.

The central activity of worship in the gurdwara is kirtan, singing of hymns from the *Guru Granth Sahib* and from the works of Guru Gobind Singh. Often there are trained musicians, ragis, who lead the faithful in the devotional music, which is a valuable means of lifting the soul to communion with God. There may be readings and exhortations. The worship generally closes with verses from a hymn by Guru Amar Das, the reading of the congregational prayer called *Ardas*, and the salutations, "Hail to the Guru's khalsa, Hail to the Guru's victory." There follows a ritual of opening the *Guru Granth Sahib* at random and reading the hymn that appears on the head of the left-hand page. This is regarded as the Guru's command (*hukam*), providing guidance for the people. As part of the concluding rituals, the worshipers receive **karah parsad**, a sacred food made of flour, sugar, and clarified butter. This is served to everyone present, Sikh and non-Sikh alike. After the worship, the people often participate in the langar, the communal meal served freely to everyone present.

Festivals and Holy Days   There are numerous festivals and holy days throughout the year for the Sikh community. It is said that Guru Amar Das commanded the Sikhs to assemble in his presence on the Hindu spring and autumn festivals of Vaisakhi (or Baisakhi) and Divali, as a way of promoting a distinctive Sikh identity. Sikhs had to choose where they belonged at these festival times, with their Hindu neighbors and kin, or with the guru. Vaisakhi is the New Year festival, held on the first day of the month of Vaisakh (in the Punjab, this is fixed by the solar calendar on April 13). Traditionally, for Hindus, this was a time of offering grain from the new crops to the Brahmans. Sikhs transformed the Hindu festival and made it a time to visit the gurdwara. Vaisakhi has historic connotations as the day on which Guru Gobind Singh instituted the khalsa, and today it is celebrated as a joyful religious and social occasion.

Divali, celebrated on the day of the new moon in the month of Kattak (October/November), is the Hindu festival of lights. Sikhs connect this festival with a story about the release of Guru Hargobind from imprisonment by the Mughal emperor. The order for his release came just before Divali, but the guru refused to accept freedom unless 52 imprisoned Hindu rajas were released with him. The Mughal emperor agreed that he could take as many rajas with him as could hold onto his cloak as he passed through the narrow gate. So the guru had long tassels attached to his cloak and, by holding on to them, all the rajas were freed. Sikhs celebrate this theme of deliverance by illuminating the gurdwaras with lights and giving presents to children.

There are also specifically Sikh festivals for various occasions, such as commemorating the birthday of Guru Nanak, the birthday of Guru Gobind Singh, the martyrdom of the fifth Guru Arjun, and the first installation of the *Adi Granth* in the Golden Temple at Amritsay. These anniversary festivals will often be observed by carrying the *Guru Granth Sahib* in procession through the community. The Holy Book is placed in a decorated palanquin carried on a flower-bedecked lorry. The joyful procession is led by men marching with drawn swords, and many enthusiastic and gaily dressed devotees participate, some in singing parties, others as sword-stick performers, and the like. Often the festival includes a common meal for the worshipers at the langar of the gurdwara.

Rituals of the Passages of Life   Sikhism does not approve of excessive ritualism. Still, there are commonly observed ceremonies relating to the main passages of life. After the birth of a child, some Sikhs follow the tradition of mixing water and honey in a steel bowl while reciting the first five verses of the *Japti*. A few drops of the sanctified water are put in the baby's mouth, and the rest is given to the mother. In the naming ceremony, the Holy Book is opened and the child is given a name starting with the first letter of the first word on the left page. Religious instruction is provided privately or at the gurdwara, and the first day when the child learns to read the *Granth Sahib* is a day of great festivity. In some families, when a boy reaches eleven or twelve he has his first turban ceremoniously tied on by a Sikh elder in the presence of the *Guru Granth Sahib*.

When Sikh boys and girls come of age they may be formally initiated into the order of the khalsa. They must be old enough to comprehend the meaning of the vows they take. In practice, many Sikhs wait until later in life to be initiated, while other Sikhs do not go through the ceremony at all. Anyone who lives a worthy life and accepts the Sikh principles may be accepted into the khalsa through the rite of initiation. All present at the initiation ceremony will be wearing the symbols of the khalsa. Five khalsa Sikhs perform this ritual, stirring sugared water (amrit) with a steel double-edged dagger accompanied by the recitation of sacred verses. The amrit is poured into the cupped hands of the initiates and they drink of it, and it is then touched to their eyes and sprinkled on their hair. All chant together, "Vahiguruji ka khalsa! Vahiguruji ki fateh!" (Hail to the Guru's khalsa! Hail to the Guru's victory!). The five officiants say together the basic creedal statement, and the initiates repeat it after them, after which the Rahit (the code of beliefs and practices of the khalsa) is explained to them. The ritual ends with prayers and the distribution of karah prasad, which all initiates share from the same dish.

Much preparation and arranging by the families involved precedes Sikh marriages. Traditionally, the groom may arrive on horseback, accompanied by the wedding party, and gifts will be exchanged. The wedding ceremony takes place in the presence of the *Guru Granth Sahib*. There are marriage instructions and the singing of hymns, and the bride's father comes forward to place the hem of the bridegroom's scarf into the bride's hand (signifying giving over his daughter). Now the person doing the reading sings the Lavan of Guru Ram Das, a hymn which the guru composed for his daughter's wedding. After each of the four stanzas, the couple walks slowly around the *Guru Granth Sahib* in a clockwise direction, the groom leading. After the rounds the couple bow down before the Holy Book, more hymns are sung, karah prasad is distributed to the congregation, and the wedding feast follows.

When a Sikh dies, the body is bathed and dressed in the emblems of the faith and taken in solemn procession to the crematorium. During the journey the family sings hymns; no wailing is permitted. A close family relative lights the funeral pyre, and the evening hymn (kirtan sohita) is sung during the cremation. Mourners may return to the family home to sing hymns and begin a complete reading of the *Guru Granth Sahib*. Since death is the removal of the last obstacle to complete union with God, the funeral is a time to consider the purpose of life, as the evening hymn encourages:

> Worldly souls who scorn your sweetness suffer pain from
>   self-conceit.
> Deeper, deeper pricks the thorn as Death prepares to strike.
> They who love your sacred Name shall break the bonds of
>   birth and death.
> Thus they find the One Eternal; thus they win supreme
>   renown.
> Poor am I and ever humble; save and keep me in your care.
> Grant the aid your Name can bring me, grant me peace and
>   wondrous joy.[10]

Sikh Practices of Healing and Medicine From the time of Guru Nanak and the other gurus, Sikhs have been active in healing and medicine in India. Stories of the gurus tell how many of them cared for the sick and participated in healing them. Furthermore, Sikhs contributed to the Ayurveda traditional practices common across that culture, and many still look to traditional medicine to supplement modern medical technology.

With their strong conviction that all of nature as well as humans are created and preserved by God, Sikhs generally have strongly supported medical research and practices that enhance and prolong life. But procedures that destroy or harm life are rejected, such as mercy-killing or suicide. Suffering is the result of one's karma, and so it should be borne, like Sikh martyrs did even though they could have escaped suffering through suicide. "Suffering is medicine," according to a Sikh saying. But because God has given humans the ability to develop and use medical practices, it is one's duty to alleviate suffering through the best medical practices.

Family planning is a wise stewardship of God's gift of life, though natural means are preferred for birth control. But abortion is not allowed, except to save the life of the mother, for that interferes in the creative work of God. Traditional Sikhs discourage experimentation on embryos and stem-cells. Overall, the best way to health is through healthful living, as set forth by the gurus: no smoking, drinking, or taking drugs that are not for medical purposes; practices of moderation and virtue in living; and meditating and worshiping God.

Aesthetic Expressions of Loving God The worship life of Sikhs gives expression to the love of God in a variety of art forms. Sikhs tended to shun sculpture because of the worship of images in India, but they have richly cultivated most of the other arts. Paintings and illustrations have focused especially on the ten gurus, providing a sense of their ongoing spiritual presence in the Sikh community. Since the word of God is central, the literary arts have been highly cultivated, especially that of religious poetry, with the powerful poems of the gurus taken as models. Architecture has taken distinct forms among the Sikhs, from the Golden Temple at Amritsar to many gurdwaras in India and throughout the world.

Of many artistic designs and symbols created by Sikhs, the *khanda* has been given special significance, and today it is a universal Sikh symbol displayed at all gurdwaras in countless artistic variations. The basic design is of an upright double-edged sword (khanda) placed on a circle (cacra), with a curved sword (kirpan) standing on either side. Many interpretations are given of this symbol. The double-edged sword may represent God's sovereign power over life and death as well as the need to distinguish truth from falsehood. This sword was used by Guru Gobind Singh to stir the amrit (nectar) in the ceremony of initiation into the khalsa. The cacra (circle) was a throwing weapon; it speaks of the oneness of God and the unity of humankind. And the two kirpans remind Sikhs of Guru Arjan's instruction to his son, Guru Hargobind, that he should wear two swords, one for spiritual authority and one for temporal authority.

One art especially beloved by Sikhs is music, used in kirtan, singing the sacred songs to uplift the soul, as well as for enjoyment in a great variety of festivals and celebrations. Guru Nanak spoke:

In the house in which men sing the Lord's praises
And meditate upon Him,
In that house sing the songs of praise
And remember the Creator;
Sing the song of praise of thy fearless Lord,
Let me be a sacrifice unto that song,
By which we attain everlasting solace.[11]

A Sikh writer explains the importance of the art of music in this way: "Music carries an individual above the mundane and helps in merging the not-Self with the Self. By music the soul is lifted into an almost mystic union with God."[12]

Society and the Good Life

Sikh Society: Khalsa and Gurdwara How should we live? A Sikh should live as befits one who belongs to the Panth (path), the Sikh community of believers, disciples of the gurus.

Many Sikhs think of themselves as part of the khalsa, the special form of the Panth founded by Guru Gobind Singh. Historically, the khalsa is the community founded by the tenth guru to keep the Sikhs in military readiness and bravery, but it has become a symbol of belonging to the Sikhs, an identity expressed concretely by the uncut hair and turban worn by men. Although there are birth rituals for Sikhs, the real entrance into the Sikh community for many is through the initiation into the order of the khalsa held when the individual comes of age. It is true that many Sikhs (perhaps the majority) do not actually go through this initiation ceremony, yet they uphold the code of beliefs and conduct of the khalsa, and they join in the oft-repeated salutation, "Hail to the Guru's khalsa! Hail to the Guru's victory!" And there are some Sikhs who belong to non-khalsa groups.

The Sikh community differs from the other religions arising from India in having no priests, mendicants, or other holy persons as worship leaders. It is an egalitarian community, and any person with reasonable proficiency in the Punjabi language, including women, can conduct congregational services and act as readers of the *Adi Granth*. Larger gurdwaras may appoint functionaries called granthis, to organize and lead the religious life of the community, take care of the gurdwara, and officiate at weddings and other ceremonies. Although some granthis may have special training, they are not "priests."

Leadership in the Sikh community is found in the committees formed to manage the gurdwaras (temples). These are local autonomous bodies, elected democratically. These groups not only manage the temples but also run many educational institutions and publish religious literature, playing a leading role in political developments as well. In modern times, Sikhs have set up a central authority, the Shiromani Gurdwara Parbandhak Committee (known as the SGPC), made up of the leaders of the major historic gurdwaras in the Punjab in India. However, the legal authority of the SGPC is limited to the Punjab, and Sikhs in other parts of India as well as in the overseas diaspora do not necessarily feel bound by its decisions. The final authority, for Sikhs throughout the world, is the *Guru Granth Sahib*.

Sikh Vision of the Ethical Life: Self-Realization Love of God and the guru is the basis of the good ethical life, leading to happiness, grace, and self-realization. And that good life is the natural life, following the highest law that is in the human heart. As Guru Nanak said, we should act according to the Universal Will that is written within one's self. The Sikh tradition is unique in India in maintaining that the highest ethical life is carried out not by renunciants, mendicants, or priests, but by householders. The three main practices of that good life are work, worship, and charity.

The primary human problem that stands in the way of the good life is the ego, that is, attachment to self apart from God. Sikhs believe that one's present life has been shaped by karma in past existences, and further that the Will of God controls all existence. However, even though much of our existence is beyond our ability to control, we do have a realm of free will in which we can cultivate the love of God and follow the guidance of the guru in order to break our attachment to selfishness. The good life is seen as the way to move away from ego to the union of the self with God and, thus, complete self-realization. This means cultivating concrete virtues and avoiding attachments to sins and vices, thus becoming a true Sikh.

There are, of course, springs of action that hinder the moral life; these are concupiscence, anger, covetousness, attachment, and pride, the "evil ones and thieves" that continuously steal away our virtues. Against these vices Sikhism does not advocate extreme asceticism or withdrawal from social relations. Rather, recognizing one's place in God's Will, one should cultivate the central virtues. Guru Nanak said that the many vices are like chains around one's neck; vices can only be removed by virtues.

Heading the list of virtues would be wisdom, as the foundation for the good life, and truthfulness, as a fundamental quality growing from the love of God and one's fellow humans. Another central human virtue is justice, regarding all others as equal to oneself, respecting their rights, and not exploiting them. Sikhs further emphasize the virtue of self-control, living one's life in moderation and governing the lower impulses by the higher, not through extreme asceticism but through moderation: eating less, sleeping less, and talking less, as Guru Nanak suggested. A related virtue would be contentment, that is, accepting both success and failure calmly.

Still one more characteristic virtue in the Sikh view of the good life is courage. Sikhs are enjoined to be fearless and unflinching in standing in their faith, no matter what the suffering. Beginning with Guru Gobind Singh, the tenth guru, the virtue of courage was extended to taking arms and struggling on the battlefield in the cause of righteousness. For when the situation is past all remedies, it is righteousness to take to the sword. Such militant courage is to be used only when all other avenues are closed and together with the other virtues of justice and love. The virtue of courage is embodied especially in the khalsa with its code of discipline and the symbolic wearing of the sword.

But how does one apply these virtues concretely to life in family and in society? Sikhism teaches that all should perform the duties associated with their particular station in life. Furthermore, all should observe the duties of right livelihood, not depending on the charity of others and not being dishonest in trade. They should help the needy, regarding such help as an act of service to the guru. Extramarital sexual relations are immoral, and intoxicants and narcotics are forbidden.

As part of their vision of the good life in human society, Sikhs reject the Hindu caste system in favor of the principle of universal equality. One concrete symbol of this social equality is the characteristic Sikh institution of the community kitchen (langar), where people of all sorts sit together and partake of the same food without any distinction between the high and the low.

With respect to gender roles, Guru Nanak and the gurus who followed generally upheld equality of women in all spheres of life. Women are to be accorded equal status and respect with men, conducting worship services, leading Sikh armies, voting in elections, and the like. Guru Nanak said,

> Of a woman are we conceived,
> Of a woman are we born,
> To a woman are we betrothed and married,
> It is a woman who is friend and partner of life,
> It is woman who keeps the race going. . . .
> Why should we consider woman cursed and condemned
> When from woman are born leaders and rulers.
> From woman alone is born a woman,
> Without woman there can be no human birth.
> Without woman, O Nanak, only the True One exists.[13]

Wives of the gurus have been strong leaders in their own right and, thus, have provided models for women in Sikhism. For example, Mata Gujri, wife of Guru Tegh Bahadur, was a strong force in holding the community together after the Guru's martyrdom, helping to infuse courage and sustain the community even through martyrdom for her grandsons, her son Guru Gobind, and even herself. Because of long-standing cultural traditions, it seems that the status of women is still not on a par with that of men in religious leadership, especially in India. But today Sikh women are active in all community spheres, including important leadership posts as secretaries or presidents of many gurdwara management committees.

To realize human brotherhood, Sikhs are taught to do away with slander of others and all enmity toward them. In a positive sense, they are to practice altruism toward all, involving themselves in social service for the poor and needy—for in serving humanity, one is serving the guru and serving God. Sikhs point to the example of Bhai Ghanaya, whose duty on the battlefield was to bring water to the thirsty soldiers. But he was found bringing water to the Hindus and the Muslims as well as the Sikhs, so the Sikhs complained to the guru that he was helping the enemy. When the guru asked him about his actions, Bhai Ghanaya explained, "O true King, I do not see who is a friend and who is a foe. I see your image in every one of them alike. They are all your Sikhs and none else, and so I served water to every one of them." When by the grace of the Guru our heart is filled with divine light, there is no enemy, and none is "other."

In the Sikh vision of the good life for the world today, peoples of all nationalities and religions are considered equal.

SIKH PRESENCE

Sikh majority

Sikh minority

AFGHANISTAN

Inset

JAMMU AND KASHMIR

Nanak's birthplace

Amritsar

HIMACHAL PRADESH

CHINA

PAKISTAN

PUNJAB

ARUNACHAL PRADESH

1947 partition of India and Pakistan

HARYANA

New Delhi

NEPAL

RAJASTHAN

UTTAR PRADESH

ASSAM

MEGHALAYA

GUJARAT

MADHYA PRADESH

BIHAR

BANGLADESH

WEST BENGAL

TRIPURA

Calcutta

INDIA

ORISSA

BAY OF BENGAL

Mumbai (Bombay)

MAHARASHTRA

20°

20°

ARABIAN SEA

ANDHRA PRADESH

15°

KARNATAKA

JAMMU

HIMACHAL PRADESH

10°

KERALA

INDIAN OCEAN

LAHORE

Lahore   Amritsar

SARGODHA

PUNJAB

Jhelum River

Indus River

Chenab River

MULTAN

Sutlej River

HARYANA

Delhi

0   300 Miles

0   300 Kilometers

70°   75°

1947 Partition

Punjab at the end of reign of Mughal Emperor Akbar (1605)

Sikh majority

All religions originated with good intentions and are like different roads leading to the same destination. Sikhs feel they should not enter into arguments about the truth of other religions. Rather the gurus encourage the cultivation of a rational attitude, finding out for oneself what is right and what is wrong. In doing so, Sikhs believe one will find that the path taught by the ten gurus is the highest path of self-realization.

Sikhism in modern times is not a missionary religion, but Sikhs do consider Guru Nanak and the other gurus as world teachers. And so Sikhs today have translated their scriptures and provided other means of education by which other peoples of the world can better understand and appreciate the Sikh vision and way of life. For example, a modern Sikh thinker, Taran Singh, has interpreted the khalsa in such a way as to transcend a narrow sectarian view. There is one universal Spirit, he holds, who belongs to all people, whatever their color, country, caste, or religion; there are no privileged people or superior faiths. He writes,

> The doctrine of the Khalsa or the Universal Brotherhood of the Pure, proceeds from the doctrine of the all-pervasive and indivisible ultimate Reality. The Wonderful Lord manifests himself in a wonderful drama . . . of the cosmos and creation. In fact all the actors in this cosmic play are Khalsa or Pure; they are all saints and no sinners. . . . So the brotherhood of the Pure is the brotherhood of the entire humanity.

And those initiated Sikhs who make up the actual khalsa are to be seen as an ideal society of humankind who have a mission to perform: "It is a society of humanity so that they might transform the world into the Kingdom of Heaven."[14]

DISCUSSION QUESTIONS

1 How did a monotheistic religion such as Sikhism develop in India in the fourteenth and fifteenth centuries C.E.?

2 What was the experience that transformed Nanak and made him a guru?

3 What is the role of the ten gurus in Sikhism? Why is the *Adi Granth* also called Guru?

4 Describe the special Sikh form of monotheism. How is this similar to, or different from, the monotheism of the Abrahamic religions?

5 How do the Sikhs maintain both the idea of God's creation of the world and belief in samsara and rebirth?

6 According to the Sikhs, what is the major human problem? What is the main movement on the path of transformation, and what is the spiritual goal?

7 What is kirtan, and why is this practice so central in Sikh worship?

8 What is the khalsa, and what is the importance of the khalsa in the Sikh community today?

9 What would you consider to be the key ethical virtues in the Sikh worldview?

10 Give examples from Sikh life showing how the principle of equality for all people is put into practice.

KEY TERMS: SIKHISM

Adi Granth "original collection," the sacred scripture of the Sikhs; *see also Guru Granth Sahib*

Arjan the fifth guru and first Sikh martyr (1563–1606)

Gobind Singh the tenth and last Sikh guru (1666–1708), who founded the khalsa

Golden Temple important Sikh gurdwara at Amritsar

gurdwara temple and meeting place for Sikhs, housing a copy of the *Adi Granth*

Guru leader and guide for Sikhs, through whom God's word is channeled; besides the ten gurus, God and the *Adi Granth* are also called Guru

Guru Granth Sahib "Sacred Collection," the Sikh sacred scriptures, with the title Guru; another name for the *Adi Granth*

Kabir a poet (1440–1518), an important predecessor of Guru Nanak, founder of Sikhism

karah parshad sacred food used in the Sikh worship assembly

khalsa a major military-type group within Sikhism, founded in 1699 by Gobind Singh, the tenth guru, with a special code of discipline

kirtan Sikh practice of singing hymns in worship of God

langar Sikh community kitchen

Nam in Sikhism, the Name of God, the total divine presence in the world

Nanak founder (1469–1539) of Sikhism and the first guru

Sikh "disciple," that is, one who follows the gurus

Singh surname taken by men who join the Sikh khalsa

Word of God in Sikh thought, God's presence that reverberates throughout creation, channeled especially through the gurus

Part 3 Religions of China and Japan

INTRODUCTION

East Asia—that vast region including the peoples of China, Korea, Japan, and Mongolia—is a very diversified cultural area with many different ethnic and linguistic groups. Moreover, it has an immense number of people—perhaps one-fourth of the people of today's world live in East Asia! In their very long and complex cultural history, the peoples of East Asia have seriously experimented with many world visions, philosophies, and ways of life. These traditions are called by different names, and there are varieties within each stream of tradition—Confucianism, Daoism, Buddhism, Shinto, and the many forms of popular religion.

In this exploration into the religions of East Asia, we will focus especially on the religions of China and Japan, a group of religious traditions that is perhaps not as closely knit historically as those arising in India or the Abrahamic religions (Judaism, Christianity, and Islam). Even within China the vast land and the variety of ethnic groups promoted a diversity of religious traditions, and Japan developed a unique culture in isolation until Chinese influence began to infiltrate in the sixth century C.E.

But there is some commonality of vision underlying all this, even in the divergent practices and teachings. It is possible in a certain sense to speak of the religious traditions of China, and Japan as a family of religions, for they do share important historical developments and religious ideas. Historically, China had developed a great civilization by the second millennium B.C.E., and its Confucian and Daoist religious traditions were passed on later to Korea and Japan and the rest of East Asia to become the heart of the common East Asian vision. And Mahayana Buddhism, though originally foreign to China, was accepted and transformed into a Chinese religious tradition, and this also was shared with Japan and the rest of East Asia to form another major component. So the common history is largely a matter of Chinese civilization, developing stage by stage, moving outward to permeate the rest of East Asia with its culture, written language, and a common religious outlook, tempered, of course, by the indigenous traditions such as Shinto in Japan.

But what are some main elements of that common East Asian religious vision? A good word to start with is *harmony*—the functioning harmony of a cosmos filled with sacred forces. There is a close interrelationship of the human and natural orders, and the sacred forces—gods, kami, spirits, yin–yang forces—stand at the heart of the sacred ecology. This is one unified world—no transcendent God or eternal world outside this unified sacred cosmos. We are a part of this one world together with all the sacred forces and all of nature, and our highest good comes in maintaining harmony and balance within it.

The natural social links to family, community, and nation are key arenas of religious involvement for the peoples of China and Japan. The family in particular is the realm of sacred power most directly and concretely affecting one's existence. And the family is founded on the ancestors, so worship of ancestors is a most characteristic form of religious expression. Many gods and spirits are associated with the home, and most religious rituals are based in the family. The pattern of family relationships is also the basis for one's relationship to the community and to the nation as a large sacred family.

The religious traditions of China and Japan are typically "this worldly," in the sense that some transcendent world or a future life after death is not the central concern. It is true that Mahayana Buddhists did bring into East Asia a concern about the fate of the souls of the dead. But the strongest emphasis is on the good, balanced life here and now. The world is good and beautiful, human nature derives from positive sacred forces like Heaven and the kami, and the religious path means achieving and enhancing the potential life of sacred harmony in the world and in human society. There is no sharp division, then, between sacred and secular parts of life, between spiritual and humanistic concerns, for all are joined together in balance.

We should note that one strong common factor throughout East Asia is the worldview of Mahayana Buddhism. Though originally a foreign religion from India, Mahayana Buddhism was thoroughly transformed into an East Asian religion, itself transforming East Asia at the same time. The key concepts of shunyata (emptiness) and the universal Dharma Body of the Buddha have permeated the culture and the arts of China and Japan in very fundamental ways, in a creative union with the Chinese notion of Dao as the source and support of all reality.

Founded on these common ideas, the cultures of China and Japan demonstrate a profound appreciation for ritual and for the aesthetic quality of life. Important aspects of life tend to be highly ritualized, for ritual helps to create and sustain harmony. Art is united with religion, for it is in the good and beautiful material of human life that the fullest expressions of the religious vision can be created. And it is not only the product of art but also the process of artistic creation—the "way" of art—that is considered important in East Asian religions.

It is tempting to put great emphasis on the common elements of the East Asian religious traditions, for this provides a basic context in which to compare and understand these particular religions. But this can be misleading if it covers up the fact that each tradition has its own special shape and integrity. Among the religious traditions of China and Japan, the interplay between common elements and distinctive traditions is somewhat complicated. First of all, the Chinese religious traditions form their own unity, and the Japanese religious traditions also make up a unified culture. But within China it is important to recognize the separate streams of tradition that are called Confucianist, Daoist, and Buddhist. And yet actual Chinese religion as practiced by the people consists of a synthesis of these traditions and includes many common popular religious practices as well. The situation is similar in Japan. Shinto represents the indigenous tradition, still alive and well today, but Buddhism also receives the allegiance of most Japanese, and Confucian values and popular religious practices are also part of Japanese religion as it is lived in local communities.

Chapter 11

Chinese Sacred Story and Historical Context

[*Note:* The pinyin spelling of Chinese names and terms, widely in use today, is adopted here. The older Wade-Giles spellings, still used in some scholarly works, will be given after the first use for important terms. We will use the name Confucius in its very familiar Western form.]

Today, people of Chinese heritage live all over the world, often maintaining their distinctive culture in Chinese communities in places such as Singapore, Bangkok, San Francisco, London, and many, many other places. In the Chinese homeland itself, the turbulent history of the twentieth century caused many disruptions and changes. But still Chinese culture remains, supported by well over a billion people in China and elsewhere who know they are Chinese.

To be Chinese is to belong to one of the most ancient societies on earth, to respect the ancestors and the land. Called the Middle Kingdom, this ancient great people and vast land were felt to be the reflection on earth of the mandate of Heaven, the society of the cultivation of the ideal human.

In speaking of Chinese religion, it has been customary to highlight the three paths that developed over many centuries in China, that is, the Confucianist, Daoist, and Buddhist traditions. For most Chinese, these three traditions are one story. Traditional Chinese honor all three paths; this is the Chinese way—the way of harmony. Underlying all three paths are the traditional Chinese practices and ideas focused on the family, the ancestors, gods and spirits, and the various forces of nature—all those elements that since ancient times have made up traditional Chinese religion.

The Chinese story begins in very ancient times with great kingdoms and ideal rulers. Important classical writings were produced that have guided Chinese thinking ever since. The story includes the diversification of the tradition in the forms of Confucianism and Daoism, and the coming of Mahayana Buddhism fills out the religious universe of the Chinese people. Each of the three great traditions underwent centuries of growth and decline and revitalization, interacting with one another and contributing to the common popular religion of most of the Chinese people. But in this diversity of traditions and schools there remains a striking unity, based on a common written language, an overriding sense of the centrality of the family, an abiding concern for the harmony of Dao, common classical writings, and an overall sense of this vast group of peoples as one national family.

FOUNDINGS OF THE CHINESE TRADITIONS

The beginnings of the Chinese story go far back to ancient China, long before **Kongzi (Confucius)** and **Laozi (Lao Tzu)**, the reputed founders of the Confucianist and Daoist traditions. China is one of the oldest continuous civilizations in the world and, thus, this story is the accumulation of wisdom over many, many centuries. Confucius, Laozi, and the other sages did not start totally new traditions—they simply reshaped and revitalized what had long been present in China.

Ancient Rulers and Worldviews

Humans have lived in China for hundreds of thousands of years. Near Beijing, important discoveries of so-called Beijing Man have been made in caves, representing the human culture of *Homo erectus* dating from about 500,000 years ago. Humans here had learned the use of fire, used tools and hunted big game animals, and had developed social structures. After the last glacial period, abundant evidence of Neolithic culture is found in China, where agricultural peoples lived in villages, made coarse pottery, used the stone-bladed hoe for agriculture, and kept domestic animals such as pigs, horses, and cattle.

Chinese traditions tell the story of important sages who lived during the third millennium B.C.E., namely, the Three Sovereigns and the Five Emperors. The Three Sovereigns domesticated animals, instituted family life, and invented agriculture. Heading the list of the Five Emperors, Huang Di, the Yellow Emperor, is traditionally seen as the symbolic ancestor of all Chinese people. Appropriately, he and his court are credited with inventing many of the cultural boons so important to later Chinese civilization: writing, music, medical arts, wooden houses, carriages, bronze mirrors, silk cloth, weapons, and the like. The great sage-king Yu, sometimes considered the last of the Five Emperors, is famous in legend for saving China from the great flood by engineering a drainage system, thus creating China's major rivers. He is credited with founding the first Chinese dynasty, the Xia (Hsia, ca. 2200–1750 B.C.E.). Although archaeological evidence has not substantiated the existence of the Xia dynasty as such, it is clear that there was a fountainhead of culture in this period, when people knew the art of casting bronze, the cultivation of the silkworm, the use of the wheel, and perhaps the value of written symbols. Surely they venerated their ancestors, and they paid great concern to the fertility of the earth and the presence of many sacred powers of nature.

The Period of the Shang Rulers History—that is, knowledge of ancient life based on written materials and supported by archaeological evidence—begins with the Shang period (ca. 1751–1111 B.C.E.). Shang kings mastered neighboring tribes in northeastern China and marched to northwestern China to incorporate the Xia alliance. Under the Shang rulers, important features of Chinese culture developed: ceramics, carving, bronze casting, the chariot, architecture, the feudal system, the calendar, and the art of writing. Typical Chinese religious practices, probably with roots in earlier periods, came to clear expression in the Shang era.

The Shang rulers established a kind of theocracy, with themselves as divine rulers who worked for the welfare of their people by worshiping the gods, the ancestors, and especially the high god, Shang Di. All the forces of the world—sun, wind, rain, rivers, and earth—are gods to be worshiped and served. But they are all part of the pantheon presided over by Shang Di, the "Lord Above," who can be worshiped only by the Shang ruler—perhaps being the ruler's primordial ancestor. The hierarchy of the ruler and his people is reflected in the hierarchy of the supreme god and the lower gods and goddesses, and that establishes a central dimension of Chinese religious tradition: the pattern of social ranks and divine ranks making up the total order of nature and society.

Besides structuring the hierarchy of the gods and of society, the story of the Shang kings establishes the model for two additional basic tendencies in Chinese religion. The Shang kings worshiped their ancestors, and they performed divination rituals to understand the will of their ancestors and of the forces of nature.

Worshiping the ancestors was a very elaborate affair, and for the Shang rulers it involved establishing a royal genealogy and a well-organized ritual cycle. Furthermore, it was important for each king to become an ancestor when he died, and so elaborate burials were performed, including burial of carriages, utensils, ritual vessels, jewelry, weapons, food, and the like. Even wives and slaves, with their chariots and horses, were buried alive with their master, to continue the total royal life into the next world when the ruler would be an ancestor. The practice of burying wives and servants with the dead ruler was stopped later, with clay representations sometimes substituted; but the important perception that the ancestor continues to live and rule in an effective way is a long-time heritage of Chinese religion.

In order to determine the will of the ancestors and the operation of the various forces of nature, the Shang rulers consulted divination experts, just as some Chinese have continued to do up to the present time. Their favored form of divination was to use bones and shells heated in a fire and plunged in water, the cracks being read by experts and the answer inscribed on the bones. These oracle inscriptions—nearly 100,000 examples from the Shang capital city—represent the first clear use of Chinese writing in pictographs and ideographs, appropriately designed as an operational method of achieving harmony with the forces of nature.

The Ideal Society: Zhou Dynasty A rebellion by the Zhou tribal alliance brought down the Shang kingdom in the eleventh century B.C.E. and inaugurated the **Zhou (Chou) dynasty** (ca. 1123–221 B.C.E.), whose early rulers created a realm remembered ever after as a model for the ideal Chinese society. The evils of the Shang nobility brought about the rebellion of the Zhou family, we are told by the early Zhou writings, *Classic of History*, *Classic of Poetry*, and inscriptions on bronze vessels. A new religious consciousness had evolved, which held that the supreme God cannot merely be a patron deity of a ruling tribe. Rather, the supreme God, which now is called **Tian** (*T'ien*, Heaven), is a universal righteous moral authority. Heaven will give its mandate to rule only to a righteous king governing a righteous state, taking the mandate away from unrighteous rulers and peoples.

> Heaven without pity sent down destruction on Yin [Shang]. Yin has lost its mandate to rule, and we of Zhou have received it. . . . Heaven's mandate is not easy to keep. It is hard to depend on Heaven. People lose its mandate because they are not able to carry out the illustrious virtue of their forefathers.
>
> (*Shujing*, Chunshi 2,4)

The sage-kings of Zhou developed the notion of the moral mandate and righteous rule into a complete feudal political system, with the king as "Son of Heaven;" and the whole Zhou society was stratified hierarchically according to the relationship with the royal family. Here is the pattern that later generations looked to as the ideal human society.

As part of this overall pattern, the Zhou rulers developed ceremonialism to a degree perhaps unknown in many other cultures. Performing the proper reverential ceremonies (**li**), according to the ancient sages, is an expression of cosmic order. The ceremonies make connections with the larger forces of existence, especially with the ancestors, so that the people continue in their blessing. According to the ancient *Classic of Poetry*, ceremonial sacrifice for the ancestors in the early Zhou era was very elaborate and meticulously done. Preparations included making fermented liquor and preparing viands for the offerings. As the rites began, the representatives of the dead were seated. Many people were involved, choosing the sacrificial victims, slaying them, attending to the cooking, and arranging the sacrifice. At a certain point, the ancestral spirits arrived and accepted the offerings, blessing their filial descendant. The sacrifices were presented in brilliant array, and all par-

took of a large number of carefully prepared dishes. "Every ceremony is according to rule; each smile and each word are in perfect decorum. . . . We have done all within our power and have performed the rites without error" (*Shijing* 2:6.5.1–6). Through the proper performance of ritual, the order of society and of the cosmos itself was upheld.

Ancient Worldviews: Yin–Yang and the Five Elements It is clear that the personal wills of the family ancestors and of the various gods were important to the ancient Chinese people, and they had elaborate rituals to stay in harmony with them. But there are also impersonal forces that shape everything humans are and do, as discovered already in ancient times. These are forces that are powerfully helpful and productive when they are in harmony but cause destruction and death when they are out of harmony. One of the most significant discoveries in the Chinese story is the bipolar activity of the **yin** and **yang** forces. All reality is made up of the interaction of two polar forces: yin forces of darkness, femininity, coldness, wetness, and passivity; and yang forces of brightness, masculinity, heat, dryness, and activity. Keeping these forces in harmony brings benefits and happiness, but disharmony causes disaster and suffering.

The Chinese also discovered that all reality operates through the *five elements* or agents, which are qualities that act and transform things. These are water, fire, wood, metal, and earth, all operational qualities that interact with each other and cause things to be the way they are. We will explore these ideas of yin and yang and the five elements further in the next chapter.

To deal with these forces of the gods, the ancestors, yin and yang, and the five elements, the early Chinese people devised methods of divination, such as the use of bones and shells by the Shang rulers. By the Zhou period, the practice of divination that came to be widely used is the system of trigrams made up of broken and unbroken lines (e.g., ⚏ and ⚎), the unbroken lines representing yang and the broken lines representing yin. Each trigram has its own referent in cosmic forces operating in this particular context. By placing one trigram on top of another, a system of sixty-four hexagrams is developed, each with a special operational meaning. Commentaries on these hexagrams are written in the *Yijing (I Ching)*, the *Classic of Changes*, begun during the early Zhou period and certainly one of the most influential books in all of Chinese history.

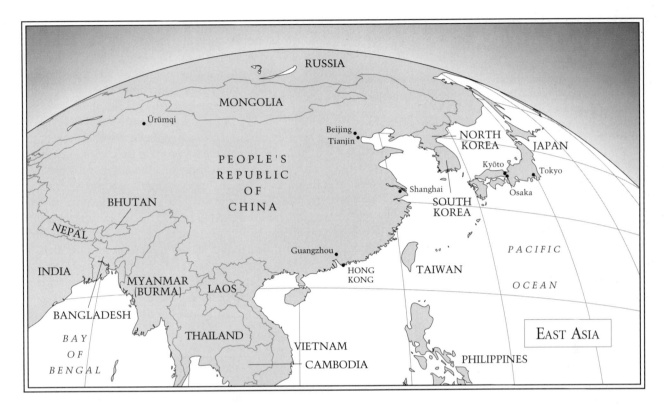

People still consult the *Yijing* today for guidance on all sorts of matters.

THE STORIES OF CONFUCIUS, LAOZI, AND THE CHINESE BUDDHA

In many religious traditions, it seems, some of the most important religious developments come when bad times overtake the stable institution that seems to be the religious ideal. So, too, in China, when the ideal Zhou kingdom fell on bad times, in the ensuing questioning and searching there was a great period of religious transformation in which many important Chinese religious traditions were founded.

Anarchy and Searching in the Middle Zhou Period
Troubles for the Zhou rulers started around 800 B.C.E. when their power dwindled with the emergence of a number of independent states headed by powerful princes. The struggle for supremacy among these states continued for

five centuries until the rulers of the Qin (Ch'in) state emerged victorious and unified China under a dictatorship in 221 B.C.E.

A striking picture of the situation in the eighth and seventh centuries is given in some of the poems in the *Classic of Poetry*, reflecting the suffering and disruption felt during these times. If the rulers are really ruling according to the Mandate of Heaven, why are all these misfortunes and wars occurring? Is Heaven really the moral force that oversees all rulers and all nations?

> I look up to great Heaven, but it shows us no kindness. We have been disquieted very long, with great afflictions sent down. There is nothing stable in the land. Officers and people alike are in distress.

(*Shijing* 3:3.10.1)

> Great and far-spreading Heaven has restricted its kindness, sending down death and famine to destroy all through the land. Compassionate Heaven now strikes terror, showing no forethought or care. Criminals rightly are punished for their crimes,

but innocent people are indiscriminately overwhelmed with ruin.

(*Shijing* 2:4.10.1)

Oh, great and far-spreading Heaven, whom we call father and mother! Though without crime or offense, I suffer from these disorders. The terrors of great Heaven are too much. Indeed, I have committed no crime. Great Heaven is very excessive. Indeed, I have committed no offense.

(*Shijing* 2:5.4.1)

The poets lamented the fact that people look to Heaven but find no clear guidance. With the questioning of the traditional beliefs came a tendency toward a more rationalistic and humanistic interpretation of life.

The middle and late Zhou periods, in spite of the troubles of society, are remembered as a classical age of ancient China, for many creative developments took place. The laws were written down for the first time, and there were important advances in agriculture and production. The earlier classical writings of poetry, history, and divination were read and memorized by statesmen and scholars. Teachers set up schools to train boys for public office, or instructed small groups of disciples in their homes. Their teachings had to do with the ancient traditions, but they also took up the burning religious, political, and social issues of the day. The words of some of these teachers were remembered and written down by their disciples. Among these teachers were sages and leaders such as Confucius and Laozi, along with Mozi (Mo Tzu), **Mengzi** (Meng Tzu or Mencius), and **Zhuangzi** (Chuang Tzu). The important religious traditions of China—later known as **Confucianism** and **Daoism**—developed from these foundations.

The Confucian Story

The man whose teachings transformed Chinese society and have guided the Chinese state and educational system for the past two thousand years was of fairly obscure birth and was not widely recognized in his own lifetime. His disciples carried on his teachings after him, transforming them in the process, and eventually in the Han period his philosophy of life was enshrined as the official way of Chinese thought. Confucian cult became the state religion of China. The heart of the story is the vision of life articulated in the Confucian tradition. But the life story of Confucius himself is also important.

The Life of Confucius   Although there is a biography of Confucius from several centuries after his lifetime, supplying a detailed ancestry that makes him a direct descendant of the Shang royal house, contemporary records say little about his background. The collection of his sayings, the *Analects*, does not give much biographical information about his life. We know nothing for sure about his parents, for they are never mentioned in the materials from Confucius' time, leading to the supposition that he was orphaned at an early age. We do know of a daughter and a son, but from the early sources we know nothing about his wife.

He was born in the small state of Lu in the northeastern part of China around the year 551 B.C.E. Confucius said of himself that he was of humble status and he owned little personal property. Yet all the traditions suppose that he came from an aristocratic ancestry, and he certainly was well educated and had leisure time to pursue such arts as music and archery. In his day there were many members of formerly wealthy aristocratic families who were not able to

An eighteenth-century portrait of the great sage Confucius.

maintain their high social status, for there were not enough government positions available for all of them. According to Mengzi, Confucius was once a keeper of stores and once he was in charge of pastures. One of his disciples said that Confucius did not have a regular teacher, so perhaps he was largely self-taught. It is clear, however, that he excelled in learning the classical writings of the past.

Like most educated people of his day, Confucius aspired to political office, and there are persistent traditions that he was a minister in the state government of Lu for a time. His special goal was to restore the culture and religion of China to what they had been under the ideal reign of the early sage-kings of Zhou. His service in public office, however, was not recognized, and he was repeatedly rebuffed in his attempts to attain responsible public positions for which he felt he was suited. He turned to teaching to make his great contribution to Chinese culture. Confucius, perhaps because of his own background, had developed a sympathy for the common people, and when he set up his own school, he resolved never to turn away an aspiring student no matter how poor he was.

Confucius had a full life teaching in his state of Lu and seeing his disciples attain government positions so as to shape culture and society. But in his fifties he was frustrated and disillusioned with the lack of moral leadership in the state, and he decided to leave and journey to other states to instruct rulers and attempt to find a way of putting his principles into practice. Although he was respected and well received by many rulers, and was even offered a position here and there, he did not find the kind of moral commitment and understanding necessary to revitalize the ideal Zhou rule and society.

Finally Confucius was invited back to the Lu state, after a decade of wandering, when he was nearly seventy. Outwardly it perhaps seemed that he had failed, for no ruler had heeded him and put his ideals into practice. But these journeys and challenges contained the sparks of the future, when other Confucianists would journey and was teach and create a society that would use this fundamental vision as the standard of culture and religion.

After several years with his disciples back in Lu, Confucius fell sick and died. We do not know the details of his death, but the *Analects* (the collection of his sayings) tell about an earlier sickness when his disciples feared he was dying. His disciple Zilu was agitated that the master

was dying and suggested that sacrifice and prayer be offered. Confucius dryly commented, "Is there such a thing?" When his disciple quoted the ancient classics to support such prayer, Confucius said simply, "My prayer has been for a long time" (*Analects* 7.34). His life was his death prayer.

Death in Chinese society is a very important communal affair, and the mourning rituals—up to three years of mourning—are a high priority for the family. Although they were not his family, Confucius' closest disciples observed the three years of mourning after his death. He is like the sun and the moon, one disciple said (*Analects* 19.24); he was the uncrowned king, in the eyes of later generations.

The Way of Life According to Confucius   Perhaps we do not know a great many certain facts about the life of Confucius. But then the most important dimension of the Confucian story is not the life of Confucius but the way of life that he taught as recorded in the *Analects*. Many Chinese see their identity in following the Way of Confucius.

The way of life that Confucius walked and taught to his students was not a new, revolutionary change from the traditional Chinese way. He felt that the main problem was a breakdown in morality and values resulting from turning away from the standards of the early Zhou society. Now rulers usurped power and oppressed their subjects, ruling by laws and punishments, and the people responded with violence and hatred. So Confucius taught that the people needed to return to the basic principles of virtue as these were enacted by the virtuous rulers of the early Zhou period, who followed the **Mandate of Heaven** and presided over realms of peace and harmony.

What does it take for people to transform themselves into people who live in peace and harmony? Confucius articulated an important goal, that of *ren* (**jen**), humane goodness. Like so many ideographs among the written Chinese characters, ren is most expressive: the sign for a person plus the sign for two—that is, two persons in harmonious interaction, representing society in harmony. Confucius felt that all humans have the capability for this basic goodness. The reason people act selfishly and harmfully toward others is the influence of social anarchy and immorality of the rulers. How can this be turned around so that the people can become people of ren?

People need a discipline, Confucius taught, and the best discipline is the deliberate cultivation of the tradition of the ancient sages. That is the key to harmony and peace and prosperity. By studying their words and modeling one's actions after their actions, a person can become humane as they were. So Confucius led his disciples in studying the classics, writings traditionally held to stem from the sage-kings of earlier times. Some traditions say Confucius even had a hand in writing or at least editing these classics, which form such an important part of the Chinese tradition. The heart of the Confucian scriptures has always been the **Five Classics**. As they took their final form in later times, these include the *Classic of History* (*Shujing*), recording words and deeds of the ancient sage-rulers from the prehistoric Yao period to the early Zhou period. The *Classic of Poetry* (*Shijing*) is a collection of some three hundred poems dating mostly from early Zhou times, exemplifying the quintessence of moral virtue and poetic beauty. The *Classic of Changes* (*Yijing*) is a book of divination that includes interpretations and commentaries explaining the patterns of the universe. A sacred text on ritual is the *Classic of Rites* (*Lijing*), giving detailed accounts and interpretations of the rituals of the ancient sage-kings, plus additional philosophical teachings. And the fifth classic is the *Spring and Autumn Annals* (*Chunqiu*), a record of events in Confucius' native state of Lu between 722 and 481 B.C.E., together with several commentaries. There apparently was a sixth classic, the *Classic of Music*, which is no longer extant. Study of these classical writings provided a full humanistic education in what we now would call the liberal arts: history, literature, natural science, religion, political science, and the fine arts. In leading his disciples into a path of self-transformation based on the study of these traditional writings, Confucius established the model that has been very influential in providing the shape of the Chinese way.

A key principle in the sages' way of life, Confucius taught, is *li*, a word that means "propriety" or "respectful ritual." This word originally referred to the sacrifices and rituals directed toward the ancestors, actions filled with respect and performed with great care and thoroughness. The heart of propriety is **filial piety** directed toward parents and ancestors. But Confucius showed how this attitude of respect can permeate all actions; we can practice propriety as we live our daily lives, performing the proper rituals and ceremonies as an outer discipline so that we transform ourselves inwardly into people of ren. Confucius

saw a close relationship between ritual and human goodness, as illustrated in this dialogue:

> Yen Yuan asked about humanity. Confucius said, "To master oneself and return to propriety is humanity. If a man (the ruler) can for one day master himself and return to propriety, all under heaven will return to humanity. . . . Do not look at what is contrary to propriety, do not speak what is contrary to propriety, and do not make any movement which is contrary to propriety."

(*Analects* 12.14)[1]

The purpose of practicing propriety, Confucius taught, is to establish the proper relationships in family and in society. As these outer relationships are in order, so the inner nature is also in order.

In teaching the discipline of study and the practice of rituals to transform people toward humaneness, Confucius knew he was putting forth a way of life that had its foundation in sacred power. He spoke of his practice as **Dao** (way), a term used from earlier times to designate a religious path. To follow Dao means to be in harmony with the ancestors and spirits, with the forces of yin and yang and the five elements, and with the will of Heaven. Yet Confucius was not overly interested in what we might think to be the "religious" aspects of Dao, that is, the gods, spirits, and natural forces. His concern was human life in family and society, not invocation of gods and spirits. Once a student asked him about worshiping gods and spirits, and his answer was: "If we are not able to serve humans, how can we serve gods?" And when the student asked about death, Confucius replied: "If we do not yet know about life, what can we know about death?" (*Analects* 11.11). The gods and spirits should not be the focus of attention; much more important is the transformation of human society into a society characterized by humaneness.

But this is not to say that Confucius had no vision of the sacred in relation to human life. He was deeply religious in his conviction that Heaven as the supreme moral authority ruled over all through its decree or mandate. And he believed that his own way was in harmony with the Mandate of Heaven, although he preferred to leave the demonstration of that to the real evidence of his life. Once, when he was in danger, he said: "If the Way is to prevail, it is Heaven's will. If the Way is to be stopped, it is Heaven's will. What can Gongbo Liao do against Heaven's will?" (*Analects* 14.38).

So it is that through Confucius' teaching and life, the Way of Heaven became a central part of Chinese identity. Even Chinese who do not call themselves Confucianists still follow his model in studying the classics, practicing the traditional rituals, cultivating the proper family relationships, and striving to live together in peace and harmony according to his teachings.

Disciples of the Confucian Way   Many of Confucius' disciples went on to become important government officials, for Confucius was particularly concerned with educating the superior person who could lead the people with virtue and propriety and, thus, help them develop their humanity. As these disciples passed on the teachings of Confucius, they also developed and shaped them. Two new writings in the Confucian tradition were produced that had a great effect and became part of the story, helping to shape Chinese identity ever since. These are the *Doctrine of the Mean* and the writings of Mengzi.

The *Doctrine of the Mean*, traditionally attributed to a grandson of Confucius and incorporated as a chapter in the *Classic of Rites*, teaches that the Way of Heaven that prevails throughout the universe also underlies the moral nature of humans. Our nature has been imparted to us by Heaven. Therefore, we can develop this Heaven-given nature, assisting in developing the nature of others, even reaching the point of assisting in the transformation process carried on by Heaven and Earth. The *Doctrine of the Mean* set forth the very influential image that humans can become a unity with Heaven and Earth in the nourishing and transforming process of the Way.

Mengzi (ca. 372–289 B.C.E.) has been accepted by many as the chief interpreter of the Confucian tradition, and his writings rank second only to Confucius in their importance for shaping the Confucian way of life. Mengzi established the philosophy that humans in their original nature are "good," and from this he drew the principle that all political and social institutions exist for the benefit of the people. We are to serve Heaven, Mengzi taught, by fulfilling human nature and living the good moral life. "He who knows his nature knows Heaven. To preserve one's mind and to nourish one's nature is the way to serve Heaven."[2] Mengzi followed the lead of Confucius in teaching a humanism rooted in the Way of Heaven—a humanism that for many centuries has been a foundation of the Chinese way of life.

Laozi and the Beginnings of Daoism

Dao has long been a central concern of Chinese people. In the experience of Confucius, the Way is realized especially in social relations, in the family structures, in ruler–subject relationships, and the like. But there were others in this fertile middle Zhou period who took a sharply different approach to harmony with Dao. These Daoists (as they later came to be called) felt the Way of Confucius was too artificial and structured. Real harmony with Dao is to withdraw from the structures of society and experience the natural rhythms of the universe itself. Daoism later developed institutions of priesthoods and rituals that identify it as a particular religion of China. But as a philosophy of life, complementing Confucianism as its polar contrast, the vision of Daoism has greatly influenced many Chinese people.

The Story of Laozi and the *Daode jing*   Who was Laozi, traditionally said to be the founder of Daoism? There are legends about his life, although many scholars suspect that these legends are collective representations of sages who protested against the tight structuring of society by withdrawing to the mountains as recluses to practice methods of harmonizing with nature. Details of his life are rather scanty. Even the great historian Sima Qian, writing in the mid-second century B.C.E., despaired of writing an accurate biography of Laozi. And that is properly so. For one who attunes himself so completely with the flow of Dao as did Laozi passes beyond the limitations of human history.

But the legend has its importance. Laozi was born about 604 B.C.E., it is said, making him an older contemporary of Confucius. He was conceived sixty-two years before this at the time when his mother had admired a falling star. When the time came for his birth, his mother gave birth while leaning against a plum tree, and he was able to speak when he was born. Since his hair was already white, he was called Laozi, "Old Master."

Later Laozi became palace secretary and keeper of archives for the court of Zhou at Louyang. Many knew of his wisdom and the spiritual depth of his meditative practices and came to be his disciples. The story reports that even Confucius came to visit Laozi in 517 and was overwhelmed by his deep insight and spirituality.

But by the time he was 160 years old, Laozi had become disgusted with the way people lived in the world, and he decided to withdraw from society to pursue the higher virtues in the mountains of the west. As he departed through the Hangu Pass, riding a chariot drawn by a black ox, the keeper of the pass recognized him as a sage and prevailed upon him to write his wisdom in a book. Laozi responded by writing down the 5,000 characters of the book called ***Daode jing*** (***Tao Te Ching***) and then he departed for immortal sagehood.

These legendary stories of Laozi's life do not connect with historical events very well. He appears to be representative of the approach developed by a group of recluse thinkers, especially in the fourth and third centuries B.C.E., who resisted the Confucian structures of society and advocated instead a simple nature mysticism. Whereas Laozi is an important character, it is not so much the legend of his life as the sacred writing associated with him, the *Daode jing*, that has profoundly shaped Chinese life and thought.

This short text with its vision of living in harmony with the flow of Dao has been a most influential book in Chinese history. People of almost all traditions in China have gone to it for inspiration. And its influence has not been limited to China—no book except the Bible has been translated into Western languages as often as this text. It is, of course, a special book of those who call themselves Daoists, the ones who follow Dao.

The title, *Daode jing*, means "Classic of Dao and Power." It puts forth a vision of the Way that stands in sharp contrast to the Confucian notion of the Way of Heaven. Dao is the sacred principle immanent in nature, that which is the source of all and that to which all returns. In a typically cryptic statement, the *Daode jing* describes Dao:

> There was something undifferentiated and yet complete,
> Which existed before heaven and earth.
> Soundless and formless, it depends on nothing and does not
>   change.
> It operates everywhere and is free from danger.
> It may be considered the mother of the universe.
> I do not know its name; I call it Tao.
>
> (Ch. 25)[3]

Everything in the world is produced by this universal Dao, so all of nature has an inherent harmony and balance in its natural process.

Since Dao is the source of all, the greatest human good is to be in harmony with Dao. And people get in harmony with Dao not by following rules of propriety or structuring

Laozi, the legendary founder of Daoism, whose philosophy is expressed in the *Daode jing*.

their activities in society, but by ***no-action*** (*wuwei*). That is, after all, how nature itself operates: passively, quietly, and in a natural rhythm. The tree grows, water flows, winter changes into spring—all without effort or striving. And so the Daoist sage will follow that pattern of no-action and nonstriving, withdrawing from the activities of society, harmonizing the inner self with the flow of Dao.

In weakness and passivity there is strength, the *Daode jing* teaches. The softest things in the world overcome the hardest things. Water washes away mighty mountain cliffs. The sage who attunes with nature, who does not use aggression and violence, who seeks not reward and position, who lives spontaneously without rules and plans, who accepts weal and woe with equanimity—such a one is kingly and free.

"One with nature, he is one with Dao. One with Dao, he is eternal and is free from danger throughout his life" (Ch. 16).

Daoist Freedom and Creativity: Zhuangzi Nearly as important as Laozi in the formation of the Daoist story is Zhuangzi (Chuang Tzu) (ca. 369–286 B.C.E.), and his life is almost as legendary and obscure. It appears that he was a government official at one time, but probably he lived most of his life as a recluse doing, apparently, some very unconventional things. The traditional story counts him as the main successor and interpreter of Laozi and, most importantly, the author of the very influential book called *Zhuangzi*. It is from Zhuangzi's stories and parables more than anything else that we have derived our image of the free, unimpeded, nonconventional, roaming Daoist saint. Zhuangzi, thus, plays a significant role as a model for the Daoist way of life.

Zhuangzi was not concerned with good government or society; he proposed no plan to remake the world to improve the human situation. Rather, he used his great literary skills to advocate emancipation from the shackles of conventional values and thought and a total identification with the very process of nature, namely, Dao. Our conventional way of thinking tells us that some things are good and others evil, that pleasure is different from pain, that life is desirable and death is undesirable. But Dao encompasses all forms of existence without such distinctions and dualities. To be in tune with Dao is to transcend ordinary judgments and emotions and attain absolute happiness by understanding the real nature of things. Dao, embracing all things, is in a constant process of change and transformation. Rather than reacting to these changes with pain or pleasure, the wise one accepts them as the natural process and goes along with them.

Zhuangzi delighted in shocking conventional wisdom by extolling creatures that (by ordinary values) were ugly, misshapen, or useless; to Zhuangzi, they display the freedom and naturalness of Dao. He told a story about a horribly deformed man, Ziyu, who had a hunched back, internal organs on top of his body, and shoulders higher than his head. But when asked whether he disliked this condition, Ziyu replied,

> No, why should I dislike it? Suppose my left arm is transformed into a cock. With it I should herald the dawn. Suppose my right arm is transformed into a sling. With it I should look for a dove to roast. Suppose my buttocks were transformed into wheels and my spirit into a horse. I should mount them. What need do I have for a chariot? When we come, it is because it was the oc-

casion to be born. When we go, it is to follow the natural course of things. Those who are contented and at ease when the occasion comes and live in accord with the course of Nature cannot be affected by sorrow or joy. This is what the ancients called release from bondage.

(Ch. 6)[4]

Living with Dao frees one from the limitations imposed by normal, conventional life. In fact, Zhuangzi told stories about the ability of Daoist sages to fly through the air above the clouds, avoiding all harm, achieving miraculous longevity, and otherwise transcending normal human limitations. So one is freed from the conventions imposed by social life, laws and rules, ceremonies and etiquette, and all other forms of artificiality. Providing an alternative to the dominant Confucian philosophy of life, Zhuangzi has embedded in Chinese tradition a vision of spontaneity and naturalness that has given a special shape to culture, art, and religion.

Development of Popular Confucianism and Daoism

The teachings of Confucius and Mengzi, on the Confucian side, and of Laozi and Zhuangzi, on the Daoist side, are very important to the Chinese religious perspective, but they do not yet represent completely what the average Chinese thinks of as Confucianism and Daoism. There is something more to these religious ways, something more involving temples and priests, altars and shrines, gods and spirits, rituals and festivals. Moreover, the story is the story of the three Ways, and we have not yet mentioned the founding of the third Chinese Way, Buddhism. It was during the Han dynasty (202 B.C.E.–220 C.E.) that beginnings were made in the direction of a more specifically religious orientation of these Ways.

Confucian Triumph and the Cult of Confucius For some centuries after the time of Confucius, the Confucian approach to the humanization of society existed as one philosophy among others. There was the Daoist alternative, of course. Another important alternative to Confucianism was the movement founded by Mozi (Mo Tzu, ca. 471–391 B.C.E.), who lived soon after Confucius and taught an approach to life that rejected certain Confucianist principles. Mozi held a strong belief in a righteous God (Heaven) who loves all people impartially. The evils of the day, Mozi taught, are directly caused by the fact that people do not love one another altruistically but only selectively and partially—as exemplified by the Confucian notion of filial piety with its concern directed mainly to one's own family and clan. This kind of unequal treatment of others must be replaced by "universal love," loving all others as oneself, equally and impartially, showing the same respect for their lives and possessions as for one's own. Mozi leveled strong criticism against the extravagant rituals dedicated to the ancestors, such as the costly funeral rites. He was outspoken in his opposition to war and violence, and he taught that the highest good is that which benefits people. Mohism had many devout followers for several centuries and provided strong competition to the Confucian vision of human life.

Another significant movement grew up within the Confucian tradition itself, stemming from **Xunzi** (Hsun-Tzu, ca. 300–238 B.C.E.). Xunzi turned away from the perception of the fundamental goodness of humans to take the more realist position that humans by nature are basically inclined toward evil. Consequently, he advocated a strict system of discipline so that people's natural evil inclinations might be overcome and peace and order might exist. He also rejected all superstitious beliefs about supernatural powers and taught a naturalistic understanding of the world and of the value of rituals and ceremonies.

Some of Xunzi's ideas found expression in the school of the **Legalists**, who advocated a system of authoritarian government with strict laws and punishment to enforce order. These Legalists managed to gain control of the state of Qin (Ch'in), and eventually it was the Qin rulers who conquered the other Chinese states and established a unified empire in 221 B.C.E. The Qin Empire lasted only a few years, but it enforced a uniform order by the repression and wholesale slaughter of all opponents. It was, in fact, made a capital crime to discuss Confucian writings and principles, and books representing all views opposed to the Legalists were burned.

Here was a profound crisis for the Confucian tradition, as well as for the other non-Legalist schools of thought. But the story tells how some scholars, at risk to their lives, managed to save some of the classic writings so that the ancient wisdom was not lost in this book-burning frenzy. The Qin dynasty fell rapidly, to be replaced by the **Han dynasty** (202 B.C.E.–220 C.E.). The first Han rulers continued to be of the Legalist persuasion, although without the violent excesses of the Qin rulers. But now Confucian scholars managed to revive their teachings and work out a complete cosmological basis for a unified state under an emperor who served as the representative of Heaven, channeling the cosmic forces and providing harmony in society.

The turning point for Confucianism came when Emperor Wu (r. 140–87 B.C.E.) ascended the throne and, realizing the need for well-educated officials, ordered scholars to appear for interviews. One of the scholars was Dong Zhongshu (179–104 B.C.E.), who convinced the emperor to practice the teachings of Confucius only and dismiss all other theories and scholars. Emperor Wu appointed Dong to be the chief minister of the state, and soon he established doctoral chairs for the classics, thus making Confucianism the state ideology. Now all state officials had to pass civil service examinations in the Confucian classics, ensuring that Confucianism would remain as the official state ideology and, thus, as the leading component in the Chinese identity—a position it held until the beginning of the twentieth century.

Together with this intellectual triumph of Confucianism went a new emphasis on the rituals and ceremonies associated with Confucianism and the state. State-supported temples for Confucian ceremonies were established all over China, Confucius' home became a national shrine, spirit-tablets of Confucius and his disciples were venerated in elaborate rituals, and the so-called state cult of Confucius was born. Soon new versions of the texts began to assert the semidivine status of Confucius, and eventually Confucius even came to be considered a god in the popular religion of China.

Through all of this, the very broad range of teachings, rituals, education, and social structures that makes up the Confucian tradition had become the central focus of the Chinese culture.

Development of Daoist Religious Paths   The Daoist vision expressed by Laozi and Zhuangzi is not the complete story of Daoism. There were other streams of practice that merged with those early Daoist insights to produce that broad, complex religious tradition that is called Daoism. We should note, perhaps, that later Chinese scholarly usage tended to distinguish between "philosophical Daoism" (*Daojia*), that is, the kind of vision expressed in the *Daode jing* and the *Zhuangzi*, and **religious Daoism** (*Daojiao*), the popular religious practices that developed later. However, recent scholarship has questioned such a sharp distinction, showing rather the complex continuities between the early Daoist texts and the various religious practices that developed in interaction with those ideas.

Many of these practices were in existence in pre-Han times, although the full development of the Daoist religious tradition, complete with its writings, priests, and sects, took many centuries. The common denominator of these Daoist streams is the concern about long life and immortality. Laozi and Zhuangzi had already made some statements about the freedom from human limitations that can be experienced by getting into complete harmony with eternal Dao. Around this central notion there began to draw together many popular practices and beliefs cultivated from ancient times by shamans, mediums, and diviners, all rooted in the fundamental idea that humans can get in tune with the larger spiritual forces of our universe. The so-called hygiene school emphasized breathing exercises and various methods of controlling the bodily processes of decay as a way of prolonging life. A search was on to use the five elements in such a way as to produce an elixir of life, a movement that later became known as alchemy. And expeditions were organized to sail across the seas and find the Isle of the Blest, where it was believed there grew a plant that could renew a person's life and vitality. The emperor of the Qin dynasty had sent out such expeditions, and they continued in the Han period.

This search for immortality began to extend also to the common people, and it combined with the ancient interest in gods and spiritual beings. For example, around the year 3 B.C.E., a popular religious movement erupted centered on a mother goddess named Xiwangmu (Queen Mother of the West). All over China people turned to her with singing and dancing, believing that by worshiping her and wearing charms with her name written on them they would be able to avoid death. As these movements spread, other gods, goddesses, spirits, and Daoist immortals (sages who were thought to have become immortal) came to be included in the powers who could grant long life and immortality. One Daoist group called itself the Way of Great Peace (Taiping Dao). Their leaders functioned as both priests and military officers, and their chief god was Lord Lao, that is, Laozi, legendary author of the *Daode jing*, now worshiped as a god and as the creator of the world. They had a sacred book, the *Scripture of Great Peace*, which revealed how to restore good government, encourage peace, and bring good health and long life to the people. Known also as the Yellow Turbans, they instigated a rebellion that helped bring an end to the Han dynasty. Another group that originated in western China during the later Han period was the Way of the Celestial Masters (Tianshi Dao), which set up its own state ruled by a Master of Heaven with priest-officials as assistants. They also worshiped Laozi as a god.

These communities, worshiping Laozi and other gods and immortals and centering on rituals performed by priests on the basis of sacred texts, display some of the features of the developing religious path of Daoism. Here the ideas of Laozi and Zhuangzi were taken over and put in concrete form through rituals, priests, techniques for attaining immortality, and community structures. Daoism developed many more scriptures, organizations, rituals, and techniques over the next centuries, but its basic role in the Chinese story was already established.

The Beginnings of Chinese Buddhism

So we have the Way of Confucius and the Way of Daoism. But when traditional Chinese think of who they really are, the Way of the Buddha also plays a part, and so we should include the beginnings of Chinese Buddhism in the foundational history. The acceptance of Buddhism came gradually, over a number of centuries, and it was the Mahayana form of Buddhism that most connected with the Chinese story.

A tradition says that Han emperor Ming (58–75 C.E.) had a dream in which he saw a golden man, taken by his wise men to be the Buddha; so he dispatched envoys to northwestern India to bring back scriptures and teachers. We know that as early as the first century C.E., Buddhist monks and laypeople made their way along the silk routes into central Asia (through present-day Afghanistan) and on into China. For a time, Buddhism flourished in central Asia, creating an impressive civilization with renowned literature, paintings, and sculptures. But this Buddhist civilization faded away under Muslim pressure around the tenth century C.E. However, from central Asia, monks and missionaries went to China, where Buddhism came to be firmly planted and rose to become one of the three great religions of China, along with Confucianism and Daoism. This remarkable development—a religion from India being adopted by the Chinese and later, through Chinese influence, also by the Koreans and the Japanese—led to rich new transformations of Buddhism.

How did it come about that such a foreign way of thinking came to be so important in China? It is not easy to answer that, for there were things about Indian Buddhism that the Chinese people could not understand or accept. What was most problematic about Buddhism as it arrived in China was the monastic system: monks and nuns leaving their families, not working but begging for their food, taking the vow of celibacy and, thus, cutting off the family line. Traditional Chinese society strongly advocated the centrality of the family and the individual's duty to respect and care for parents and to continue the family by marrying and having children. Chinese values affirmed living in society, seeking happiness, and working productively for the good of all. Buddhist monks were accused of being lazy and idle because they went about begging and did nothing for the welfare of society. The notion that life is suffering and that worldly pleasure should be renounced also seemed strange to the Chinese, as did the "no-self" teaching of Buddhism. And Chinese scholars pointed out that Buddhism was a foreign, barbarian philosophy, not mentioned in the Chinese classical writings.

And so Buddhism was not widely accepted at first in China. But the incursion of Buddhism continued. Mahayana scriptures were brought in and translated into Chinese, and gradually the Chinese came to understand what Buddhism was about, transforming it in the process to fit better into the Chinese worldview. The upheaval that came with the end of the Han dynasty (220 C.E.) led many Chinese to turn away from Daoism and Confucianism and embrace Buddhism. From the fourth to the sixth centuries C.E., Buddhism consolidated its place and then became, for a time, the most powerful and vital religious force in the country.

The appeal of Buddhism was manifold and soon outweighed the initial negative reactions on the part of the Chinese. The disunity and warfare surrounding the end of the Han dynasty induced many to turn to the relative security and peace of the Buddhist monasteries, escaping, among other things, serving in the armies. And Buddhism in China showed itself not to be opposed to the importance of family life. By becoming a monk or nun, a child could actually fulfill a great amount of filial piety, praying for the family, accumulating merit for the welfare of the ancestors of the family, erecting pagodas to perpetuate the memory of the parents, chanting scriptures for their welfare, and performing the funeral rituals and the rituals for the release of the ancestral souls from purgatory. The monasteries in China tended to be like settled communities, supported by landholdings, serving as art centers, hostels, retreats, and centers of life. Although joining a monastery meant leaving one's family, it was like becoming part of a new family, especially in the filial-like relationship with one's Buddhist master.

When Buddhism came to China, it brought important new ideas about human existence that were enlightening to the people of China. The Chinese traditions had virtually nothing to say about life after death or the causes of one's present existence, and here Buddhism was influential. The law of karma, for example, helped to explain why people were born in particular circumstances, whether slave or king. The Buddhist doctrine of samsara helped people to understand that there are rebirths for all in future existences, on many different planes. In addition, Buddhist tradition supplied a great variety of conceptions about Buddhas and bodhisattvas, heavens, and hells. The cult of Buddhas and bodhisattvas could be added to other popular Chinese cults, and the idea of rebirth in the heavens was not unattractive. The Mahayana notion that each person possesses the Buddha-nature and is capable of salvation appealed to the common people. Buddhism from India contributed great scriptures and works of art to enrich Chinese culture and religion.

One way in which Buddhism was transformed in China was through the translation of Buddhist scriptures into Chinese. At first Theravada scriptures were translated, but as time went on, the great Mahayana texts of India were translated into Chinese or—scholars think some of them may actually have been composed in China—attributed to a translator. The high regard the Chinese have for the ancient classics led them to respect these translations and seek more. At the same time, putting Indian texts into Chinese inevitably meant coloring those ideas by Chinese vocabulary and concepts. Perhaps the greatest translator was Kumarajiva (344–413), who translated or revised translations of most of the popular Mahayana sutras and treatises from Nagarjuna's school, thus introducing the very important philosophy of emptiness into Chinese thought. Kumarajiva's translations are still in use today.

TRANSFORMATIONS IN THE CHINESE TRADITIONS

The shape of Chinese religion reached its fullness with the triumph of Confucianism as the state ideology and cult, the rise of religious forms of Daoism, and the acceptance of Buddhism as one of the foundations of the Chinese story—all of this integrated with the continuing popular religious practices focused on family, gods, and nature. So by the end of the Han period or not too long afterward, the main components of Chinese identity were in place. But Chinese tradition, like Dao itself, is dynamic, changing and restructuring itself with the flow of time. Religion in Chinese history, from the end of the Han period up to the present, has been characterized by the persistence of ancient ideas and practices and the continual interaction of the great religious traditions, even as new influences are encountered and integrated.

After the disintegration of Han rule around 220 C.E., China entered into a period of political disunity until the end of the sixth century. During this time Buddhism gained in acceptance and vigor, and Daoism was also in ascendancy, whereas Confucianism was gradually eclipsed. A high point of Chinese culture came in the Tang (T'ang, 618–907) and Song (Sung, 960–1280) eras, when there was a brilliant flowering of literature, art, and philosophy that signaled China as perhaps the greatest world civilization of the time. Winds of change came with the Mongols ruling all of China in the Yuan era (1280–1368). Chinese rule was temporarily reestablished with the Ming dynasty (1368–1644), and Neo-Confucian orthodoxy won the day.

Buddhist Expansion and Crystallization

Part of the reason for the great success of the Buddhist way in China was its acceptance by various emperors, such as Emperor Wu of the Liang dynasty (r. 502–549), who abolished Daoist temples and built Buddhist ones and who himself entered a monastery as a lay servitor. The Sui emperors (581–618) and the Tang emperors (beginning in 618) continued imperial support of Buddhism. The emperors were particularly attracted to the intellectual systems of the Buddhist schools, which could serve as a unifying ideology.

The whole Chinese cultural landscape was being made over under Buddhist influence. Thousands of monasteries and shrines were built, tens of thousands of people became monks and nuns, and often the monasteries had huge land holdings. Elaborate Buddhist rituals came to supplement the Confucianist and Daoist ones, and Buddhist festivals such as the Lantern festival, the Buddha's birthday, and Ullambana (All Souls' Day) came to be universally observed. Monasteries became social centers for money lending and medical care, serving also as hostels and retreats. Buddhist influence fostered literature and art, with particularly significant contributions in Buddhist sculpture.

Schools of Chinese Buddhism: **Tiantai** and **Huayan** Very important and characteristic of Chinese Buddhism was the development of a number of different schools or "lineages" that took place during the sixth and seventh centuries. Mahayana teachings had opened the way for a variety of different practices to reach the goal of liberation, whether by help from Buddhas and bodhisattvas or by one's own discipline and meditation—and many combinations in between these two paths. And it had produced many scriptures, purporting to be the Buddha's own word, explaining these paths. Why there are so many scriptures and paths was easily explained: The Buddha used skillful means and, thus, taught different doctrines and practices to suit the condition of the audience. So monks and nuns could devote their attention to one or several of the great scriptures and develop a school that would specialize in certain teachings and practices. While some ten such Chinese Buddhist schools are recognized, a number were of relatively minor importance, and only two continued past the persecutions at the end of the Tang period—that is, Pure Land and Chan (Ch'an). Two others did contribute a great deal to Chinese thought, however, and also to Buddhist developments in Japan: **Tiantai** (T'ien-t'ai) and **Huayan** (Hua-yen).

The Tiantai school, founded by Zhiyi (Chih-i, 538–597) at the monastery on Mount Tiantai, can be seen as a synthesis and harmonization of all Buddhist teachings and practices. According to this school, the great mass of scriptures taught by the Buddha can be classified into five periods in which the Buddha taught the different scriptures.

In the earlier periods he taught the Theravada scriptures and then, when the people were more enlightened, the elementary Mahayana scriptures; finally in the last period he taught that all paths leading to salvation are united in the one path as taught in the *Lotus Sutra*, which is the full and perfect teaching.

The Huayan school devoted its attention mainly to the *Garland Sutra*, teaching that the absolute reality and the temporary phenomenon are completely interfused with each other and that all phenomena interpenetrate each other. Thus, every thing or event in this passing world is a manifestation of the absolute, which means that everyone possesses the Buddha-nature and, thus, each is related to all other beings. Both Tiantai and Huayan, harmonizing many basic strands of tradition, deepened the Mahayana sense of the Buddha-nature as a universal reality present in all beings.

Practical Schools: Pure Land and Chan   The cultural climate of China lent itself to the creation of simpler and more direct versions of Buddhism, which had greater appeal to the masses than the complex philosophical teachings of Tiantai and Huayan. The inspiration for both these new forms, Jingtu or **Pure Land** Buddhism, and **Chan** (Ch'an) or Meditation Buddhism, came from India, of course, but as they developed in China they took on special Chinese characteristics and greatly increased the popular appeal of Buddhism in China. They developed strongly in the Tang era, partly as reformist reactions against the increasing worldliness of the powerful monastic establishment.

Amitabha Buddha (called *Amituo fo* in Chinese), the compassionate heavenly Buddha who created the beautiful and peaceful Pure Land paradise and assisted living beings to be reborn there, had been known in China from earlier texts, and meditation on Amitabha was practiced in monasteries. In the Tang era, teachers like Tanluan (476–542) and his successors began to focus on the recitation of the Buddha's name as their central practice, teaching that salvation in the Pure Land came through the power of Amitabha, open to all who recite his name orally with a concentrated and devout mind. By saying Amitabha's name over and over with faith in his vows to save all beings, even sinful people could hope for rebirth in the Pure Land paradise. It is easy to understand that the Pure Land school appealed directly to the common people with its simple but effective teachings and practices, and

its influence also permeated the other schools. Here was a form of Buddhism that could spread throughout the populace and be practiced in independent communities and societies outside the monasteries. Pure Land Buddhism soon became the most popular form of Buddhism in China and was taken also to Japan, where some centuries later it likewise became immensely popular. As it developed, Pure Land Buddhism became a characteristic form of East Asian culture.

Another distinctively Chinese school of Buddhism to develop in the early Tang era was Chan (meditation) Buddhism, likewise simple and direct and popularly supported. Chan was a thoroughly Chinese creation, drawing on the early Indian practices and texts that emphasize meditation. Meditation was, of course, practiced in all the schools but as only one aspect of many disciplines of study and ritual. The concern of the Chan masters was to make meditation the central practice to be vigorously pursued to reach enlightenment. In this sense it was a reform and simplification, somewhat parallel to the Pure Land movement.

According to Chan tradition, the founder of this school was Bodhidharma, an Indian meditation master who came to China around 470 C.E. When Emperor Wu of Liang asked him what merit he had earned by his donations and temple building, Bodhidharma answered, "No merit at all." Banished by the emperor, Bodhidharma went to northern China and settled in a mountain temple, where he spent nine years sitting in meditation gazing at a wall, it is said, until his legs fell off. He also, the story says, cut off his eyelids so that his gaze would not falter. Among the successors of Bodhidharma, the most famous was Huineng (638–713), known as the sixth patriarch, who supposedly was illiterate but demonstrated a flair for the direct, sudden awakening taught in Chan. His legendary career provided a model for Chan life, and all later masters claim to be descended from him. Two schools of Chan eventually became particularly influential, Linji (Linchi) and Caodong (Ts'ao-tung), differing on whether enlightenment should come suddenly or as a gradual process.

Chan is characteristically Chinese in the way it brings Buddhism into contact with Chinese ideas and practices, especially those of Daoism. The emphasis on meditation carries with it a certain anti-intellectual tendency, for, according to Chan, thoughts and concepts cloud the mind and, therefore, the mind must be emptied so that we can see directly into our Buddha-nature. In order to empty out the mind and see the truth directly, relationship with a master is crucial, for there is a special transmission of the truth outside the scriptures that goes from mind to mind, without words. Sayings and dialogues of the masters were collected and came to be used as themes for meditation. These "public documents" (*gongan*; Japanese *koan*) were used to show that ordinary logic must be transcended in order to see directly into one's real nature (see p. 302–303).

This school of Buddhism first became influential in the Tang era, advocating group meditation in the context of disciplined communal life in a monastery. Monasteries were established in remote areas, and frugality and shared work characterized the communal life. While Chan did not become a "popular" movement in the sense of great numbers of people joining the monasteries, it did achieve widespread support among the people of China. The Chan form of Buddhism is distinctively a creation of China, and in the stories about the masters, the iconoclastic attitude toward rituals and doctrines, the practice of meditation to realize Buddhahood, and the poems and paintings by Chan artists, we find some basic shadings of Chinese identity.

The golden age of Buddhism in China was glorious—but brief. Although it enjoyed wide support from all levels of society, there remained opponents among the Confucianists and Daoists, some of whom thought of Buddhism as a "foreign" religion. And the relative independence and growing wealth of the monasteries were often seen by the rulers of the state as a distinct threat. Finally, in 845, an ardent Daoist emperor, Wuzong (r. 840–846), ordered the suppression of Buddhism, leading to the destruction of most of the Buddhist monasteries and temples across the empire, and forcing tens of thousands of monks and nuns to return to lay life. Wuzong died the next year and the order was rescinded, but Buddhism never regained its former prestige and position. The only schools that survived the persecution were the popularly supported Pure Land and Chan schools, and they did continue to exercise considerable influence on Chinese culture.

A new development in the Song era (960–1280) was the emphasis on the compatibility of the two Buddhist schools.

Bodhidharma, the legendary founder of Chan Buddhism in China, crossing the Chang (Yangtze) River on a reed. 'Bodhidharma Crossing the Yangzi River on a Reed'. China, Yuan dynasty, 1279-1368. Hanging scroll, ink on paper, 89.2 x 31.1 cm. © The Cleveland Museum of Art, John L. Severance Fund, 1964.44.

In the monasteries, both meditation and recitation of Amitabha's name came to be employed together as two techniques toward achieving the same end of emptying the mind and reaching awakening. Another important development was the growth of lay Buddhist societies, including both men and women, both gentry and commoners, who devoted themselves to good works and recitation of the Buddha's name.

Maturing of the Daoist Religious Path

Interest in Daoist philosophical ideas revived in the post-Han period, as thinkers like Wangbi (226–249) wrote commentaries on the *Daode jing* and the *Zhuangzi*, while other Daoists involved themselves in artistic pursuits and practiced a free, naturalistic way of life. But the search for long life and immortality continued to dominate the Daoist movement throughout the period of disunity following the Han era and also during the Tang and Song periods. Sometimes patronized by the rulers, Daoist masters perfected a great variety of ritual techniques for controlling cosmic operations, reversing the forces of decay, and establishing the forces of renewal. Great scriptures were revealed, written down, and memorized for use in the rituals. Many sects developed, founded by recognized masters based on a particular scripture, and each sect developed its own ritual experts or priests.

Daoist Religious Experts: Interior Gods and Alchemy Daoist religious masters focused on *qi* (*ch'i*), the primordial breath or substance from which humans, like all nature, evolve. Qi comes ultimately from Dao, and it is present especially in the cosmic gods, the astral bodies of the universe, and the other manifestations of nature. The problem is that under the conditions of our existence our vital breath becomes stale and exhausted and, thus, our life becomes weak and short. Daoist experts developed various techniques for renewing and restoring that vital qi, so that long life and even immortality may be achieved. A key idea is that the human body is a microcosm of the great cosmos of nature, and so within each organ of the body there reside gods, and furthermore the great forces of the cosmos can be called down and actualized within the human body. Daoist priests developed ritual techniques by which they could visualize these interior gods of the body and the cosmic bodies and planets as they descend into the body, purifying and preserving the vital organs.

Carrying over the interest from ancient China in the five elements and how these can be used to promote long life, Daoist experts cultivated various techniques for creating substances to be ingested into the body to renew the vital breath. The science of alchemy developed, based on the idea that the ingestion of gold and other chemicals can renew the vital breath and prolong life.

But there were also the "inner elixir" techniques for renewing and prolonging life. Ritual techniques were developed by Daoist priests involving breathing techniques and gymnastics. By special breathing and bodily exercises, the breath could be circulated through the various zones of the body to nourish the vital powers. At the same time, it was felt that much care should be given to diet, especially avoiding grain foods that, coming from the yin earth, nourish the three "worms" or principles of death in the body. Some advanced adepts practiced ritual techniques of sexual intercourse, the idea being that the forces of yin (female) and yang (male) nourish each other and, thus, restore the vital forces.

Development of Daoist Sects Something new happened in the development of Daoism: There arose communities or congregations of Daoists led by priestly authorities, something unheard of in the Chinese tradition up to this point. The community called the Way of Great Peace, mentioned earlier, was one of the first such group religious movements. The other early group movement established about the same time was more lasting. This was the Way of the **Heavenly Masters** (Tianshi Dao), which established a state in northern Sichuan that was organized like a church, having a Celestial Master at its head and local parishes under the authority of "libationers" or priests. The first Heavenly Master was Zhang Daoling (died between 157 and 178 C.E.), who received revelations from Laozi, now thought of as a god, and instituted various communal rituals. Zhang Daoling is often considered the "founder" of Daoism as a religious path, since almost all Daoist sects trace themselves in some manner back to him. Faith-healing was practiced in this sect, based on the idea that sickness was caused by sin and, therefore, repentance, confession, and good deeds were part of the healing process. Documents inscribed with the sins and the penances were transmitted to the rulers of

Heaven, earth, and the waters to ensure healing and blessing. This communal Daoist movement had a strong emphasis on moral, virtuous living as part of the requirement for healthy, long life. Following this precedent, one of the characteristics of religious Daoism in general has been the emphasis on the practice of moral virtues in addition to the rituals and ceremonies.

During the Tang era (618–907), Daoism received considerable support from some of the emperors, enabling it to flourish and develop. Emperor Gaozong (r. 649–683) conferred on Laozi the title of emperor, thus confirming Laozi's divine status and claiming him as a royal ancestor. The political power of Daoism reached its zenith with the suppression of Buddhism and other non-Chinese religions in 845.

The most important Daoist order during the Tang era was the Maoshan sect, based on the mountain of Maoshan, where many temples were built, scriptures edited, and disciples trained to be priests. There, under the direction of a hierarchal priesthood headed by "masters of doctrine," they carried on ritual activities of purgation and cosmic renewal, calling down the gods of the stars and practicing ritual meditation. Their outstanding leader was Sima Chengzhen (647–735), who authored many works and was well known for his calligraphy. He emphasized ritual meditation focused on "emptiness," teaching that only the emptied heart can be the dwelling place for Dao.

Among the many new sects of Daoism that developed in the Song era (960–1280), two were lasting and are still influential in the twenty-first century. A scholar named Wang Zhe (1113–1170) became the founder of the Quanzhen (*Total Perfection*) sect in northern China. Wang studied Confucian texts in his youth and practiced Buddhist disciplines for a time. He experienced two mysterious encounters with Daoist immortals that led him to dig a grave and live in it for three years, after which he lived in a thatched hut for four years before burning it down and setting out to start the new Daoist order. He selected seven disciples who lived as eccentric ascetics, but they attracted lay followers from all classes, including women. Influenced by Chan Buddhism, this sect spiritualized some of the ritual practices. Wang taught celibacy and sitting in meditation to control the mind and the will and to nourish one's nature and life force. As the first Daoist sect to base itself in monasteries, the Total Perfection sect aimed for a rigorous

life of simple monastic discipline, including celibacy and abstinence from wine and meat. Founder Wang stressed practices of inner alchemy and self-perfection as well as Confucian and Buddhist doctrines, teaching the unity of the three religions.

One of Wang's disciples made a three-year trek to visit Chinggis Khan (Genghis Khan) at his central Asian court in 1222, ensuring the continuation of imperial support for this Daoist sect even into the time of the Mongol rule. For a while, the Total Perfection sect was favored over Buddhism by the Mongol rulers, but a conflict developed when the Daoists started to teach that the Buddha was one of the eighty-one transformations of Laozi. After a series of debates, Khubilai Khan ordered the Daoist Canon burned and the Daoist priests returned to lay life, and the sect went into a long eclipse. But the monastic basis of the Total Perfection sect survived through many tumultuous times, including the **Cultural Revolution** of the twentieth century. Today there still are monks and nuns of the Total Perfection sect active especially in the People's Republic of China, with their seat and training center at the White Cloud Monastery in Beijing.

The other major Daoist sect that came to influential status during the Song era was the Zhengyi (Orthodox Unity) sect, which was a continuation of the Way of the Heavenly Masters of earlier times. Its patriarchs were believed to be descendants of Zhang Daoling, and they based their headquarters at Dragon-Tiger Mountain (Longhu Shan) in Jiangxi (Kiangsi) Province. The thirty-sixth generation Heavenly Master, Zhang Zongyan, was invited to the capital by the emperor in 1277 to perform a "Grand Offering of the Entire Heaven," and shortly after that the emperor appointed him head of all Daoists in southern China. Then in 1295 the emperor decreed that Heavenly Master liturgical texts be used throughout the empire, and since then this sect has generally had the highest influence in ritual and liturgical matters. Under the first Ming emperor, toward the end of the fourteenth century, the Heavenly Masters were put in charge of all Daoist affairs.

In contrast to the celibate monks of the Total Perfection sect, the priests of the Orthodox Unity sect do not live in monasteries nor do they restrict themselves to a vegetable diet. They hand down their esoteric ritual arts in their families. Since they marry and live with their families, they are sometimes called "fire dwellers," that is, living by the family hearth. This sect of the Heavenly Masters continues to the present day, although the Heavenly Master in 1949 had to leave the Dragon-Tiger Mountain and flee to Taiwan to lead this organization of religious Daoism from there.

Other Daoist sects arose in the Song era and afterward, and many of the sects contributed new works to the burgeoning Daoist Canon. The compilation of the present **Daoist Canon** was commissioned and completed by 1447, under the Ming emperors. The emperors brought the growing sectarianism under control by decree of the court, limiting to three the monastic centers authorized to grant licenses of ordination, without which the local Daoist masters were forbidden to practice. But popular, unauthorized Daoist movements continued to rise and spread throughout the Ming (1368–1644), Qing (Ch'ing) (1644–1912), and even modern periods. This created a polarization between the traditional classical orders and the popular Daoist priests of local origin. The traditional orders were given the title "orthodox," whereas the newer popular groups were called "heterodox."

Resurgence of the Way of Confucius: Neo-Confucianism

The Confucian way, of course, remained a strong component of Chinese government and family life, the main foundation for morality, social custom, and status even after the fall of the Han dynasty. But as a vital religious force it was eclipsed by Buddhism and Daoism for many centuries, as the best philosophical and religious thinkers of China devoted themselves to Buddhism, and Daoism attracted government support because of its expertise in rituals of health and long life. To be sure, there were a few Confucian philosophers, such as Han Yu (768–824), who reasserted the central Confucian theme of the goodness of human nature and sharply attacked both Daoists and Buddhists for belittling humanity and human relations. But in general there was not much fresh thinking in Confucian circles from the fourth to the tenth centuries.

However, in the eleventh century, during the Northern Song dynasty, a series of important thinkers appeared who attempted to revive Confucianism as a philosophical vision of life. They were influenced by Buddhism and Daoism, but they turned back to Confucian sources to articulate a new philosophy of life, focused on a positive view of human nature, family life, and social reform. This **Neo-Confucianism** movement arose vigorously in the Song era, became dominant in the Ming era, and controlled Chinese thought throughout the Qing era down to the twentieth-century revolutions.

The Northern Song Masters of Neo-Confucianism
The beginnings of a Confucian revival can perhaps be seen in the Tang era, centered in the class of people known as **literati** (*ru*). The Tang government kept a huge bureaucracy to administer its vast empire, and the examination system required that higher status in the government was won by those who mastered the study of the Confucian classics. In the following Song era these literati established themselves as dominant in the political and intellectual spheres. Many of the literati, of course, got caught up in the expediency of government politics, but there was a minority who devoted themselves to study and teaching in an attempt to recover the ancient Confucian ideal of the **noble person** (*junzi*), the one who perfects his moral qualities.

Actually the Neo-Confucians went further than the noble person ideal, cultivating themselves to become "sages" like the ancient sages who had revealed the truth of the Way in the classics. The true sage, they believed, reaches the ultimate of true humanity by complete identification with the nature of all things. This is possible, they believed, because the heavenly principle is universal, possessed both by the self and by all things. One who meditates on that universal principle becomes more wise, mature, and in control, so that he can help to bring order and harmony to family, society, and government.

In the eleventh century there was a group of outstanding Confucian thinkers who worked out a Neo-Confucian cosmology and metaphysics based on redefining concepts from the Confucian classics. For example, Zhou Dunyi (1017–1073), sometimes considered the real founder of Neo-Confucian philosophy, taught that the Great Ultimate (*taiji*) generates yin and yang, which, through their alternation, give rise to the five elements, which in turn produce myriad things, of which humans are the most intelligent. But the many are actually the *one* reality, and the one is differentiated in the many. Zhang Zai (1020–1077) identified material force (*qi*) with the Great Ultimate, functioning through yang and yin; he also redefined the gods (**shen**) and evil spirits (**gui**) as positive and negative spiritual forces involved in the expansion and contraction of material force. Zhang is famous for his short essay called the Western Inscription, which he inscribed on a panel in the western window of his study, reflecting on the ethical implications of the doctrine that all creation is united by the universal underlying principle (see p. 274).

These early Neo-Confucianists often referred to the one unified reality as "principle" (*li*). The Cheng brothers (Cheng Hao, 1032–1085, and Cheng Yi, 1033–1107) based their teaching entirely on principle, which they conceived of as self-sufficient, extending everywhere, and governing everything. It is that by which all things exist, and it is possessed by everyone and all things, binding all together into a unity. The great philosopher **Zhu Xi** (Chu Hsi, 1130–1200) likewise taught that the whole universe is but one principle, the Great Ultimate, which is prior to form and which contains all principles and is the source of all principles. At the same time each phenomenon has its own defining principle. Zhu Xi explained this by using the metaphor of the single moon that is reflected in many lakes and rivers; everything has the Great Ultimate, yet the Great Ultimate remains one. But, according to Zhu Xi, principle never exists in isolation but always is attached to material force (qi), that which exists within form. Principle is one, but its manifestations are many. Since the one principle is identical with all things and with one's mind and nature, moral and spiritual development comes through the investigation of things, both in the external world and within oneself.

Later Neo-Confucian thinkers put more emphasis on the mind as morally self-sufficient, innately endowed with knowledge of the good and ability to do the good. This Mind School of Neo-Confucianism, represented especially by Wang Yangming (1472–1529), has as its central thesis the view that principle and mind are one. Since the mind, which innately contains all principles, is the master of the body, to cultivate oneself one need only follow the impulses of the mind's innate knowledge. Thus, Wang argued, the way to self-cultivation is not through the investigation of external things, as Zhu Xi taught, but through the cultivation and extension of the innate knowledge of the mind, through inner moral and spiritual cultivation.

The idealistic concern for awakening the moral consciousness of the mind, as put forth by Wang Yangming, continued to have influence in later generations of Neo-Confucianists, but Zhu Xi's more rationalistic concern for the ordering principle tended to remain dominant. The Manchu rulers, who conquered China in 1644 and inaugurated the Qing dynasty, affirmed Zhu Xi's Confucianism as the orthodox ideology of their reign, and so it remained until the onslaught of Western imperialism and the revolutionary forces of the twentieth century both brought down imperial rule in China and put the whole Confucianist tradition in jeopardy.

Persistence and Transformation of Popular Religion

The Chinese story highlights the Confucianist, Daoist, and Buddhist traditions as they developed to their full space by about the end of the Song era, continuing more or less in that form down to the modern era. But we need to emphasize again that vast area that overlaps with these three religious streams but includes much more—what is sometimes called popular religion. The popular religious traditions go back as far as the records go, and they include a great variety of religious activities. The term *popular religion* can refer to common Chinese practices associated with the family, such as funeral and memorial services and the New Year's festival, observed by virtually all traditional Chinese but not the sole possession of any of the three major traditions. *Popular religion* also refers to many additional beliefs and practices for dealing with various supernatural forces, accepted by the majority of the people although sometimes discounted by the educated elite, the strict Confucian scholars, Buddhist monks, orthodox Daoist priests, and state officials in their public roles.

In ancient times most Chinese participated in religious activities such as ancestor worship, exorcism, use of spirit mediums, divination, sacrifices to spirits, and belief in ghosts and demons. These activities were based in family, clan, and village, and they continued effectively even as the major religious traditions developed. Eventually the vaguely defined stream of popular religion incorporated Buddhist ideas about karma and rebirth, Buddhas and bodhisattvas, as well as Daoist and Confucian conceptions, forming the more or less coherent popular religious system that has continued to the present day.

Although popular religion does also promise salvation from hell and a favorable rebirth, generally it has focused on practical, immediate human concerns such as protection of property, health and long life, expulsion of evil spirits, obtaining favor from the gods, peace and harmony in the home, good livelihood, repose of ancestors, and the like. For these benefits, the most important sacred powers are the ancestral spirits and the popular gods. These powers bring benefits and protection in life and in death.

Most of the gods of popular religion were originally human beings who were gradually deified over time as more and more people recognized their power and efficacy. The gods have a reciprocal relationship with the humans: They understand the needs of the worshipers, and they need the offerings and recognition of the worshipers if they are to keep their position as gods. New gods are recognized as their power and fame are effective, but gods can also be demoted and forgotten if their benefits no longer are felt. The gods of popular religion were organized into a bureaucratic system with each one having a particular function, such as protecting fishermen, bringing children, causing rain, protecting the village, and so on. The **Jade Emperor** presides over the gods, parallel to the emperor in the human realm, and the Jade Emperor appoints the various gods to their offices, promoting them for effective help but also demoting them when their effectiveness fails.

The popular gods maintain order over and against the vast array of demons and ghosts that can bring sickness and death. These demons (*gui*) usually are spirits of the restless dead who died unjustly or who were not cared for by their descendants, and they need to be expelled by a spirit-medium or a Daoist priest in the name of a powerful god. Harm can also come from ancestors who have been aggrieved, and harmony can be restored by a medium communicating with the ancestor to learn what the family should do to make amends.

Popular religion has always been carried on in the midst of the family, village, and city neighborhood, and so there are usually no full-time specialists. The temples are run by local people who have other jobs. Some people have special talents as spirit-mediums, spirit-writers, healers, and the like, and Daoist priests and Buddhist monks can also be employed to perform special rituals. Popular religion practices include a rich cycle of annual festivals, funeral rituals, and rituals of **feng shui**, the process of establishing the proper locale for a house or a grave. We will look more closely at some of these ideas and practices later.

These activities of popular religion have given a special character to most Chinese families and communities, even as the people also pursued Confucianist, Daoist, and Buddhist practices. In modern times, some aspects of popular religion have been questioned and ranked as superstition in the People's Republic of China, but these practices are still significant to many people in Taiwan, Hong Kong, and other overseas Chinese communities.

WESTERN INCURSION AND REVOLUTIONARY CLIMATE

One major foreign influence that transformed traditional China was, of course, Buddhism, but Buddhism was indigenized and contributed much to the shape of Chinese religion. More disruptive were the incursions of religions and ideas from the West, followed in the nineteenth century by foreign imperialism in China. The upheaval in traditional Chinese society culminated in the Revolution of 1911, ending two millennia of imperial rule and inaugurating the Republic of China. More disruption followed the Communist takeover of the mainland, with the result that Chinese religion today is somewhat diminished in the People's Republic, although it is still alive in other Chinese communities.

Foreign Religions and Western Domination

We should note that other foreign religions besides Buddhism did play a part in China's religious history. During the Tang period, for example, Zoroastrianism and Manicheism (teaching a cosmic dualism) came into China as a result of contact with Persia, and they dealt some influence on Daoism and Buddhism.

During the Tang and Song periods, increased Muslim dominance of the western edges of China led to the presence of a significant Muslim community in northwestern China. When the Mongols established the Yuan dynasty in China (1280–1368), Muslim merchants, soldiers, and religious leaders settled throughout China, and numerous Chinese converted to Islam during this period. But Muslims maintained the purity of their faith, refusing to blend it with other Chinese religions, and adherents of Islam tended to be from minority non-Han tribal groups, lumped together as the Hui peoples. Generally they retained their own language and culture, thus maintaining a separate religious and ethnic identity. Today, Muslims total perhaps thirty million people in China. In general, they have been given a good bit of autonomy under the Communist government. While they, like other religious groups, suffered during the Cultural Revolution, they have revived quickly and today practice their religion actively. Yet, because they have stood aloof from the syncretistic tendencies of the traditional Chinese religions, the overall impact of Islam on Chinese religion has been limited.

There is also an interesting though brief story of Jewish presence in traditional China. During the Song dynasty, a Jewish community was established in Kaifeng, and an impressive synagogue was built there in the style of a Chinese temple. But cut off from contact with other Jews, the small Jewish communities in China eventually lost their identity and were totally assimilated.

Traces of Christian presence in China go back as far as the Tang period, when Nestorian Christians came to China. And in the thirteenth century, the pope at Rome dispatched Franciscan monks overland to China, during the time when the Mongols ruled all of central Asia and Marco Polo had made Europe aware of China. But with the fall of the Mongol dynasty, the Ming rulers closed the door to foreigners, and the fledgling Christian communities died out.

The more lasting Western Christian impact on Chinese culture came with the Jesuit mission in the sixteenth and seventeenth centuries. Around 1500 Portuguese traders came to southern China, and Christians started entering China especially from the Spanish Philippines. The newly founded Jesuit order devoted itself to a missionary-scholar approach, both in Japan and in China. The first Jesuit missionary in China was **Matteo Ricci** (1552–1610), who went to China in 1582 and set out to learn the ancient Chinese writings, accommodating Christianity to the best of classic Chinese culture. The Jesuits took on the role of Chinese literati, wrote works in Chinese, and proved helpful to the Chinese rulers by providing maps and Western learning in science and astronomy.

The Jesuits found acceptance in the scholarly, governmental circles partly because they tried to integrate Christianity into what they considered the best of Chinese culture. They made Christianity acceptable to many

Chinese by, for example, using the Chinese words **Shang Di** and **Tian** for God in the Christian sense, adopting the ceremonies of respect for Confucius, teaching that Confucian ethics were consonant with Christian faith, and interpreting the ancestral rituals as acceptable within the Christian understanding. But before long, rival Christian religious orders attacked the Jesuit methods of accommodation, accusing them of not imposing fasting and not teaching that Confucius was in hell. After much discussion of this so-called rites controversy, the pope at Rome finally decided against the Jesuit position, leading to the breakdown of the Jesuit relationship with the Chinese emperor and the suppression and expulsion of Christian priests.

Around the beginning of the nineteenth century came English and Dutch traders to China, and with them the first Protestant Christian missionaries arrived. These missionaries tended to work with the working classes, not the literati. The Western presence was fortified by military power, which forced the Chinese to open up ports and allow foreigners to travel in the interior and teach Christianity. By the end of the nineteenth century, there were some two thousand Christian missionaries in China. Some mission groups, like the China Inland Mission in particular, began to adapt more to Chinese customs and carried on much educational and medical work, which had a considerable impact on Chinese society. But the close association with Western imperialism and the general failure to recognize the drastic changes in modern China kept Christianity from gaining wide favor, and the revolutionary movements of the twentieth century turned against the Christian movement.

Revolutionary Movements and Communist Society

Reacting against the burdens of the decaying Qing dynasty, as well as responding to the West and to Christianity, China was gripped by new religious movements, rebellions, and revolt against its own traditional imperial system.

Rebellions and Revolution   An early people's rebellion, influenced to some decree by Christianity, was the **Taiping Rebellion** in the middle of the nineteenth century. A farm boy named Hong Xiuquan, influenced by Christian pamphlets, had visions of ascending to heaven, where he learned that Confucius had confused the people and that he himself was the Father's son next younger to Jesus. Hong organized a religious movement based on some Christian ideas, baptizing, throwing out the ancestral tablets, and destroying shrines and temples. The movement drew on the centuries-old peasant frustration with the old hierarchical system; it advocated an egalitarian social structure, equality of the sexes, and the redistribution of land. In 1851, Hong proclaimed himself the Heavenly King of the Heavenly Kingdom of Great Peace (Taiping Tianguo). The movement grew rapidly and started to attack armies in Beijing and elsewhere, but in 1864, the whole group, now 100,000 strong, was defeated and massacred. But the rebellion had devastated China and almost toppled the Qing dynasty.

The winds of change blew strongly as the twentieth century began. The abortive Boxer Rebellion in 1899–1900, an extensive antiforeign movement that tried to drive out Western influences and attacked Christian missions in the name of Chinese gods, was symptomatic of the growing conflict between traditional values and the impact of the West. The imperial government, humiliated by defeat at the hands of the Japanese in 1894–1895, was not able to stem the growing tide of dissatisfaction. Reforms were attempted, such as abolishing, in 1905, the long-standing Confucian examinations for government service. But it was too little too late, and the Qing government fell in the 1911 revolution, the final end of many centuries of imperial rule.

While the majority of Chinese continued their traditional religious practices, many intellectuals turned to Western ideas and philosophies, including Marxism. The leader of the revolution and of the republican government that followed, Sun Zhongshan (Sun Yat-sen) (1866–1925), had received a Western, Christian education, as did his successor as leader of the Nationalist party, Jiang Jieshi (Chiang K'ai-shek). Sun and Jiang followed a kind of modern, liberal Protestantism; Jiang even promoted the revival of ancient Confucian virtues during his leadership of the Nationalist government. Other leading intellectuals were influenced by the antireligious attitudes of Western liberal thinkers such as John Dewey and Bertrand Russell and took a strong stand against all traditional religion. The famous May 4, 1919, student protest, for example, demanded a New China based on humanistic liberal principles, free of all old literature, education, and religion.

Mao and the Communist Party Western liberalism could not control the spirit of anarchy that had developed, and in 1920 a group of Marxists secretly formed the Communist Party. The Communists cooperated for a number of years with the Nationalist Party, but by 1928 an irrevocable split had occurred. Jiang Jieshi led the Nationalist government, relying on rural landlords and the urban business class, whereas the Communist Party built support among the peasantry. The Nationalists began a notorious "bandit extermination" campaign against the Communists, but under the leadership of **Mao Zedong** (1893–1976) the Communists escaped to the north in the famous Long March of 1934, creating a mythology that supported Mao's domination of the Chinese Communist Party. In the chaos following World War II, Mao and his followers successfully carried through a revolution and established the People's Republic of China in October 1949, sweeping Jiang's forces out of the mainland and into an exiled Nationalist government on the island of Taiwan.

The religions of China have been subjected to more disruption under Maoist rule than in any previous period in Chinese history. The constitution of the People's Republic does establish the freedom both to practice religion and to be atheist. In practice, however, sharing the Marxist attitude that religion is an instrument that oppressive overlords use to pacify and exploit the energies of the people, the Chinese government mounted a series of campaigns to turn people's loyalty away from the traditional religions to support the new Chinese order. People were encouraged to "struggle against Confucius," for that system of thought supported the old hierarchical state. Popular Daoist practices were denounced as superstitions, not to be condoned in the modern society. For a time, state-controlled Buddhist and Christian associations were tolerated. But during the so-called Cultural Revolution, which began in 1966, all religious institutions were subjected to intense persecution by fanatical Red Guards in the struggle to rid China of the "four olds": old habits, old ideas, old customs, old culture. The Red Guards invaded homes to expose people practicing religion and to destroy religious art, scriptures, and literature. Temples and churches were closed, images destroyed, leaders returned to lay life, and books burned. All over China there was an attempt to get rid of everything that looked like a remnant of the "bad old days" before the 1949 revolution. It seemed that the thousands of years of religious tradition in China had come to an abrupt end.

Coinciding with the attack on the traditional religions, there grew up a new "religion" in China: the cult of Mao. The philosophy of Marxism, as has often been pointed out, has some of the characteristics of a religious philosophy, with its call for repentance, conversion, and unconditional commitment, and also with its view of history moving toward the consummation of a classless society. In China, communism took over some of the traditional religious forms: Mao was revered almost like a state deity, and national holidays were celebrated complete with popular music, art, drama, parades, and banners to create the atmosphere of a sacred state. During the Cultural Revolution, Maoism went further in taking on many of the characteristics of a religious cult. Some people looked to Mao almost as a god, and young people carried the "bible" of his sayings around, studying, memorizing, and reciting his teachings. It was in the intolerant furor of this cult of Mao that the excesses against everything having to do with the "old" religions and institutions were carried out.

The Cultural Revolution came to an end with the death of Chairman Mao in 1976 and with the downfall of his wife and three other leaders (the Gang of Four) who tried to continue these policies. Though traditional religious ideas had been drastically shaken and reduced in influence, they were not dead. Under more moderate leadership, China entered into a new phase in which more relaxed and practical programs were emphasized in order to attain the "Four Modernizations": science, agriculture, industry, and defense. Along with all this came a liberalization of government policies toward religion. Hundreds of temples, churches, and mosques reopened, and the government has even paid back rent for the religious buildings that were confiscated during the Cultural Revolution. The key guideline established by the Chinese government for all religious organizations is that they be compatible with patriotism and national unity.

Religion in China Today

Today in the People's Republic of China one senses a certain revival of interest in the traditional religions. There are significant numbers of monasteries, seminaries, and religious colleges to train leaders in the different religious communities. Although a whole generation of religious leaders was lost during the Cultural Revolution years, today

a new, young generation of priests, monks, nuns, ministers, imans, and other religious leaders is seen in increasing numbers. Sacred scriptures and other religious books are being published, and one sees increasing worship activities at temples, churches, and mosques. At Chinese universities, scholars again are doing research and publishing writings about religious subjects.

A revival of Buddhism in the People's Republic is apparent today, as temples all over China are again bustling and some monasteries and educational centers are training young men and women into the monastic life. Buddhists are recognized by the government under the Buddhist Association of China, with a stated goal of contributing to social stability and national unity. Actually there are three broad communities of Buddhists in China, namely, the Chinese language Buddhists, the Tibetan language Buddhists (especially in the Tibetan and Mongolian regions), and the Pali language Buddhists (smaller ethnic communities). When the Republic of China was established in Taiwan in 1949, some of the senior Buddhist leaders moved there from the mainland, and over the last half century, Buddhism has thrived on the island. Well over ten thousand monastics have been ordained in Taiwan—the majority of them women. Besides meeting the spiritual needs of the people, Buddhist organizations in Taiwan are making large contributions in social services, medical care, education, and world peace.

Daoism, with its traditional religious rituals, scriptures, and priests, has not shared as much in the general revival of religion in the People's Republic, partly because some traditional practices that were associated with popular Daoism are still looked upon as superstitions harmful to the new society. Yet Daoist temples are bustling with worshipers who come to pay devotion to the many Daoist gods and participate in Daoist ceremonies. The Chinese Taoist Association, which oversees Daoist activity in China, is headquartered at the White Cloud Temple (Baiyun guan) in Beijing, which also is home to the China Daoist College where young men and women are training to be Daoist priests. And there are hundreds of local Daoist associations in the various cities and provinces of China, as well as in Hong Kong, Taiwan, Malaysia, and Singapore.

Confucianism, that is, the whole religious, ethical, and literary tradition based on the Confucian canon, was deeply damaged by the persistent Maoist attack on it as the backbone of Chinese "feudal" civilization. Today there is more appreciation of the value of the Confucian tradition as a foundation of Chinese identity. And certainly Confucian virtues such as respect for the family and for elders, loyalty to the community and the nation, and the acceptance of reciprocity as the basis of human relations continue in present-day China, evidence that deeply based religious attitudes persist even in drastically changed conditions. Scholars again are studying and writing about the Confucian heritage of China. Some Chinese philosophers are working on what they call the New Confucianism, an attempt to integrate Western philosophy and logic into Confucian thinking with the idea that Eastern and Western forms of thought can supplement each other.

Today in China there is a general flourishing of Christianity. In addition to overflowing churches in some of the cities, there are countless "house church" groups throughout China guided by lay leaders. Protestant churches do not have denominations but belong to the Three Self Movement, or to a similar Protestant organization, the China Christian Council. They pledge to be self-governing, self-supporting, and self-propagating—that is, they are free from control of foreign church bodies and dedicated to the ideals of the new China. The Catholic Church in China is recognized under the Chinese Catholic Patriotic Association, which officially is to be independent from Roman papal authority. This has caused tension among Catholics in China, since there have been ordinations of Chinese bishops that were not authorized by the pope in Rome. There is a sizable "underground" Catholic Church in China made up of priests and laypeople who want to remain under the pope's authority, some of whom probably overlap with the Chinese Catholic Patriotic Association. Recently there have been attempts, both from the Chinese government and from the pope, to ease the tensions by allowing for compromise because of the extraordinary situation of the Catholic Church in China.

Muslims, as a recognized ethnic group in China made up mostly of Hui and Uighurs, did not suffer as drastically during the Cultural Revolution and have managed to continue their religious practices somewhat outside the mainstream of Chinese social and political life. Muslims run a number of Islamic colleges, including one at the headquarters of the Chinese Islamic Association in Beijing and a grand, well-equipped one in Yinchuan, the capital of the Ningxia Au-

tonomous Region of the Hui people. There are some 42,000 mosques in China, most with imams who conduct classes in Islam for the people. Thousands of Muslims from China make the Hajj (Pilgrimage) to Mecca each year.

On the popular level in China, there is some evidence of a renewed interest in traditional religious practices such as ancestor worship and funeral rituals, and colorful local festivals are making a comeback, especially in rural areas. Many people today are quite interested in traditional Chinese medicine and healing, as well as the whole array of **qigong** practices—traditional Chinese meditation, exercises, and breathing techniques, to bring health and a better life—developed on the basis of the traditional Chinese worldview.

However, while there is a sense of openness and freedom in religious practice in China today, at the same time the government has tended to be intolerant of religious and quasi-religious groups that operate outside the recognized and approved structures, particularly if they engage in practices considered superstitious and detrimental to the new China. The best-known example, perhaps, is the Falun Gong movement, a large but somewhat secretive group that draws on Buddhist and Daoist ideas and claims to practice a form of qigong. The founder of Falun Gong, Li Hongzhi, is said to possess special powers that he can transmit to the followers, and he warns of a coming world disaster from which Falun Gong practitioners will be saved. Falun Gong, which apparently numbers in the millions, has been banned and some of its leaders arrested by the Chinese government on the grounds that it is harmful to the Chinese people.

It must still be said that religious activities, though significant, take place only on a fairly small scale in the People's Republic of China today, and that the majority of the people seem to have rather little interest in religious matters. Their concern is for good jobs, education for their children, modern housing, and working to better Chinese society. Whether the basic human religious questions and concerns will again play a major part in their lives appears to be an open question.

The religious situation in Hong Kong, Taiwan, Singapore, Malaysia, and other overseas Chinese communities is quite different, of course. Religious practices differ somewhat from place to place, and modernization affects their religious beliefs as elsewhere in the world. But, in general, traditional religion still flourishes, based in a strong family system and community support of temples, monasteries, festivals, and various popular religious ceremonies.

DISCUSSION QUESTIONS

1 How was the origin of writing in China related to religious practices of the Shang era?

2 How did the beginnings of Confucianism and Daoism reflect the social situation in the middle Zhou period?

3 How can the cultivation of ren and li, and study of the tradition, bring personal transformation, according to Confucius?

4 It is sometimes said that Confucius' ideas were humanistic, not religious. How would you define the matter?

5 What does the *Daode jing* put forth as its basic perspective on the world?

6 How did the Confucian way triumph and become the leading ideology of the Chinese state? What is the "state cult of Confucius"?

7 What were the streams that went into the making of "religious Daoism"? How were these related to the ideas of the *Daode jing* and *Zhuangzi*?

8 Discuss factors that worked for and against the Chinese acceptance of Buddhism.

9 Describe the major Buddhist schools or lineages in China during the Tang period. Why were Pure Land and Chan able to survive the persecutions of 845?

10 Explain the Neo-Confucian idea of universal principle (*li*).

11 Why must we include a category such as "popular religion" in addition to Confucianism, Daoism, and Buddhism in China? Explain some of the features of popular religion.

12 How did Christianity rise to become influential in the sixteenth and seventeenth centuries? What caused its subsequent decline?

13 What were the roles of Sun Zhongshan, Jiang Jieshi, and Mao Zedong in twentieth-century events?

14 What happened to the traditional religions under the People's Republic of China after 1949? How did the Cultural Revolution affect the religious traditions?

15 Discuss reasons for the current revival of religious interest among the people of China. What do you see in the future?

Chapter 12

Chinese Worlds of Meaning

SACRED REALITY IN THE CHINESE VISION

What's it all about? Where do we look for the sacred center, the real? Several thousand years of searching and experimenting in China have yielded answers to these kinds of questions that are diverse and yet fit together in a vibrant world of meaning.

The early Chinese worldview was naturalistic. The whole universe was felt to be a dynamic sacred organism, following the basic laws of cyclical processes, growth and decline, and the bipolar operation of the forces of yin and yang. In a sense, the world itself was ultimate reality, operating in harmony and following the natural laws without any supreme creator or lawgiver. This overall conception of a dynamically functioning sacred universe has remained central to Chinese experience and has colored all thinking about sacred beings and powers.

Divine Powers: Shang Di and Tian

Within this self-governing natural order, as we saw earlier, there was belief from early times on in a supreme being called Shang Di (Ruler Above) or Tian (Heaven), and these terms have figured centrally in the Chinese conception of sacred reality ever since. Shang Di, as worshiped by the rulers of the Shang dynasty, was not the ultimate or unlimited god over all, of course, but did function as the power of conspicuous importance that controlled nature and brought both good and evil on the Shang rulers. Although Shang Di may have been the special god of the Shang rulers, perhaps even thought of as the high ancestor of the ruling house, this was not just a tribal god. Shang Di had control over all the natural forces and over human welfare, bringing the benefits of rain, military victory, and building cities, but also the punishment of drought, defeat, and ruin of cities. The texts show that Shang Di was felt to have divine personality and intelligence, could issue orders to the wind and rain and other natural forces, and could bring things and events into being.

Beneath Shang Di there was a full pantheon of gods of nature—Sun, Moon, Wind, Rain, Earth, Mountain, River, and gods of the Four Directions—functioning as divine subordinates of the supreme god. In addition, all the ancestral gods of the house of the Shang rulers were members of Shang Di's pantheon. The deceased kings of the Shang dynasty were worshiped especially as mediators to approach and obtain Shang Di's approval. It seems that deceased queens were also worshiped as accompanying Shang Di, and perhaps even the ancestral dukes, ministers, and diviners found their place among the ancestral gods. The sacred powers of nature and of human ancestry were linked in harmony around the center provided by the supreme god.

Tian (Heaven), as worshiped by the rulers of the Zhou dynasty, was assimilated to Shang Di and was conceived as the all-powerful, all-knowing, purposeful god who sent down blessings or disasters in accordance with divine pleasure or displeasure with the people. When kings prospered, it was believed that they had received the mandate of Heaven; in the case of corrupt or unworthy rulers, Heaven would withdraw the mandate and the ruler would fall.

Texts from the *Classic of Poetry* and the *Classic of History* describe the cosmic moral operation of Heaven:

> Be reverent. Be reverent! Heaven's will is evident, but its mandate is not easily preserved. Do not say that Heaven is far distant above. Concerned with our affairs, it ascends and descends, and it daily inspects all our doings.
>
> (*Shijing* 4:1.3.1)

Heaven inspects the people below and considers their right-eousness. It bestows on them length of years, or the contrary. Heaven does not destroy people; they bring their lives to an end themselves.

(*Shujing*, Gaozong 3)

Here there is a strong emphasis on the universal moral authority of Heaven along with the notion of Heaven as an impersonal governing authority. When we live in accord with Heaven's will, we prosper, but when we go against that will, our lives are short and bitter.

Chinese ideas and feelings about Heaven are colored by the sayings of Confucius, who emphasized this universal moral power. Confucius had a strong belief in the mandate of Heaven, and he was convinced that he had a sacred mission that had been conferred on him by this purposeful supreme power. To Confucius, Heaven was the guardian of humanistic culture. Once, mistreated by the people of Kuang, he said,

Since the death of King Wen [founder of the Zhou dynasty], is not the course of culture in my keeping? If it had been the will of Heaven to destroy this culture, it would not have been given to a mortal [like me]. But if it is the will of Heaven that this culture should not perish, what can the people of K'uang do to me?

(*Analects* 9.5)[1]

Some leading thinkers continued to emphasize the personal character of Heaven as a supreme being to be loved and worshiped. Mozi (late fifth century B.C.E.) described Heaven as the father who loves all people equally, who accepts sacrifices from all and is concerned about the moral conduct of the people. Others emphasized more the impersonal qualities of Tian. Xunzi (ca. 300–238 B.C.E.), for example, denied that Heaven acts in response to human actions or pleas. Rather, Tian is simply the operation of the physical universe according to its inherent laws.

Since the time of these ancient thinkers, many have continued to ask the question whether Heaven is personal and interactive with humans or whether Heaven operates impersonally and naturally. For example, the Neo-Confucianist Liu Yuxi (772–842 C.E.) wrote *A Treatise on Heaven* describing the two traditional theories. Some say Heaven and humans really influence each other, Liu wrote, meaning that calamities will surely descend on us because of our wrongdoings, but blessings will surely come because of our good deeds. If we cry out in distress we will be heard and, thus, it definitely seems that there is someone who rules over us. On the other hand, according to Liu, some say that Heaven and

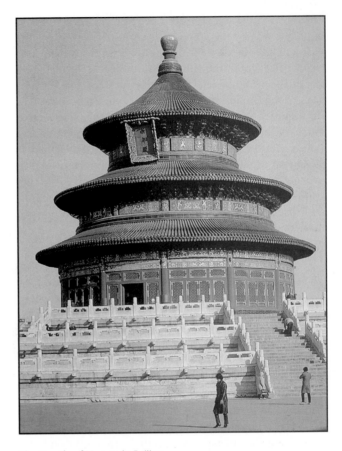

The Temple of Heaven in Beijing.

humans are really different and have no effect on each other. Lightning hits and destroys without anyone committing any wrongdoing, and bushes flower in the spring without any good deeds being rewarded; thus, it seems there is no one ruling over us. So Liu proposed his own theory about the mutual interaction of Heaven and humans, with Heaven's way lying in producing and reproducing, and humanity's way lying in moral order and regulation.[2] As suggested by this example, thinkers in the Confucian tradition did a lot of speculating on the nature of Heaven, the powerful reality that somehow is involved in controlling, or at least interacting with, human existence.

The importance of Heaven can be seen in the emperor's practice, continued down to the twentieth century, of making a special sacrifice to Heaven each year at the winter solstice. The sacrifice to Huang Tian Shang Di (August Heaven Supreme Ruler), which began before dawn on this longest night of the year (the peak of yin forces), could only be made by the emperor, the son of Heaven, for the well-being of the whole people. The ceremony also included sacrifices to all the subordinates of Heaven, including imperial ancestors, celestial deities of stars and planets, gods of mountains and rivers, and so on. On another day, the summer solstice, the emperor would offer sacrifice to Earth as the counterpart of Heaven. From long Chinese tradition and practice, it is clear that Heaven, whether personal god or naturalistic power, has an important role in holding everything together for human benefit. And, according to the established Chinese belief, the emperor as the representative of humans shares in the responsibility of nourishing the process of life with sacred power.

The Way of Nature: Dao

The ancient conception of Dao, or the way of nature, has also played an important part in Chinese views of sacred reality. The word *Dao*, "path" or "way," is used in various Chinese traditions to describe religious teachings and practices. But within their vision of ultimate sacred reality, Chinese thinkers have described Dao as the source and origin of everything and also as that power that maintains harmony and balance in the world. This eternal Way of the universe can be thought of at many different levels, as reflected in different religious traditions of China. But it is the philosophers of early Daoism that have most deeply explored this dimension of ultimate reality.

Dao as the Undifferentiated Source of All   Chinese thinkers and searchers from early times have talked of a primordial source of all reality, itself undivided and prior to all the multiplicity of things that make up our existence. The famous passage in Chapter 25 of the *Daode jing*, in its mysterious, cryptic language, sets forth this understanding:

> There was something undifferentiated and yet complete,
> Which existed before heaven and earth.
> Soundless and formless, it depends on nothing and does not change.
> It operates everywhere and is free from danger.
> It may be considered the mother of the universe.
> I do not know its name; I call it Tao.
> If forced to give it a name, I shall call it Great.
> Now being great means functioning everywhere.
> Functioning everywhere means far-reaching.
> Being far-reaching means returning to the original point.[3]

So Dao is one, prior to all differences. Nothing produced Dao, nor is it limited or affected by anything. Whereas everything else is dependent on Dao, Dao only follows its own nature. It is that eternal, primordial reality that contains within itself the inexhaustible source and creativity of the whole universe. It is the "mother" of all and operates within everything, pervasive and invincible, producing all and regenerating all.

This rich description of Dao in the *Daode jing* uses many terms and qualities that might be ascribed to God in other religions, although it is said that Dao contains all within itself and is immanent in all—far different from the monotheistic concept that the creator is transcendent beyond the creation. But Daoists hold that such terms and qualities are only pointers to a deep, mysterious reality that cannot be grasped by word or concept. It is important that Laozi's 5,000-character description of Dao in the *Daode jing* begins with the assertion that such a description is impossible:

> Dao that be spoken is not eternal Dao;
> Name that can be named is not eternal name.
> Nameless is the origin of Heaven and Earth;
> Named is the mother of all things.

Once Dao is named and described, it is limited and, thus, no longer primordial Dao. Dao is immanent in heaven and earth and all things as the undifferentiated stuff out of which all namable things are articulated—but Dao in itself can only be known intuitively by getting one's mind and whole being in harmony with the movement of Dao.

Dao operates as the inner source of all things, even the most common and insignificant, as we see in this dialogue in the *Zhuangzi*:

> Tung-kuo Tzu asked Chuang Tzu, "What is called Tao— where is it?"
> "It is everywhere," replied Chuang Tzu.
> Tung-kuo Tzu said, "It will not do unless you are more specific."
> "It is in the ant," said Chuang Tzu.
> "Why go so low down?"
> "It is in the weeds."
> "Why even lower?"
> "It is in a potsherd."
> "Why still lower?"
> "It is in the excrement and urine," said Chuang Tzu.
> Tung-kuo gave no response.[4]

So Dao, prior to everything, operates in even the most insignificant realities. How does it operate? Not through power and coercion, not through commands or absolute structures, but simply as the innermost universal way of nature. "Dao does nothing at all, yet there is nothing that is not done" (*Daode jing*, Ch. 37). Dao is really the operation of the way of the universe in its totality.

> The Great Tao flows everywhere.
> It may go left or right.
> All things depend on it for life, and it does not turn away
>   from them.
> It accomplishes its task, but does not claim credit for it.
> It clothes and feeds all things, but does not claim to be master
>   over them.
> (Ch. 34)[5]

Zhuangzi describes Dao, formless and without action, as the ultimate source, support, and continuing power for all realities, all forms, even all gods:

> The Way has its reality and its signs but is without action or form. You can hand it down but you cannot receive it; you can get it but you cannot see it. It is its own source, its own root. Before Heaven and earth existed it was there, firm from ancient times. It gave spirituality to the spirits and to God; it gave birth to Heaven and to earth. It exists beyond the highest point, and yet you cannot call it lofty; it exists beneath the limit of the six directions and yet you cannot call it deep. It was born before Heaven and earth, and yet you cannot say it has been there for long; it is earlier than the earliest time, and yet you cannot call it old. . . . The Big Dipper got it and from ancient times has never wavered. The Sun and Moon got it and from ancient times have never rested.[6]

Not only those who call themselves Daoists but also most Chinese have been deeply impressed by this vision of Dao as the source of existence. Even as many adhere to other views of ultimate reality, those views somehow cohere with the worldview represented by Dao.

The Daoist Gods of the Prior Heavens To the priests and experts of the Daoist religious groups, the abode of the transcendent, eternal Dao is most associated with the stellar constellations, the Prior Heavens, and in these Prior Heavens there are great gods who are exempt from the changes that take place in the visible world (the Posterior Heavens). The great gods are one with the eternal Dao and, thus, are the source of life, primordial breath, and blessing for our visible world.

At the summit of the gods are the Three Ones. These are the "three primordial breaths" that were breathed forth from Dao and rule heaven and earth. In present-day Daoist rituals, these **Three Pure Ones** or Three Heavenly Worthies are Yuanshi, the Primordial Lord of Heaven; Lingbao, the Lord of Earth; and Lord Lao, the Lord of Humans. The Three Heavenly Worthies head a pantheon of gods that includes the Five Primordial Spirits, the Five Great Mountains of China, and many more deputies and helpers.

In the Daoist conception of reality, these great gods are not only resident in the Prior Heavens. Since our world and our human body make up a microcosm (small cosmos) corresponding to the macrocosm (great cosmos), these gods are also present within our world and within our body. For example, the Lord of Heaven is also Lord of the head and the primordial breath; the Lord of Earth is also Lord of the chest and the spirit; the Lord of Humans is also Lord of the belly and the seminal essence. The power that originates in the primordial Dao is very present and active in the several spheres of our existence. Since favorable activity of these gods is essential for human happiness and success, people look to the Daoist experts to summon and revitalize these powers within the community.

Gods of Popular Religion Some Daoist texts identify one of the Three Heavenly Ones as the Jade Emperor; other texts seem to think of the Jade Emperor as another sacred being. In any case, popular religion in China has looked to the Jade Emperor as the supreme arbitrator over life in this changing, human world—perhaps as the deputy of the Lord of Heaven in administering the heavenly bureaucracy and in governing the world of humans. It is widely believed among traditional Chinese that the Jade Emperor is the head of the heavenly court, and that he has many helpers and deputies to govern our world. There is, for example, the god of Tai Shan, the great mountain of the East, who is the Jade Emperor's regent on earth. Then there are the city gods (the Gods of Moats and Walls) who have been given the administration of particular villages and cities. Another important local god is **Tudigong** (T'u-ti kung), the earth god, guardian of the local community in all its fortunes and misfortunes. Then there are important household gods, including especially **Zaojun** (Tsao-chun), God of the Cooking Stove, who keeps the ledger of good and bad deeds committed by the members of the family and, in general, looks after the welfare of the home.

All these deputy gods, it is believed, come to the Jade Emperor's court once a year to report and hand in accounts of their administration over the past year. And then they are promoted or punished accordingly, for their beneficial administration must harmonize with the work of the human emperor and the local administrators. If the larger good of human society is not served, the fault must lie somewhere within these human and divine bureaucracies.

Where did all these gods come from? Many, of course, are gods of nature or gods imbued with social functions. But many other gods were originally humans who died and as ancestral spirits displayed such power and benefit that they were promoted to the ranks of the higher gods. The simple test of divine status is efficacy—does this god really come through with beneficial power or not? This approach is very practical-minded. When sacred power from a particular deceased human is experienced by many in the community and beyond, clearly an important god is in the making, for the gods are channels of sacred power as it is dispersed for the welfare and growth of the human community.

As important among the divine powers, we should mention two outstanding gods who are worshiped all over the Chinese communities, **Mazu** (Ma Tsu) and **Guanyin** (Kuan-yin). Mazu is a favorite goddess, "Old Granny." Her story is especially important, for it illustrates how a human soul becomes a most universal, beneficial channel of sacred power. The story originates on an island in southern China, where a teenaged girl showed special powers in communicating with and helping fishermen at sea. She knew when her father and brothers were experiencing a horrible shipwreck, and she flew to them in spirit to save them. She carried her brothers to safety in her arms but lost her father, for she was carrying him in her mouth and had to open her mouth in reply to a question from her mother. She died as a young woman, but soon other fishermen experienced her assistance, and then still others, until before long, all across southern China, Mazu was revered as a most efficacious sacred power. Eventually even the emperor recognized her powers and she was raised to the status of Imperial Consort of Heaven—certainly a high position in this whole realm of sacred beings. Mazu provides much help in the practical circumstances of life—childbirth, healthy children, happy marriages, and much more.

Gods can make their appearance from many different directions, and Guanyin is one who came in with Bud-

dhism. As the great Bodhisattva Avalokiteshvara in India, this sacred being was widely known for saving and helping people, and in China the power continued and increased. Now known as Guanyin, the Lord Who Looks Down (a translation of the Sanskrit name), this bodhisattva has become one of the most widely worshiped gods in China. The compassion and mercy of this bodhisattva have come to be expressed in feminine symbols and images, and many think of Guanyin as the great goddess of mercy who grants help in the most critical areas of life.

Mazu, Guanyin, and many more—Chinese people know that these gods, goddesses, and spirits are not ultimate and universal in their power, but they represent the ways, the avenues, in which ultimate Dao shows effective presence within daily human existence. These sacred powers are tangible and real elements of the operating everyday universe, and to stay in harmony with them is a most important practice of life.

The Inner Principle of All: Neo-Confucian Metaphysics

What really holds everything together? The Confucian tradition made important intellectual advances in China during the Song era, and this Neo-Confucian philosophical attitude became central to the vision of ultimate reality held by many Chinese, as we saw in the previous chapter. What we call Neo-Confucianism was really known as the school of "Principle," that is, the underlying Principle that holds everything together; thus, it is precisely what we are looking for in this investigation—ultimate reality as Chinese understand it. The theory of **principle** (**li**) attaches itself to the earlier views, incorporating the concepts of Heaven and Dao. These terms flow together in the Neo-Confucian notion that all is principle and that the mind itself reflects and resonates with this principle.

We can take Zhu Xi's (1130–1200) synthesis of Neo-Confucian thought about ultimate reality as representative, though, of course, there were alternate ideas and emphases in some of the other thinkers. As the very source of all, Zhu Xi posits the Great Ultimate (**taiji**), another term used from ancient times. The Great Ultimate transcends time and space. It is both the sum total of the principles of all things and also the highest principle within each. As the repository for all actual and potential principles, the Great Ultimate is present in the universe as a whole and in each thing individually. Zhu Xi explained this relationship in this way:

> The Great Ultimate is merely the principle of heaven and earth and the myriad things. With respect to heaven and earth, there is the Great Ultimate in them. With respect to the myriad things, there is the Great Ultimate in each and every one of them. Before heaven and earth existed, there was assuredly this principle. . . . Fundamentally there is only one Great Ultimate, yet each of the myriad things has been endowed with it and each in itself possesses the Great Ultimate in its entirety. This is similar to the fact that there is only one moon in the sky but when its light is scattered upon rivers and lakes, it can be seen everywhere. It cannot be said that the moon has been split.[7]

So the real center of all, that which holds all together, is ultimate principle, both transcendent and completely within all things.

But how can we understand principle within each individual thing? Zhu Xi made a distinction between principle, *li*, and material force, *qi*. Principle is eternal, unchanging, indestructible, and incorporeal. On the other hand, material force is transitory, changing, destructible, and corporeal. Yet these two do not exist separately. Principle needs material force to adhere to, and material force needs principle as its essence. Understandably, someone asked Zhu Xi which came first, principle or material force. Principle has never been separated from material force, Zhu answered, even though if we talk about origins we would have to say that principle is prior.

But what about the Lord Above and Heaven? What about gods and spirits? In answer to questions like these, Zhu Xi consistently interpreted all such ideas as simply the operation of principle. One questioner referred to passages in the classics about Heaven's creative activity and said: "In passages like these, does it mean that Heaven has no personal consciousness and that the passages are merely deductions from principle?" Zhu Xi's answer was direct: "These passages have the same meaning. It is simply that principle acts this way."[8] Thus, in their view of ultimate reality, Neo-Confucianist teachers have effectively excluded the idea of a personal God who rules over all. Finally, it is principle that holds things together and keeps the world running.

Chinese Buddhist Vision of the Ultimate

If the Chinese perspective on the ultimate is not too complicated already, we should add that many Chinese also have accepted the Mahayana Buddhist view of ultimate reality as emptiness and as the Dharma Body of the Buddha (discussed in Part 2). Many distinctive Chinese ideas associated with the sense of cosmic harmony and Dao have colored Buddhist views of the ultimate in China. The Huayan school, for example, articulated a complicated teaching about the interpenetration of the transcendental Dharma (suchness) and the dharmas of the conditioned world of rebirth, so that all phenomena enter into and are identical with each other. To illustrate this, one great Huayan master placed a Buddha image illuminated with a lamp in the middle of a hall, setting up mirrors in all the ten directions (the four cardinal directions, the four intermediate directions, and up and down). Each mirror thus reflects the Buddha image—and each also reflects the Buddha image as reflected in all the other mirrors, showing the interpenetration of all reality infused with the Buddha nature.

Chan Buddhism perpetuated the basic Mahayana conceptions of the ultimate and presented them in direct, forceful form in China: nirvana as nondifferent from samsara, the Buddha essence of all reality, and the Dharma Body (equated with Dao) as universal. The Chan masters used all kinds of stories, illustrations, and paradoxical sayings to assert that the deepest principle of the truth is "utter nondifference." Ignorance and wisdom are the same without any difference. Form and emptiness are nondifferent. The practical message of Chan is that ultimate reality is no different from the suchness of life in every moment as we live it.

So the Chinese tradition puts forth a number of important answers to the question about what is ultimate, what really holds everything together. One may believe in the Lord Above, Heaven, as the power that runs the world. Or one may look to Dao of nature as the center of all. Again, one may find that the great gods of the Prior Heavens, together with their deputies on earth, provide the real center and support for existence. Or one may take the view that all these forces are really the natural, impersonal functioning of Principle. Finally, there is the Buddhist view of ultimate reality as the Dharma Body of the Buddha and as emptiness. The truth of the matter is that many Chinese have held to all these views in varying degrees. Chinese religious thought has produced many creative visions of ultimate reality on the basis of these fundamental patterns.

COSMOS AND HUMANITY

So what sense or meaning is there in life? What is this world all about anyway? Ancient Chinese thinkers spent a great deal of time speculating and arguing on precisely questions such as these, and their positions have influenced Chinese religion ever since. There are ancient myths of the evolving of the universe from chaos to order. And there are philosophical theories about the origin of all and about how the sacred forces operate together in this world. All these stories and theories point to a cosmology in which humans are closely interwoven with the various aspects of the world in the harmony of sacred power that is within, not outside, nature.

Origin of the Cosmos and Human Nature

From Chaos to Cosmos The origin of all things in a condition of chaos, called *hundun*, is an ancient and widespread Chinese idea. It is, of course, found in other religious traditions also, such as the ancient Babylonian and Hebrew stories of the creation of the cosmos from a condition of chaos. Hundun is the great void, the undifferentiated, formless, watery source that through a process of differentiation engendered our universe. This chaos is prior to all categories, characterized by flexibility, simplicity, and spontaneity, with inexhaustible potency to create the cosmos. As an eternal reality, it underlies the cosmos as the perpetual source of regeneration.

To help us understand this traditional Chinese worldview, let us consider the **Pangu** myth of cosmic origins. The ancient myth, from a third-century C.E. Chinese text, relates how Heaven and Earth were in the chaos condition (hundun). Gradually as Heaven and Earth were separated, pure yang formed the Heaven and murky yin formed the Earth. Pangu stood between them and grew to cosmic proportions, with his head supporting Heaven and his feet stabilizing Earth, until Heaven and Earth came to be separated by their present distance. Other versions of the myth tell that after Pangu died he was transformed into the universe. His breath became the wind and the clouds, his voice the thunder, and his eyes the sun and moon. His

blood became the rivers, his flesh the soil, his hair and beard the constellations, his skin and body hair the plants and trees, and his teeth and bones the metals and stones. And the parasites on his body, impregnated by the wind, became human beings.

The Pangu myth describes chaos as a chicken's egg, a notion that is widespread in ancient China and also in many other cultures. The symbolism is appropriate, for the egg contains creative potentiality, with all the aspects of life already present, ready to evolve and burst out. All the multiplicity of things, all opposites, even yin and yang, are united in this source of creativity. The cosmic person, Pangu, is engendered and nurtured within chaos to become the universe itself. There is no creator god here, working from the outside, as in the Hebrew creation story. Rather creation grows organically from within as that which is born in the chaos-womb grows to become the universe. There is a continuing process of transformation, as Pangu grows and Heaven and Earth become established. The transformation continues with the death of this cosmic Person. Pangu, the macrocosm (great universe), becomes all the various aspects of the world, so that each part of the world is organically linked to the whole.

Here is a self-evolved world. The original chaos is completely unified with the resultant world in a continuous process of creation and regeneration.

World Process: Dao, Yin–Yang, and Five Elements Laozi and later Daoist thinkers identified the primordial chaos as none other than Dao. They held that Dao is not only the origin of all but also the inner source of the continual transformation of the whole universe. That process involves generation and evolving forth; it also involves devolving and returning to the source, the "uncarved block," Dao. How does Dao operate? The *Daode jing* says,

Dao produced One.
One produced two.
Two produced Three.
And Three produced the ten thousand things.
The ten thousand things bear yin and embrace yang, and by the
    blending of material force they achieve harmony.

(Ch. 42)

Dao here is the original source and root of all, engendering the one chaotic, undifferentiated reality that is replete with creative material and energy, giving rise to a separation between the finer and brighter elements, which became Heaven (yang), and the coarser and darker elements, which became earth (yin), together with all that is in between. From yang come fire and the sun, from yin water and the moon—and so on in the total operation of the world, Dao functioning in the interaction of yin and yang. All of this is closely related to human welfare and happiness:

> Therefore the yin and the yang are the great principles of Heaven and Earth. The four seasons are the great path of yin and yang. Likewise, punishment and reward in government are to be in harmony with the four seasons. When punishment and reward are in harmony with the seasons, happiness will be produced; when they disregard them, they will produce calamity.[9]

As we see from the four seasons, Dao operates in yang–yin cyclical processes of rise and decline. We can also understand Dao as the operation of the five elements or forces. The five elements are wood, fire, earth, metal, and water, but these are identified with many other sets of five: planets, weather, seasons, cardinal directions, sense organs, tastes, viscera, moods, and so forth. These are dynamic operational agents that are continually moving in cyclical changes from one to the other. Each element has its time to rise, flourish, decline, and be taken over by the next. The relationships are complicated processes of mutually producing, conquering, and transforming. Thus, for example, wood conquers earth, metal conquers wood, fire conquers metal, water conquers fire, earth conquers water. In this whole cyclical process, an ecological balance is maintained. For example, overforestation would be stopped by forest fires, which would be stopped by rain. On the other hand, water can produce forests faster than metal cuts the trees down. This ecological balance is extended into all facets of personal, social, and political life.

The Human Position in the World   Where do we come from and why are we here? The Pangu myth, describing how everything in the world came from different parts of the cosmic Pangu, tells how the parasites on Pangu's body were impregnated by the wind and became human beings. This may seem to be a rather modest view of human origins and of human function in the world, unlike the view in the three Abrahamic religions that humans were made specially as the crown of creation to be God's representative over all. Actually, the point of the Pangu story of human origins does not seem to be that humans are parasites on the world. Rather, humans are from the same one source as the whole universe, organically related to the rest of nature. Humans are not masters of the universe, but they are evolved from the same source and share the common process of life with all.

Chinese farmers working in the rice paddies. The sense of the rhythms of nature is prominent in Chinese religious experience.

The early classic writings and the Confucian and Daoist philosophers provide much discussion on the nature of humans and their position in the world. There is general agreement that human nature is intricately related to all the sacred forces inherent in the universe. One of the clearest statements of human nature is in the *Classic of Rites*: "Humanness is consistent of benevolent virtue of Heaven and Earth, the co-operative union of Yin and Yang, the joint assembly of ghost [*gui*] and spirit [*shen*], and the finest breath contained in the Five Elements."[10] Human nature is the finest cooperative product of the universe itself, containing the basic substance and elements of the universe.

This passage from the *Classic of Rites* refers to "the joint assembly of *gui* and *shen*" within human nature. Chinese traditionally conceived of two souls within humans, appropriately, since humans are the "cooperative union of yin and yang." One soul is the yang soul (*hun*), which comes from Heaven, the realm of pure yang. The other soul is the yin soul (*po*), from the pure yin source, Earth. The yang dimension is also thought of as the spiritual aspect, and the yin as the physical aspect, of a person. During life, yin and yang are united, but at death they again separate. The yang soul, stemming from Heaven, becomes shen, a spiritual being or god. The yin soul becomes gui, an earthly spiritual force to be returned to its original source, the earth, in burial. If the gui is not properly buried and cared for by descendants, it may become an unhappy wandering spirit, or "ghost."

Thus, we see that human nature is a microcosm of the great universe itself. Human nature reflects all those powers writ large on the cosmic scale, now active and focused on the human scale. Many philosophical texts delight in spelling out the correspondences between the human body and the forces of Heaven and Earth, yin and yang, and the five elements. One text says,

> The roundness of the head imitates Heaven, and the squareness of the foot imitates Earth. Like Heaven has four seasons, Five Elements, nine divisions and 360 days, human beings also have four limbs, five viscera, nine orifices and 360 joints. Like Heaven has wind, rain, cold, and heat, human beings also have the qualities of accepting, giving, joy and anger. Therefore gall corresponds to clouds, the lung to vapor, the spleen to wind, the kidneys to rain, and the liver to thunder. Thus human beings form a trinity with Heaven and Earth, and the human mind is the master.[11]

The suggestion here that humans form a triad with Heaven and earth is an important idea in the Chinese view of human nature and makes it clear that humans have an important role to fill. Philosophical discussions of human nature inevitably come to that question of what special role humans have in the universe.

For Confucius and his followers, the ideal human position in the world could best be characterized by the concept of *ren*, "humanness," a notion that puts strong emphasis on interrelationship between people, in kindness and morality. It is this morality that makes humans different from animals; humans have the Heaven-given qualities of love or commiseration, righteousness, propriety, and wisdom; and they have the potential of fulfilling these qualities. Dong Zhongshu (178–104 B.C.E.), a great Confucianist who synthesized the ideas of yin–yang, five elements, and Dao within Confucianism, had a bit to say about the high position of humans in the universe.

> Of the creatures born from the refined essence of Heaven and Earth, none is more noble than man. Man receives the mandate from Heaven and is therefore superior to other creatures. Other creatures suffer troubles and defects and cannot practice humanity and righteousness; man alone can practice them.... From this we can see that man is distinct from other creatures and forms a trinity with Heaven and Earth....
>
> The beauty of humaneness is found in Heaven. Heaven is humaneness. Heaven shelters and nourishes the myriad things. It transforms and generates them. It nourishes and completes them. Heaven's affairs and achievements are endless. They end and begin again, and all that Heaven raises up it returns to serve humankind.... Since human beings receive their lives from Heaven, accordingly they appropriate Heaven's humaneness and are thereby humane.[12]

In this Confucianist interpretation is summed up a high view of the role of humans in the world, to be in union with Heaven and earth not only physically but also spiritually and, thus, help to maintain harmony in the universe through moral life.

Thinkers in the Daoist tradition have defined human roles a little differently. According to Laozi and Zhuangzi, human beings have received a special quality of virtue or power (*de*) from Dao, the life principle inherent in each individual. Therefore, humans simply need to discover that virtue or power within and live according to it. In any case, Chinese from all traditions see human good in the balanced, creative interaction with the sacred forces of the universe—morally, spiritually, and physically.

Realities of Human Existence in the World

Why do things seem so uncertain and confused? Why is there so much evil and suffering in the world? What keeps us from living the way we should? Since ancient times Chinese philosophers have debated questions about why humans seemingly do not reach their full potential in their own nature and in society. Sometimes, usually among Confucian thinkers, the discussion focuses on the question of whether humans are good or evil by nature, seen within the social context. Those inclined toward the Daoist vision see the problem more in terms of humans trapped in artificiality and conventional strictures instead of living in full harmony with Dao. Buddhists emphasize the problems of ignorance, desire, and karma. Those concerned about our relation to the gods and spirits feel that problems arise because humans forget them or fail to make use of their power of renewal. Whichever view is chosen, there is consensus on one thing: we humans do not live the full life of happiness, because we are out of harmony with the sacred power(s) at the heart of our existence.

Life in Community: Confucian Concerns   It is not hard to see that things are not right in the world. True, there have been eras of relative peace and harmony—Chinese thinkers often took a nostalgic look back to the early Zhou period (starting ca. 1100 B.C.E.) as a time when sage-kings ruled according to the mandate of Heaven in an era of peace and prosperity. But even that peaceful era was short-lived. Both Confucius and Laozi lived in a time of upheaval and anarchy. At no time could it be said that humans reached their full potential in peace and prosperity.

Chinese thinkers of all persuasions have offered theories as to why humans fail to live up to their possibilities. There are many possible theories, but it is characteristic of Chinese thinking that good and evil behavior is seen as a human problem, not something that is determined by divine forces, whether god or evil power. Of course, humans do interact with many spiritual forces, and hungry wandering spirits can cause suffering and misfortune. But in the final analysis the human problem of failure lies within humanity itself—in the individual, in society, or in both.

It is a time-honored view in China to consider human nature as essentially good and positive, in spite of the reality of evil and suffering in human society. This was the view suggested by Confucius and articulated clearly by Mengzi. Confucius based his whole approach on the educability of human beings, including the common people whom he accepted in his school. He held that it was lack of moral leadership and the attempt to rule by laws and penalties that prevented the people from developing a sense of honor. It is not that people by nature are hurtful and cruel; it is the anarchy of society and especially the greed and brutal power of rulers that turn human behavior to negative and harmful directions.

Mengzi articulated clearly the basic notion that humans are essentially good by nature but turn to evil because society and its leaders fail to cultivate and nourish that goodness of nature. All people have inborn virtues and potentials for developing goodness and humaneness. Famous in this discussion is Mengzi's parable of a child falling into a well:

> Here is why I say that all human beings have a mind that commiserates with others. Now, if anyone were suddenly to see a child about to fall into a well, his mind would always be filled with alarm, distress, pity, and compassion. That he would react accordingly is not because he would use the opportunity to ingratiate himself with the child's parents, nor because he would seek commendation from neighbors and friends, nor because he would hate the adverse reputation. From this it may be seen that one who lacks a mind that feels pity and compassion would not be human; one who lacks a mind that feels shame and aversion would not be human; one who lacks a mind that feels modesty and compliance would not be human; and one who lacks a mind that knows right and wrong would not be human.
>
> The mind's feeling of pity and compassion is the beginning of humaneness (*ren*); the mind's feeling of shame and aversion is the beginning of rightness (*yi*); the mind's feeling of modesty and compliance is the beginning of propriety (*li*); and the mind's sense of right and wrong is the beginning of wisdom. Human beings have these four beginnings just as they have four limbs.[13]

These four beginnings are motivations and possibilities that are inherent in everyone. Starting with commiseration, these originating impulses in human nature motivate us to become humane, righteous, proper, and wise.

But, Mengzi holds, these beginnings of goodness need to be nurtured and developed—and for many people that fails to happen. It seems that what we call evil in human nature is really due to lack of completion and development of the innate goodness. Mengzi likens human nature to Ox Mountain, which now is bald and denuded; once trees flourished there, but they no longer grow because of constant cutting down and lack of cultivation. So people think it never had any trees—but can that be the nature of a mountain? So too some people think humans are evil and selfish by nature—but like Ox Mountain humans are innately capable of producing good. "Therefore," Mengzi says, "with proper nourishment and care, everything grows, whereas without proper nourishment and care, everything decays."[14] So evil does not arise within human nature but comes, in a sense, from without, from lack of nourishing by society. The tendency of human nature is to do good, Mengzi said, like water flowing downhill. Of course, you can interfere and splash water uphill, but this is due not to the nature of water but to the force of circumstances. Similarly, humans may be brought to do evil, but that is because something has been forced onto human nature. Lack of nourishment of our good nature, corrupting influences from outside—from these arise the human problem of evil and suffering.

But there is an alternate way of looking at the problem, and this was best articulated by another disciple in the Confucian tradition, Xunzi (ca. 300–238 B.C.E.). Xunzi, taking a "realist" position, held that human nature is essentially selfish and hateful, and that any kind of goodness can only be acquired by training or enforced through laws and punishment. Heaven—which to Xunzi is a mechanistic force without moral qualities—produces a human nature that loves profit, envies and hates, and strives and plunders selfishly. Xunzi wrote,

Human nature is evil; its goodness derives from conscious activity. Now it is human nature to be born with a fondness for profit. Indulging this leads to contention and strife, and the sense of modesty and yielding with which one was born disappears. One is born with feelings of envy and hate, and, by indulging these, one is led into banditry and theft, so that the sense of loyalty and good faith with which he was born disappears. One is born with the desires of the ears and eyes and with a fondness for beautiful sights and sounds, and, by indulging these, one is led to licentiousness and chaos, so that the sense of ritual, rightness, refinement, and principle with which one was born is lost. Hence, following human nature and indulging human emotions will inevitably lead to contention and strife,

causing one to rebel against one's proper duty, reduce principle to chaos, and revert to violence.

(Ch. 23)[15]

If left to itself, our evil human nature would destroy any goodness in our civilization. Yet, for all his pessimistic view of human nature, Xunzi was optimistic that humans could be reshaped through the laws and training produced by the sages.

Since Mengzi and Xunzi seem to hold opposite positions, it is inevitable that there might be a view of human nature somewhere between the two. Some later Confucianists argued that both Mengzi and Xunzi were right; human nature is partly good and partly evil. If the good aspect is cultivated and nourished, the goodness increases; but if the evil aspect is cultivated, the badness increases. One thinker put it this way: "Man's nature is a mixture of good and evil. He who cultivates the good in it will become a good man and he who cultivates the evil in it will become an evil man."[16] This additional perspective suggests that Mengzi and Xunzi were perhaps not as far apart as might appear at first glance. The basic problem is still a genuinely human one: evil tendencies (whether from society or from human nature) often grow and spread, whereas good tendencies (whether from human nature or from society) often wither and diminish. And the struggle goes on not in the cosmos but on the stage of human life in society. The Confucian path of transformation is designed to reverse that human situation so that humaneness and righteousness prevail.

Daoist Views: The Problem of Artificiality and Coercion There is still another position on the question of whether humans are good or evil by nature. One thinker challenged Mengzi by claiming that there is no distinction between good or bad in human nature: "[Human] nature is like swirling water. Open a passage for it in the east, and it will flow east; open a passage for it in the west, and it will flow west. Human nature does not distinguish between good and non-good any more than water distinguishes between east and west."[17] Perhaps asking whether human nature is good or evil is the wrong approach, for that very judgment is artificial and may in fact contribute to the problem. Perhaps our basic problem is that we pass such judgments about good and evil!

This is the general approach to the human problem taken by Daoist philosophers. It is artificiality and coercion that lie at the root of our problems in the world. Dao by nature grows and wanes, operating in everything in harmony, and the good life is always to be in complete harmony with Dao. But our human tendency is to try and take charge of our lives, change things in accordance with our own strategies, and force structures onto nature and ourselves. We judge wealth and power to be good, and we judge poverty and weakness to be evil—and we spend our lives struggling for one and trying to escape from the other. But in doing so we are alienated from the harmony of Dao. Zhuangzi stated the problem with his characteristic flair for imagery:

> The duck's legs are short, but to stretch them out would worry him; the crane's legs are long, but to cut them down would make him sad. What is long by nature needs no cutting off; what is short by nature needs no stretching. That would be no way to get rid of worry.[18]

It is in going against the givenness and spontaneous fitness of nature that we experience suffering, frustration, and defeat. All of our problems come from trying to force things in artificial, unnatural ways.

Where does this human tendency come from? Laozi and Zhuangzi do not really say whether it is inherent in human nature or whether it stems from institutions of society. Probably even these distinctions are false and misleading. Nature itself is the operation of Dao, and evil embodies all that resists pristine nature through coercion, artificiality, and intellectual skill. However they originate, these tendencies at least are promoted by social institutions such as laws, education, ceremonies, rules of morality and etiquette, and the like. This means that the people who do the most to worsen our human problems are the law enforcers, the teachers, and the ritualists—all of them imposing restraints on what should be natural and free.

Of course, this Daoist perspective pertains most directly to those following the path put forth by Laozi and Zhuangzi. But the same basic notion flows over into the more widespread religious Daoist view of the human problem: we are out of balance with the cosmic forces that support and sustain us. These forces are the great gods of the stellar constellations, managing the operation of yin–yang and the five elements. Through neglect and ignorance we often live out of harmony and bring deprivation and evil upon ourselves. In popular religious understanding, these forces are the gods and goddesses that make up the pantheon of the state and the local community; they are the ancestral spirits that oversee the family and dispense weal

or woe in accordance with our harmony with them. One need only look at one's failures and frustrations, conflicts and tragedies, to recognize that the general disharmony with Dao and yin–yang is reflected in daily life in family and community.

Chinese Buddhist Views of Human Existence In bringing to China ideas of karma arising out of ignorance and desire, the wheel of existence, rebirth, and so forth, Buddhists contributed much to the Chinese conception of human nature and the human problem. The Mahayana Buddhist schools of China emphasized the classical doctrine of the universal Buddha-nature that all people possess, holding that it is human ignorance that keeps us from seeing this Buddha-nature, with the result that we remain trapped in suffering. For example, Zongmi (780–841), the fifth patriarch of the Huayan school, wrote an essay on the origin of human nature (*Yuanren lun*). He emphasized that all sentient beings possess the true mind of natural enlightenment—that which is also called Buddha-nature and Tathagatagarbha. This true spiritual nature neither comes into existence nor goes out of existence; from time immemorial it has always been there, clear and pure. However, from time immemorial, sentient beings have been deluded and asleep, not knowing their true Buddha-nature, clinging to the self and filled with ignorant desires, thus accumulating karma and suffering the pain of life and death.[19]

One tendency that developed among some Chinese Buddhists was to view the present world-age as particularly degenerate compared to earlier ages, thus making it much more difficult to follow the disciplines of the Buddhist path. An old Buddhist teaching about the **Three Ages of the Dharma** was popularized and influenced many. Basically, the first age, the first five hundred years after the lifetime of the Buddha (some held it was one thousand years), was the age of the Perfect Dharma, when the Buddha's Dharma was correctly preached and human minds were clear, so that many could follow the holy path to nirvana. The second age (the next one thousand years) declined into the age of the Counterfeit Dharma, when minds were clouded and following the holy path was much more difficult. But then comes the age of the End of the Dharma, in which all humans have become so degenerate in intellect and will that it is no longer possible to follow the former disciplines to reach the goal of enlightenment. Since Chinese Buddhists generally dated the Buddha's death as having occurred in 949 B.C.E., the feeling arose among some Buddhists that the world had entered into the age of the End of the Dharma in the year 552 C.E. Consequently, it was now extremely difficult if not impossible for humans to make progress on the path. Not all Buddhists agreed that human nature had degenerated to this extent, but those who did started advocating new, simpler solutions to the human problem, such as the Pure Land path.

Chinese popular imagination was fascinated by Buddhist ideas about bad karma accumulated during one's existence and rebirth in purgatories and hells, and lurid descriptions of the horrors of those purgatories abound in popular literature. Buddhist notions of purgatory were expanded by Chinese notions of trial and punishment for the guilty.

For example, one popular tract first issues a plea for sinners to repent and then presents a portrait of what is in store for them if they do not. The Judges of the Ten Courts of Purgatory agree that all who led virtuous lives shall be escorted at their death to the land of the Immortals. Those with a balance of evil against them will be dragged by horrid devils through all the Courts, suffering bitterly as they go, and will again be born to endure in life the uttermost poverty and wretchedness, in death to return to the tortures of purgatory. Those who are disloyal, unfilial, who commit suicide, take life, or disbelieve the doctrine of karma are simply handed over to the everlasting tortures of hell. After a long description of the most horrid punishments imaginable, the tract reflects on the foolishness of human nature, illustrated by those who, having passed through the purgatories and through the Terrace of Oblivion (where they are caused to forget all that has happened to them), now rejoice at the prospect of being born again as humans. They all rush on to birth like an infatuated or drunken crowd, and they act lustfully and destroy life, and finally they bring themselves once more to the same horrible state.[20]

PATHS OF TRANSFORMATION

How can we start living the life that is real? How can we find power for renewal and transformation? The portrayals of the human problem in the Chinese traditions, against the background of the human potential for goodness and happiness, help to set the stage for the Path of Transformation, the kind of praxis that leads to renewal of harmony with Dao, the gods, the spirits, and the innermost sources of life.

The Confucian Path of Study and Ritual

The Confucian tradition, disdaining as it does some of the usual religious practices such as calling on the gods for help, has sometimes been considered not a religious path at all but rather a kind of philosophy for improvement of self and society. Are these questions, having to do with the search for real life and renewal, even applicable to the concerns of Confucianists?

Of course they are, for these are basic, universal, human concerns. Confucianists are just as concerned as anyone else about real, authentic life and self-transformation. The emphasis is not on life after death or salvation through help from the gods, it is true. But perhaps for that very reason there is a very strong emphasis on achieving the life that is truly human and fulfills our full potential for peace, harmony, and happiness—according to the design of Heaven. Confucianism is clearly a path of spiritual transformation, stressing both the intellectual pursuit of education and study and also the practical and social pursuits of ritual behavior and propriety. We look more closely at the Confucian rituals and ethical actions later; here we want to understand the theoretical basis of the path: How can study, ritual, and moral behavior be the basis of self-transformation, the path to real life?

Transformation Through Study and Moral Cultivation
Confucius was above all an educator, and those following in his tradition have always stressed the path of study and education as the means toward transformation. The human problem, as we have seen, is that our fundamentally good nature gets stunted for lack of nourishment and even misdirected by the anarchy that tends to rule in society because of selfish rulers, repressive laws, and wrongful social relationships. But we have the potential to realize our humanness and become noble people if we have noble teachers and rulers, if we allow ourselves to be educated, and if we study our own nature and the nature of things as determined according to the will of Heaven. This means using the intellect for education, study, and moral self-cultivation.

Confucius taught that the sage-kings of old had deep insight into the will of Heaven and perfected their own humanity in harmony with Heaven. Therefore, the classics that tell about their sayings and their lives can mediate that wisdom and perfection to those who read and study these sacred writings, for through such study and education one's human goodness can be nourished and perfected.

In a famous passage in the *Analects*, Confucius points to the way of learning as a lifelong process of self-cultivation:

> When I was fifteen, I set my heart on learning. At thirty, my character was established. At forty, I no longer had doubts. At fifty, I knew Heaven's will. At sixty, I listened to it. At seventy, I could follow my inmost desire without going astray from the path.

(2.4)

There is no quick fix here, no sudden conversion and transformation. The path is a long, gradual movement of study and learning, awakening the inner knowledge of the will of Heaven and growing into that will so that the very springs of motivation are in complete harmony with it. So study is not just for knowledge's sake but also for inner cultivation and growth in realizing the will of Heaven—thus becoming a true noble person (*junzi*).

The study of the classics actually involves all the major liberal arts, providing a thorough humanistic education. The six disciplines are based on the Six Classics, and they include study of poetry for refinement of thought and expression, study of history for understanding the tradition and refining moral judgment, study of ritual for understanding propriety, study of music for inner transformation, study of politics for social transformation, and study of cosmology to harmonize with the sacred forces. By such study and practice it is possible to cultivate the innate human capabilities to become good and noble and superior; such noble persons can then lead and guide others to become humane and good.

The Neo-Confucianists developed the path of study into a total system of moral and spiritual self-cultivation, and to many Chinese this Neo-Confucian model of the path has been their highest aspiration. We recall Zhu Xi's teaching about universal principle. Humans have principle, *li*, as their original nature, good and humane. But principle needs to be attached to material force, *qi*, to be actualized, and this aspect of human nature is often characterized by selfish desires, clouding principle and leading to evil results. Therefore, it is important, Zhu Xi taught, for humans to cultivate themselves by penetrating to the underlying principle and, thus, rectifying the mind. The way to do this is through learning and the investigation of things, both in the external world and within oneself.

So learning and knowledge cross over into transforming the will and mind and personal life, and this strength of personal character influences the whole social setting of the family, the community, and even the world. One of the most important descriptions of this path of self-cultivation is in the *Book of Great Learning*:

> The Way of learning to be great consists in manifesting the clear character, loving the people, and abiding in the highest good. . . . The ancients who wished to manifest their clear character to the world would first bring order to their states. Those who wished to bring order to their states would first regulate their families. Those who wished to regulate their families would first cultivate their personal lives. Those who wished to cultivate their personal lives would first rectify their minds. Those who wished to rectify their minds would first make their wills sincere. Those who wished to make their wills sincere would first extend their knowledge.

So all the good expressions of character depend on steps of self-cultivation that finally rest on extending one's knowledge, as the very first movement. The text continues:

> The extension of knowledge consists in the investigation of things. When things are investigated, knowledge is extended; when knowledge is extended, the will becomes sincere; when the will is sincere, the mind is rectified; when the mind is rectified, the personal life is cultivated; when the personal life is cultivated, the family will be regulated; when the family is regulated, the state will be in order; and when the state is in order, there will be peace throughout the world.

Here are eight steps toward the transformation of human society in the world! The last three have to do with family and society—reflecting the importance of parents, teachers, rulers, and others on the path of transformation. But the focal point still is the cultivation of personal life. The text goes on to say, "From the Son of Heaven [the emperor] down to the common people, all must regard cultivation of the personal life as the root or foundation. There is never a case when the root is in disorder and yet the branches are in order."[21]

So the important question is, how can one cultivate personal life so as to become a noble person? The text lays out some basic steps, namely, investigation of things, extension of knowledge, the will becoming sincere, and the rectification of the mind. These form the heart of the path of transformation, leading to the moral and spiritual cultivation of personal life. The investigation of things means to study the nature of the world and of oneself, arriving at true understanding of the underlying moral principles of the universe. In this process the will becomes sincere, resolving on the goal with calmness and unflagging determination. The path of transformation specifically involves rectification of the mind, becoming one with the whole universe by understanding its principles and looking upon the whole cosmos as one's own self. All of this adds up to cultivation of personal life, that is, self-discipline and practice with diligence and zeal, in study, meditation, and cultivation of moral virtue.

Transformation Through Ritual In addition to the mental disciplines of study and extension of knowledge, the Confucian path places great emphasis on the practical disciplines of self-transformation. In some religions, such as Judaism and Islam, ritual and ethical behavior according to God's law play a major part in the path of transformation. Confucianism does not think in terms of God's law, but it finds ritual and ethical behavior (propriety) in society to be powerful instruments of self-transformation. Both ritual and the rules of propriety, in fact, correspond to the patterns immanent in the whole of reality.

It is important to understand that what we are calling ritual and ethical behavior are the same word in Chinese: *li*. As the inherent ritual pattern of the universe, *li* is followed and practiced both in the various traditional rituals and in one's proper roles in family and society.

In traditional China there were rituals for almost every purpose—sacrifice to the ancestors, political occasions, family events, great public occasions, receiving a guest, and so on. And many great thinkers have written about the meaning of ritual, following the lead of the *Classic of Rites*, the ancient text that describes many rituals and also provides important ideas about the meaning of the rituals. Chinese have always thought of ritual as closely connected with the underlying principles of the whole universe. In ancient China, for example, rituals of divination were used to connect with the sacred powers of the world and even to direct and control them. Thus, by performing ritual correctly, we are harmonizing ourselves with the forces of Heaven and earth.

Xunzi, a Confucian thinker who wrote a lot about ritual, has this to say about the origin of ritual:

> Rites have three roots. Heaven and Earth are the root of life, the ancestors are the root of the human species, and rulers and teachers are the root of order. . . . Thus rites serve Heaven above and Earth below; they honor ancestors; they exalt rulers and teachers.

So ritual has both a cosmological origin and a social origin. It issued forth from Heaven and earth as part of the very principle of the universe. And it also was transmitted by ancestors and shaped by teachers and rulers. Indeed, it is ritual that upholds and unifies the whole realm of the world. Because of rites, Xunzi says,

> Heaven and earth find harmony,
> The sun and moon become bright,
> The four seasons follow in order,
> The stars and constellations move,
> The rivers and streams flow,
> And all things flourish.
> Likes and dislikes are regulated;
> Joys and hates are made appropriate.[22]

Therefore, ritual can effect the great transformation of harmonizing us with the world, so that we humankind do become, as the classics state, a trinity with Heaven and earth. Through rituals our innate goodness is nourished and we conform ourselves more and more into the pattern of Heaven and earth, becoming people of humanity.

Moral Cultivation Through Propriety in Society Confucius taught that we can become people of humanity (*ren*) especially by practicing the rules of *li*, "propriety" (the same word as ritual). Here the focus is on relationships in society, in accordance with the will of Heaven, transforming ourselves by practicing and fulfilling our proper roles.

The Confucian tradition talks about the **rectification of names**, that is, transforming oneself so as to practice one's proper roles in family and society. Confucius said, "Let the prince be prince, the minister be minister, the father father and the son son" (*Analects* 12.11). Each person is related to all the others in society, so each needs to fulfill the particular role and duty that he or she has. Much of the breakdown in society today results from people not fulfilling their proper roles, usurping the roles of others, rulers looking after their self-interest, teachers misleading students, and all the rest. Many people do not live according to their proper role in family and society—they usurp the authority of their elders, they fail to respect and obey the rulers, they consider themselves above their teachers. To transform ourselves into our potential human goodness, we need the discipline and practice of rectifying our social roles, Confucius taught. We need to discipline ourselves to live as a father, a son, a sister, a ruler, a subject. Only in this way will we be able to inject humaneness (*ren*) into our lives and into our relation with others.

What makes this pursuit of ritual and propriety a religious path is the deep sense that the elaborate systems of ritual and the rules of propriety are based in the pattern originating in the cosmic principle of the universe, according to the mandate of Heaven. "Not knowing the will of Heaven, it is impossible to be a superior person," Confucius said. "Not knowing propriety, it is impossible for one's character to be established" (20:3).

Paths of Transformation in the Daoist Tradition

How can we start living *real* life? Where do we find power for life and immortality, beyond failure and death? The Daoist tradition is very much concerned with these questions, and it proposes one fundamental answer: Get into harmony with Dao!

The basic human problem from the Daoist perspective, as we recall, is forcing our lives against the flow of Dao, engaging in the human tendency of artificiality, judging others, planning strategies, forcing people into roles, and generally struggling selfishly against the stream. This is what causes evil and misery, war and violence, sickness and early death.

So what can one do to transform all this? The path offered by those of the Daoist persuasion consists of ideas, disciplines, and practices to lead to harmony with Dao and with all the spiritual forces that operate within our universe. According to the early Daoist philosophers, the way to ultimate transformation involves the practice of meditation, inaction, and withdrawal from society's constraints. Daoist priests and ritual experts offer many more rituals and practices that restore the powers within our bodies, call down the great cosmic gods, all together balancing yin and yang forces to bring blessed life and immortality.

Returning to Dao Through No-Action The kind of existence that can be attained, according to Laozi, Zhuangzi, and other Daoist thinkers, is one beyond all limitations, hindrances, and finite borders. We can become transcendental, realizing our body as part of the universe. That means we need have no worries or anxieties, for the real truth tran-

scends normal knowledge and moral principles. Invincible and immortal, we can live fully in tune with Dao.

A most important movement on the path of transformation, according to the *Daode jing*, is to practice "no-action" (*wuwei*). This seems like a contradiction in terms—how can you practice no action? Of course, what the path prescribes is a way of life in which nothing is done against the course of nature, no actions are forced, no mental concepts are imposed on Dao, and judgments about good and bad or desirable and nondesirable are completely avoided. Dao in itself is neither good nor bad, neither right nor wrong, so there is no need for actions on our part to resist or change the natural transformations. The course of Dao is simply the natural, universal course of Dao—and our highest good is to be in harmony with that Dao just as it is. That calls for a life in which we dedicate ourselves to disciplines and practices that open us up toward Dao—disciplines of nonstriving, noncontrol, nonstructure, and nondirection. Never do anything that is against the natural flow of Dao—that is the basic meaning of *wuwei*, no-action. Stated positively, it means to do everything in accord with the flow of Dao.

This kind of life requires practice. And the Daoist texts put forth a program designed to cultivate the no-action type of life: withdrawing from society, living simply, cultivating one's inner nature. Early Daoists were hermits and recluses, following Dao in the mountains and valleys, through winter and summer, alone and in groups, practicing the discipline of no-action. Central to this is meditation, emptying out the plans, structures, and strategies of the mind so that the natural flow of Dao might fill the whole being. An important text in the *Daode jing* says:

> Attain complete vacuity,
> Maintain complete quietude.
> All things come into being,
> And I see thereby their return.
> All things flourish,
> But each one returns to its root.
> This return to its root means tranquility.
> It is called returning to its destiny.
> To return to destiny is called the eternal.

(Ch. 16)[23]

What is proposed here is a type of meditation that empties the mind of all ideas and concepts that limit and restrain, so that the mind can directly experience the flow of

Dao, the rise and return of all things to the root and source of all. Zhuangzi talks about a "fasting of the mind," a "listening with the spirit" that creates the emptiness in which Dao is experienced (Ch. 4). Through such meditation we harmonize ourselves with Dao so that we are not affected by change, by feelings of good and bad, even by death. By being one with Dao we can live totally freely and spontaneously, letting everything happen as it will.

This path of transformation does not involve study and learning in the traditional sense, for such activities only serve further to cloud over our minds so that we cannot open ourselves to the flow of Dao. Nor does this path mean learning our proper roles in society, for such structures only increase artificiality and convention. Rather the ideal path would be that of a mountain hermit, roaming about freely and carelessly, fully attuned to the rhythms of nature, acting only in full harmony with the flow of Dao. It is possible to follow this path without becoming a mountain hermit, of course, but the method of withdrawing from societal structures and meditating in harmony with nature is still important even for those who remain in society.

Since words and concepts do not help on the path of Dao, it is misleading to offer too many rationalized explanations. Zhuangzi once said:

> The fish trap exists because of the fish; once you've gotten the fish, you can forget the trap. The rabbit snare exists because of the rabbit; once you've gotten the rabbit, you can forget the snare. Words exist because of meaning; once you've gotten the meaning, you can forget the words. Where can I find a man who has forgotten words so I can have a word with him?

(Ch. 26)[24]

Fortunately, Zhuangzi was a great storyteller, and through these stories we can develop some sensitivity for what it means to practice no-action and follow Dao. Once, Zhuangzi said, Prince Wenhui's cook Ding was cutting up a bullock. "Every touch of his hand, every shift of his shoulder, every tread of his foot, every thrust of his knee, every sound of the rending flesh, and every note of the movement of the chopper was in perfect harmony." Prince Wenhui was impressed and praised him for his perfect skill, but the Cook Ding replied:

> What I care about is the Way, which goes beyond skill. When I first began cutting up oxen, all I could see was the ox itself. After three years I no longer saw the whole ox. And now—now I go at it by spirit and don't look with my eyes. Perception and

understanding have come to a stop and spirit moves where it wants. I go along with the natural makeup, strike in the big hollows, guide the knife through the big openings, and follow things as there are. . . . A good cook changes his knife once a year—because he cuts. A mediocre cook changes his knife once a month—because he hacks. I've had this knife of mine for nineteen years and I've cut up thousands of oxen with it, and yet the blade is as good as though it had just come from the grindstone.

Now the prince understood and said, "Excellent. I have heard the words of Cook Ding and learned how to care for life" (Ch. 3).[25] This way of cultivating life is the way of no-action, that is, not scheming and forcing things but working spontaneously with one's spirit in harmony with Dao. That approach brings success and happiness in life. In fact, one completely in tune with Dao overcomes the normal human limitations, as Zhuangzi says somewhat playfully:

> I'm going to try speaking some reckless words and I want you to listen to them recklessly. How will that be? The sage leans on the sun and the moon, tucks the universe under his arm, merges himself with things, leaves the confusion and muddle as it is, and looks on slaves as exalted. Ordinary men strain and struggle; the sage is stupid and blockish. He takes part in ten thousand ages and achieves simplicity in oneness. For him, all the ten thousand things are what they are, and thus they enfold each other.

(Ch. 2)[26]

Daoist Religious Path   There is no sharp division between the Daoist path of transformation as understood by the philosophers and that practiced by the priests and experts. The masters and priests of the religious sects start from the basic perspective of Laozi and Zhuangzi and offer a path that relates more concretely to the human concerns of health, material happiness, well-being of family and community, and even immortality. Whereas the path of the philosophers is mostly a private pursuit of individuals, the path of religious Daoism is a community concern and focuses on experts and priesthoods, temples and festivals and rituals, for the welfare and transformation of the community. Still, the priests and experts follow the path for their own personal transformation, for only in that way can they share the transforming power with others. The religious path of Daoism really operates at two levels, then: the level of the expert or priest and the level of ordinary people in the community.

The Daoist view of the human situation holds that our problems arise because we are out of balance with the cosmic forces that support and sustain us. These forces can be seen as the great gods of the stellar constellations who manage the operation of yin–yang and the five elements, related also to the ancestral spirits and the gods and goddesses of everyday life. So to start living real life means to follow the path that restores one's balance with these cosmic forces.

An important factor in the Daoist path is the microcosm–macrocosm relationship. The macrocosm or "great cosmos" is Dao operating through the gods of the stellar constellations, yin–yang, and the five elements. The microcosm or "small cosmos" is our limited world, our local temple, and even our human body, a small-scale replica of the great cosmos. This means that the regions of the temple and of the human body correspond to the regions of the cosmos. And the forces of the cosmos are also present within the temple and the human body, or they can be called down to inhabit them.

The path of the Daoist adept or priest is first of all a path of study and discipline, for it is necessary to memorize the spirit registers and the appropriate rituals for summoning the gods. Typically a priest would pass this knowledge and expertise on to one of his sons—the rule being one priest in each generation of the family. So through a long discipline of study and practice, the Daoist priest becomes adept at the rituals, able to summon the great powers into this realm and into his own body to bring about renewal and transformation.

In ancient times, the path included the practice of alchemy, creating a kind of gold-dust fluid to drink for the purpose of nourishing the inner forces and prolonging life. More important for Daoists today, the path includes various practices of bodily exercises and meditation designed to nourish the life forces. It is believed that the most important elements in the body are spirit, breath, and spermatic essence. These are present throughout the body but are especially concentrated in the three Cinnabar fields, namely, the head, the heart, and just below the navel. These three fields are also the special realms of the Three Pure Ones, the great stellar gods that inhabit the body. The processes of yin and yang are also at work in the body, for the yang soul came from Heaven and the yin soul from earth. As life goes on, yang gradually is used up and yin increases, leading to an imbalance. And finally spirit, breath, and seminal essence are dissipated in death.

The path followed by the Daoist adept is designed to reverse this process, to renew the heavenly yang forces and, thus, restore vitality. There are methods of inner contemplation in which the One Dao is meditated upon, and through a visualization technique the Three Pure Ones are summoned into the three fields of the body to bring renewal. There is also visualization of the gods who dwell in each point and each organ of the body, and visualization of the heavenly bodies and planets that also descend into the body. Furthermore, there are breathing techniques, gymnastics, and dietetics to free the body of impurities, clear the channels of circulation throughout the body, and nourish the primordial breaths. One important practice is guiding the breath through the different fields of the body to nourish the vital forces.

Since it is only the Daoist priests who know the names and characteristics of each of these spiritual forces, together with the elaborate techniques for summoning them to provide renewal, this is a path of transformation that is followed by the priests and adepts, not by the common people, even though they also reap benefits from it.

But what about the average person? Does the average person have no path of transformation, no way to find the life that is whole and blessed with harmony? Of course, an important part of the religious path for ordinary people is relying on the priests and experts for their services in the great festivals, critical life events such as marriages and funerals, and times of sickness and other need. The priests and experts can restore the balance of sacred forces by exorcising the evil spirits and calling down the great gods to renew life force and restore harmony. In this respect religious Daoism resembles other religions, such as some forms of Christianity or Hinduism, in which there is reliance on the authority of ritual experts to effect the desired transformations. For example, only those with proper training and authority can say the Christian mass or chant the Hindu Vedas for the desired transformation. So, too, in religious Daoism, one part of the path for laypeople is to respect and rely on these ritualists and experts in Dao.

But ordinary people themselves have appropriate involvement on the path, for the sake of maintaining a balance of sacred forces in their personal lives, in family, and in community. These practices go beyond religious Daoism strictly speaking, including Buddhist and Confucian elements together with long-held local folk traditions. The popular religious path has many variables, but it centers around the cult of popular gods and goddesses, the ancestral cult, and personal spiritual cultivation.

Whereas the priests summon the great cosmic gods of the Prior Heavens that bring renewal and harmony to the universe, there are other powers in our world that have a lot to do with health and happiness in our lives, and when we are out of balance with these powers we suffer in various ways. So people can go to the local temple and worship the gods who have demonstrated their power and importance. For example, Guanyin, a Buddhist bodhisattva of great mercy, is to many people a compassionate mother, the giver of children, and a source of help in time of need. The Jade Emperor, a Daoist cosmic god, is also the supreme god to whom all the local gods report. The path of the laypeople means invoking and worshiping these gods and many more, so that the sacred balance may be maintained in their personal lives.

The theory of the ancestor cult is rooted in the conviction that the souls of the dead ancestors continue existence after death, and that the original family relationship remains in full force, with the ancestors possessing even more spiritual power than they had in life. The dead and the living are mutually dependent on each other, the living providing sacrifices and care for the graves, the ancestors providing blessings. To maintain harmony in this reciprocal relationship, people need carefully to fulfill the requirements for proper funerals and graves, offer continuing sacrifices to the ancestors, and observe the seasonal visits to clean and repair the graves. In all of these activities, the family and clan maintain and renew a sense of wholeness and cohesion, bound together in the love and remembrance of the ancestors.

Buddhist Paths of Transformation in China

The path followed by Chinese people has been significantly influenced by Buddhism as by the other Chinese religions. We discussed (in Part 2) the basic Buddhist path, but we need to take note of important Chinese contributions to the shaping of the Mahayana path of transformation. We can focus on the two major Chinese schools, Pure Land and Chan.

The Pure Land Path   Worship of Buddha Amitabha (Amituo fo) was known from early Buddhist times in India, but the main emphasis had been on the discipline of meditation, since the early Pure Land sutras talked of con-

centrating on Amitabha as a meditative discipline. In China, the practice of chanting the Buddha's name, with the formula *namo Amituo fo*, became a central practice in the meditative exercises. Through the chanting exercise, which might proceed through different rhythms and tonal patterns, the worshiper could abandon all worldly thoughts and attain to realization of the nonduality of the Buddha.

As some Chinese Buddhists adopted the idea that the world had now entered into the degenerate Age of the End of the Dharma, they began to seek new solutions that did not depend on the ability to practice the disciplines. Two major new ideas were introduced by the Chinese Pure Land masters to make this path more appealing and more usable by the common people. Amitabha's original vows were interpreted to mean that simply reciting the name of Amitabha with faith in one's heart is sufficient to attain rebirth in the Pure Land through Amitabha's power. And, based on the vows taken by Amitabha, the Chinese Pure Land masters taught that even those who have committed evil deeds and atrocities can be reborn in the Pure Land if they sincerely desire it and chant the Buddha's name.

So here is a Chinese path of salvation open to everyone, based in traditional Buddhist meditative disciplines but developed into a chanting practice that everyone can participate in. The efficacy of this path is based in the Mahayana notions of universal Buddha-nature and transfer of merit. Through the chanting of Amitabha's name, with faith in his vows, the Buddha's great storehouse of merit is made available to cancel evil karma and make possible rebirth in the Buddha's own realm, the Pure Land.

The Way of Chan   The path of transformation offered by the Chan school focuses primarily on meditation, with many similarities to early Buddhist practices in this regard. Becoming totally aware of the true nature of reality is what brings transformation. But meditation in the Chan school is based on Mahayana principles—that all reality is the universal Buddha-nature, that nirvana is not different from samsara, and that one's original nature is the Buddha-nature. Through meditation it is possible for anyone, learned or unlearned, to awaken to this true Buddha-nature. Scriptures and orthodox doctrines are not necessary, for the Chan masters held there was a special transmission of the truth outside doctrines, a direct transmission from mind to mind. The basic path was simply to strive constantly to have no ego-centered notions but to see directly into one's nature.

Buddist monks at Lama Temple in Beijing in 1966.

ries, it seems, is part of Chan discipline.

It appears that the Chan masters were influenced considerably by the Daoist path, meditating through emptying the mind, cultivating free and spontaneous living in the world. Chan masters emphasized that one need not try to escape from the change and flux of the world. The path itself is enlightenment and freedom. The Buddha-nature is universal and can be realized without any special searching, in the commonness of daily existence. Often-quoted words of Master Linji Yixuan make this point in a dramatic way:

> Seekers of the Way. In Buddhism no effort is necessary. All one has to do is to do nothing, except to move his bowels, urinate, put on his clothing, eat his meals, and lie down if he is tired. The stupid will laugh at him, but the wise one will understand. . . .

> Seekers of the Way, if you want to achieve the understanding according to the Law, don't be deceived by others and turn to [your thoughts] internally or [objects] externally. Kill anything that you happen on. Kill the Buddha if you happen to meet him. Kill a patriarch or an arhat if you happen to meet him. Kill your parents or relatives if you happen to meet them. Only then can you be free, not bound by material things, and absolutely free and at ease. . . . My views are few. I merely put on clothing and eat meals as usual, and pass my time without doing anything. You people coming from the various directions have all made up your minds to seek the Buddha, seek the Law, seek emancipation, and seek to leave the Three Worlds. Crazy people! If you want to leave the Three Worlds, where can you go? "Buddha" and "patriarchs" are terms of praise and also bondage. Do you want to know where the Three Worlds are? They are right in your mind which is now listening to the Law.[28]

Therefore, the master–disciple relationship was crucial in the Chan path. In private interviews, the master would teach and provoke the disciple, until finally, at a critical moment, the disciple would experience a spontaneous awakening to the Buddha-nature. Stories about these master–disciple encounters were later collected and became a characteristic part of Chan literature. A typical example is the story told about Linji Yixuan (d. 867). Linji went to talk with Master Huangbo, asking him the real meaning of Bodhidharma coming from the West (a standard question in Chan interviews). Immediately Huangbo struck him. Linji came back to visit the master three times, but each time he received blows. Finally, on Master Huangbo's advice, Linji went to visit another master, Dayu, who asked him what Huangbo had taught him. Linji told him how, when he asked for the real meaning of Buddhism, Huangbo struck him, three times over. "I don't know where I was at fault," said Linji. But Master Dayu cried out, "Your master treated you entirely with motherly kindness, and yet you say you do not know your fault." Upon hearing this, Linji experienced sudden enlightenment, stating, "After all, there isn't much in Huangbo's Buddhism!"[27] Understanding these sto-

The path in the Chan tradition is not a matter of striving to escape the samsara world and achieve nirvana. Given the universal Buddha-nature, the path itself is enlightenment. Awakening means getting in touch with one's original nature, one's true mind. And that Buddhist insight, born in India, resonates creatively with the Chinese traditions.

DISCUSSION QUESTIONS

1 Dao is the Mother of all—what do you think this means?

2 What is the difference between the Daoist gods of the "Prior Heavens" and the gods of popular religion?

3 How do yin and yang and the five elements operate as part of the world process?

4 What are some basic implications about the world to be drawn from the Pangu myth?

5 What does it mean to say the human body is a "microcosm" of the great universe itself?

6 Review the discussion in the Confucian tradition about whether humans are basically inclined to good or evil. Which view becomes dominant? What do you think?

7 What view does Daoism (represented by the *Daode jing* and the *Zhuangzi*) put forth as to the nature and problem of human existence?

8 How can study be transformative? How can ritual and the practice of social propriety be transformative?

9 Explain the Daoist principle of no-action (*wuwei*). How can this be transformative?

10 Describe the path of transformation as taught in Pure Land and in Chan Buddhism.

Chapter 13

Ritual Practices and the Good Life in China

RITUAL PRACTICES AND WORSHIP

How can we renew power for life? How can we restore balance and harmony? Through agelong experience, Chinese people have created various forms of ritual and worship as the means for renewing power and harmony in life.

Ritual has always been very important in Chinese society—after all, one of the ancient texts is the *Classic of Rites*. Confucian thinkers have taught and written a lot about the proper practice of ritual and what it means. From time immemorial, Chinese have ritualized all facets of family life as well as life within the state's political community, and there are frequent public ceremonies and festivals. Since the religious traditions of China are so interwoven, it is not possible to draw sharp distinctions between the rituals of the different traditions in all cases. We look first at what are generally recognized as Confucian, Daoist, and Buddhist rituals, and then we consider the more general festivals and the rituals of the life cycle.

Ritual in the Confucian Tradition

The term *ritual* or *propriety* (*li*) as used by Confucius goes back to the ritual sacrifices offered to the ancestors. Confucian scholars thoroughly investigated the function of ritual to show how it serves to transform and renew life. In fact, as we saw earlier, ritual is a cosmological principle for Confucian thinkers like Xunzi. Performance of ritual helps to uphold the whole universe, to stay in communion with the ancestors, and to harmonize human society.

Ritual in the Family and the Cult of the Ancestors The Confucian emphasis on ritual is most apparent in aspects of family and community life that have to do with the principles of hierarchy and reciprocity. It is through ritual that the relationship is maintained between parent and child, between ancestor and descendant, between friend and friend. Perhaps the most important rituals are those that hold the family together in proper order, that is, the rituals expressing and cultivating filial piety. The idea of reciprocity, of mutual dependence of younger and elder, of living and dead, is basic to these ritual actions.

Traditional Chinese homes have an altar on which the ancestral tablets are kept and also where images of the gods important to the family are worshiped. Incense is offered on the table before the altar daily, usually by a woman of the house. On important occasions, the central ritual actions in worshiping the ancestors and the gods include offerings of food, offering of spirit money, acts of reverence such as *ketou* (kowtow, that is, prostrating oneself), and prayers. Since the ancestors are kinspeople, they are offered food in much the same form as the family's guests. The table in front of the altar is set with rice bowls, chopsticks, spices and condiments, and fully prepared dishes hot from the stove, including cooked rice. Food offerings are also made to the gods in the home, and on certain occasions meals are offered to the homeless spirits—but these are always placed outside the house. Paper spirit money is also sometimes offered at the altar, usually silver for ancestors and gold for the gods. Performing ketou before the ancestors and the gods is an essential act of reverence, and the number of ketous depends on the status of the spirit being worshiped—a person may bow four times before ancestors, for example, only twice before the Stove God, and a hundred times before Lord Shang Di. Furthermore, bowing is done in the proper order in the family hierarchy.

Ritual in State and Community   Beyond the family, the Confucian principle of ritual permeates government and community life. At the local level, officials, magistrates, and governors perform rituals for the harmony and happiness of the community. And at the highest levels, up until the twentieth century, the emperor and the supreme officials performed rituals directed to Heaven and earth and the royal ancestors, for the harmony and welfare of the whole people.

An example of worship in the state cult would be the emperor's sacrifice to Heaven at the winter solstice, during the longest night of the year. The emperor and his officials arose before dawn and climbed to the top of a great stone altar south of the city (the direction of yang). The ancestors and other gods were represented by inscribed tablets on the altar, and food was placed before them. A young red bull (a symbol of yang) was offered to Heaven, and wine, incense, and silk were presented together with music from bells and drums. It was important that all the ritual be done well on the emperor's part, so that Heaven and the ancestors would do their part and assist in the rebirth of yang and the coming of spring once again, for the benefit of all nature and society.

In traditional China, official magistrates were assigned by the imperial government to have charge over a particular district, and it was each magistrate's job to worship the spiritual powers for the welfare of his territory. Important in the local capital was the Confucian temple, whose main hall contained the spirit-tablets of Confucius and other sages. Sacrifices were held here twice yearly, in midspring and midautumn, with the city magistrate as the chief celebrant and the senior officials in attendance. At dawn, sacrifices were placed before the tablet of Confucius, including a roll of silk, chalices of wine, bowls of soup, other food dishes, an ox, a pig, and a sheep. The officials lined the sides of the courtyard below the hall, and six ranks of young students in traditional costume postured with long wands tipped with pheasant feathers. Drums and an orchestra playing an ancient melody accompanied the ceremonies, as the celebrant made each offering, together with ketous and hymns of praise. An observer remarked that it is "one of the most impressive rituals that has ever been devised. The silence of the dark hour, the magnificent sweep of the temple

lines, with eaves curving up toward the stars, the aged trees standing in the courtyard, and the deep note of the bell, make the scene unforgettable to one who has seen it even in its decay."[1]

Of primary importance at the district level was the city god, also called the god of moats and walls (Chenghuang shen). The city god was the divine counterpart of the district magistrate, ruling in the invisible realm just as the magistrate ruled over affairs in the local district. So the city god had a temple just like the magistrate's headquarters, rode in the same kind of sedan car, and had similar kinds of attendants. The magistrate often visited the city god to pray for the welfare of the people, for good harvest, protection from evil powers that would bring famine and plague, and general wellness and prosperity. Not only the magistrate but also all the people, even the commoners, worshiped the city god to seek help in all kinds of situations. Even people accused of crimes would go before the city god to seek a sign of innocence. The annual festival of the city god was a great community celebration, full of crowded and colorful events.

The highly structured imperial cult, of course, is no more today. And there are no more district magistrates worshiping city gods. But popular cults of these gods continue in various part of China and Taiwan. Below the level of the city god are many forms of the local earth god, Tudigong. Still today in towns and villages, local officials go out on new and full moons to worship and burn incense to Tudigong and to pray for the welfare of the whole community. Like a local mayor, Tudigong sees to the spiritual forces that promote health and prosperity for the local community. The god is responsible for warding off spiritual bandits and unhappy ghosts, tending to the needs of the community in weddings, births, good business, and much more. The birthday of Tudigong is typically the occasion for a grand communal celebration, providing worship and entertainment for the divine dignitaries as well as a time of refreshment and renewal for the human community.

Daoist Rituals and Popular Religion

Just as some aspects of worship and ritual are linked with Confucian ideas and principles, we can identify other kinds of rituals more specifically with Daoist traditions. Of course, the line between Daoist practices and the more general popular religious rituals and festivals is indistinct and there is no particular need to separate them rigorously. Some of the rituals are performed specifically by priests or experts for their own transformation, but most of them are to help and benefit the people whom the priests serve. Reciprocity is also a principle of Daoist religious ritual, involving mutual exchange of gifts and benefits between people and gods and setting up a reciprocating contract or relationship.

Summoning the Gods: Cosmic Renewal Daoist priests are recognized primarily by the level of their command of the sacred powers. The people are also served by exorcists, those who are familiar with the local gods and can use rituals to bring their power to bear on evil spirits that cause sickness and ill fortune. Daoist priests (**daoshi**), in addition, are familiar with the great gods of the universe, knowing their names and their characteristics, able to summon them when needed. Daoist priests chant scriptures and use written formulas, ritual implements, and ritual dances to accomplish what is necessary for repulsing evil spirits and obtaining boons from the higher gods. In addition, the priest makes use of internal rituals such as meditation, visualization, and ritual breath control.

The rituals used by Daoist priests have a long history, going back to the methods for attaining immortality practiced by the Heavenly Master sect and other sects from the later Han era on. The rituals are based on the belief that the priest's body is a microcosm of the great cosmos and that, therefore, the great gods of the stellar constellations can be summoned into the body to supply power of renewal. Today the main ritual that still contains the purely Daoist rituals is the *Jiao* (Chiao), the Rite of Cosmic Renewal, performed in Taiwan by Daoist priests to renew a particular community's covenant with the highest gods. Jiao are held at different intervals depending on the community, and they may last from one to as many as seven days, although three days is the most likely duration.

What makes the Jiao different from the many other popular rituals and festivals is that the powers addressed are not the gods of local popular religion but the Three Pure Ones, the threefold primal expression of Dao. The Three Pure Ones receive only "pure" offerings (wine, tea, cakes, and fruit), in contrast to the meat sacrifices offered to the popular gods. And they are worshiped by the Daoist priests inside the temple, unseen by the people who carry on their own popular religious rituals outside in the community during this festival. Occasionally the two celebrations come together when the Daoist entourage emerges to perform some rituals for the people, but essentially what goes on inside the purified temple is something that can be done only by qualified Daoist priests: summoning the great gods and renewing the whole community through the primordial power of Dao. The people's participation is in the form of contributions and support for the Daoist experts.

To prepare for the Jiao, the temple is sealed except for one door, and the gods of the people are removed from their places of honor along the north wall and placed on the south, to prepare for the coming of the Three Pure Ones and the other Heavenly Worthies from the realm of pure yang. The temple area is set up as a model of the Prior Heavens, with scrolls representing the Three Pure Ones on the north wall and other important gods represented on the east and west walls. In the center is an altar at which the priests stand, with a brass bowl on the east side giving forth yang sounds when struck and a hollow wooden sphere on the west side to give forth yin sounds when struck. The chief priest stands in the center, while acolytes to the east and west chant the liturgy alternately, representing the alternation of yin and yang in the universe. The vestments worn by the priests are symbolic of the powers of the universe, including the flame-shaped golden pin on top of the chief priest's crown, showing that he is lighted from within by the eternal Dao.

The rituals performed by the priests are very elaborate and complicated. They include summoning all the spirits to attend and then the very dramatic ritual of purifying the sacred area, sealing it off so no forces of yin can enter. Perhaps some sense of the intense religious drama can be felt in Michael Saso's description of a Jiao, drawing both on Daoist texts and his own experience as a Daoist priest. There are many elaborate rituals to prepare the temple, invite the gods and spirits, and purify the participants. Then come the dramatic rituals that purify the sacred *Tan* area where the key ceremonies will take place:

> The Taoist then calls upon the orthodox spirits of the seven Pole Stars to come and fill the body; he asks specifically that the three

Pole Stars of the Dipper's handle, which control man's destiny, come and fill the three realms of the body, upper, middle and lower, in order to give birth to, nourish, and protect the "*Tao*-life" conceived within. It is specifically into the Taoist's body that the spirits are called; and with the Taoist as mediator, they are infused into the bodies of all those present.

Next the Taoist performs a sacred dance called the "Steps of *Yu*," based upon the nine positions of the magic square called *Lo Shu*, dragging one foot behind the other, imitating the lame pace of *Yu* when he stopped the floods, wearied by endless meritorious wanderings. . . .

As he performs the steps, the Taoist again purifies the four directions by blowing the sprays of purified water from his mouth, standing first in the northeast, the Devil's Gate, and purifying the east; then from the southwest, the Door of Man, he purifies the west; finally from the northwest, the Gate of Heaven, he purifies the north, asking each time that the true, realized *Tao*-breath be implanted in the sacred area. Then, he steps to the center, and facing the northwest, the Gate of Heaven, begs that the "realized breath of the center" come down into the sacred *T'an* area.

Now the climax has been reached, as the Taoist begins to trace another heavenly dance step, that of the seven stars of the Great Dipper, in the center of the area. He summons the exorcising spirits of the north to close all entrances to the sacred area from spirits of malevolence, *Yin*, or death. Next, he summons all the heavenly spirits [and a long list of all the great sacred powers] to assemble now at once in the sacred area, right at the devil's door, and seal it forever.

Taking the great sword in his right hand, the Taoist then draws a circle on the floor, three revolutions from left to right, that is, clockwise, going toward the center. Then over this he draws another circle, this time from right to left, counterclockwise. Over these two concentric circles he then draws seven horizontal lines, representing heaven, and seven vertical lines, representing earth. By thus sealing the Gate of Hell, that is, the northeast position, the primordial breath of earth and the seminal essence of wood can no longer flow away, but they with the *Tao* (spirit) can now be kept within, that is, in the Yellow Court of the center. Finally, he draws the character for demon, "*Kuei*," in the center of the figure, and runs it through with the sword, spraying the purifying water on it from his mouth. The Gate of Demons is now sealed, with primordial breath, semen, and spirit kept within, and the evil influences of *Yin* locked without. The sacred *T'an* area having been purified, the members of the entourage are filled with the orthodox *Yang* spirits of the heavens, the five elements are now in their life-giving order bearing "*Yang*," and the liturgy of the encounter with the spirits of the Prior Heavens may begin.[2]

The liturgy goes on with continuous reading of scriptures, offerings to the heavenly guests, and lighting of the new fire of yang. As physical rituals are performed by the assistants, the chief priest performs internal meditation, summoning the great gods of the universe, visualizing within himself the process of restoring the universe to the pristine vigor of yang. The high priest has special audiences with the Three Pure Ones to make them present, and finally he brings the Three together in the center to offer them a great banquet accompanied by a heavenly ritual dance. Then the petitions of the whole community are sent off to the assembled gods by burning the paper slips on which they were written. Finally, the priests go outside the front of the temple and present the petitions of the community to the Jade Emperor and the other gods who rule this changing world. The whole community has now been renewed through the powers of the heavenly world of pure yang.

In addition to these essential Daoist rituals, the Jiao contains many rituals promoting the welfare of the people. The presence of the ancestors is especially felt, for they have been invited to attend by the Daoist priests, and there is a great procession to float paper lanterns in the rivers, to summon the souls from the underworld. After the presentation of the petitions to the Jade Emperor outside the temple, a twenty-four-course banquet is laid out for the ancestors and the orphan spirits, and the Daoist priests come out to perform the ritual to release all souls from hell. The great celebration that follows is a fitting conclusion to the Rite of Cosmic Renewal; meantime, the Daoist priests alone in the temple send off the gods to the realms from which they came.

Rituals of Exorcism and Divination Whereas the Jiao, held only occasionally, is the special time for the advanced Daoist priests to perform their highest role, much more common are the other rituals that the priests and exorcists perform for the service of the people in their everyday needs. The most important needs concern illness, bad luck, and death, already experienced or anticipated. A Daoist priest, for example, will perform a brief ceremony for one in need, presenting a written memorial calling on the gods in charge, in exchange for offerings, to cause good fortune to come to the one named in the memorial. The memorial is read and then transmitted to the gods by burning. Mediums offer the service of communicating with the dead for various purposes, and both exorcists and priests perform rituals to deliver souls imprisoned in hell.

A most important occasion for Daoist ritual, of course, is a time of sickness. A Red-head Daoist priest on Taiwan, for example, in curing a child's sickness, first computes from the daily almanac the relative yin and yang influences for the child, depending on the date of birth, and then he determines the cause of illness (both natural and supernatural). The Daoist then summons the various gods at his command. On a piece of yellow paper he draws a talisman and signs it with a special seal. Lighting a candle, he recites an exorcistic mantra commanding the demons causing the sickness to leave. The priest casts the divination blocks, and once he receives a positive answer from the blocks the talisman is burned. Water with some of the ashes mixed in it is given to the child to drink, along with a prescription for medicines the priest thinks will cure the natural causes of the illness.

Some forms of exorcism pit the priest or exorcist against the power of the evil spirits causing the trouble. A major source of trouble is the soul of a person who has died violently or tragically and, thus, becomes a wandering spirit, and in such cases dramatic rituals of exorcism are needed. For example, a child drowned in a village pond in Taiwan and, since it happened while the image of the chief god of the village was away for a different village's festival, people thought an angry ghost had pulled the child in. But now the child's spirit would also become very harmful, having died so tragically. So the village leaders prepared an exorcism using divination chairs. These are small chairs each held by two bearers. Gods descend on these chairs and cause them to move about, sometimes violently, providing instructions on how to perform the exorcism by tracing out characters on a tabletop with one of the protruding arms. In this ritual, a local god became present on one chair and instructed the people to avoid speaking bad words to each other, since the death had caused disharmony in the village; furthermore, they should keep their children away from the fish pond. Then a second chair was possessed by the chief village god, who gave them instructions for the exorcism. The two gods would go into the pond to drive out the "bad thing" (avoiding the word "water ghost," which should not be spoken), and the people should stay away so that it would not lodge in their bodies. The wielders of the chair were instructed to carry spirit money signed by one of the gods—who proceeded to cause the arm of the chair to dip in ink

and make a blot on sheets of spirit money that had been laid out on the table. The anthropologist's report becomes vivid:

> The men stuffed these into their pockets and left in a great hurry for the fish-pond, following the two wildly swinging divination chairs, which fairly dragged their wielders along the road. Upon arrival at the pond the chairs ran madly about the perimeter of the pond, then hurled themselves and their bearers into the water, where they circled the pond several times more swinging up and down into and out of the water to drive out the bad thing. At the same time the onlookers shouted high-pitched shouts, hurled burning firecrackers over the pond, and threw handfuls of sesame seeds into the water. The shouting, the rain of sesame seeds, and the continual and ubiquitous explosions of firecrackers were all calculated to terrify the ghost, and added to this were the chairs of the gods ploughing through the water, hot on the trail of the startled ducks. When the gods climbed out at one bank, they would leap in wildly elsewhere and beat the water with renewed vigor.[3]

The key force for the exorcism is the command from the village god to the ghost—in this case conveyed rather dramatically to that ghost.

As seen in this example, rituals of divination are important in many Chinese ceremonies, for it is through divination that communication is established with the spirits, gods, and sacred forces. They can make their will known through a divination chair held by two bearers writing on a table, as we have just seen. Again, they can speak through a Y-shaped stick suspended above a shallow tray of sand, handled by a stick-wielder possessed by a particular god, scratching out characters that are "read" by a trained expert. Much of the revelation received from the gods comes through such **spirit writing**.

There are other forms of divination based on reading the forces of yin and yang. The system contained in the *Yijing* (*Classic of Changes*) has been used continuously in China since ancient times. This system began as eight trigrams, consisting of all the possible combinations of three broken lines (yin) or unbroken lines (yang). This developed into sixty-four hexagrams by placing one trigram on another, working out all the possible combinations of six broken or unbroken lines. These patterns can be divined in various ways, such as by throwing coins to determine the yin or yang character of each line. The *Yijing* then is consulted, for it contains judgments and commentaries on each of the hexagrams, helping people understand how the universal forces are operating and how to stay in harmony with them.

Another example of rituals of divination is the practice of *feng shui* (wind and water), which is the science of reading the interaction of the yin–yang forces at a particular place, to determine the best location and shape of an ancestral grave or a house or even interior decoration in a house. The feng shui expert ritually determines where the yin and yang "breaths" are pulsating, finding the outlines of the azure dragon (yang) and the white tiger (yin) in the landscape and devising the best way to retain the breaths in maximum harmony and vitality. To accomplish this, additional landscaping may be needed, such as planting trees behind the house to counteract evil exhalations and placing a freshwater pond in front. Nowadays, feng shui experts are consulted also in planning the construction of large hotels, office towers, and banks in large Chinese cities.

But much worship and divination need not involve priests or experts. Anyone can go to the temples to visit the local gods, give offerings to them, and seek their help. After all, they are in their position as gods because they have shown that they can provide benefits to the people as they worship them. The whole community—people and gods—are bound up in a reciprocal relationship. The gods are housed in temples, their official residences, lesser gods first and then the principal god in the center. The temple doors are open at all times, and people can go in at any time to bring personal problems to the gods.

In worshiping at the temple, typically the worshiper lights several sticks of incense and places them in the brazier on the altar. The worshiper bows before the altar to show respect, sometimes burning paper spirit money or offering different kinds of food. Then the worshiper consults the god about personal problems or questions, and for this he or she can use rituals of divination to see what the divine answer is so that he or she knows what course of action to take. One simple ritual is to throw two divination blocks on the floor before the altar. The blocks are rounded on one side and flat on the other (like the halves of a banana that has been split lengthwise). A flat side down signifies yin in the ascendancy, and a rounded side down signifies yang in the ascendancy. So it is when one rounded side and one flat side are up together that yin and yang are in harmony—and that is an affirmative answer from the god. Another method of divination is to shake numbered sticks out of a vase, taking the first stick to fall out to the attendant, who matches the number with a slip of paper and interprets one's destiny for the occasion from what is written on the paper.

Buddhist Influences in Chinese Ritual Practices

Buddhist rituals and worship in the home and at temples or monasteries, as described in Part 2, have been a part of Chinese worship life for many, even those who also participate in Confucian and Daoist rituals. In popular religious practices, Buddhist rituals and prayers—for example, those dedicated to the great bodhisattva Guanyin—mingle with non-Buddhist rituals. Some temples have room for Buddhas and bodhisattvas along with Confucian and Daoist deities, so rituals can be directed to whichever one or ones are appropriate for the current need. Among people more specifically committed to the Buddhist path, many have altars in their homes, near the shrine that holds the ancestral tablets, and they offer incense to the Buddha image and recite sutras. In addition to worship in families and in temples, some join lay societies that meet together regularly for worship, reciting favorite Buddhist scriptures or chanting Buddha Amitabha's name, sometimes six or seven hours a day.

Ritual and worship at Buddhist monasteries in traditional China developed some characteristic Chinese forms. The ritual of tonsure symbolizes the beginning of life as a novice monk or nun. In the presence of other monks and novices, the master and the candidate prostrate themselves before the Buddha image and offer incense. Then the candidate hands a razor to the master, renouncing lay life and pledging to become the master's dependent. The master shaves off the hair, and the novice changes into a monk's gown.

Full ordination in Chinese Buddhism involves elaborate rituals. According to the traditional pattern, after a training period of several weeks at the ordaining monastery, a first ordination is held in which the ordainees recite the Three Refuges and the Ten Precepts. After a night of penance, followed by ritual bathing, they process to a secluded ordination platform and accept the monastic vows collectively, then go up to the platform in groups of three to be examined and accepted as monks or nuns by the three ordination masters. A week later they recite the "Bodhisattva Vows," which impose a commitment to lead all sentient beings into nirvana before attaining it themselves. A special feature of Chinese Buddhist ordination is the ritual of burning "incense scars" into the scalp at the end of the ordination ceremonies. Cones of moxa are placed on wax on the novice's head and then lighted by a head monk. As the cones burn down into the scalp, other monks or nuns hold the novice to help con-

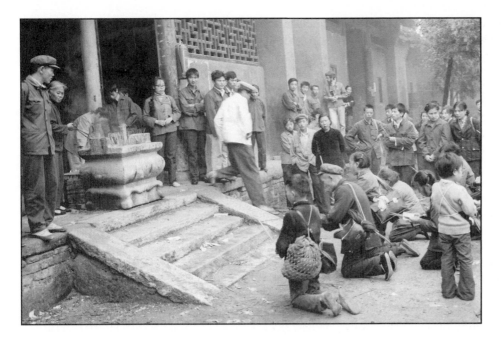

Chinese pilgrims praying at the Buddhist shrine on Heng Mountain in Hunan Province.

legs, while a meditation patrol observes carefully. If someone dozes, the patrol goes before him and strikes him with the incense board on the upper part of the back as a reminder. At 8:00 there begins another cycle of "running" and then sitting in meditation. At 9:00 they go to the refectory for some rice and then, back at their seats, are served tea, the first of three teas served to them during the day. There is a "noon meditation" period, followed by yet another meditation period, lasting until 2:00. Then comes another meal, after which the monks may go to the apartment of the abbot or an instructor for discussion about their progress. Around 3:00 comes the afternoon worship in the great shrine hall, the liturgy including the reading of the Pure Land sutra. For about two hours the monks have a rest period in the meditation hall, but then comes the longest and most important meditation period of the day, lasting an hour and a half. At 8:00 a meal is served to them in their seats, followed by "running," an exhortation by the abbot, and still another period of sitting in meditation, ending at 10:00 with lights out.

During special intensive training for seven weeks starting on the fifteenth of the tenth month, the daily regimen is much stricter, with monks leaving the meditation hall only for meals and once a week to bathe. Their running and sitting cycles add up to fifteen hours a day.

In addition to their monastic rituals, the monks are often called on to perform rituals of chanting scripture on various occasions for laypeople, especially for funerals and for anniversaries of deaths.

Sacred Times in the Chinese Traditions

Although much of the worship and ritual in China depends on the specific needs of the people, one major need is to have regular times for renewal of life—that is, seasonal

trol the pain, and all chant prayers until the ordeal is over—and the new monk or nun is branded for life.

Buddhist rituals are most fully practiced in the monastic setting, and Homes Welch has provided a detailed description of the daily ritual routine in a Chan monastery.[4] The monks are awakened at 3:00 A.M. to wash and march to the great shrine hall to recite morning devotion to the accompaniment of a liturgical orchestra of monks sounding a handchime, wooden fish, bell-and-drum, cymbals, and hand-gong. The liturgy consists of scriptures, poems of praise to the Buddha, the Three Refuges, and reciting the Buddha's name. Then the monks recite Buddha Amitabha's name while processing in a serpentine course around the shrine hall and in the courtyard. At breakfast an acolyte takes seven grains of rice from a bowl in front of a Buddha image and places them out for the hungry ghosts, after which the monks eat in silence, meditating on the debt they owe to those who provided the food. After visiting the latrines, the monks join in circumambulation, a rapid walking or "running" while swinging their arms, meditating all the while.

At 7:00 A.M. they go to the meditation hall, sitting in exact order of rank. They sit erect in silence with crossed festivals, special holy days, and sacred times that occur periodically to revitalize life and the bonds with family, ancestors, and community.

Birthday Festivals of the Gods   One of the favorite days of communal celebration is the birthday festival of the god, whether this is one of the great gods traditionally worshiped throughout China or one of the local gods worshiped especially by the people of the local community. Widely celebrated with great excitement, for example, are the birthday festivals of the Jade Emperor (ninth day of the first lunar month); Laozi (fifteenth of the second month); Bodhisattva Guanyin (nineteenth of the second month); Mazu, the goddess of seafarers and Consort of Heaven (twenty-third of the third month); the Buddha Shakyamuni (eighth day of the fourth month); Guan Gong, the warrior-protector (twenty-fourth of the sixth month); and Confucius (twenty-seventh of the eighth month). But each community also celebrates the birthday of its own local Tudigong (earth god) and the other important gods of the village or community.

These divine birthday festivals have colorful processions in the city streets, packed with sightseers and worshipers. There are offerings of food, lighting of candles and incense, and burning of spirit money. The honored god is carried in a large sedan chair, with firecrackers to announce his or her coming and a band playing traditional music. Multitudes join in the parade, dressed in court clothes and carrying placards. People hail the god as she or he passes by, holding infants in arms to be blessed and protected. All such festivals include standard theatricals or operas to entertain the gods as well as their human audiences.

The festival of the Buddha's birthday, unlike the other birthday festivals, is completely Buddhist in orientation. A small image of the Buddha is placed in a basin of fragrant water with flower petals. Worshipers ladle dippers of water over the image in honor of the gods bathing the Buddha immediately after his birth.

New Year's Festival and Other Annual Festivals   The New Year, of course, has important symbolic meaning for all peoples as the renewing of time and of life that has run down in the course of the past year. In China, the New Year's Festival has long been the most important and elaborate of all the festivals. The Chinese New Year, fixed according to the lunar

calendar, comes in late January or early February, a time of renewal and celebration before the start of spring planting. Events begin ten days earlier with housecleaning and closing of business offices. About a week before New Year's eve, the God of the Cooking Stove, Zaojun, is sent off to heaven to report to the Jade Emperor on the behavior of the family members for the past year. It is traditional to take his printed image from the wall and smear his mouth with syrup before sending him off by burning, so that he will only tell sweet things. He returns home on New Year's eve, when a new picture is pasted up over the stove, to be present for the main event of the New Year festival: the family feast on New Year's eve, when important rituals of family bonding are held.

On New Year's eve, the family members worship Heaven and earth, the tutelary gods of the home, and the family ancestors. At the conclusion of these rites, all family members who can possibly be there—but no outsiders—join in the family feast. Then, to show respect for the living elders, each family member comes forward in order of precedence to bow to the family head and his wife. Firecrackers are set off, and on New Year's day and several days afterward, courtesy visits are made to relatives and friends. The season ends at the full moon (fifteenth day of the first month) with a celebration of light called the Lantern Festival.

Two other major annual festivals are the Dragon Boat and the Mid-Autumn Festivals. The Dragon Boat Festival ("double fifth," i.e., fifth day of the fifth lunar month), popular in southern China, features dragon boat racing and making triangular-shaped rice dumplings wrapped in bamboo leaves. These rituals are said to be connected with the story of a third-century B.C.E. poet and official who, when a corrupt king refused to accept his advice, committed suicide in a river. The rituals have to do with searching for his body and nourishing his spirit by throwing rice into the river. The festival also has to do with the summer solstice that occurs about this time, the high point of yang and the beginning of its displacement by yin. The Mid-Autumn Festival (fifteenth of the eighth lunar month), celebrating the autumn harvest as in many cultures, features enjoyment of the beauty of the harvest moon and round sweet pastries called "moon cakes."

Two other main festivals have to do primarily with honoring the ancestors: the **Qing Ming** (Ch'ing Ming, clear and bright) Festival on the third of the third lunar month (early April), and the Feast of Souls on the fifteenth of the seventh lunar month (late August). For the Qing Ming Festival, the people bathe in flowing streams to wash away the dirt and harmful forces that have accumulated during the winter, and they put out all old fires for three days before starting new fires by rubbing two sticks together—the rebirth of spring yang power. Most importantly, family members spend the day at the ancestral graves, cleaning the tombs, offering food to the ancestors, and renewing family ties with a joyful, hearty picnic feast.

The Feast of Souls (Yulanpen or **Ullambana**) was influenced by Buddhist ideas of souls in purgatory. The souls of the ancestors are worshiped on the fifteenth day, when family members give offerings and sometimes burn spirit money and other paper equipment for the comfort of the dead souls. But during the whole month it is believed the gates of purgatory stand open and the souls from purgatory—the hungry ghosts—wander about before being sent back to purgatory on the last day of the month. Out of compassion for their plight and in recognition that one's own ancestors might be suffering in purgatory, families set out offerings of food for them. During this festival, many rituals are performed by Buddhist monks (and Daoist priests, to a lesser extent). In the great services in the middle of this month, the monks recite the Chinese Buddhist scripture that tells how the monk Mulian descended to the deepest hell to rescue his mother from her miseries there and how this festival was instituted to save the ancestors, at least temporarily, from the tortures of purgatory. The ritual performed by Buddhist monks is called *pudu*, "ferrying all souls across," indicating a scope of universal liberation. All the people join in the extensive ceremonies and general festivities.

Rituals of the Life Cycle in China

Since the family is the locale of meaning in an individual's life, the rituals connected with the important passages in a person's life—birth, puberty, marriage, and death—are, as in most cultures, closely connected with the family. And since the family is focused on the ancestors, these rituals are performed with close attention to the ancestors.

Customs associated with birth include rituals having to do with propitiating hungry ghosts that could cause harm during pregnancy and birth. And, naturally, offerings are made to the ancestors, the God of the Cooking Stove, all the gods in the family shrine, and the local patron god. Not much attention is paid to individual birthdays in China—the real birthday for everyone is New Year's day, when everyone is counted a year older. After years of education involving training both for livelihood and for carrying on the family traditions socially and ritually, young people enter into adulthood. Years ago there were special ceremonies of initiation, giving a new adult name and cap to a man in a "capping" ceremony, and providing a special hair-do and new clothes for a woman. In recent times, the coming-of-age ceremonies tend to be celebrated just before marriage.

As befits the strong emphasis on family and ancestors, the two most important celebrations in a lifetime are at marriage and death. A traditional Chinese marriage consists essentially in the ritual transfer of the bride from her own patrilineal group to that of her husband-to-be, accompanied by exchange of gifts and agreements between the two families. They will consult a diviner to make sure the horoscopes of the couple are compatible and to set an auspicious date for the wedding ceremony. Then they formalize the engagement with exchange of gifts and visits of the young man and woman to their future parents-in-law. Gifts from the bridegroom's family go toward the woman's dowry, especially to buy furniture and other items for the new household. On the day of the wedding, the woman's dowry is sent to the man's home in a procession through the streets. The groom's family hires a special red sedan chair to be sent to the bride's house to receive the bride, the groom himself riding in a blue sedan chair. This ritual leave-taking is full of the symbolism of separation, as shown in this description from Taiwan:

> The arrival of the groom and his party to claim the bride quickens the pace of activity.... The go-between then calls the couple to the family altar to bow first to the gods and then to the girl's father's ancestors. At this point the sedan chair ... is carried into the living room, and parents and daughter begin to exchange the ritual formulas of farewell, wishing each other long life, wealth, happiness, and for the bride, many sons. By this time mother and daughter are weeping uncontrollably.... The chair is closed, and the bearers carry it out of the house. The house doors are quickly slammed behind the bride's chair to prevent the wealth of the family from following the bride. Her brother spits or throws water on the departing chair to indicate that just as spilt water cannot be returned to the container, so the bride cannot return to her natal home.[5]

When the sedan chair procession arrives at the groom's home, the couple bows before the gods of Heaven and earth, the God of the Cooking Stove, and the ancestors, indicating that the bride is now part of her husband's lineage. Then the couple pays respects by bowing before the groom's parents, uncles, aunts, older brothers and sisters-in-law, and any other senior relatives. A great many guests have been invited, and the feasting may go on for several days.

Death rituals represent the culmination of life—the safe passage to ancestral status, with the soul secure in the family grave (the yin soul) and in the tablet kept on the ancestral altar (the yang soul). These funeral rituals are the most serious and protracted of all traditional Chinese rituals, and they are described only in brief outline here. Chinese are well aware of death and begin to prepare a proper coffin and a grave long before, though the actual duty of making funeral arrangements falls on their sons. When a person is near death, he or she is moved into the main hall of the home, where the ancestral tablets are kept. When the person dies, the body is covered with a coverlet red on top and white (the color of death) on the bottom, and food offerings are placed at the feet. The family dons mourning garments and washes the body; they send out cards announcing the death to relatives and friends, who come to wail and mourn. A soul-tablet is made with the name of the deceased and set up by Daoist or Buddhist priests to receive the prayers of the mourners. The grave jacket (longevity jacket) is put on the body, the corpse's mouth may be filled with rice, and the deceased is placed in a coffin together with paper spirit money. The family is in no hurry to remove the body from the home; they may wait weeks or even months for the auspicious day chosen for taking the coffin out for the final funeral rites.

After the coffin is taken outside, sacrifice is offered to the deceased and the coffin is sealed. Then the funeral procession is organized with a banner, musicians, and many symbolic palanquins. Most important is the sedan chair for the soul-tablet, followed by Daoist or Buddhist priests and then the coffin itself, carried by four or more pallbearers. The oldest son walks behind the coffin, followed by the other sons and all the rest of the mourners. The mourning clothes typically are of sackcloth, with different colors and types showing different relationships to the deceased. At the grave, the soul-tablet is placed on an altar and the coffin is lowered into the pit. The filial son kneels with the soul-tablet, and it is dotted with a brush dipped in vermilion ink, signifying that it is now the actual residence of the soul of the deceased. This soul-tablet is carried home by the eldest grandson, seated in the sedan chair; finally the tablet is placed in the main hall to join the other ancestors.

Mourning continues for quite some time, showing proper respect and ensuring that the deceased person's soul will be in a beneficial relationship to the family as an important ancestor. The intensity of mourning and the length are determined by how closely one is related to the deceased; traditionally there were five degrees of mourning. First-degree mourning is for the sons, daughters, and spouse of the dead person, lasting from two to three years, in which they eat simple food and wear coarse clothing. Others are to observe mourning in a lighter tone; for example, the great-grandsons wear clothes of joyous colors showing that the lineage of the dead ancestor will continue on.

Chinese Medicine and Healing Practices

Traditional Chinese religious practices have always aimed at "health" in its broad sense, that is, maintaining well-being in harmony with the ancestors, gods and spirits, natural forces, and the human community. For many centuries, scholar physicians drew on the main ideas and practices of the religious traditions, such as the operation of yin and yang and the five elements, techniques of meditation, methods for controlling the breath and circulatory systems, and dietary practices. And important medical and pharmacological texts were written, some claiming great antiquity. The earliest and perhaps most cited text is the *Huangdi Neijing* (*The Yellow Emperor's Classic of Internal Medicine*), ascribed to the legendary Yellow Emperor who brought benefits of civilization to the Chinese people already in the third millennium B.C.E. This text and others were known already in the Han era, and over the next centuries sages of medicine developed the whole system of traditional Chinese medicine. Today, the traditional system is taught at Chinese medical schools, along with Western medicine, and some aspects, such as acupuncture and herbal medicines, have become well-known also in the Western world today.

A central key in Chinese medicine is the healthy balance of qi, the vital energy which flows in the universe and in the human body and includes not only physical but also mental and spiritual energy. Imbalances cause qi to dwindle and weaken, or to be congested and obstructed, while proper balance maintains vigor and well-being. Now, Chinese medicine sees the body as a constellation of qi in which the vital functions are concentrated in the organs, and there are a number of meridians or pathways for the flow of qi. The organs are classified according to yin and yang and the operation of the five elements. The solid organs (liver, heart, spleen, lungs, and kidneys) are associated with yin because they create and store energy. The hollow organs (gallbladder, small intestine, stomach, large intestine, and bladder) are yang in that they pass and distribute energy. Furthermore, each of the five elements is associated with specific organs: wood is linked to the liver and the gallbladder, fire is linked to the heart and small intestines, earth is linked to the spleen and stomach, metal is linked to the lungs and large intestine, and water is linked to the kidneys and bladder. Moreover, the five elements and the organs are connected with other key aspects of life, such as certain colors, tastes, odors, emotions, times of the day, weather, particular seasons, and much more. For example, the heart (fire) produces spiritual energy (shen), so it contributes clarity of vision and structure to the person; it is associated with bitter taste, sweaty fluid, a burning or pungent odor, a mood of joy, the color scarlet, noontime, and summer. So also with all the other organs.

The five elements and their related organs and components are dynamic, operating in sequences of creating or subduing. In the creative cycle, wood (potential activity) leads to fire (full activity), followed by earth (transitional), then metal (potential settling), then water (actual settling), which again produces wood, and so on. At the same time, to balance the process, the subduing sequence is going on, in which metal subdues wood, fire subdues metal, water subdues fire, earth subdues water, and wood subdues earth.

In the Chinese perspective, then, the operation of yin and yang through the sequences of the five agents is the basis of health and vitality. Healthy life is experienced when all these factors are normal and balanced. But when they are disrupted by some cause, the normal flow of qi becomes stopped up and congested in some areas and weak in other areas—and sickness results.

For diagnosing disorders and for treatment, Chinese doctors turn to the theory of arterial pathways or meridians, linking the organ fields together in a complex network that transmits qi throughout the body. There are many impulse points (*xue*) on these meridians that are close to the surface, where changes in the flow of energy can be detected and induced. Through centuries of experience, Chinese doctors have mapped out these pathways and classified the characteristic symptoms that arise when the normal flow of energy in each of these pathways is disrupted. For example, the stomach meridian starts near the nostrils, descends through the chest and belly, turns outward in the groin area, and runs down the front of the leg, ending in the second toe. Symptoms caused by the disruption of energy in this pathway include shivering, high fever, groaning, swelling of the body, and boils. This pathway has forty-five impulse points that can be used in acupuncture treatment. So too the characteristic symptoms for disruptions in all the other pathways have been classified.

Physicians use holistic and time-consuming methods of diagnosis, for every aspect of the person's body, life, and environment is significant. There is inspection of various parts of the body, including eyes, skin color, tongue, even the person's demeanor and spirit. Certain sounds and odor of breath, body, and excreta can be indicators of imbalance of energy. The physician questions the person about the disease and also about his or her whole physical, social, emotional, and spiritual context. Pulse diagnosis is especially extensive, for there are three important pulse points on each wrist, and each pulse is characterized as being superficial, deep, slow, rapid, depleted, overflowing, slippery, or stringlike—each type telling something about the organ fields and their balance of energy. Physicians distinguish diagnostic patterns such as yin disorders, yang disorders, coldness disorders, heat disorders, lack of energy, congestion of energy, and so forth. And the probable pathological agents include dampness, dryness, wind, cold, as well as worry, desire, anger, fear, improper diet, physical overexertion, overindulgence in sex, and the like.

Chinese medicine includes a wide variety of remedies and treatments, tailored to the specific diagnosis. There are many drug and herbal remedies designed for treatment strategies such as to induce sweating, clear heat away, bring about purgation, harmonize antagonistic functions, warm the patient, cool the patient, increase the flow of energy, or clear away congested energy. Acupuncture done at the impulse points along the affected meridian is especially useful for increasing the flow of energy or dissipating blocked energy. As a complement to acupuncture, physicians use moxibustion, which consists of burning a ball or cone of dried mugwort on one or more of the impulse points to provide heat stimulation. And doctors prescribe many supplementary treatments, such as prescribed diet to balance yin and yang, and Chinese massage to balance qi energy flowing through the body. Another widely used treatment is qigong, "energy work," a combination of bodily movement and meditation; slow, graceful movements together with mental visualizations direct the flow of qi through the affected areas to promote healing and balance.

In modern times, Chinese doctors have supplemented the traditional methods with new technologies such as electrostimulation and laser acupuncture. Western doctors have adapted acupuncture for specific purposes such as producing an anesthetic effect or for treating drug addiction. Many Western physicians prefer to endorse the use of acupuncture on the basis of proven scientific results, rather than relating the benefit of acupuncture to traditional Chinese theories of yin and yang, five agents, qi, and meridians. However, for many Chinese and other East Asians, as well as some Westerners, the traditional Chinese medical theories make sense, for they constitute a holistic approach to health and well-being based on long experience and wisdom.

Artistic Expression in Chinese Religions

As in all cultures and religions, art forms have always been intricately bound up with religious expression in China. Since the goal of religion in China is the fullest harmony with the natural forces, art enters in to express and perhaps even to create that harmony. Furthermore, since our human existence is a microcosm of the great cosmic processes, artistic endeavors can present those sacred processes on our human scale.

Each of the great religious traditions of China had significant influence in the development of the aesthetic perspective and interest of the Chinese people. For example, the Daoist sense of letting the innermost truth of the sacred process of nature express itself became a key principle of art. Confucianism, especially Neo-Confucianism, put emphasis on self-cultivation and self-transformation through the disciplines of study and ritual. From this view, the artistic pursuit itself can become a way of life that transforms oneself. And Buddhists brought the experience of spontaneity, emptiness, and the universal Buddha-nature to add its distinctive flavor to the arts—they can become ways of enlightenment.

Many art forms developed in China under the direct influence of these three religious traditions. For example, sculptures and paintings of Daoist gods and immortals, as well as Buddhas and bodhisattvas, were created in great numbers, so that they seem almost as numerous as worshipers in China's many temples. Stories told by Buddhist monks eventually gave rise to the full-length Chinese novel, the most famous of which is *Journey to the West*, a series of tales about a famous Chinese Buddhist monk's pilgrimage to India. Through the trials of this journey, he and his companions (a monkey, a pig, and a water monster) eventually attain spiritual transformation and receive heavenly ranks in reward for the merit achieved on their difficult journey.

The ancient Chinese emphasis on ritual led to the full cultivation of the aesthetics of movement, dance, drama, chanting, clothing, and especially music. The ancient texts particularly extol the art of music—meaning music and dance together—as expressive of full human emotions. Xunzi had this to say about the art of music:

> This is the symbolism of music: the drum represents a vast pervasiveness; the bells represent fullness; the sounding stones represent restrained order; the mouth organs represent austere harmony; the flutes represent a spirited outburst; the ocarina and bamboo whistle represent breadth of tone; the zither represents gentleness; the lute represents grace; the songs represent purity and fulfillment; and the spirit of the dance joins with the Way of Heaven.
>
> The drum is surely the lord of music, is it not? Hence, it resembles Heaven, while the bells resemble the earth, the sounding stones resemble water, the mouth organs and lutes resemble the sun, and the scrapers resemble the myriad beings of creation.[6]

The ideal music–dance performance evokes and expresses various human qualities as well as cosmic features. In fact, it helps assure the harmonious working of the whole universe.

Chinese poetry is known as far back as the *Shijing*, the *Classic of Poetry*, an anthology containing 305 poems dating from between 1100 and 600 B.C.E. The poems cover a great variety of subjects, but some are addressed to royal ancestral spirits, and many are concerned with Shang Di or Tian in relation to human experience. The tradition of songs and hymns dedicated to the various deities continued throughout the Zhou and Han eras. After the Han period, many poets tended to be syncretistic, drawing their inspiration and imagery from all of the religious traditions. The three greatest poets of the golden age of Chinese poetry, the Tang era (618–907), are said to represent, respectively, the three great religious traditions. Du Fu (712–770), the Sage of Poetry, wrote poems with a strong emphasis on Confucian ideals of morality and compassion. A favorite image for him was the phoenix, the bird of fire and a powerful yang symbol, appropriate for the Confucian perspective. Li Bo (701–762), the Immortal of Poetry, adopted a Daoist view of life, embracing naturalism—a favorite image is the moon reflected on the water at night. He fully indulged in the sensual pleasures of life, but his poems are full of Daoist mythology and a yearning for the realm of the immortals. Wang Wei (701–761), the Buddha of Poetry and also a renowned landscape painter, used some of his poems for direct Buddhist teaching. In other poems, he conveys more subtly an overall Buddhist vision of human existence, a contemplation of nature with the sense both of tranquility and of sadness.

Architecture in China, as we already noted in discussing the technique of feng shui, has been greatly influenced by ideas about the sacred cosmic forces, especially yin and yang, and the sense that the human space is a microcosm of the great cosmic order. Temples, often combining popular religion with Daoist, Confucianist, and Buddhist shrines and images, typically have their major halls built on a north–south (yin–yang) axis, with other halls on parallel north–south lines or on east–west lines. The whole compound is surrounded by an outer wall, and there is a high, decorated main gate (often a triple-gate) opening from the south, where creative yang influences come from. The main halls have their back to the north, the direction of baleful yin influences. As one progresses from the south into the compound, there usually are inner gates, and then comes the main hall in the central position—where the main god's throne and altar are set, facing south. There are halls of lesser importance to the sides and back of the main hall, balancing each other in a configuration of harmony, all reflecting cosmic order.

This same sacred temple space is illustrated in Beijing's famous Forbidden City, the capital of the Ming and Qing dynasties. First, the whole city of Beijing was built in a balanced concentric pattern, with outer walls enclosing the entire city, an inner square walled area marking the limits of the imperial city, and within that yet another very large inner walled area, the Forbidden City. The main gate of the

Forbidden city, Tiananmen Gate, opens from the south, and all the main halls are on the north–south axis. The imperial throne halls are in the center, with the imperial palaces behind. This was not only the center of government but also the ceremonial center of Chinese religion, with the emperor maintaining the harmony of the gods and sacred forces for the benefit of all the Chinese people.

Temples that are specifically Buddhist follow the same architectural patterns, with the particular Buddha image and attendants enshrined in the main hall in the posture of the Chinese emperor. These temple compounds typically include multistoried pavilions dedicated to individual Buddhas and bodhisattvas, sutra repositories, storage rooms for temple treasures, ceremonial gates, lecture halls, and residences for monks and nuns. Characteristic Buddhist architecture in China includes also the towering pagoda, a form imported from India. These pagodas loom over the lower Chinese buildings (the tallest pagoda in China is over 67 meters) to give a definite signal of the presence of Buddhism, with its foreign origins, in the midst of Chinese society.

A striking Chinese art form is monochrome ink landscape painting (plain black ink against a plain white background). Early Daoist painters strove to capture the authentic spontaneous forms of nature, and later Chan Buddhist painters brought the ink landscape painting to a peak of naturalness and simple harmony. One of the main principles of Chinese painting was called "Spirit Resonance and Life Movement," and painters interpreted this to mean being filled with the creative power of nature (Dao) so that it could be expressed in spontaneous brushstrokes that were not so much skills of the painter but movements of Dao itself. A few comments Su Shi (1036–1101) made about Yuko (d. 1079) help us see the attitude:

> When Yu-k'o painted bamboos he was conscious only of the bamboos and not of himself as a man. Not only was he unconscious of his human form, but sick at heart he left his own body, and this was transformed into bamboos of inexhaustible freshness and purity. . . .
>
> In his earlier years Yu-k'o painted his bamboos whenever he found some pure white silk or good paper. He grasped the brush quickly, brushing and splashing with it freely. He simply could not help (doing) it. . . .
>
> Painters of to-day draw joint after joint and pile up leaf on leaf. How can that become a bamboo? When you are going to paint a bamboo, you must first realize the thing completely in

Landscape painting and calligraphy on a hanging scroll from the Yuan period (1280–1368). National Palace Museum, Taipei, Taiwan, Republic of China.

your mind. Then grasp the brush, fix your attention, so that you see clearly what you wish to paint; start quickly, move the brush, follow straight what you see before you, as the buzzard swoops when the hare jumps out. If you hesitate one moment, it is gone. Yu-k'o taught me thus.[7]

To paint bamboo, one should first sit down and meditate, harmonize one's spirit with Dao, become a bamboo—then pick up the brush and let the bamboo paint itself!

This Daoist approach to painting was further shaped by Confucianists into a way of self-cultivation and by Chan Buddhists into a way of enlightenment. Chan painters in particular influenced the Chinese theory of painting with Chan ideas of spontaneity and emptiness. The effortlessness and sudden insight of Chan meditation are reflected in the quick, spontaneous creation of a painting. And Chan painters sometimes made use of empty space more than brushstrokes, reflecting their experience of the "emptiness" of reality. Reality is formless and, thus, the function of what has form in the painting is to help one experience formlessness.

SOCIETY AND THE GOOD LIFE

How should we live? One who is Chinese belongs to a huge, multiethnic grouping of peoples speaking a variety of dialects, yet unified around traditions of the family and the nation. The good life consists in fitting into this society at appropriate places and observing the moral principles taught in the religious traditions.

Structure of Chinese Society

Sometimes it is said that in the Asian religions, in contrast to the Abrahamic religions, the individual is not important, for only the group has value. That is, of course, not true. The individual is very important in China, so much so that rituals of individual life passages such as marriage and funerals are the focus of much attention. And personal, individual self-transformation is the goal of the path as set forth in Daoism, Neo-Confucianism, and the different schools of Chinese Buddhism. The value and the religious needs of the individual are surely not forgotten in China.

Yet the individual is seen in balance with the larger community in Chinese society. Individual worth and meaning are closely tied to roles within the social nexus of family, local community, and nation. What meaning would a person have if he cut himself off from these reservoirs of meaning to move out as an "individual" into some new world? The key to Chinese social tradition is that full personal worth and belonging comes with the cultivation of fellow-humanness—in family, in community, in nation.

Family, the Heart of Chinese Society   In China, religious affiliation is not primarily a matter of belonging to a particular religion or a denomination (although there are such things in China, too), but it centers on the family or clan. We have already seen how the cult of the ancestors has formed the basis of Chinese society both historically and theoretically. In practical terms, the ongoing life of the ancestors and their continued influence comes in the arena of the family, as each family elder who dies becomes a shen and is enshrined in the spirit-tablet on the family altar. Within the family, the virtue of filial piety is all-important, and it is this virtue that underlies all the different roles of the various individuals within the family structure—the head of the family and his wife, the oldest son and his younger brothers, the daughters, the sons-in-law and daughters-in-law, the oldest grandson, the other grandchildren, the various uncles and aunts, and the rest. All have their proper roles in the family structure, and by fulfilling this role each individual realizes personal fulfillment.

The family structure is based on the patrilineal clan or lineage, those who share a common surname and a shared descent from common ancestors, usually supported in written proof in genealogical records. Within this larger clan, the individual households revolve around a male of the older generation who was a part of the original household, one who "shared the stove" of the house. The family is multigenerational. And those who have died are present as ancestors, and those yet unborn are present in potential in the lives of the young people who cultivate their bodies and grow up to marry and produce offspring who will carry on the family and its life. The sons will keep the family surname and continue the family into the next generation. The daughters are brought up in order to be transferred into other lineages through marriage contracts.

The family, thus, is the primary focus of meaning and identity for all members. The worst imaginable tragedy is

to be cut off from the family with its network of obligations and support; this would be to lose all meaning and purpose while living and to become a "hungry ghost" after death.

The National Family   The Confucian tradition built on the family structure with its central value of filial piety and, in fact, extended the basic structure to the larger community groupings, to the village or town, and especially to the nation. The family is the prototype of all these concentric circles of human relationships. A filial son will certainly also be a good citizen, and a ruler or superior who lives as a good parent will also be an ideal ruler. During the long successions of dynasties in China (from the third century B.C.E. up to the twentieth century), the state was conceived as a "national family," with the emperor fulfilling the role of "father" and the guiding principles being filial piety and paternal love. As the head of the national family, the emperor was concerned both with the welfare of the people and with the spiritual welfare of the national ancestors.

Along with this ideology of the national family, the Confucian state also developed a centralized bureaucracy based on the principles of ceremonials and penalties. Under the emperor there was a large bureaucracy made up of Confucian scholars from the gentry, chosen on the basis of an examination in the Confucian classics.

Even though the national family was considered sacred, this is not completely a "chosen people" ideology. The emperor, called the **"Son of Heaven,"** was thought to be given a mandate from Heaven to rule as long as he kept order and prosperity for his people. He, therefore, was held responsible both for mismanagement in government and also for natural disasters that befell the nation. If disasters occurred, it was believed that the mandate of Heaven was being taken away from the emperor.

There are other religious communities besides the family and the state, certainly. The village or town is an important social unit, with respected local leaders performing the important rituals on occasions of community festivals. The people of the community unite in support of the local temples, and often there are special gods whose duty it is to guard the community and bring prosperity to its people. Furthermore, there are special voluntary religious groups, such as Buddhist monasteries or nunneries, lay Buddhist associations, and the various orders of Daoist priests.

Religious Leaders in China Religious leaders correspond to the major social groupings in China. Perhaps most important of all is the head of the family, the one responsible for continuing close communion with the ancestors, governing the activities of the family, presiding over the important family rituals, and so forth. It is imperative that the head of the family have a wife to perform many of the important household rituals. And many duties fall to the oldest son, who in a special way is the representative of his grandfather and, thus, is very important for carrying on the worship of the ancestors and the family well-being.

In the traditional feudal hierarchy in China, those responsible for governing at the different levels also had corresponding roles of religious leadership. The village elders, the city administrators, and the province governors all had specific roles to play in the local and state cults. They were ranked in a hierarchy just as the gods are accorded different ranks. At the top, corresponding to Heaven and earth, is the emperor, the father of the nation and the only one empowered to perform the essential rituals that bring renewal and harmony to the whole land.

Among the other important religious leaders are the Confucian scholars, the literati, who attained their leadership by virtue of mastering the classics and passing state examinations, who also presided at important Confucian rituals, often connected with the state cult. Then there are the various types of ritual specialists, especially the Daoist priests, who go through long training in the secretive scriptures and rituals and receive an ordination rank depending on how extensive their command of the spirit world is. Today there is generally recognized a distinction between the monastic Daoist priest who pursues the Daoist disciplines for his own transformation, and the "fire-dwelling" priest, that is, one who has a family and serves as a ritualist for the community. In Taiwan today, those fire-dwelling priests who can perform the great festivals in the "orthodox" way are sometimes called Black-head priests (from their black head-dresses), whereas the priests performing the more popular rituals and exorcisms are called Red-head priests. Finally, there are also Buddhist monks and nuns who pursue their own spiritual growth but who also have special spiritual powers that they can share for the benefit of the laypeople in chanting scriptures, saying prayers, and the like.

A type of religious leader that cuts across religious traditions in China is the "master," one who has reached a high level of spiritual achievement and who takes a small number of disciples. Unlike a teacher who simply passes information to students, the master imparts something of himself, his secret insights, and his special disciplines to the disciples. And he remains in that master–disciple relationship with them as long as they live. Great masters established "lineages" that continued for many generations as the conduit for transmitting advanced spiritual insights and practices. In modern times, abbots of Buddhist monasteries, Chan masters, and Daoist chief priests still fulfill this important religious role of master.

Women in Religious Leadership Women, as is clear from our discussion here, have always had subordinate roles in Chinese society, starting from the Confucian patriarchical image of the family, with excesses like footbinding to ensure the marriageability of the family's daughters. We need to point out, of course, that even in the Confucian system, Chinese women did take a strong and even dominant role in family life and the religious traditions associated with it. And, in contrast to Confucian thought, the Daoist tradition places high value on the feminine side of human activity. Dao is the Mother of the universe, and the yin-like feminine qualities of human existence (the soft, pliant, mysterious, intuitive, natural, and bodily qualities) are those to be cultivated for high spiritual achievement.

There are some powerful divine exemplars for women in the Chinese religious tradition, starting with the Queen Mother of the West, worshiped by Daoists as the source of immortality, the Queen of all Immortals. And there is Mazu, the fisherman's daughter who became a goddess after death and eventually was elevated to the rank of Consort of Heaven, rescuing those in need in all places and circumstances. Still another model, from the Buddhist side, is Guanyin (Avalokiteshvara in India), the most widely worshiped deity in all of China, manifesting the great compassion of the bodhisattva, most appropriately depicted in feminine form.

A fascinating example of a powerful Chinese woman is Empress Wu Zetian (625–705) of the Tang dynasty, the only woman to hold the title and absolute power of emperor in China. She skillfully used both Confucianism and Buddhism, even to the point of understanding herself as a bodhisattva in human form. She was a highly competent and shrewd ruler, and Chinese Buddhism was brought to its highest status with her imperial support.

Through the centuries many Chinese women chose to disengage from the Confucian family structures and find personal fulfillment in the alternative provided in the Buddhist order of nuns. Buddhist nuns have been highly influential in political and cultural affairs. Some nuns were known as great teachers who gave lectures on the Buddhist sutras to groups of nuns and large congregations of laypeople. Some wrote commentaries and treatises on Buddhist doctrines. They acted as spiritual guides to the emperor and other members of royal families. There are even instances of nuns who publicly debated famous monks—and defeated them. A few women are represented in the various master–disciple lineages of the Chan school.

In religious Daoist circles, as elsewhere, women played important roles even while being on the margins of the organized institutions. They have frequently been mediums for priests, individual healers, spirit-writers, and so forth. Individual women have gained fame as Daoist masters and adepts, and a number of famous alchemists were women.

As China moved into the twentieth century, women often provided strong leadership in the revolution and still do in the People's Republic today. As writers, intellectuals, workers, and political leaders, women are helping shape the future of Chinese society. Whatever the future of Chinese religion may be, women's roles and experiences will be central.

The Confucian Vision of the Good Moral Life

We saw earlier how the Confucian tradition sees Heaven (Tian) as the ultimate moral authority by whose mandate all human decisions and actions are measured—not as an external law-giver and judge but as the cosmic law that is also inherent in our human nature. We also saw that Confucianists have generally considered human nature as basically good and positive, so that living according to our moral nature is possible. The famous opening passage of the *Doctrine of the Mean* sums it up succinctly: "What Heaven has endowed is called the nature. Following the nature is called the Way. Cultivating the Way is called instruction. The Way cannot be departed from for so much as an instant. If it were possible to depart from it, it would not be the Way."[8]

What does it mean to cultivate the Way in day-by-day situations? The place to start is by molding all one's actions to the principle of filial piety. Moving out from there, the same basic attitude of respect and reciprocity is extended to all others through acts of propriety (*li*) as the humanizing force in social relationships.

In spite of the practical bent of Confucian principles, they are not based simply on utilitarian motivations. It is true that the influential thinker Mozi, or at least his disciples, advocated a form of utilitarianism: "Any word or action that is beneficial to Heaven, spiritual beings, and the people is to be undertaken. Any word or action that is harmful to Heaven, spiritual beings, and the people is to be rejected."[9] And that kind of practical test of moral actions—whether they bring good and happiness to the people—is often used to evaluate a ruler's actions. But Confucius spoke strongly against doing a moral action simply because of the reward that would be received: "The gentleman understands what is right; the inferior man understands what is profitable" (*Analects* 4.16).

The Good Life of Filial Piety Confucius often described the ideal moral life as the life of humaneness (*ren*), that is, fully displaying one's innate human goodness in relationship to others. The very root of that humaneness, he taught, is in filial piety (*Analects* 1.2). The Chinese character used for filial piety (*xiao*) is very illuminating, made up of the graph for old person, supported by the graph for son placed underneath it. According to the *Classic of Filiality*, the filial son should be as reverent as possible to his parents when they are living, take care of them with all possible joy, be extremely anxious about them when they are sick, be stricken with grief when burying them, and display the utmost solemnity when making sacrifices to them after their death. Having performed these five duties in full measure, one can say he truly served his parents (*Xiaojing* 10). Out of all crimes and wrongs, there is none worse than being unfilial—in traditional China, such a crime, in fact, could be punished by death.

Among the primary obligations of filial piety is the duty to marry and have offspring, so that the ancestral sacrifices can be continued and the family line will not die out. But beyond the duty to honor and support parents, perform the sacrificial rites for the ancestors, and produce offspring to continue the family, filial piety is a moral virtue that permeates how one lives all of life. Mengzi lists some of the things that are unfilial:

There are five things which in common practice are considered unfilial. The first is laziness in the use of one's body without attending to the support and care of one's parents. The second is chess-playing and fondness for wine, without attending to the support and care of one's parents. The third is love of things and money and being exclusively attached to one's wife and children, without attending to the support and care of one's parents. The fourth is following the desires of one's ears and eyes, thus bringing his parents to disgrace. And the fifth is being fond of bravery, fighting, and quarreling, thus endangering one's parents.[10]

The last point is interesting: in what way do bravery and fighting endanger one's parents? Getting oneself killed or maimed is, in effect, to cut off filial service to one's parents. A dead son will not get married to produce offspring. Even to be maimed in some part of the body is to do dishonor to the parents who gave one one's body in a state of wholeness. Therefore, a pious son avoids climbing to great heights, going near precipices, or moving about in darkness; he avoids reckless sports or fighting. What a person does with his personal life is no private matter, for reckless life or even careless accidents are slaps at one's parents.

Filial piety, thus, forms the heart of practicing the good ethical life. And it extends beyond considerations of parents and family to the other areas of life. "Filiality is the root of virtue and the wellspring of instruction. . . . Thus filiality begins with service to parents, continues in service to the ruler, and ends with establishing oneself in the world [and becoming an exemplary person]."[11]

The Good Life of Propriety   But what about the rest of life besides considerations of parents and family? What are the basic ethical principles having to do with community, business, politics, and the rest? In a sense, these principles are derived by extending the respectful, serving attitude of filial piety to embrace all other relationships. At the heart of his ethical system Confucius put the practice of rites (*li*), usually translated as "propriety" when it refers to social relationships. As we have seen, this word originally was used for the sacrificial rites offered to the ancestors. The Confucian tradition held that even Heaven and earth are upheld by li as a cosmological principle, and so it makes sense to pattern social relationships after this: one should always treat others with respectful reverence.

When asked exactly what were the essential ingredients of the principle of propriety or respectful reverence, Confucius stated that it all was based on reciprocity (*shu*) and loyalty (*zhong*) (*Analects* 4:15). In explaining these basic principles, the *Analects* give two versions of a golden rule:

What I do not want others to do to me, I do not want to do to them. . . . A man of humanity, wishing to establish his own character, also establishes the character of others, and wishing to be prominent himself, also helps others to be prominent.

(5:11; 6:28)[12]

The first statement is expressed negatively and the second positively, but both together show that propriety is really the expressing of mutual, reciprocal relationships of trust, loyalty, and respect, in which one is actively concerned for the well-being of the other.

Confucian thinkers have generally defined these reciprocal relationships in a hierarchical scheme, for there needs to be an orderly structure so that trust, loyalty, and respect can prevail and confusion and anarchy can be avoided. And where there is structure, there is superior and inferior, older and younger. Such hierarchy does not mean arbitrary power, for the superior in each case must show the appropriate moral virtues. Of course, there are many types of human relationships, but Confucian thinkers since Mengzi have talked about the **five** basic human **relationships**—that is, five fundamental patterns into which all social relationships fit so that the proper forms of propriety can be practiced. These five paradigmatic relationships are father–son, husband–wife, elder brother–younger brother, ruler–subject, and older friend–younger friend. In each of these relationships there is a particular quality of propriety that is to be shown. The son is to show filial piety to the father, for example, and the wife should show obedience to the husband. The younger brother shows respect to the older brother, the subject shows loyalty to the ruler, and the younger friend should show deference to the older friend. But these are reciprocal relationships, so the appropriate virtues should also be shown by the superior party: The father should show kindness, the husband caringness, the older brother nobility, the ruler benevolence, and the older friend humaneness.

Within this structure, the moral principles can be brought into daily life, for these reciprocal relationships provide the basic patterns for all social involvement. For example, the father–son relationship is the pattern for parents and children and also for ancestors and descendants. And the ruler–subject relationship is the pattern for all cases in which one is in authority and the other is under that authority. And all of this, Confucius teaches, corresponds with the will of Heaven for living the good life in human society.

Live According to Your Place in Life The Confucian tradition has a positive, life-affirming outlook. One should not withdraw from society in favor of some higher, purer spiritual pursuits. Political and economic involvement is necessary and good, and wealth and success do not corrupt the morally superior person. Physical needs and desires are not evil and should be fulfilled through the proper social means for food and provisions, clothing, and sexual relations with one's spouse. Always the guiding principle is the welfare of the family and the community.

The ethical philosophy expressed in the *Doctrine of the Mean* might be summed up as doing one's best according to one's place in life.

> The superior man does what is proper to his position and does not want to go beyond this. If he is in a noble station, he does what is proper to a position of wealth and honorable station. If he is in a humble station, he does what is proper to a position of poverty and humble station. If he is in the midst of barbarian tribes, he does what is proper in the midst of barbarian tribes. In a position of difficulty and danger, he does what is proper to a position of difficulty and danger. He can find himself in no situation in which he is not at ease with himself.[13]

The Confucian ethical vision has a strong interest in the leaders and rulers of society, for these people set the tone for all the rest. An evil ruler will fail to promote the goodness of the people and will create anarchy and disaster, but a good leader will educate and nourish the moral nature of the people. One of Confucius' sayings hits this point directly:

> Lead the people with governmental measures and regulate them by law and punishment, and they will avoid wrongdoing but will have no sense of honor or shame. Lead them with virtue and regulate them by the rules of propriety (*li*), and they will have a sense of shame and, moreover, set themselves right.
>
> (*Analects* 2.3)[14]

There were Legalists in ancient China who tried to rule the people with strict laws and punishment, based on the theory that people are evil by nature. But the Confucian tradition advocates the power of moral action as the key principle for social and political ethics.

Daoist Perspectives on the Good Life

The good life seen from a Daoist perspective has quite a different hue from that of Confucians, though it is not as fully articulated. The thrust toward withdrawal, no-action, and meditation tends toward a more quietistic and natural type of life, at least for those looking to the vision of Laozi and Zhuangzi. A fundamental principle of Daoist religious teaching would be the need to maintain a balance in all activity; giving in unduly to the senses can lead to an exhausting of life powers and an unhealthy imbalance.

No-Action, Freedom, and Spontaneity as a Basis for Living Whereas the Confucian approach has definite principles of right and wrong, good and evil, in human behavior, it is characteristic of the Daoist view to take a relative position on such issues, as we saw. To a duck, short legs are good, but to a crane, long legs are good. Making judgments about right or wrong is forcing something artificial on the natural process. Thus, the fundamental Daoist approach to the good life would be to do everything in the natural way, freely and spontaneously, without artificiality or coercion. That is, no-action should be one's basic principle. This does not necessarily mean withdrawal to a life of reclusion and quietism, although some Daoists have done that. In family and in community, in work and in play, it means always to act spontaneously and naturally, not according to plans or schemes or strategies.

This approach to the good life works best, it is true, at the personal level, although even then it may strike others as bizarre or even immoral. The Seven Sages of the Bamboo Grove (ca. 210–263 C.E.) were notorious because they flouted customary mores to live their lives freely and spontaneously. They dropped out of politics, lived impulsively, and had drinking parties in which they drank wine from a common bowl on the floor, sharing it even with pigs.

Of course, Daoists do not advocate simply giving in to every whim, but cultivating a style in which the natural events of life are not stifled through emotional judgments about good and bad but are simply accepted and lived for what they are. A good example of this approach to life is Zhuangzi's behavior when his wife died. A friend came to offer condolences, but he found Zhuangzi squatting on the ground and singing, beating on an earthen bowl instead of performing the mourning rites. The friend was scandalized and rebuked him: "You lived with her, she brought up your children and grew old," he said. "It should be enough simply not to weep at her death. But pounding on a tub and singing—this is going too far, isn't it?" "You're wrong," replied Zhuangzi.

> When she first died, do you think I didn't grieve like anyone else? But I looked back to her beginning and the time before she was

born. Not only the time before she was born, but the time before she had a body. Not only the time before she had a body, but the time before she had a spirit. In the midst of the jumble of wonder and mystery a change took place and she had a spirit. Another change and she had a body. Another change and she was born. Now there's been another change and she's dead. It's just like the progression of the four seasons, spring, summer, fall, winter. Now she's going to lie down peacefully in a vast room. If I were to follow after her bawling and sobbing, it would show that I don't understand anything about fate. So I stopped.

(Ch. 18)[15]

One should not let emotional judgments about good and bad, happiness and grief, or other things stand in the way of living the authentic natural life.

Of course, Daoist philosophers did provide certain guidance about ideals and virtues in life, even about relationships with others, even though the emphasis is on the individual's style of life. Like Confucianists, Daoists are also concerned with how leaders and rulers should live their lives for the benefit of their people. But, in contrast to the Confucian ideal of a ruler who leads with the rules of propriety, the Daoist notion of a good ruler is one who lets the people develop naturally. Already in the *Daode jing* is this statement about the good ruler:

Govern the state with correctness.
Operate the army with surprise tactics.
Administer the empire by engaging in no activity.
How do I know that this should be so?
Through this:
  The more taboos and prohibitions there are in the world,
    The poorer the people will be.
  The more sharp weapons the people have,
    The more troubled the state will be.
  The more cunning and skill man possesses,
    The more vicious things will appear.
  The more laws and orders are made prominent,
    The more thieves and robbers there will be.
Therefore the sage says,
  I take no action and the people of themselves are
    transformed.
  I love tranquility and the people of themselves become correct.
  I engage in no activity and the people of themselves
    become prosperous.
  I have no desires and the people of themselves become
    simple.

(Ch. 57)[16]

A leader who uses laws and punishments, weapons and force, even cunning and strategy will inevitably rule by force and coercion, thus doing injury to the natural flow of life. A leader who follows the Daoist vision will rule through no-action, that is, practicing the virtues of Daoism and, thus, allowing the people also to live freely and spontaneously.

It is true, of course, that most rulers in Chinese history have been Confucianists.

Daoist Ethics: A Life of Balance   In that large realm of Chinese life that we have associated loosely with the more religious Daoist stream, there is attention to living in the right kind of way. The scriptures in the Daoist canon put forth basic principles for the good and wholesome life, arising from the Daoist concern for the balance of sacred forces in the universe and in the body. Some of these principles have to do with the notion that certain types of actions, such as immoral and pleasure-seeking actions, use up the vital forces of the body and should be avoided. One Daoist text states, for example, that when the five organs are ruled by the mind and a regulated will, then seminal essence and spirit flourish and life breath is not dissipated. But when the organs are seduced by sensual pleasure, they become shaken and unstable. Then breath and blood overflow and are wasted, seminal essence and spirit gallop away, and calamity strikes.[17]

There is an ancient Daoist tradition that the inner gods will be beneficial for renewal only if the adept practices virtues and good works. So Daoist adherents would do good deeds like repairing bridges, endowing orphanages, and caring for the poor and sick. Still today, in preparation for a Daoist festival, the people of the community will give attention to alleviating their wrongdoings and to doing good deeds, such as giving money to repair temples, giving alms to the poor and the crippled, and presenting offerings of food to the hungry ghosts who flock about on the last day of the festival. The underlying motivation is that of maintaining harmony and balance among the forces that affect the lives of all. When someone suffers, whether through poverty or as a hungry ghost, all the people are responsible in some way, and the baleful effects of that suffering are felt also in their lives. When people help those unfortunate ones, the benefits of that are also shared because of the enhanced harmony and peace that result.

Patterns and Paradigms for World Society

The religions of China, except for Buddhism, have traditionally been seen simply as Chinese religions, of benefit specifically to those varied peoples who came to call China their sacred land. In theory, both Confucianism and Daoism are universal religious traditions—that is, the basic principles apply to the whole world and even the whole universe, although the Chinese have not attempted to draw other peoples of the world into the Chinese religions. In modern times, attempts to reform and better Chinese society have often included breaking the hold of the traditional religious system, especially of Confucianism. But there are modern thinkers who believe the traditional wisdom of China has some important things to contribute to the peace and welfare of the whole world.

Throughout the centuries, the Chinese religious traditions have held up the ideal of harmony and balance in the universe and in society. And the model structure for living that harmony is the family. The lineage, the community, even the state have been structured after the paradigm of the family. Within the paradigm of the family, the notion of reciprocal relationships is central; when conflict arises, when injustices become apparent, when needs change, the whole structure works toward reconciliation so that the harmony can be restored.

This model was extended to all of society in China, operating slowly to bring reforms and changes, all the while maintaining harmony and balance. The big question is whether it can continue to work today. The heavy blows to this Confucian-based ideal have been modernization and the Communist movement in China, both purporting to liberate the people from the shackles of tradition. The future of the traditional models of society is indeed clouded in China, although in Taiwan, Hong Kong, and overseas communities the pattern has remained more intact. But, at least according to some observers, the basic paradigm of family, reciprocity, and reconciliation to maintain harmony still plays a central role even in the People's Republic of China. Maoism has been described as a quasi religion, patterned very much after the Confucian tradition, with Mao taking the part of the sage-father, and the state (or the party) of the family. However the new China develops, it appears that the ideals of reconciliation and harmony will always play a key role.

Containing nearly a quarter of the world's population, China is a not-so-small world in itself, and with its own problems there has been little time to think of responsibility for the rest of the world. But since ancient times the theme of a "grand unity," not just of humanity but also of the whole universe, has fascinated Chinese thinkers, and these visions can still excite imagination today and suggest an enduring world message of China's wisdom. Here are two well-known passages presenting the Confucian vision of a grand unity.

In this passage from the *Classic of Rites*, these words were purportedly spoken by Confucius (though scholars think they were probably composed at the time of the Han dynasty), reflecting on the primordial age of grand commonalty (*datong*). This passage is one of the most celebrated in Confucian literature, representing Confucius' ideal social order and often invoked by modern Chinese leaders. The ancient age of grand commonalty is followed by our less perfect order in which people pursue selfish interests, and so the leaders who civilize them through government, ritual, and moral guidance in this age of Lesser Prosperity are our heroic figures, as Confucian ideals are applied to our real world situation.

> The practice of the Great Way, the illustrious men of the Three Dynasties—these I shall never know in person. And yet they inspire my ambition! When the Great Way was practiced, the world was shared by all alike. The worthy and the able were promoted to office and men practiced good faith and lived in affection. Therefore they did not regard as parents only their own parents, or as sons only their own sons. The aged found a fitting close to their lives, the robust their proper employment; the young were provided with an upbringing and the widow and widower, the orphaned and the sick, with proper care. Men had their tasks and women their hearths. They hated to see goods lying about in waste, yet they did not hoard them for themselves; they disliked the thought that their energies were not fully used, yet they used them not for private ends. Therefore all evil plotting was prevented and thieves and rebels did not arise, so that people could leave their outer gates unbolted. This was the age of Grand Commonalty.
>
> Now the Great Way has become hid and the world is the possession of private families. Each regards as parents only his own parents, as sons only his own sons; goods and labor are employed for selfish ends. Hereditary offices and titles are granted by ritual law while walls and moats must provide security. Ritual and rightness are used to regulate the relationship between ruler and subject, to ensure affection between father and son,

peace between brothers and harmony between husband and wife.... Therefore intrigue and plotting come about and men take up arms. Emperor Yu, Kings Tang, Wen, Wu, Cheng, and the Duke of Zhou achieved eminence for this reason: that all six rulers were constantly attentive to ritual, made manifest their rightness, and acted in complete faith. They exposed error, made humanity their law and humility their practice, showing people wherein they should constantly abide.[18]

Over a thousand years later, another passage famous in Chinese tradition is the "Western Inscription" by Zhang Zai (1020–1077), which he inscribed on a panel of his west window. Zhang Zai eloquently expresses the ethical implication of the Neo-Confucian vision that all reality is unified

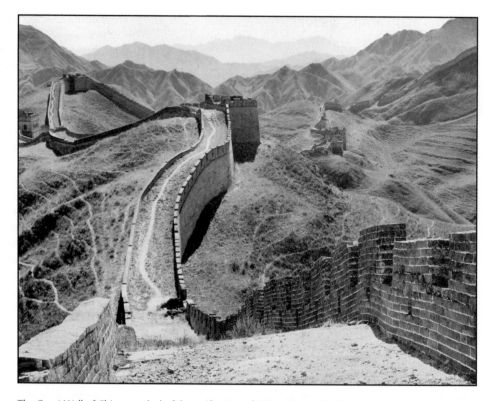

The Great Wall of China, symbol of the unification of China during the Qin dynasty (ca. 210 B.C.E.).

by the single underlying principle. Drawing on classic Confucian ideas, Zhang Zai provides a moving expression of the basic humanism, warmth, and compassion inherent in Chinese tradition.

Heaven is my father and Earth is my mother, and even such a small creature as I finds an intimate place in their midst. Therefore that which fills the universe I regard as my body and that which directs the universe I consider as my nature. All people are my brothers and sisters, and all things are my companions. The great ruler [the emperor] is the eldest son of my parents, and the great ministers are his stewards. Respect the aged—this is the way to treat them as elders should be treated. Show deep love toward the orphaned and the weak—this is the way to treat them as the young should be treated. The sage identifies his character with that of Heaven and Earth, and the worthy is the most outstanding man. Even those who are tired, infirm, crippled, or sick; those who have no brothers or children, wives or husbands, are all my brothers who are in distress and have no one to turn to....

One who disobeys [the Principle of Nature] violates virtue. One who destroys humanity (*ren*) is a robber. One who promotes evil lacks [moral] capacity. But one who puts his moral nature into practice and brings his physical existence into complete fulfillment can match [Heaven and Earth].

One who knows the principles of transformation will skillfully carry forward the undertakings [of Heaven and Earth], and one who penetrates spirit to the highest degree will skillfully carry out their will.... Wealth, honor, blessing, and benefits are meant for the enrichment of my life, while poverty, humble station, and sorrow will be my helpmates to fulfillment. In life I follow and serve [Heaven and Earth]. In death I will be at peace.[19]

In spite of its idea of a Grand Unity, the Confucian vision has fallen on hard times in the modern secular, liberated, Marxist-oriented world of China. Yet there are promises of renewed interest in this grand vision. Some modern Chinese philosophers, for example, are talking about the New Confucianism, a way of philosophy that integrates elements from Western philosophy while seeking to make traditional Confucian ideals available for promoting peace and unity in the modern world.

The Daoist tradition is also in some trouble today, because many religious Daoist practices are considered superstitious and, thus, antimodern. But the fundamental Daoist contribution—a philosophy and practices promoting balance and harmony—is still of great interest to Chinese people. And it has also been heard by numerous other people in the world today—through the many translations of the *Daode jing*, through overseas Chinese who still consult the Almanac and the *Yijing*, through people who are interested in arts like taiji, through practices of traditional Chinese medicine, and more.

It is not that Chinese people are missionaries to other peoples of the world. Rather, many people throughout the world are discovering a vision of life and a practice of harmony that fascinate and compel them—not to become Chinese but to accept something of lasting value from that ancient wisdom.

DISCUSSION QUESTIONS

1 Describe the various rituals by which a Chinese family maintains relations with the ancestors.
2 What goes on in a Daoist Jiao festival? Describe both the actions of the Daoist priests and the community celebration outside the temple. Are they connected at all?
3 In an exorcism ritual, who are the main antagonists?
4 What is the purpose of divination, such as use of the *Yijing*, divination blocks, and *feng shui*? Do you think these practices can have some results?
5 Do you think the daily regimen in a Chan monastery is conducive to spiritual development?
6 What attitudes about the ancestors are expressed in the Ullambana festival? Do you find anything similar in other religions, such as Christianity?
7 What do you see as the key activities in a Chinese wedding? What do these activities signify about the relationships involved?
8 What is accomplished through the extensive rituals of a Chinese funeral?
9 Show how traditional Chinese medicine is rooted in the traditional Chinese religious worldview. Why do

you think Chinese medicine has become so popular also in the Western world?
10 Show how Chinese monochrome ink landscape painting is especially expressive of Daoist and Chan ideas.
11 What was the position of women in traditional Confucian thinking? In what ways did Daoist and Buddhist traditions provide some positive leadership roles for women?
12 Why is filial piety such an important virtue for Chinese? Why are such things as sports and partying considered unfilial?
13 What are the five basic patterns of reciprocal social relations, according to the Confucian tradition?
14 How does Zhuangzi's behavior when his wife died illustrate Daoist perspectives?
15 What advice might come from Confucianists, on the one hand, and Daoists, on the other, for bettering government and education? Which advice would you tend to agree with more?

KEY TERMS: CHINESE RELIGIONS

Note: Chinese terms are given in the pinyin spelling, with the Wade-Giles spelling in parentheses.

Analects compilation of the sayings attributed to Confucius

Chan school of meditation Buddhism in China, Korea, Vietnam, and Japan (Zen in Japan), influential in the arts

Confucianism Western term for the broad and pervasive religious tradition involving the learned scholars (literati), study of Confucius' *Analects* and the Five Classics, and traditional rituals involving especially the family and the ancestors

Confucius, Kongzi teacher (ca. 551–479 B.C.E.) whose philosophy of life became dominant in Chinese culture

Cultural Revolution the period from 1966 to 1976 in China during which Red Guards attempted to destroy all forms of "old" religion and culture

Dao (Tao) "way," Chinese term for a spiritual path; for Daoists, the indefinable source of all reality, the way of nature

Daode jing (***Tao Te Ching***) "Classic of Dao and Its Power"; earliest and very influential text of Daoism

Daoism broad term for Chinese tradition based on the *Daode jing* and the *Zhuangzi*; and also the variety of

Daoist practices involving rituals, priests, scriptures, and techniques for prolonging life

Daoist Canon (Daozang) library of sacred texts and commentaries produced in Daoist religious movements, numbering over one thousand volumes

daoshi (tao shih) Daoist priest

feng shui geomancy, the Chinese art of reading forces of yin and yang so as to determine the most beneficial location for graves and houses

filial piety, xiao (hsiao) primary Confucian virtue of respect toward parents and ancestors

Five Classics the heart of the Confucian scriptures, including the *Shujing* (*Classic of History*), the *Shijing* (*Classic of Poetry*), the *Yijing* (*I Ching, Classic of Changes*), the *Lijing* (*Classic of Rites*), and the *Chunqiu* (*Spring and Autumn Annals*)

five elements or five agents Chinese idea of five modes of energy in the universe that mutually influence each other: wood, fire, earth, metal, and water

five relationships Confucian teaching of proper reciprocal roles and moral norms in the basic human relationships: father and son, husband and wife, elder and younger brother, ruler and subject, and friend and friend

Guanyin (Kuan Yin) Bodhisattva Avalokiteshvara, widely worshiped in China as a god/goddess of great mercy (Kannon in Japan)

gui (kuei) earthly yin spirits; malevolent spirits in Chinese popular thought

Han dynasty period in China (from ca. 202 B.C.E. to 220 C.E.) during which Confucianism became the state ideology and cult, Buddhism made its entry, and religious Daoism developed

Heavenly Masters early sect of Daoism whose lineage continues today as the Orthodox Unity sect

Huayan (Hua Yen) a Chinese school of Mahayana Buddhism based on the *Garland Sutra*

Jade Emperor supreme god in Chinese popular religion

Jiao (Chiao) important festival in religious Daoism, the Rite of Cosmic Renewal

Laozi (Lao Tzu) legendary author of the *Daode jing* and founder of Daoism (according to tradition, born in 604 B.C.E.)

Legalists school of thought in China that emphasized the need for strict law and order

li rites, propriety; the Confucian code of ceremonial behavior

li *see* principle

literati (ru, ju) learned Confucian scholars

Mandate of Heaven in Chinese religion, the expression of Tian's moral will, especially in granting prosperity to virtuous rulers and cutting short evil ones

Mao Zedong (Mao Tse-tung) leader (1893–1976) of the Chinese Communist movement and of the People's Republic of China

Matteo Ricci first Jesuit missionary to China (1552–1610)

Mazu (Ma Tsu) widely worshiped goddess of Chinese seafarers; known as the Queen of Heaven

Mengzi (Meng Tzu, Mencius) leading thinker (ca. 372–289 B.C.E.) whose writings shaped the Confucian tradition

Neo-Confucianism revival of Confucian thought in the eleventh century C.E., with emphasis on the underlying principle of all things

no-action (wuwei) basic Daoist principle of not doing anything contrary to the flow of nature

noble person (junzi) ideal Confucian goal; a noble person defined by moral character

Pangu (P'an Ku) in Chinese tradition, mythic primordial person out of whom the whole universe developed

principle (li, different word from *li* meaning "rites") Neo-Confucian teaching that identifies principle as the underlying source of all phenomena, operating together with *qi* (material force)

Pure Land school of Buddhism focusing on worship of Amitabha Buddha (Chinese: Amituo fo), with hope of rebirth in the Pure Land Buddha realm

qi (ch'i) material force, breath, flowing vital energy, in Chinese traditions

qigong broad term for variety of Chinese physical exercises to cultivate qi in body and spirit

Qing Ming (Ch'ing Ming) "clear and bright" festival; spring festival of visiting and renovating ancestral tombs in China

rectification of names Confucian program for the development of a moral society by properly structuring social relationships

religious Daoism variety of Daoist practices involving rituals, priests, scriptures, and techniques for prolonging life

ren (jen) humaneness, an important ideal in Confucianism

Shang Di (Shang Ti) supreme god worshiped by the Shang rulers in ancient China

shen in Chinese tradition, heavenly yang spirits; benevolent and honored spirits, including ancestors

Son of Heaven title of Chinese emperor

spirit writing in Chinese religion, writing on a tray of sand or on paper by a spirit who moves the pen

taiji (t'ai-chi) Great Ultimate that underlies and generates all things; a popular Chinese exercise is called taiji quan (fist of the Great Ultimate)

Taiping Rebellion (T'ai P'ing) abortive popular movement in the mid-nineteenth century in China, based on religious ideas, attempting to change the hierarchical structure of society

Three Ages of the Dharma Buddhist teaching of increasing decline and degeneracy in humans' ability to follow the Buddhist path: the age of the Perfect Dharma, the age of the Counterfeit Dharma, and the age of the End of the Dharma

Three Pure Ones designation for highest gods summoned by Daoist priests

Tian (T'ien) "heaven," from ancient times in China considered an ultimate power that rules especially through the moral order

Tiantai (T'ien T'ai) a school of Mahayana Buddhism in China, based on the *Lotus Sutra*

Total Perfection Daoist sect from the Song era that practices monastic life, still existent today

Tudigong (T'u Ti Kung) local earth god in Chinese religion

Ullambana Buddhist festival in China and Japan worshiping the souls of ancestors and providing for souls temporarily released from purgatory; called Obon in Japan

wuwei *See* no-action

Xunzi (Hsün Tzu) important Confucian thinker (ca. 300–238 B.C.E.) who advocated a realistic understanding of the human inclination toward evil

Yijing (*I Ching*) the Classic of Changes, an ancient Chinese divination manual based on sixty-four hexagrams (each of six unbroken and broken lines)

yin and **yang** Chinese idea of polarity of forces in the universe; yin is passive, earthly force, and yang is active, heavenly force

Zaojun (Tsao Chun) God of the Cooking Stove in Chinese religion

Zhou Dynasty (Chou) long dynasty (ca. 1123–221 B.C.E.) during which the classics were compiled and the Confucianist and Daoist traditions developed

Zhu Xi (Chu Hsi) leading thinker of the Neo-Confucian movement (1130–1200 C.E.)

Zhuangzi (Chuang Tzu) important early teacher (ca. 369–286 B.C.E.) whose book bearing his name has been very influential for the Daoist movement

Chapter 14

Japanese Sacred Story and Historical Context

In visiting Japan today, one sees a highly modern and technologically advanced people, and one gets the impression that they have become very westernized and secular in their outlook on life. Are traditional Japanese culture and religion merely relics of the past? We need to understand that from ancient times the Japanese people have made a habit of accepting new ways but not throwing away the old. So beneath the highly modern surface, many aspects of traditional culture still persist, including the religious traditions.

To be Japanese is to have one's real identity in this ongoing story of Japan, bound up with the land and the cultural and religious heritage of the people. Japanese religious identity is complicated, made up of perhaps half a dozen important religious traditions from earlier times. Some of these traditions have developed institutional forms, but Japanese people characteristically find no problem in sharing in a number of religious traditions simultaneously.

The life story of a typical person can illustrate this. When the person is born, her parents take her to the family **Shinto** shrine to dedicate her to the **kami** (gods, sacred beings) traditionally worshiped by the family. She regularly goes to the shrine on New Year's Day and other holidays, and she is married in a Shinto wedding ceremony. But the wedding date is determined in accordance with lucky and unlucky days according to the Daoist calendar. In family relationships she strives to uphold the Confucian virtue of filial piety toward parents and relatives, and her associations in school and business build on the Confucian attitude of loyalty. She studies Christian teachings and especially respects Christian morality, finding the Christian idea of love even for the poor and downtrodden a most commendable attitude for modern society. She likes the local festivals, legends, and other activities of her hometown, folk religious practices unique

to her region and dating from who knows when. She turns to Buddhism as she remembers her parents and ancestors who have died. Her intellectual commitment is to the Buddhist vision of life and the final goal of liberation and the peace of nirvana.

Shinto, Buddhism, Confucianism, Daoism, Christianity, folk religion—a Japanese person often is involved in the sacred stories of all of these religious traditions. We discussed the major traditions of Confucianism and Buddhism in previous chapters, but we need to see the distinctive Japanese form that these traditions have taken. And we need to pay particular attention to the indigenous Shinto tradition. It should be kept in mind that "Shinto" (*shendao,* "way of spirits") is a word taken over from Chinese to designate the early religious practices of Japan. Throughout early history, Shinto was not an organized religion but included both the traditions of the ruling family and the various practices throughout the different localities of Japan. Today the Association of Shinto Shrines is an organization that includes the main part of those who consider themselves Shinto, but generally various local popular practices and new religious movements are also included in this designation.

STORY OF THE JAPANESE PEOPLE

Although the early Japanese did not have any system of writing to record their sacred stories, they did pass them on orally generation by generation in the different clans and communities. In early Japan there was no organized religion, so the stories about the kami and the origins of the people varied from place to place. Many of these stories were never written down, whereas others were collected and shaped into larger narratives that focused on the imperial clan and the important families and localities. These stories have provided a general national story of origins for many generations of Japanese. The sacred stories about the kami go back to the time of the beginnings and tell of the creation of the world, moving without a break into the origins of the land of Japan and the sacred people.

Prehistoric Foundations of Japan

To provide some orientation, it is helpful to set the stories of the kami and the people into historical context. The very late development of writing in Japan means that essentially everything before the eighth century C.E. is in the prehistoric period. The first Japanese writings—the *Kojiki* (712) and the *Nihon shoki* (720)—were written in Chinese characters under considerable influence from Chinese civilization and the political developments of the imperial rule in Japan.

Origins of the Japanese: Hunters and Rice Planters   The Japanese story goes far back into prehistoric times in Japan, to the Jomon period (ca. 4500–250 B.C.E.) when the early humans in this land lived by hunting and fishing. Since the Japanese islands are bounded on all sides by seas, a somewhat unified cultural sphere developed. They lived in pit dwellings and made pottery with a rope pattern. Some people in the ancient period perhaps had matriarchal clans. When family members died, they placed flexed bodies decorated with red ochre in burials, indicating some hope of a passage to the afterlife. Apparently they had a special sense of the power of the sun, building many stone circles used apparently for rituals related to the sun. The kami associated with the sun, we know from the myths, is a dominant kami in the Japanese story. Other religious ideas are indicated by ritual objects similar to ones found in China, especially curved beads, swords, and mirrors—symbols of the emperor later on. They also made ritual use of phallic stones, clay masks, and fertility figurines. While we do not

A female figurine from the late Jomon period (ca. 500 B.C.E.). 'Female Figure'. Japan, Aomori Prefecture; Final Jomon period (1000 - 300 B.C.E.). Earthenware with traces of pigment (Kamegao Ka type) H. 9 7/8 in. (25.1 cm.). Photograph by Lynton Gardiner. The Asia Society, New York, Mr. and Mrs. John D. Rockefeller 3rd Collection.

know a lot about the religious vision of these Stone Age ancestors of the Japanese, we can recognize some later Japanese ideas and practices as having had their origins in this dim past.

But new migrations of people came into Japan during the Yayoi period (ca. 250 B.C.E.–250 C.E.), and now an important new development becomes central: wet-rice cultivation. Later it is taken for granted that growing rice is the heart of the Japanese way of life, and many festivals and rituals have to do with planting and harvesting rice. Traditional Japanese religion, associated with the cultivation of rice, is concerned with fertility, growth, birth, and renewal. In the communal religion of the Yayoi peoples, we can discern the origins of the Japanese way of life. Probably the Japanese language was developing in this period, and the artistic expressions of the people show many of the aesthetic characteristics of later Japanese art. These people are Japanese.

Some of the descriptions in the records of Chinese dynasties provide illuminating details about the people in this formative period. We are told that men tattooed their faces and decorated their bodies with designs, and women wore their hair in loops. They enjoyed liquor and practiced a form of divination to tell whether fortune would be good or bad. Whenever they went on a sea voyage, they would select a man who did not comb his hair, rid himself of fleas, or wash his clothes, also abstaining from meat and lying with women. This man behaved as a "mourner," and he would be rewarded if the voyage met good fortune or killed if ill fortune occurred. Earlier these people of "Yamatai" had been ruled by a man, but after much warfare they accepted as their ruler a woman, Pimiko, who remained unmarried and practiced magic. When she died, a great mound was raised in her honor, and more than a hundred attendants followed her to the grave, according to the Chinese account.

Such glimpses into ancient Japanese society show that communication with the kami through divination and reliance on shamans and shamanesses were part of Japanese religion from very ancient times.

Clan System and the Imperial Rule   The formation of Japanese society and religion was completed in the Kofun (tomb mound) period (ca. 250–550 C.E.), characterized by the large mounds that served as tombs for rulers and their attendants. Possibly there were new migrations of peoples from the continent and from the southern islands of the Pacific Ocean during this era, and the people now were made up of many large families and clans. Before long, one clan attained dominance over the others, and this became the imperial clan. The head of this clan was the ruler, the emperor—and gradually traditional Japanese society made up of emperor and people took shape. The head of each clan served as priest of the kami of the clan, and the emperor, as head of the whole people, was recognized as high priest of the kami for the sake of all the people.

As the imperial clan established its rule, a new cultural impetus developed. The emperors built huge mound-tombs for their burials, and the art produced for these tombs is strikingly Japanese in character. Of particular significance are the dogu, clay representations of animals and people, which were placed in the tombs to accompany the deceased ruler. Archaeological evidence makes it clear that by the end of the prehistoric period the imperial family was firmly in place in this central area of Japan, ruling over a people whose religion and culture are the fountainhead of Japan as we know it from the historical period. The mythology recorded in the *Kojiki* and the *Nihon shoki* seems to reflect the religious ideas and practices of this formative period, at least from the point of view of the imperial clan.

Sacred Nation: Stories of the Kami

The Japanese sense of identity as a people in this sacred land was influenced by traditions of interaction with the kami of the land—the kami of the mountains, the rivers, the rice fields, and the rest of nature, together with the kami of ancestors and families. The story has many local variants, but important versions are told in the *Kojiki* and *Nihon shoki*, bringing together mythologies about the kami who created the world and the land. The story includes the origin of the imperial family and of all Japanese from the kami. It tells how sacred government spread over the land and how many festivals and rituals originated. The myths reflect the basic Japanese way of looking at nature, the land, the kami, and the people.

Izanagi and Izanami: Creating the Land and Culture Among the kami generated on the Plain of High Heaven in the beginning time, **Izanagi and Izanami** are most important because they are the ones whose creative power brings forth the land and Japanese civilization. The myths tell how Izanagi and Izanami, descending to the Floating Bridge of Heaven, stir up the brine below and, thus, create an island to which they then descend to give birth to the various kami of the world. The whole world is interpenetrated with kami power—the myths talk of eight hundred myriads of kami on the Plain of High Heaven, to say nothing of the kami of earth.

We know that Japanese people have much concern for purity, that they venerate the sun kami as special among all the kami, and that they celebrate festivals at shrines with prayers, music, dancing, and the like. These age-old traditions have models in the mythical stories.

When Izanami died (after giving birth to the kami of fire), she went to the underworld. Izanagi descended there to try and bring her back, impetuously breaking in to see her in her state polluted by death, which made her rather angry so that she pursued him. Escaping from her, now Izanagi needed to purify himself from the pollutions of the underworld, so he washed in a river, purifying and exorcising the evil from himself. Here Japanese people see the model for purification rituals so important in their traditional religion.

Finally, when Izanagi washed his left eye, **Amaterasu** (Heaven Illuminating Kami, that is, Sun Kami) was born, and from washing his right eye and his nose, Tsukiyomi (Moon Kami) and **Susanoo** (Valiant Raging Male Kami) were born. Izanagi rejoiced at these kami of the sun, moon, and storm, and he gave his necklace to Amaterasu and entrusted her with this mission: "You shall rule the Plain of High Heaven." To Tsukiyomi he gave the mission of ruling the night, and to Susanoo the rule of the seas. Thus it is that Amaterasu, the sun kami, born in this sacred land, became the ruler of all the heavenly kami.

The mythic narrative goes on to tell of the conflict that developed between Amaterasu and Susanoo, her boisterous storm kami brother. Amaterasu withdrew to the rock cave of heaven, so that now constant night began to reign on the Plain of High Heaven and in the Central Land of Reed Plains, with cries rising everywhere and all kinds of calamities occurring. So the eight hundred myriads of heavenly kami held a great festival. They set up a sasaki tree and hung strings of curved beads, a large mirror, and white and blue cloth in its branches. Then they presented offerings and intoned prayers. And Kami of Heavenly Headgear performed a shamanistic dance on a bucket, exposing her breasts and genitals and entertaining the kami so that the Plain of High Heaven shook with kami laughter. Intrigued by the raucous festival, Amaterasu was enticed out of the cave, and the Plain of High Heaven and the Central Land of Reed Plains were illuminated once more. Following this heavenly model, Japanese perform festivals of entertaining the kami at the shrines, so that the blessing of kami power will continue.

The Divine Descent of the Imperial Family   In the beginning times, the story says, the kami of the earth were unruly, so from time to time heavenly kami were sent down to pacify and subdue them. Finally, the Central Land of Reed Plains was subdued, and Amaterasu decided to send down her descendants to rule the land. To her grandson **Ninigi** she gave the commission: "The Land of the Plentiful Reed Plains and the Fresh Rice-Ears has been entrusted to you to rule. In accordance with the command, descend from the heavens." Then Amaterasu gave Ninigi the three symbols of divine rule: the myriad curved beads, the mirror, and the sacred sword, saying, "You have this mirror as my spirit; worship it just as you would worship in my very presence"(*Kojiki* Chs. 38–39). Then came the great descent: Ninigi pushed through the myriad layers of the trailing clouds of heaven until he stood on an island by the Heavenly Floating Bridge. Then he descended from the heavens to the peak of Mount Takachiho to inaugurate kami rule on earth. Emperor Jimmu, the legendary first emperor, was the great-grandson of Ninigi.

According to the traditional way of thinking, all emperors of Japan are direct descendants from this line, descendants of the great kami Amaterasu, and, thus, they are fit to rule the land and people, also descended from the kami.

Many Japanese people today, of course, do not understand these myths in a literal, factual way. But the myths do say something important about land, people, and emperor: all are bound together in the sacredness of Japan.

People and Kami in Communion   In early times in Japan, life centered on family, clan, hunting, planting and harvesting rice, the people responding to the goodness of the kami in the rhythm of the seasons, the beauty of mountains and forests, and the fertility of the land. The head of the family or clan acted as a priest for the kami of the clan, worshiping and honoring the kami at a shrine on a hill or in a forest. The shrine probably had no building, at least in early times, but a rope boundary was stretched around the sacred space and the kami was called down to be present there to receive gifts of prayer and food and to give blessings to the people. The chieftain of a large clan would sometimes set up a special pure house near the shrine and appoint a female relative to be priestess for the kami, communicating with the kami through shamanistic trances and providing information for the chieftain.

The *Nihon shoki* tells how the emperors, chieftains of the ruling clan, at first worshiped Amaterasu, their kami ancestor, right in the imperial palace. But Sujin, the tenth legendary emperor, was not at ease living with such awesome power in the palace, so he established a special shrine for Amaterasu to reside in and appointed Princess Toyosukiiri to act as high priestess. Later, at the time of the next emperor, the sun kami revealed that she wished to dwell in the pleasant and secluded land of the province of Ise. So the shrine for Amaterasu was built at **Ise**, the most important shrine in all of Japan for the worship of the sun kami, the divine ancestress of the emperor.

All of Japan was dotted with shrines for worshiping the kami, both the kami of the various clans and also many other kami of various localities, of mountains, trees, waterfalls, rice fields, and the like. Each community had seasonal festivals at these shrines, during which the kami came to provide their powerful presence for the people and grant blessings so the rice crops would grow and the people would be healthy and prosperous. When calamities struck, great purification ceremonies would be conducted to rid the community of the pollution and restore purity for the continued blessing that comes through the kami.

CHINA

RUSSIA

HOKKAIDO

Sapporo

NORTH
KOREA

SEA

OF

JAPAN

40°

HONSHU

Sendai

YELLOW

SEA

SOUTH
KOREA

JAPAN

PACIFIC

Korea Strait

Tokyo

Yokohama

Mt. Fuji

35°

Kamakura

Hiroshima

Mt. Hiei

Kyoto

Nagoya

Kitakyūshū

Kobe

Nara

Ise

OCEAN

Fukuoka

Osaka

SHIKOKU

Mt. Koya

Nagasaki

KYUSHU

EAST

30°

CHINA

SEA

PHILIPPINE

SEA

JAPAN:
MAJOR CITIES
AND
RELIGIOUS SITES

25°

125°   130°   135°   140°

0   100   200 Miles

0   100   200 Kilometers

The Coming of Buddhism and Chinese Culture

In the sixth century C.E., this early Japanese world was penetrated by a very different religion and culture, a way of looking at existence that seems quite contrary to the early Japanese vision. Buddhism, with its view of the passing nature of this world and the goal of nirvana, made its appearance in Japan, together with other aspects of Chinese culture such as Confucianism, Daoism, scriptures, art, and writing. Now the story of Japan was transformed and drastically redirected—yet that story goes on, as the Japanese absorbed Buddhism and the other aspects of Chinese culture while continuing the main lines of their traditional society.

Buddha Images and Scriptures   In 552 C.E., according to the *Nihon shoki*, a provincial king in Korea sent gifts to Emperor Kimmei, and among these gifts were a Buddha image and Buddhist scriptures. Of course, something was known about Buddhism before this, since Korean immigrants had recently come to Japan. But now for the first time the Japanese emperor, father of the people and high priest of the kami, was confronted directly with the claims for the superior power of this new teaching of the foreign Buddha.

Along with the gifts, the Korean king sent a message praising the Buddhist teaching as a precious treasure, even though it is hard to understand. Moreover, he stated, from distant India all the way through Korea there are none who have not accepted the Buddhist teaching with reverence. Now the Japanese leaders were in a dilemma—they had always looked to Amaterasu and the kami as the divine forces who bring all good and blessing in the world. They had never seen this mysterious kami in seated position with eyes closed, so contrary to the Japanese tradition that did not have humanlike images or statues of the kami. And they had never used any form of writing, so they could not understand these mysterious scriptures.

Emperor Kimmei was overjoyed at this gift, but he was undecided about what he should do, so he consulted his three trusted ministers as to whether they should worship this Buddha or not. Soga no Iname felt the superiority of the Chinese culture should determine the answer, pointing out that all the western lands without exception do worship the Buddha; should Japan alone refuse to do so? But the other two ministers were from the Mononobe and the

Nakatomi families, both hereditary priesthood families, and they saw a potential risk. Since it has always been the custom of the emperors to worship the Japanese kami, they argued, should a foreign kami be worshiped instead, it might incur the wrath of the kami of the Japanese nation. In this dilemma, Emperor Kimmei compromised, giving the Buddha image to Minister Soga to worship privately as an experiment. Soga was overjoyed; he enshrined the Buddha image in his house and began to follow Buddhist disciplines and practices in worshiping the Buddha. This was a momentous step—a court minister worshiping the foreign kami, the Buddha. Shortly after this, a pestilence prevailed in the land, and the Mononobe and Nakatomi ministers petitioned the emperor, saying that this pestilence had broken out because their advice had not been followed; now happiness could only be secured by throwing the Buddha image away. So the emperor ordered the Buddha image to be thrown into a canal—whereupon a sudden fire swept away the great hall of the imperial palace! Thus, the dilemma of how to respond to the power of the Buddha continued to rage in the land of the kami.

But the attraction of the new religion was not to be denied, even as the question of its relation to the traditional way of Japan was unresolved. The next year people reported hearing Buddhist chants coming like thunder from the sea, together with a great light from the west. Investigating this, they found a piece of shining camphor wood floating on the water, and the emperor ordered an artist to make images of the Buddha from this wood. In the following years, more Buddhist images and scriptures came from Korea, and also Buddhist monks and nuns who could teach the Buddhist disciplines, meditation, making of images, and building of Buddhist temples. The Soga family in particular continued its dedication to Buddhism. Soga no Umako, son of Soga no Iname, worked tirelessly for the acceptance of Buddhism and for Japanese to study the Buddhist scriptures and disciplines. Gradually the teaching of this "foreign kami" attained a foothold among the leading families of Japan.

Transformation of Japan Through Buddhism and Chinese Culture   One of the most brilliant rulers in Japanese history, Prince **Shotoku** (573–621), who administered the nation as prince regent, was a key figure in the Buddhist transformation of Japan. Shotoku continued the traditional worship of the kami, issuing an edict saying that all ministers should pay homage to the kami of heaven and earth from the bottom of their hearts. But Shotoku also studied Buddhism and Confucianism and attained deep understanding of both. In 604, he issued the famous Seventeen Article Constitution, in which he advocated the Confucian virtues of harmony, propriety, and loyalty to the emperor. And he also stated that the people should sincerely reverence the Three Treasures, namely, the Buddha, the Dharma, and the Sangha. Prince Shotoku was strongly committed to the Buddhist teachings and even gave lectures on the Buddhist sutras. For this he has won veneration in the sacred story as the founder of Buddhism in Japan. Thus, the transformation came about that set Japanese culture firmly on three foundations: the kami way, the Buddhist way, and the Confucian way. The relationship among these foundations has been debated through the centuries and is still debated today. But Japanese life and culture have been shaped by these traditions.

As Japan moved into the Nara period (710–784), with the capital no longer shifting about with each new emperor but now set permanently at Nara, Buddhism and other aspects of Chinese culture became ever more an integral part of the Japanese story. The city of Nara was laid out in the style of the current Chinese capital city, for example. And the structure of government, with bureaucracies and systems of ranks, was modeled after the Chinese pattern.

The Confucian influence from China was pervasive, especially in its emphasis on social harmony through a system of hierarchical relationships in which the subordinate one is loyal and benevolent. The Japanese sense of family was reinforced with the Confucian notion of filial piety. And Confucian teachings supported the traditional respect for the emperor as the head of the leading family by its notion of loyalty of subjects to rulers. One difference retained in Japan was that the emperor, the son of Heaven in the Chinese Confucian view, ruled not only according to the mandate of Heaven but also according to his descent from Amaterasu. Whereas Chinese emperors could be deposed if they lost the mandate of Heaven, the traditional Japanese story makes the imperial line permanent and eternal.

The influence of Daoism from China was subtle but extensive. Following the Chinese bureaucratic model, the Japanese government set up a Bureau of Divination, officially incorporating Daoistic practices of divination for determining auspicious dates for government activities and

interpreting good and bad omens. Gradually, Daoist religious ideas and practices merged with traditional Japanese ideas of kami and nature and filtered into all the Japanese religious traditions.

The importation of Buddhism by means of monks and nuns, images and scriptures, masters and searchers continued strongly in the Nara period, when the first important Buddhist philosophical schools developed in Japan. Important for the story is the increasing acceptance of the Buddhist way first by the nobility and the imperial court, followed by a general turn to Buddhism also by the common people of the land. Wandering shamans and charismatic leaders adopted the new Buddhist vision and became evangelists for the new teaching. One shamanistic Buddhist priest, Gyogi, had no education or ordination but because of his zeal and ability to unify the people around Buddhism was made archbishop of Buddhist priests in Japan. In 752, Emperor Shomu decided to build a great Buddhist temple in Nara as the central temple for all Japan, and he enlisted Gyogi and others to raise money from the common people for erecting a colossal statue of Lochana (Vairochana), the Sun Buddha, there.

But what about the sun kami, Amaterasu? What did the imperial Ancestress feel about this foreign sun deity? The story says that the emperor sent Gyogi to inquire of Amaterasu at the Grand Shrine of Ise, and the august Ancestress communicated that the Sun Buddha Lochana was really a manifestation of the kami and could be worshiped as identical with the sun kami, Amaterasu. Since the protection provided by the Buddha was now considered important, the emperor also set up temples in all the provinces where monks and nuns could live and pray for the welfare of the nation.

Thus, the sacred history was transformed to include both Confucianist virtues and Buddhist worship. The Japanese story is based on relationship to the kami. But it is also the story of Confucius, and it is especially the story of the Buddha who came to the Japanese land.

CONTINUING TRANSFORMATIONS OF THE JAPANESE WAY

After the formative periods in the prehistoric and Nara eras, the Japanese tradition has seen many further transformations. These have resulted both from internal developments and from influences on Japan from the outside.

Integrating the Buddhist Way into Japanese Religion

The Japanese path, now including Buddhism and Chinese culture as part of the story, widened and deepened during the Heian (974–1185), Kamakura (1185–1333), and Muromachi (1333–1600) periods. One of the chief characteristics of Japanese history is the way the Japanese responded to the periodic waves of influence that came from the Chinese mainland, reflecting religious and cultural developments taking place in China. Another characteristic is the coming forth of powerful religious personalities during these times to provide dynamic leadership and found Buddhist movements that transformed religious life in Japan.

Firming Up the Foundations: Heian Era   When the capital city was moved to Heian (Kyoto) in 794, a classical period of refinement and deepened religious understanding commenced, under imperial courtly rule. The emperor was the nominal ruler, but real power was held by the Fujiwara family, which cultivated a courtly style of elegance and taste well illustrated, for example, in Lady Murasaki's *Tale of Genji*, a masterpiece of early Japanese literature. Much of the stimulus for culture came from two new Buddhist schools imported from China, **Tendai** and **Shingon**. Each established an important monastic center in Japan and acted as a wellspring for Buddhist education and the transmission of culture.

A young monk named **Saicho** (767–822) studied at the Tiantai (Japanese Tendai) monastery in China and upon his return to Japan established a Tendai monastery at Mt. Hiei near Kyoto. Tendai Buddhism in Japan actually included practices from some of the other schools, like Chan, Pure Land, and Tantric Buddhism. The Tendai monastery on Mt. Hiei set forth a strenuous training program for monks and nuns and, thus, shaped generations of Japanese Buddhist leaders. This monastery flourished for a number of centuries and became a fountainhead for many of the later developments in Japanese Buddhism.

The founder of the Shingon school of Buddhism, **Kukai** (773–835), is considered to be one of the most gifted and brilliant religious leaders in Japanese history. Trained first for government service, Kukai spent years in austere Buddhist practices. He studied the Chenyan (Tantric or esoteric) form of Buddhism in China and advocated these practices for the Japanese people, greatly influencing the emperor and others of the court from his monastery at Mt. Koya. The Shingon practices included the use of mantras (sacred chanted formulas), mudras (ritual gestures), mandalas (paintings of cosmic Buddha symbols), and other forms of meditation and ritual. Kukai excelled in the arts and literature, and he established a special school that gave instruction in both religious and secular education. His writings describe the development of all religions through ten stages, with Shingon as the highest level, and he taught the doctrine of becoming a Buddha in this very body through the Tantric practices. Shingon became a kind of national religion for Japan, and literature and the arts were widely promoted under Kukai's influence.

Now that Buddhism was firmly established as a central factor in the Japanese way, the indigenous Shinto tradition also went through some new transformations. In earlier times, there was simply a variety of folk beliefs and practices loosely held together by the leading clans and their mythologies. Now there was an attempt to create a more self-conscious Shinto tradition based on the ancient way of the kami. Imperial edicts called for the people to be pure, bright, and upright, in accordance with the kami way, and a work on history as transmitted in a Shinto priestly family was compiled, the *Kogoshui* (Gleanings from Ancient Accounts). Rules were put forth regulating the shrines and priests and designating a number of important shrines as "specially privileged," receiving support from the court. Now Shinto, at least as represented by the larger shrines and their priesthoods, was becoming an institutionalized religion.

But important internal transformations of Shinto were also occurring. Shinto priests were not oblivious to the powers of the Buddha and of Chinese culture. The feeling eventually developed that the kami themselves could benefit by the help of the Buddha, and in some shrines Buddhist chapels were set up and Buddhist scriptures recited before the presence of the kami. These popular attitudes were reinforced by ideas that the kami were "protectors of the Buddha's Law." Therefore, kami were enshrined in Buddhist temples. Before long, the idea developed that Buddhahood was the "original essence" of the kami, and so the kami could be worshiped as manifestations of the Buddha, some of them even given the title *bosatsu*, bodhisattva.

As Shinto was transformed by Buddhist influence, Buddhism was also being influenced by the Japanese traditions, especially the this-worldly attitude of the Shinto way. Many people took to a path that combined ideas and practices from both Shinto and Buddhism. For example, popular religion featured many shamanistic men and women who went about healing and helping people, using rituals and practices from both Shinto and Buddhism. Some, called *yamabushi* (literally, those who sleep in the mountains), underwent spiritual disciplines in the mountains to acquire sacred power, and they used that power in healing and exorcisms for the people. Typically they based their practice in esoteric Buddhist rituals. But they also practiced Shinto rituals of purification and abstinence and made retreats to Shinto holy mountains.

During the later Heian period, the worship of Amida Buddha (Amitabha) grew rapidly in Japan, permeating both the Tendai and the Shingon schools and becoming very popular with the aristocrats. Shamanistic Buddhists such as Kuya (903–972) took the gospel of Amida to the masses, teaching them to sing the **Nembutsu** chant, "Namu Amida Butsu" (Praise to Amida Buddha), to a popular tune. Also extremely popular among the common people was the Bodhisattva **Jizo** (Kshitigarbha), who had taken a vow not to attain Buddhahood until the last soul was redeemed from hell. Since fear of suffering in hell was very real, especially among the peasants, Jizo was a good figure to which to turn in anxiety and distress, for he mediates on behalf of the souls destined to descend to the lower world, particularly the souls of infants and children who die. The worship of Amida Buddha and of Jizo was not confined to any particular school or locality, being absorbed into the general religious system of the people.

Salvation in Uncertain Times: Kamakura and Muromachi Eras   Rule by the aristocracy of the imperial court came to an end in the twelfth century with the rise of the **samurai** (warrior) classes and the new feudal system in which landed barons called *daimyo* with their samurai retainers and vassals vied with one another for power and control. The strongest military leader, Minamoto Yorimoto (1147–1199), moved the center of power to Kamakura and ruled as shogun (military dictator). The imperial house continued to exist and to exercise ceremonial leadership, but the real power from now until the nineteenth century was in the hands of such feudal shoguns.

Himeji Castle, typical of castles in Japan from the medieval period.

The collapse of the aristocratic culture of the Heian era and the outbreak of more or less continual fighting between the various daimyo brought a sense of uncertainty and hopelessness among the people, leading to new religious searchings. How can we find order and meaning in life? How can we be delivered from this passing world and attain assurance of salvation in the next world? Such questions were foremost to the religious in these uncertain times.

The Buddhist traditions that came to the fore in this period had already been present in Japan for some time, but now they resonated to the new urgency of the situation. In the eyes of many, this was a particularly degenerate age. The old Buddhist idea of the three ages of the Dharma (Perfect Dharma, Counterfeit Dharma, End of Dharma), which had already played a significant role in China, now became popular in Japan. The feeling developed that the third age, End of Dharma, had begun in Japan about the year 1052—a feeling corroborated by the collapse of Heian society and the upheavals inaugurating the feudal era in

Japan. In this third age of Dharma, many felt, it was no longer possible to reach salvation by the traditional path. So people were looking for new assurances of deliverance and salvation, which the older practices seemingly could no longer provide. The new schools that developed in this period are clear expressions of a Japanized Buddhism, emphasizing salvation and enlightenment through simple faith and practice.

Worship of Amida Buddha, popular already in the Heian era as part of the Tendai system, now became the only way to salvation in the eyes of many. **Honen** (1133–1212), considered the founder of the **Pure Land** sect in Japan, frequently declared that, for ordinary mortals living in this degenerate world, there is no way to reach the Pure Land except by depending on the saving power of Amida. Honen was one of the most persistent advocates of the path of salvation by calling on Amida's name with the words, "Namu Amida Butsu." This *Nembutsu* formula, he taught, should be said over and over with firm faith in Amida's vows to save all beings. The Pure Land sect became a movement devoted to the exclusive worship of Amida Buddha for the gift of rebirth in the paradise of the Pure Land.

Shinran (1173–1262), one of Honen's disciples, laid even greater stress on the total inability of humans in this degenerate age to move toward salvation by their own merit or efforts. The highest path is simply to accept the gift of salvation promised through Amida's vow to save all beings and, out of thankfulness, to chant Amida's name and rely completely on his grace. To emphasize that humans can have no merit in this degenerate age, Shinran gave up monastic life, married, and raised a family—starting the tradition of married Buddhist priests in Japan. The sect founded by Shinran, the True Pure Land, became very popular in medieval Japan and has continued to be the religious practice of a large segment of the Japanese people to the present day.

A similar answer to the question of salvation was provided by **Nichiren** (1222–1282), a humble fisherman's son who became, in the eyes of many, "the pillar of Japan, the eye of the nation, and the vessel of the country." Nichiren was convinced that the woes Japan was experiencing resulted from the abandonment of the true Buddhist path. The true path is the teaching of the *Lotus Sutra*; this is the supreme teaching of the Buddha Shakyamuni, revealing

the one and only way to salvation both for individuals and for the whole nation. Now, Nichiren felt, the different Buddhist schools had abandoned this pure and simple truth, and because of that Japan was suffering various misfortunes. To return to the true path, people need only to take on their lips the name of the *Lotus Sutra* through the formula, "Namu myoho rengekyo" (Praise to the wondrous truth of the *Lotus Sutra*). Nichiren himself was identified as an incarnation of a bodhisattva, and he made it his mission to save Japan from the political and social evils that he felt came from wrong Buddhist teachings. He condemned the other Buddhist schools, caused great difficulty for the government, was twice exiled, and narrowly escaped execution. But he received considerable recognition when the Mongol invasion that he predicted actually occurred, and many were attracted to his simple religion and his vision of Japan as an earthly Buddhaland. Nichiren's zeal and his straightforward path appealed to many in this broken age, and the Nichiren sect grew to a large movement. Through the centuries Nichiren Buddhism has been a special Japanese form of Buddhism, and today many people in Japan belong to Nichiren groups.

Not all people were looking for salvation through sacred power that comes from outside, whether from Amida Buddha or from the *Lotus Sutra*. Some in this turbulent period were looking to Buddhist roots for something that would transcend the disorder and anxiety and restore calmness in the heart. And they found this in the practice of **Zen** (Chinese Chan) Buddhism. The Zen meditation type of Buddhism was known in Japan in the Nara and Heian periods along with the other forms of Chinese Buddhism, but the impetus for developing Zen as a separate school in Japan came from fresh importations from China. **Eisai** (1141–1215) is credited with bringing Zen anew to Japan; he found favor with the military rulers and emphasized the nationalistic value of Zen, as in his tract, "Propagate Zen, Protect the Country." It was **Dogen** (1200–1253) who provided the intellectual foundation for Zen in Japan. As a Tendai monk, he was bothered at an early age with the question that if all living beings have the Buddha-nature, then why does one have to engage in religious practices to gain enlightenment? His search took him to China, and when he returned he established a monastery where he taught the single practice of **zazen** (sitting in meditation). It is not by "other power" that one is saved, Dogen taught;

rather it is through self-power, simply sitting in meditation, that one reaches enlightenment. Since one already possesses the Buddha-nature, all one has to do is awaken to that nature.

Dogen founded the Soto (Chinese Caodong) Zen sect in Japan, which advocates "gradual enlightenment," that is, an unhurried, purposeless, nonstriving practice of zazen, which gradually deepens one's experience of enlightenment. The other main school that developed is Rinzai (Chinese Linji), the "sudden enlightenment" school. Rinzai masters typically gave their disciples **koans**, Zen questions and riddles from the sayings of the Chinese masters. The disciple would concentrate on this koan, eventually experiencing a sudden breakthrough, an awakening.

Zen monasteries in Japan practiced an austere mode of life with heavy emphasis on meditation as the path to enlightenment. Critical of the "easy paths" of Pure Land and Nichiren Buddhism, Zen adherents cultivated a strong-minded approach to the spiritual life that brought calm and control in the midst of the troubles of the age. There is no need to rely on the Buddha from far off or to long to be reborn in the Pure Land of the West. The Pure Land is right here; the Buddha is within oneself! Anyone, taught Dogen, even women and common people, can sit in meditation and realize Buddhahood.

Of course, the common people were not drawn to Zen as they were to Pure Land and Nichiren, but one important class did find the Zen approach most attractive—the samurai. This newly rising class of warriors and military lords found meaning in the discipline, self-reliance, strong commitment, and mental control involved in Zen practice. The strong sense among Zen masters of enlightenment directly within the pursuits of the ordinary world gave strong impetus to martial arts such as swordfighting and archery, and it likewise contributed greatly to other traditional arts such as poetry, classical **Noh** drama, and the tea ceremony. Although the total number of Zen adherents during these times was perhaps never large, through the important Zen monasteries and the dedication of the warrior class and artists, Zen had a transforming effect on all Japanese society and culture.

The Zen movement also provided a new avenue for Confucian teachings to permeate Japanese society—now the Neo-Confucianism of the late Song period in China—as many Zen priests also adopted Confucian learning and ideals. They were especially attracted to the Neo-Confucian emphasis on self-cultivation through discipline and study. With its teaching of total loyalty to superiors, Neo-Confucianism helped to shape the samurai ethic, providing the foundation for what later (in the Tokugawa era) was systematized as *bushido*, the "way of the warrior." Samurai became retainers of a particular daimyo master and dedicated themselves with total loyalty to that master, practicing military discipline as a kind of spiritual training. Bushido placed a heavy emphasis on bravery, duty, and being fearless to meet death in the service of one's lord.

The Shinto path continued to be an important influence during the medieval era, existing both in its local popular forms and in the amalgamation with Buddhism. For the first time in Japan, leading thinkers tried to articulate the Shinto basis of the Japanese way, acknowledging the contributions made also by Confucianism and Buddhism but beginning the intellectual process that eventually attempted to separate Shinto from Buddhism.

This cultural synthesis involving Shinto, Buddhist, and Confucian religious traditions formed the basis for the aesthetic pursuits that blossomed in the Muromachi era (1333–1600). So much of what we consider to be typically Japanese cultural forms in architecture, literature, and the other arts grew out of this synthesis. Main elements were contributed by the different religious traditions: the sense of the purity, beauty, and goodness of nature (Shinto); the realization of enlightenment or emptiness through art forms (Zen Buddhism); and the experience of self-cultivation and transformation through artistic practice (Neo-Confucianism). Such elements as these combine in the Japanese *geijutsu-do*, the "**way of art**," which we will look at in more detail later. Among the arts widely practiced as spiritual aesthetic paths were poetry, painting, Noh drama, calligraphy, the tea ceremony, flower arranging, gardening, and even martial arts such as swordfighting and archery. The heritage from the medieval religio-aesthetic synthesis has been a strong factor in shaping Japanese identity.

Unification of Japan and the Modern Period

Starting in the mid-sixteenth century, the unification of Japan under the Tokugawa shogunate, together with the encounter with the West and with Christianity, brought strong influence on the Japanese religious traditions.

Unification, Christian Impact, and Reaction The close of the Muromachi period was signaled in the gathering strength of three military dictators who finally unified Japan during the last thirty years of the sixteenth century: Nobunaga, Hideyoshi, and Tokugawa Ieyasu. The long medieval period of wars and conflicts ended when Tokugawa Ieyasu (1542–1616) established the Tokugawa Shogunate, instituting a peaceful period for Japan from 1600 to 1867.

By the time Oda Nobunaga (1534–1582) came to power, the various Buddhist groups had attained considerable land and even military power in Japanese society, and there was also much fighting between the Pure Land and the Nichiren groups, each with its own army of soldier-monks. With power, of course, came a tendency toward political involvement, and a power struggle ensued between Nobunaga and the Buddhists, especially the Pure Land group. In several attacks, Nobunaga massacred tens of thousands from this sect. The violence of these events considerably weakened the influence of the Buddhist groups, at least for a while.

But the religious situation during the unification of Japan was complicated by the intrusion of a new foreign religion: Christianity. European explorers and traders began to arrive in the 1540s, and the Jesuit missionary Francis Xavier arrived in 1549, followed by other Jesuit missionaries and priests of the Franciscan and Dominican orders. Christian and European influence rose sharply for half a century and then just as sharply declined and virtually disappeared in the Japanese reaction that led to the closing of Japan. But the Christian story, so foreign to Japan, touched and contributed to the Japanese story.

The Society of Jesus, formed by Ignatius Loyola in 1540, sent forth an army of Christian monk-soldiers into the Asian world. Pursuing a policy of accommodation to the best of the local cultures, Francis Xavier and other Jesuits attempted to convert the Japanese feudal leaders to Christianity, with some success for a time. Following the lead of certain feudal lords, tens of thousands of people took over the Christian vision. The spread of Christianity was aided perhaps by Nobunaga's hostility toward the organized Buddhist groups.

But suspicions about the connections of Christians with the foreign European powers soon surfaced, and Nobunaga's successor Hideyoshi (1537–1598) turned against the Christians and instigated the first persecutions, to be followed by the more systematic attempts by the early Tokugawa rulers to control and wipe out the European-Christian intrusion. There were heroic martyrdoms and even a peasant-based revolt of some 37,000 people, mostly Christian, in Shimabara on the coast of Kyushu in 1637–1638, who stood against government forces for several months before being massacred. Finally, the Tokugawa authorities enforced their ban on all Christian priests and Christian activities. Responding to the threat of foreign intrusion and domination, they closed Japan to Western contact and influence, and the Christian century was over. The ban on Christianity was enforced by requiring all people to register with their local Buddhist temples, and reports of continuing involvement in Christianity were investigated and the offenders punished. A number of Christian families and groups in more remote areas did manage to continue practicing Christianity in secret; some groups of these "**Hidden Christians**" (*kakure kirishitan*) still existed two hundred years later when Westerners again were permitted into Japan.

Floating World and Shinto Resurgence While the Tokugawa government made Buddhist temples into the guardians of the state against Christianity, the ideological leanings of the regime were toward Neo-Confucianism. A strict separation and ranking of the classes of society were developed, with duties assigned to each: the samurai, the farmers, the artisans, and the town merchants. No mobility between these classes was permitted.

But changes were coming. Because the Tokugawa regime was in total control and permitted no opposition,

Famous Shinto shrine at Nikko which enshrines Tokugawa Ieyasu, the founder of the Tokugawa Shogunate.

the samurai class became idle and relatively nonproductive. The farmer-peasant class became impoverished under their tax burden. But the merchant class rose to create a flourishing urban culture with new religious and artistic dimensions. In the Genroku era (ca. 1675–1725), this new urban world of art and pleasure was called the "Floating World" (*ukiyo*), made up of a lively interaction of painters, playwrights, performers, and geishas, supported by the flourishing merchants. Novels and bunraku (puppet theater) plays on themes of love and urban life were widely popular. Novels such as *The Life of a Man Who Lived for Love* and *Five Women Who Chose Love*, both by Saikaku, and bunraku plays such as *The Love Suicides at Sonezaki*, by Chikamatsu, suggest the sorts of themes that caught the interest of the merchant class. Japan was entering into the modern era, even though its social structures were still based in the medieval world.

Interest in Neo-Confucianism inspired Japanese scholars to go back to the original classics of China. But before long these same scholars were also going back to the early Japanese classics, and the Shinto Restoration movement was born. Earlier medieval scholars had begun to resist the dominant theory that kami were reflections of the original Buddha reality; they suggested instead that the kami represented the sacred essence, and the Buddhas were but reflections of this original reality. Now a **School of National Learning** developed to promote the study of original Shinto writings and to attempt to restore an authentic Shinto way purified of foreign (Buddhist) influence.

A leading scholar of the National Learning movement was **Motoori Norinaga** (1730–1801), who came from a merchant-class family. He had training in Pure Land Buddhism and Confucianism, but he became interested in ancient Shinto as the source of the special Japanese spirit. So he devoted his life to the study of the ancient Japanese way, as set forth in the *Kojiki* and the *Nihon shoki*, and also in early poetry such as the *Manyoshu* collection. He argued, for example, that the *Kojiki* provided the best and universal principle for Japan and for humankind. And he advocated the restoration of a "natural," pure Shinto based on the ancient texts. Motoori further articulated the unique Japanese outlook on life in aesthetic terms, as *mono-no-aware*, a "sensitivity to things," which he explained as an emotional, aesthetic openness to both the beauty and the pathos of life. The Shinto Restoration movement exerted much influence on the political scene and helped to create the climate that led to the restoration of imperial rule.

Meiji Restoration and Nationalistic Shinto   In the middle of the nineteenth century, internal pressure from the Shinto Restoration movement and from peasant uprisings combined with pressure from the West to bring great changes. After Commodore Matthew Perry's ships appeared off the shore of Japan in 1853, events moved swiftly: Japan was opened to the West, the Tokugawa regime fell, and imperial rule was restored in 1868 under Emperor Meiji. The **Meiji Restoration** combined two quite different tendencies. On the one hand, Japan became a modern nation and adopted many Western forms of government and education, including freedom of religion. On the other hand, the government attempted to restore a kind of "pure" Japanese society on the basis of the classic Shinto texts. The emperor was thought of as the father of the nation. And Shinto was separated from Buddhism and taken over under the administration of the state. So that there could be freedom of religion and still universal participation in Shinto, the government declared that state Shinto was not a religion but rather the cultural heritage of all Japanese. Even Buddhists and Christians were expected to participate in Shinto rituals to show their loyalty to the emperor and the nation.

In the rising tide of Japanese nationalism, especially in the 1920s and 1930s, the government used the educational system to teach the Shinto mythology as the basis of its claim to the divine origin of Japan and its manifest destiny to rule Greater Asia. There were dissenting voices to this misuse of the Shinto tradition, but they were considered unpatriotic and were dealt with harshly. After the defeat of Japan in World War II, the Occupation Forces insisted on the complete disestablishment of Shinto, removing government support of the shrines and making Shinto simply one religion alongside Buddhism and Christianity in Japan. The emperor remained as the symbolic head of the nation, but he renounced the nationalistic use of the Shinto traditions.

Religion in Japan Today

Survival of the Religious Traditions   In the trauma and ferment following Japan's defeat in World War II and occupation by the Allied forces, many of the traditional values and religious practices were questioned and a period of strong westernization and secularization set in. Yet, though their strength was diminished, the religious traditions continued to survive and to adjust to the context in Japan today.

After the great disruption caused by its disestablishment, Shinto was stabilized and continues to find support in the local communities. The Association of Shinto Shrines sees to it that priests are educated in the Shinto traditions and rituals, assigning them to shrines as needed. Although many smaller shrines do not have resident priests, they still can be administered by local people and served by priests from time to time. Even though many people no longer keep a *kamidana* (household shrine) in their homes, they visit the shrines on festival days and participate in Shinto community activities.

Buddhism still holds the intellectual allegiance of most Japanese, even though they may not actively take part in Buddhist activities. Many who are quite secular still turn to Buddhism in times of crisis or when a family member dies. The major sects of Japanese Buddhism today, based in the schools of **Tendai, Shingon, Pure Land, Nichiren**, and **Zen**, appear to have weathered the crises of postwar Japan: defeat, economic loss, westernization, secularization, and growth of New Religions. Large numbers of people still look to Buddhist temples and priests for guidance in life crises and for comfort and ritual when death strikes in the family. The intellectual life in Japanese Buddhist circles has been particularly lively, and numerous Japanese Buddhist scholars have contributed significantly to the revival of Buddhist scholarship in the world. Many Japanese scholars working out of the Buddhist intellectual tradition have achieved international reputation, such as the founder of the famous Kyoto school of philosophy, Nishida Kitaro (1870–1945), as well as his leading successor, Nishitani Keiji (1900–1990), and many others. Buddhist scholars and leaders are also much engaged in dialogue with leaders of other religions and with movements seeking peace throughout the world.

One of the most striking developments in Japanese religion in the modern period has been the emergence of many **New Religions**, which have captured the imagination of a good portion of the Japanese people. While it is difficult to be precise, it is estimated that as many as 30 percent of Japan's population participate in one way or another in the activities of these New Religions. They represent one of the most vital sectors of Japanese religion today. Some of these started in the nineteenth century, but most are more recent movements, and the real spurt of growth has come in the postwar period. In a sense, these are not really "new" religions, for they generally adopt elements from the traditional religions and combine them in new ways. Some draw mainly on Shinto traditions, others stem from Buddhism, and still others draw from a variety of traditions, including Christianity. In fact, one characteristic of many New Religions is their syncretistic character—their main teachings and practices typically come from a number of religious traditions and, in addition, often draw on modern science and technology as well.

A central characteristic of the New Religions is a strong, charismatic founder or leader who has new revelatory experiences. Another characteristic is their emphasis on concrete, this-worldly benefits and goals, especially healing from sickness and success in life. They have simple teachings and practices, and above all they offer a caring community in which people, lost in the frustrations of modern life, can find identity and meaning.

These New Religions run the whole range of traditional religious emphases in Japan. One movement that has many Shinto and shamanistic elements is **Tenrikyo**, founded by a farmwoman, Nakayama Miki (1798–1887), through whom a monotheistic God spoke, providing a narrative of the creation of the world and establishing rituals to bring humankind back to God. Many groups have arisen from Nichiren Buddhism, among them **Soka Gakkai**, a lay movement that emphasizes chanting the name of the *Lotus Sutra* for immediate health, happiness, and success in life. Yet another type is represented by P. L. Kyodan (Perfect Liberty Order), which advocates a balanced life and graceful rituals in keeping with its slogan, "life is art." In recent years, a "new" New Religion type has emerged in Japan, borrowing Western religious notions of apocalyptic destruction leading to a new order. One such group, Aum Shinri-kyo, attracted much attention through actions such as spreading poison gas in a subway system. Such groups are tiny and isolated, however, and the great majority of New Religions advocate peace and communal values.

The Story Today and Future Prospects The Japanese sacred story still goes on today, with many changes and transformations. Japan is a very modern, technologically advanced nation, and the people are highly educated and outwardly very westernized. Secularization has played a big role in Japan in recent years, and many people find it unimportant to participate in the traditional religious activities. Modern urban life does not lend itself to the family and clan-centered focus that was the heart of so much of the religious activity in the past. It could be said, perhaps, that many Japanese have experienced a loss of their traditional story that provided identity since ancient times.

Yet this does not mean that religion is dead in Japan today—far from it. Religious questions still abound, and people still turn to traditional religious sources in their searching. For example, there is much discussion over the role of the emperor and the relation of Shinto practices to the modern state. The trauma of having an abortion or the fear of becoming senile draw many people to seek help at Buddhist temples. Young people flock to Shinto shrines to celebrate Adults Day or to get help in passing university examinations. The sense of being trapped in work and not feeling fulfillment in life impels some to a variety of traditional religious practices as well as to new religious movements.

It is difficult, of course, to predict the future in the Japanese context. Certainly, the Shinto and Buddhist paths will continue, and perhaps renewal and revitalization will take place. And just as certainly the widespread secular attitudes of many people will continue and perhaps grow. Less certain is the future story of the New Religions, whose growth has stabilized after the great surge in the early postwar period. Perhaps these religions will mature, enter into associations with others, and become a continuing part of the Japanese religious story.

DISCUSSION QUESTIONS

1 What are the half-dozen religious traditions that share in making up the identity of many Japanese?
2 In what ways has the mythic tradition about the creation of the world and the rule of Amaterasu provided identity for the Japanese people?
3 What does the story about the first introduction of a Buddha image into Japan reveal about the early Japanese reaction to Buddhism?
4 What was Prince Shotoku's importance for Buddhism in Japan?
5 Explain the importance of the Buddhist schools founded in the Heian period, namely, Tendai and Shingon.
6 Outline the teachings of three Buddhist sects that developed in the Kamakura period: Pure Land, Nichiren, and Zen. What concerns did they have in common?
7 What changes took place in the Shinto tradition as Buddhism became integrated into Japanese culture?
8 What might account for the success of Christianity in the sixteenth century in Japan? And why was it soon banned?
9 What were the concerns of the leaders of the Shinto Restoration movement in the Tokugawa period?
10 What are some main characteristics of the so-called New Religions of Japan?
11 Do you see signs of a revival of religion in Japan today, or do you think religion will fade more to the sidelines?

Chapter 15

Japanese Worlds of Meaning

SHINTO VIEWS OF SACRED REALITY AND HUMAN LIFE

As we have seen, Shinto and Buddhist views are intertwined in the overall Japanese perspective. But, as we seek to understand the Japanese perspective on the central human questions about ultimate reality, existence, and the path of transformation, it will be helpful to look first at the Shinto worlds of meaning. Then we will take up the Buddhist view once again, specifically to identify how Buddhists in Japan have shaped the Japanese world of meaning—and have in turn been shaped by it.

What's it all about? What is really the meaning and purpose of life? Where do we look for the power that transforms us? The basic Shinto answer to questions such as these centers on the kami and our relationship to the kami.

Myriads and Myriads of Kami

The word *Shinto*, formed from Chinese terms, means in native Japanese terms *kami no michi*, "Way of the Kami," that is, a way of life according to the will of the kami. But the Japanese people have never given much concern to working out theoretical doctrines about kami nature. It was not until the Shinto Restoration movement in the Tokugawa era that Shinto theoreticians articulated basic teachings about the nature of the kami. More important to Japanese understanding are ancient myths about the kami preserved in classical texts such as the *Kojiki* and *Nihon shoki* and the numerous other stories and beliefs passed on in the various shrines in Japan.

Myths About the Kami: Generation of Sacred Life Are the kami eternal, or where did they come from? The myths do not concern themselves about whether the kami are related to some eternal transcendent being or principle. Rather, the emphasis is on the generation of kami as a continuous rhapsody of sacred life, from an indescribable and inexhaustible source.

The myths telling the origin of the kami begin quite simply with primordial chaos and a spontaneous generation of a series of kami:

> In the time of the beginning of heaven and earth, on the Plain of High Heaven there came into existence first Lord of the Heavenly Center Kami, then High Generative Force Kami, and then Divine Generative Force Kami. These three kami came into existence as single kami, and their forms were invisible. When the world was young, resembling floating oil and drifting like jellyfish, something like reed-shoots sprouted forth, and from this Excellent Reed Shoots Male Kami and Heavenly Eternal Standing Kami emerged. These two kami also came into existence as single kami, and their forms were invisible. These are the Separate Heavenly Kami. Then there came into existence Earth Eternal Standing Kami and Abundant Clouds Field Kami. These two kami came into existence as single kami, and their forms were invisible. Next there came into existence the Clay Male and Female Kami, Post Male and Female Kami, Great Door Male and Female Kami, Complete Surface Kami and his spouse, Awesomeness Kami; and Izanagi and his spouse, Izanami. These are the Seven Generations of the Kami Age.

(*Kojiki*, Chs. 1–2)

The kami sprang forth without progenitors, independently, in some mysterious generation out of the fertile, primordial, divine chaos. The last pair, Izanagi and Izanami, became the bearers of sacred life as they created the first land and descended to it to begin the creation of everything.

For understanding the kami nature, it is important to realize that everything that Izanagi and Izanami gave birth to is called kami—rivers, sea, wind, trees, mountains, plains, and fire. They overflowed so much with kami power that they spontaneously generated many more kami from their tears, blood, purification water, and so forth, in complete continuity with the originating kami.

Japanese generally make a distinction between the Kami of Heaven—such as those in the myths discussed so far—and the Kami of Earth. The Kami of Heaven are the powerful kami of the Plain of High Heaven, headed by Amaterasu, connected with the greater forces of nature such as the sun, moon, wind, and the like. The Kami of the Earth are those myriads of kami who are resident in all facets of nature throughout the earth, usually associated with certain localities.

The myths provide a large canvas of kami activity on earth, with stories about various kami of the different regions and their interaction with the people. Already in the Age of the Kami, Susanoo, too unruly for the Plain of High Heaven, was forced to descend to the region of Izumo, and Susanoo's descendant O-Kuninushi (Great Land Master Kami) held sway in the Izumo region and finally agreed to accept the rule of the descendant of Amaterasu. But the divisions between the Kami of Heaven and the Kami of Earth are not rigid. Even the sun kami herself, though she rules the Plain of High Heaven, is in close relation to the people; the stories tell how the emperor enshrined his August Ancestress in the shrine at Ise. Ever since that time the emperor has performed special ceremonies of worship to Amaterasu at Ise for the welfare of the whole people.

Nature and Role of the Kami   These myths in the *Kojiki* and *Nihon shoki*, and many stories and rituals associated with the kami at the thousands of shrines throughout Japan, provide a general view of the kami. Japanese have a personal, intuitive sense of the kami as the center of existence, without trying to define fully who or what they are. Still, there are some basic ideas that can be expressed about the nature of the kami and especially about their role in our world.

Scholars have often attempted to find the etymological meaning of the ancient word *kami*, but there are no theories that have gained widespread consensus. The only way

The "Wedded Rocks" at Futamigaura in Mie Prefecture, linked with sacred straw ropes, revered as the kami of the Futami Okitama Shrine. Beautiful spots of nature often are considered sacred to the kami.

to understand the word is to pay attention to how the people feel and act toward the kami. Perhaps the best definition was given by the famous Shinto scholar Motoori Norinaga (1730–1801), who wrote that kami means "anything whatsoever that seems strikingly impressive, possesses superior power, or inspires a feeling of awe." So kami are defined principally by the awesomeness and striking impressiveness that they demonstrate, calling forth feelings of respect, fear, and appreciation of beauty and goodness. Of course, Motoori Norinaga also included all kami that appear in the *Kojiki*, as well as the spirits that are worshipped at all the shrines. In principle, then, human beings, birds, animals, trees, plants, mountains, oceans—all may be *kami*.

Thus, anything that seems imbued with kami quality is thought of as kami. This can include the qualities of growth, fertility, and productivity; various natural phenomena and objects, such as wind and thunder, sun, mountains, rivers, trees, and waterfalls; animals, such as the fox and the dog; and ancestors, especially the ancestors of the imperial family. Furthermore, kami can include the guardian spirits of the land and of occupations; the spirits of national heroes; and even spirits that are pitiable and weak, such as those who have died tragic deaths.

Unlike conceptions of the creator God in the Abrahamic religions, and unlike Indian and Chinese conceptions of transcendent gods or eternal principles, Shintoists believe the kami, even the Kami of Heaven, to be entirely immanent within the forces and qualities of the world. They are not preexistent beings who create the world and then stand above it. Rather the kami are the inner power of all nature, constituted from the sacred nuclei of the world itself. As such, they are the forces that bestow and promote all life, growth, and creativity.

Some distinction in rank among the various kami can be made, but only in terms of how they contribute to life and growth. There is some tendency to think of the Kami of Heaven as superior, with Amaterasu having the leading position of all the kami. Yet even Amaterasu is not absolute in her power and authority. She pays her respects to other kami and consults them; even though Japanese revere her, they also worship other kami and go to them for concerns that fall under their functions. And certainly there are kami that are inferior, such as kami of flora and fauna, who also need to be respected and appeased with religious rites when their domain is impinged upon. The kami who are negative and destructive are also respected—those who bring vengeance and calamity on humans. For these kami, too, are manifestations of life-power, turned to the destructive side, and they also are worthy of reverence and worship.

The kami sometimes communicate important knowledge to those who worship them. It was taken for granted in ancient Japan, for example, that the kami communicated their will to the clan leader and to the people through oracular means, usually through a shamanistic priestess. This revelation would be kept and passed on as important truth for the family and community.

Under Buddhist influence there was some tendency in medieval Shinto to look for some kind of kami essence or principle that could be compared to the Buddhist notion of the universal Buddha-essence. Some, for example, thought of the kami as local reflections or forms of the Buddhas, all of whom really go back to the one Buddha-reality. Later some Shinto scholars, as we saw, held that the Japanese kami are really the "original essence" and the various Bud-

dhas are the reflections of this. And there was a tendency to regard one particular kami, such as Heavenly Center Lord Kami, the first kami to be generated in the mythological account, as the supreme original kami who existed before the creation of the world. But today Shinto leaders reject any notion of a supreme creator kami, affirming instead the independent dignity of each kami in the Shinto pantheon, still giving the central position, of course, to Amaterasu.

What holds it all together? Monotheistic religions have one absolute God, and monistic or nondualistic religions have some one principle that holds everything together in a unified whole. It is sometimes said that a polytheistic religion necessarily understands the world in a fragmented way, with the different aspects of the world under the domain of different gods. But Shintoists believe that the myriads of kami function together in complete harmony so there is no division of the cosmos against itself. The kami generate all life, growth, happiness, and creativity, also all suffering and destruction. The way of the kami is a dynamic cosmic harmony.

Shinto Perspectives on the World and on Humans

How can we make sense out of this world and our lives? Why are things so filled with confusion and violence? Questions about the meaning of life and the cause of evil and suffering have been felt by the Japanese long before atomic bombs exploded over Japanese cities. Buddhist views of the nature of the world and human existence are, of course, widely accepted by the Japanese. But the ancient Shinto tradition also has a particular vision of the world and of humans, a vision that even today forms part of the Japanese way of looking at human existence.

A World Replete with Kami   The world in its essence is good, pure, and beautiful, as we learn from the myths and from the unsystematized traditions.

This is because the kami are good, pure, and beautiful, and the world originated from them. The Shinto myths of the creation of the world really do not tell how the world was created; rather they tell how the kami of everything in the world came into existence, and that is equivalent to the origination of the things themselves. We are told how the kami of the mountains were born, how the kami of forests came into existence, and how the kami of the sun, moon, and storm were engendered. In this vision there is no such thing as neutral matter that makes up the world; all operates in the will and activity of the various kami.

The main cosmology assumed in the early myths is a vertical, three-layered one, consisting of the Plain of High Heaven, the Manifest World, and the World of Darkness. The Plain of High Heaven is the locale of the spontaneous generation of the first series of kami, but how the Plain of High Heaven itself originated is not told. The unformed world is described as "resembling floating oil and drifting like jellyfish," and some of the kami were born from reed-like shoots that sprouted from the floating chaos.

The beginnings of the Manifest World came when Izanagi and Izanami, from the Floating Bridge of Heaven, stirred the brine below with their Heavenly Jeweled Spear and, when they lifted the spear, the brine dripping from it heaped up and formed an island. Descending to the island, they had sexual intercourse and bore as kami-children the Great Eight-Island Land (Japan) and then the other lands and the various kami of all other things. Even when Izanagi died after giving birth to the kami of fire, more kami came into existence from her vomit, feces, and urine—all these things are highly charged with kami power.

The overall sense we get from the myths of creation is that the whole world is replete with kami essence, symbolized by the phrase, "800 myriads of kami." This is a kami-saturated cosmos, for all the kami are immanent within the world. There is no such thing as nature in distinction from the sacred power, as is the case in monotheistic religions. An early poem from the *Manyoshu* expresses this feeling of kami presence within nature:

> Lo! There towers the lofty peak of Fuji
> From between Kai and wave-washed Suruga.
> The clouds of heaven dare not cross it,
> Nor the birds of the air soar above it.
> The snows quench the burning fires,
> The fires consume the falling snow.
> It baffles the tongue, it cannot be named,
> It is a god [kami] mysterious.
> The lake called Se is embosomed in it,
> The river we cross, the Fuji, is its torrent.
> In the Land of Yamato, the Land of the Rising Sun,
> It is our treasure, our tutelary god.
> It never tires our eyes to look up
> To the lofty peak of Fuji! [1]

Lofty, snow-covered Mt. Fuji is a silent kami presence providing beauty, mystery, and a treasure of blessing for the land of Yamato.

Furthermore, the world gradually progresses from chaos to order, from confusion and conflict to harmony and unity, as the kami engender the whole world and then bring it all into peaceful functioning under kami rule. All things, organic and inorganic, fit together in this divine harmony—humans, animals, mountains, rivers, forests, and so forth. The whole universe is essentially a sacred community of living beings, all together contributing to the development of inexhaustible kami power. This-worldly values are not negated in Shinto, for there is no need to transcend the Manifest World for a different kind of world. This world—the only world for humans—is inherently good, pure, and beautiful.

Humans as Children of the Kami   Unlike the creation stories of the Abrahamic religions, the creation of humans does not receive special attention in the Japanese myths. Humans are "children of the kami," just like the mountains, rivers, animals, and all the rest. There really is no sharp line separating humans from kami, for in a sense all humans have the kami nature. After death humans can be thought of as kami, though this term is usually reserved for great and important ancestors. Since humans received life from the kami, they have that kami essence within themselves. They are originally pure and clean.

Shinto: Nature and Ancestor Spirits

The meaning and purpose of life are implied in the truth that humans are children of the kami. Owing life to the kami, humans should show gratitude by contributing to the continuing evolution of the kami-based world.

Reality of Human Existence: Pollution and Failure Why do we fail to live in harmony and happiness? For all its optimism, the Shinto perspective does know of human failure and inadequacy. Although this does not stem from the essence of human nature, it still is real and often felt in our lives. Where does it come from?

The Shinto tradition is realistic about life in this good and beautiful world. The myths of origins describe how the world evolved slowly from chaos, as even the originating kami experienced failure and suffering in the process of generating this world and humans within it. Izanagi and Izanami failed in their first attempt at producing kami-land offspring, giving birth to a leech-child because of a ritual failure when Izanami spoke before Izanagi. And the dark specter of death and the World of Darkness rose up when Izanami died amid vomit and feces and descended to the underworld, where she was seen by Izanagi with maggots squirming around her body amid great pollution. Failure and death, it appears, are bound up with the generation of life.

As the world evolves through kami-generation, a persistent theme in the myths is the unruliness of many aspects of the world. This is symbolized by Susanoo, the storm-kami brother of Amaterasu. Whereas Amaterasu represents the purity and sovereignty of the sun, Susanoo rages against her, plays dirty tricks, and instigates Amaterasu's withdrawal into a cave, which brings about a disastrous darkness over the whole world. The kami of the Plain of High Heaven depose Susanoo—to, of all places, the Central Land of the Reed Plains (the human world, specifically Japan), where he and his descendants continue their unruly ways and are only gradually pacified so that finally Amaterasu's grandson Ninigi can descend to inaugurate kami-rule on earth. The world evolves toward peace and harmony—but unruliness, failure, suffering, and death are always present in the process.

To get a picture of the realistic Shinto view of human existence, we can turn to the ancient ritual prayers (**Norito**), to the prayer for the great exorcism to be celebrated on the last day of the sixth month, to purify the whole nation from defilements. Included in the prayer is this statement illustrating human existence in a realistic way:

> The various sins perpetrated and committed
> By the heavenly ever-increasing people to come into existence
> In this land which he [Grandson of Amaterasu] is to rule tranquilly as a peaceful land:
> First, the heavenly sins:
> Breaking down the ridges,
> Covering up the ditches,
> Releasing the irrigation sluices,
> Double planting,
> Setting up stakes,
> Skinning alive, skinning backwards,
> Defecation—
> Many sins [such as these] are distinguished and called the heavenly sins.

> The earthly sins:
> Cutting living flesh, cutting dead flesh,
> White leprosy, skin excrescences,
> The sin of violating one's own mother,
> The sin of violating one's own child,
> The sin of violating a mother and her child,
> The sin of violating a child and her mother,
> The sin of transgression with animals,
> Woes from creeping insects,
> Woes from the deities of on high,
> Woes from the birds of on high,
> Killing animals, the sin of witchcraft—
> Many sins [such as these] shall appear.[2]

This interesting listing of the various offenses among the descendants of the heavenly kami (that is, the nobles and officials of the land) seems to indicate that people have always been the same: greedy, selfish, unruly, and thoughtless of others. That's just the way humans are—and that's why, of course, the Great Purification ritual was necessary twice every year.

But the Shinto view does not find evil and offense as something inborn in human nature. This listing of offenses is realistic, but there is no idea here of some original, innate sinfulness. Shinto texts do talk of offense or sin, but the word for this, *tsumi*, suggests defilement or **pollution** (*kegare*), as well as sickness, error, and disaster. These offenses are harmful because they pollute the community, and pollution stands in the way of life, harmony, and happiness. Since the kami are pure, they dislike impure deeds and, thus, our pollution hinders the flow of blessing and life from the kami.

There are some suggestions in Shinto tradition that even evil happenings stem from the kami, that is, the evil and violent kami. When Izanagi fled from the World of Darkness, he brought pollutions with him, and from these pollutions were born the Kami of Great Evils. To counteract this evil, the Kami of Great Good were also born at the same time. Some Shinto thinkers have interpreted these kami as the origin of all evil and all good events in the world. The great Shintoist Motoori Norinaga explained it like this:

> All things in life—great and small, their very existence in the universe, even man himself and his actions—are due to the spirits of the gods [kami] and their dispositions of things. In general, there are various kinds of gods—noble, mean, good, bad, right, and wrong. So it is that things in life are not always lucky and good: they are mixed with the bad and the unfortunate. Internecine

wars break out occasionally and events not in the interest of the world or of mankind take place. Not infrequently, good or bad fortune befalls a man contrary to the principles of justice. Such things are the acts of the evil deities. The evil deities are those who do all manner of evil, moved by the spirit of the deity Mag-atsubi who was born of the pollution of the land of death, of which the God Izanagi had cleansed himself. When such evil deities flourish and are unchecked, there are times when even the protective powers of the shining deities prove inadequate. This has been true since the Divine Age.[3]

Norinaga's reason for emphasizing this is to advocate the Shinto attitude of accepting evil and death as part of life without resorting to foreign teachings (as in Buddhism and Christianity) that deny death by hoping for some kind of life after death. There is nothing sadder than death, Norinaga noted; but the authentic human emotion, knowing that death is caused by evil kami, is to weep and mourn, respecting and pacifying the malevolent kami. Other Shinto thinkers like Hirata Atsutane (1776–1843) have held that the Kami of Great Evils are those who hate pollution and, therefore, become violent and rough when there are pollutions and wrongdoing. In this view, kami do not originate evil, but they do become rough and violent when humans commit defilements and pollution.

The Shinto tradition sees human nature as originally pure but also imperfect and limited. Humans are not at war with kami, there is no fall into sin, and evil is not a cosmic force overpowering us. But evil and pollution are accumulated in the ordinary course of living, like dirt and dust. Since humans are finite and imperfect, they do sometimes act with a black heart rather than with a bright pure heart; they make errors and mistakes, bringing pollution and shame upon themselves, hindering the flow of life and happiness from the kami. These pollutions affect not only the individual but also the whole community, for relation to the kami is always a social affair, and almost all offenses are social offenses.

Consequently, what humans need to move toward better and fuller life is the path of purification.

Shinto Path of Purification

A Pure and Bright Heart   How can we start living the life that is *real*? Where do we find sacred power to give meaning and goodness in life? The Shinto tradition has not worked out theories of how people become transformed

and in harmony with the kami. Rather it is in myths, rituals, and poems that we understand the path of **purification**. The primordial model for purification is Izanagi, who was polluted when he visited Izanami in the world of darkness. He bathed in a stream, washing his body with water and, thus, cleansing the pollution from himself. In a certain sense, all pollution originates in the world of darkness, and people repeat Izanagi's act of purification every time they purify themselves with water or by other means.

Something of a theory of how pollution is done away with is found in the Great Purification Ritual of the sixth month. According to the *Norito* (ancient prayers), this is a national, communal purification to cleanse all Japan from pollution. In this ritual the defilements of the nobles and officials are transferred to narrow pieces of wood and sedge reeds, which are then thrown into the river and carried out to the sea. When this exorcism is performed, the liturgy says, the kami of the various river shoals and the kami of the ocean depths cooperate in carrying the pollution from the river to the sea and to the distant ocean depth. Then the kami of the ocean depths swallow the pollution and blow it away to the world of darkness from which it originally came. Then,

> The deity called Haya-sasura-hime,
>   Who dwells in the land of Hades, the underworld,
> Will wander off with them and lose them.
> When she thus loses them,
>   Beginning with the many officials serving in the Emperor's court,
>   In the four quarters under the heavens,
>   Beginning from today,
>   Each and every sin will be gone.[4]

Pollution comes from the world of darkness, and the kami assist in cleansing the world by returning pollution to the world of darkness.

But Shinto teaches that outward purification of the body and community should be accompanied by inner purification, a cleansing of the heart that restores it to its original uprightness. Very frequently in imperial edicts, poems, and other Shinto literature, terms like "the bright and pure heart" or "the honest and sincere heart" are used. The Shinto scholar Kitabatake Chikafusa (1293–1354) quoted a kami oracle that called on the people to prepare themselves purely and fairly with a bright, red heart and not a dirty, black heart, and he explained that the true way of purity consists in discarding one's own desires and keeping oneself lucid and clear in any situation, just as a mirror reflects objects—alluding to the bright mirror of Amaterasu, the sun kami, that she transmitted to her grandson Ninigi when she commissioned him to descend and establish kami rule on earth.[5]

Dedication to the Kami   Purification of the body and a bright and pure heart are required before coming into the presence of the kami. Further transformation comes from worshiping the kami through rituals of dedication, as people offer sprigs of the sacred sasaki tree and other offerings, present music and dance, and read the solemn prayers. The prayers are permeated with praise of the kami, petitions for protection and blessing, dedication to the will of the kami, and vows to live an upright, pure life.

Shinto believers do not try to formulate a theory of what happens when one comes into contact with the kami. But as one approaches the kami, the inner heart changes, bringing a sense of awe and reverence and a strong feeling of appreciation and gratitude. In and through these forms of worship of the kami, people are helped to regain their original purity and brightness and to live life in reverence for the kami. Fellowship with the kami helps one discover the inexhaustible sacred life that has its source in them, for renewal and transformation, enabling one to contribute to the continuing evolution of the kami-based world.

The need for transformation extends to the family and the community as well, and so the path provides family rituals as well as communal festivals. The family rituals serve especially to bond the family together with the ancestors, as people renew their sense of gratitude to the ancestors for giving life, protection, and blessing; and they resolve to realize their hopes and ideals by passing love and care to their descendants. Many of the rituals of worshiping the ancestors are Buddhist rituals, but reverence and gratitude to the ancestors and the continued transformation of the family through their blessings is certainly also a central Shinto concern. Festivals also have a transformative effect on the community, for these are sacred times when the whole community purifies itself and renews its life and harmony by joyful communion with the kami.

So the path of transformation begins with purification of the physical world and of the inner heart, and it leads to renewal of individual and communal life in harmony with the kami, the source of all goodness and blessing.

ULTIMATE REALITY AND THE PATH IN JAPANESE BUDDHISM

Universal Buddha-Nature

The perspective of Mahayana Buddhism plays an important role in Japanese thinking about ultimate reality. The ideas of the Dharma Body of the Buddha and emptiness (*shunyata*) are central, and Japanese thinkers reinforced the Mahayana nondualistic interpretation of reality: samsara is nirvana. In a series of writings, Dogen, for example, argued forcefully that there is a universal Buddha-nature. Whereas Mahayana scriptures had said that all beings have Buddha-nature, Dogen wrote that all beings *are* Buddha-nature. Thus, Buddha-nature is not some unchanging entity beyond the world but it is precisely inseparable from the transiency common to all beings. In fact, Dogen wrote, impermanence and even birth-and-death—the conditioned character common to all beings—are Buddha-nature. In this way Dogen pushed the Mahayana teaching that samsara is nirvana to a radical level of understanding.

One tendency in Mahayana Buddhism, to elevate a particular Buddha toward ultimate status, may be seen in some of the Japanese sects. For Pure Land Buddhists of Shinran's school, Amida is the supreme Buddha for this age, the only saving power available; and his Pure Land paradise is almost identified with nirvana itself. For Shinran, Amida is not just one Buddha among others, limited to his period of enlightenment ten kalpas ago. Rather, he is the eternal Buddha, the formless Dharma Body that took form to manifest his essential nature, making his eternal compassion and wisdom available for the salvation of living beings.

Tantric Buddhism in Japan, that is, Kukai's Shingon school, elevated Mahavairochana, the Sun Buddha (*Dainichi*, Great Sun), to the status of the all-encompassing Buddha reality whose body is the whole universe. Shingon thinks of Mahavairochana as the eternal Dharma Body of the Buddha. But whereas the Dharma Body was traditionally thought of as formless and totally beyond conceptualization, Mahavairochana's attributes are represented in the Buddhas and gods of the universe. Mahavairochana transcends the universe, yet this material universe is his body. Kukai wrote, "The Buddha Dharma is nowhere remote. It is in our mind; it is close to us. Suchness is nowhere external. If not within our body, where can it be found?"[6] So the

At Sanjusangendo Temple in Kyoto, one thousand and one statues of the thousand-armed bodhisattva Kannon (Avalokiteshvara) provide a strong sense of sacred presence.

Whereas Shinto teaches that nature and humans are originally bright and pure, Japanese Buddhists stressed, for example, the notion of "original enlightenment" (*hongaku*), the innate enlightenment or Buddha-nature that all people, and even plants and animals, possess. This means that there is a Buddha quality about life and nature—a quality that was aesthetically explored in poetry, painting, and other arts. But, as Shinto holds that pollution and impurity obscure the original nature, Japanese Buddhists teach that original enlightenment is obscured by ignorance and desire. As Kukai said, "All sentient beings are innate bodhisattvas; but they have been bound by defilements of greed, hatred, and delusion."[7]

Dharma Body is the ultimate pantheistic-monotheistic reality with personality, wisdom, and compassion, who is found in the world and in our mind.

For the Nichiren Buddhists of Japan, it is the *Lotus Sutra* that embodies all the power and perfection of Buddhahood. Shakyamuni Buddha is the eternal reality, of whom all other Buddhas are emanations. But the absolute truth of Shakyamuni Buddha and the whole universe is embodied in the **Daimoku**, the sacred title of the *Lotus Sutra* that is chanted in the formula "Namu myoho rengekyo" (Praise to the wondrous truth of the *Lotus Sutra*).

Japanese Buddhist Perspectives on Human Existence

Though Japanese culture is permeated with the Shinto sense for the world and human nature, Japanese people have also been deeply influenced by the perspective of Buddhism on topics of the universal Buddha-nature, impermanence, no-self, conditioned arising, and karma. This perspective operates for many people in a complementarity (or in a certain tension) with the Shinto perspective.

Some schools of Japanese Buddhism, as we saw, have taken over the notion of the "three ages of the Dharma" from China, holding that we are now living in the third, totally degenerate age of this world cycle. Consequently, life in the world is depicted as corrupt and degenerate, and the purgatories and hells awaiting after death are described or painted in pictures with gory details. Other schools resist such a gloomy picture of human existence. But all agree on the basic Buddhist perspective that it is ignorance and clinging that cause suffering and continued samsaric existence.

Japanese writers have provided striking portrayals in literature of this human problem. For example, *The Spider's Thread*, a short story by Akutagawa Ryunosuke, tells how one day the celestial Buddha, sauntering by the lotus pond of paradise, happened to look down through the crystal water and saw hell far below. Among the sinners squirming on the bottom of hell he spotted Kandata, a great murderer and robber. The Buddha remembered that, among his innumerable crimes, Kandata had one good deed to his credit: One day he had spared a spider's life rather than step on it. Thinking he might deliver him from hell, the Buddha took some silvery thread from a spider of paradise and let it down to the bottom of hell. Below, Kandata chanced to see the thread and, wearied though he was from all the torments, began to climb with all his might to get out of hell. He was having a fair amount of success and began to think he might even climb to paradise, although hell is myriads of miles removed. Finally he stopped to rest, but now he noticed to his horror that countless other sinners were climbing eagerly after him, like a procession of ants. How could this slender spider thread support these hundreds and thousands of sinners without breaking? He cried to them that this thread was his and they should get off. At that moment, the thread, which had shown no signs of breaking, snapped above Kandata and he fell headlong back into the Pool of Blood at the bottom of hell.

Selfish struggle and desire are common human tendencies, but they do not lead to liberation.

Buddhist Paths of Transformation in Japan

Many, if not most, Japanese follow in some degree the Mahayana Buddhist paths of transformation, either exclusively or together with the Shinto path. Buddhists in Japan have taken over the full path from India and China, and they have given it characteristic Japanese accents. We find these accents in the path as taught, for example, in Shingon, Pure Land, Nichiren, and Zen, and carried over into some New Religions of today.

Resonating to the concrete, this-worldly emphasis of Japanese culture, one strand of the Buddhist path in Japan has long focused on the possibility of achieving Buddhahood in this very body, this very existence. Kukai, founder of Shingon, provided particular emphasis on this goal, as he taught the esoteric (Tantric) form of Buddhism, but these basic perspectives came to permeate other schools of Japanese Buddhism as well. The whole universe is really the body of the great cosmic Buddha, Mahavairochana or Dainichi (Great Sun), Kukai taught. Since our real nature is the great Buddha, it is possible by meditation and ritual action to realize one's Buddhahood. The body, speech, and mind of Mahavairochana—the Three Mysteries— permeate the whole cosmos. But these three mysteries are innate to all living beings and, therefore, it is possible through meditation and ritual to integrate the microcosmic activities of our body, speech, and mind into the Body, Speech, and Mind of Mahavairochana. This is done in meditation by symbolic ritual acts of body, such as sitting in meditation and use of hand gestures (mudras); by recitation of mantras, symbols of Mahavairochana's cosmic speech; and by rituals of the mind involving thinking, imagining, and visualizing, focusing especially on symbolic paintings of the sacred cosmos (mandalas). Kukai wrote:

> If there is a Shingon student who reflects well upon the meaning of the Three Mysteries, makes mudras, recites mantras, and allows his mind to abide in the state of samadhi [meditative trance], then, through grace, his three mysteries will be united with the Three Mysteries [of Mahavairochana]; thus, the great perfection of his religious discipline will be realized. . . . If there is a man who whole-heartedly disciplines himself day and night according to the prescribed methods of discipline, he will obtain in his corporeal existence the Five Supernatural Powers. And if he keeps training himself, he will, without abandoning his body, advance to the stage of the Buddha. The details are as explained in the sutras. For this reason it is said, "When the grace of the Three Mysteries is retained, [our inborn three mysteries will] quickly be manifested." The expression "the grace . . . is retained" indicates great compassion on the part of the Tathagata and faith on the part of sentient beings. The compassion of the Buddha pouring forth on the heart of sentient beings, like the rays of the sun on water, is called *ka* [adding], and the heart of sentient beings which keeps hold of the compassion of the Buddha, as water retains the rays of the sun, is called *ji* [retaining]. If the devotee understands this principle thoroughly and devotes himself to the practice of samadhi [meditation], his three mysteries will be united with the Three Mysteries, and therefore in his present existence, he will quickly manifest his inherent three mysteries.[8]

Kukai's words reflect the characteristic Japanese Buddhist double emphasis on the compassion or power of the Buddha and on faith and discipline on the part of the meditator. These two emphases are reflected, in somewhat different configurations, in the Pure Land and Zen paths of transformation.

One strand of the path takes over the Chinese Pure Land tradition of depending on the power of Amida Buddha. Honen, considered the real founder of the Pure Land movement in Japan, felt deeply that humankind had entered into the third age of the Dharma, the "latter end of the Dharma," the period of hopeless degeneracy. In this situation, it is no longer possible to follow the path of meditation and discipline and reach enlightenment, so the only hope is to rely on the power of Amida Buddha, on the basis of Amida's original vows to save all those who have faith in him and call on his name. The power of Amida is made available through his name, so it is by repeating the *Nembutsu,* that is, the phrase "Namu Amida Butsu" (Praise to Amida Buddha), that the mind becomes fixed on Amida and, at death, one is reborn in the Pure Land paradise. Honen taught:

> The method of final salvation that I have propounded is neither a sort of meditation, such as has been practiced by many scholars in China and Japan, nor is it a repetition of the Buddha's name by those who have studied and understood the deep meaning of it. It is nothing but the mere repetition of the *"Namu Amida Butsu,"* without a doubt of His mercy, whereby one may be born into the Land of Perfect Bliss.[9]

Shinran, a disciple of Honen, articulated this emphasis on help from Amida into a full theology of salvation by grace and faith. If we have feelings of merit, Shinran felt, these can stand in the way of total dependence on Amida's saving grace. Likewise, if we feel we first need strong faith and goodness before Amida helps us, we will despair. Rather, Shinran taught, even before we are moved to recite Amida's name, we are already embraced by Amida's saving light from which we will not be forsaken. Faith is really a gift from Amida, transforming our minds and giving hope and confidence of salvation. It matters not whether one is saint or sinner—Amida's original vow saves all. Honen had taught that since Amida can save even an evil person, surely he can easily save a good person. To make his point effectively, Shinran turned this saying around: "Even a good person can attain birth in the Pure Land, so it goes without saying that an evil person will." And he explained:

> This is because a person who relies on the good that he does through self-power fails to entrust himself wholeheartedly to Other Power and therefore is not in accord with Amida's Primal Vow, but when he abandons his attachment to self-power and entrusts himself totally to Other Power, he will realize birth in the Pure Land.[10]

Self-confidence and reliance on "self-power" (*jiriki*) are grand illusions, for in this degenerate age good deeds are impossible for mortal beings. In place of such pride and illusion, Shinran urged complete reliance on the "other power" (*tariki*) of Amida, for it is through the Buddha's act of compassion and his gift that faith arises in our hearts, and that is none other than attaining the Buddha-nature.

At the moment that faith arises in the mind, according to Shinran, one has total assurance of salvation, for one has entered into the company of the assured, to remain in this state of nonretrogression until one is born into the Pure Land paradise. So the moment of faith brings salvation now, determining once and for all the destiny of the individual and thus assuring salvation. Thus, the life of faith is marked by joy, gratitude, and thankfulness.

In contrast to the "other power" emphasis of Pure Land, Zen masters in Japan have self-consciously cultivated an approach to transformation that relies on one's own powers and abilities to see the Buddha-nature within. The Japanese Zen master Dogen complained that many people fall back on the excuse that the world is in the degenerate third age of the Dharma and, therefore, they cannot follow the Buddhist discipline but need an easier path. But that is a misunderstanding of the Buddhist teaching, said Dogen; rather, every human being has the capacity to follow the Dharma, and any person at any time can attain enlightenment.[11] There is no need to fall back on the "easy path," relying on other power and looking to future rebirth in the faraway Pure Land paradise. The Buddha is our own mind; the Pure Land is here this very instant. Practicing zazen in accordance with the Buddha's teaching will invariably bring to actualization the innate capacity for enlightenment.

Like Chan in China, Japanese Zen teaches a path of transformation that is without goal or purpose. There is no goal to be attained, no purpose to strive for. Goal, purpose, future reward, striving for—all such concepts suggest that the Buddha-nature is something other than the immediate here-and-now existence. All such concepts of the mind need to be discarded, for they only stand in the way of direct seeing. Just sit quietly and do nothing, Dogen counseled, emptying the mind and seeing directly into your own nature. This is to realize the pure mind of Buddhahood and to experience awakening—satori. There is no difference between the practice of meditation and enlightenment itself; doing zazen is itself experiencing enlightenment.

Dogen's school of Zen, the Soto school, teaches the path toward a "gradual enlightenment," a deepening experience of awakening arising from daily zazen. The Rinzai school has traditionally practiced the path with a view toward "sudden enlightenment," an intense experience of awakening that comes suddenly after much practice and floods the consciousness. To help disciples toward the experience, Rinzai masters make use of the koan, a question or riddle often taken from the sayings of the early Chinese Chan masters, as we saw in our discussion of Chinese Chan Buddhism. For example, a favorite koan tells how Zhaozhou, when asked about the Buddha-nature of a dog, replied simply: "Wu" (nothingness). One koan often used in Japan stems from Japanese master Hakuin: "Listen to the Sound of the Single Hand." Hakuin explained: "What is the Sound of the Single Hand? When you clap together both hands a sharp sound is heard; when you raise the one hand there is neither sound nor smell."[12] The disciple meditates on the koan, striving to understand it and explain it in daily interviews with the master. Since the koan cannot be answered by ordinary rational, or logical thinking, gradually the conceptual operation of the mind breaks down, and the disciple may experience the "great doubt" and the "great death," which culminates in the "great enlightenment," in Master Hakuin's words.

> If you take up one koan and investigate it unceasingly your mind will die and your will will be destroyed. It is as though a vast, empty abyss lay before you, with no place to set your hands and feet. You face death and your bosom feels as though it were afire. Then suddenly you are one with the koan, and both body and mind are cast off. This is known as the time when the hands are released over the abyss. Then when suddenly you return to life, there is the great joy of one who drinks the water and knows for himself whether it is hot or cold. This is known as rebirth in the Pure Land. This is known as seeing into one's own nature.[13]

Whether through gradual enlightenment or sudden enlightenment, the Zen path leads to the transformation of life that results from seeing the "suchness" of reality, the Buddha quality that is inherent in every moment of existence.

So we see that, with the Mahayana emphasis on realizing Buddhahood, Japanese Buddhists shaped paths that emphasize either "other power" or one's own discipline and meditation—with many different shadings of these possibilities. We should remember that many Japanese have retained a sense of the basic identity of kami and Buddhas and that the Confucian path of transformation has also remained influential for many Japanese. So it is typical in Japan not to remain strictly within the confines of the Shinto path or the Buddhist path but also to integrate elements of Shinto, Buddhism, and Confucianism in a "way" (*michi*) of self-cultivation. Examples of such syntheses abound, such as the way of the warrior (bushido) or the way of the mountain priests. Even though most of the "New Religions" tend to fall into either the Shinto or the Buddhist tradition, the way as practiced in many of them combines elements from Shinto, Buddhism, Confucianism, and folk traditions. Finally, we might mention that for some Japanese even the practice of the traditional arts, such as poetry, Noh drama, the tea ceremony, and flower arranging, is filled with disciplines and rituals and is considered a "way" of self-transformation.

DISCUSSION QUESTIONS

1 Describe the origin of the kami, according to the Japanese mythology. Explain Motoori Norinaga's view of the nature of kami.

2 Describe the generation of the world through Izanagi and Izanami. What does it mean to say this is a "kami-saturated" cosmos?

3 What does it mean to say humans are "children of the kami"? Why are there evil and suffering in the world, in the Shinto view?

4 What is the importance of "purification" in the Shinto path of transformation? Describe the Great Purification ritual and its meaning.

5 What is meant by a "pure and bright heart"? How does dedication to the kami bring inner transformation?

6 What does the Buddhist idea of the Three Ages of the Dharma imply about the nature of human existence?

7 Explain Kukai's view of the use of the Three Mysteries in the path of transformation.

8 What is the double emphasis in the Japanese Buddhist path of transformation, as exemplified in Pure Land and Zen?

9 Explain the Pure Land path of transformation, as taught by Honen and Shinran.

10 What are meant by "gradual enlightenment" and "sudden enlightenment" in the Zen school? What is a koan and how is it used?

Chapter 16

Ritual Practices and the Good Life in Japan

JAPANESE RITUAL PRACTICES

How can we find new power for life? How can we find meaning in the commonplace events of daily existence? Answers to questions like these are given through ritual worship and sacred times in Japan as elsewhere. Japanese religion is practical more than theoretical. Colorful ceremonies, exuberant sacred dances, quiet meditation sessions, pilgrimages to sacred mountains—more than articulating doctrines and beliefs, Japanese traditionally have *performed* their religion.

Rituals and ceremonies from the Confucian and Daoist traditions are intertwined in varying degrees in Japanese religious life. But most characteristic of Japan are the specifically Shinto practices of worshiping the kami and Buddhist worship of Buddhas and rituals of meditation. For many Japanese these are not exclusive practices. For example, traditional families often have both a *kamidana* (altar for the kami) and a **butsudan** (altar for the Buddha) in their home, with appropriate daily rituals performed at both.

Ritual in the Rhythm of Daily Life

Worshiping the Kami Because all life, growth, and goodness come from communion with the kami, the Japanese have from ancient times cultivated the art of worshiping the kami, based on the patterns given in the mythology. When, for example, Amaterasu, the sun kami, withdrew into a cave, all the myriads of kami celebrated a **matsuri** (festival) to please her and entice her to come out of the cave. Shinto worship and festivals today are patterned after that event. The main ingredients of worshiping the kami are purification, an attitude of respect and gratitude, presenting offerings, and saying prayers—accompanied, of course, with a dedication of one's life in harmony with the will of the kami.

Actually, because all life is lived in communion with the kami, even ordinary daily life is thought of as matsuri, service to the kami. But it is important to maintain harmony and unity with the kami by specific rituals of worship growing out of a sincere heart, in a sacred time and a setting of purity.

Where does one worship? Wherever the presence of kami is felt it is appropriate to worship them. Primarily this will be at home, at the shrines, on neighborhood streets during community festivals, and, of course, in beautiful places of nature.

Devout Japanese often begin the day by worshiping the kami at the kamidana in the central room of the home, a high shelf with a miniature shrine containing talismans of the kami, with a rope stretched over the shrine. The ritual of worship is very simple. The worshiper washes the hands and rinses the mouth and then places fresh offerings before the kami, consisting of clean rice, water, and salt. On special occasions, rice cakes, sea fish, fowl, seaweed, vegetables, or fruit might also be offered. Facing the shrine, a slight bow is made, followed by two deep bows. A brief prayer may be offered audibly or silently. Then the worship is ended with two deep bows, clapping the hands together twice, another deep bow, and a slight bow. Later, the special food offerings may be served at mealtime, when a special act of reverence would again be made.

On many special occasions, individuals or families go to a public **shrine (jinja)** to worship the kami, and the general attitude of worship is the same as at home. Proceeding on foot, the worshipers pass through the first **torii** (shrine gate) with a sense of entering sacred space. At the ablution pavilion, they purify their mouth and hands with water from a wooden dipper. Standing in front of the worship hall, they jangle a bell, toss a coin into the offering box, and then perform the bows, hand claps, and prayers. On occasions of special significance, such as starting a new business venture or entering college, they may go inside the worship hall with a priest for a more formal ritual before the kami, with offerings and a prayer. Before leaving the shrine they may obtain a printed oracle that tells what fortune or misfortune lies ahead, and after reading these they usually twist them around a twig of a tree or some other convenient object, as a petition to the kami for fulfillment (or warding off, if a misfortune is predicted). They leave the shrine with an inexpressible feeling of peace and renewal.

Some of the most joyous and renewing times come when the whole community shares in a Shinto festival. It is said that many people in Japan today are secular, and perhaps not a large percentage would call themselves Shinto believers. But when a community festival comes along, many of these people join in. Communal worship at a shrine typically includes four major movements: purification, presentation of offerings, intoning of prayers, and communal participation.

In preparation for a festival, the priests do many acts of purification, cleaning the shrine and abstaining from forbidden acts. The people also purify themselves with water upon entering the shrine. The festival typically begins with the priests appearing in their special garments, and one of them performs a formal purification, waving a purification wand with sweeping arm movements and sprinkling salt.

As all bow deeply, the chief priest opens the doors of the inner sanctuary (where the symbol of the kami is kept) to the accompaniment of music and a special "oo-ing" sound. Then the special food offerings, having been ceremonially prepared and purified and arranged on trays with exquisite aesthetic taste, are passed from one priest to another until they are placed before the kami. The food items typically consist of rice, rice wine, salt, vegetables, seafood, and fruit. There may also be other special offerings of silk, money, or other items from the Association of Shinto Shrines or, in the case of some shrines, from the Imperial Household.

With the offerings in place, the priest recites the ancient prayers (*Norito*) in a dignified, high, chanting voice. The prayers thank the kami for benefits over the past year, asking for continued health and prosperity. After the prayers, the offerings are removed, later to be consumed

The Gion Festival held during July in Kyoto is one of the most famous festivals in Japan. Originating in the ninth century to seek divine protection against an epidemic, the festival features many large floats pulled through the main streets of the city.

by the priests and their families, and the chief priest closes the doors to the inner sanctuary, accompanied by the "oo-ing" sound.

At this point the fourth movement of the matsuri begins, the communal participation. Laypeople may come forward to make offerings and receive a sip of the wine offered previously to the kami. Often there will be a dance (kagura) performed by the young shrine maidens, both solemn and colorful, according to the tradition of the local shrine. Another special dance is the ancient Chinese court dance called *bugaku*. In addition, there will usually be a variety of other entertainment presented at the festival, such as horse races, archery, folk dancing, Japanese wrestling (sumo), pageants, and processions—all designed to entertain the kami and the human participants as well. A special part of local shrine festivals is the procession of the palanquin with the kami-symbol through the streets of the community. These processions can be solemn, but nowadays one may see sturdy young men carry the palanquin on their shoulders, zigzagging down the street shouting "*washo, washo*," under the watchful eyes of the shrine priests. Usually the people go to visit the kami; during the procession the kami comes to visit the people and bless the community with divine presence.

Buddhist Ritual Activities in Japan   Traditional homes also have a butsudan in the central room, a lacquered cabinet containing images of Buddhas and small containers for offerings. Offerings are made to the Buddhas, and prayers and sutras are recited in daily devotions. The butsudan also typically contains the wooden tablets representing the spirits of the family ancestors, so worshiping at the butsudan is at the same time venerating the ancestors, praying to them to ensure their continued blessing for the family.

Worship at Buddhist temples has a somewhat different character from that at Shinto shrines. Whereas shrines are usually simple and natural, without statues, in Buddhist temples there are usually elaborate altars and statues of Buddhas and bodhisattvas, the inner darkness of the ornate temple rooms illuminated with candles that reflect light off the gilded statues and decorations. Many villages and neighborhoods have parish Buddhist temples, where not only Buddhas but also the ashes of ancestors of parish families are enshrined. Often these parish temples have cemeteries where families erect memorial stones dedicated to the ancestors. As at the butsudan in the home, so also at the temple people make offerings and speak prayers and sutras

before the altars. Priests associated with these temples perform worship services, commemorative rituals, memorial rites, and the like, for their own needs and for the welfare of the laypeople. The temple cultic life is especially active, of course, during the major annual and seasonal festivals.

The ultimate purpose of Buddhist worship is to attain enlightenment and Buddhahood, but, as we have seen, the path toward the ultimate transformation is broad and can find expression in many types of ritual and worship. One prays before the Buddhas and ancestors to achieve ends such as the protection of the nation, success in life, healing of the sick, or repose for the dead. Whereas such acts of worship are directed toward immediate needs, we should remember that the power for these benefits comes from the wisdom and compassion of those beings who have achieved Buddhahood and who are believed, through various means, to lead their devotees toward that goal. Several of the Buddhas and bodhisattvas are widely worshiped for such benefits. Very popular is **Kannon** (the bodhisattva Avalokiteshvara), the "goddess of mercy," who provides help in almost any kind of need, such as conceiving a child, easy childbirth, safe travel, and much more. In times of sickness, people pray and recite scripture before a statue of Yakushi, the healing Buddha. And to request repose and merit for the dead, people pray before statues of Jizo, patron saint of the spirits of the dead, especially of dead children.

There are some Buddhist activities of worship that can be carried out by laypeople with little or no priestly help. Sometimes a group of laypeople will form their own association for the purpose of worshiping a particular Buddha, holding regular meetings in their homes during which they have simple services and social gatherings.

Japanese following the popular Pure Land and Nichiren traditions exemplify typical patterns of group worship, whether at home or temple, with or without priests participating. The Pure Land worship service includes the usual elements of Buddhist worship, but a special focus is on reciting the *Nembutsu*, "Namu Amida Butsu," for this is the formula by which the worshipers receive the merit and compassion of Amida Buddha. Worship might include chanting verses from Shinran's writings, reading Shinran's biography, listening to sermons, and discussing the teachings.

Buddhists following the Nichiren tradition, one of the most lively and populous of the various traditions in modern Japan, follow Nichiren's special design for worship, focusing on the *gohonzon* as the object of worship and using the daimoku chant. The gohonzon, as designed by Nichiren, is a kind of mandala without pictorial images; it is a scroll inscribed with names of leading Buddhas and bodhisattvas of the *Lotus Sutra*, with the sacred words of the daimoku chant at the center. This is the chief object of worship both in homes and in temples. The daimoku is the formula, "Namu myoho rengekyo" (Praise to the wonderful truth of the *Lotus Sutra*), which Nichiren considered to contain the universal Buddha nature. Nichiren worship, thus, consists of reciting the daimoku before a gohonzon, to the accompaniment of drums, with worshipers often fingering the particular Nichiren rosary of 108 beads. The worship is dramatic and intense and is felt to produce many spiritual benefits as well as benefits for everyday life. Modern Nichiren groups in Japan often include informal small group discussion sessions that provide opportunity for individuals to share their personal problems and receive Buddhist insight in dealing with them.

In contrast to the Pure Land and Nichiren forms, the characteristic Zen Buddhist meditation rituals are carried on primarily by Zen monks and nuns, although certain laypeople may also participate on occasion. Of course, priests of Zen temples perform the usual types of Buddhist worship for the benefit of the laypeople, but the distinctive Zen ritual discipline is meditation. The typical daily ritual in a Chan (Zen) monastery in China was discussed earlier (p. 259). Here let us look more closely at the actual practice of zazen, sitting in meditation. The simplicity of the meditation hall and rituals of sutra-chanting, bowing, and offering incense before a statue of the Buddha help set the atmosphere for the period of quiet sitting. Practitioners in the Soto tradition sit facing the wall; in the Rinzai tradition, the meditators face into the room, looking down to the floor in front. The basic ritual discipline is the art of sitting itself. From his manual for Zen meditation (Shobogenji), here is Master Dogen's famous description of how to sit:

> In the place where you regularly sit, spread out a thick mat and put a cushion on top of it. Sit in either the full cross-legged or half cross-legged position. For the full position, first place your right foot on your left thigh, and then place your left foot on your right thigh. For the half position, simply rest your left foot on your right thigh. Loosen your robes and belt, and arrange them in order. Next, put your right hand on your left foot, and

your left hand on your right palm, with thumb-tips touching. Then straighten your body and sit erect, without leaning to the left or right, forward or backward. See that your ears are in line with your shoulders and your nose in line with your navel. Press your tongue against the front of your palate, having teeth and lips shut. Keep your eyes always open. Breathe gently through the nose. After adjusting your posture, take a breath and exhale fully. Rock your body to the left and right. Settle down into a steady sitting position. Think of not thinking. How do you think of not thinking? Nonthinking. None other than this is the essential art of zazen.

During the meditation session, which may last thirty to forty minutes, one monk may walk slowly among the seated meditators carrying the long flat *keishaku* stick; when someone feels drowsy or unalert, he or she may bow toward the monk, who will then strike him or her sharply on the shoulders, an act of compassion to assist in meditation. In the Soto tradition, the meditator simply practices zazen and empties the mind, without effort, without purpose. In the Rinzai tradition, the meditator may work on such koans as "The sound of one hand clapping," "What was your face before you were born?" or simply "Mu!" (nothingness), allowing that koan to break through ordinary dualistic notions of self and object. Regular interviews with the master for testing and growing insight also form part of the meditation discipline and ritual.

Sacred Times in Japan

There are a great number of festivals in Japan, depending on the region and specific community, and these festivals may be predominantly Shinto or Buddhist, often containing elements from both traditions together with many local popular traditions. Probably the most highly ranked festivals are those at the Grand Shrines of Ise where Amaterasu is enshrined: the Spring Festival, the Autumn Festival, and especially the Niiname-sai (November 23–24), at which the emperor offers the first fruits of the grain harvest. The Niiname-sai is modeled on the ancient ceremony in which a newly enthroned emperor first offers the new food to Amaterasu and the other kami. Other important local Shinto festivals are widely attended by tourists, such as the Aoi Matsuri in Kyoto on May 15, involving a procession through the streets with ox-drawn carts, horses with golden saddles, and everything decorated with wisteria. Again, the Gion Festival in Kyoto in the middle of July presents a grand spectacle, with huge colorful palanquins from all the major shrines pulled through the streets by hundreds of devotees, to bring health to the whole city and to entertain the kami.

Among the universally celebrated festivals are some that no longer have specific religious significance, such as the Doll Festival (for girls) on March 3, Boys' Day on May 5 (now Children's Day, a national holiday), and the Star Festival on July 7. Of important religious significance are the Great Purification celebrated at local shrines on June 30 and also the spring and fall festivals for the tutelary kami. There is also the festival of the Buddha's birthday, celebrated in Japan on April 8, when temples perform a special ritual of pouring sweet tea over a statue of the infant Buddha, in memory of the story of Shakyamuni's birth when flower petals and sweet tea rained from the sky. More solemn than this festive springtime celebration is the observance marking the Buddha's attainment of enlightenment, generally held on December 8. At this time, Zen monasteries hold specially intensive training sessions over a seven-day period, culminating in all-night sitting until the dawn of December 8.

The **Obon Festival (Ullambana)**, celebrated in the middle of the seventh lunar month (today most Japanese observe it in the middle of July), is Buddhist inspired and related completely to the ancestors, like the similar festival in China discussed earlier. The spirits of the ancestors are welcomed in the home at the butsudan with special offerings, and the families visit the ancestral graves and clean the area and place new flowers. Although the festival has to do with the dead, it tends to be joyful, with the spirits warmly welcomed on the night of the thirteenth day of the month, entertained with colorful dances and singing, and then, after two days, sent off by fires to the graveyards. In some places lanterns are floated on a nearby river. Obon festivals often conclude with people dancing around a temporary tower holding singers and drummers. During the festival, Buddhist priests hold memorial services in temples and homes. Services remembering the dead and visits to the family graves also take place during the spring and autumn equinoxes (Higan-e); rituals include repenting of past sins and praying for enlightenment in the next life.

The New Year Festival, now almost universally observed at the beginning of January (the old lunar calendar has it in February), is the most vigorously celebrated festival of the year and the most important family event. Toward the end of December there is much bustle as workers leave the cities to journey back to the country to be with their families. Business and industry shut down for a number of days, and the perpetual smog over industrial cities even lifts a bit. Shrines perform a great purification to purify people of defilements from the previous year. Each family cleans and symbolically purifies the house, putting a pine branch on the outside gate and hanging a straw rope over the entrance. Special New Year foods are prepared, especially dried fish and o-mochi, a sticky rice cake. Offerings are made to the ancestors, the family eats, drinks, and relaxes together, and with midnight the cry goes up, "Akemashite omedeto gozaimasu!" (Happy New Year!). At Buddhist temples, at midnight, the temple gongs are struck 108 times, signifying the 108 kinds of blind passions that should be purged out in the coming year.

On New Year's Day people make their first visit of the New Year to the local shrine, wearing traditional kimonos, to begin the New Year with luck and happiness. Buddhist temples are also visited, but the bulk of the seventy million people who make the New Year visit go to Shinto shrines. Many buy new shrine symbols and paper to place in their household shrines, since the old ones have been used up in absorbing all the bad luck and illness in the past year. For the next few days there is general relaxing and visiting of family and friends. Gradually the festivities end, people journey back to the cities, and around January 15 in a bonfire celebration the New Year decorations are burned. So the people have purified the home and the community, renewed family bonds and contacts with the ancestors, visited the kami and Buddhas anew, and now they start off the new year with fresh vitality.

Besides these rituals and festivals there are still other opportunities for personal spiritual growth. People can go individually to the shrine and apologize to the kami for wrongdoing, or, for stronger penance, perform the ritual of the "hundredfold repentance"—walking between two stone markers one hundred times reciting repentance. Going on pilgrimages to special temples, shrines, sacred mountains, and the like is another well-used ritual of spiritual transformation. Since the Heian era (794–1185), there have been people who engaged in special training and practices on sacred mountains, combining Buddhist practices with local Shinto traditions, and these mountain priests (yamabushi) would serve as guides to pilgrims going on retreats to these mountains. Today there still are some Shinto organizations that continue the traditions of these earlier mountain ascetics, and there are in addition many formal and informal mountain pilgrimage groups. A popular Buddhist pilgrimage takes the devotee to eighty-eight special temples on the island of Shikoku, worshiping the main Buddhas enshrined in these temples. The main emphasis on the Shikoku pilgrimage is "walking with Saint Kukai," the holy man born in Shikoku who founded Shingon Buddhism in Japan and is widely believed to be alive yet today, walking with the pilgrims and helping those who need assistance. The pilgrimage is made by individuals, family groups, groups of friends, and even more formally organized pilgrimage groups.

Rituals of the Passages of Life

At the great moments of life passages or crises, many Japanese look especially to the assistance of guardian kami, whose protective arms enfold all their children. Unlike Western ideas of change and decay, the Shinto view is of life as a clear and pure river with endless change, freshness, and renewal. And so the main passages of life are dedicated to the kami for purification and renewal.

The kami are frequently invoked to assist couples who want to have a baby. In earlier times there were many avoidances associated with childbirth, an impure situation especially because of the blood involved. After a month the child is considered free from impurities and is taken to the shrine of the tutelary kami, to be dedicated to the kami who is affirmed as the source of life and protection. There are special events the family celebrates with the young child—on the first birthday, for example, or the first participation in the Doll Festival or Boys' Day. A special festival on November 15 is "Seven-Five-Three Festival"—for girls of seven and three and boys of five—when the children dress up in their best and visit the shrine.

The passage from childhood to adulthood is marked in a number of ways—for example, when a young man first participates in the local festival by helping to carry the portable shrine. For many Japanese youth, the "examination hell," which finally leads to entrance to a good university, is a critical passage in life, and there are visits to the kami for help in learning. Today, Japan has a national holiday on January 15 called "Adult Day," on which all twenty-year-olds are formally recognized as adults and show their gratitude by visiting a local shrine. This very modern tradi-

At a modern Shinto wedding ceremony, the bride and groom worship the kami.

tion is a good example of how Shinto has adapted its institutions to modern-day life.

Marriage is an important affair, joining not only two lives but also two families. Even in modern Westernized Japan, many families prefer to arrange marriages for their children, using a family friend as a "go-between," with, of course, considerable input from the young people about the prospective mate. Weddings traditionally occurred in the home, and the crucial ceremony was the ritual exchange of o-sake (rice wine) between the bride and groom. In modern times it has become customary to have the wedding ceremony at a shrine with very formal Japanese (or Western) dress. The couple sit before a priest in the presence of family and close friends. The priest waves the purification wand and offers prayers that they may be free of ill fortune and blessed by good things. And all present receive some o-sake as a sharing with the protective kami who have been invoked. If and when the new couple is able to build their own house, they will have a Shinto priest perform a purification ritual at the site, and there will also be a framework-raising ceremony to thank the kami and invoke their continued protection.

While Japanese turn to the kami during the changes in the flow of life, when death approaches their thoughts turn to Buddhist teachings, and most observe Buddhist funeral practices. In a sense, Shinto has to do with life, fertility, and growth; Buddhism in Japan has to do especially with death and the ancestral existence after death. So the funeral service is conducted by Buddhist priests, reciting Buddhist scriptures at the wake, in the funeral service, and at the cremation. A Buddhist posthumous name is given to the deceased and written on a memorial tablet, which is set up in front of the butsudan in the home. The family is in mourning for forty-nine days, after which the dead person is considered to be transformed into an ancestral spirit. After this, memorial masses are held on the anniversary days of the death, often ending with the thirty-third anniversary, when the deceased joins the more general generations of ancestors.

Healing and Medicine in Japan

The Japanese people have access to all the benefits of modern, scientific medicine. Still, various traditional forms of medicine and healing practices are widely popular in Japan. Like many societies, the Japanese practice a kind of medical pluralism. Western medicine is supplemented with two other healing traditions: kampo, which is the Japanese form of traditional Chinese medicine, and the healing practices offered by many shrines and temples throughout Japan. Many people look to all three of these for their needs of healing and health maintenance, covering the ground from the latest scientific medical care to the time-tested religious healing practices.

Having been in the Chinese cultural orbit for many centuries, the Japanese have always made use of kampo, Chinese medicine. Characteristically, however, the Japanese have shaped kampo in distinctive ways through their long experience with these healing practices. They have developed a large variety of herbal and animal medicines, designed specifically to treat every kind of ailment. And they use acupuncture and also moxibustion, burning young

mugwort leaves on selected parts of the body to provide stimulus from heat. Though these practices were restricted under the Allied occupation of Japan after World War II, in recent years kampo has gained much popularity as the distinctively Japanese approach to health. The government supports research and training in kampo, and many health insurance plans cover these treatments as complementary to Western medicine, used especially for chronic illnesses and pain.

It has always been popular in Japan to seek healing at particular Shinto shrines and Buddhist temples, some of which are widely known for their healing efficacy. In recent years this practice has mushroomed, as busloads of people come daily to shrines and temples that specialize in different kinds of help. Certain kami and Buddhas or bodhisattvas are known to be especially effective in healing particular ailments, like diseases of the eyes, throat, stomach, lungs, hips, and all the rest. Many shrines and temples specialize in illnesses of the elderly, such as stroke, hemorrhoids, incontinence, and so forth. But younger people come for help also, especially for health in pregnancy, an easy childbirth, health and growth for children, protection from traffic accidents, recovery from surgery, and much more.

In visiting these sacred sites, the people offer worship and prayer to the appropriate kami and Buddhas, as well as engage in additional activities. There is great interest in acquiring *omamori* (amulets and talismans) from the shrine or temple for recovery from illness and health maintenance. An omamori might be, for example, a paper image of the Jizo of Easy Childbirth, to be swallowed or placed on the body. Or it might be an amulet of the Kami of the Hip, to be wrapped in white paper and rubbed against the ailing part. Pregnant women can visit Nakayama Temple, which specializes in obstetrics and gynecology, to receive a special sash to be worn during pregnancy. At Ishikri Shrine in Osaka, worshipers can build up healing power by performing the *ohyakudo* ("hundred times"), walking back and forth between two sacred stones.

Recent years have seen a great increase in two types of Buddhist rituals, reflecting conditions of life in modern Japan: memorial services for aborted fetuses and rituals for a speedy death. Certain Buddhist temples have become very popular in offering memorial services for *mizuko* (water-child), unborn children aborted by their mothers. The rituals provide repose for the agitated soul of the aborted child, and the mother receives a sense of peace in fulfilling her obligations to her unborn child. Similarly, there has been a dramatic increase in elderly people visiting certain temples that offer rituals for the prevention of old-age diseases and debilitating senility. In modern Japan, aged people particularly dread the prospect of becoming a burden for their children by being bedridden, and so they go to these temples to perform rituals for prolonging their physical health, to obtain efficacious underwear for incontinence, and to pray for *pokkuri shinu*, dying a timely and speedy death.

Art in Japanese Religion

A deep aesthetic sense permeates Japanese culture, and this sense has roots both in Shinto and in Buddhist-Confucianist-Daoist traditions from China. Many of the arts are closely related to Buddhism, especially Zen, but the indigenous Japanese outlook on life first established the integration of art and religion that is so characteristic of Japanese culture.

The Shinto attitude is that the elements of nature are the pure and beautiful children of the kami, and humans are to cooperate with the kami to promote this goodness and beauty. The land itself is pure, sacred, and beautiful as created by the kami and, therefore, the presence of the kami is revealed not only by words but also especially by aesthetic awareness of the beauty of nature. Leaders of craft guilds in ancient times acted as priests, invoking the kami of the tree and the metal before cutting wood or forging metal to create cultural objects. Still today carpenters may intone prayers to the kami when raising the head beam of a building. Furthermore, the idea that human cultural creations are made in service to the kami inspires artists to create the most aesthetically pleasing houses, shrines, clothing, food, and the rest. The Shinto perspective has contributed an emphasis on the natural and the simple in art forms, a reflection of the true pure heart.

The Shinto tradition has not done much with iconography—rarely have there been statues or images to represent the kami, for example. Rather, the arts to which Shinto has contributed are those related to ritual, such as dance, music, drama, poetry, clothing, food, and so forth.

In Shinto worship, the kami are summoned to this world and this shrine, entertained here, and then sent away again—and the arts flourished in this setting, as entertainment for the kami and the people as well. The shrine dance-drama, kagura, has its origins in the mythology of the kami, when one of the heavenly kami performed an ecstatic dance, entertaining the kami so as to entice Amaterasu out of the rock-cave into which she had withdrawn. In ancient times, shamanesses drew on that heavenly model as they performed kagura, to the accompaniment of music, for entertaining the kami in worship festivals. Today, kagura has many different forms throughout Japan, performed by young women of the shrine, called miko, as a central part of shrine festivals.

Japanese poetry likewise grew up in a strong Shinto world, with poems in the classical uta or waka form (with five- and seven-syllable lines) found already in the mythological texts and in the eighth-century poetic collection, the *Manyoshu*. These poems express the free interchange between kami and humans, reflecting the seamless, natural early Japanese world of meaning.

Buddhist art in Japan is influenced both by developments in China and by the pre-Buddhist Japanese sensitivity for the natural and the simple as appropriate for sacred power. Much use is made of art in Buddhist practice in Japan, serving to enhance rituals, create a sense of sacred time and space, make present the Buddha power, or assist in realizing the Buddha-nature. Chinese Buddhist art was carried over into Japan—iconography, including sculptures and paintings of Buddhas and bodhisattvas, paintings of mandalas, temple architecture, literature, music, drama, and the like. But in appropriating this art, the Japanese also transformed it in keeping with the Japanese aesthetic tradition, as is evident in the simple, natural, and open architecture of some monastery halls, slender and graceful sculptures of Buddhas and bodhisattvas, simple gardens of rocks and sand, and Buddhist poetry inspired by nature.

Kukai, the founder of Shingon Buddhism in Japan and himself an excellent calligrapher, laid a strong foundation for the use of art in Japanese Buddhism by emphasizing the universal Buddha-nature in all of nature. Using the art of poetry, Kukai wrote:

The three Mysteries [body, speech and mind of
  Mahavairochana] pervade the entire universe,

Adorning gloriously the mandala of infinite space.
Being painted by brushes of mountains, by ink of oceans,
Heaven and earth are the bindings of a sutra revealing the
    Truth.
Reflected in a dot are all things in the universe;
Contained in the data of senses and mind is the sacred book.[1]

Kukai influenced the arts especially by promoting the Tantric idea that through ritual and art forms one experiences the universal Buddha-nature. Since, as he taught, all the world is the Dharma Body, identical with the cosmic Sun Buddha Mahavairochana, through aesthetic forms such as hand gestures, chanted formulas, paintings, and the like, it is possible to experience that Buddha-nature. One must take care, Kukai cautioned, not to take the finger pointing to the moon for the moon itself. The highest truths cannot be expressed in words or forms. Yet through ritual use of speech and forms, especially paintings of mandalas, in meditative practice, one can act out the cosmic drama of Mahavairochana's self-activity, "entering self into Self [Mahavairochana] so that the Self enters into the self."[2] The aesthetic forms, thus, aid in awakening to the Buddha nature.

Zen Buddhist art in Japan, deeply influenced by Chinese aesthetic developments in the Song era, uses restraint, empty space, and natural materials to heighten the Mahayana awareness that "form is emptiness, emptiness is form," as stated in the widely used *Heart Sutra*. A painting such as Sesshu's (1420–1506) misty landscapes often leaves much empty space and merely suggests the lines of the form. Zen temples may have rock gardens, such as the one at Ryoanji Temple in Kyoto, created from scattered rocks on a base of raked sand; here emptiness and form seem to interact with each other, creating an atmosphere of stillness and tranquility resonating with the "suchness" that underlies all reality.

Buddhist art in Japan, like Shinto art, has always reflected a concern for the natural and the simple, bringing to fruition the notion that life is art lived beautifully and purely. Under Buddhist influence, many of the traditional Japanese arts are thought of as "ways," complete with spiritual training and discipline—for example, the way of poetry, the way of painting, the way of Noh drama, the way of flowers, the way of tea, and the way of the sword. Basic to these arts is the Mahayana Buddhist sense of the nonduality of samsara and nirvana—that is, the experience of the Buddha-nature can be expressed aesthetically in the com-

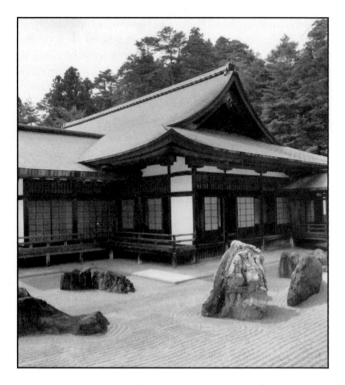

Composed of rocks and raked gravel, a Japanese garden expresses qualities of enlightenment in the Zen Buddhist sense.

monness of daily life, whether in the sparse brushstrokes of a landscape painting, a few common words put together in a short poem, or a social gathering for a cup of tea.

The poems of Japanese Buddhist poets attain a deep sense of impermanence and of the immediacy of the nirvanic experience in the midst of natural life. For example, the poet-monk Saigyo (1118–1190) wandered about in isolated mountain settings, composing poems that both celebrated the beauty of natural life and the evanescence of all things. In one waka poem (thirty-one syllables) he reflected on a famous passage from the *Nirvana Sutra*, "All phenomena are fleeting, / this is the law of birth and death / When you have wiped out birth and death / nirvana is your joy." This is Saigyo's poem:

I think of past times,
So swift
In their vanishing,
The present soon to follow—
Dew on the morning-glory.[3]

In even terser form, haiku poems (seventeen syllables) present a snapshot of reality that can only be understood intuitively by the mind, as in Basho's (1644–1694) celebrated haiku:

furu ike ya	An ancient pond, ah!
kawazu tobikomu	A frog leaps in—
mizu no oto	Water's sound.

Such a poem presents the suchness of reality in its undivided immediacy, devoid of our mental and emotional interpretations; it returns one, for a moment at least, to the "original mind" of enlightenment.

Japanese culture produced a rich set of theater arts, evolving from the kagura dance-drama and various kinds of popular plays and drama, further influenced by Buddhist ideals. Lively, colorful kabuki plays and bunraku (puppet theater) are well-known theater arts that are still flourishing and popular among the Japanese. An important form of theater that developed early in medieval times is Noh drama, a sophisticated art of traditional drama and music brought to its height by master Zeami (1363–1443). Noh is closely connected to the classical literary tradition as well as to the ritual tradition of music and dance. But it also came under the strong influence of Zen Buddhism in the creation of its aesthetic ideals. The goal, according to Zeami, is for the actor to use his spiritual strength (developed through long, intense discipline) to take the audience beyond the outer appearance, revealing the inner essence and depth of reality. The term *yugen* ("sublime beauty") is used to speak of this form of beauty through which we experience the profound, ineffable, inner qualities of existence. The long, piercing flute sound that opens the play transports us beyond the normal world; the chanting of the chorus and the music of flute and drums; the elaborate costume and masks of the actors; and the slow, exquisite dance movements of the actors all reveal a spiritual quality of great profundity. To the actors (and the well-informed audience), the way of Noh is a spiritual path as well as an artistic pursuit.

Besides the artistic ideals, the plots of Noh dramas typically express religious meaning, with the appearance of kami, bodhisattvas, demons, priests, and various spirits and themes of karma, reincarnation, spirit possession, worshiping the Buddha, and attainment of salvation. The typical plot would have a troubled ghost first appear, drawn to a particular place because of attachments and passions still remaining from life. The ghost then is induced to tell her or his story, often reenacting those crucial parts that have to do with the continuing passions and attachments. Through all of this, a deliverance occurs and the ghost (and perhaps the audience) is granted release and salvation.

The way of tea (**chanoyu** or **chado**) is perhaps the epitome of a "secular" Japanese art that was interpreted by some great masters of the art as a way of enlightenment. The way of tea is a way of life focused on the tea ceremony, encompassing many of the traditional arts such as gardening, architecture, flower arranging, and calligraphy. It involves stringent training and discipline, and it moves toward self-transformation and awakening. But the materials of the art are precisely common everyday experiences: rustic utensils (highly valued, of course, for their rustic beauty) for preparing tea, a simple hut, a tranquil garden, a sprig of flowers, some food, and a cup of tea shared between friends.

Wabi is an essential aesthetic quality sought after in the practice of the tea ceremony art. It is the aesthetic experience of poverty and insufficiency, of the bare bone of reality, of the pith or essence that underlies the abundance. Wabi, one great tea master said, is seeing the moon dimly shining through a veil of clouds. It is the appreciation of the cold and withered branch in winter. The great master Sen Rikyu (1521–1591), considered the main founder of the tea ceremony art, taught the meaning of wabi by means of this poem:

> To those who await
> only the cherry blossoms—
> how I would like to show
> the first patches of green grass
> through the snow of the mountain village.

The art of chanoyu involves a whole way of life, with years of discipline and practice required to master all the arts and cultural knowledge and to develop the aesthetic sensitivity required of a tea master—and of a guest. Training typically includes Zen discipline as well as training in all the cultural arts of Japan. The tea ceremony gathering itself is a very slow, deliberate affair—a formal tea ceremony with a full meal and two servings of tea lasts four hours. The host and the handful of invited guests are co-actors in a kind of plotless drama as they share food, drink tea, and enjoy the unique experience of this particular moment. The ritual art of the tea ceremony slows down this common everyday experience, as it were, savoring the aesthetic quality of each movement, sound, sight, and taste. Every action, every sense, every aesthetic form is attuned to the real. The tea ceremony is "a one-time meeting once in a lifetime"—that is, it focuses all of life's experience in the timelessness of the present moment, touching that depth of reality that, to Buddhists, is none other than the Buddha-nature. Sen Rikyu is said to have expressed the spiritual meaning of the tea ceremony art in this way:

> The essential meaning of *wabi* [Rikyu's style of tea ceremony] is to manifest the Buddha-world of complete purity free from defilements. In this garden path and in this thatched hut every speck of dust is cleared out. When host and guest together commune direct from the heart, no ordinary measures of proportion or ceremonial rules are followed. A fire is made, water is boiled, and tea is drunk—nothing more! For here we experience the disclosure of the Buddha-mind.[4]

To the twenty million people today, in Japan and elsewhere, who involve themselves to some extent in chanoyu, this art has many meanings. In a primary way, it represents to them an important and authentic piece of traditional Japanese culture. But it is perhaps unique among the arts in that what appears to be a purely secular social gathering can be in fact a disciplined way to experience qualities of enlightenment.

SOCIETY AND THE GOOD LIFE

How should we live? To be Japanese means to live as part of the Japanese people. The sense of community in Japan has been strong from ancient times, and the good life means living in accordance with the role one has within the family, the community, and the nation.

Structure of Japanese Society: Sacred Community

An outstanding feature of Japanese society is the strong group solidarity, as in China. The sense of individualism does not predominate; it is the social nexus that provides identity and meaning. Perhaps because of insular isolation, Japanese society is more homogeneous than Chinese society. Emigrants from outside were assimilated during the prehistoric period, and since that time there have been only a few divisions in Japanese society along ethnic or cultural lines. So the concentric circles of group solidarity move out without disruption from family to clan to village/town to the whole people as one large family.

The importance of the family in Japan is much like that in China, and indeed the influence of Confucianism imported from China played a big part in structuring the family values of Japan. But even before Confucian influence, ancient Japanese society was already based in clans (*uji*) that bound familial groups together around tutelary kami, clan shrines, and a clan leader. The clans in ancient Japan each had their own family kami (*uji-gami*), which they worshiped through the head of the clan, acting as the priest of the kami. This tradition of tutelary kami has continued in a modified form up to the present, at least in areas where families have maintained connections with their family shrines or with local tutelary shrines. Children, for example, are taken to the family shrine a month after birth to be dedicated to the tutelary kami. The family is certainly the keystone of Japanese society and religion; in fact, most participation in society and in religious practices is based in the family.

The traditional family often includes at least three generations, the oldest son of a family continuing the primary line and the other sons setting up branch families. The importance of the family for one's personal identity is illustrated by the common practice of referring to family members by their particular position or roles in the family. The cohesion of the family is closely linked to the ancestors. A traditional family will place ancestral tablets on a butsudan (Buddhist altar) in the home and make offerings and prayers to the ancestors in household rituals. They believe that the ancestors make special visits to the family homes during the New Year celebrations and during the festival of the dead in late summer. In this way the ancestors provide blessing and protection within the ongoing family unit.

The family naturally broadens out through participation in the local community, which traditionally was the village but in modern Japan is often a city or an urban district. In the rural areas a number of farming families form a village community for economic and religious cooperation, making practical decisions for the welfare of the community and sponsoring the village shrines and festivals. Neighborhood groups in the cities sponsor local shrines and festivals in which many of the people participate.

The notion of the Japanese people as a sacred nation (*kokutai*) has been a long and powerful tradition, reaching back to the ancient mythology of the descent of people from the kami and continuing in varying forms up to the disestablishment of Shinto after World War II. Throughout much of Japanese history religion has been closely bound up with the nation, focusing on the emperor as the head of the people, descended from Amaterasu, the sun kami. Often this was expressed in terms of a "father–child" relation between emperor and people, with the people expected to dedicate themselves wholeheartedly to the welfare of the emperor and the whole nation. It is true that this ideology of loyalty to the emperor and the nation was abused as a tool of totalitarianism in the hands of military expansionists in the World War II tragedy. But at the end of the war Emperor Hirohito issued an Imperial Rescript to renounce the emperor's "divinity," broadcast over the radio on January 1, 1946. The emperor reinterpreted his relationship with the Japanese people by saying that the ties between emperor and people have always stood on mutual trust and affection; they do not depend on mere legends and myths.[5] And under the Allied occupation, the disestablishment of Shinto and the separation of government and religion in Japan were carried out.

But even today the nation has a semireligious character for many Japanese. Many have deep respect and reverence for the emperor as the symbol of the unity of the whole people. They recognize that the state no longer supports religious activities but feel it is important nevertheless, for example, that the special shrine of Amaterasu at Ise is maintained, that the emperor performs the special thanksgiving rites at harvest time for the welfare of the whole nation, and that those who died for the nation be remembered through special rituals at Yasukuni Shrine (the national shrine for war dead). Most Japanese took much interest in the funeral rites for Emperor Hirohito in 1989 and in the rituals associated with the enthronement of the new emperor, Akihito. National ritual observances like these are somewhat controversial today, given the official separation of state and religion. But the important point is that the Japanese people are more than just people who

happen to live in a certain place; there still is some special sense of belonging to a sacred community.

There are, of course, other kinds of community identity in Japan. In the early Tokugawa period, following Neo-Confucian ideas, the samurai (warriors) cultivated loyalty to superiors into a path of self-transformation called bushido (way of the warrior). Bushido involved an elaborate code of ethical honor and spiritual conduct, focusing on unlimited loyalty to one's lord (daimyo), bravery and self-sacrifice to the point of death, and a rigorous spiritual discipline often based in Zen meditation. That same kind of group loyalty focused on a master or leader can be seen in schools of the traditional arts, where the head of the lineage (the *iemoto*) is the focus of intense group tradition and loyalty. Some sociologists have pointed out that a similar type of group loyalty operates in many modern Japanese corporations.

Other groups are more specifically religious. There are Buddhist lay societies, for example. Community identity is especially important for members of the New Religions—the recently formed religious movements that have incorporated many of the traditional religious forms but offer to the believers a more personal and intimate sense of belonging to a large family of like-minded believers. These New Religions usually have a powerfully charismatic founder or leader, and the new believers can enter into a "parent–child" relationship with that leader. Typically there are many group activities, including regular meetings, pilgrimages, and even sports events, to recreate the sense of belonging that perhaps has been lost with the decline of the traditional communities in Japan. These New Religions grew tremendously in Japan in the period after World War II, and for many Japanese still today they appear to provide a most important sense of community identity and belonging.

Religious Leadership in Japan From ancient times there has not been a sharp line separating kami and humans, and Japanese have always looked on great ancestors and powerful leaders as personifications of kami. In certain periods the emperor was considered "manifest kami" as a direct descendant of Amaterasu and as father of the Japanese national family. Through the centuries, the role of the emperor waxed and waned, but in general he (or she, in some early cases) always had the double role of being the chief of state and the chief priest of Shinto, since politics and religion were closely bound together. Even though Shinto is disestablished from state support today, the emperor still performs certain rituals such as the harvest thanksgiving ceremony, acting in his capacity as the spiritual head of the traditional Japanese religion.

In early times, the head of each clan had special responsibilities to act as priest in worshiping the kami, sometimes communicating with the kami through a priestess or shamaness. Gradually, special families of Shinto priests developed, regulated by the government. Today the priests of most of the shrines are educated and certified under the auspices of the Association of Shinto Shrines. During the wartime shortage of priests, wives of some priests performed the priestly duties in place of their husbands, and today women make up nearly 10 percent of the approximately 20,000 certified Shinto priests registered with the Association of Shinto Shrines.

Of course, as in other Buddhist lands, Buddhist monks and nuns are also holy persons who provide important religious leadership for the Japanese people. A special characteristic of Japanese Buddhism is the tradition, starting with Shinran of the Pure Land school, of married Buddhist priests. Shinran broke with the Buddhist tradition of celibacy for monks because of his conviction that in this degenerate age such practices bring no merit and are not helpful. Following Shinran's example, the tradition of a "household Buddhism" developed in all Japanese Buddhist schools, with married Buddhist priests in charge of local temples.

Among the holy persons in Japan is also the shaman or medium who lives among the people and serves as healer and exorcist apart from the organized religions. One important tradition in northern Japan was the blind shamaness who received special training and was able to communicate with the dead. Founders of some of the New Religions have also shown shamanistic traits, believed to be possessed by sacred power and, thus, qualified to give revelation and guidance. It is not unusual that the leader of a New Religion is considered to be a "living kami" (*ikigami*).

Women in Religious Leadership Roles   It is abundantly clear that throughout Japanese history, and even today to a large extent, women have had roles subordinate to those of men in religious affairs as well as in all other areas of public life. Women's focus has been on the home and the family, and in that role they have always been essential in overseeing the household religious rites, family trips to the shrines and temples, and so on. Additionally, concerns over pollution through menstrual blood and women's sexual powers no doubt contributed to restrictions on their participation in religious activities. For example, women—even nuns—were not permitted to set foot in certain sacred places and monastic complexes.

In spite of this subordinate, domestic focus, there are certainly many examples in Japanese history of powerful leading women, both divine and human. The early mythologies describe a number of awesome and powerful female kami. Foremost among them is Amaterasu, the sun kami—the divine ancestor of the imperial family, the Ruler of the Plain of High Heaven. It seems that in prehistoric times the Japanese had women rulers who often had shamanistic powers. Chinese records describe the ruler Pimiko, who was renowned as a shamanic diviner and was attended by more than a thousand female servants as she lived in seclusion. When she died the people built a huge grave mound, and when they rejected the male successor to the throne, a female relative of Pimiko named Iyo, a girl of thirteen, became queen and restored order. Later, Empress Jingu was a powerful ruler, effectively promoting the cultural development of early Japan. And there was the tradition of the princess-priestess, rooted in ancient shamanism in Japan. A woman relative—niece, sister, or wife—of the clan chieftain would be consecrated and would live apart to maintain absolute purity. She would go into trances, possessed by the kami of the clan, giving advice to the chieftain. This system was institutionalized by the emperor, with the Ise princess-priestess performing this function with relation to the great kami Amaterasu. But after Chinese culture and Confucian ideas arrived in the eighth century, women seldom attained leadership roles.

Women did attain proficiency in the literary arts, indicating a degree of cultural education at least for some women. Many of the early Japanese poems were written by women. In the feudal era, court women were well educated and strong, at the center of court intrigues. One of Japan's greatest literary works, the *Tale of Genji*, was written by a woman, Lady Murasaki, providing a look at court life and with that a glimpse into men's and women's lives in the centers of power in the Heian era.

Throughout the centuries there have continued to be shamanesses (*miko*), especially in rural areas, playing heroic roles, healing the sick, helping those in need, and telling fortunes. The alternative of becoming a Buddhist nun has been chosen by many women in Japanese history, providing an avenue for spiritual development and leadership, although the status of nuns has always been below that of monks in Japan as elsewhere. A famous Zen nun was Ryonen Genso (1646–1711). She was a well-educated court woman, admired for her elegant accomplishments in poetry, painting, and calligraphy; but after ten years of marriage and several children, she became a disciple of Master Haku-o, who considered her his leading disciple and confirmed her enlightenment. Later, as abbess of her own convent, she was well known for her scholarship and her educational work. It is interesting that requirements for nuns have remained stricter than for monks, even today. For example, following the example set by Shinran, many Japanese priests have married without losing their status as religious leaders, but it is generally expected that a nun will remain celibate, or, if she marries, will lose her spiritual status.

It is significant that many of the so-called New Religions, such as Tenrikyo, Omoto, and Tensho-kotai-jingu-kyo, have been founded by women. These women often gained their transformatory experiences later in life, having gone through the whole life cycle of a woman. Some of these women are considered by their followers to be ikigami, "living kami." Much of the success of these new religions is due to the zeal and effective leadership of women. However, the tendency has been that, once the new religion has become established, religious leadership drifts back to the males of the leading families, and women revert to their more traditional roles.

The Good Life in the Japanese View

How should we live? What is the good life for us and our community? It is typical of the Japanese to be directed more toward actually living the good life than toward discussing what it is. It goes without saying that the Buddhist and Confucian ethical views, discussed earlier, are very important for most Japanese. But the Japanese understanding

of Buddhist and Confucian ethics has been tempered and shaped by the traditional Shinto outlook on life.

The Shinto Perspective on the Good Life Unlike many religions, in the Shinto tradition there has never been any standardized written law code to guide behavior, nor are ideas of morality and ethics discussed in the sacred texts. Once, in Tokugawa times, a Confucian scholar argued that the lack of such codes showed that the ancient Japanese were morally deficient: "As proof of this there is the fact that no native Japanese words exist for the concepts of humanity, righteousness, decorum, music, filial piety, and fraternal affection." A leading scholar of the Shinto restoration movement, Hirata Atsutane (1776–1843), responded indignantly:

> Humanity, righteousness, filial piety, and the rest are all principles governing the proper conduct of man. If they are always automatically observed and never violated, it is unnecessary to teach them.... The ancient Japanese all constantly and correctly practiced what the Chinese called humanity, righteousness, the five cardinal virtues and the rest, without having any need to name them or to teach them.[6]

It is Shinto belief that a moral sense is a natural property of human beings. In proper harmony with the kami, people will naturally do what is good and right in their personal lives and in family and community.

Not only does the Shinto tradition not have any written moral code, but it also does not have sharp definitions of what is right and what is wrong or what is good and what is evil. Nothing is unconditionally evil; good and evil are relative notions, to be understood in the context of family, clan, community, nature, and the rest. The meaning and value of a particular action depend on the motivations, purpose, circumstances, time, and place. In the myths and legends about the kami and the early ruling families, there is considerable violence, fighting, sex, and the like. But a situation becomes evil when a kami becomes angry and rough and obstructs the processes of life, and good occurs when the kami is quieted down and brings benefits. Similarly, something is good when fortunate things happen and bad when unlucky things happen, apart from considerations based on some standard of morality.

This is not to say that the Shinto outlook is immoral or amoral. Traditions of proper behavior have been passed on in families and communities, and there is wide consensus on the general outlines of the good life. It is recognized, according to Shinto scholar Sokyo Ono, that "that which disturbs the social order, causes misfortune, and obstructs worship of the kami and the peaceful development of this world of kami is evil." There is also consensus on what is good: "Generally speaking, however, man's heart must be sincere; his conduct must be courteous and proper; an evil heart, selfish desire, strife, and hatred must be removed; conciliation must be practiced; and feelings of goodwill, cooperation, and affection must be realized."[7]

The emphasis here is on the inner motivation, the need for a sincere and pure heart. Thus, the important moral quality of an act depends on intentionality, on the sincerity or honesty (*makoto*) of the heart. That sincerity is common to kami and to humans, and if one is in harmony with the kami and acts in sincerity, one will be doing the best, being "true" to the whole situation.

From this perspective we can see that the Shinto view of right behavior is not only situational and intentional; it is also naturalistic. Since our nature, and the nature of all the world, is pure and good as given from the kami, the good life is also the most fully natural life. There is no fundamental breach between humans and the natural world. This means that all natural needs, instincts, desires, and passions are also good and can be indulged in with a sincere and honest heart—sexuality, acquiring wealth, drinking and eating, playing, and the rest. It further means that the good life brings people into close harmony with nature itself, for together the world and humans are siblings, children of the kami. So the good life means an ecological balance, with respect and love for nature as well as for human society. One aspect of this ethical harmony with nature is the value Japanese have always placed on art; part of human responsibility is to assist the kami in making human life and nature as beautiful as possible.

Buddhist Ethical Contributions in Japan   The Buddhist ethical system has also been very influential in Japan, of course. The most characteristically Japanese developments in Buddhism—Pure Land, Nichiren, and Zen—have each contributed to the shaping of the Japanese view of the good life. Shinran, a leader of the Pure Land school, placed much stress on the gratitude that should permeate the life of one who knows he or she is

saved by Amida's power. He said that when he thought about Amida Buddha's Vow to save all beings, he would feel that Amida did this specifically for Shinran alone, the greatest of all sinners (as he called himself), and he would be filled with deep gratitude and thanksgiving. The sense of gratitude for the compassion of the Buddha is to find expression not only in reciting the Nembutsu but also in showing sympathy for others and in refraining from speaking ill of others. Later interpreters of Pure Land ethics tended somewhat toward a passive quietism, based on the view that human life is inevitably under the sway of passion even for those who have faith in Amida. Rennyo (1414–1499), for example, constructed a theory of two levels of moral truth: The believer should obey the conventional morality, at the same time knowing that he or she is free from such obligations because his or her destiny is determined solely through faith in Amida.

Nichiren Buddhism, at least in some of its sects, has tended to emphasize the positive value of the world and ordinary human activities, arising from the Mahayana equation of nirvana and samsara. The Nichiren perspective often includes a wholehearted affirmation of the positive benefits offered by the modern world, with its science and technology, its opportunities for a happy, prosperous life. Some of the new Nichiren movements of today, such as Soka Gakkai, explicitly direct concern toward human fulfillment and worldly benefits that accrue to the person following the Nichiren path.

Zen Buddhism, in a somewhat different way, also affirms a this-worldly ethical outlook, building on the Mahayana idea that the ultimate truth transcends all dualities, including those of right and wrong or good and evil. Of course, Zen masters do not promote immorality, but they remind Buddhists that all moral values are relative. Right conduct does not result from following rules but from the spontaneous expression of inner awakening. A popular figure in the Japanese Zen tradition is Ikkyu Sojun (1394–1481), an eccentric Zen master who gained a reputation for tavern and brothel hopping, claiming they were far better places for attaining enlightenment than the corrupt establishment temples. But despite his flaunting of accepted standards of morality, Ikkyu pursued the rigors of the meditative life in preference to the pomp and rewards that could have been his through the established Zen institutions. The ideal Zen life transcends standards of right and wrong—but it results in a life of selflessness and compassion.

Principles of the Good Life: Filial Piety and Loyalty
We have emphasized the personal, subjective aspect of the good life. But we cannot forget that the main context for this life is the community—the community that includes the kami and the Buddhas, the family together with the ancestors, and the larger community and nation. In traditional Japan, questions about how one should live are inseparable from the welfare of family and nation. This does not mean that the individual is sacrificed to the group—although that mentality did have some backing during the nationalistic World War II period. The central paradigm, as in China, is the family, writ large as the national family, and the twin ethical principles are filial piety and loyalty. These principles the Japanese learned from China and Confucianism, but they are simply ways of expressing deeply held ancient Japanese values. Hirata Atsutane, a Shinto thinker deeply influenced by Neo-Confucian values, summed up this context by writing that, since the people originally came out of the creative spirit of the kami, they have the innate capacity to venerate the kami, the emperor, and their parents, and to carry out other obligations.[8] Here we see the concentric circles of the good life, with duties to family and nation simply extensions of worship of the kami. The good life is really a way of showing gratitude to the kami by contributing to the continuing evolution and welfare of the kami-based family and nation.

Duties within the family have tended to be defined in Confucian terms, with the virtue of filial piety as the core. This is broadened to put emphasis on each person's responsibility upward toward seniors or superiors. There is, of course, a family hierarchy, and the specific grade of privilege and responsibility of each member is clearly understood—whether that be where to sit for meals, in what order to bathe, what subtleties of speech formality to use, or the degree of authority over the family budget. A major obligation, as a member of the family, is to live up to the standards of the family and do nothing to discredit it. Such "loss of face" for the family would be a serious affront to one's parents and ancestors.

The traditional Japanese idea of the good life maintains the centrality of the family, while at the same time incorpo-

rating the nation itself as the larger context. Here the Confucian key term is loyalty. Since early times the political rule of Japan has been closely united with religion, and loyalty to the rulers, especially the emperor, has been highly valued. This sense of loyalty to one's superior was highly cultivated in bushido, the way of the samurai.

One of the reasons Japanese society has never needed strong law enforcement is the deep sense of reciprocal social obligation and duty that forms the heart of the social system. A key term is **giri**, the social obligation to help those who have helped one and to promote the welfare of the group of which one is part. Each person has obligations to live up to the standards of his or her family, rank, class, or group and to do nothing to discredit them. To fulfill these obligations, no matter what the cost, is the highest moral worth. To fail in this is *giri-shirazu*, "not knowing *giri*"—one of the worst insults imaginable. This system of reciprocal obligations works in many contexts. One important arena is the workplace, where a person is a part of a large family, the business company. Here loyalty to the company and to superiors in the company takes on important moral force. As in the family and in the nation, there are reciprocating relationships in the company structure, with duties going both ways among superiors and employees.

Concern for the Betterment of Human Society The strong Japanese sense of group loyalty translates into a feeling of responsibility for the welfare of society. The most dramatic evidence of that is the way the person in charge assumes complete responsibility when misfortune or disaster befalls the people—whether the person is a government official or a company head. In present-day Japan, the ethic of productive work for the welfare of the group (the company) and the whole nation is likewise strong. Each company employee has responsibility for the good of the whole.

According to modern Shinto thinkers, there is in the Shinto outlook a vision that lends itself to social change and progress. As children of the kami, people show their gratitude to the kami by working toward the fuller goodness of this evolving kami-world. As one modern Shinto author says,

> It is further believed that the *kami* who created this land are those who bless and sustain life in this world and that human participation in and advancement of this life

constitute at once a realization of the will of these deities and the fulfillment of the meaning and purpose of individual existence. . . .

Some people, not yet understanding Shinto, criticize it as a religion that has a primary interest in this-worldly benefits. From a Shinto perspective, however, an interest in tangible benefits that will promote life in this world is regarded as a perfectly natural consequence of its esteem for the *kami* that bestow and enhance life.[9]

From this Shinto point of view, Japanese people can participate wholeheartedly in promoting the betterment and further evolving of life in the world, realizing it as the unfolding of kami-life that is infinite and inexhaustible.

In a land that has had its share of bloody violence down through the centuries, many Japanese today draw on the harmony promoted in Shinto and the pacificism of Buddhism to present to the world a voice for peace and reconciliation. Like all religions, the Japanese religions also have in the past been used to lend support to violence and war. But many religious leaders today, freed from political ideology, continue to support the unique heritage of Japan while seeking the betterment and harmony of the whole world. The Association of Shinto Shrines has strongly emphasized that maintaining the Japanese Shinto heritage includes working for the peace and prosperity of the whole world. And many Buddhist groups in Japan have been engaged actively in promoting interreligious cooperation and in efforts to end the risk of nuclear war in the world. Interestingly, one of the groups leading the peace movement is Rissho Koseikai, a new religious movement in the Nichiren tradition. Nichiren groups have traditionally been known for their nationalism and exclusive claims to truth, but Rissho Koseikai has launched an international movement for attaining world peace through interreligious cooperation. With Japan's unique status as the only country to have suffered from nuclear bombing, these Japanese voices for peace carry a compelling message to the rest of humankind.

DISCUSSION QUESTIONS

1 What are the four main movements of matsuri (Shinto shrine festivals)?

2 Explain the different purposes of Buddhist rituals of worship in Japan. What is the meaning of rituals for *mizuko*?

3 What is the main worship for Pure Land Buddhists? For Nichiren Buddhists?

4 Describe the ritual practice of zazen by Zen adherents.

5 Describe some of the main religious festivals for the Japanese, noting the interplay of Shinto and Buddhist traditions.

6 Outline the interaction of Shinto and Buddhism in the rituals of life and death in Japan.

7 Discuss how key Japanese concerns about sickness and healing are based in their religious perspectives.

8 What are some of the principles and practices of art in the Shinto tradition?

9 In what sense are the artistic ways in Japan, such as poetry, Noh drama, the tea ceremony (chanoyu), and others, considered to be ways of spiritual transformation?

10 Explain the Japanese view of the family and the nation as sacred communities.

11 Portray the roles of women in Japanese traditional society. What is the situation today?

12 In what senses is the Shinto vision of the good life situational, intentional, and naturalistic?

13 Why is there so little crime in Japan? Discuss the importance of family and group loyalty in Japan, as well as the sense of *giri*, in terms of Shinto and Confucianist ideals.

KEY TERMS: JAPANESE RELIGIONS

Amaterasu sun kami, ruler of the Plain of High Heaven, ancestress of the Japanese emperors

Amita Buddha of infinite light (Amitabha) presiding over the Pure Land Buddha realm

bushido "way of the warrior," the Japanese code of self-discipline for warriors based on Zen, Shinto, and Neo-Confucian ideals

butsudan in Japan, Buddhist altar in the home

chado *see* chanoyu

chanoyu the art of the Japanese tea ceremony; also called chado, "the way of tea"

Daimoku formula used in Nichiren Buddhist worship: "Namu myoho rengekyo" (Praise to the wonderful law of the *Lotus Sutra*)

Dogen important thinker (1200–1253) and founder of Soto Zen in Japan

Eisai founder (1141–1215) of Rinzai Zen in Japan

giri important Japanese sense of social obligation and duty

Hidden Christians Christians in Japan who continued to practice their religion secretly after Christianity was outlawed in the mid-seventeenth century

Honen founder (1133–1212) of Pure Land Buddhism as a separate sect in Japan

Ise Shrine shrine of Amaterasu, the Japanese sun kami

Izanagi and Izanami the pair of kami who created the world, according to Japanese mythology

Jizo popular Buddhist divinity in Japan known as the savior of the dead and helper of dead children

kami spirits or divinities in Shinto, including mythological beings, powerful and awesome aspects of nature, and important humans

kamidana kami altar in the home in Japan

Kannon bodhisattva Avalokiteshvara, popular goddess of mercy in Japan (Guanyin in China)

koan Zen Buddhist saying or riddle used in meditation (gongan in China)

Kojiki *Records of Ancient Matters*, earliest writing in Japan, a compilation of stories about the age of the kami and the beginnings of Japan

Kukai great Japanese Buddhist thinker (773–835) and founder of Shingon

matsuri Shinto shrine festival

Meiji Restoration restoration of imperial rule in Japan in 1868

Motoori Norinaga leading scholar (1730–1801) of the National Learning movement that advocated the restoration of Shinto as Japan's central religion

Nembutsu (nianfo in China) Japanese formula of calling on Amida Buddha with the words, "Namu Amida Butsu" (Praise to Amida Buddha)

New Religions in Japan, term used for new religious movements, often drawing on and combining aspects of Buddhism, Shinto, and folk religion

Nichiren Japanese Buddhist sect based single-mindedly on the *Lotus Sutra*, founded by the monk Nichiren (1222–1282)

Nihon shoki (Nihongi) chronicles of Japan, compiled shortly after the *Kojiki* and containing stories about the kami and early emperors

Ninigi grandson of Amaterasu, sent to earth to begin kami rule on earth, ancestor of first legendary Japanese emperor

Noh classical Japanese theater, closely linked to the religious traditions, especially Zen

Norito ancient Shinto ritual prayers

Obon (Ullambana) festival of the seventh month in Japan welcoming the ancestors

pollution in the Shinto view, anything that hinders life and fertility by causing separation from the kami

Pure Land school of Buddhism focusing on worship of Amitabha Buddha, with hope of rebirth in the Pure Land paradise, founded in Japan especially by Honen and Shinran

purification rituals, important in Shinto, to remove pollution and reinstate harmony and communion with the kami

Saicho founder (767–822) of Tendai Buddhism in Japan

samurai the Japanese class of warriors influenced by Zen and Neo-Confucianism

School of National Learning Shinto restoration movement during the Tokugawa period

Shingon esoteric (Tantric) Buddhism in Japan

Shinran disciple (1173–1262) of Honen and founder of the True Pure Land Buddhist sect in Japan

Shinto term designating the indigenous Japanese "way of the kami," from the Chinese term *shendao*

Shotoku prince regent (573–621) who advocated Buddhism as one of the pillars of Japan

shrine (jinja) Shinto sacred place focused on the presence of a kami; usually has appropriate buildings where a symbol of the kami is housed and where worshipers can consult priests

Soka Gakkai largest New Religion in Japan, based on Nichiren Buddhism

Susanoo storm kami in Japanese mythology, unruly brother of Amaterasu

Tendai important school of Buddhism in Japan (Tiantai in China)

Tenrikyo the oldest of the existing New Religions in Japan, founded in 1838

torii characteristic gateway to the Shinto shrine

way of art in Japan, practice of an art (such as poetry, Noh drama, or the tea ceremony) as a way of self-cultivation

zazen Japanese term meaning "sitting in meditation," central practice in Zen Buddhism

Zen important school of meditation Buddhism in Japan (Chan in China)

Chapter *17*

Epilogue

In these first years of the twenty-first century, the world is changing in many ways. What of the religions—those paths that have guided, shaped, and inspired our human adventure throughout the many millennia of human life?

As we reach the end of our study of the sacred paths of the East, we need to remember that our journey has been only a beginning and that a vast store of these paths remains to be explored. We have discovered a multifaceted human pilgrimage made up of many communities of people, each one with its own path that provides full and compelling meaning for life. We have seen that these individual religious traditions are dynamic, changing homes for communities of peoples, sources of identity and meaning, reservoirs of values, and storehouses of motivation and action.

The Religions and the Future of Humankind It is perhaps important to reflect for a moment on the significance of these religious paths in the world today and in the future. Things have changed; it is a new day in our common human history. Each of us can make our own list of what is new today, different from the past, in the areas of life that are of central concern to religion. Here are some starters.

As never before, the peoples of the world are bound together into a global village, through interconnections of communications, economy, politics, and concerns of common survival.

As never before, people come into daily contact with those of other religions and cultures.

As never before, the peoples of the world are being bombarded with rapid change, unimagined secularity, rampant materialism, and competing ideologies.

As never before, people who practice the religious paths are educated in a modern secular way and taught knowledge and value judgments that are often in basic conflict with their traditional worldview.

As never before, at least in recent human history, women are becoming aware of their own religious experience and religious heritage, and both women and men are recognizing how patriarchal religious traditions have oppressed women and how there is need today to revive the feminine aspects of religious experience.

As never before, there are forces in the world that have the very real potential of devastating the human community: overpopulation and starvation, dwindling natural resources and greater competition for their use, nuclear weapons of awesome and incomprehensible destructive power, and terrorist groups willing to destroy masses of people to enforce their will. Never before (since the early stages of human evolution) has the human race faced such imminent threat of widespread devastation.

Enough—let the reader go on with her or his own list. Given all of this, what significance do the religious traditions have in the world of the twenty-first century? There are different possibilities, of course.

In the view of some, the sacred paths are in the process of withering and dying. We face, they say, a religionless future. Perhaps, some think, that future will be humankind coming of age, throwing off the shackles of religion and superstition; perhaps, others warn, it will be the Brave New World of totalitarian thought control through nameless bureaucracies and technological forces. This view of a withering away of religion has, however, become less persuasive with the obvious revival going on in most religious traditions of the world. More likely, some say, religion will remain but will be a part of a continuing slide into a one-dimensional, secular, materialistic world culture, with religion as one of the diversions to make people think they have some control and meaning in their lives.

The point of view suggested here, which of course cannot be proved, is that the religious traditions will continue to play a vital role in the future. To have religious experience appears from our study to be a central dimension of being human and, thus, we might suppose that religion will continue in changing and adapting forms as long as humans exist. Religious traditions, as we have seen, possess great adaptability to new needs and pressures. Every religious tradition, in fact, is an organic composite of developments over many years in changing circumstances, always managing to maintain a continuity of identity in the midst of transformations.

So the real question is not whether there will be religion in the future. It is whether the sacred paths can help shape the future of humankind in a creative, beneficial, hopeful way. Each religious tradition has done this among its own sacred peoples and within its own sacred lands. But what of the future of this interconnected global community?

One fear for the future is a rise in nationalistic and fanatical religious groups that could foment conflict and violence. It is true that recent years have seen growing *fundamentalistic* movements within most of the world religions. This term has been used to refer to revivals that push for a strict and literal adherence to what are considered the orthodox scriptures, doctrines, and ethical requirements of the religious community. The Christian fundamentalist movement has been well known for many years; recently much attention has been given to Muslim fundamentalists. But there are also Jewish fundamentalists, as well as Hindus and Buddhists and others. Now we need clearly to recognize that religious fundamentalism as such is an authentic way of following one's religious path, and it does not necessarily bring with it intolerance, aggression, or violence toward others. But one possible scenario is a bloody eruption of holy wars as people are pressed closer and closer together but revert all the more strongly to fundamentalistic exclusive religious claims.

Such a pessimistic outlook, however, is not warranted by our study of the sacred paths. For all the intolerance, conflict, and violence that each of the major religious traditions bears in its history, there is peace and reconciliation at the heart of each. And most of the religious paths we have studied are "universal." That is, claims are made for some kind of universality for the whole human race. Each one embodies a vision for the welfare and happiness of the whole world, with important blueprints for achieving that. So how can these great religious resources be tapped in the common human search for hope and welfare? There are many ways, and there are dedicated people in each of the religions today who are utilizing these resources in their efforts toward justice, peace, and reconciliation in the world. This book is dedicated to the view that studying, learning, and understanding the different religions will make some contribution toward world peace and reconciliation. The guideposts and crossings on the paths represent high points and interconnections in the common human religious experience, and the better people come to know and understand these, the more consciously they can join others in using these resources to work toward peace and well-being for all. Here are four suggestions as to how the resources of the religious paths could contribute to the common human welfare.

There is pressing need in our world today for mutual understanding and respect among the different peoples of the world. In spite of the increasing globalization of all societies today, world peace and cross-cultural harmony still seem elusive. Much of the conflict in the world today stems from, or is worsened by, lack of understanding between the peoples involved. Every culture has been influenced by religious traditions, so understanding another culture means understanding the religious vision that the culture is bound up with. Some tragic mistakes have been made—and are still being made—simply by the failure of one people or government to understand and respect the values and religious commitments of another people. As examples of conflict in which religious factors have come into play, one need only mention the conflict in Vietnam, the Arab–Israeli conflict, the struggles between India and Pakistan, the strife in Northern Ireland, the tragic conflicts in Bosnia, in Kosovo, in the Sudan, in Iraq—and the list goes on. Sometimes it is said that religions cause conflict, but that is most often not the case. Most of these conflicts developed over nonreligious issues. It is not religion but rather ignorance and lack of understanding about religion that lend support to the conflict. Conversely, better understanding and mutual respect among the peoples of different religious traditions would contribute greatly to world peace.

A second point of importance is that there is within each religious tradition a compelling vision of the good world, of the ideal goal of peace and happiness for all humankind. No religious tradition advocates evil and destruction on the other peoples of the world—such perversions have indeed occurred at infamous points in the history of each tradition, but that does not negate the honest, peaceful, compassionate motivation at the heart of each. There are many and various approaches, to be sure, to the question of how to create a better world. We might say that the religions from India tend toward pacifism and self-sacrifice; the Abrahamic religions advocate justice, love, and equality; the religions of China and Japan emphasize harmony and reconciliation; and sacred paths of indigenous peoples express community of people and environment. By now we have learned, of course, that such characterizations are oversimplifications, and that within each religious path there are many variant tendencies. But each approach is important and helpful, and through better understanding of one another these resources can become more effective in our interconnected global village.

A third point is the transnational character of religious commitment. While religious values and commitments, even of people of the global religions, are always located in specific communities and even nations, religious commitment has the quality of transcending national or group loyalties and ideologies. "Is it better to serve God or humans?" (asked by followers of Jesus Christ in a situation of conflict between religious and national commitment) is a question found in some form in all religious communities, especially in the world religions that transcend national boundaries. While religions can be, and often have been, used by the state or other groups to indoctrinate, and for selfish, even violent purposes, religious commitment can also be the motivation for people to say no, to pursue values and goals different from those of the ruling authorities. Most governments, in fact, have recognized that religion can be a subversive force. Drawing on their religious resources, people can challenge and guide governments and other groups in their societies to act with justice and concern for the welfare of all.

A fourth related point is the potential for people of all religious traditions to cooperate across religious, ethnic, national, and ideological lines to deal with our common human concerns, which seem so overwhelming today. The secularization of all values, the great god of materialism, the devaluing of human life, the oppression and exploitation of minorities and women, the rape of our natural resources and degradation of our environment, and the great threat to humanity posed by the militarizing and nuclearizing of our global village—people in each religious tradition do have important things to say in common about all such concerns. A paradigm of such interreligious cooperation might be the worldwide peace movement, in which people from all the different religious traditions work together to achieve reconciliation, peace, and disarmament throughout the world. It is urgent that those who are steeped in the religious ideal of a peaceful and whole world rather than those who trade in weapons and conflict be the visionaries who shape the future of humankind.

Dialogue: Crossings on the Paths These suggestions about the contribution people of the religions can make to the future of humankind are based on the presupposition that people will get to know and understand their own religious traditions and the traditions of others better. In spite of the explosion of knowledge today about every conceivable topic, many people still remain surprisingly in the dark about the different religions of the world. Once other people's religions (and also one's own, in many cases) were shrouded in mystery and lack of knowledge and, therefore, misguided religious prejudices abounded. Today there is no longer any excuse for that, for accurate information and opportunities abound for contact with peoples of the different religions.

In fact, one of the striking developments in recent religious history, at least within some of the traditions, is the increase of meaningful conversation or *dialogue* between people of different religions. Since this has the potential of creating new levels of intercultural understanding, let us look more closely at the attitudes and movements that are involved in understanding through dialogue.

Dialogue can take place on different levels, of course. Important dialogue takes place today between leading scholars and experts in the different religious traditions, each representing her or his own tradition and entering into conversation with those of different traditions on a deep religious–theological level. But dialogue also can take place as ordinary people of the different paths meet each day as neighbors, fellow employees, students, or tourists. In particular, dialogue occurs between people of different paths as they face the common concerns and problems of daily life together, working toward understanding and dealing with the social, political, and economic issues that affect all of us.

There are difficulties and misunderstandings about such dialogue between people of differing religions. Some people have the naïve notion that all religions are essentially the same, with somewhat differing outer forms and trappings. A related attitude, widespread today, is that we can pick and choose among the religions, adopting elements that suit us and discarding all the uninteresting or unappealing elements. In this way new religious movements are begun—or at least we tailor our own brand of religion. But these attitudes neglect the wholeness and integrity of each religious tradition. As we have seen, each religious tradition is a whole meaning system with its own central and primary symbols. To simply flatten all the religions into one shape or arbitrarily to pick and choose some elements without regard to the rest is to do injustice to that religious tradition's full integrity.

Another kind of attitude is that dialogue is not desirable or not really possible among people of different religious commitments. This attitude is often associated with religious fundamentalism, the attitude that one's own religion is the exclusive truth and, therefore, truth claims of another religion can only be argued against and shown to be false. From another perspective, drawing on postmodern thought, certain cultural-linguistic theories of religion also suggest that people of different religions have differing linguistic systems and, therefore, cannot really understand the vocabulary and semantics of another religion. A Hindu, a Christian, and a Daoist may all use the English term *God*, but the term carries incommensurate meaning for each. If we cannot understand each other's words, real dialogue would seem impossible. Both of these views remind us of important characteristics of religion. It is well to remember that claiming to be the *real* truth is essential to any particular religion. And it is also important to realize that each religious tradition is a unique cultural-linguistic system,

whose terms and concepts cannot simply be interchanged with those of another tradition.

But it is not necessary to press these ideas to the conclusion that real dialogue among people of different religions is impossible. One can claim to possess the real truth and still listen to, and even understand, the truth claims of others. Our religious traditions are differing cultural-linguistic systems, yet there is a common quality of human experience and rationality that does allow cross-cultural communication and understanding. All humans have lived on the same mother earth, under the same sky and sun, experiencing birth, sex, food production, fellow-human relationships, and death in common. It is not necessary to suppose there is a common essence of religion in order to believe that it is possible for humans to communicate their religious ideas to one another.

Furthermore, there have been and continue to be many crossings on the paths—for millennia, as we have seen in our study, peoples of different religious traditions have interacted, learned from others, and adopted elements from other religions into their own. Today, of course, the interaction is more intense and widespread, but there is plenty of evidence from the past that people can communicate across the cultures, and that they can learn and grow through such communication.

The Attitude and Process of Dialogue   The process of meaningful conversation and dialogue among people of different religious traditions has been tried and tested in many settings today. It is generally agreed that a number of basic attitudes are important, so that the process of dialogue can take place. Among the most important attitudes are the following:

1 Real dialogue presupposes a firm standing in one's own religious tradition. It is interesting to float above all religions, coming down only where something useful is found. But dialogue means to share that which is most essential and innermost to oneself, and that comes from deeply held religious convictions. This does not mean there are no doubts, questions, or dissatisfactions with one's own tradition—we have seen that such doubt and questioning are essential to change and development within each tradition. But dialogue means

"talking through to another," presupposing one sharing her or his religious commitment with one of another faith—not people with no commitments looking around for what suits them best.

2 The goal is to grow in understanding of the other religions and of one's self. The goal is not to convert the partners in dialogue, nor is it to convince oneself to convert to the other religious viewpoint.

3 Dialogue presupposes a respect for the people of the other religious traditions and a willingness to see how those traditions really make sense to the people who live by them.

4 Dialogue involves the readiness to share at a deep level one's own religious commitments and convictions about truth, yet without arrogance or defensiveness. Such sharing means a willingness to be vulnerable, to let others in on one's inner beliefs and values.

5 Dialogue presupposes a willingness to learn from the other, taking the risk of growing and changing in one's own understanding.

It may seem difficult to bring these attitudes into an area as personal and as subject to strong feelings as religion. It is in the nature of religious belief to make claims to truth. If I was not convinced that my religion is the truth about existence, it would no longer be my *religion*. Each religious person has experienced the sacred by means of a particular religious tradition, and based on that there are certain absolute and irreducible convictions by which he or she lives. The whole issue then of competing truth claims cannot be avoided when two people of different religions talk together: Is one religion true and the other not? Are they both true? Do they both possess partial truth? These are important questions to think about and to discuss.

The experience of people engaged in dialogue today is that it is possible to remain firm in one's own religious tradition and still respect the truth claims of others. One can acknowledge the fact that each religious tradition claims to be the real truth about human existence—and leave open the question whether such claims have to be exclusive. The attitude of dialogue is based on the realization that in religion we enter into the sacred mystery of life (remember our definition of religion in Part I), and that the sacred can

never be fully grasped or limited by our own understanding or experience. However much we are convinced of the truth of our own religious understanding, we can acknowledge that the sacred mystery is still greater and deeper, and that others may have valid religious experiences, which, if we but listen to them, may be illuminating also to us.

Of course, it is not necessary to give up critical thinking in order to enter into conversation with people of different religions. Dialogue involves a give-and-take that includes questions and challenges as well as respect and acceptance. Comparing religious ideas and practices calls for accurate information and good critical thinking. But experience has shown that this can be done in an atmosphere of respect and willingness to learn and grow.

The process of dialogue between people of different religious beliefs involves four main movements:

1 It is important, first, to become aware of one's own religious values and commitments. It is possible, then, to "bracket" them so as to enter into the other person's religious world, as much as possible, without preconceived notions and prejudices.

2 Next comes a movement of passing over to enter into the universe of symbols that makes up the other person's religion, seeing it from the inside as the other person does.

3 The next movement is returning to one's own worldview, but bringing new ideas and comparisons from the other person's religious tradition.

4 Now integration and growth can take place, seeing one's own religious ideas more clearly and deeply.

These movements, of course, are essential for learning and growth in all areas of life—moving outside ourselves to experience something new, then returning and integrating that with what we already are, as the process of growth goes on. The four movements listed take place over and over again, sometimes occurring simultaneously, as the conversation with people of other religions goes on.

The increase of interreligious dialogue today coincides with revival and renewed vitality in most of the world religions. As dialogue between the peoples of the different religions continues and deepens, on all levels, the potential contribution of the sacred paths to the common life and well-being of humankind and of our whole world will become stronger. What this will bring cannot be fully predicted, of course, but it appears as one hopeful sign in the outlook for the future of humanity.

DISCUSSION QUESTIONS

1   In what ways is the present age a new critical time for the religions—and for humanity?
2   Divisions and conflict in the world often seem to involve religion. Do you think that some religions cause conflict and violence, or do you think that all world religions have peace at their center?
3   Does what is common and universal to the religions seem more important to you, or do you focus on what is unique and particular to each tradition?
4   Do you see any conflict between holding to one's own religious convictions, on the one hand, and attempting to understand and respect the faith of others, on the other hand?
5   What kinds of attitudes are presupposed for conversation and dialogue among people of different religious traditions? What are the main movements by which that kind of dialogue process can lead to deeper understanding?
6   What, do you think, are some resources of the world religions that could contribute to the common human welfare and the welfare of our whole world?

Glossary

Note: Chinese terms are given in the pinyin spelling, with the Wade-Giles spelling in parentheses

Adi Granth "original collection," the sacred scripture of the Sikhs; *see also Guru Granth Sahib*

Advaita nondualism, Shankara's school of Vedanta, emphasizing the all-encompassing one ultimate reality, Brahman

aesthetic concerning beauty or artistic perception, important for religious expression

Agamas main scriptures of the Jains

Agni Vedic god of fire

agricultural revolution the widespread changes in human culture when ancient humans learned to produce their own food in Neolithic times

ahimsa "nonviolence," one of the most important Jain principles; also emphasized in Buddhism and Hinduism

Amaterasu sun kami, ruler of the Plain of High Heaven, ancestress of the Japanese emperors

Amida Japanese name for Buddha of infinite light (Amitabha) presiding over the Pure Land Buddha realm

Amitabha heavenly Buddha who presides over the Pure Land Buddha realm

Analects compilation of the sayings attributed to Confucius

ancient civilizations the great civilizations that developed after the agricultural revolution, with cities, temple cults, kings, commerce, and often systems of writing

animism belief in spirits; theory that religion originated in reverence for spirits of living beings and inanimate objects

arhat (Pali: arahant) "worthy one," a perfected saint who has reached nirvana and will be released from samsara at death

Arjan the fifth guru and first Sikh martyr (1563–1606)

Aryans peoples related to the Indo-Europeans, who migrated into India in ancient times

Ashoka great Buddhist king in India (r. ca. 272–236 B.C.E.), the "second founder" of Buddhism

ashramas the four stages of life for higher-class males in Hinduism: student, householder, forest-dweller, and renouncer; ashrama is also a hermitage or place for meditation

atman in Hinduism, the soul or self, considered eternal

avatara descent or incarnation of a god, as Krishna and Rama are avataras of the great God Vishnu

Ayurveda traditional system of medicine in India

Bhagavad Gita important scripture from the *Mahabharata*, containing Krishna's teaching to Arjuna and summing up the fundamental ideas of Hinduism

bhakti devotion, self-surrender to one's god

bhikkhu, bhikkhuni Pali terms for Buddhist monk and nun (Sanskrit, bhikshu, bhikshuni)

Birthday of the Buddha joyful festival usually celebrated in May (in April in Japan); *see also* Vesakha

Bodh Gaya the place where Siddhartha Gautama attained enlightenment

bodhisattva being who is intent on becoming fully enlightened; in Mahayana Buddhism, one who reaches enlightenment but vows to continue rebirths in samsara to assist others

Brahma designation for the creator god in Hindu thought

Brahman Hindu term for ultimate reality; the divine source and pervading essence of the universe

Brahmanas ritual commentaries, part of the Vedas

Brahmans highest-ranked, priestly class in Hindu society

Buddha   "Enlightened one"; Siddhartha Gautama (ca. 563–483 B.C.E.) became the Buddha for our present age

bushido   "way of the warrior," the Japanese code of self-discipline for warriors based on Zen, Shinto, and Neo-Confucian ideals

butsudan   in Japan, Buddhist altar in the home

chado   *see* chanoyu

Chan   school of meditation Buddhism in China, Korea, Vietnam, and Japan (Zen in Japan), influential in the arts

chanoyu   the art of the Japanese tea ceremony; also called chado, "the way of tea"

Confucianism   Western term for the broad and pervasive religious tradition involving the learned scholars (literati), study of Confucius' *Analects* and the Five Classics, and traditional rituals involving especially the family and the ancestors

Confucius, Kongzi   teacher (ca. 551–479 B.C.E.) whose philosophy of life became dominant in Chinese culture

cosmogonic myth   sacred story that tells of the creation or founding of the world and of basic human realities

Cultural Revolution   the period from 1966 to 1976 in China during which Red Guards attempted to destroy all forms of "old" religion and culture

Daimoku   formula used in Nichiren Buddhist worship: "Namu myoho rengekyo" (Praise to the wonderful law of the *Lotus Sutra*)

Dalai Lama   head of the Geluk Tibetan Buddhist school, traditionally recognized as spiritual and political leader of Tibetans; the current Dalai Lama (b. 1935) is the fourteenth

Dao (Tao)   "way," Chinese term for a spiritual path; for Daoists, the indefinable source of all reality, the way of nature

***Daode jing* (*Tao Te Ching*)**   "Classic of Dao and Its Power"; earliest and very influential text of Daoism

Daoism   broad term for Chinese tradition based on the *Daode jing* and the *Zhuangzi*; and also the variety of Daoist practices involving rituals, priests, scriptures, and techniques for prolonging life

Daoist Canon (Daozang)   library of sacred texts and commentaries produced in Daoist religious movements, numbering over one thousand volumes

daoshi (tao shih)   Daoist priest

darshana   in Hinduism, the ritual act of being granted the "seeing" of a sacred image, person, or place; also, the six "viewpoints" or traditional schools of philosophy

dependent co-arising (pratitya-samutpada)   central Buddhist teaching that everything is conditioned by something else, that all reality is interdependent

Devi   Hindu term for goddess, sometimes meaning the great Goddess, often under many other names

Dharma   in Buddhist usage, the truth; the teaching of the Buddha

Dharma   in Hinduism, the cosmic order, social duty, and proper behavior

dharmas   in Buddhism, the most basic constituents of all phenomena

Digambara   "sky-clad," renouncing the use of clothing; one of the two major groups among the Jains

diksa   initiation ceremony for Jain monks and nuns

Divali   autumn festival of lights and good fortune in India

Dogen   important thinker (1200–1253) and founder of Soto Zen in Japan

dukkha   "sorrow," characteristic of all conditioned reality as stated in the First Noble Truth of Buddhism

Durga   great, fierce Hindu goddess, often considered a form of Devi

Eightfold Path   the fundamental path toward nirvana as taught by the Buddha, involving eight interrelated practices: right views, right resolve, right speech, right conduct, right livelihood, right effort, right mindfulness, and right concentration

Eisai   founder (1141–1215) of Rinzai Zen in Japan

emptiness   *see* shunyata

ethics   thought and study about moral decisions on the basis of traditions of right and wrong

feng shui   geomancy, the Chinese art of reading forces of yin and yang so as to determine the most beneficial location for graves and houses

filial piety, xiao (hsiao)   primary Confucian virtue of respect toward parents and ancestors

First Council of Buddhism   held at Rajagriha shortly after the Buddha's parinirvana, where, according to tradition, the Buddha's sayings were recited and compiled

Five Classics   the heart of the Confucian scriptures, including the *Shujing* (*Classic of History*), the *Shijing* (*Classic of Poetry*), the *Yijing* (*I Ching*, *Classic of*

Changes), the *Lijing* (*Classic of Rites*), and the *Chunqiu* (*Spring and Autumn Annals*)

five elements or five agents   Chinese idea of five modes of energy in the universe that mutually influence each other: wood, fire, earth, metal, and water

Five Precepts   the basic Buddhist moral precepts: to refrain from destroying life, from taking what is not given, from wrongful sexual behavior, from wrongful speech, and from drugs and liquor

five relationships   Confucian teaching of proper reciprocal roles and moral norms in the basic human relationships: father and son, husband and wife, elder and younger brother, ruler and subject, and friend and friend

Four Noble Truths   basic teachings presented in the Buddha's first sermon: the truths of sorrow, of the cause of sorrow, of the overcoming of sorrow, and of the path to follow

Four Sights   sickness, old age, death, and a wandering hermit; seeing these motivated Siddhartha Gautama to seek enlightenment

Gandhi   leader of the Hindu independence movement emphasizing spiritual preparation and nonviolent resistance (1869–1948)

Ganesha   son of Shiva, popular elephant-headed Hindu god who overcomes obstacles and brings good fortune

giri   important Japanese sense of social obligation and duty

Gobind Singh   the tenth and last Sikh guru (1666–1708), who founded the khalsa

Golden Temple   important Sikh gurdwara at Amritsar

great goddesses   feminine sacred beings, source of life and power, worshiped at least as early as the Upper Paleolithic period (starting ca. 35,000 B.C.E.)

Guanyin (Kuan Yin)   Bodhisattva Avalokiteshvara, widely worshiped in China as a god/goddess of great mercy (Kannon in Japan)

gui (kuei)   earthly yin spirits; malevolent spirits in Chinese popular thought

gurdwara   temple and meeting place for Sikhs, housing a copy of the *Adi Granth*

Guru   leader and guide for Sikhs, through whom God's word is channeled; besides the ten gurus, God and the *Adi Granth* are also called Guru

guru   spiritual guide and master

Guru Granth Sahib   "Sacred Collection," the Sikh sacred scriptures, with the title Guru; another name for the *Adi Granth*

Han dynasty   period in China (from ca. 202 B.C.E. to 220 C.E.) during which Confucianism became the state ideology and cult, Buddhism made its entry, and religious Daoism developed

healing rituals   religious rituals devoted to promoting health, often complementary to modern medical practices

Heavenly Masters   early sect of Daoism whose lineage continues today as the Orthodox Unity sect

Hidden Christians   Christians in Japan who continued to practice their religion secretly after Christianity was outlawed in the mid-seventeenth century

Hinayana   *see* Theravada

Holi   popular festival in northern India with a carnival atmosphere

Homo erectus   human species about 500,000 years ago; lived in communities, had many stone tools, and engaged in cooperative hunts

Homo sapiens sapiens   modern human species, dating back to Upper Paleolithic period

Honen   founder (1133–1212) of Pure Land Buddhism as a separate sect in Japan

Huayan (Hua Yen)   a Chinese school of Mahayana Buddhism based on the *Garland Sutra*

impermanence   basic Buddhist doctrine that change is characteristic of everything that arises

Indo-Europeans   groups of pastoralist peoples who migrated from the steppes of Asia and founded ancient civilizations in Europe, Persia, and India

Indra   Vedic storm-warrior god

Indus valley civilization   urban-agricultural civilization that flourished in the third millennium B.C.E. in the Indus River valley and influenced Hinduism

International Society for Krishna Consciousness   new Hindu movement, founded by Swami Bhaktivedanta Prabhupada (1896–1977), worshiping Krishna as the supreme manifestation of the divine; known as ISKCON, this movement has drawn many Westerners as devotees

Ise Shrine   shrine of Amaterasu, the Japanese sun kami

Izanagi and Izanami   the pair of kami who created the world, according to Japanese mythology

Jade Emperor   supreme god in Chinese popular religion

jati   "birth"; one's caste or closed social group as determined by birth in India

Jiao (Chiao)   important festival in religious Daoism, the Rite of Cosmic Renewal

Jina   "conqueror," Jain idea of one who has reached total liberation; *see also* Tirthankara

Jizo   popular Buddhist divinity in Japan known as the savior of the dead and helper of dead children

Kabir   a poet (1440–1518), an important predecessor of Guru Nanak, founder of Sikhism

Kali   goddess of death and destruction in Hinduism, often considered a form of Devi

kami   spirits or divinities in Shinto, including mythological beings, powerful and awesome aspects of nature, and important humans

kamidana   kami altar in the home in Japan

Kannon   bodhisattva Avalokiteshvara, popular goddess of mercy in Japan (Guanyin in China)

karah parshad   sacred food used in the Sikh worship assembly

karma   "action," law that all deeds and thoughts, according to one's intentions, will have set consequences, including rebirth, according to the religions from India

karma   Jain idea of subtle form of matter that clings to the soul because of the soul's passion and desire, causing rebirths

karuna   Buddhist ideal of compassion

kenosis   "emptying out"; in ritual, the movement of separation or doing away with the old state; *see* plerosis

kevela   the highest state of enlightenment, according to Jainism

khalsa   a major military-type group within Sikhism, founded in 1699 by Gobind Singh, the tenth guru, with a special code of discipline

kirtan   Sikh practice of singing hymns in worship of God

kirtana   in Hinduism, devotional group worship through song and dance

koan   Zen Buddhist saying or riddle used in meditation (gongan in China)

Kojiki   *Records of Ancient Matters*, earliest writing in Japan, a compilation of stories about the age of the kami and the beginnings of Japan

Krishna   avatara of the great Hindu god Vishnu; hero of the *Bhagavad Gita* and popular god in Vaishnavite devotional movements

Kshatriyas   the warrior class in Hindu society

Kukai   great Japanese Buddhist thinker (773–835) and founder of Shingon

lama   "master" or spiritual leader in Tibetan Buddhism

langar   Sikh community kitchen

Laozi (Lao Tzu)   legendary author of the *Daode jing* and founder of Daoism (according to tradition, born in 604 B.C.E.)

Legalists   school of thought in China that emphasized the need for strict law and order

li   *see* principle

li   rites, propriety; the Confucian code of ceremonial behavior

liminal   in ritual, the state between separation (kenosis) and restoration (plerosis)

lingam   phallic pillar that symbolizes the great God Shiva

literati (ru, ju)   learned Confucian scholars

Lotus Sutra   important early scripture of Mahayana Buddhism

Madhyamika   early school of Mahayana Buddhism that emphasized shunyata (emptiness)

magic   attempt to control forces of nature through rituals and incantations

Mahabharata   one of the two great epics of Hinduism

Mahavairochana   the great sun Buddha

Mahavira   the twenty-fourth and last Jina of the present world half-cycle, who according to Jain tradition lived from 599 to 527 B.C.E.

Mahayana   the "great vehicle," form of Buddhism that arose in India beginning in the second century B.C.E. and eventually spread to East Asia

mandala   painting of cosmic Buddhas or a symbolic cosmos, used especially in Vajrayana Buddhist ritual and meditation

Mandate of Heaven   in Chinese religion, the expression of Tian's moral will, especially in granting prosperity to virtuous rulers and cutting short evil ones

mantra   powerful sacred words, formula, or verse chanted as a focus for meditation and devotion

Mao Zedong (Mao Tse-tung)   leader (1893–1976) of the Chinese Communist movement and of the People's Republic of China

matsuri   Shinto shrine festival

Matteo Ricci   first Jesuit missionary to China (1552–1610)

maya   in Hinduism, appearance, illusion; term to indicate that which prevents one from seeing truly

Mazu (Ma Tsu)   widely worshiped goddess of Chinese seafarers; known as the Queen of Heaven

Meiji Restoration   restoration of imperial rule in Japan in 1868

Mengzi (Meng Tzu, Mencius)   leading thinker (ca. 372–289 B.C.E.) whose writings shaped the Confucian tradition

moksha   liberation from bondage to samsara and karma; the goal of Hindu spiritual practice

monism   view that all reality is one unified divine reality

monotheism   belief in one almighty God, separate from the world

Motoori Norinaga   leading scholar (1730–1801) of the National Learning movement that advocated the restoration of Shinto as Japan's central religion

mudra   hand gesture or pose with symbolic meaning

myth   story about sacred beings in the beginning time, telling how existence came to be as it is and providing the pattern for authentic life

Nagarjuna   important philosopher (ca. 150–250 C.E.) of the Madhyamika school of Buddhism

Nam   in Sikhism, the Name of God, the total divine presence in the world

Nanak   founder (1469–1539) of Sikhism and the first guru

Neanderthal   human species ca. 100,000 to 35,000 years ago, with clear archaeological evidence of religious activities

Nembutsu   (nianfo in China) Japanese formula of calling on Amida Buddha with the words, "Namu Amida Butsu" (Praise to Amida Buddha)

Neo-Confucianism   revival of Confucian thought in the eleventh century C.E., with emphasis on the underlying principle of all things

Neolithic   period beginning after the last ice age (ca. 10,000 years ago) when planting was discovered and villages and cities founded

New Religions   in Japan, term used for new religious movements, often drawing on and combining aspects of Buddhism, Shinto, and folk religion

Nichiren   Japanese Buddhist sect based single-mindedly on the *Lotus Sutra*, founded by the monk Nichiren (1222–1282)

Nihon shoki (Nihongi)   chronicles of Japan, compiled shortly after the *Kojiki* and containing stories about the kami and early emperors

Ninigi   grandson of Amaterasu, sent to earth to begin kami rule on earth, ancestor of first legendary Japanese emperor

nirvana   "blowing out" the fires of life, liberation from suffering and rebirth, the spiritual goal of Buddhist practice

no-action (wuwei)   basic Daoist principle of not doing anything contrary to the flow of nature

noble person (junzi)   ideal Confucian goal; a noble person defined by moral character

Noh   classical Japanese theater, closely linked to the religious traditions, especially Zen

nondualism   view that ultimate reality and the phenomenal world are not different

Norito   ancient Shinto ritual prayers

no-self (an-atman)   the basic Buddhist doctrine that there is no permanent, absolute self

Obon (Ullambana)   festival of the seventh month in Japan welcoming the ancestors

ordination   *see* upasampada

Paleolithic   Old Stone Age; in the Upper Paleolithic period (ca. 35,000 to 10,000 years ago) the modern species of *Homo sapiens sapiens* appeared

Pangu (P'an Ku)   in Chinese tradition, mythic primordial person out of whom the whole universe developed

parinirvana   full nirvana; complete liberation attained at the death of a Buddha

Parshva   the twenty-third Jina of the present world half-cycle, who lived in the mid-ninth century B.C.E.

Path of Action (karma-marga)   Hindu path toward liberation based on acting according to Dharma, without desire for the fruits of action

Path of Devotion (bhakti-marga)   Hindu path toward liberation based on devotional practices directed toward one's god

Path of Knowledge (jnana-marga)   Hindu path toward liberation based on knowledge, emphasizing meditation

path of transformation   practice in a religious tradition that changes one from the wrong or inadequate state to the ideal state

plerosis   "filling up"; fulfillment or restoration movement of ritual; *see* kenosis

pollution   in the Shinto view, anything that hinders life and fertility by causing separation from the kami

polytheism   belief that many divine powers share in the world's operation

prasad   in Hinduism, gift from the deity consecrated in ritual, especially food, shared by the devotee

prehistorical   before written records

principle (**li**, different word from li meaning "rites")   Neo-Confucian teaching that identifies principle as the underlying source of all phenomena, operating together with *qi* (material force)

puja   in Hinduism, ritual worship of the image of a god by offering food, flowers, music, and prayers

Puranas   late Hindu scriptures that developed from popular theistic devotional movements

Pure Land   Mahayana school of Buddhism focusing on worship of Amitabha Buddha, with hope of rebirth in the Pure Land paradise, founded in Japan especially by Honen and Shinran

purification   rituals, important in Shinto, to remove pollution and reinstate harmony and communion with the kami

qi (**ch'i**)   material force, breath, flowing vital energy, in Chinese traditions

qigong   broad term for variety of Chinese physical exercises to cultivate qi in body and spirit

Qing Ming (**Ch'ing Ming**)   "clear and bright" festival; spring festival of visiting and renovating ancestral tombs in China

Rain Retreat (*Vassa*)   important three-month time of study and discipline for Theravada Buddhist monks and nuns, when lay people also make offerings and perform service for the monastics

Rama   avatara of Vishnu, divine hero of the *Ramayana*

Ramakrishna   modern Hindu holy man (1836–1886) whose teachings were brought to America by his disciple Vivekananda (1863–1902), who established the Ramakrishna Mission (Vedanta Society)

Ramanuja   Hindu philosopher and advocate of the Vaishnavite bhakti tradition (ca. 1017–1137)

Ramayana   story of Rama, one of the two great epics of Hinduism

rebirth   belief that after a person's death, the accumulated karma will cause another rebirth to take place

rebirth   in the Jain tradition, belief that after the death of its body, the accumulated karma causes the soul to take on another body from the almost infinite range of possibilities, including one-sense bodies

rectification of names   Confucian program for the development of a moral society by properly structuring social relationships

religious Daoism   variety of Daoist practices involving rituals, priests, scriptures, and techniques for prolonging life

religious traditions   sacred stories and basic ideas and practices that religious communities "hand over" from generation to generation; that which is handed over (Latin *traditio*) is thought to maintain a recognizable unity even while changing over time

ren (**jen**)   humaneness, an important ideal in Confucianism

restraints   the Jain vows of nonviolence, not lying, not stealing, refraining from wrong sex, and nonpossession or nonattachment

Rig Veda   the earliest and most important collection of Vedic hymns in Hinduism

rites of passage   rituals connected with the critical changes or passages in a person's life, especially birth, puberty, marriage, and death

rituals   activities of many kinds that connect people with sacred realities, including prayer, sacrifice, chanting, pilgrimage, festivals, disciplines of meditation, and much more

sacred space   space that is made special by connection with the sacred, providing orientation and rootedness for a people

sacred story   master story of a religion, providing identity for the adherents; *see* myth

sacred, the   what is experienced as ultimate reality, the mysterious Other that is the ground of ultimate value and meaning

sacred time   special time of ritual and festival, when mythic events are made present once more

Saicho   founder (767–822) of Tendai Buddhism in Japan

Samhitas   "collections" of early Vedic hymns and verses; there are four collections: *Rig-Veda*, *Sama-Veda*, *Yajur-Veda*, and *Atharva-Veda*

Samkhya one of the classical schools of Hindu philosophy stressing an absolute distinction between matter and spirit

samnyasin one who has renounced the cares and concerns of the world; samnyasa is the fourth stage of life in Hinduism

samsara the rebirth cycle of existence

samskaras in Hinduism, rituals performed at the critical changes and passages of life

samurai the Japanese class of warriors influenced by Zen and Neo-Confucianism

sangha the communities of Buddhist monks and nuns

sati in Hinduism, self-sacrifice of a widow on her husband's funeral pyre; outlawed in modern times

School of National Learning Shinto restoration movement during the Tokugawa period

Shakti in Hinduism, divine energy, personified as a goddess; female aspect of a god, especially of Shiva

Shakyamuni a title of Siddhartha Gautama the Buddha: the wise one of the Shakya clan

Shang Di (Shang Ti) supreme god worshiped by the Shang rulers in ancient China

Shankara great philosopher of Advaita (nondual) Vedanta (788–820 C.E.), in Hinduism

shen in Chinese tradition, heavenly yang spirits; benevolent and honored spirits, including ancestors

Shingon esoteric (Tantric) Buddhism in Japan

Shinran disciple (1173–1262) of Honen and founder of the True Pure Land Buddhist sect in Japan

Shinto term designating the indigenous Japanese "way of the kami," from the Chinese term *shendao*

Shiva one of the two great Hindu Gods, symbolized by the lingam; focus of the Shaivite devotional movement

Shotoku prince regent (573–621) who advocated Buddhism as one of the pillars of Japan

shrine (jinja) Shinto sacred place focused on the presence of a kami; usually has appropriate buildings where a symbol of the kami is housed and where worshipers can consult priests

Shruti in Hinduism "that which is heard," the eternal truth, that is, the Vedas

Shudras classical servant class in Hindu society, the fourth class

shunyata "emptiness," Mahayana Buddhist teaching that all things are devoid of any substantial or independent reality

Shvetambara "white clad," accepting the use of clothing; one of the two major Jain groups

Sikh "disciple," that is, one who follows the gurus

Singh surname taken by men who join the Sikh khalsa

skandhas "heaps" or aggregates; the Buddhist teaching that a person is really a changing process in five aggregates: physical matter, sensations, perceptual activities, impulses to action, and bits of consciousness

Smriti in Hinduism, "that which is remembered," the tradition, that is, the scriptural writings after the Vedas

Soka Gakkai largest New Religion in Japan, based on Nichiren Buddhism

Son of Heaven title of Chinese emperor

spirit writing in Chinese religion, writing on a tray of sand or on paper by a spirit who moves the pen

stupa memorial Buddhist shrine or reliquary

Susanoo storm kami in Japanese mythology, unruly brother of Amaterasu

symbols words, pictures, ideas, rituals, and so on that evoke deep meanings by connecting with sacred reality

taiji (t'ai-chi) Great Ultimate that underlies and generates all things; a popular Chinese exercise is called taiji quan (fist of the Great Ultimate)

Taiping Rebellion (T'ai P'ing) abortive popular movement in the mid-nineteenth century in China, based on religious ideas, attempting to change the hierarchical structure of society

Tantrism movement using initiation, rituals, imagination, and sexual symbolism as spiritual practices leading toward liberation; *see also* Vajaryana

Tathagata title for the Buddha meaning the "Thus Come One," that is, the perfected one

Tendai important school of Buddhism in Japan (Tiantai in China)

Tenrikyo the oldest of the existing New Religions in Japan, founded in 1838

Theravada "teaching of the elders," term for the early Buddhist tradition and practice still followed in South and Southeast Asia. Theravada is generally used in place of the term *Hinayana*, "lesser vehicle," a pejorative term that Mahayana Buddhists applied to the early Buddhist sects

Three Ages of the Dharma   Buddhist teaching of increasing decline and degeneracy in humans' ability to follow the Buddhist path: the age of the Perfect Dharma, the age of the Counterfeit Dharma, and the age of the End of the Dharma

Three Body Teaching   Mahayana teaching of three dimensions of Buddha: Dharma Body (universal Buddha essence), Bliss Body (heavenly Buddhas), and Transformation Body (human manifestations of Buddha)

Three Pure Ones   designation for highest gods summoned by Daoist priests

Three Refuges   the ritual formula, "I take refuge in the Buddha, I take refuge in the Dharma, I take refuge in the Sangha,"

Tian (T'ien)   "heaven," from ancient times in China considered an ultimate power that rules especially through the moral order

Tiantai (T'ien T'ai)   a school of Mahayana Buddhism in China, based on the *Lotus Sutra*

Tipitaka   see *Tripitaka*

Tirthankara   "ford builder," Jain idea of one who has reached total liberation and shows the way across the ocean of suffering; *see also* Jina

torii   characteristic gateway to the Shinto shrine

Total Perfection   Daoist sect from the Song era that practices monastic life, still existent today

transformation   the act of reaching the ideal state of wholeness, perfection, or salvation

Tripitaka (Pali: *Tipitaka*)   the scriptures of the Pali Canon of Buddhism, meaning "Three Baskets"; they include the Vinaya Pitaka, the Sutra Pitaka, and the Abhidharma Pitaka

Tudigong (T'u Ti Kung)   local earth god in Chinese religion

Ullambana   Buddhist festival in China and Japan worshiping the souls of ancestors and providing for souls temporarily released from purgatory; called Obon in Japan

understanding   "standing under" another's way of thought and life, comprehending it by reference to one's own experience

upanayana   initiation of high-class boy into the student stage of life in Hinduism; he is given a sacred cord to wear over his left shoulder and taught the appropriate mantras

Upanishads   in Hinduism, collection of teachings about the self and ultimate reality that makes up the last part of the Veda (Shruti)

upasampada   ordination, important Buddhist ritual marking the beginning of life as a monk or nun

uposatha   fortnightly Buddhist holy day when temple meetings for teaching, ritual, and meditation are held

Vaishyas   the classical producer-merchant class in Hindu society

Vajrayana   Diamond Vehicle, the Tantric tradition of Buddhism especially in Tibet and Japan, using initiation, rituals, imagination, and sexual symbolism as spiritual practices leading toward liberation

varna   "color," term for the classes in the system of Hindu society

Varuna   Vedic god of the heavens, in Hinduism

Vedanta   "end of the Vedas"; influential school of philosophy in Hinduism, based especially on the Upanishads

Vedanta Societies   Hindu groups in America and Europe following the teaching of Swami Vivekananda (1863–1902) and Sri Ramakrishna (1836–1886)

Vedas   most important scriptures of Hinduism, the Shruti; they consist of the Samhitas, Brahmanas, Aranyakas, and Upanishads

Vesakha   in Theravada communities, a grand festival in May celebrating the Buddha's birth, enlightenment, and parinirvana

Vinaya   texts containing rules for Buddhist monastic life and discipline

vipassana   central Buddhist meditation practice focusing on calming the mind and seeing true reality

Vishnu   one of the two great Gods in Hinduism, worshiped also in his avataras Rama and Krishna

way of art   in Japan, practice of an art (such as poetry, Noh drama, or the tea ceremony) as a way of self-cultivation

Word of God   in Sikh thought, God's presence that reverberates throughout creation, channeled especially through the gurus

worship   respectful ritual activity in special times, directed toward sacred beings or realities of ultimate value

wuwei   *see* no-action

Xunzi (Hsün Tzu)   important Confucian thinker (ca. 300–238 B.C.E.) who advocated a realistic understanding of the human inclination toward evil

Yijing (*I Ching*)   the Classic of Changes, an ancient Chinese divination manual based on sixty-four hexagrams (each of six unbroken and broken lines)

yin and **yang**   Chinese idea of polarity of forces in the universe; yin is passive, earthly force, and yang is active, heavenly force

Zaojun (Tsao Chun)   God of the Cooking Stove in Chinese religion

zazen   Japanese term meaning "sitting in meditation," central practice in Zen Buddhism

Zen   important school of meditation Buddhism in Japan (Chan in China); *see also* Chan

Zhou Dynasty (Chou)   long dynasty (ca. 1123–221 B.C.E.) during which the classics were compiled and the Confucianist and Daoist traditions developed

Zhu Xi (Chu Hsi)   leading thinker of the Neo-Confucian movement (1130–1200 C.E.)

Zhuangzi (Chuang Tzu)   important early teacher (ca. 369–286 B.C.E.) whose book bearing his name has been very influential for the Daoist movement

Notes

PART 1 EXPLORING THE SACRED PATHS

Chapter 1 Perspectives on the Religious Path

[1] See, for example, Daniel L. Pals, *Seven Theories of Religion* (New York: Oxford University Press, 1996).

[2] Rudolph Otto, *The Idea of the Holy*, trans. John Harvey, 2nd ed. (London: Oxford University Press, 1982).

[3] Joachim Wach, *Sociology of Religion* (Chicago: University of Chicago Press, 1944), pp. 17–34.

[4] Mircea Eliade, *The Sacred and the Profane: The Nature of Religion*, trans. Willard R. Trask (New York: Harcourt, Brace & World, 1968).

[5] The terms *kenosis* and *plerosis* are used by Theodor H. Gaster, *Thespis: Ritual, Myth, and Drama in the Ancient Near East* (New York: Doubleday, 1961), pp. 23–49.

[6] The structure of the rites of passage was first analyzed by Arnold van Gennep, *The Rites of Passage*, trans. Monika Vizedom and Gabrielle Caffee (Chicago: University of Chicago Press, 1960).

[7] Eliade, *The Sacred and the Profane*, pp. 20–65.

Chapter 2 Beginnings of the Human Religious Adventure

[1] For some examples of the current discussion, see *What Is Religion? Origins, Definitions, and Explanations*, ed. by Thomas Idinopulos and Brian C. Wilson (Leiden: Brill, 1998); *Guide to the Study of Religion*, ed. by Willi Braun and Russell T. McCutcheon (London: Cassell, 2000); and *The Craft of Religious Studies*, ed. Jon R. Stone (New York: Palgrave, 2000).

PART 2 RELIGIONS ARISING FROM INDIA

Chapter 3 Hindu Sacred Story and Historical Context

[1] Wendy Doniger O'Flaherty, trans., *The Rig Veda: An Anthology* (New York: Penguin Books, 1981), pp. 211–212.

[2] Ibid., p. 149.

[3] Ibid., p. 99.

[4] Ibid., p. 134.

[5] Ibid., p. 25.

[6] Taken with editing from *The Satapatha-Brahmana*, trans. Julius Eggeling, vol. 43 in *The Sacred Books of the East*, ed. F. Max Müller (reprinted Delhi: Motilal Banarsidass, 1966 [first edition Clarendon Press, 1897]), pp. 381–390.

[7] Robert Ernest Hume, trans., *The Thirteen Principal Upanishads Translated from the Sanskrit*, 2nd ed. (New York: Oxford University Press, 1931), p. 76.

[8] Barbara Stoler Miller, trans., *The Bhagavad-Gita: Krishna's Counsel in Times of War* (New York: Columbia University Press, 1986), p. 39.

[9] Ibid., p. 87.

[10] See John M. Koller, *The Indian Way* (New York: Macmillan, 1982), p. 257.

Chapter 4 Hindu Worlds of Meaning

[1] O'Flaherty, *The Rig Veda*, pp. 25–26.

[2] Hume, *The Thirteen Principal Upanishads*, pp. 119–120.

[3] Ibid., pp. 117–119.

[4] Ibid., p. 147.

[5] Ibid., p. 210.

[6] *The Vedanta-Sutras with the Commentary by Sankaradarya*, trans. George Thibault, vol. 34 in *The Sacred Books of the East*, p. 61.

[7] Miller, trans., *The Bhagavad-Gita*, pp. 99–105.

[8] Ramanuja on Bhagavad Gita 6.47, in R. C. Zaehner, *Hinduism* (London: Oxford University Press, 1962), p. 99.

[9] See the poems of the Virashaivite saints in A. K. Ramanujan, trans., *Speaking of Shiva* (Baltimore: Penguin Books, Inc., 1973), p. 84.

[10] Swami Nikhilananda, trans., *The Gospel of Sri Ramakrishna* (New York: Ramakrishna-Vivekananda Center, 1952), pp. 134–135.

[11] Hume, *The Thirteen Principal Upanishads*, p. 81.

[12] Ibid., p. 248.

[13] Ibid., p. 140.

14 Ibid., pp. 413–414.
15 Ibid., p. 143.
16 Ibid., p. 140.
17 Ibid., pp. 83–84.
18 Ibid., p. 142.
19 Ibid., p. 353.
20 Ibid., p. 141.
21 Ibid., p. 393.
22 Miller, *Bhagavad-Gita*, pp. 52, 43.
23 Ibid., p. 87.
24 Ibid., p. 79.
25 David R. Kinsley, *The Sword and the Flute* (Berkeley: University of California Press, 1977), pp. 52–53.
26 Wendy Doniger O'Flaherty, *Shiva: The Erotic Ascetic* (Oxford: Oxford University Press, 1981), p. 149.
27 *Manikka Vasagar*, quoted in R. C. Zaehner, *Hinduism*, pp. 133–134.
28 See Ramprasad's poems translated in Leonard Nathan and Clinton Seely, *Grace and Mercy in Her Wild Hair: Selected Poems to the Mother Goddess* (Boulder: Great Eastern, 1982), pp. 62, 25.
29 Swami Nikhilananda, *The Gospel of Sri Ramakrishna*, pp. 261–262.

Chapter 5   Hindu Ritual and the Good Life

1 McKim Marriott, "The Feast of Love," in *Krishna: Myths, Rites, and Attitudes*, ed. Milton Singer (Chicago: University of Chicago Press, 1968), p. 212.
2 See, for example, V. K. Duvvury, *Play, Symbolism and Ritual: A Study of Tamil Brahmin Women's Rites of Passage* (New York: Peter Lang, 1991), pp. 117–132; and Julia Leslie, ed., *Roles and Rituals for Hindu Women* (London: Pinter Publishers, 1991).
3 Mariasusai Dhavamony, *Classical Hinduism* (Roma: Università Gregoriana Editrice, 1982), pp. 181–183.
4 Miller, *Bhagavad-Gita*, p. 149.
5 *Law-code of Manu*, 3:55; 9:3–4, 11, 26, in Ainslie T. Embree, ed., *Sources of Indian Tradition*, 2nd ed. (New York: Columbia University Press, 1988), I, pp. 228–229.
6 *Law-code of Manu*, 6:2, in Ibid., p. 229.
7 *Law-code of Manu*, 6:33, 42, in Ibid., pp. 229–230.
8 *Law-code of Manu*, 6:45–81, in R. C. Zaehner, *Hinduism*, p. 113.
9 Charles White, "Mother Guru: Jnanananda of Madras, India," *Unspoken Worlds: Women's Religious Lives*, eds. Nancy Auer Falk and Rita M. Gross (Belmont, CA: Wadsworth, 1989), pp. 15–24.
10 Written in *The Harijan* for December 8, 1946; in Troy Wilson Organ, *Hinduism: Its Historical Development* (Woodbury, NY: Barron's Educational Series, 1974), p. 368.
11 S. Radhakrishnan, *Eastern Religions and Western Thought* (Oxford: Clarendon Press, 1939), p. 327.

Chapter 6   Buddhist Sacred Story and Historical Context

1 From *Suvarnaprabhasa*, a Mahayana text, in Edward Conze, trans., *Buddhist Scriptures* (Baltimore: Penguin Books, 1959), pp. 24–26.
2 From *Buddhacarita*, a Sanskrit poem said to have been composed by Ashvaghosha between the first and second centuries C.E., Wm. Theodore de Bary, ed., *The Buddhist Tradition in India, China, and Japan* (New York: Vintage Books, 1972), p. 58. We follow the main outlines of the *Buddhacarita* in telling the Buddha's story.
3 Ibid., p. 59.
4 Ibid., pp. 61–62.
5 Ibid., p. 66.
6 Henry Clarke Warren, *Buddhism in Translation: Passages Selected from the Buddhist Sacred Books* (Cambridge: Harvard University Press, 1947), pp. 60–61.
7 de Bary, *Buddhist Tradition*, p. 68.
8 Warren, *Buddhism*, p. 76.
9 Stephan Beyer, *The Buddhist Experience: Sources and Interpretations* (Belmont, CA: Dickenson Publishing, 1974), p. 197.
10 From *Samyutta Nikaya*, in Ainslie T. Embree, ed., *Sources of Indian Tradition*, 2nd ed. (New York: Columbia University Press, 1988), I, p. 101.
11 From Mahaparinibbana Sutta, *Digha Nikaya*, ibid., pp. 111–112.
12 From *Digha Nikaya*, ibid., p. 112.

Chapter 7   Buddhist Worlds of Meaning

1 Wapola Rahula, *What the Buddha Taught* (New York: Grove Press, 1974), p. 37.
2 Edward Conze, *Buddhism: Its Essence and Development* (New York: Harper and Row, 1959), p. 40.
3 From *Samyutta Nikaya*, in Rahula, p. 27.
4 *Digha Nikaya*, in Embree, *Sources of Indian Tradition*, I, p. 128.
5 See Conze, *Buddhist Scriptures*, pp. 222–224.
6 From *Samyutta Nikaya*, in Embree, *Sources of Indian Tradition*, I, p. 101.
7 Taken with editing from *The Questions of King Milinda, Part II*, trans. by T. W. Rhys Davids, vol. 36 in *The Sacred Books of the East*, pp. 196–197.
8 From *Majjhima Nikaya*, in Bhikkhu Nanamoli, *The Middle Length Discourses of the Buddha: A New Translation of the Majjhima Nikaya*, edited and revised by Bhikkhu Bodhi (Boston: Wisdom Publications, 1995), pp. 534–535.
9 Rahula, *What the Buddha Taught*, p. 73.

[10] Shantideva, *The Bodhicaryavatara*, trans. Kate Crosley and Andrew Skilton (New York: Oxford University Press, 1995), pp. 20–21.

Chapter 8 Buddhist Ritual and the Good Life

[1] In Melford E. Spiro, *Buddhism and Society: A Great Tradition and Its Burmese Vicissitudes* (New York: Harper and Row, 1972), p. 210.

[2] Ibid., p. 212.

[3] Stephen Beyer, *The Buddhist Experience: Sources and Interpretations* (Belmont, CA: Dickenson Publishing, 1974), p. 241.

[4] *Suttanipata*, I, 8, in Rahula, *What the Buddha Taught*, pp. 97–98.

[5] Siksasamuccaya, in Embree, *Sources of Indian Tradition*, I, p. 162.

[6] *Dhammapada*, vss. 3, 50, 223, in Rahula, *What the Buddha Taught*, pp. 125–132.

[7] *Majjhima Nikaya*, 2:147ff., in Embree, *Sources of Indian Tradition*, I, pp. 140–141.

[8] *Sutta Nipata*, v. 136, in ibid., p. 139.

[9] *Digha Nikaya*, 3:180ff, in ibid., p. 124.

[10] *First Pillar Edict*, in ibid., p. 144.

[11] *Twelfth Rock Edict*, ibid., p. 147.

Chapter 9 The Path of the Jains

[1] Paul Dundas, *The Jains* (London: Routledge, 1992), p. 49.

[2] Embree, *Sources of Indian Tradition*, I, p. 80–82.

[3] Ibid., pp. 62–63.

[4] Jyotiprasad Jain, *Religion and Culture of the Jains* (New Delhi: Bharatiya Jnanpith Publication, 1975), p. 114.

[5] Ibid., p. 176.

Chapter 10 The Way of the Disciples: The Sikhs

[1] C. Vaudeville, *Kabir* (London: Oxford University Press, 1974), pp. 154–155.

[2] Trilochan Singh et al., trans., *Selections from the Sacred Writings of the Sikhs* (London: George Allen and Unwin, 1960), p. 28.

[3] Trilochan, *Selections*, pp. 103–105.

[4] Trilochan Singh, *Selections*, p. 91.

[5] Ibid., p. 203.

[6] Ibid., p. 102.

[7] Taran Singh, quoted in W. Owen Cole, *The Guru in Sikhism* (London: Darton, Longman and Todd, 1982), p. 89.

[8] Gopal Singh, *The Sikhs: Their History, Religion, Culture, Ceremonies, and Literature* (Madras: M. Seshachalam, 1970), p. 64.

[9] Trilochan Singh, *Selections*, p. 56.

[10] Hew McLeod, *Sikhism* (New York: Penguin Books, 1997), p. 298.

[11] Trilochan Singh, *Selections*, p. 60.

[12] Pritam Singh Gill, *Heritage of Sikh Culture: Society, Morality, Art* (Jullundur: New Academic Publishing Co., 1975), p. 229.

[13] Trilochan Singh, *Selections*, p. 93.

[14] Quoted in Cole, *The Guru in Sikhism*, pp. 93–94.

PART 3 RELIGIONS OF CHINA AND JAPAN

Chapter 11 Chinese Sacred Story and Historical Context

[1] Wing-tsit Chan, *A Source Book in Chinese Philosophy* (Princeton, NJ: Princeton University Press, 1969), p. 38.

[2] Ibid., p. 78.

[3] Ibid., p. 152.

[4] Ibid., p. 197.

Chapter 12 Chinese Worlds of Meaning

[1] Chan, *A Source Book in Chinese Philosophy*, p. 35.

[2] Wing-tsit Chan et al., comps., *The Great Asian Religions: An Anthology* (London: Macmillan, 1969), p. 135.

[3] Chan, *A Source Book in Chinese Philosophy*, p. 152.

[4] Ibid., p. 203.

[5] Ibid., p. 157.

[6] Burton Watson, trans., *The Complete Works of Chuang Tzu* (New York: Columbia University Press, 1968), p. 81.

[7] Chan, *A Source Book in Chinese Philosophy*, p. 638.

[8] Ibid., pp. 635–636.

[9] *Guanzi*, ch. 40, in Milton Chiu, *The Tao of Chinese Religion* (New York: University Press of America, 1984), pp. 147–148.

[10] Ibid., p. 173.

[11] From *Huainanzi*, ibid., p. 176.

[12] In Chan, *A Source Book in Chinese Philosophy*, p. 280, and Wm. Theodore de Bary and Irene Bloom, comps., *Sources of Chinese Tradition*, vol. I, 2nd ed. (New York: Columbia University Press, 1999), p. 301.

[13] de Bary and Bloom, *Sources of Chinese Tradition*, p. 129.

[14] Chan, *A Source Book in Chinese Philosophy*, p. 57.

[15] de Bary and Bloom, *Sources of Chinese Tradition*, pp. 179–180.

[16] From Yang Xiong (53 B.C.E.–18 C.E.), in Chan, *A Source Book in Chinese Philosophy*, p. 289.

[17] de Bary and Bloom, *Sources of Chinese Tradition*, p. 147.

[18] Watson, *The Complete Works of Chuang Tzu*, pp. 99–100.

[19] Chan et al., *The Great Asian Religions*, pp. 208–212.

[20] See Herbert A. Giles, *Strange Stories from a Chinese Studio* (Shanghai: Kelly & Walsh, Ltd., 1926, 4th rev. ed.), pp. 467–485; quoted in Laurence G. Thompson, *The Chinese Way in Religion* (Belmont, CA: Dickenson Publishing, 1973), pp. 187, 195.

[21] Chan, *A Source Book in Chinese Philosophy*, pp. 86–87.

22 de Bary and Bloom, *Sources of Chinese Tradition*, p. 175.

23 Ibid., p. 147.

24 Watson, *The Complete Works of Chuang Tzu*, p. 302.

25 de Bary and Bloom, *Sources of Chinese Tradition*, pp. 103–104.

26 Burton Watson, trans., *Chuang Tzu: Basic Writings* (New York: Columbia University Press, 1964), p. 42.

27 Chang Chung-yuan, trans., *Original Teachings of Ch'an Buddhism: Selected from the Transmission of the Lamp* (New York: Vintage Books, 1971), pp. 116–117.

28 Chan, *A Source Book in Chinese Philosophy*, pp. 446–448.

Chapter 13   Ritual Practices and the Good Life in China

1 John K. Shryock, *The Origin and Development of the State Cult of Confucius* (New York: Paragon Book Reprint Corp., 1966; originally printed 1932), pp. 175–176.

2 Michael R. Saso, *Taoism and the Rite of Cosmic Renewal* (Pullman: Washington State University Press, 1972), pp. 70–72.

3 David K. Jordan, *Gods, Ghosts and Ancestors: Folk Religion in a Taiwanese Village* (Berkeley: University of California Press, 1972), pp. 56–59.

4 Holmes Welch, *The Practice of Chinese Buddhism*, 1900–1950 (Cambridge: Harvard University Press, 1967), pp. 53–77.

5 Margery Wolf, *Women and the Family in Rural Taiwan* (Stanford: Stanford University Press, 1972), pp. 135–136.

6 Burton Watson, trans., *Basic Writings of Hsun Tzu* (New York: Columbia University Press, 1967), pp. 117–118.

7 Osvald Siren, *The Chinese on the Art of Painting: Translations and Comments* (New York: Schocken Books, 1963), pp. 54–56.

8 de Bary and Bloom, *Sources of Chinese Tradition*, p. 334.

9 Chan, *A Source Book in Chinese Philosophy*, p. 226.

10 Ibid., p. 77.

11 deBary and Bloom, *Sources of Chinese Tradition*, p. 326.

12 Chan, *A Source Book in Chinese Philosophy*, pp. 28, 31.

13 *Doctrine of the Mean*, ch. 14, in ibid., p. 101.

14 Ibid., p. 22.

15 Watson, *The Complete Works of Chuang Tzu*, p. 73.

16 Chan, *A Source Book in Chinese Philosophy*, p. 166.

17 Saso, *Taoism and the Rite of Cosmic Renewal*, pp. 48–51.

18 de Bary and Bloom, *Sources of Chinese Tradition*, p. 343.

19 Ibid., p. 683.

Chapter 15   Japanese Worlds of Meaning

1 *The Manyoshu: The Nippon Gakujutsu Shinkokai Translation of One Thousand Poems* (New York: Columbia University Press, 1965), p. 215.

2 Donald Philippi, *Norito: A Translation of the Ancient Japanese Ritual Prayers* (Princeton: Princeton University Press, 1990), pp. 46–47.

3 Ryusaku Tsunoda et al., comps., *Sources of Japanese Tradition*, vol. II (New York: Columbia University Press, 1964), pp. 24–25.

4 Philippi, *Norito*, p. 48.

5 See Tsunetsugu Muraoka, *Studies in Shinto Thought*, trans. by Delmer Brown and James Araki (Tokyo: Ministry of Education, 1964), p. 37.

6 Yoshito S. Hakeda, trans., *Kukai: Major Works* (New York: Columbia University Press, 1972), p. 93.

7 Ibid., p. 218.

8 Ibid., pp. 230–232.

9 Wm. Theodore de Bary et al., *Sources of Japanese Tradition*, vol. I, 2nd ed. (New York: Columbia University Press, 2001), p. 226.

10 Ibid., p. 228.

11 See Chan et al., *The Great Asian Religions*, p. 287.

12 Philip B. Yampolsky, trans., *The Zen Master Hakuin: Selected Writing* (New York: Columbia University Press, 1971), pp. 163–164.

13 Ibid., pp. 135–136.

Chapter 16   Ritual Practices and the Good Life in Japan

1 Hakeda, *Kukai: Major Works*, p. 91.

2 Ibid., p. 98.

3 Burton Watson, trans., *Saigyo: Poems of a Mountain Home* (New York: Columbia University Press, 1991), p. 130.

4 From *Namboroku*, in *Chado koten zenshu*, Vol. IV, ed. Sen Soshitsu (Kyoto: Tanko Shinsha, 1956–1962), p. 264.

5 See H. Byron Earhart, *Religion in the Japanese Experience*, 2nd ed. (Belmont: Wadsworth Publishing Company, 1997), pp. 43–44.

6 Tsunoda et al., *Sources of Japanese Tradition*, vol. II, pp. 42–43.

7 Sokyo Ono, *The Kami Way* (Tokyo: International Institute for the Study of Religions, 1959), pp. 106–107.

8 See Chan, *The Great Asian Religions*, p. 300.

9 Kenji Ueda, "Shinto," in Ichiro Hori et al., eds., *Japanese Religion: A Survey by the Agency for Cultural Affairs*, trans. by Yoshiya Abe and David Reid (Tokyo: Kodansha International Ltd., 1972), pp. 38–41.

Suggestions for Further Reading

PART 1 EXPLORING THE SACRED PATHS

Note: Extensive articles on all religious studies topics and on all facets of the world religions can be found in *The Encyclopedia of Religion*, edited by Mircea Eliade, 15 vols. (New York: Macmillan, 1987). Now the revised and updated edition of this reference work is available: *The Encyclopedia of Religion*, 2nd edition, edited by Lindsay Jones (New York: Macmillan Reference, 2005).

Perspectives on the Religious Path

Brockman, Norbert C. *Encyclopedia of Sacred Places*. New York: Oxford University Press, 1998.

Brown, Frank Burch. *Good Taste, Bad Taste, and Christian Taste: Aesthetics in Religious Life*. New York: Oxford University Press, 2003.

Christ, Carol P., and Judith Plaskow, eds. *Womanspirit Rising: A Feminist Reader in Religion*. Revised edition. San Francisco: Harper & Row, 1991.

Comstock, Gary L. *Religious Autobiographies*. Second edition. Belmont, CA: Wadsworth, 2004.

Denny, Frederick M., and Rodney L. Taylor, eds. *The Holy Book in Comparative Perspective*. Columbia: University of South Carolina Press, 1985.

Doniger, Wendy. *Splitting the Difference: Gender and Myth in Ancient Greece and India*. Chicago: The University of Chicago Press, 1999.

Eastman, Roger, ed. *The Ways of Religion: An Introduction to the Major Traditions*. Third edition. New York: Oxford University Press, 1999.

Eliade, Mircea. *A History of Religious Ideas*. 3 vols. Translated by Willard R. Trask. Chicago: University of Chicago Press, 1981–1988.

———. *Patterns in Comparative Religion*. Translated by Rosemary Sheed. Lincoln: University of Nebraska Press, 1996.

Falk, Nancy Auer, and Rita M. Gross, eds. *Unspoken Worlds: Women's Religious Lives*. Second edition. Belmont, CA: Wadsworth, 2000.

Ferguson, Marianne. *Women and Religion*. Englewood Cliffs, NJ: Prentice Hall, 1995.

Lovin, Robin W., and Frank E. Reynolds, eds. *Cosmogony and Ethical Order*. Chicago: University of Chicago Press, 1985.

Pals, Daniel L. *Seven Theories of Religion*. New York: Oxford University Press, 1996.

Sharma, Arvind, ed. *Religion and Women*. Albany: State University of New York Press, 1994.

Sharma, Arvind, and Katherine Young, eds. *Her Voice, Her Faith: Women Speak on World Religions*. Boulder: Westview Press, 2003.

Smart, Ninian. *Dimensions of the Sacred: An Anatomy of the World's Beliefs*. Berkeley: University of California Press, 1996.

Stone, Jon R., editor. *The Craft of Religious Studies*. New York: Palgrave, 2000.

Weaver, Jace, ed. *Native American Religious Identity: Unforgotten Gods*. Maryknoll: Orbis Books, 1998.

Whaling, Frank, editor. *Theory and Method in Religious Studies: Contemporary Approaches to the Study of Religion*. Berlin: Mouton de Gruyter, 1995.

Beginnings of the Human Religious Adventure

Adams, Richard E. W. *Prehistoric Mesoamerica*. Revised edition. Norman: University of Oklahoma Press, 1996.

Bahn, Paul G. *Journey Through the Ice Age*. Berkeley: University of California Press, 1997.

Benard, Elisabeth, and Beverly Moon, eds. *Goddesses Who Rule*. New York: Oxford University Press, 2000.

Clottes, Jean, et al. *The Shamans of Prehistory: Trance and Magic in the Painted Caves*. Translated by Sophie Hawkes. New York: Harry N. Abrams, 1998.

Fagan, Brian M. *People of the Earth: An Introduction to World Prehistory*. Tenth edition. Upper Saddle River: Prentice Hall, 2000.

Scarre, Christopher. *Exploring Prehistoric Europe*. New York: Oxford University Press, 1999.

Sharer, Robert J. *The Ancient Maya*. Stanford, CA: Stanford University Press, 1994.

Wenke Robert J. *Patterns in Prehistory: Humankind's First Three Million Years*. Fourth edition. New York: Oxford University Press, 1999.

PART 2 RELIGIONS ARISING FROM INDIA

General

Embree, Ainslie T., ed., *Sources of Indian Tradition*. Second edition. New York: Columbia University Press, 1988.

Hardy, Friedhelm. *The Religious Culture of India: Power, Love, and Wisdom*. New York: Cambridge University Press, 1994.

Koller, John M. *The Indian Way*. New York: Macmillan, 1982.

Lopez, Donald S. *Religions of India in Practice*. Princeton, NJ: Princeton University Press, 1995.

Hinduism

Blurton, T. P. *Hindu Art*. London: British Museum Press, 1992.

Brockington, J. L. *The Sacred Thread: Hinduism in Its Continuity and Diversity*. Revised edition. New York: Columbia University Press, 1996.

Coward, Howard G., Julius Lipner, and Katherine Young, eds. *Hindu Ethics: Purity, Abortion, and Euthanasia*. Albany: State University of New York Press, 1991.

Davis, Richard. *Worshipping Siva in Medieval India: Ritual in an Oscillating Universe*. Delhi: Motilal Banarsidass, 2000.

Dimmit, Cornelia, and J. A. B. van Buitenen, trans. *Classical Hindu Mythology: A Reader in the Sanskrit Puranas*. Philadelphia: Temple University Press, 1978.

Eck, Diana L. *Banaras: City of Light*. New York: Columbia University Press, 1998.

Flood, Gavin. *An Introduction to Hinduism*. Cambridge: Cambridge University Press, 1996.

Freed, Stanley A., and Ruth S. Freed. *Hindu Festivals in a North Indian Village*. Seattle: University of Washington Press, 1998.

Fuller, C. J. *The Camphor Flame: Popular Hinduism and Society in India*. Princeton, NJ: Princeton University Press, 1992.

Haberman, David L. *Journey Through the Twelve Forests: An Encounter with Krishna*. New York: Oxford University Press, 1994.

Harlan, Lindsey, and Paul B. Courtright, eds. *From the Margins of Hindu Marriage: Essays on Gender, Religion, and Culture*. New York: Oxford University Press, 1995.

Hartsuiker, D. *Sadhus, the Holy Men of India*. London: Thames and Hudson, 1993.

Hawley, John Stratton. *At Play With Krishna: Pilgrimage Dramas from Brindavan*. Princeton, NJ: Princeton University Press, 1985.

———. *Sati, the Blessing and the Curse: The Burning of Wives in India*. New York: Oxford University Press, 1994.

Hawley, John Stratton, and Donna Marie Wulff, eds. *Devi: Goddesses of India*. Berkeley: University of California Press, 1996.

Kinsley, David R. *Hindu Goddesses: Visions of the Divine Feminine in the Hindu Religious Tradition*. Berkeley: University of California Press, 1985.

———. *Hinduism: A Cultural Perspective*. Second edition. Englewood Cliffs, NJ: Prentice Hall, 1993.

———. *The Sword and the Flute: Kali and Krishna, Dark Visions of the Terrible and the Sublime in Hindu Mythology*. Berkeley: University of California Press, 1977.

Klostermaier, Klaus K. *A Survey of Hinduism*. Second edition. Albany: State University of New York Press, 1994.

Knipe, David M. *Hinduism: Experiments in the Sacred*. New York: HarperSanFrancisco, 1991.

Kramrisch, Stella. *The Hindu Temple*. 2 vols. Delhi: Motilal Banarsidass, 1976.

Leslie, Julia. *Roles and Rituals for Hindu Women*. London: Pinter Publishers, 1991.

Lipner, Julius. *Hindus: Their Religious Beliefs and Practices*. London: Routledge, 1994.

Michaels, Axel. *Hinduism: Past and Present*. Princeton: Princeton University Press, 2004.

Miller, Barbara Stoler, trans. *The Bhagavad-Gita: Krishna's Counsel in Time of War*. New York: Columbia University Press, 1986.

Mittal, Sushil, and Gene R. Thursby, eds. *The Hindu World*. New York: Routledge, 2004.

O'Flaherty, Wendy Doniger, ed. *Karma and Rebirth in Classical Indian Traditions*. Berkeley: University of California Press, 1980.

———, trans. *The Rig Veda: An Anthology*. New York: Penguin Books, 1981.

———. *Siva: The Erotic Ascetic*. Oxford: Oxford University Press, 1981.

Pearson, Anne MacKenzie. *"Because It Gives Me Peace of Mind": Ritual Fasts in the Religious Lives of Hindu Women*. Albany: State University of New York Press, 1996.

Pechilis, Karen. *The Graceful Guru: Hindu Gurus in India and the United States*. New York: Oxford University Press, 2004.

Perrett, Roy W. *Hindu Ethics: A Philosophical Study*. Honolulu: University of Hawaii Press, 1998.

Pintchman, Tracy. *The Rise of the Goddess in the Hindu Tradition*. Albany: State University of New York Press, 1994.

———, ed. *Seeking Mahadevi: Constructing the Identities of the Hindu Great Goddess*. Albany: State University of New York Press, 2001.

Sax, William S. *Mountain Goddess: Gender and Politics in a Himalayan Pilgrimage*. New York: Oxford University Press, 1991.

———. *The Gods at Play: Lila in South Asia*. New York: Oxford University Press, 1995.

Sharma, Arvind. *Classical Hindu Thought: An Introduction*. New York: Oxford University Press, 2001.

————. *Modern Hindu Thought: The Essential Texts*. New York: Oxford University Press, 2001.

Shattuck, Cybelle. *Hinduism*. Upper Saddle River: Prentice Hall, 1999.

Sil, Narasingha P. *Ramakrishna Revisited: A New Biography*. Lanham, MD: University Press of America, 1998.

Singer, Milton, ed. *Krishna: Myths, Rites, and Attitudes*. Westport: Greenwood Press, 1981.

Smith, Brian K. *Classifying the Universe: The Ancient Indian Varna System and the Origins of Caste*. New York: Oxford University Press, 1994.

Venkatesananda, Swami. *The Concise Bhagavatam*. Albany: State University of New York Press, 1989.

Buddhism

Bushwell, Robert E. *The Zen Monastic Experience: Buddhist Practice in Contemporary Korea*. Princeton, NJ: Princeton University Press, 1992.

Cabezon, Jose Ignacio. *Buddhism, Sexuality, and Gender*. Albany: State University of New York Press, 1992.

Coleman, James Williams. *The New Buddhism: The Western Transformation of an Ancient Tradition*. New York: Oxford University Press, 2002.

Conze, Edward, et al., eds. *Buddhist Texts Through the Ages*. Oxford: Oneworld Publications, 1995.

Fisher, Robert F. *Buddhist Art and Architecture*. New York: Thames and Hudson, 1993.

Friedman, Lenore, and Susan Moon, eds. *Being Bodies: Buddhist Women on the Paradox of Embodiment*. Boulder: Shambhala, 1997.

Gethin, Rupert. *The Foundations of Buddhism*. New York: Oxford University Press, 1998.

Goldstein, Melvyn C., and Matthew T. Kapstein, eds. *Buddhism in Contemporary Tibet: Religious Revival and Cultural Identity*. Berkeley: University of California Press, 1998.

Gombrich, Richard. *Theravada Buddhism: A Social History from Ancient Benares to Modern Colombo*. London: Routledge & Kegan Paul, 1988.

Gross, Rita. *Buddhism After Patriarchy: A Feminist History, Analysis and Reconstruction of Buddhism*. Albany: State University of New York Press, 1993.

Habito, Ruben L. F. *Total Liberation: Zen Spirituality and the Social Dimension*. Maryknoll: Orbis Books, 1989.

Hardacre, Helen, and Alan Sponburg, eds. *Maitreya, the Future Buddha*. New York: Cambridge University Press, 1988.

Harvey, Peter. *An Introduction to Buddhism: Teachings, History and Practices*. Cambridge: Cambridge University Press, 1990.

Hawkins, Bradley K. *Buddhism*. Upper Saddle River: Prentice Hall, 1999.

Heine, Steven, and Charles S. Prebish, editors. *Buddhist in the Modern World: Adaptations of an Ancient Tradition*. New York: Oxford University Press, 2003.

Kabilsingh, Chatsumarn. *Thai Women in Buddhism*. Berkeley, CA: Parallax Press, 1991.

Kalupahana, David J. *Ethics in Early Buddhism*. Honolulu: University of Hawaii Press, 1995.

Keown, Damien. *Contemporary Buddhist Ethics*. New York: Routledge, 2000.

————. *Buddhism and Abortion*. Honolulu: University of Hawaii Press, 1998.

Klein, Anne Carolyn. *Meeting the Great Bliss Queen: Buddhists, Feminists, and the Art of the Self*. Boston: Beacon Press, 1995.

Kraft, Kenneth. *The Wheel of Engaged Buddhism: A New Map of the Path*. New York: Weatherhill, 1999.

Levenson, Claude B. *The Dalai Lama: A Biography*. New York: Oxford University Press, 2004.

Lopez, Donald S., ed. *Buddhism in Practice*. Princeton, NJ: Princeton University Press, 1995.

————, ed. *Religions of Tibet in Practice*. Princeton, NJ: Princeton University Press, 1997.

————. *The Story of Buddhism: A Concise Guide to Its History and Teachings*. New York: HarperSanFrancisco, 2002.

Murcott, Susan. *The First Buddhist Women: Translations and Commentaries on the Therigatha*. Berkeley, CA: Parallax Press, 1991.

Nakasone, Ronald Y. *Ethics of Enlightenment: Essays and Sermons in Search of a Buddhist Ethic*. Fremont, CA: Dharma Cloud, 1990.

Powell, Andrew. *Living Buddhism*. Berkeley: University of California Press, 1995.

Powers, John. *Introduction to Tibetan Buddhism*. Ithaca, NY: Snow Lion Publications, 1995.

Prebish, Charles S. *Luminous Passage: The Practice and Study of Buddhism in America*. Berkeley: Uuniversity of California Press, 1999.

Prebish, Charles S., and Kenneth K. Tanaka, eds. *The Faces of Buddhism in America*. Berkeley: University of California Press, 1998.

Queen, Christopher S., and Sallie B. King, eds. *Engaged Buddhism: Buddhist Liberation Movements in Asia*. Albany: State University of New York Press, 1996.

Rahula, Walpola. *What the Buddha Taught*. Revised edition. New York: Grove Press, 1974.

Reynolds, Frank E., and Jason A. Carbine, editors. *The Life of Buddhism*. Berkeley: University of California Press, 2000.

Robinson, Richard H., and Willard L. Johnson. *Buddhist Religions: A Historical Introduction.* Fifth edition. Belmont, CA: Wadsworth, 2004.

Schaeffer, Kurtis R. *Himalayan Hermitess: The Life of a Tibetan Buddhist Nun.* New York: Oxford University Press, 2004.

Seager, Richard Hughes. *Buddhism in America.* New York: Columbia University Press, 2000.

Shaw, Miranda. *Passionate Enlightenment: Women in Tantric Buddhism.* Princeton, NJ: Princeton University Press, 1995.

Singh, Iqbal. *Gautama Buddha.* Second edition. New York: Oxford University Press, 1997.

Strong, John S. *The Experience of Buddhism: Sources and Interpretations.* Belmont, CA: Wadsworth, 1995.

Suzuki Shunryu. *Zen Mind, Beginner's Mind.* New York: Weatherhill, 1986.

Tsomo, Karma Lekshe. *Buddhist Women Across Cultures: Realizations.* Albany: State University of New York Press, 1999.

Tucci, Giuseppe, *The Religions of Tibet.* Translated by Geoffrey Samuel. Berkeley: University of California Press, 1980.

Williams, Paul. *Mahayana Buddhism: The Doctrinal Foundations.* London: Routledge & Kegan Paul, 1989.

[*See also* Religions of China and Religions of Japan.]

Jainism

Babb, Lawrence A. *Absent Lord: Ascetics and Kings in a Jain Ritual Culture.* Berkeley: University of California Press, 1996.

Cort, John E. *Jains in the World: Religious Values and Ideology in India.* New York: Oxford University Press, 2001.

Dundas, P. *The Jains.* Second edition. New York: Routledge, 2002.

Jain, Jyotiprasad. *Religion and Culture of the Jains.* New Delhi: Bharatiya Jnanpith Publications, 1975.

Jaini, Padmanabh S. *Gender and Salvation: Jaina Debates on the Spiritual Liberation of Women.* Berkeley: University of California Press, 1991.

————. *The Jaina Path of Purification.* New edition. Delhi: Motilal Barnsidass, 2001.

Pal, Pratapaditya. *The Peaceful Liberators: Jain Art from India.* New York: Thames and Hudson, 1994.

Roy, Ashim Kumar. *A History of the Jainas.* New Delhi: Gitanjali, 1984.

Sangave, Vilas Adinath. *Aspects of Jaina Religion.* New Delhi: Bharatiya Jnanpith, 1990.

————. *Jaina Community: A Social Survey.* Second, revised edition. Bombay: Popular Prakashan, 1980.

Sikhism

Cole, W. Owen. *The Guru in Sikhism.* London: Darton, Longman and Todd, 1982.

———— and Piara Singh Sambi. *The Sikhs: Their Religious Beliefs and Practices.* London: Routledge & Kegan Paul, 1985.

Grewal, J. S. *The Sikhs of the Punjab.* New York: Cambridge University Press, 1998.

Harbans Singh, S. *The Message of Sikhism.* Delhi: Guru Nanak Foundation, 1984.

Khushwant, K. S. *A History of the Sikhs.* 2 vols. Reprint with corrections. Delhi: Oxford University Press, 1999.

Mann, Gurinder Singh. *Sikhism.* Englewood Cliffs: Prentice Hall, 2003.

McLeod, W. H. *Exploring Sikhism: Aspects of Sikh Identity, Culture, and Thought.* New York: Oxford University Press, 2001.

————. *Sikhism.* New York: Penguin Books, 1997.

————. *The Sikhs: History, Religion, and Society.* New York: Columbia University Press, 1989.

Oberoi, Harjot. *Construction of Religious Boundaries: Culture, Identity and Diversity in the Sikh Tradition.* New York: Oxford University Press, 1997.

Shackle, Christopher, Gurharpal Singh, and Arvand-pal Mandair. *Sikh Religion, Culture and Ethnicity.* Surrey, England: Curzon Press, 2000.

Singh, Avtar. *Ethics of the Sikhs.* Third edition. Patiala: Punjabi University, 1996.

Singh, Pashaura. *The Guru Granth Sahib: Canon, Meaning and Authority.* New York: Oxford University Press, 2001.

Singh, Paushaura, and N. Gerald Barrier, eds. *Sikhism and History.* New York: Oxford University Press, 2004.

PART 3 RELIGIONS OF CHINA AND JAPAN

General

Brannigan, Michael C. *Striking a Balance: A Primer in Traditional Asian Values.* New York: Seven Bridges Press, 2000.

Ikels, Charlotte, ed. *Filial Piety: Practice and Discourse in Contemporary East Asia.* Palo Alto: Stanford University Press, 2004.

Religions of China

Bays, Daniel H., ed. *Christianity in China: From the Eighteenth Century to the Present.* Palo Alto: Stanford University Press, 1996.

Berling, Judith. *A Pilgrim in Chinese Culture: Negotiating Religious Diversity.* Maryknoll: Orbis Books, 1997.

Berthong, John H. *Transformations of the Confucian Way.* Boulder: Westview Press, 1998.

Bodenkamp, Stephen R. *Early Daoist Scriptures.* Berkeley: University of California Press, 1997.

Chappell, David W., ed. *Buddhist and Taoist Practice in Medieval Chinese Society*. Honolulu: University of Hawaii Press, 1987.

Ching, Julia. *Chinese Religions*. Maryknoll: Orbis Books, 1993.

———. *Mysticism and Kingship in China: The Heart of Chinese Wisdom*. New York: Cambridge University Press, 1997.

Clart, Philip, and Charles B. Jones, eds. *Religion in Modern Taiwan: Tradition and Innovation in a Changing Society*. Honolulu: University of Hawaii Press, 2003.

Cole, Alan. *Mothers and Sons in Chinese Buddhism*. Stanford, CA: Stanford University Press, 1998.

Dean, Kenneth. *Taoist Ritual and Popular Cults of Southeast China*. Princeton, NJ: Princeton University Press, 1993.

de Bary, Wm. Theodore, et al., eds. *Sources of Chinese Tradition*. 2 vols. Second edition. New York: Columbia University Press, 2000–2001.

Dumoulin, Heinrich. *Zen Buddhism: A History*. Vol. I (India and China). New York: Macmillan, 1988.

Ebrey, Patricia, and Peter Gregory. *Religion and Society in T'ang and Sung China*. Honolulu: University of Hawaii Press, 1993.

Feuchtwang, Stephan, *Popular Religion in China: The Imperial Metaphor*. Surrey, England: Curzon Press, 2001.

Girardot, N. J., *Myth and Meaning in Early Taoism: The Theme of Chaos*. Berkeley: University of California Press, 1983.

Goldstein, Melvyn C., and Matthew Kapstein, eds. *Buddhism in Contemporary Tibet: Religious Revival and Cultural Identity*. Berkeley: University of California Press, 1998.

Hall, David, and Roger Ames. *Thinking Through Confucius*. Albany: State University of New York Press, 1987.

Ivanhoe, Philip J., and Bryan W. van Norden, eds. *Readings in Classical Chinese Philosophy*. New York: Seven Bridges Press, 2000.

Jochim, Christian. *Chinese Religions: A Cultural Perspective*. Englewood Cliffs, NJ: Prentice Hall, 1996.

Jones, Charles Brewer. *Buddhism in Taiwan: Religion and the State, 1660–1990*. Honolulu: University of Hawai Press, 1999.

Jordon, David K., and Daniel K. Overmyer. *The Flying Phoenix: Aspects of Chinese Sectarianism in Taiwan*. Princeton, NJ: Princeton University Press, 1986.

Kohn, Livia. *Early Chinese Mysticism: Philosophy and Soteriology in the Taoist Tradition*. Princeton, NJ: Princeton University Press, 1992.

———. *The Taoist Experience: An Anthology*. Albany: State University of New York Press, 1993.

———, and Harold D. Roth, eds. *Daoist Identity: History, Legend, and Ritual*. Honolulu: University of Hawaii Press, 2002.

Kwong-Loi Shun. *Mencius and Early Chinese Thought*. Stanford, CA: Stanford University Press, 1997.

Lagerwey, John. *Taoist Ritual in Chinese Society and History*. New York: Macmillan, 1987.

Lopez, Donald S., ed. *Religions of China in Practice*. Princeton, NJ: Princeton University Press, 1996.

Macinnes, Donald E. *Religion in China Today: Policy and Practice*. Maryknoll: Orbis Books, 1989.

Madsen, Richard. *China's Catholics: Tragedy and Hope in an Emerging Civil Society*. Berkeley: University of California Press, 1998.

Oldstone-Moore, Jennifer. *Taoism*. New York: Oxford University Press, 2003.

Overmyer, Daniel L. *Religions of China: The World as a Living System*. Prospect Heights: Waveland Press, 1998.

Overmyer, Daniel L., and Richard Edmonds. *Religion in China Today*. New York: Cambridge University Press, 2003.

Palmer, Martin. *Travels Through Sacred China*. San Francisco: HarperCollins, 1996.

Paper, Jordan, and Lawrence G. Thompson. *The Chinese Way in Religion*. Second edition. Belmont, CA: Wadsworth, 1998.

Robinet, Isabelle. *Taoism: Growth of a Religion*. Translated by Phyllis Brooks. Stanford, CA: Stanford University Press, 1997.

Shahar, Meir, and Robert P. Weller, eds. *Unruly Gods: Divinity and Society in China*. Honolulu: University of Hawaii Press, 1996.

Sommer, Deborah, ed. *Chinese Religion: An Anthology of Sources*. New York: Oxford University Press, 1995.

Taylor, Rodney L. *The Religious Dimensions of Confucianism*. Albany: State University of New York Press, 1990.

———. *The Way of Heaven: An Introduction to the Confucian Religious Life*. Leiden: E.J. Brill, 1997.

Teiser, Stephen. *The Ghost Festival in Medieval China*. Princeton, NJ: Princeton University Press, 1988.

Thompson, Laurence G. *Chinese Religion: An Introduction*. Fifth edition. Belmont, CA: Wadsworth, 1996.

Tu, Wei-ming. *Confucian Thought: Selfhood as Creative Transformation*. Albany: State University of New York Press, 1985.

Tu, Wei-ming, Milan G. Hejtmanek, and Alan Wachman, eds. *The Confucian World Observed: A Contemporary Discussion of Confucian Humanism in East Asia*. Honolulu: University of Hawaii Press, 1992.

Tucker, Mary Evelyn, and John H. Berthrong, eds. *Confucianism and Ecology: The Interrelation of Heaven, Earth, and Humans*. Cambridge: Harvard University Press, 1998.

Weidner, Marsha, et al. *Latter Days of the Law: Images of Chinese Buddhism, 850–1850*. Honolulu: University of Hawaii Press, 1994.

Weinstein, Stanley. *Buddhism Under the T'ang*. Cambridge: Cambridge University Press, 1987.

Wright, Arthur F. *Buddhism in Chinese History*. Stanford, CA: Stanford University Press, 1983.

Religions of Japan

Andreasen, Esben. *Popular Buddhism in Japan: Shin Buddhist Religion and Culture*. Honolulu: University of Hawaii Press, 1998.

Bodiford, William M. *Soto Zen in Medieval Japan*. Honolulu: University of Hawaii Press, 1993.

Brandon, Reiko Mochinaga, and Barbara B. Stephan. *Spirit and Symbol: The Japanese New Year*. Honolulu: University of Hawaii Press, 1994.

Breen, John, and Mark Teeuwen, eds. *Shinto in History: Ways of the Kami*. Honolulu: University of Hawaii Press, 2000.

Clarke, Peter B. *Japanese New Religions in Global Perspective*. Surrey, England: Curzon Press, 2000.

Davis, Winston Bradley. *Japanese Religion and Society: Paradigms of Structure and Change*. Albany: State University of New York Press, 1992.

de Bary, Wm. Theodore, et al, editors. *Sources of Japanese Tradition*. Vol. 1. New York: Columbia University Press, 2002.

Dobbins, James C. *Jodo Shinshu: Shin Buddhism in Medieval Japan*. Bloomington: Indiana University Press, 1989.

Dumoulin, Heinrich. *Zen Buddhism: A History*. Vol. II (Japan). New York: Macmillan, 1988.

Earhart, H. Byron. *Japanese Religion: Unity and Diversity*. Fourth edition. Belmont, CA: Wadsworth, 2004.

———. *Religion in the Japanese Experience: Sources and Interpretations*. Second edition. Belmont, CA: Wadsworth, 1997.

Elison, George. *Deus Destroyed: The Image of Christianity in Early Modern Japan*. Cambridge: Council on East Asian Studies Harvard University, 1988.

Hardacre, Helen. *Kurozumikyo and the New Religions of Japan*. Princeton, NJ: Princeton University Press, 1986.

———. *Shinto and the State, 1868–1988*. Princeton, NJ: Princeton University Press, 1989.

Heine, Steven, and Dale S. Wright, eds. *The Koan: Texts and Contexts in Zen Buddhism*. New York: Oxford University Press, 2000.

Hirota, Dennis, ed. *Wind in the Pines: Classic Writings on the Way of Tea as a Buddhist Path*. Fremont, CA: Asian Humanities Press, 1995.

Kageyama, Haruki. *The Arts of Shinto*. New York: Weatherhill Press, 1973.

Kane, Paula, and Robinson Arai. *Women Living Zen: Japanese Soto Buddhist Nuns*. New York: Oxford University Press, 1999.

Kato, Genichi. *A Historical Study of the Religious Development of Shinto*. New York: Greenwood Press, 1988.

King, Winston L. *Zen and the Way of the Sword: Arming the Samurai Psyche*. New York: Oxford University Press, 1993.

Kitagawa, Joseph M. *On Understanding Japanese Religion*. Princeton, NJ: Princeton University Press, 1987.

———. *Religion in Japanese History*. New York: Columbia University Press, 1966.

Kraft, Kenneth, ed. *Zen: Tradition and Transition*. New York: Grove Press, 1988.

LaFleur, William R. *Liquid Life: Abortion and Buddhism in Japan*. Princeton, NJ: Princeton University Press, 1992.

Leggett, Trevor. *The Spirit of Budo: Old Traditions for Present-Day Life*. London: Kegan Paul International, 1998.

Littleton, C. Scott. *Shinto and the Religions of Japan*. New York: Oxford University Press, 2002.

Machida Soho. *Renegade Monk: Honen and Japanese Pure Land Buddhism*. Translated by Joannis Mentzas. Berkeley: University of California Press, 1999.

Mullins, Mark R. *Christianity Made in Japan: A Study of Indigenous Movements*. Honolulu: University of Hawaii Press, 1998.

Myodo, Satomi. *Journey in Search of the Way: The Spiritual Autobiography of Satomi Myodo*. Translated by Sallie B. King. Albany: State University of New York Press, 1993.

Nefsky, Marilyn F. *Stone Houses and Iron Bridges: Tradition and the Place of Women in Contemporary Japan*. New York: Peter Lang, 1991.

Nobutaka Inoue et al, editors. *Shinto: A Short History*. New York: Routledge Curzon, 2003.

Payne, Richard K., ed. *Re-envisioning "Kamakura" Buddhism*. Honolulu: University of Hawaii Press, 1998.

Picken, Stuart D. B. *Essentials of Shinto*. New York: Greenwood Publishing Group, 1994.

Reader, Ian. *Religion in Contemporary Japan*. Honolulu: University of Hawaii Press, 1991.

———. *Simple Guide to Shinto*. London: Global Books, Ltd., 1998.

———, Esben Andreasen, and Finn Stefansson. *Japanese Religions: Past and Present*. Honolulu: University of Hawaii Press, 1993.

———, and George J. Tanabe, Jr. *Practically Religious: Worldly Benefits and the Common Religion of Japan*. Honolulu: University of Hawaii Press, 1998.

Schnell, Scott. *The Rousing Drum: Ritual Practice in a Japanese Community*. Honolulu: University of Hawaii Press, 1999.

Sered, Susan. *Women of the Sacred Groves: Divine Priestesses of Okinawa*. New York: Oxford University Press, 1999.

Sonoda, Koyu, and Yusen Kashiwahara, eds. *Shapers of Japanese Buddhism*. Rutland: Charles E. Tuttle, 1994.

Stone, Jacqueline I. *Original Enlightenment and the Transformation of Medieval Japanese Buddhism*. Honolulu: University of Hawaii Press, 1999.

Suzuki, Daisetz T. *Zen and Japanese Culture*. Princeton, NJ: Princeton University Press, 1970.

Suzuki, Shunryu. *Zen Mind, Beginner's Mind*. Tokyo: John Weatherhill, 1970.

Tamaru, Noriyoshi, and David Reid, eds. *Religion in Japanese Culture: Where Living Traditions Meet a Changing World.* New York: Kodansha International, 1996.

Tanabe, George J., Jr., ed. *Religions of Japan in Practice.* Princeton, NJ: Princeton University Press, 1999.

Unno, Taitetsu. *River of Fire, River of Water: An Introduction to the Pure Land Tradition of Shin Buddhism.* New York: Doubleday, 1998.

Varley, H. Paul. *Japanese Culture.* Fourth edition. Honolulu: University of Hawaii Press, 2000.

Epilogue

Almond, Gabriel A., R. Scott Appleby, and Emmanuel Sivan. *Strong Religion: The Rise of Fundamentalisms Around the World.* Chicago: The University of Chicago Press, 2003.

Chapple, Christopher Key. *Ecological Prospects: Science, Religion, and Aesthetic Perspectives.* Albany: State University of New York Press, 1993.

Juergensmeyer, Mark. *Terror in the Mind of God: The Global Rise of Religious Violence.* Third edition. Berkeley: University of California Press, 2003.

Kinsley, David. *Ecology and Religion: Ecological Spirituality in Cross-Cultural Perspective.* Englewood Cliffs, NJ: Prentice Hall, 1995.

Kosmin, Barry A., and Seymour P. Lachmin. *One Nation Under God: Religion in Contemporary American Society.* New York: Harmony Books, 1993.

The Meaning of Life in the World Religions. Oxford: Oneworld Publications, 1999.

Sharma, Arvind, and Kathleen Dungan, eds. *A Dome of Many Colors: Studies in Religious Pluralism, Identity, and Unity.* Harrisburg, PA: Trinity Press International, 1999.

Smith-Christopher, Daniel L., ed. *Subverting Hatred: The Challenge of Nonviolence in Religious Traditions.* Boston: Boston Research Center for the Twenty-first Century, 1998.

Thumma, Scott, and Edward R. Gray. *Gay Religion.* Walnut Creek, CA: AltaMira Press, 2004.

Tucker, Mary Evelyn, and John A. Grim, eds. *Worldviews and Ecology: Living Sustainably on a Fragile Planet.* Maryknoll: Orbis Books, 1994.

Twiss, Sumner B., and Bruce Grelle. *Explorations in Global Ethics: Comparative Religious Ethics and Interreligious Dialogue.* Boulder: Westview Press, 1998.

Acknowledgments

TEXT

From *The Middle Length Discourses of Buddha*, trans. Bhikkhu Nanamoli © Bhikkhu Bodhi, 1995. Reprinted from *The Middle Length Discourses of the Buddha: A Translation of the Majjhima Nikaya*, with permission of Wisdom Publications, 199 Elm Street, Somerville, MA 02144 U.S.A., *www.wisdompubs.org*.

From *What the Buddha Taught*, by Walpola Rahula. Reprinted with permission from Grove Press.

From *The Gospel of Sri Ramakrishna*, translated by Swami Nakhilananda. Reprinted with permission from the Ramakrishna-Vivekananda Center.

From *Taoism and the Rite of Cosmic Renewal*, by Michael Saso. Reprinted by permission of Washington University Press.

From *The Tao of Chinese Religion*, by Milton Chiu, Ithaca, NY. Reprinted with permission from Milton Chiu.

From *Manyoshu: Nippon Gakujutsu Shinkokai Translation of One Thounsand Poems* (New York: Columbia University Press, 1965). Reprinted with permission from Japanese Society for the Promotion of Science.

From *The Chinese on the Art of Painting: Translations and Comments* by Osvald Siren. Reprinted by permission of Schocken Books, distributed by Pantheon Books, a division of Random House, Inc.

From *The Buddhist Tradition in India, China and Japan*, edited by William Theodore de Bary. Copyright © 1969 by William Theodore de Bary. Vintage Books edition 1972. Reprinted by permission of Pantheon Books, a division of Random House.

From *Bhagavad-Gita*, translated by Barbara Stoler Miller, copyright © 1986 by Barbara Stoler Miller. Used by permission of Bantam Books, a division of Random House, Inc.

From *The Rig Veda: An Anthology*, translated by Wendy Doniger O'Flaherty (Penquin Classics, 1981). Copyright © Wendy Doniger O'Flaherty, 1981. Reproduced by permission of Penquin Books Ltd.

From *Sikhism* by Hew McLeod (Penquin, 1997) Copyright © W H McLeod, 1997. Reproduced by permission of Penquin Books Ltd.

From *The Buddhist Experience: Sources and Interpretations*, 1st edition by Beyer. © 1974. Reprinted with permission of Wadsworth, a division of Thomson Learning: *www.thomsonrights.com*. Fax 800 730–2215.

From *A Source Book in Chinese Philosophy*, by Wing-tsit Chan. Chan , Wing-tsit; *A Source Book in Chinese Philosophy*. © 1963 Princeton University Press, 1991 renewed PUP. Reprinted by permission of Princeton University Press.

From *Norito: Ancient Japanese Ritual Prayers*, translated by Donald Philippi. Reprinted with permission from Princeton University Press.

From *Sword and the Flute: Kali and Krsna: Dark Visions of the Terrible and the Sublime in Hindu Mythology*, by David Kinsley. © 1975 The Regents of the University of California. Reprinted by the University of California Press.

From *Buddhism and Society: A Great Tradition and Its Burmese Vicissitudes*, by Melford E. Spiro. Second, expanded edition. Copyright © 1982 Melford E. Spiro. The Regents of the University of California. Reprinted by the University of California Press.

From *Sources of Indian Tradition*, edited by Ainslie T. Embree. Copyright © 1988. Columbia University Press. Reprinted with permission of the publisher.

From *Sources of Chinese Tradition*, vol. 1, 2nd edition, edited by William Theodore de Bary and Irene Bloom. Copyright © 1999. Columbia University Press. Reprinted with permission of the publisher.

From *Basic Writings of Hsun Tzu*, translated by Burton Watson. Copyright © 1967. Columbia University Press. Reprinted with permission of the publisher.

From *The Complete Works of Chuang Tzu*, translated by Burton Watson. Copyright © 1968. Columbia University Press. Reprinted with permission of the publisher.

From *Sources of Japanese Tradition*, vol. 1, 2nd edition, edited by William Theodore de Bary, et al. Copyright © 2001. Columbia University Press. Reprinted with permission of the publisher.

From *Sources of Japanese Tradition*, vol. 2, edited by Ryusaku Tsunoda, et al. Copyright © 1964. Columbia University Press. Reprinted with permission of the publisher.

From *Kukai: Major Works*, translated by Yoshito S. Hakeda. Copyright © 1972. Columbia University Press. Reprinted with permission of the publisher.

From *The Zen Master Hakuin: Selected Writings*, translated by Philip B. Yampolsky. Copyright © 1971. Columbia University Press. Reprinted with permission of the publisher.

From *Saigyo: Poems of a Mountain Home*, by Burton Watson. Copyright © 1991. Columbia University Press. Reprinted with permission of the publisher.

From *Ascetism and Eroticism in the Mythology of Siva*, reprinted as *Siva: The Erotic Ascetic* (1973) edited by Wendy Doniger O'Flaherty. By permission of Oxford University Press.

From *Hinduism* (1996) by Zaehner, R.C. By permission of Oxford University Press.

From *The Bodhicaryavatara* (1996) edited by Kate Crosley and Andrew Skilton, (Translators). By permission of Oxford University Press.

From *Kabir*, translated by C. Vaudeville. Reprinted with permission of Oxford University Press.

From *The Thirteen Principal Upanishads*, by Robert Ernest Hume. Reproduced by permission of Oxford University Press India, New Delhi.

IMAGES

Chapter 1; Page 7, Air India Library; **p. 12,** Israel Ministry of Tourism, North America; **p. 17,** AP Wide World Photos; **p. 21,** Paul Gauguin, French, 1848–1903 'Christ on the Cross' ca. 1900. Woodcut, printed in brown ink. 15 7/8 × 5 3/8 in. The Metropolitan Museum of Art, New York. Harris Brisbane Dick Fund, 1929.

Chapter 2; Page 31, Egyptian Tourist Authority; **p. 32,** Museum of Natural History.

Chapter 3; Page 46, Rama, India, Tamil Nadu; Chola period, 11th century. Copper alloy. H. 37 3/4 in. (95.9 cm.). Photograph by Susuma Wakisaka, Idemitsu Museum of Arts, Tokyo. The Asia Society, New York, Mr. and Mrs. John D. Rockefeller 3rd Collection; **p. 53,** Mary Evans Picture Library/Photo Researchers, Inc.

Chapter 4; Page 59, Corbis/Bettmann; **p. 61,** Shiva as Lord of the Dance (Shiva Nataraja) India, Tamil Nadu; Chola period, 12th century. Copper alloy. H. 29 1/4 in. (74.3 cm) 1979.29. Photograph by Susuma Wakisaka, Idemitsu Museum of Arts, Tokyo. The Asia Society, New York: Mr. and Mrs. John D. Rockefeller 3rd Collection; **p. 71,** 'The Rainy Season (Varsha)'. India, Gujarat or the Deccan; late 17th century. Temple hanging (pichhavai); opaque watercolor, gold, and silver on dyed cotton 80 3/4 × 86 /2 in. (205.1 × 219.7 cm) Photograph by Otto Nelson. The Asia Society, New York, Mr. and Mrs. John D. Rockefeller 3rd Collection.

Chapter 5; Page 75, Ganesha. India, Uttar Pradesh; 8th century. Sandstone. H. 49 1/2 in. (125.7 cm). Photograph by Lynton Gardiner. The Asia Society, New York: Mr. and Mrs. John D. Rockefeller 3rd Collection; **p. 80,** Bernard Pierre Wolff/Photo Researchers, Inc.; **p. 87,** Air India Library.

Chapter 6; Page 96, AP/Wide World Photos; **p. 101,** Denis Gray/AP Wide World Photos; **p. 105,** Japan National Tourist Organization.

Chapter 7; Page 111, AP Wide World Photos; **p. 116,** Hideo Kurihara, Getty Images Inc.-Stone Allstock; **p. 121,** 'Bodhisattva'. Nepal; Early Malla period, 13th century. Gilt copper with inlays of semiprecious stones. H. 18 3/4 in. (47.6 cm). Photograph by Lynton Gardiner. The Asia Society, New York, Mr. and Mrs. John D. Rockefeller 3rd Collection.

Chapter 8; Page 125, Dinodia Picture Agency/R.A. Acharya/The Image Works; **p. 132,** Corbis/Bettmann.

Chapter 9; Page 144, Jehangir Gazdar/Woodfin Camp & Associates; **p. 150,** Alex Webb/Magnum Photos, Inc.

Chapter 10; Page 157, Corbis/Bettmann; **p. 163,** Marc Riboud/Magnum Photos, Inc.

Chapter 11; Page 176, Charles Phelps Cushing/PhotoEdit; **p. 180,** © Bettmann/CORBIS; **p. 187,** 'Bodhidharma Crossing the Yangzi River on a Reed'. China, Yuan dynasty, 1279–1368. Hanging scroll, ink on paper, 89.2 × 31.1 cm. © The Cleveland Museum of Art, John L. Severance Fund, 1964.44.

Chapter 12; Page 199, Carl Purcell/Photo Researchers, Inc.; **p. 205,** Bruno Barbey/Magnum Photos, Inc.; **p. 217** Paolo Koch/Photo Researchers, Inc.

Chapter 13; Page 225, Robert E. Murowchick/Photo Researchers, Inc.; **p. 232,** National Palace Museum, Taipei, Taiwan, Republic of China; **p. 240,** Fritz Henle/Photo Researchers, Inc.

Chapter 14; Page 245, 'Female Figure'. Japan, Aomori Prefecture; Final Jomon period (1000–300 B.C.E.). Earthenware with traces of pigment (Kamegao Ka type) H. 9 7/8 in. (25.1 cm.). Photograph by Lynton Gardiner. The Asia Society, New York, Mr. and Mrs. John D. Rockefeller 3rd Collection; **p. 252,** Japan National Tourist Organization; **p. 255,** Corbis/Bettmann.

Chapter 15; Page 260, Japan National Tourist Organization; **p. 266,** Japan National Tourist Organization.

Chapter 16; Page 271, Japan National Tourist Organization; **p. 275,** Japan National Tourist Organization; **p. 278,** Robert A. Isaacs/Photo Researchers, Inc.

Index